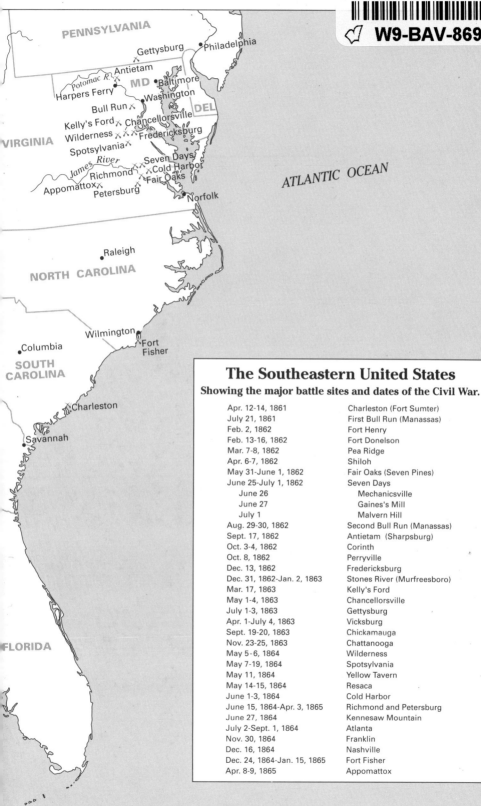

PENNSYLVANIA

Gettysburg • Philadelphia

Potomac R. Antietam
Harpers Ferry MD • Baltimore
Bull Run × • Washington
DEL
Kelly's Ford × Chancellorsville
Wilderness × × Fredericksburg
VIRGINIA
Spotsylvania ×
James River Seven Days
Richmond Cold Harbor
Appomattox × Fair Oaks
Petersburg
• Norfolk

ATLANTIC OCEAN

• Raleigh

NORTH CAROLINA

Wilmington
• Columbia Fort Fisher
SOUTH CAROLINA

Charleston

Savannah

FLORIDA

The Southeastern United States
Showing the major battle sites and dates of the Civil War.

Apr. 12-14, 1861	Charleston (Fort Sumter)
July 21, 1861	First Bull Run (Manassas)
Feb. 2, 1862	Fort Henry
Feb. 13-16, 1862	Fort Donelson
Mar. 7-8, 1862	Pea Ridge
Apr. 6-7, 1862	Shiloh
May 31-June 1, 1862	Fair Oaks (Seven Pines)
June 25-July 1, 1862	Seven Days
June 26	Mechanicsville
June 27	Gaines's Mill
July 1	Malvern Hill
Aug. 29-30, 1862	Second Bull Run (Manassas)
Sept. 17, 1862	Antietam (Sharpsburg)
Oct. 3-4, 1862	Corinth
Oct. 8, 1862	Perryville
Dec. 13, 1862	Fredericksburg
Dec. 31, 1862-Jan. 2, 1863	Stones River (Murfreesboro)
Mar. 17, 1863	Kelly's Ford
May 1-4, 1863	Chancellorsville
July 1-3, 1863	Gettysburg
Apr. 1-July 4, 1863	Vicksburg
Sept. 19-20, 1863	Chickamauga
Nov. 23-25, 1863	Chattanooga
May 5-6, 1864	Wilderness
May 7-19, 1864	Spotsylvania
May 11, 1864	Yellow Tavern
May 14-15, 1864	Resaca
June 1-3, 1864	Cold Harbor
June 15, 1864-Apr. 3, 1865	Richmond and Petersburg
June 27, 1864	Kennesaw Mountain
July 2-Sept. 1, 1864	Atlanta
Nov. 30, 1864	Franklin
Dec. 16, 1864	Nashville
Dec. 24, 1864-Jan. 15, 1865	Fort Fisher
Apr. 8-9, 1865	Appomattox

NONE DIED IN VAIN

Books by Robert Leckie

HISTORY

None Died in Vain: The Saga of the American Civil War
Delivered from Evil: The Saga of World War II
The Wars of America: Updated and Revised, 1609–1980
American and Catholic: The Catholic Church in the U.S.
Challenge for the Pacific: The Struggle for Guadalcanal
With Fire and Sword (edited with Quentin Reynolds)
Strong Men Armed: U.S. Marines Against Japan
Conflict: The History of the Korean War
The March to Glory: 1st Marine Division's Breakout from Chosin

AUTOBIOGRAPHY

Helmet for My Pillow
Lord, What a Family!

BELLES LETTRES

These Are My Heroes: A Study of the Saints
Warfare: A Study of War
A Soldier-Priest Talks to Youth

FICTION

Ordained
Marines!
The Bloodborn
Forged in Blood
Blood of the Seventeen Fires

FOR YOUNGER READERS

The Battle for Iwo Jima
The Story of Football
The Story of World War Two
The Story of World War One
The War in Korea
Great American Battles
The World Turned Upside-Down
1812: The War Nobody Won
The Big Game
Keeper Play
Stormy Voyage

NONE DIED IN VAIN

The Saga of
the American Civil War

Robert Leckie

■ HarperCollins*Publishers*

FIRST EDITION

Designed by Alma Orenstein

Cartographer: Mapping Specialists, Ltd.

Library of Congress Cataloging-in-Publication Data

Leckie, Robert.
    None died in vain : the saga of the American Civil War / Robert Leckie.
        p.   cm.
    Includes bibliographical references.
    ISBN 0-06-016280-5
    1. United States—History—Civil War, 1861–1865.   I. Title.
E468.L45   1990
973.7—dc20   89-45832

---

90 91 92 93 94 CC/RRD 10 9 8 7 6 5 4 3 2 1

To my Grandfather
Patrick Leckie,
who came over from Ireland
to fight for the South
until he learned
that the British Crown
favored the Confederacy
whereupon
he switched sides

It is rather for us to be here dedicated to the great task remaining before us; that from these honored dead we take increased devotion to that cause for which they here gave the last full measure of devotion; that we here highly resolve that these dead shall not have died in vain; *that the nation shall, under God, have a new birth of freedom; and that government of the people, by the people, for the people, shall not perish from the earth.*

—Concluding sentence of Lincoln's Gettysburg Address

Contents

Maps

Acknowledgments

I WOULD LIKE to express my appreciation to the staffs of the New York City Public Library and the Daniel Library at The Citadel, Charleston, South Carolina; to my editors M. S. "Buz" Wyeth and Daniel Bial for their courteous criticism and suggestions which did so much to improve this book; to my good friend Austin Drukker of Upper Montclair, New Jersey, for generously lending me so many books from his splendid Civil War library; and to my dear wife who typed this manuscript while wearing— from among her collection of hats as wife, mother, chef, chauffeur, financier, etc.—her secretary's chapeau. For such fidelity I forgive her her perverse pleasure in asking me how to spell all those words she says I've misspelled.

—Robert Leckie
Polliwog Pond
Byram Township, New Jersey

October 8, 1989

NONE DIED IN VAIN

1

.

Mexico:
The Divisive Victory

O N THE MORNING of September 9, 1847, General Winfield Scott realized that he had to attack Mexico City. His position, though not exactly desperate, was at least serious. Here he was on the outskirts of the Mexican capital, his little invading army dwindled down to 7,000 men, at the end of a supply line running 250 miles through hostile territory to Vera Cruz on the Gulf, with no hope of reopening this base until the dread *vomito* fever vanished in November. Before General Antonio de Lopez Santa Anna became alive to the possibilities of this vulnerable supply line—how he might sever it at will and starve the invading gringos into submission—Scott simply had to destroy him.

At a conference that day with his volunteer generals, and his cherished regular army staff officers such as Captain Robert E. Lee, Captain Joe Hooker, and Lieutenant G.P.T. Beauregard, the towering Scott—at six feet five inches and 250 pounds easily the most commanding presence in the U.S. Army—explained that there were two approaches: one to the west and the other to the south. His generals and Lee favored the southern route, but Beauregard—the Little Creole, as he was called—argued cogently for striking the fortress of Chapultepec in the west. This, he said, would unmask two readily traversed causeways into the city. Hearing him, General Franklin Pierce changed his vote to Chapultepec. Scott agreed. Clapping on his head the plumed hat that, with his fastidious nature, had earned him the unwelcome nickname of Old Fuss 'n Feathers, Scott arose and said: "Gentlemen, we shall attack by the western gates."

It was a happy choice. On the morning of September 12, the Americans seized the vacant Molino del Rey and Casa Mata on the western end of the Chapultepec complex. The most furious American bombardment of the Mexican War began battering the castle. Inside General Nicolas Bravo

1

called for reinforcements. But Santa Anna had no desire to send any of his remaining 6,000 soldiers into what might become a slaughter pen. Bravo had to hold the fortress with fewer than 1,000 men, of whom a hundred were young cadets of the Mexican Military College in Chapultepec.

Against them came General Gideon Pillow's division issuing out of the Molino and General William Worth's division striking the bastion's eastern end. Pillow's men, rushing whooping through a cypress grove, were scythed by a withering fire, and he was himself wounded. Lieutenant James Longstreet, rushing up with a flag in his hand, went down, and the colors were caught and carried forward by Lieutenant George Pickett. On the left Mexican musketry routed the men around Lieutenant Tom Jackson as he tried to manhandle a gun forward single-handed. "There's no danger!" Jackson cried. "See, I'm not hit!" But his gunners remained under cover until a column of regulars appeared. Among them was Lieutenant Ulysses S. Grant, making a mental note that the humorless Jackson also had no fear.

On the east General John Anthony Quitman was taking heavy casualties. The fight was hand-to-hand with crossed swords and clubbed muskets. For a time, the Mexicans held firm, but then gave way—all but the cadets, many of whom fought on to the death and entered Mexican history as "Los Ninos," or the Little Ones. Six of them, aged thirteen to nineteen, gave up their lives rather than surrender. Agustín Melgar fought the Americans step-by-step up the stone stairs of the college until he reached the roof, where Yankee bayonets ended his gallant young life. Lieutenant Pickett stepped over his dying body to haul down the green-red-and-white Mexican tricolor and run up the Stars and Stripes. Cheers rose from the rooftop. Chapultepec had fallen.

The battle was now a race for the city. Quitman had the shorter route. His men smashed through the Belen Gate into the capital's outskirts. The Mexicans under Santa Anna fought back savagely from the Citadel and Belen Prison. The Americans hung on against mounting casualties, some of them taking refuge in the network of canals. As night fell, General Quitman fell into a canal, losing his left shoe. In the morning, September 14, 1847, his uniform still damp, his left foot bare, Quitman drew his sword and led his men forward. He expected a bitter battle. But the Citadel was silent. A flag of truce waved from its ramparts. During the night Santa Anna, aware that his outer defenses had been breached, had retired from his position to Guadalupe Hidalgo in the north. Before leaving, he freed some 2,000 convicts to prey upon the detestable gringos.

Quitman quickly occupied the Citadel. But then, hearing that the freed criminals were plundering the city, the half-shod general marched his men into the Grand Plaza. He formed them in the great square in the shadow of the Cathedral and sent a detachment of U.S. Marines under Lieutenant A. S. Nicholson into the National Palace to clear it of brigands.

Atop the Palace itself, the legendary "Halls of Montezuma," Nicholson cut down the Mexican flag and flung the red-white-and-blue to the breeze, thereby giving his famous corps the first line of its stirring battle hymn. Shortly after there came the blare of bugles and the clatter of horses' hooves. Winfield Scott, superbly uniformed and splendidly mounted, swept into the Plaza escorted by dragoons with bared sabers. A stream of staff officers galloped after him. Bands played, Scott's soldiers presented arms and whooped, and even the rooftops black with Mexican citizens echoed the cheers of the Americans, while ladies at the windows of the surrounding buildings waved handkerchiefs.

If military success is to be measured by the extent of land captured, then Winfield Scott had won one of the greatest victories in the history of warfare—certainly the most momentous in the annals of American arms. He and his little army, which the great Duke of Wellington had long ago given up as "lost," had added 1,193,061 square miles of territory—an area five times the size of France, the largest nation in Europe—to the national domain of the United States. With Texas, this area included the present states of Arizona, Nevada, California, and Utah, and parts of New Mexico, Colorado and Wyoming.*

All this was ceded to the United States by the Treaty of Guadalupe Hidalgo, under which payment of $15,000,000 was to be made to Mexico while Washington also promised to pay $3,250,000 in claims against that country filed by American citizens. The treaty was signed on February 2, 1848, and seventeen days later, after a remarkably rapid journey, a courier came cantering down the broad muddy surface of Pennsylvania Avenue with the document in his saddle bag. He delivered it to Secretary of State James Buchanan, who gave it to President James Knox Polk.

President Polk was not at all happy with it. It had been negotiated by Nicholas Trist, the chief clerk of the State Department, whom he had sent to Mexico for that purpose, but whom he had recalled on October 25. Trist, however, had deliberately ignored the order, seeing in the abdication of Santa Anna a golden opportunity to obtain California and the Southwest, Polk's original objectives.

---

*In 1853 the Gadsden Purchase added another 29,640 square miles to round out the southern parts of Arizona and New Mexico and to make way for a southern railroad to the Pacific.

Democrat Polk's reasons for removing Trist were that he had learned that Trist was being "lenient" with the Mexicans and had become the warm friend of Winfield Scott, an ardent Whig. Polk hated Whigs more than he hated Mexicans, and he had moved quickly to squelch the popularity that might carry the war hero into the White House in 1848 by replacing him with a Democratic general. James Knox Polk was like that: vindictive and mean, a lonely, tough little squirrel of a man whose friends called him Little Hickory while his enemies derided him merely as Little Jimmy. Another reason for Trist's dismissal was that Polk had been preparing to raise the price of peace. Influenced by the "screaming-eagle" expansionists in his own party, most of them from the South, he was no longer satisfied with California and the Southwest, but now wanted to annex all of Mexico and perhaps Cuba and the other islands of the Caribbean along with it.

But the Mexican War was, with Vietnam, one of the two most unpopular wars in American history, and Polk was denounced as a warmonger whose unjustified invasion of Mexico was made to extend the area of slavery. Whigs controlling the House had passed a resolution stating that the war had been "unnecessarily and unconstitutionally begun by the President of the United States."

Polk was in a dilemma. If he repudiated this unauthorized treaty as he wished to do, he would prolong this detested war and magnify the erosion of Democratic popularity, while also plunging himself into an all-out battle with the Whigs for funds to maintain the army in Mexico, a conflict he could lose and thus risk the loss of California and the Southwest. So he sent the treaty to the Senate, where it was ratified on February 23 by a vote of 38 to 14. A motion to add to it the controversial Wilmot Proviso, which flatly stated that slavery was to be prohibited in any territory acquired from Mexico, was defeated by 38–15. It seemed to the Democrats who rejected it—proslavery senators from the South, Northerners with Southern sympathies known as doughfaces—that this persistent attempt to limit "Southern rights" had finally been laid to rest, and that the country could now turn to the presidential election of 1848.

Polk was true to his word not to seek reelection, but his fear of a Whig war hero winning the White House was justified when General Zachary Taylor of Louisiana, Old Rough 'n Ready as he was known after his victories in northern Mexico, swept to victory over Lewis Cass, a doughface from Michigan. A coalition of antislavery Whigs and Democrats, assisted by a third party of antislavery Free-Soilers, received enough votes in New York to take that vital state away from Cass. Thus, for the fourth time in its sixty-year history the supposedly antimilitarist American nation had conferred its highest office on a military hero.

Taylor's inauguration in 1849 seemed to launch what was literally an American Golden Age, for the discovery of gold in California had brought a flood of "Forty-niners" pouring into the Sacramento Valley. It was glamorous with the gleaming white sails of the American clipper ships, then the admiration of every sea, and bright in the hopes of thousands of Old World immigrants moving west along the new roads and railroads leading into the lands taken from Mexico and the Indians. In the North the Industrial Revolution gave manufactures a golden shove, while Europe's devouring hunger for cotton crowned that staple king of the South. Eli Whitney's invention of the cotton gin seemed to guarantee that the South would maintain economic as well as political domination over the North, and none but a few thoughtful Southerners could perceive that it had rescued the "peculiar institution" of slavery from that slow death they had desired for it.

America was then the envy of the world, if not the admiration of it. In its sixty brief years of history, the thirteen little seagoing republics on the Atlantic seaboard had not, as European savants confidently predicted, become a congeries of quarreling states unable to unite, but had continued to expand, organizing sixteen more states by the power of Congress, so that those which had created the Federal Union were now outnumbered by those which had been created, and would eventually be overwhelmingly so when the United States, now a continental power stretching from sea to sea, began to organize so many more out of the lands taken from Mexico and the Indians and the remaining territories of the Louisiana Purchase.

Outwardly this development seemed not to have altered the nature of the Union—between 1804 and 1865 the Constitution was not once amended—but inwardly it had wrought vast changes, so that many forms of cultural and economic interdependence were making the country more national than Federal. Indeed, it could hardly have been otherwise during the fever of nationalism that had seized the Western world. Thus the sections had unconsciously developed *separate* nationalisms, each with a different image of the Union not grasped by the other side. If the Southern states displayed a fierce devotion to the Union, it was only insofar as it benefited themselves, and they were with equal passion convinced of their right to *leave* it if such better served their purposes. The North, with its new-state allies only dimly suspicious of this, was possessed by a contrary and just as powerful conviction that the Union must be preserved at all costs, even war—and of this the South in turn had little inkling. Here was the classic formula for war: one side believing the other side won't fight, or one side believing the other will not throw down the gauntlet. The spark that would ignite the powder keg—slavery—was indeed present, had always been present; but in mid-nineteenth-century America both sides were still pretending that the thing that divided them most and about which they cared most—human bondage—was not worth arguing about.

Indeed by 1850 Americans had much to distract them from this vital question, much to be proud of. They had doubled their population every two decades, so that by 1850 it stood at 29 million souls, one million more than the old Mother Country; their merchant fleet and their science were challenging the leading nations of the Old World for global supremacy, and they were developing a national art and literature. Although major cities the equal of those in Europe were emerging in Boston, New York, Philadelphia and Baltimore, and Washington one day would fulfill L'Enfant's splendid design to become a gleaming white city "of magnificent distances," most Americans at mid-nineteenth century were small farmers or mechanics and clerks dwelling in rural peace and plenty. They lived better than their parents had and expected their children to do better. More than all this, they were free men, guaranteed the liberating right to vote by universal manhood suffrage. So they were indeed proud—even bumptious—confident of a secure future bright with progress. How could they perceive that organization of the new lands would reopen the old question of slavery expansion, that Thomas Jefferson's dreadful "firebell in the night" would then renew its clanging with a clangor that could never again be silenced? How were they to know—as their president and secretary of state did not know—that the fruits of the great victory in Mexico were already rotten with the seeds of a terrible and bloody civil war?

2

■

The Crisis of Slavery

DEMOCRACIES are prone to face perilous problems with their heads in the sands. Thus in 1820 the "sacred" Missouri Compromise had been passed, and hosannas were raised to the skies in praise of this final solution of the slavery question. Under it, slavery was prohibited in territory north of 36°30′. Never mind that the South led by Senator John Calhoun of South Carolina had protested that the compromise was unconstitutional. Calhoun maintained that Congress had no power to limit the extension of slavery, while insisting that it had the positive duty to protect it. Slaves were property, just like cattle, and slave-owners had the right to take their property anywhere in the Union. Slavery, said Calhoun, followed the flag.

Such was the Southern position, and although it begged the question of the evil of one man *owning* another, it was allowed to do so because there were powerful men in Congress who feared that to press the South any further would end in disunion and probably civil war. Moreover, both sections were embroiled in a politico-economic power struggle. For sixty years the South, beginning with the "Virginia Dynasty"—which included the two Adamses from Massachusetts—had controlled the Federal government. It now hoped to cement that ascendancy by gaining the allegiance of the new states today known as the Midwest through trade up and down the Mississippi and its tributaries. But then the new railroads began tying the bread basket of America to the Eastern ports and bankers. Calhoun saw clearly that the North—the Midwestern and Eastern states—was becoming stronger. Its population was rapidly increasing, chiefly because immigrants had no wish to go south to compete with slave labor but preferred to remain in the East or migrate to the West. Finally, if slavery were to be put to the ban north of Missouri's southern border, the ranks of the free-soil states would be swelled and the North would become all-powerful.

7

Here was the sectionalism gnawing away at the vitals of the national union. But sectionalism was only the symptom of the deeper cause and infection: slavery. If there had been no black African slaves in the United States there would have been no danger of civil war. Because the slaves were black, the white slavery of antiquity having long since vanished, the South would be able to develop, as it did develop, the defensive doctrine of racial superiority. Without black slavery, of course, there would still have been sectionalism, as there must always be in any federation. In the America of that time, although the Union was universally beloved, citizens were much more prone than nowadays to take pride in their native state, often speaking of it as "my country." The theory of states' rights was advanced not only in the South by leaders such as Calhoun; as recently as the War of 1812 New England had seized upon state sovereignty to defend the Hartford Convention at which outright secession was discussed as a means of protecting economic benefits reaped by the region through the British enemy's deliberate indulgence of it.

Despite widespread protests that the real cause of division was the various differences coalescing in a struggle for power, slavery was the root cause. Without slavery, North and South would indeed have remained almost as different as people sharing the same language, political philosophy, and generally the same race and religion could possibly be. The Southern society was agricultural, aristocratic and fixed, the Northern industrial, democratic and mobile. The North wanted high tariffs to protect its manufactures, the South wanted lower or no tariffs to cheapen the products imported from Europe in exchange for its cotton. Moreover, the South financed its crops with money borrowed in the North. But most important of all, the South employed slave labor, while its capitalist creditor in the North hired free men. Here it was again: the basic difference. Without black slavery the South could indeed have remained agricultural. It also could have hired free men; but if it did, it would not have remained aristocratic. There would have been no "po' white trash" to be despised by aristocrat and black servitor alike. It might be that the wealthy planters who dominated the South could have grown wealthier by such change, but to have accepted such an economy would have reduced the planters in status, would have tarnished the gloss on those mythical descendants of Cavaliers, superior in blood and breeding to all other Americans. Yet, when the South scornfully cried that the so-called free wage-earner of the North was hardly more than an industrial serf, it pointed with much truth to a social evil that would not for another half century be placed on the path to correction. Nevertheless, the free wage-earner did have the vote, and that dignified him. His exploiters could not enslave him, and they had to be careful not to make his life too miserable lest his ballot put some troublesome reformer into political power. Also, the last thing this semi-serf desired was to have his smallest corner of economic freedom erased by the introduction of slave labor into the North.

There it was again, finally: slavery. The South, or rather that class of rich planters who exploited and dominated the region, regarded bondage as the basis of their wealth, power and privilege. They desired, in a phrase that runs through the history of the Slavocracy like the recurrent theme of a fugue, that it be "fixed, controlled and protected by law." Nor did this class differ from any of the other exploiters in human history—human leeches bloated on the blood and sweat of helot and peon, slave and serf, from antiquity to their own time—in that they had no intention of surrendering their position. Thrones and high seats, history shows, are never vacated but must always be emptied. So the apologists of slavery, like the British introducing their infamous, religion-based Penal Code into Ireland, evolved the doctrine of "inequality," through which, by a supreme casuistry, they could proclaim the foul results of a foul policy as the reason for continuing it. Aiming at the degradation of a race by forbidding its members to be free or educated or skilled in any civilizing pursuit, they could then point to the beastliness of their lives as proof that they were subhuman. This was the belief underlying the Dred Scott decision, and in fairness to the South it must be stated that it was also widely held in many of the free states of the North, many of which had either laws barring free blacks from residing within their territory, or habits of hostility that effectively did the same. But the slavery based on this belief was not the economic system of the North, and it was bondage, regularized and enforced, that was the divisive issue, the one sticking point, always seeming to aggravate or magnify all the other sectional differences and rivalries, *because it was a moral issue*—the difference between right and wrong—and thus the slavery question was made sharper and then irreconcilable by the shift from the economic to a moral plane. Why this is so can be understood only if the institution itself is understood.

3
■
Slavery in History and the South

S LAVERY BEGAN when the warrior races of antiquity ceased to torture, kill and sometimes eat their captives and instead put them to work for them. As such, bondage could then be considered a great humanitarian advance, especially when the custom of manumission—freeing a trusted slave as a reward for faithful service—was introduced. Slavery was the economic base of the Greco-Roman civilization and was nowhere criticized or condemned as immoral, but rather approved and justified by such thinkers as Plato and Aristotle. Jesus Christ lived and died in a colony of the Roman Empire and spoke not a word against the institution. When St. Paul wrote in his letter to the Colossians, "Servants, obey in all things your masters," and "Masters, do to your servants that which is just and equal," the word "servants" actually meant slaves. Slavery in ancient times was both cruel and kind: chained men working in mines, on farms and aboard galleys were driven mercilessly until they were broken, but in the homes of the wealthy where they were servants, nurses and even tutors they were held in high esteem. Cicero's letters were edited by his manumitted slave, Tiro. Nevertheless, Roman bondage was revolting, as may be seen in the pages of Cato, Juvenal, Seneca, and even Julius Caesar, who sold 53,000 captured Aduatuci into immediate slavery. Gradually, under the ameliorating influence of Christianity, bondage shed many of its most horrifying customs—especially the chief evil of one man owning another—until it emerged as the far less repulsive medieval institution of serfdom. Slavery seemed to have vanished.

But then came the great age of exploration by European navigators, followed by the scramble among these nations for colonies and profits in the less advanced nations of Asia and Africa and the New World of North and South America. Slavery experienced a rebirth. At first those enslaved

10

were the Indians of the New World, compelled to work in mines and on farms. The practice was denounced by Pope Paul IV in a papal bull insisting that the Indians were true human beings entitled to all the rights and privileges of free men, but papal bulls in those days often were left lying unpublished in episcopal cellars, while the efforts of missionaries to protect the savages earned them the enmity of the colonizers of Catholic France, Spain and Portugal. But then both Catholic and Protestant imperialists realized that the Indians, hunters and food-gatherers unfamiliar with agricultural labor, often collapsed under the pressure. With this came the discovery that the black slaves of West Africa were accustomed to agricultural labor and could be bought cheap from the warlike black races that enslaved them—chief among them the Dahomey, Ashanti and Yoruba. Most of these West African nations, though not nearly as advanced as the Europeans, possessed better-than-primitive economic systems based not only on plantations worked by slave gangs but a significant division of labor, a regulated trade system and craft guilds. Among the Ashanti there was a system of land tenure that placed a brake on the accumulation of land. Nor could a slave-owner accumulate wealth by profiting from the economic surplus produced by slaves: bondsmen worked for themselves and could save enough money to buy freedom. They could also be adopted into friendly families as free men, the ease with which this could be accomplished varying in time and place. Status, then, rested primarily on political and social rather than economic criteria. Moreover, both masters and slaves were black, as they had been mostly white in the Western world of antiquity and the early Middle Ages. Therefore one of the most debasing tenets of American slavery—the doctrine of the black bondsman's natural racial inferiority to his white master—did not exist. True enough, an African slave was still a thing, a chattel, which could be sold from place to place. But there were ameliorations, which never softened the brutal system in the American South. The worst that an African slave had to fear was to be chosen as one of the victims for ritual human sacrifice. These usually occurred during celebrations of military victories. In Dahomey, slaves were slain to provide the late king with a retinue of ghostly servants. These, then, were not the naked, berry-picking cannibals of superstition and vicious legend still present in some American white supremacists' minds. There were indeed African blacks answering that description, but they never either owned slaves or were considered slaveworthy, acting only as slave-catchers for the European powers.

Of these the combined British, French, Dutch, Portuguese and Danish, by the end of the eighteenth century, had no fewer than forty slave depots on the African coasts for the shipment of slaves to their colonies. These white Europeans did not capture the slaves themselves, but rather bought them from individual slave-catchers or those warlike black kingdoms engaged in the slave traffic, usually through the sale of war prisoners. This is not to absolve the whites of guilt in this evil commerce, but only to set the record straight on the source of supply: the brethren of the bondsmen. At the same time American slave ships from the Yankee ports of New England—home of the Abolitionists—were a common sight on the Atlantic Ocean. The colonies of Spain, Portugal, France, Holland and Britain became strongholds of slavery, and the institution flourished in the American North until, beginning with Massachusetts in 1780 and ending with New Jersey in 1804, the Northern states one by one abolished bondage. It was hoped that Dixie would do likewise, especially in the Cotton Kingdom of the Lower South, where the time lost separating the cotton from its seeds was making this staple too expensive to produce. But then in 1794 Eli Whitney of Massachusetts patented his famous cotton gin, a device that did the job so rapidly and cleanly that cotton plantations began to proliferate, with a corresponding rise in the demand for slaves.

Meanwhile slavery was being abolished elsewhere, so that by 1860 the European colonizers, under pressure of both Protestant and Catholic churches and outraged public opinion, had also put the pernicious institution to the ban. In Latin America, all the newly independent nations except Brazil and the Spanish colony of Cuba had freed their slaves. In this they were influenced by the outspoken insistence of the Roman Catholic Church that all races were equally the children of God, as well as by the traditional color-blindness of the mother countries of Spain and Portugal. Huge numbers of the citizens of Latin America were nonwhite: native Indians and mestizos of mixed Indian and white blood. They welcomed a general emancipation, although peonage—a status between slavery and freedom—remained. Yet by 1860 even the Russian czar was contemplating freeing the serfs, so that by then the only places in which men were owned by other men were Brazil, Cuba and the American South.

Of all the abuses of Southern slavery none was more evil than the slave trade. There had always been a certain amount of buying and selling of bondsmen locally but after Congress outlawed the African slave trade in 1808 and the rich cotton lands in the West were opened, a thriving interstate slave trade developed in buying the surplus bondsmen of the Upper South—where some planters sold them to buy fertilizer—and driving them to the Lower South. Slave gangs moving south were a common sight on the main north-south arteries. The men were chained together in pairs to prevent escape, while the women followed behind, leading their children and carrying their possessions in big bundles. Mounted slave dealers armed with long blacksnake whips rode alongside. Although slavery in the North was supposed to have ended in 1804, there still existed as late as 1818 a steady traffic in bondsmen centered in New York and New Jersey.

Auctions usually were held outside the county courthouse, but some were in the dealers' auction rooms and even, in New Orleans, in the lobby of the St. Louis Hotel. Buyers carefully examined slaves standing on the auction block, inspecting their teeth, fingers, muscles and especially their backs for telltale flogging scars that would suggest either indolence or unruliness. Dealers often "merchandised" their "wares," that is, spruced them up with new clothes, oiled skin and blackened gray hairs. As the demand for bondsmen rose, and the inevitable new evil of slave farms appeared, chiefly in Kentucky and Virginia, the price of slaves rose. In 1795 a prime field hand (a male eighteen to twenty-five) brought less than $300 in Virginia and South Carolina, but by 1860 he fetched $1,250 in Virginia and $1,800 in New Orleans. Women were sold at about three-quarters the value of men, although a "fancy girl"—another abuse of the peculiar institution—was worth as much as $2,500 or more.

Auction blocks were often stages for poignantly real scenes of human suffering. One Memphis buyer wrote in his journal: "One yellow woman [mulatto] was sold who had two children. She begged and implored her new master on her knees to buy her children also, but it had no effect, he would not do it. She then begged him to buy her little girl (about 5 years old) but all to no purpose, it was truly heart rending to hear her cries when they were taking her away." He did not specify what happened to the children, although it is probable that they were bought for a low price by a planter or perhaps the owner of a slave farm. Slave children were not considered workable until they were ten.

Slaves also might be sold in the settlement of the estates of dead owners or in mortgage foreclosures, or by planters put in need of money by the extravagance common to their class or even by a college student placing his supposedly beloved slave valet on the block to finance his education. Usually these desperate people lamented the cruel necessity of having to traffic in human flesh, or promised to redeem and free the slaves so sold if their fortunes improved, but none condemned the institution itself. As a rule, slave traders were detested, although some, such as Nathan Bedford Forrest, the mayor of Nashville, Tennessee, and later a famous Confederate cavalry leader, were respected members of their community.

Generally, the huge profits of the slave trade—like the drug traffic of today—attracted clever, avaricious and unscrupulous men. There was even an unholy alliance between traders and planters of the Upper South, who would sell their slaves to the dealers after their crops had been harvested. They were taken to the Lower South, where most of them were quickly sold and the remainder rented out until a more favorable market appeared. Slave smuggling was also widespread, most of the ships being based in New Orleans although some were fitted out in New York City. Such vessels, like the legal African slavers before them, were floating hells with slaves crammed into stinking holds like herrings in a barrel, gasping in the foul air and squirming in their own filth. Fed starvation rations and unattended medically, sometimes as many as one-third of these miserable human beings perished, and yet there was not a jury in the South that would convict a sea captain accused of slave smuggling.

Slave-owning in the South, however, was not nearly as widespread as might be suspected from the region's impassioned defense of the system and the North's scathing denunciation of it. The census of 1850 states that among a white population of 6,184,477, only 347,525 were owners. Even this number is an exaggeration, for a single owner of slaves in more than one place would be entered more than once, and the census lumped slave-hirers together with slave-owners. Probably the figure is closer to 250,000. Taking the more generous number of 300,000, this must be multiplied by five to include the owner's immediate family, which, together with the white overseers and white employees on the estate and their families, comes to a generous total of 2,000,000 Southerners engaged in the ownership or management of slaves. Thus, not a third of the people of the South in 1850 had an interest in slavery; and by 1860 not a fourth had such concern.

Among those owning or hiring bondsmen the vast majority possessed fewer than ten apiece and a clear majority fewer than five each. Only 11 persons were listed in the census of 1850 as owning five hundred or more slaves, and only 254 possessing two hundred or more. In all, 8,000 persons in the South could be classified as "planters," that is, farmers with fifty or more slaves.

Plantation slavery was chiefly the slavery of the Lower South. On the smaller farms the black slaves usually worked under the direct supervision of the owner, and sometimes alongside him. On the bigger plantations, an overseer was usually employed. At an annual salary ranging from $1,000 to $1,500—and for an especially good manager, up to $2,000—it was his duty to see to the sowing, cultivation and harvesting of the crop; to take care of equipment, land and outbuildings; and to regulate the entire economy of the place. He planned and apportioned the labor, maintained discipline by punishing the lazy or unruly, while rewarding the productive slave; issued rations, provided clothing and fuel, and attended to the sick. He was also expected to keep careful records of his expenditures, which, of course, an unscrupulous overseer, especially one employed by an absentee owner, might manipulate for his own profit. Most big planters relying on overseers believed that one man could not handle more than fifty or sixty slaves, and thus, there could be several overseers. Almost all of them were white, although a trusted black driver might be raised to that position. A driver— always black, muscular and masterful—handled a gang of about twenty slaves and was responsible for their productivity.

Surprisingly, few plantations had more than a third of its total force working in the fields. On Episcopal Bishop Leonidas Polk's plantation in Louisiana only a third of his 396 slaves were effective field hands. Productivity was graded by "hands." Thus, quarter-hands were children and the elderly; half-hands the middle-aged; and full hands the mature and able-bodied. Because of the short life expectancy of both whites and blacks in those days, there were relatively few "aunties" and "uncles" for the planter to support. Only 1.2 percent of the blacks lived past seventy, and most of these were house hands.

There was a great distinction between field and house hands. House blacks ate better food, usually from the master's kitchen; wore the cast-off finery of the master and his family; and because they imitated the manners of the masters were often regarded with contempt by the field blacks. House hands often slept in a blanket at the foot of the master's bed. They also had a hierarchy in which the driver, servant and skilled craftsman ranked at the top. Among the female servants the nurse or "Mammy" ranked highest. Because so many house hands were mulattoes they often adopted a superior attitude toward their darker brethren in the fields. Life in the "big house" was thus not nearly as harsh as in the fields, and this sometimes produced a real affection toward the master and his family. When he returned from a trip he might be welcomed with great joy, and on Sundays and holidays there was a kind of reception with the master and mistress standing at the foot of the mansion steps to shake hands with bowing and curtsying house blacks. At least at the big house of the antebellum South there was a much closer integration of blacks and whites. Small children of both races played together happily. Black nurses often suckled the master's children and blacks and whites attended church together, joining in the singing of hymns. Only after the Civil War and the beginning of segregation in the 1890s did the blacks voluntarily withdraw into their own churches. It was at the big house, then, that the myths of the happy, laughing, singing darky and "moonlight and magnolias" was born.

Thus it was upon the field hand that the brutality of American slavery chiefly fell, especially those who had been slaves in their African homeland. There, with the partial exception of Dahomey, bondage had been milder and patriarchal. Even slaves from a conquered tribe might be adopted into a new culture. They could become free human beings in a new homeland. The black slave arriving in America found nothing like this. Ripped from his loved ones, he had, with other half-naked unfortunates, been herded aboard a floating cesspool to be taken thousands of miles from home to a new land which offered him nothing but hard blows. He could not profit from his labor; he could not buy his freedom; he dared not attempt to escape for, without knowledge of a new language and with his black skin, there was no place to hide; and not until he did learn to speak English did he discover that there was indeed a sanctuary in the North either just across a river or fifteen hundred miles away. But this last act of desperation was an option reserved only for his children, brave and hardy enough to risk the terrible penalties that would be exacted upon recapture.

In Africa there had been racial prejudice, of course, but only the antipathy of one tribe for another. But it was not based on color as it was in this hated new homeland. Here he was not a human being but rather a beast of burden, and was treated hardly better than those lower animals.

Field slaves were issued clothing of the coarsest, cheapest fabric. Small children wore a shirt and nothing else. Men were given two cotton shirts and pants in summer, and in the fall a pair of woolen pants, a jacket, a hat, a pair of rough brogans, and every second or third year a blanket. Women received cloth to make their dresses, bonnets and kerchiefs. Some women wove their own cloth. Field slaves were required to take a bath once a week and wear clean clothes on Sunday. Food, though plentiful, was tasteless, monotonous and undernourishing.

Slave quarters were usually a cluster of cabins lying behind the big house. On large plantations the cabins were in rows along a street with the overseer's house at the end. Black drivers policed the area. As usual, a cabin's comfort and cleanliness—or lack of both—depended on whether the master was kind or cruel. Considerate planters built cabins of brick or plank-and-clapboard, providing the family with two or even three rooms on the first floor and a loft above. The best were as large as twenty-one by twenty-one feet with fireplaces and comfortable if rude furniture. But then there were the little, windowless log cabins, twelve by twelve, dark, dirty, and verminous. There was little privacy in these dwellings. Patrols roaming the roads on the lookout for "suspicious persons" or runaway slaves might burst into the cabins unannounced, searching for firearms or explosives.

Discipline on the plantations was maintained by the overseer, the black slave-driver and the master himself. Punishment was usually by flogging, although there were many planters like Jefferson Davis who forbade the whip, invoking other penalties such as depriving a slave of his meat. Davis's brother Joseph even introduced slave juries, which tried their accused brethren, frequently reducing the sentences or even pardoning the convicted culprit. But most planters believed that flogging was necessary to maintain discipline. A Louisiana cotton planter named Bennett Barrow personally flogged his slaves two or three times a week, either for picking "trashy" cotton, for laziness, for running away or for allowing themselves or their cabins to become filthy. At times Barrow was cruel, especially with runaways. One he "ran and trailed about a mile, treed him, made the dogs pull him out of the tree. Bit him very badly, think he will stay home a while." Of another: "dogs soon tore him naked, took him Home Before the other negroes at dark & made the dogs give him another overhauling." But Barrow also provided incentives for good work, by giving his slaves holidays or a store-bought suit of clothes. He often donated whiskey for a slave dance or made money gifts at Christmas. At Louisiana Governor A. B. Roman's plantation dances were held in the sugar house every Sunday, and the girls appeared in white crinoline dresses with pink sashes.

Some plantations had strict codes governing the punishment of slaves. Whipping was never to be done in anger or to exceed twenty lashes. But this did not seem to bind overseers, either white or black, as much as masters. Thus slaves on absentee plantations were more liable to harsh treatment than those living under the eye of the master. On the whole, most planters seem to have been considerate of their slaves, if only for economic reasons. Thus both master and mistress were diligent in attending to sick slaves. Some of their remedies, however, might have been the envy of a witch doctor.

But there were also cruel masters, among them Dr. Richard Eppes, a Virginia aristocrat who owned three plantations. A graduate of the University of Virginia and a devout Episcopalian, Eppes nevertheless seems to have been unrivaled in the variety of personal reasons for reaching for the whip. On April 2, 1852, he whipped William for leaving the plantation without a pass; on April 16 he whipped George "for not bringing over milk for my coffee, being compelled to take it without"; on July 2, he flogged Dick for stealing sugar and telling a lie; on August 18, 1859, he ordered Miles whipped for allowing the cows to get into a cornfield, while "correcting"

Tom in an unknown manner for galloping one of his carriage horses; and on September 2 he personally gave Henry fifteen stripes for violation of plantation rules.

Maintenance of discipline among the slaves, then, undoubtedly depended on the whip—perhaps used a bit too readily, but never to the extent suggested by Abolitionist literature. To injure or maim one's bondsmen simply did not make economic sense. Indeed wherever possible slave labor was protected from dangerous occupations. Risky handling of bounding bales of cotton sliding down chutes onto steamboats was kept from slaves and given to immigrant Irish. Masters might hire out slaves to dig tunnels, but kept them away from blasting. Nor were they hired out to clear malarial swamps.

Hired slaves were used extensively to build railroads and public projects. They were also rented to work in factories, although their masters looked askance at the practice once they began to receive privileges suggestive of racial equality or learned to run machinery like white men. Factories might also become schools for subversion, but the planters closed their eyes to this possibility once the rising rates for hired slave labor reached 10 percent a year of a slave's purchase price. Thus a slave earning $150 or $180 annually could turn a tidy profit for a master spending only about $21 or $22 a year for his keep.

In a system in which a slave was regarded as a valuable economic unit, there were an astonishing number of blacks murdered by angry mobs. In June of 1854 a slave accused of rape near Ryalia, Mississippi, was seized by a mob which castrated him, hung him by his heels and then emptied shotguns into him. In the following month another black charged with the same crime was tortured, mutilated, tied to a tree and then burned to the ground before a crowd of two thousand onlookers. Late in 1855 a slave was burned for attempted rape near Lexington, Mississippi, while in the spring of 1856 another was reduced to ashes for murder at Mount Meigs, Alabama. Two more such burnings occurred in Alabama and Missouri in 1858. No master is known to have participated in these barbarities; indeed, for a master to kill a slave, even in a fit of passion, would be a kind of economic suicide. These atrocities were mob vengeance for the unforgivable sin: a crime against a white, especially a woman. It is also possible that the slaves' masters received compensation for the loss of their bondsmen. If the slaves had been tried, convicted and executed, under Southern law their masters would have been recompensed. Finally, it must be emphasized that similar atrocities also occurred in the North in colonial times—specifically in New York and New Jersey—and that the evils of slavery did not proceed from fundamental flaws in the character of Southerners but sprang from the institution itself. Northerners and Europeans who settled in the South behaved toward slaves exactly like the native-born.

Another vice of the system—miscegenation—cannot be so easily explained or dismissed. According to the census of 1860 there were some 588,000 mulattoes among the 4,441,800 blacks in the country. Probably this figure is far too low. On the plantations owned by Jefferson Davis and his brother Joseph—two men of extreme moral rectitude—among Jefferson's 113 slaves, 31 were mulattoes; and among his brother's 355, there were 104. This ratio of more than one-quarter is far larger than the 13.2 percent for the 1860 census and 7.7 for the one in 1850.

Responsibility for this light-skinned black population rests almost entirely with white males—chiefly Southerners—for though more mulattoes were born of white mothers than is commonly supposed, they were comparatively few. It was notorious that the blood of some of Dixie's most aristocratic families flowed in the veins of slaves. Wives were heartbroken by their husband's attachment to their black mistresses, anguished when their sons fell into the same vice. Southern women petitioning for divorce frequently complained that their husband was cohabiting with a colored woman. One woman who reproached her errant spouse received this rebuke: "Damn you, if that sticks by you, I will bring her here tomorrow in the gig by the side of me in style." Not only planters and their sons frequented the slave quarters. Overseers were just as promiscuous. Rachel O'Connor, a remarkable woman planter in Louisiana, complained that one of her most distressing problems came from her overseers "sneaking after those negro girls." In disgust she made two of her black slaves overseers, and found them better than their white predecessors.

Miscegenation outraged the fathers and brothers of slave girls, embittered jealous wives, made trembling neurotics of unwilling recipients of the planter's favor, and filled those children condemned to a harsh life of slavery with resentment for the better life led by their lighter-skinned half-brothers and half-sisters. It was a custom so deeply embedded in the mores of the ruling class that few voices were raised to criticize it. One of them, the Reverend J. D. Paxton of Kentucky, cried:

"The condition of female slaves is such, that promises and threatenings and management can hardly fail to conquer them. They are entirely dependent on their master. They have no way to make a shilling, to procure any article they need. Like all poor people they are fond of finery, and wish to imitate those who are above them. What now, are not presents and kind treatment, or the reverse, if they are not complying, likely to effect on such persons? That the vice prevails to a most painful extent is proved from the rapid increase of mulattoes. Oh, how many have fallen before this temptation: so many, that it has almost ceased to be a shame to fall!"

Another evil, not so readily perceptible and thus even less frequently denounced, was slave breeding. It is said that nothing could anger the great Henry Clay more than charges that his state of Kentucky, and Virginia as well, were centers of slave breeding. There is no proof that *organized* farms for the breeding of slaves existed, but there is no doubt that many owners found the *incidental* profits of slave increase irresistible. They deliberately sought "rattling good breeders," that is, especially fertile women, and mated them early, anticipating a doubling of population in fifteen years and a quadrupling in thirty. Some undoubtedly conducted a breeding business. John C. Reed in his book *The Brothers' War* claimed that this "was what the master thought of and talked of all day long."

In 1859 an attorney from Wilmington, North Carolina, en route to Georgia by train to hire slaves, talked openly of his breeding business. He bought girls of sixteen or so, hired them out for $6 a month, and mated them. They might lose a few months hire by confinement, but their children paid handsomely for the lost time: $1,000 for a girl of eighteen, $1,500 for a boy of twenty. "So you see, it's a moneymaking business. Why, our richest men have made their fortunes from it. There's old Squire Brown, who didn't use to be worth a red cent, and always was as poor as could be, now lives in one of the biggest houses in Wilmington, keeps his carriage and toddles off to the springs every summer. And when people wonder how he got rich so fast, he tells them that they forget that his niggers increase as fast as other people's."

As may be expected, the breeders sought strength and size in the mating; and, where possible, beauty, in hopes that the baby would be a female and grow up to be one of those high-priced fancy girls. Traffic in fancy girls was centered in New Orleans, where they were bought for immoral purposes by saloonkeepers, gamblers and dissolute young men of wealth.

Thus three of the radical defects of slavery: the maltreatment and misery of the bondsmen, their inability to rise above their low station and the sexually immoral treatment of their women by their white masters. But there was a fourth, perhaps the worst of all in its far-reaching effects— effects that remain to this day: the system's hostility to family life among the blacks.

■　　■　　■

In slavery disruption of the family life of the slaves was common, springing from a general lack of respect for marriage and enforced sales which often broke up a family. White cohabitation with black women was also a factor. Binding ties in slave marriages were not recognized by law, and although some planters wished that such unions be made as valid as those among whites, most found this to be inimical to their economic interests, for much of the value of slave property depended on its fluidity. Thus the breakup of families was common under the system. A humane master might keep slave families united while he lived, but after his death ruthless executors were prone to send them to the auction block in the way most profitable: to wit, singly. Just as pernicious was the Southern rule that the child followed the mother. If it had been that the child followed the father, a strong incentive might have existed to make the slave marriage legal and permanent, and this, in turn, would have encouraged the master to develop a stronger bond with the family. Thus, when slaves were united in a true religious ceremony, the minister omitted the phrase "until death do ye part," substituting "unless you are unavoidably separated."

Slave marriage could not have been more casual, often celebrated by merely jumping over a broomstick. Large planters discouraged marriages between slaves of differing plantations, claiming that they interfered with efficiency, but they were common among the smaller slaveholders. Easily made, they were just as quickly undone, although conjugal fidelity was observed while they lasted. Most Southerners believed that chastity was uncommon among the blacks. But such "immorality" sprang as much from their low station as from any moral defect. Where no attempt was made to enforce a moral standard, where almost all children were born out of wedlock and innocent amusements were few, it could hardly have been otherwise. Moreover it ill became the fathers of all those mulattoes to preach continence. "The whole commerce between master and slave," said Thomas Jefferson, "is a perpetual exercise of the most boisterous passions, the most unremitting despotism on the one part, and degrading submission on the other." Jefferson, of course, had a black mistress of his own.

Promiscuity also militated against the dignity of the father. A male slave might at one time be the father of two or more children, all of whom, of course, followed the mother and were thus reared without benefit of a figure of authority. There was also the practice, born, it appears, of a pity flowing from a sense of guilt, of selling mothers with their children, thus bereaving a father and husband. But mothers were also frequently disregarded, their infants literally torn from their breasts and sold. Although ten was generally considered the age at which a slave child could commence work, it was often begun at eight. Most dealers dealt in children ten to twelve and would advertise for those age six to nine. A child sold forty or fifty miles away from his mother was lost.

Slavery was far less productive than the free labor of the North. Slave gangs on the big plantations worked reasonably well under close supervision, but to assign to them more than one or two operations was prohibitively expensive. All contemporary observers and students of the antebellum Southern economy seem agreed that slaves produced about a third as much as free Irish and British laborers. They were at best indifferent workers. They broke tools and abused livestock. A hoe in the South had to be three times as strong as the Northern one used by free laborers and small farmers. After it was found that mules and horses plowed better than oxen, the North used horses because they were the most productive, but the South chose mules because they could endure more abuse. An English traveler has recorded seeing a slave trying to make a mule move by throwing stones at its feet. Livestock were so neglected that hogs averaged 200 pounds and more in the North but barely reached 140 in the South.

How could it have been otherwise? How could a black man held in contempt as no better than a beast of burden possibly care about excellence? Where was his profit? Incentives there were, yes, but the highest of these rewards were not the equal of what a free worker in the North could earn by his own toil. Of course the black field slaves loafed, abused equipment and livestock, feigned illness, and were guilty of slowdowns, waste and self-inflicted injuries. They were not stupid or unaccustomed to hard work, as the contemporary explanations of their indifference maintain. They knew what they were doing. They were sabotaging a system that made a duke of the man in the big house and gave them $22 a year worth of sustenance. This was passive resistance—"playing dumb"—the one way in which exploited colonials or enslaved people can express their resentment of such injustice. Nor did the black slaves fear any terrible reprisal, for they understood economic values and were quite aware that chained though they were, it was upon them that their lordly master depended.

Whether consciously or not, the so-called Cavaliers of the South—that is, the planter class, farmers with fifty or more slaves—seemed to have borrowed from the British aristocracy which they so much admired and imitated the device for dominance that can only be described as king worship. When the sovereign who sits atop the blue-blood pyramid is frequently seen in public crowned and clothed in satins and ermine, guarded by armed and colorfully uniformed soldiers, surrounded by elegant and fawning courtiers, bands playing, banners waving—all the paraphernalia of royalty designed to inspire respect, reverence and even awe—he will still produce this reaction among the people if he appears among them alone and casually dressed. This is because the outward ornaments of wealth and power have made of him an awesome being. So too did the Southern planters use conspicuous consumption to invest themselves with a similar aura. They have been called squanderers and spendthrifts, but every dime they invested in satins and silks, jewelry and perfume for their women, in college education for their children, beautiful horses, fine wines, Havana cigars, handsome clothing for themselves, trips abroad for the entire family together with balls and cotillions and lavish barbecues for their friends and neighbors, was money well invested in maintaining their political and social control of the South. Trained in two skills—politics and statecraft—they dominated the state legislatures and thus were easily able to perpetuate their system at home while retaining such command of the White House and the Capitol that they could contain the menace from the North.

Although the planter was fond of describing himself as a capitalist, he and his system were actually the antithesis of capitalism. Usually capitalism is described as a system involving the interaction of four parts of a free society. These are a democratic government of free men by and for themselves, an open market, a commercial-industrial class and a moral-cultural order embracing the churches, academia, the media and critical intellectuals. So long as these four remain in fruitful tension, with none of them alone or in combination achieving an ascendancy over the others, the society remains free and productive. But in the South what may justly be called the Slavocracy of the planters everywhere strangled or retarded the development of each of these features of capitalism. There was nowhere any opposition strong enough to break the grip of this class.

A bourgeoisie such as arose in Europe to challenge the power of the nobility and give birth to capitalism was in Dixie but a small commercial class, either aspiring to the status of planters themselves, or else content to serve the planters. Southern yeomanry, unlike their European counterparts, lacked the purchasing power to sustain industrial development. All the planters wanted from the factories was cheap slave clothing and cheap farm implements. Because of the agrarian nature of the Slavocracy there were no large cities—saving New Orleans, built by Spanish and French Creoles—to draw unto themselves a coterie of subversives: writers, dissidents, intellectuals and other dangerous innovators. Southern banking also served the planters. Banks put prominent planters on their boards of directors and were closely regulated by the planter-dominated legislatures. Like the Southern industrialist and merchant, the banks were never a middle-class counterweight to the power of the planters but rather their servants. From the moral-cultural dimension which is probably the most vital counter-vailing power of a truly free capitalist society, there came not a word of criticism or a sign of opposition, but rather enthusiastic support of the system. The churches busied themselves only in comforting the slaves, not in attacking the injustice of their condition, while quoting biblical texts to justify the doctrine of white supremacy evolved by Southern intellectuals.

Planter values were aristocratic, not capitalist. The planter empha-sized family and status, a high code of honor and a life of luxury and ease. Capitalist values of thrift and hard work were abhorrent to him, and he detested the crass commercialism, vulgarity and bustle of the North. Though he did not despise the acquisitive spirit—loving luxury as he did—he could not abide the Yankee's worship of the dollar. His attitude is best expressed by the axiom: "The Northerner loves to make money, the South-erner to spend it."

Planters were intensely proud of their social graces, their admitted poise, grace and dignity proceeding from their independence and unques-tioned habit of command. But they were also ashamed of their dependence for all of their status and wealth on a despised race which they and their sycophants defined as subhuman. This accounts for their Jekyll-Hyde na-tures: strength, grace and gentleness concealing violence, hatred and insta-bility. Mrs. Mary Chesnut of Charleston in her famous *Diary from Dixie* describes the planter best: "My husband's father is kind, and amiable when not crossed, given to hospitality on the grand scale, jovial, genial, courtly in his politeness. But he is as absolute a tyrant as the Czar of Russia, the Khan of Tartary, or the Sultan of Turkey." Of his love for his beautiful plantation and host of slaves, she writes: "These are his Gods; he worships his own property."

Most planters could not abide criticism, and rejected the appeals of such perceptive agrarian innovators as Edmund Ruffin of Virginia, who advocated diversifying crops like the prosperous Yankee farmers or at least saving money by producing home-grown foods to feed the slaves. Instead they stuck to their one-crop system and set aside their worst land to grow food.

The phrase "soil depletion" was anathema to them. Although the soil of the "Black Belt"—so-called because slaves outnumbered whites three to two—was among the finest in the world and cotton was not an especially exhausting crop, the rapidity of the depletion of the Southern soil astonished and frightened many planters. It was the basis of their ardor for an expansionist policy, once it also became clear that there would come a day when the moving frontier came to a halt and there would be no more virgin soil to exploit. Although soil science was not in those days a highly developed discipline, it was known by 1850 that artificial manures may maintain soil fertility for long periods; that crops require phosphates and salts of alkalis; that non-leguminous crops such as the Southern staples require a supply of nitrogenous compounds and that fallowing produces an increase in them. Reformers like Ruffin pleaded with the planters to reform their practices, recommended deep plowing, crop rotation, the use of legumes and manuring. These suggestions also were ignored, although in fairness to the planters it must be observed that there was really no way they could implement them. Slavery would not permit it.

The one-crop system perpetuated by slavery prevented crop rotation; the planter's fondness for expensive status symbols put him always in debt and thus unable to obtain the capital to buy fertilizers, artificial or otherwise; his slaves' abuse of livestock left him with insufficient manure to cover his vast fields, and even if he had the money to buy livestock to produce manure, that would be as economically feasible as burning down a barn to roast an egg; the poor quality of the only farm equipment he dared to entrust to the slaves obviated deep plowing; while the general carelessness and waste of the slaves made all attempts at soil reclamation unlikely to succeed.

There it was again: slavery. The planter's independence depended on these despised beings, as they well knew. He also knew that they were sabotaging him, which is why he was always reaching for the whip. Two-thirds of plantation corporal punishment was meted out for negligence and carelessness; but it didn't change a thing. Perhaps more severe punishment might have produced a salutary fear in the hearts of these black people, but one does not improve the output of an expensive labor force by whittling it down. The Romans and Nazis could work slaves to death because their victorious armies provided them with dirt-cheap bondsmen. Planters could not.

The system of slavery, then, was the chief cause of soil depletion and low productivity. However, it is extremely difficult to assess slavery's profitability because of so many variables, such as the tendency to assign slaves to food crops during a period of low prices, or the extent of the output of slaveless white farmers or of white farmers with fewer than fifty bondsmen, which was the criterion for belonging to the planter class. Planters had many problems: the loss to bad weather and pests of anywhere to half or a quarter of the anticipated yield; substantial crops but low prices; an epidemic carrying off a large part of the labor force; high interest rates; sustained periods of low profits and even loss; and the necessity of supporting the labor force during bad times when a Northern manufacturer might retrench through layoffs. Probably the only way to suggest—not prove—low productivity in the slave system is to compare the Northern and Southern standards of living.

Slavery gave the South a valuable exportable surplus of cotton, rice, sugar and tobacco. It is doubtful that free white labor could have produced the quantity of staples that the slave-gang system did. But most of the profits from these exports went to a small proportion of the people in the South. Southerners below the planter status did not compare in wealth to those below the rank of tycoon in the North. Travelers below the Mason-Dixon line and the Ohio River testify to this fact again and again in their diaries and letters. Northern farms were neat and prosperous and worth more than twice as much an acre as the run-down farms of the South. Farmers in Dixie lived only slightly better than their grandfathers had, occupying the same rough log cabins and eating the same tasteless diet, whereas those in the North were much better off than their fathers. Frederick Law Olmsted, who traveled extensively in the South, reported that in the homes he visited between the Mississippi and the upper James nine times out of ten he slept with others in a bed that stank, with but one sheet, if any; he washed with utensils common to the entire household; he saw no gardens, no fruit, no flowers, no tea, no cream, no sugar, no wheat bread; no curtains, no couch, no lifting windows; and in the living rooms no carpets or mats. All of these houses were the homes of slaveholders, some of small planters, and all were verminous. He also did not see, except in one or two towns, a thermometer, a copy of Shakespeare, an engraving, a piano or a sheet of music.

It was slavery and the Slavocracy that made the South so much poorer than the North. A few perceptive planters were aware of this, and knew that the system was doomed. But they had no intention of becoming the first dominant class in human history to step down voluntarily from their pedestals. Even when they clamored for expansion so as to provide new fertile soil or insisted on their right to take their human property anywhere they wished, they knew that nature had already begun to toll the death knell for the peculiar institution. The semi-arid lands in Utah and New Mexico, territories opened to slavery by the Compromise of 1850, were unsuited to the practice, and if they had been rich in soil instead, Southern slavery would have been unable to compete with cheap Mexican labor. By 1860 not a single slave lived in New Mexico, only two in Kansas and fifteen in Nebraska Territory. Slavery might have thrived in southern California except that the residents of that state had outlawed the institution. Only the "black waxy" lands of central Texas could have supported slavery, but it did not appear because of the lack of wood for fencing (barbed wire had not yet been invented), the fear of droughts and the absence of railroads.

Yet the Southern leaders continued to clamor for the "right" to extend slavery into territory they knew to be inimical to the system. Perhaps exclusion of slaves seemed to them to attach a stigma to slaveholding and by extension to the entire South, always so sensitive on a point of honor. Surely the refusal to extend slavery meant denial of equal protection of the laws. Whatever the reason, when the dispute shifted from the economic to the moral plane it became insoluble.

4
■
The House Divides

DOWN DEEP the problem *was* moral. If slaves were property, then a slaveholder did have the right to take his slaves into any corner of the Union and expect the government to protect him in his possession of them there. But if it was wrong to make chattels of human beings, then at the very least the nation could not permit this evil to spread. Outright abolition, of course, was hardly even discussed by those Northern leaders who wished to preserve the Union. The South had some $2 billion invested in slaves and followed a way of life that despised labor as fit only for bondsmen. Southerners considered their society superior to the North's, and it is highly doubtful that they would have accepted even compensatory emancipation—that is, to have the government repay them at the "market value" of their freed blacks. To remove the "peculiar institution" from the fabric of Southern society was just not possible, because that fabric was woven with the thread of slavery. Many Northern leaders, then, recognized this seemingly ineluctable fact, just as they preferred to ignore or remain indifferent to the question of the morality of slavery.

The Abolitionists of the North were not indifferent. At first they were temperate in their criticism of slavery. They considered it an incongruity in a free society and resented the fact that much of the South's political power sprang from the fact that three-fifths of the slave population was counted in apportioning slave-state representation. Gradually, however, the moderates gave way to sincerely outraged crusaders such as William Lloyd Garrison, who founded his anti-slave newspaper in 1831 with the declaration: "On this subject I do not wish to think, or speak, or write, with moderation . . . I will be harsh as truth and as uncompromising as justice. . . . I am in earnest—I will not equivocate—I will not excuse—I will not retreat a single inch. AND I WILL BE HEARD."

He was heard, and eventually the South began censoring Abolitionist literature pouring through the mails and proposed a gag on anti-slavery petitions in Congress. But the Abolitionist movement grew, and as it did it grew less temperate. In ever more strident tones its disciples denounced slavery as a crime and a curse and quoted the Bible as well as the Declaration of Independence to prove that all men were created equal. They harried the slave-catchers who were sent north by the masters of escaped slaves (and who sometimes also kidnapped free blacks under the pretext that they were fugitives), and they organized the famous Underground Railroad by which escaped blacks were passed from house to house at night until they reached some far northern sanctuary or even crossed into Canada. They were not always popular in the North, these crusaders burning with a thirst for justice, and Ralph Waldo Emerson once advised them to love their neighbors a little more and their black brethren less. But they would not leave their more apathetic neighbors alone so long as slavery flourished in the United States. Hating bondage with such a fierce, deep hatred that they sometimes seemed just a little hateful themselves, disdaining compromise and ready to accept even disunion as a consequence of their goal of abolition, these fanatics nevertheless made more and more Americans realize that slavery was both a social injustice and a dreadful moral evil; and if they rubbed some delicate natures the wrong way, they also kept the public conscience awake.

They also drove the South to the position of defending slavery as a moral right and a social good. The glories of those ancient civilizations that had rested on slavery were extolled, while the Bible was quoted not only to sanction bondage but to demonstrate that God had deliberately created inferior races such as the blacks to be the servants of superior people such as the white Cavaliers of the South. In the South the wants of the blacks were more than cared for, it was argued, while in the hypocritic North a wage-earner was rarely paid enough to purchase the necessities of life.

So the gap widened. More and more Southerners became willing to pick up the gauntlet of disunion thrown down by the Abolitionists, and the South began to dream of a great slaveholding republic stretching from sea to sea. Then, in 1849, California decided to skip the territorial phase of organization and requested admission to the Union as a free-soil state with a constitution prohibiting slavery—and with that the South talked openly of secession.

Henry Clay, the "Great Pacificator" who had brought off the Missouri Compromise, came forward once again to preserve the Union. Clay realized that the Union was not yet capable of dealing with secession. In January of 1850 he proposed a set of this-for-that compromises which touched off one of those great debates that have been characteristic of American history from the time of the Federalists to the Truman-MacArthur controversy during the Korean War.

It took place in the Senate, among the old lions—Clay, Calhoun, Webster—and such rising young leaders as Jefferson Davis of Mississippi, Stephen Douglas of Illinois, William Seward of New York and Salmon P. Chase of Ohio.

With all his conciliatory skill, Clay pleaded with the North not to insist on the Wilmot Proviso prohibiting slavery in the new territories, and to return fugitive slaves. He told the South that secession was not constitutional and would not be tolerated.

After Clay spoke, Calhoun's ultimatum was issued. "I have, Senators, believed from the first that the agitation of the subject of slavery would, if not prevented by some timely and effective measure, end in disunion." The words were spoken by Calhoun's friend, Senator James M. Mason of Virginia. Calhoun himself sat silent, wrapped in his cloak like a ghostly hawk, dying of catarrh. But his words were a clarion to the South: the North must "cease the agitation of the slave question."

Now it was the turn of Daniel Webster. It was his last great appearance. He spoke once again with that marathon grandiloquence which was typical of his time, with all his old oratorical skill: the thunderous voice and the imposing figure and massive head, the pointing finger and the questioning eye. "I wish to speak today," he began, "not as a Massachusetts man, not as a Northern man, but as an American. . . . I speak today for the preservation of the Union. 'Hear me for my cause.' " Webster supported Clay's compromise proposals, even a more stringent Fugitive Slave Law, repugnant as it was to him. And he warned the South that it could not expect secession without strife. "Sir, your eyes and mine are never destined to see that miracle! . . . There can be no such thing as a peaceable secession."

Senator Seward, a spokesman for the antislavery faction, and a leader-to-be of the yet unborn Republican Party, opposed the compromise and appealed to "a higher law than the Constitution." Seward's appeal to the Almighty—which disgusted Webster—had little effect on the debate. Webster's masterly speech and the powerful support of Douglas of Illinois carried the day for what has been called the Compromise of 1850.

A resolution was adopted providing (1) admission of California as a free-soil state; (2) organization of the territories of New Mexico (including Arizona) and Utah without reference to slavery; (3) a new and stringent fugitive slave law; (4) abolition of the slave trade in the District of Columbia.

President Taylor did not like the Compromise, and might have vetoed it—except that as the debate raged he fell victim to a combination of Fourth of July oratory and medical exuberance. After listening to a two-hour speech in the boiling sun, Old Zack tried to cool off with large helpings of cucumbers washed down with cold milk. He became ill with acute gastroenteritis, from which he might have recovered had not his doctors sprung to his side to stuff him full of calomel, opium, ipecac and quinine, after which they bled and blistered him until, on July 9, 1850, the Angel of Death came to his rescue.

His successor, Vice President Millard Fillmore of Buffalo, was a man more friendly to compromise. He was also the perfection of mediocrity. The measure of his outlook and insight was his expressed hope that the slavery question had reached its "final settlement."

Although the new Fugitive Slave Law all but silenced secessionist talk in the South, it stuck in Northern throats. "This filthy enactment," Emerson called it, and declared: "I will not obey it, by God." Actually the law defeated the purpose of the Compromise. In placating the South it infuriated the North, and thus guaranteed that "agitation of the slave question" would not cease—as the South demanded as the price of union—but would increase. And then, in 1852, Harriet Beecher Stowe published *Uncle Tom's Cabin.*

No book written in America has even approached *Uncle Tom's Cabin* in its influence on American history.* Serialized in a magazine at first, each installment was eagerly awaited by millions of readers. In book form it sold 300,000 copies in less than a year, and eight presses were kept busy day and night catching up with the demand. *Uncle Tom* was also translated across the world, and plays based upon it gave additional millions the opportunity to hear Mrs. Stowe's message. Slavery, she said, debases all: master as well as slave and the society that permits it. She said this in a style that was ordinary, and through characters who were crude caricatures of the good and gentle slave and the cruel, crass master, yet her theme erupted in the American conscience with titanic force; and after it was published it was no longer possible for Northerners to remain indifferent to slavery or for Southerners to pretend that the problem had been settled.

Alarmed and angered as the South was, it still kept its political head. In 1852, the year of *Uncle Tom's* publication, the all-powerful Democratic

*When Mrs. Stowe visited the White House during the Civil War, Lincoln greeted her with the remark: "So this is the little lady who made this big war."

Party bowed to Southern wishes and nominated Franklin Pierce for president. Although Pierce was from New Hampshire, he was regarded as a doughface. His opponent was his old military chief from Mexico City days, General Winfield Scott. The Whigs, torn by factions, had decided to go with the old war-hero formula again. But Franklin Pierce won by a margin wide enough to contain the corpse of the expiring Whig Party, and Scott's defeat—his second—seems to have demonstrated that, except for the unique George Washington, generals seeking to be president had better be rough-and-ready rather than full of fuss-and-feathers.

Pierce was the third mediocre president in a row. Without real convictions of his own and always persuaded by the last man to talk to him, especially if it were Secretary of War Jefferson Davis, he was the butt of friend and foe alike. Yet his was one of the stormiest of administrations, chiefly because Stephen Douglas, the senator from Illinois who had once hailed the Missouri Compromise as a "sacred thing, which no ruthless hand would ever be reckless enough to disturb," lifted his own to kill it.

Stephen Arnold Douglas, the Little Giant from Illinois, five feet full of bounce, brilliance and belligerence, was born in Brandon, Vermont, in 1813. Shortly afterward the family migrated to Illinois, where, in Jacksonville, Douglas hung up his shingle to practice law before he was eligible to vote. He had also by then attained his full height, exactly sixty inches. But his body was thick and durable, crowned by a massive head on which a shock of luxuriant black hair was combed backward in a lionesque mane. Indeed there was much of the lion in Stephen Douglas, and when he did turn twenty-one he leaped into politics with a roar. At that age he was elected Illinois state's attorney, and it is a measure of how far sheer determination shorn of little knowledge of the law and none of jurisprudence might carry a lawyer in those days that at twenty-eight he was a judge on the Illinois supreme court. At thirty he began two terms as a Democratic representative in Congress and at thirty-four embarked on his meteoric career in the Senate.

Douglas was self-educated, but he had none of that wide-ranging knowledge which, with perception and reflection, makes a politician a statesman. Masterful politician that Douglas was, he was nothing more. He read only lawbooks, government manuals and accounts of debates. He could not generalize and had little power of abstract thought. Seldom writing letters, keeping no diary, he was so ignorant of so many fields that he became ill-informed on all of them. Yet, he was driven by two deep and burning convictions: one, that it was the destiny of the United States to push across the plains and over the Rockies to the shores of the Pacific; the other, his almost religious faith in popular self-government.

Few senators could withstand Stephen Douglas in debate. John Quincy Adams gaped in astonishment when the short, stocky Illinoisan arose in the House, stripping off his cravat and unbuttoning his jacket to deliver one of his first speeches, gesticulating wildly, his face convulsed and his deep booming bass voice reverberating around the chamber so that Adams thought he had "lashed himself into such a heat that if his body had been made of combustible matter, it would have burnt out." One of Douglas's great strengths was in drawing useful friends to him. He could seize a man's hand, fix him with a piercing eye, and then, his face relaxing in a charming smile, remark: "Remember, I'm counting on you." He was also the improviser par excellence. Never operating on a general plan, he met each crisis with a rapidly devised improvisation, relying upon his personal drive to overcome it, which he often did. But the improviser takes no thought of the consequences of his actions, of which there can be no more serious defect in a political leader, and this great flaw in Douglas was to lead to disaster. A lesser evil was his willingness in debate to twist logic or misstate facts.

He also drank too much. It was not uncommon to see him stride from the floor of the Senate where he had demolished some unwary opponent to enter the nearest saloon and there find a crony with whom, arm in arm, he would empty a bottle of whiskey. At Toledo one day he staggered into a sleeping car half drunk, bottle in hand, and tried to drag William Seward outside to address a crowd. Finally, Douglas tended to exalt material factors over the moral, and thus he could dismiss the problem of slavery as late as 1860 as "one of climate, of political economy, of self-interest."

His own self-interest was unfortunately at work, when, in 1854, he introduced his infamous Kansas-Nebraska Act. Douglas was by then a heavy speculator in western lands and so friendly with the Illinois Central Railroad that he was given a private railroad car. He also aspired to the Democratic presidential nomination in 1856. On the first two counts he wanted a proposed transcontinental railway to follow the central route from Chicago, and on the third he wanted an explosive political issue for 1856.

To gain approval of the central railway route he needed the support of Southern senators. So in a bill to divide the territory through which the railroad would pass into the future states of Kansas and Nebraska, he introduced the idea of "popular sovereignty." This meant that local residents could decide whether or not their regions would be free- or slave-soil. However, Nebraska and Kansas lay north of the Missouri Compromise line and were thus "forever" closed to slavery. In order to open them to that possibility, the "sacred" Missouri Compromise would have to be repealed. Douglas wanted this done by implication, but the Southern senators whose support he needed for the central railway route insisted that it be repealed outright. Douglas consented, and when he did he got a political issue explosive enough to blast the Union in two.

Pride and passion, the twin terrors of human nature, were newly roused by the proposal to repeal the Missouri Compromise. This was the one agreement which had kept the peace between the sections for a generation. To attempt to overturn it, even to touch it, as Douglas seems to have known before he became blinded by ambition, was to break that peace. And it was broken: Southern pride now demanding that slavery follow the flag further inflamed Northern passion already aroused by the Fugitive Slave Act.

Yet Democratic Party discipline pushed the Kansas-Nebraska Act through Congress, and the Compromise was repealed.

Next day in Boston an angry mob tried to prevent the return of a fugitive slave. A battalion of artillery, four platoons of Marines and twenty-two companies of militia were required to get the runaway down to the ship. Thousands of civilians lined the streets, hissing and groaning and crying, "Kidnappers! Kidnappers!" Buildings were hung with crepe and church bells tolled—tolled the death of the Fugitive Slave Act, for henceforth in the hardening antislavery North a man felt it was his duty not to obey that law but to violate it.

Douglas's moral obtuseness had other results powerful for change. On February 28, 1854, antislavery forces met in a schoolhouse at Ripon, Wisconsin, to recommend formulation of a "Republican party." On July 6, that party was formally organized at Jackson, Michigan, gathering to its standard Whigs, Free-Soilers and anti–Kansas-Nebraska Democrats. That very fall these astonishing new Republicans gained a majority in the House. Most important of all, Kansas-Nebraska brought out of retirement an Illinois lawyer-politician named Abraham Lincoln.

5

■

The Rail-Splitter

L IKE SO MANY frontier families, the Lincolns were westward-moving people. They had sailed west from old England to New England and then, the setting sun in their eyes again, had migrated to Pennsylvania and thence to Virginia. It was here that Captain Abraham Lincoln of the Virginia militia worked his 210-acre farm in Rockingham County in the Shenandoah Valley, and here that he took to wife Bathsheba Herring, who bore him three sons and two daughters. After the guns fell silent at Yorktown, Captain Lincoln had become captivated by his friend Daniel Boone's tales of the beautiful and productive Kentucky land that could be bought for 40 cents an acre, and in 1782 he moved his family there, filing a claim for more than 2,000 acres.

Two years later Abraham and his three sons were at work in a field when they heard a musket crack and Abraham sank to the ground. "Indians!" the boys cried in horror. Mordecai, the eldest, sprinted toward a nearby cabin; Josiah, the next, ran toward a fort for help; and six-year-old Tom stooped helplessly over his dying father. Came a shadow between them and terrified Tom glanced up to see an Indian standing above him. Then the crouching boy heard another shot and the ugly sharp *spat!* of lead striking flesh and the Indian fell with a groan. Mordecai had found a musket in the cabin and avenged his father. But Abraham was gone and the Lincoln family had to break up to survive. Little Tom lived in different places in Kentucky, usually with relatives, at first hiring out as a farm laborer before becoming a journeyman carpenter and cabinet maker.

At maturity Tom Lincoln stood five feet, nine inches, weighing a solid, muscular 185 pounds. His hair was thick, black and coarse, and his dark hazel eyes could go morose with dislike or twinkle merrily when he cracked a joke or told a story. He served a bit in the Kentucky militia, became a constable in Cumberland County, and bought a 238-acre farm in Hardin County for "the sum of 118 pounds in hand paid." His next venture was to take a flatboat loaded with merchandise down the Ohio and Mississippi rivers to New Orleans, earning enough money to marry.

The bride was Nancy Hanks, the illegitimate daughter of the unwed Lucy Hanks of Virginia. There is no record anywhere of Nancy's father, although it is widely believed that he was a married Virginia planter who gave Lucy enough money to clear out with her unwelcome daughter. So the lighthearted Lucy joined the flood of settlers flowing down the Wilderness Road and through the Cumberland Gap into Kentucky, carrying her little bundle of life all the way. Such tales did not trouble Tom Lincoln, who had fallen deeply in love with tall, slender, dark-complexioned Nancy, and on June 12, 1806, they were married. On February 10, 1807, their first child— Sarah—was born. Two years later—February 12, 1809—Tom told his neighbors "Nancy's got a boy baby." He was named Abraham, after his murdered grandfather.

Although Thomas Lincoln was a skillful carpenter, able by his trade to care for his little family and to acquire so much land that by the time of Abraham's birth he held nearly 600 acres, he seems to have been an indifferent farmer. And he was always moving, always seeking richer soil or more neighbors. He found both on a 230-acre farm on Knob Creek, alongside the famous Cumberland Trail. Here he built a one-room log cabin, and here, as little Abe began to grow, showing early promise of tall stature, he would see the road thronged with caravans of covered wagons, peddlers bumping along with cartloads of utensils and trinkets—and gangs of blacks in chains being driven from the Kentucky slave farms to the auction blocks in Louisville and Nashville. Abe was then too young to comprehend the misery of slavery; in fact, his only recollections of Knob Creek were of sowing pumpkin seeds in a big field just before a rainstorm washed them all away, and of the "blab" school—so called because the pupils crouching on their puncheon benches read their lessons out loud to show that they were studying—which he attended with his sister. It was a one-room structure built of logs with one door and a dirt floor. But here Abe learned to read and write and to "cipher." Writing he loved best of all, fascinated by the words he could form with charcoal on paper, in the dust with his big toe or in snow with his finger. As his vocabulary grew, so did the slave traffic on the Cumberland, to the intense dismay of his slavery-hating father.

By 1816 there were 1,238 slaves on the Hardin County tax lists, and Tom Lincoln was by then embroiled in lawsuits aimed at dispossessing him of his property. So he decided to move to Indiana, as Abe later wrote, "partly on account of slavery; but chiefly on account of the difficulty in land titles."

In a brutally cold December Tom and Nancy, with their two children, four horses, and their most valuable household goods, turned their faces into the north wind blowing down from Canada. It was a nightmare journey, over rolling hills so dense with every manner of tree and bush that Tom— and sometimes Abe—had to climb down from the wagon, ax in hand, to clear a path. "It was a wild region," Abe wrote later, "with many bears and other wild animals still in the woods . . ."

The Lincolns' journey ended at Little Pigeon Creek about sixteen miles from the Ohio. Here they pitched a pole shed or "half-faced camp," with one side open to the weather and the protected side warmed by a constantly burning log fire. Helped by neighbors and little Abe, not yet quite eight, Tom built an eighteen-by-twenty-foot cabin with a loft. Upon the arrival of spring they began to clear the land, felling trees and busting the sod with plows, subsisting, meanwhile, mostly on game in which the woods abounded, or on the nuts and fruits that barefoot Sarah and Abe could bring home. At night the cabin was lighted by blazing logs or merrily popping pine knots and sometimes sizzling hog fat. At times Tom would smoke out a bee tree for the honey and then there would be great excitement.

All this building and plowing and planting took place on land that Tom did not yet own. Like so many of his neighbors he was a squatter, until he made a ninety-mile trip to Vincennes in October 1817 to pay a $16 first installment on his 160-acre homestead. In December he paid another $64, giving him title to a quarter-section. Before he could acquire the rest, Nancy came down with "milk sick," a fever believed to have come from cows which ate white snakeroot or other growths that poisoned their milk.

A thick white coating appeared on Nancy's tongue, and as she took to her bed it turned brownish, while the fever shrank her thin body. Nancy knew that she was dying and called for her children, clasping their hands in her cold fingers and gasping out her last words. On October 5, 1818, she died and was taken to the little cemetery and buried in a pine box made by Tom and fastened by pegs whittled by Abe. The year that followed was "pretty pinching times" for a family without a wife and mother to comfort and care for them, and then it appeared that little Abe would join Nancy after a horse kicked him in the head. But he survived to watch his father disappear down the road back to Kentucky, headed for the cabin of the widowed Sarah Bush Johnston. "I have no wife and you have no husband," Tom said straight out. "I knowed you from a gal and you knowed me from a boy. I've no time to lose, and if you're willin' let it be done straight off." Sarah replied: "I've got a few little debts." Tom paid them and they were married December 2, 1819.

Tom and Sarah arrived at Pigeon Creek with four horses drawing a wagon filled with her household goods, themselves and her three children. With Tom's nephew, Dennis Friend Hanks, there were now eight people inside the little cabin. "Aunt Sairy" took charge of this crowded household with all the love and firmness without which few frontier families could survive. She had no favorites, although she did find it difficult to conceal her fondness for Abe, at eleven no longer quite so little. His love of learning impressed her, and it has been described by his cousin Dennis: "I never seen Abe after he was twelve 'at he didn't have a book some'ers around. He'd put a book inside his shirt an' fill his pants pockets with corn dodgers, an' go off to plow or hoe. When noon come he'd set down under a tree, an' read an' eat. In the house at night, he'd tilt a cheer by the chimbly, an' set on his backbone an' read. I've seen a feller come in an' look at him, Abe not knowin' anybody was around, an' sneak out again like a cat, an' say, 'Well, I'll be durned.' It didn't seem natural nohow to see a feller read like that. Aunt Sairy'd never let the children pester him. She always said Abe was goin' to be a great man some day. An' she wasn't goin' to have him hendered."

Even at eleven Abe suspected that the desultory nature of "schoolin' " at Pigeon Creek would never satisfy his enormous appetite for learning. School kept when a teacher appeared, usually in winter when he was looking for food and shelter, and ended after he drifted out following the spring thaw. Abe wrote later that "all his schooling did not amount to one year."

Naturally enough, the defect of Abe's virtue of loving learning was his dislike of hard work. The neighbors thought him lazy. "Abe Lincoln worked for me," a neighbor said. ". . . didn't love work half as much as his pay. He said to me one day that his father taught him to work, but he never taught him to love it." What Abe really detested was hoeing and plowing, the twin drudges of farm labor; but he really loved to cut down trees and split rails. As an admiring neighbor put it: "He can sink an ax deeper into wood than any man I ever saw." Abe liked nothing so much as to be alone in the woods with his flashing blade, making the forest ring with his blows and silencing the wildlife around him. For such work he possessed the ideal physique. At eighteen he was already fully grown: six feet, four inches tall, an unusual height for those days. His feet were so big that when he put aside his birchbark shoes for leather boots he needed a specially made size fourteen, while an ax in his huge, hard hands seemed as light as a hatchet. Evidently he had inherited his mother's height and also her slenderness. Abe's chest and shoulders were narrow, his neck scrawny and his long legs thin. Seated he looked no taller than other men, but when he arose he seemed to unfold above them. His arms were also long, but here he had inherited some of his father's muscular build: his biceps were immense, made even larger by his prowess as an axman. Yet, at no time did he ever weigh more than 180 pounds.

Because of his strength and quickness Abe excelled at sports. He was also something of a scrapper. When William Grigsby challenged him to a fight, Abe smiled and said he'd do better against his smaller stepbrother John Johnston, but when he saw Johnston faltering, he shoved Grigsby's supporters aside, seized him, and threw him out of the ring. "I'm the big buck of this lick!" Abe yelled, ruffling up his coarse black hair, his calm gray eyes challenging the Grigsby youths while rallying his own friends. "If any of you want to try it, come on and whet your horns." A wild scuffle ensued, and both sides claimed victory, but Abe Lincoln's narrow head remained steady above the crowd.

Abe was fond of pranks, one day putting barefoot boys to wading in a puddle and then walking their muddy feet across the ceiling. Aunt Sairy joined the general laughter, allowing that she ought to give big Abe a good spanking—yet pleased to see him clean the ceiling standing flat-footed beneath it. Abe Lincoln was undoubtedly homely with his angular head, wide mouth and long nose. Yet his face was incredibly expressive, especially when he was recounting a droll story. In repose it was sunk in an ineffable sadness. Lincoln would always be subject to melancholia, born of his preoccupation with death and his unspoken shame of his mother's base birth. At eighteen it was only natural for him to sample the whiskey that was as plentiful as game on the frontier, and he found he didn't like what it did to his mind and body. He also abstained from tobacco. But he was no prig, and might have been a little too fond of bawdy songs and earthy jokes. Usually he told his smutty stories to make a point.

When Abe was nineteen tragedy again struck the Lincoln family: his sister, Sarah, died in childbirth a year after she married Aaron Grigsby. For some unknown reason, Abe was bitter toward Aaron, and when his two brothers were married on the same day and didn't invite Abe to their wedding, he circulated a hilarious "Chronicle" relating how the Grigsby brothers mistakenly crawled into bed with each other's wife.

Now nineteen, Lincoln was anxious for adventure, hoping to break away from the dreary toil at Pigeon Creek and also to escape parental obligations. He had never been close to his father and in later years would speak slightingly of him, contemptuous of his lack of education; his great capacity for compassion apparently was not large enough to include a father whose family held his freedom hostage, consigning him to a "life of quiet desperation." It was James Gentry, the richest man in Pigeon Creek, who rescued Lincoln from his own frustration. He had seen him handle a ferry on the Ohio River and concluded that he would be just the man to take a flatboat of produce down to New Orleans. Lincoln built the boat and made the oars and steering poles and, with Gentry's son Allen in charge, shoved off for the Crescent City. Below Baton Rouge they were sleeping when a gang of seven blacks boarded their craft to kill the crew and steal the cargo. Lincoln knocked two of them into the river with a crab-tree club and with young Gentry chased the others ashore and into the woods. Both returned to the flatboat bleeding and the gash over Lincoln's eye left him scarred for life. But they reached New Orleans safely, sold their cargo and lingered for a few fascinating days in that riotous, raucous city of many tongues and shades of skin. But they were wise enough not to sample its dubious delights, and also repelled by the sight of black slaves in chains being herded by mounted slave drivers toward the great plantations. Their passage north on an elegant Mississippi steamboat was paid for by James Gentry, and they arrived home a pair of experienced travelers just a bit "too fine-haired" for the less sophisticated settlers of Pigeon Creek. According to the law and customs of the day, Lincoln paid his father what remained of the $24 he received for three months' work.

Tom Lincoln had the wanderlust again. A milk-sick scare had frightened the neighborhood, and John Hanks had written about the richer land and better crops in Illinois. Once more the Lincolns spent a winter building wagons and on March 1, 1830, they were ready for the journey west. The clan had grown: there were sixteen people, many of them grandchildren, aboard the three wagons piled high with household goods. Big Abraham was the wagon master. He was in high spirits, for he had attained his "majority" of twenty-one less than two weeks previously. Now he could vote and need not turn his wages over to his father. But he stayed with the family during the spring and summer of 1830, splitting thousands of rails and working as a sodbuster for John Hanks's brother, Charles. After a terrible winter, when Tom Lincoln prepared to move his family again—a hundred miles southeast to Coles County—his tall and ambitious son shook his head emphatically. He was going somewhere else: on his own.

■   ■   ■

Remembering his successful trip to New Orleans, Lincoln with John Hanks and John Johnston headed for the Sangamon River in Illinois to build a flatboat to haul cargo down to New Orleans. This trip was without incident, although the sight of the slaves in chains once again depressed him. Slave dealers' advertisements of their human wares infuriated him. They might as well have been farmers selling pigs! So he hurried north again, this time to the little village of New Salem on the Sangamon River. Here he helped to build a store, becoming its clerk at $15 a month. Soon the villagers were talking about the honesty of the big store clerk, how he walked six miles to return the few cents a woman had overpaid him, or, finding he had accidentally sold tea to another woman using a four-ounce instead of an eight-ounce weight, had walked miles to give her the four ounces due her.

Lincoln's prowess as an athlete also made him famous, especially among the wild Irish from nearby Clary's Grove. Matched against Jack Armstrong, their wrestling champion, he threw him and flattened his shoulders. This angered Armstrong's men and they came raging against big Abe, who put his back to a wall and challenged them all. At this point, Armstrong pushed his men aside and took Lincoln's hand, saying he was "the best feller that ever broke into this settlement." At New Salem Lincoln began his self-education, making friends with a schoolmaster who told him where he could find a copy of Kirkham's *English Grammar.* He walked six miles to borrow it and spent his nights poring over it by the light of pine shavings. Making friends fast, Lincoln at twenty-three made his first bid for public office, offering himself in 1832 as a candidate for the Illinois state legislature. Asked what his ambition was, he replied: "I have no other so great as that of being truly esteemed of my fellow men, by rendering myself worthy of their esteem." Fawning was not one of Lincoln's finer skills, and he could see that he had not impressed his rough-hewn audience. Before he could resume his true character, however, the Black Hawk War erupted. The Sauk and Fox chief had led his people back over the Mississippi into their ancient Illinois lands where they began to kill settlers and burn their homes. Governor John Reynolds called for 400 ninety-day volunteers from Sangamon County. Aware that the store he was running was failing, Lincoln borrowed a horse and rode nine miles to Richland Creek, where a company composed mainly of Clary Grove boys was forming. To his amazement, they elected him captain and he led them to Beardstown to join the 1,600-man Illinois "army."

In the way of all American militia since King Philip's War, Lincoln's men were not easily disciplined. The first time he gave an order, the "soldier" so addressed snapped, "Go to hell!" His troops never saw combat, making "war" on hen roosts and cow pastures, and after the capture of Black Hawk they were discharged. Lincoln went back to New Salem just in time to be roundly defeated at the polls. He was crushed, remarking: "Well, I feel just like the boy who stubbed his toe—too damned badly hurt to laugh and too damned proud to cry." He used the $95 he was paid for eighty days' service to buy a half interest in a store, which, he said, "winked out." He had not liked his partner's attempt to survive by selling liquor, although his distaste for such trade did not prevent him from making whiskey "in a little still house up at the head of a hollow."

Lincoln's defeat at the polls in 1832 had convinced him that he must educate himself further, in the law if he could, because there lay the road to both prosperity and political preferment. The dying store in New Salem gave him all the time he needed, and he buried himself in a copy of Blackstone he had bought at a Springfield auction. "His favorite place of study," a local observer wrote, "was a wooded knoll near New Salem, where he threw himself under a wide-spreading oak. . . . Here he would pore over Blackstone day after day, shifting his position as the sun rose and sank so as to keep in the shade, utterly unconscious of everything but the principles of common law. People went by, and he took no account of them; the salutations of friends were returned with a silence or a vacant stare . . ."

His reading and his knowledge of what was happening in the Illinois legislature and in Congress were given free rein after he was appointed New Salem postmaster at the absurd pay of about $50 a year in commissions on receipts. But the freedom to read and the mountains of "public prints" available! If he needed more money, he could always earn it splitting rails, as a farm or mill hand or helping out in another store. So he devoured the massive works of historians such as Gibbon and Volney, and practically memorized Tom Paine's *The Age of Reason.* His retentive memory enabled him in the fall of 1833 to accept the job of surveyor in his part of Sangamon County. Within six weeks he mastered Gibson's *Theory and Practice of Surveying* and Flint's *Treatise on Geometry, Trigonometry and Rectangular Surveying,* an incredible feat not only of memory but of comprehension by a twenty-four-year-old youth of "about a year's schoolin'." True, he was helped by a schoolmaster, but to move so quickly from two-plus-two to logarithms and the use of mathematical instruments and all the nice calculations of the trade was indeed the leap of an exceptional mind. He paid for it physically, looking like a drunk on a two-month tear. "You're killing yourself," people told him. But he persevered and got the job. Soon he was able to buy a horse, saddle and bridle, and after an admirer presented him with a set of surveying instruments, he was in business solid.

Lincoln's surveying trips to the towns of north Sangamon County expanded his circle of friendships, a not inconsiderable asset when, on April 19, 1834, he offered himself again as a candidate for the state legislature. He made no more servile attempts at ingratiating himself with the electorate, and although he was a Whig, did not disdain the help of Jacksonian Democrats who liked him, speaking little but shaking many hands face-to-face, and once stepping into a fistfight and ending it. In the August 4 elections he ran second among thirteen Sangamon County candidates, and in the last week of November took the two-day, seventy-five-mile stage trip to Vandalia, then the state capital. He was twenty-five.

Vandalia had been the state capital for fourteen of its fifteen years. It was a town of some eight hundred people overlooking the Kaskaskia River on the edge of the rolling prairie. Its "streets" were 80 feet wide covered with grass, lined with log cabins to either side fronted by "sidewalks" which were actually footpaths worn through the grass. There were about a half dozen larger buildings in which taverns and boarding houses were located, the latter beginning to fill up with legislators and lobbyists. Here Abraham Lincoln was to meet many young men, some with fewer years than himself, who were to become western governors or U.S. representatives and senators. Among them was twenty-one-year-old Stephen A. Douglas, who had come to lobby for appointment as state's attorney for the First Circuit.

At first Lincoln was a bit overwhelmed by the "finery" and "high life" of this rustic capital. Many members had brought their families, and there were parties and cotillions, orchestra music, fancy food and drink, and the ladies and gentlemen elegant in silks and satins. But when the General Assembly convened on December 1 in a dilapidated brick building the surroundings were more to his liking. Members of the House meeting on the lower floor sat on movable chairs three to a table, quill pens, cork inkstands, and writing paper on each table with a sand spittoon on the floor. Heat came from a stove and fireplace and there were three tin dippers hung above a pail of water. Debate was often punctuated by shouts warning of falling ceiling plaster. Such an unpretentious atmosphere was made for the homely, gangly yokel with his droll stories and fund of bucolic but pointed aphorisms, and Lincoln quickly established a reputation as a born politician.

Because legislative sessions in those days were remarkably brief, rarely more than a month or six weeks, Lincoln was able to devote most of his time to reading law. He did so with typical single-mindedness. As he advised a student later: "Get the books, and study them till you understand them in their principal features, and that is the main thing. . . . Your own resolution to succeed is more than any other thing." By the summer of 1835 he was ready for his bar examination, postponing it after deciding to run for reelection. Perhaps the greatest triumph of his campaign occurred in Springfield, the home of George Fourquer, a lawyer who had switched from Whig to Democrat in order to gain an appointment as register of the land office at $3,000 a year. Affluent now, Fourquer built a fine house to which he attached Springfield's first lightning rod, a marvel for those days. After hearing Lincoln speak in the courthouse, he decided to "take down" this high-flying youngster, mounting the platform to deliver a "slasher-gaff" attack. Lincoln stood quietly listening with folded arms. Returning to the platform, he said: "I desire to live and I desire place and distinction; but I would rather die now than, like the gentleman, live to see the day that I would change my politics for an office worth three thousand dollars a year, and then feel compelled to erect a lightning rod to protect a guilty conscience from an offended God." Whooping and laughing, Lincoln's friends carried him out of the courthouse on their shoulders, and it was with that kind of campaigning that New Salem's favorite son emerged with the highest vote of seventeen candidates in the county.

Soon after this triumph he appeared before two justices of the state supreme court and passed easily. On October 5, 1836, he received his long-sought license to practice law.

Lincoln was never that still persistent myth of the simple prairie lawyer, if not naive at least too trusting, whose patent honesty and undeceived and undeceiving intelligence marked him as a paragon of truth and virtue among all that crowd of posturing self-seekers. Except for the intelligence, he was none of this, but rather a tough-minded realist who realized that his high ideals and principles were useless without the power to execute them. He accepted party discipline and the give-and-take of politics, less than angelic though they might be, as the practical paths to power, and was thus a loyal Whig and an astute floor manager. One incident in his legislative career in Illinois bears this out.

In 1836 the Whigs were determined to move the state capital from Vandalia to Springfield. Lincoln as party floor manager worked ceaselessly at making bargains or doing favors for votes needed to make the change. Through Lincoln's strategy a bill for the "permanent location" of the capital passed in the Senate, where the Democratic edge was only 22 to 18. But the House, with 64 Democrats and 27 Whigs, was a far more formidable obstacle. His first move was to get an amendment passed stating that the new capital must donate $50,000 and two acres for a new state house, a tactic favorable to the more populous and affluent Springfield. But then a flood of amendments threatened to sink his bill. A snowstorm raging outside caused many members to leave the chamber, thus siphoning off strength the badly outnumbered Whigs could not afford to lose. Came a bill to postpone action "until next Fourth of July" and it passed by 39 to 38! The move to Springfield seemed doomed.

But that night Lincoln called his Sangamon County colleagues—the "Long Nine" as they were called for their unusual height—into session. Then he sent them out into the storm to remind some opponents of the bill authorizing the railroads and canals that Lincoln had helped to steer their way. Five members who had voted to table were persuaded to change their mind. Democrats who had secured political plums for friends with Whig help were reminded of their obligation, and others eagerly awaiting bridges or railroad terminals for their districts were warned of stern Whig opposition. Absentees who would have voted for Lincoln's bill were notified to be on hand for sure in the morning. A motion to "reconsider" the bill squeaked through 42 to 40. One vote shifting from Yea to Nay would have killed it. A new motion to table "until next Fourth of July" was beaten 46 to 37. Then after a bill to select a permanent capital passed by the same vote, Springfield was chosen 73 to 16 over Vandalia, with four other towns trailing behind and one member with a sense of humor plumping for "Purgatory."

Abraham Lincoln had played his delicate and dangerous game with an iron nerve, and he had won.

For years Lincoln had been thinking of marriage. He was not a ladies' man, in fact was very shy in the presence of single women. At his boarding house in New Salem he always ate at tables free of women, and in his store preferred to wait on men and boys. His temperament was far from romantic, certainly nothing like the mythical Lochinvar first presented in print by William Herndon, his law-partner-to-be, and then embellished by the poet Carl Sandburg. According to this figment, Lincoln was deeply in love with a pretty nineteen-year-old girl named Ann Rutledge. When she died of a mysterious fever in August 1835, Lincoln was supposed to have been devastated, running through the woods shrieking like a man demented, or flinging himself across her grave in grief. He certainly knew Ann Rutledge, but it is doubtful if the relationship even reached the stage of close friendship.

But he did propose to Miss Mary Owens, the daughter of a rich Kentucky farmer, who had come to New Salem in December 1833 to visit her sister, Mrs. Bennett Abell, at whose house Lincoln was staying. Mary was four months older than Lincoln, five feet five inches tall, plump, with dark curly hair and large Delft blue eyes. Lincoln seems to have fallen for her, but nothing happened and she returned to Kentucky. They corresponded, and Lincoln's "love" letters to her were about as ardent and sensual as a lawyer filing a brief. Three years later Mary was back in New Salem, and Lincoln saw with some dismay that she had gained weight and lost teeth. She was, as Thomas More said of his second wife, "neither a girl nor a pearl." Yet they came to some vague understanding of marriage; but after she went back to Kentucky again, the lonely and despondent Lincoln in 1837 wrote her a quixotic letter exaggerating the poverty she would embrace if she married him and "releasing" her from her promise. In these dry dispassionate lines one can almost see the lonely Lincoln writing before a fire and hear his quill pen scratching on parchment. Mary quite understandably never replied.

This letter was written from Springfield, to which Lincoln had moved in April 1837. New Salem had been his home for six eventful years, but the shallow and frequently unnavigable Sangamon River could never float the ambition of the little hilltop village and it was fading into a ghost town. In Springfield Lincoln rode up to the general store owned by Joshua Speed and asked the cost of bedclothes for a single bed. Speed figured it at $17 and Lincoln said: "Cheap as it is, I have not the money to pay. But if you will credit me until Christmas, and my experiment here as a lawyer is a success, I will pay you then." Speed was astonished at the sepulchral tone of Lincoln's voice. "I thought I never saw so gloomy and melancholy a face in my life." But he agreed, offering to share his double bed over the store. Lincoln unstrapped his saddle bags and carried them upstairs. He came down beaming and said: "Well, Speed, I'm moved." Thus a lasting friendship was begun.

Lincoln's law partner was John T. Stuart, a prominent county Whig. Their office was a little room over the circuit courthouse. In the beginning of Lincoln's "experiment" in law it seemed that he was fated to the typical county lawyer's portion of deeds, titles and wills, with an occasional domestic dispute or argument over ownership of land going to court. Yet the youthful lawyer was already known in Springfield and had been honored at a banquet attended by about seventy guests at which one toast declared: "Abraham Lincoln: he has fulfilled the expectations of his friends, and disappointed the hopes of his enemies." His reputation grew after he delivered a speech in January 1838 deploring the violence visited on Abolitionist ministers and the growing number of antislavery editors in the state. He said the men who had fought the Revolution had risked death to win the liberties now being violated, declaring, "whenever the vicious portion of the population shall be permitted to gather . . . and burn churches, ravage and rob provision stores, throw printing presses into rivers, shoot editors and hang and burn obnoxious persons at pleasure and with impunity—depend upon it, this government cannot last."

This was Abraham Lincoln's first expression of his burning belief in the American experiment in popular self-government. For the first time in what he would one day call "the last best hope of earth" a people was demonstrating to the world that they could govern themselves while enjoying a complete freedom that could never flourish in a privileged monarchy or aristocracy. To him the Declaration of Independence was the highest of all political credos, that men were created equal and entitled to life, liberty and the pursuit of happiness. He knew that this was true, for he had himself been born into grinding poverty, the son of a base-born mother and a failure of a father barely able to sign his name, and yet there had been no social chains on him fixing him to that station in life: he had been free to rise. Lincoln's devotion to these truths was like a religion nourishing his soul, and this is one of the reasons that he hated slavery so fiercely. He knew that many of the Founders he admired had been slave-owners, and he resented this ugly stain on the otherwise shining escutcheon of the land of liberty. But he was no Abolitionist. Their manners and intemperate language repelled him, and his subtle mind—yes, subtle, for all his outward yokelisms—could never accept their absolutism. At this time, however, Lincoln remained silent on slavery and abolition, although in the year before this speech he did say that the peculiar institution was "founded both on injustice and bad policy."

In that summer of 1838 Lincoln was again a candidate for the state legislature, while his partner Stuart ran for Congress against Stephen Douglas. Lincoln stumped more for Stuart than for himself in a literally rough-and-tumble campaign during which Stuart once seized Douglas by the neck and dragged him around the Springfield square, while the Little Giant bit him so deeply on the thumb that it left a lifelong scar. Stuart won by only 36 votes out of a total of 36,495, while Lincoln led a field of seventeen.

By then Lincoln and Stuart were confronting Douglas in another duel, a sensational murder case that had rocked Springfield. Two Democrats—Jacob Early and Henry Truett—had quarreled over a political office. Meeting in a Springfield hotel, they exchanged angry threats, and when the smaller Truett drew a pistol the burly Early picked up a chair—whereupon Truett shot him dead. Lincoln and Stuart with three other Whig lawyers represented Truett, while Stephen Douglas appeared as the prosecuting attorney. With feeling against Truett running high, his lawyers were able to postpone the trial from March 14 until October 9, to allow tempers to cool. During the trial, Lincoln and Stuart maintained that their client believed that the chair in Early's hand was a lethal weapon and that he fired in self-defense, while Douglas insisted that Truett came to the hotel armed and determined to pick a fight with Early. Truett was acquitted, chiefly because of Lincoln's penetrating plea to the jury.

Lincoln's two triumphs over the Little Giant, as well as his third victory at the polls, put him on the road to the high station in life which he sought with an ambition so boundless that it astonished his friends. Once again this was not the Abe Lincoln of mythology, a common man seeking only truth and justice. Nor was he the legendary tireless traveler of the circuit courts, but rather well on his way to becoming a lawyer's lawyer who did most of his work in the Illinois Supreme Court, participating in 243 cases and winning most of them. Far from evoking grins and chuckles, his tall black-clad figure made taller by the six-inch stovepipe hat that he wore always commanded great respect among his colleagues. No one dared call him Abe to his face, because he loathed the nickname and could show his displeasure either by the sharpness of his wit or the strength of his arms.

His fees were fair and reasonable, but he expected prompt payment. He was fond of quoting the Dutch justice who married people and then asked, "Now, vere ish my hundred dollars." If clients tried to trim his fee or avoid paying it, he sued for the exact amount—as the Illinois Central Railroad learned to its dismay. Lincoln had won for them a case so vital and involving so many millions of dollars that to win or lose meant survival or bankruptcy. To his retainer of $200 he added a bill of $4,800. The railroad refused to pay and Lincoln sued and won. Illinois Central next delayed payment for thirty-eight days, until an execution was issued directing a sheriff to seize its assets, whereupon it paid, sheepishly explaining its conduct as the result of its general counsel in New York refusing to approve payment of so large a fee to a nobody western lawyer.

There is no doubt that Lincoln liked money, and he worked hard for it. By the 1850s he was a wealthy man, earning as much as $5,000 a year, the equivalent of at least a hundred times as much today. He made wise real estate and financial investments. But he never used his position for personal gain. Lincoln's head-to-head with the Illinois Central eventually led to his becoming known as a railroad lawyer. Once his enemy, the road began to hire him to represent it regularly, and his reputation led to employment by other roads. This was a time of enormous railroad expansion in the Midwest, where the iron horse had replaced the steamboat as the hauler of produce from the American breadbasket.

Lincoln's reputation as a speaker grew apace with his fame as a lawyer. He was not an impromptu orator, as indeed few great speakers are, almost always writing out his speeches beforehand. Short, sharp and shining, sturdy and penetrating, his prose was like the sword of a Roman soldier. His shrill, high-pitched voice, far from being weak or irritating, had great carrying power and could hold large audiences spellbound. Of histrionics he had none, except, when making a point, to lean his head to one side and level a finger; or, expounding on the great truths of liberty or justice, when his little gray eyes would gleam as though lighted by an inner and holy fire, he would raise both of his long arms high in the air as though calling upon the approbation of the Almighty.

In religion, Lincoln appears to have been a deist. Sectarian faith did not appeal to him, although he had an almost deterministic and even superstitious belief in a Divine Providence guiding the affairs of men. During his congressional campaign of 1846 when it was said against him that he was "a scoffer against Christianity," he felt it necessary to issue this defense: "That I am not a member of any Christian Church is true; but I have never denied the truth of Scriptures; and I have never spoken with intentional disrespect of religion in general, or of any denomination of Christians in particular." Nevertheless, in 1860 twenty-one of twenty-four Christian ministers in Springfield voted against him as an unbeliever.

No man was more tolerant. Though he abstained from alcohol, he did not mind being with people who drank. He believed that alcoholics—then bluntly called drunks—should be understood rather than condemned and ostracized. In 1844 he took the hard-drinking William Herndon into his office as a partner with the remark, "Billy, I can trust you and you can trust me." Herndon's grandfather had freed his slaves in Virginia and he hated slavery almost as much as he hated immigrants, especially the Irish. This was a curious dichotomy common to the Abolitionists, and an article of faith with Nativists and Know-Nothings, who believed that the pope was planning to plant a nation of Catholic foreigners in the Mississippi Valley. Lincoln despised their credo, writing to his friend Joshua Speed: "Our progress in degeneracy appears to be pretty rapid. As a nation, we began by declaring that *'all men are created equal.'* We now practically read it 'all men are created equal *except negroes.'* When the Know-Nothings get control, it will read 'all men are created equal, except negroes, *and foreigners and Catholics.'* When it comes to this I shall prefer emigrating to some country where they make no pretence of loving liberty—to Russia, where despotism can be taken pure, and without the base alloy of hypocrisy."

Lincoln's wit was legendary, and he often turned it against himself to make a point. Accused of hypocrisy he retorted: "If I were two-faced, would I be wearing this one?" Or when he attacked his own country for coveting the territory of its neighbors, he quoted the story of the farmer who said: "I ain't greedy for land—I just wants what jines mine." Lincoln was fond of making what are now called "Spoonerisms," that is, exchanging the first letters of two words. One day he handed a court bailiff the following: "He was riding *bass-ackward* on a *jass-ack,* through a *patton-cotch,* on a pair of *baddle-sags* stuffed full of *binger-gred,* when the animal *steered* at a *scump* and the *lirrup-steather* broke and throwed him on the *forner* of the *kence* and broke his *pishing-fole.* He said he would not have minded it much, but he fell right in a great *tow-curd;* in fact, he said it gave him a right smart *sick* of *fitness*—he had the *moler-corbus* pretty bad. He said, about *bray-dake* he come to himself, ran home, seized up a *stick of wood* and split the *axe* to make a light, rushed into the house and found the door *sick abed* and his wife *standing open.* But thank goodness she is getting right *hat* and *farty* again."

Like many men of wit and humor Lincoln had a dark side to him. He was intense and brooding, given to fits of melancholia then called the "hypo," for hypochondria. Preoccupied with death, he was saddened by the wounded nature of creation, by mortality. He often muttered the lines of "Mortality" by William Knox, concluding: "From the gilded saloon to the bier and the shroud/Oh, why should the spirit of mortal be proud?" Lincoln also was terribly afraid of insanity. A boyhood friend of his had gone mad, locked, in Lincoln's phrase, "in mental night." He feared that he too would lose his mind, a gibbering, drooling, living organism more than a vegetable but less than an animal without the power to know. Many of his friends were troubled by his fits of depression and they believed that his folksy stories were a defensive device intended to "whistle down sadness." He said himself: "I laugh because I must not weep—that's all, that's all." Wit, he said, had the same effect on him as "a good square drink of whisky has on an old toper: it puts new life into me."

In 1840 Abraham Lincoln at last found happiness and a "new life" when he met and fell in love with Mary Todd of Kentucky.

Mary Todd was twenty-one, ten years younger than Lincoln, when they first met at the home of Mary's sister, Elizabeth Edwards. She was also fourteen inches shorter than he—five feet two—fashionably plump, gay and vivacious with her velvety pink skin, light brown hair, flashing blue eyes and turned-up nose. Lincoln found her a radiant, exciting creature indeed. He was fascinated by her breeding: her father was a well-known banker and politician in Lexington, and Mary had been to a genteel nuns' school where she learned to speak and write French and to comport herself like a lady, while also developing an interest in literature and poetry. Mary found this shy and towering suitor to be unlike anyone she had ever met before. It was as though while Lincoln made love with his eyes she was doing the same with her ears, finding his "the most congenial mind she had ever met" and becoming deeply interested in his political career. His ambition delighted her, and she eagerly returned his affection so that they became engaged in December 1840, setting the marriage date for New Year's Day 1841.

But then the black dog of despair began trotting in sinister silence around Lincoln's self-doubting soul. He became conscious once again of his pioneer past. He had thought he had shucked it, as men often do; but one's past is the one thing a person can surely hold, and it cannot be buried. So Lincoln compared backgrounds and concluded he was reaching too high.

So did Mary's sister and her husband Ninian Edwards. Neither of them liked Lincoln, and they mocked his "vulgar" frontier language: "kin" for can, "sot" for sat, "airth" for earth or "heered" for heard. They spoke of his lack of "larnin' " or "eddication" and derided his habit of addressing the head of a committee as "Mr. Cheermun." Mary was told that she was throwing herself away on a nobody with a "nebulous" future. None of this bothered Mary, who was absolutely devoid of snobbery, but the Edwardses' attempt to sabotage the engagement got to Lincoln.

Then he was devastated when Joshua Speed, the one friend in whom he could confide, sold his store and moved back to Kentucky. Lincoln not only had to find new quarters at a trying time, but had lost the counsel and love of the one man who could have reassured him. Thus annihilated, he broke off the engagement. For a week he lay alone in his room in the depths of despair, finally writing an associate: "I am now the most miserable man living." Recovering some of his self-esteem, he visited Speed, who was also having doubts about an impending marriage. They discussed their common problem, and after Lincoln returned to Springfield, Speed went ahead with the wedding. His letters full of the joy of the married state encouraged Lincoln, who began seeing Mary again—but in secret lest the implacable Edwardses learn of the renewed courtship. They were married November 4, 1842. Lincoln gave Mary a wedding ring inscribed "Love Is Eternal."

There were naturally habits born of differing backgrounds that had to be overcome or tolerated. Lincoln liked to lie on his back in the front room reading newspapers aloud; or he came to the dining table in shirtsleeves, eating his meal absently with his mind far away; or else, rather than let the servant answer the front doorbell, he would go there himself in slippers and shirtsleeves. Once when he opened the door for two fine ladies, Mary upstairs was mortified to hear him say: "She'll be down soon as she gets her trotting harness on."

Mary was herself imperious and impetuous, hot-tempered enough to scream angrily at a tradesman she suspected of cheating her. If she detected a weakness or learned of something uncomplimentary in a person whom she disliked she pounced on it like a tigress. She was also fond of fancy clothes and unstable in money matters. Yet her sometimes uncharitable assessment of others sprang from her keen insight into human nature: she could quickly scent the true motives of some "friend" who wanted to use her husband. Mary was also an immense help to Lincoln. Having chased his self-doubts she also stimulated him to seek higher and higher places in life. She gave him four sons of whom he was extremely fond and whom he spoiled as outrageously as she did. Theirs was a powerful love, physical, tender, and intimate; and although Mary was seriously injured during the birth of their fourth son in 1853, thus ending all sexual relationship, it remained ardent and undiminished.

After her children, Mary Lincoln's greatest pleasure was in sharing her husband's political career. He depended on her judgment, her insight into human nature, and although in those days, with woman's suffrage far over the horizon, no wife could accompany her husband during a campaign, she gave him much encouragement and advice. Thus she was overjoyed when in 1846 Lincoln was elected to the House of Representatives. In October 1847 they left Springfield bound for Washington, with a stopover in her home town of Lexington. There she proudly showed off her congressman husband, and there Lincoln discovered a new and unsuspected evil in the system of buying and selling human beings.

Among the most shocking stories he heard was the sale of a beautiful girl named Eliza. One sixty-fourth black, with creamy skin, straight black hair and large luminous eyes, she was nevertheless a slave. Two men among the buyers were bidding for her: one a thick-necked Frenchman from New Orleans, the other an Abolitionist minister named Calvin Fairbank, who had been authorized by a pair of antislavery Cincinnati bankers to bid as high as $2,500 to buy and free the girl. After the bidding rose to $1,200, the Frenchman asked Fairbank: "How high are you going?" and was told: "Higher than you, monsieur." The Frenchman hesitated and the anxious auctioneer opened Eliza's dress to bare her breast and shoulders, crying:

"Who is going to lose a chance like this?" A gasp came from the crowd and the Frenchman bid $1,465 only to be topped by ten dollars. Again a lull, the auctioneer seized the hem of Eliza's skirts, lifting them to bare her body from toe to navel. "Who is going to be the winner of this prize?" At once the Frenchman raised his bid to $1,580. Raising his gavel the auctioneer began to chant, "One . . . two . . . three . . ." Eliza turned her piteous face on Fairbank, who yelled, "One thousand five hundred and eighty-*five!*" Turning to the Frenchman, the auctioneer asked: "Are you going to bid?" He shook his head and Eliza sank to the block in a faint. "You've got her damn cheap, sir," the auctioneer snarled at Fairbank. "What are you going to do with her?" Fairbank shouted, "Free her!" and the crowd whooped and yelled in glee.

When Lincoln heard this story he was pleased to learn of the crowd's reaction. He had sensed a steadily growing opposition to slavery in the state of his birth and childhood, and this seemed to confirm it. But he was also shocked by the leering auctioneer's crass appeal to prurience. Heretofore he had despised slavery as the evil of one man owning another, but now he realized that slavery debased both master and slave.

But the tall young congressman from Illinois continued to keep his own counsel on the peculiar institution when he took his seat in the House. He did, however, introduce a resolution expressive of his deepest hope that slavery actually could "be put on the road to extinction." He proposed that no new slaves could be brought into Washington and only those who served government officers from the South be allowed to remain there. After January 1, 1850, all children born of slave mothers would be free, cared for by their mothers' owners and "reasonably educated." Thus, in time the pernicious institution would vanish from the District of Columbia, and this would be a model for the entire country. But after Whig support fell away from Lincoln, nothing came of it and no actual bill was offered.

Although Lincoln was a tireless worker, missing only seven roll calls during his term, he did not otherwise distinguish himself. A loyal party man, he joined the Whig opposition to "Mr. Polk's War." After his term ended in 1848 he decided not to run for reelection, returning to Springfield to resume his law practice. There he gradually evolved a position on slavery which, if not chimerical or at least naive, was at best wishful thinking. It was based on a policy of colonizing the slaves in Africa, an idea that he got from his idol, Henry Clay.

Lincoln still sympathized with the majority of Southern whites, whom he believed to be inherently patriotic and humane. "They are just what we would be in their situation," having "human sympathies, of which they can no more divest themselves than they can of their sensibility to physical pain." Because of these sympathies, he believed that the South would accept a program of compensated emancipation, after which the slaves would be deported to Africa and settled there. This assumed that the Federal government would be willing to spend the vast sums required for such a program and also that the South would not only consent to sell its labor force but also, at least among the Slavocracy, accept a lesser social status. How could a realist such as Lincoln have conceived of such an unrealistic program? Probably because his anguish at the thought that the hateful institution might continue to make a mockery of the Declaration overwhelmed his better judgment, and also because he could see no other solution short of civil war. Thus he could say in 1852 that if the Federal government could buy the slaves' freedom and restore "a captive people to their long-lost fatherland," there would then ensue a "glorious consummation" of the problem.

In Springfield also Lincoln became a devoted family man, although in February 1850 the happiness he shared with Mary was shattered by the death of their four-year-old son, Edward. Lincoln, who always lived at the edge of sadness, felt this tragedy drive his melancholia deeper into his soul, touching what he called "the sore spot." He did not, of course, turn away from politics, remaining abreast of events in Washington and Springfield. But it did not seem that he would ever again seek public office, until the Kansas-Nebraska Act ended forever his hopes that rational, peaceful men could adopt a plan like his own to put slavery "on the road to extinction." He saw in this pernicious legislation nothing less than a revolt against the Founding Fathers and his own dream of popular government unstained by bondage, and he came out of retirement to fight it.

6

■

The First Violence:
Senator Sumner and John Brown

THE INCREDIBLE Republican victory in the House elections of 1854 was widely attributed to the national scandal of "bleeding Kansas." Even before Douglas's bill became law, proslavery groups from Missouri had moved into Kansas and antislavery settlers from the Ohio valley and New England followed. Both sides sent representatives to Congress, both sides drew up constitutions and awaited admission to the Union—and both sides were armed. Civil war ensued, a minor dress rehearsal for the titanic struggle that was to convulse the nation. On balance it seems that the "Border Ruffians," as the Free-Soilers called the Missouri men, were guilty of more violence; although the Abolitionists were not averse to squeezing the triggers of their "Beecher's Bibles," as the new, breech-loading Sharps rifles were called after the Reverend Henry Ward Beecher declared them of more value to an antislavery man than a Bible. Thus, popular sovereignty became a matter of voting slavery in or out, not by the ballot but with bullets. In Washington, a Northern senator denounced the sorry spectacle of bleeding Kansas as a plot of the Southern Slavocracy.

Senator Charles Sumner of Massachusetts was as imposing physically as, in his own mind, he was morally. At six feet two inches tall and powerfully built, he was able to carry off an equally formidable paunch born of a fondness for fine dining which he had acquired during his extensive travels in Europe. He was also highly cultivated: many of the great names of Western culture were his friends. At forty-five he was still unmarried. In truth, if he had any love it was his hatred of slavery. As he told his friends, he dealt not in politics but "in morals." On the morning of May 19, 1856, this man of pitiless truth informed a friend that he would in the Senate that day "pronounce the most thorough philippic ever uttered in a legislative chamber." It was entitled "The Crime Against Kansas."

The desk in front of Senator Sumner was empty. It belonged to Senator Andrew Butler of South Carolina, an ardent apologist for slavery. When Sumner was a freshman senator, Butler had been so cordial and kind to him that Sumner could say that the old gentleman had taught him "to shun harsh and personal criticisms of those from whom I differ." But that had been before the Kansas-Nebraska Act. Today Sumner directed his diatribe against the absent Butler, sneering at him as a chivalrous knight who "has chosen a mistress to whom he has made his vows, and who, though ugly to others, is always lovely to him; though polluted in the sight of the world, is chaste to his sight—I mean the harlot slavery." There was more of the same, so much that it was not until the next day that this paragon of moral rectitude had exhausted his immense vocabulary of unclean epithets in a polemic that offered no solution, changed not a single mind or vote and succeeded only, as its author wished it to succeed, in widening the gulf of sectional hatred toward that point at which, in his own words, "every citizen will be not only spectator but actor." In short, civil war.

Next day the blood of brothers actually did flow in the antislavery settlement of Lawrence, Kansas. Here was a piece of New England set down on the great prairie not far from the Missouri border. Here was a concentration of New Englanders and other Kansas settlers grimly determined to halt the flow of slavery at that border. These men not only had guns, they had a fortress: a brick hotel built with that purpose in mind.

But there was a proslavery territorial grand jury sitting in Kansas which had called upon the sheriff to jail the town's leading citizens on charges of treason, to suppress its newspapers as public nuisances and to tear down this hotel-fort. On May 21—the day after Sumner ended his speech—a posse of a thousand men, many of them proslavery Border Ruffians from Missouri, arrived in Lawrence to enforce the grand jury's will. They too were armed, and had brought along five cannon with which to demolish the hotel. They were addressed by Senator David Atchison of Missouri, the West's great advocate of slavery, who cried: "Be brave, be orderly, and if any man or woman stand in your way, blow them to hell with a chunk of cold lead." With wild yells the sack of Lawrence was begun. After it had ended, the hotel was on fire, the newspapers' printing presses were in the river, homes were ransacked, the one owned by a man who had dared to style himself the Free-Soil governor of Kansas was burned and two innocent bystanders were dead. All this execution of justice had been accomplished by the sort of wild, whooping enthusiasm that comes in bottles, and so far from striking a decisive blow for slavery it had provoked a counter-attack of antislavery denunciation from the corps of Abolitionist news correspondents who came pouring into town only hours after the sheriff's posse went staggering out. Thus, more fuel was poured on the flames of sectional hatred.

Next day was May 22, and Charles Sumner was almost alone in the adjourned Senate. He was busy writing, his great body cramped inside a desk fastened to the floor. Hearing someone speaking to him, he glanced up and saw Congressman Preston Brooks of South Carolina standing over him. Brooks was also a big man, six feet tall and brawny. He was a nephew of Senator Butler and had served as a cavalryman in the Mexican War. In his hand was a gutta-percha cane which he held like a trooper's saber.

"I have read your speech twice over, carefully," he said in his soft Southern voice. "It is a libel on both South Carolina and on Senator Butler, who is a relative of mine."

With this he lifted his cane high and brought it down hard on Sumner's head. Again and again he struck in his practiced dragoon's stroke, while Sumner struggled to break away from the desk that trapped him. "Oh, Lord!" he gasped, as the rain of blows continued, finally with a great convulsive heave wrenching the desk free and struggling erect. But he made no attempt to attack his assailant, and more blows fell upon his bloody head until the cane broke—and even then Brooks flailed him with the stump. Now Sumner sank to the floor, and at last men came running to succor him. Brooks glanced contemptuously at the fallen senator, and murmured: "I did not intend to kill him, but I did intend to whip him." Then he left the chamber, still clutching his stub of cane.

Sumner was helped to his feet and taken to a sofa in the lobby where a doctor cleaned and dressed his wounds. He did not seem to be seriously injured, but upon returning to his rooms and finding his clothes saturated with blood he summoned another physician who took a graver view. It may have been that his spine had been affected, or at least this was the diagnosis of specialists in France and England who treated him. Also, he walked and spoke for some time like a man who had suffered a partial stroke, and he did not return to his Senate seat for four years. Hailed in the North as a martyr to the antislavery cause, in the South he was derided as a faker, and his failure to close with Brooks was offered as proof that here was another of those cowardly Yankees who, deploring physical violence, believe it permissible to wound with words. The South's hero, of course, was "Bully" Brooks, the recipient of encomiums and a shower of new canes, one of which was inscribed: "Hit him again!"

But the entire affair had disastrous consequences. Senator Sumner's invective had produced a predictable reaction by a proud and passionate Southerner, but in using force Brooks had severely widened the gulf of hatred between the sections, and it was to grow still wider and deeper after a murderous fanatic named John Brown lifted not a cane but a sword.

By the time John Brown reached middle age, he was an accomplished failure. He was born in 1800 in Torrington, Connecticut, into a family that could trace its ancestry to the *Mayflower,* but which was also strongly streaked with insanity. His mother and grandmother had died insane, while three maternal uncles and a maternal aunt suffered from the same affliction. His father, an ardent Abolitionist and a devout church-goer, was a roving handyman full up to the eyes in the bile of prejudice. His son John was just like him, but less educated because he hated school.

John Brown tried everything: farming, tanning, land-speculation, sheep-growing and a wool brokerage, all in that order and all failures. He was frequently sued, often accused of dishonest practices, and once of outright embezzlement. He could not earn enough to care for his huge family of twenty children by two wives. He was not a hard-working man but rather an uncouth and unpleasant Micawber always looking for some quick, golden and usually harebrained scheme that would make his fortune, and always blaming someone or something else when it failed. In 1848 his antislavery beliefs led him to settle his family among an Upstate New York community of free blacks organized by a wealthy Abolitionist named Gerrit Smith. In exchange for Brown's promise to clear and farm the land and "be a kind of father" to the blacks, Smith gave him two farms on generous terms; but the venture came to nothing and he moved on to Akron, Ohio.

Here he became more and more obsessed with the notion of liberating the slaves. He organized a black "League of Gileadites" to resist the Fugitive Slave Act, preaching to them the gospel of violence. In the spring of 1855 five of his sons migrated to Kansas, chiefly to claim homesteads but probably also to join the fight for free soil. Their father followed them in a wagon loaded with guns and ammunition. Among his weapons were artillery broadswords, relics from the days when gunners used blades to defend themselves against cavalry attacks. They had belonged to the Grand Eagles, one of those lunatic secret societies of which Americans of that age were fond. The Grand Eagles had a crackbrained plan to conquer Canada, but when Brown came along they thought he could put the weapons to better use in bleeding Kansas.

The attack on Lawrence found John Brown at fifty-six gaunt and graying and bent beneath the hard lash of misfortune. Ignorant and narrow-minded, egotistical and fanatical, cruel and unscrupulous, he was by then living proof of the wisdom of keeping the Bible away from violent men of unbalanced mind; for John Brown was by then, as his contemporaries agreed, on the one point of slavery completely crazy. One man spoke of the "little touch of insanity about his glittering gray-blue eyes," and the Reverend S. L. Adair of Osawatomie, at whose home Brown often stayed, described him as "a man that had always been from his childhood impressed with the idea that God had raised him up on purpose to break the jaws of the wicked."

This, after Lawrence, was exactly what John Brown intended to do. In some mysterious way he had gotten the idea that five antislavery men had been killed then—not two—and he would avenge them. He would kill five proslavery "barbarians." Did not the Holy Bible say, "An eye for an eye, a tooth for a tooth"? To extend it to "A life for a life" was not in John Brown's overheated brain an irrational leap from corporal to capital punishment, nor could the admonition, " 'Vengeance is mine,' saith the Lord" apply to the chosen instrument of the God of Battles. So he told his seven followers—four of whom were his sons—that "something must be done to show these barbarians that we too have rights." When an alarmed neighbor urged him to be cautious, "Old Brown" growled: "Caution, sir! I am eternally tired of hearing that word caution. It is nothing but the word of cowardice!" Rather he preferred the God of Battles' instructions to the Israelites on how to treat the enemy: "Thou shalt slay them with the edge of the sword." What better means, then, than the artillery broadswords? So Brown and his men honed them razor sharp on a grindstone, and on the night of May 24, with the blades gleaming faintly in the starlight, they climbed the wooded ravines leading to the proslavery settlement at Pottawatomie Creek.

En route they met a man who had read telegraph despatches describing Bully Brooks's beating of Senator Sumner. "The men went crazy—*crazy,*" one of them recalled. "It seemed to be the finishing, decisive touch."

At the cabin of a poor white family from Tennessee named Doyle, Brown hammered on the door. Doyle opened it. Brown—his sword raised—ordered him and two sons outside. They obeyed. There were screams and then silence. In the morning, the hideously mutilated bodies of the three Doyles were found lying near the road. A well-known proslavery leader named Wilkinson was next. Another knock, again the door was opened, and Wilkinson, ready-for-bed in stocking feet, was taken outside and murdered. His death cries rose above the plaintive pleading of his wife, sick in bed with the measles. William Sherman, a Border Ruffian known as Dutch Bill, was the fifth and final victim. Apparently he fought back, for his body was found lying in a stream with his head split open, a gaping hole in his chest and one hand cut off.

Lawrence had been avenged. It was now past midnight, May 25, 1856. In the South the complimentary canes were already en route to Bully Brooks. In Kansas, John Brown and his followers washed their swords in the waters of Pottawatomie Creek.

Now it was the South that seethed with rage. The name John Brown was uttered like an epithet, just as "damn-Yankee" became a single word and a curse. The gulf between the sections widened: Southerners traveling in the North felt uneasy, Northerners visiting the South sensed hostility. In the South especially there developed a rising current of nationalism. Students enrolled in Northern schools came home to study, the myth of the Cavalier South and the peasant or plebeian North was extended and exaggerated, and Southerners were exhorted to eschew all that was not of Southern origin. In effect, two distinct nations were beginning to emerge within the boundaries of the United States. The North would not—could not—cease agitating the slavery question; and the South, driven back on itself, grew ever more rigid and inflexible in slavery's defense. The cleavage even cut the Presbyterian, Baptist and Methodist churches into Northern and Southern branches.

Yet the sectional showdown was avoided for another four years because the Democrats gave the South another doughface for President. This time it was James Buchanan of Pennsylvania, for neither Franklin Pierce nor his party desired his renomination. The "black Republicans" named John Charles Frémont, a famous and popular explorer. Frémont's campaign slogan was: "Free speech, free soil and Frémont." If he had won, the South probably would have seceded then and there. But victory went to the ponderously vacillating Buchanan, the fourth successive mediocrity to occupy the White House and the one who, having done most to get there, did least after his arrival. Nevertheless, the sectional storms were also to howl around his ears—and this was because even before his inauguration he connived at the Dred Scott decision.

Dred Scott was a slave whose master took him from Missouri to Illinois and Minnesota Territory for two years. Upon his return, Scott sued for liberty in the Missouri courts on the ground that residence in a free state and a territory north of the Missouri Compromise line automatically conferred freedom on him. The case reached the U.S. Supreme Court, and

Buchanan and Chief Justice Roger Taney with four Southern justices saw in it the opportunity to extend slavery throughout the nation. In a decision announced March 6, 1857, only a few days after Buchanan took office, the Court denied Dred Scott's claim on three grounds: (1) blacks could not be United States citizens, therefore they could not sue in Federal courts; (2) the laws of Illinois could not affect him in Missouri, where he now lived; (3) his residence in Minnesota Territory north of the Missouri Compromise line could not confer freedom because the Compromise was unconstitutional.

The Dred Scott decision shook the North like a thunderclap, and the area simply refused to be guided by it. Legislatures repudiated it, and New York proclaimed the freedom of any slave who reached its precincts and promised up to ten years in prison to anyone who even passed through the state attended by a slave. To the young Republican Party the decision brought another increase of power, while to the South it brought determination to ram Kansas into the Union as a slave state.

In that year of 1857 the free-soil residents of Kansas outnumbered the proslavery settlers by nearly ten to one. Yet the Senate had rejected an antislavery constitution for the state-to-be and accepted one permitting bondage. Here Stephen Douglas, who had done so much to unsettle the Union, rose to the heights to preserve it. He led the fight to allow the people of Kansas the right to vote on the proslavery constitution, and when they rejected it by a margin of six to one they fulfilled the Little Giant's prediction: "Kansas is to be a free State." For his stand on principle, Douglas became known as "a traitor to the South." In the following year, 1858, Douglas ran for reelection to the Senate against Abraham Lincoln.

7
.
The Gulf Widens

K ANSAS-NEBRASKA changed the mind of Abraham Lincoln, and he came out of retirement attacking the immorality of slavery itself: "Slavery is founded on the selfishness of man's nature—opposition to it in his love of justice. These principles are in eternal antagonism, and when brought into collision so fiercely as slavery extension brings them, shocks and throes and convulsions must ceaselessly follow."

Sorrowfully convinced now that the peculiar institution would not be restricted to the South where it would eventually vanish, a hope he shared with the Founding Fathers, he saw that the "Slave Power" was going to grow and expand under the leadership of the Southern-controlled Democratic Party—which dominated the White House, the Senate and the Supreme Court. All talk of its being inhibited by hostile climate, soil or terrain had been but a smokescreen, for it was now obvious that the Slavocracy intended to herd manacled black men into the new lands and there set them to work in mines or ranches or in ports, for bondage was actually just as adaptable to any environment as the wage labor of free men. One more proslavery decision by the Supreme Court would nationalize the institution, ringing freedom round with slavery, and America—"the last best hope of earth"—would sink back into a state worse than feudalism or the foulest of the monarchies.

Such views were far from extreme to any thoughtful Northerner listening as Lincoln was listening to the rising shriek of hysterical anger issuing from the minds of proslavery apologists in Dixie. The Declaration of Independence and its proclamation of racial equality was derided as a "self-evident lie." The extremist George Fitzhugh called upon the South to destroy capitalistic or free society. Return to feudalism! he cried. Enslave all workers, white as well as black. Abolitionists were the sneaking allies of "uncouth, dirty, naked little cannibals from Africa." "Free society" was "unnatural, immoral, unchristian" and must inevitably "fall and give way to a slave society—a system as old as the world." From an Alabama newspaper came the blast: "Free society? We sicken of the name! What is it but a conglomeration of greasy mechanics, filthy operatives, small-fisted farmers and moonstruck theorists?"

To fight the Slave Power Lincoln joined the Republican Party and became the Illinois state chairman. He embarked upon a series of speeches directed to the Southern people, whom he believed now to be in the clutches of the slave-power firebrands. He pleaded with them to put aside all talk of disunion, to restrict slavery to the South where the Founding Fathers had placed it in the hope of its eventually vanishing. "Let us turn slavery from the claims of 'moral right' back upon its existing legal rights . . . and there let it rest in peace. Let us re-adopt the Declaration of Independence, and with it, the practices, and policy, which harmonized with it. Let North and South—let all Americans—let all lovers of liberty everywhere—join the great and good work. If we do this, we shall not only have saved the Union; but we shall have so saved it, as to make, and to keep it, forever worthy of the saving."

But the South was not listening, probably could not listen, if only because since the publication of *Uncle Tom's Cabin* local postmasters had begun to "censor"—that is, destroy—all literature likely to inflame the slaves. Laws making such publication a crime had been passed by all the Southern states, and even by border states such as Maryland. Newspaper reports of Lincoln's impassioned appeal therefore reached few Southern readers, and within that climate of hatred of the North few of them indeed were eager to discuss them. It was not until Lincoln challenged Douglas for his Senate seat in 1858 that the South at large learned that there had appeared in the North—not the customary raving, ranting, strident clamor of the Abolitionists—but one small voice pleading without passion or rancor for reason and restraint, and a return to mutual love and the principles of the Declaration. On June 16, 1858, Lincoln declared:

" 'A house divided against itself cannot stand.'

"I believe this government cannot endure permanently half slave and half free.

"I do not expect the Union to be dissolved—I do not expect the house to fall—but I do expect it will cease to be divided.

"It will become all one thing or all the other.

"Either the opponents of slavery will arrest the further spread of it and place it where the public mind shall rest in the belief that it is in the course of ultimate extinction; or its advocates will push it forward until it shall become alike lawful in all the States, old as well as new, North as well as South."

With this speech Lincoln became the Republican candidate challenging the Democrat, Douglas. Eventually the two agreed to discuss the issues in a series of debates across the state. Famous for their cogency, the Lincoln-Douglas debates might be equally celebrated for the contrasts in the debaters. Here was Douglas, a bristling bulldog dressed in fine clothes, the man of power and position riding into town on a special train and very likely firing off signal cannon to herald his arrival. There was Lincoln, six feet four inches tall, his big bony hands and feet sticking out from his ill-fitting trousers as he awkwardly rides a horse toward the platform. If anyone impresses, it is Douglas, with his powerful bark and sure movements of the hands; but then, as one observer reported, Lincoln speaks and "his eye glows and sparkles, every lineament, now so ill-formed, grows brilliant and expressive, and you have before you a man of rare power and of strong magnetic influence." His rough good humor softens the bite but not the point of his logic and he *"takes* the people every time."

The outstanding meeting was at Freeport, where 15,000 people heard Lincoln ask Douglas how he could square his doctrine of popular sovereignty with the Dred Scott decision that slavery follows the flag. Douglas replied that residents of a territory had it in their power to prevent or protect slavery by local police regulations. This was the Freeport Doctrine, by means of which Douglas sidestepped the moral issue of the right or wrong of slavery. It guaranteed his reelection, but also so mortally offended the South that he lost all chance of gaining the Democratic presidential nomination in 1860.

In the intervening period, the North continued to agitate and the South to protest until fanatical old John Brown ended all hope of moderation.

8

■

The Raid on Harpers Ferry

A FTER THE Pottawatomie massacre John Brown began to regard anti-slavery as the purpose of his life. With Christ, he could say: "It was for this that I came into the world." For three years—from 1856 to 1859—he gave up all other pursuits to concentrate on plans for military operations against slavery, in Kansas or elsewhere. During this period the death of his son Frederick at the hands of proslavery men and the Dred Scott decision hardened him in his resolve. From his reading of Wellington's *Memoirs* he had learned that a handful of men in difficult terrain could hold off an army, and in his trip to Europe in 1851 he had inspected battlefields—especially Waterloo—and fortifications. By 1859 John Brown had come to fancy himself as a leader of guerrilla forces.

By then he had also evolved a plan for a slave revolt. He would strike a blow from Maryland into Virginia or beyond, where he would establish a base. From all over the South slaves would flock to his standard, and so would the free blacks of the North. They would all be armed. If the South sent militia against him, his forces would easily rout them. He would also defeat Federal troops. Armed raids deep into Tennessee and Alabama would provide booty and more black recruits. All slaveholders who tried to resist Brown would be killed or taken back as hostages. Secure in his Appalachian fastness, he would lead his freedmen in the formation of a mountain state. Its presence in Dixie would draw off so many slaves that eventually the slave states would be compelled to emancipate their bondsmen.

Only the mad imaginings of a monomaniacal mind could have conceived such a preposterous plan. It was wishful thinking at its worst: the idea that all the slaves were eager for revolt, that his original handful could defeat militia or Federal troops, that he could rob and kill with impunity in the name of his glorious cause and bring untold suffering and death upon his followers. None of this daunted him, for he had already become convinced that it was better for an entire generation of Americans to pass away violently than that slavery should endure. Most fantastic of all, John Brown had no men and no money.

Undaunted, he spent thirty months traveling across the northern United States. He made seven trips to Boston, then the intellectual capital of the country; five trips to Upstate New York to see the Abolitionist Gerrit Smith; and many more to other places, pleading for financial aid. His greatest triumphs were in Boston. Here his rough frontier clothing and, in his boot, the sturdy bowie knife taken from a murdered proslavery man, his grim countenance and his obvious contempt for words rather than deeds captivated these perfumed and cultivated Brahmins, who found in him the "man of action" that they could never be—a warrior prophet out of the Old Testament, a Highland chieftain rebuking his son for his "soft" habit of rolling a snow pillow for his head, or a fierce but pious Cromwellian Covenanter killing the innocent with Bible in one hand and sword in the other, and praise of the Lord on his lips. If Brown had ever doubted his fantasy as a messianic leader, these eminent dupes made it a reality for him—and he was quick and cunning enough to play the role up to the hilt as he met the leading men of Boston. Franklin Sanborn, the young schoolmaster who was a favorite of Ralph Waldo Emerson, took him to meet Dr. Samuel Gridley Howe, the philanthropist famed for his work with the blind. He also met Theodore Parker, probably the most famous clergyman in the United States; as well as Amos Lawrence, the wealthy textile magnate who had founded the settlement of that name in Kansas, together with George Stearns, another rich man. Thomas Wentworth Higginson, a young Unitarian minister of Puritan origin and later Emily Dickinson's "dear preceptor," became an enthusiastic friend. Later Old Brown of Pottawatomie, the man with what the widow Doyle called "the face of a snake," was welcomed into the homes of Emerson and Henry David Thoreau. Thoreau called him "a man of rare common sense and directness of speech," Emerson saw him as a noble savage: "A shepherd and herdsman, he learned the manners of animals and knew the secret signals by which animals communicate." The transcendentalist philosopher Bronson Alcott wrote: "I am accustomed to divine men's tempers by their voices—his was vaulting and metallic, suggesting repressed force and indomitable will."

It is not unusual for men of thought, perhaps embarrassed by the comfort and safety of their own lives, to lionize men of action; but what was remarkable in Brown's Boston reception was that these perceptive intellectuals did not seem to notice that their hero's burning eyes—without hint of humor or compassion—betrayed the mad purpose of the paranoid. Equally surprising was Brown's naive belief that he could squeeze any real money out of this crowd of fawning Yankee penny-pinchers. A plan to get $100,000 for him from the Massachusetts legislature failed, after which he had to be content with small donations in the neighborhood of a few hundred dollars. Stearns made a contingent promise of $7,000 for use to raise one hundred volunteers in Kansas. Nothing came of it, although a committee to help him was formed including Stearns, Sanborn, Higginson, Parker and Howe. With Gerrit Smith they became "the Secret Six," dedicated to giving Brown limited aid. All of them were militant Abolitionists and hoped most fervently for civil war. But in Kansas, not in the South.

When Brown's true plans became known to them by accident they were terrified. They feared exposure. Although they agreed that arms bought for Brown for use in Kansas could be employed elsewhere, they also stipulated that "they in future not know his plans." Uninformed, of course, they could not be prosecuted. Still, they urged him on, these intrepid Yankee coat-holders—and on the night of October 16, 1859, he struck at Harpers Ferry.

It was a dark, moonless night, chill and damp, when at eight o'clock John Brown led his men from their headquarters on a Maryland farm toward the Federal arsenal at Harpers Ferry five miles away. There were seventeen of these "officers," mostly youthful adventurers, including three more of Brown's sons. They moved two by two, each carrying a Sharps rifle and two revolvers. Brown himself drove a one-horse wagon loaded with pikes, a crowbar and a sledgehammer. The vehicle's creak and rattle rose above the rustle of boots moving through dry leaves and grass. Upon sight of the town's lights some of the men became nervous. At once Brown sent two men to cut the telegraph wires while the main body moved on to seize the wagon-and-railroad bridge, capture the watchman and post two more men as guards. The end of the Shenandoah Bridge was also secured. Next the watchman at the armory gate was overpowered and both armory and arsenal were overrun, after which the rifle works were taken.

Brown now held all the Federal property at Harpers Ferry, together with millions of dollars' worth of arms and ammunition. But he had yet to sound the tocsin bidding Virginia's bondsmen to rally to him; indeed he had not even let them know beforehand that he was coming. From this point forward, everything that John Brown did or omitted to do appears to be not the work of an accomplished incendiary leader but the confused and hopeful fumbling of a madman looking for a martyr's crown. Even after he sent detachments about a half dozen miles into Virginia to capture two slaveholders and ten of their slaves he spoke not of his mission or even mentioned his name. One of those captured was Colonel Lewis Washington, the great-grandnephew of George Washington. His most cherished heirloom, the ceremonial sword given Washington by Frederick the Great, was brought in with him when the details returned at daybreak. Brown was delighted with it, as he was by the black men into whose hands he pressed pikes, ordering them to guard the hostages and taking no notice of their bewildered and frightened demeanor. Nor was he bothered by the inadvertent killing of a free black baggage master when a Baltimore and Ohio railroad train was stopped at 1 A.M. and then allowed to continue, a monumental mistake that enabled the conductor to warn Baltimore. By midmorning President Buchanan, Governor Henry A. Wise of Virginia and the Maryland militia commander all knew that a white-led slave insurrection was under way at Harpers Ferry. The last two officials quickly ordered militia and volunteers to the scene, while Buchanan called upon brevet Lieutenant Colonel Robert E. Lee of the U.S. Cavalry to lead a force to the arsenal.

It is a measure of the fatuous antimilitarism that still guided the American people of that day that in all the nation's capital there was available to Lee only about ninety-odd United States Marines. They left by train ahead of Lee, under the command of Lieutenant Israel Green. Lee, still in civilian clothes, followed them, accompanied by Lieutenant J.E.B. Stuart. By the time they arrived at Harpers Ferry that night, the militia and volunteers, with a verve and skill rare in such troops, had seized all of the arsenal's key points while mortally wounding four of Brown's men, including his son Watson, after which they drove Brown and his survivors into a fire-engine house. Brown was trapped, and he knew it.

Lee preferred to attack in the morning rather than risk harming Brown's captives in the dark. But first, mindful of protocol, he offered the honor of assault to the militia and volunteers. All demurred, deferring to the professionals. Lee next called upon Lieutenant Green to form a storming force of a dozen picked men, with another such unit in reserve. They would use the bayonet only, again to protect the prisoners. But first they would have to batter down the engine house's heavy double wooden doors. So sledgehammers were issued to the Leathernecks, standing ready in blue trousers, darker blue frock coats, white belts and blue caps. Now Lieutenant Stuart seized a white flag of truce and strode forward to demand the insurgents' surrender. Lee had told him that if they stalled, he should wave his broad-brimmed cavalry hat as a signal for the Marines to charge.

Stuart was astonished when, peering through a crack in the doors, he saw and recognized white-bearded John Brown, whom he had met three years before on the Kansas prairie. At once aware that Brown's attempts to bargain were but delaying tactics, he stepped aside, swung his hat, and Green's Marines came trotting forward with sledgehammers. But their blows failed to break those stout doors. Exasperated, Green caught sight of an abandoned ladder and ordered his men to use it as a battering ram. On the second thrust, made while Brown's men fired through the door, a hole was opened. Brown fired at the intruding ladder and it was withdrawn. But then Green crawled into the murky engine house followed by his men and a brief fight ensued.

Green saw Brown kneeling to reload his carbine and struck at him with his dress sword. A true blade would have killed him, but this one merely opened a cut in Brown's neck and knocked him down. Green next thrust at Brown's body, but the sword bent double. In frustration the Marine beat upon Brown's head with its hilt, finally stretching him sense-less—and it was all over at Harpers Ferry.

Brown's men had killed four people—one a Marine—and wounded nine. He had lost ten dead or dying, including another son, Owen; seven had been captured and five escaped. As commander in chief of the Provisional Army of the North he had proved himself so incredibly inept, incompetent and disorganized that it is difficult to escape a growing conviction that John Brown had come to Harpers Ferry not to set alight and lead a great slave rebellion but rather to court a national martyrdom that might better serve his Abolitionist cause.

First, did he actually believe that with an "army" of twenty-two idealistic but romantic youths he could withstand the combined armed forces of Virginia and the Federal government? Second, leading this "se-cret" assault upon slavery, why had he brought with him to his Maryland farm a carpetbag loaded with four hundred confidential letters from his co-conspirators which could and would be turned against them so that no fewer than forty-seven of them were compromised. Third, granting that the character of his operation should have compelled him to contemplate a siege, why did he not bring with him to Harpers Ferry the requisite food and entrenching tools? Indeed, why did he give so little thought toward feeding his men and his hostages that he had to order forty-five breakfasts from the Wagner House; and why did he, if he actually expected 250 to 500 slaves to rally to him the first night, sit down in the engine house without even the barest, the most rudimentary commissary or quartermaster to provide for them? Finally, if he were so unskilled militarily that he allowed himself to be trapped between two rivers, why did he also—oh, travesty of travesties!—seek to incite a slave rebellion without letting the slaves know about it, and then expect them to rally to him without knowing that he was there?

Mad though he was—especially on the point of slavery—was he really that insane, that naive, that incompetent? Is it not more likely that the cunning he had shown in his association with the adulatory literati of Boston could not also have been present here; that he understood the impossibility of destroying slavery with the puny means at his disposal, and that a much better weapon against the detested institution would be his own death—his own martyrdom—at the hands of the defenders of human bondage? This explains his keeping his identity secret and his failure to warn the slaves. There wasn't really going to be any uprising, but rather only a provocation ending in an Abolitionist bloodbath, and when the news that the body of the sainted John Brown of Pottawatomie had been found among the slain broke like a thunderclap in the North—like the very voice of the Almighty crying out for vengeance—it would send coursing into the South a tidal wave of wrath that would at last cleanse American soil of this foulest of evils. What? Would he really have sacrificed his own people, his own sons, in such a megalomaniacal design? Why not? Was he not the chosen instrument of the Great Jehovah? Had he not frequently prophesied that it would be better for an entire generation of Americans to perish rather than to allow slavery to endure? When God speaks, his servants must not hesitate, no more John Brown than Abraham with his knife poised above the bared breast of Isaac.

Speculative though this indeed may be, it is no more conjectural than the insistence of most historians upon the insanity of John Brown as an explanation of his monumental neglect of the most basic requirements for an insurrection. But if he were mad, so were all those Abolitionists and Northern intellectuals who shared his belief that the slaves were writhing with discontent, waiting only for a signal to rise in revolt—bloody revolt, as most of these genteel agitators hoped. How did Brown and all these people come to this conclusion? From reading Abolitionist literature and *Uncle Tom's Cabin,* that was how, for not one of them ever traveled in the South or had the slightest acquaintance with the true relationship between masters and slaves. They simply could not or would not credit the possibility that loyal slaves and kind masters might exist in the South, preferring rather to believe their own propaganda. Thus Theodore Parker could write after Harpers Ferry that the "fires of vengeance" burning in a black man's heart could be put out only by "the white man's blood," and Thomas Wentworth Higginson went so far as to warn Southern whites of the danger of being shaved by black barbers. If John Brown were a lunatic, then, as the Boston *Post* wryly observed, "one fourth of the people of Massachusetts are madmen."

Insanity therefore does not suffice to explain John Brown's incredibly bungled attempt to raise the slaves, simply because he was at the very least intelligent enough to know that he could not succeed. Actually he wanted failure, because failure could be transformed into success of a much more brilliant and glorious character—a martyr's crown—that would raise the Northern antislavery movement to the level of a holy crusade. Israel Green's fragile sword ended that hope only temporarily, for John Brown was quick to perceive that in his trial, conviction and execution God had given him a matchless opportunity for a martyrdom exceeded only by the unjust trial, conviction and execution of his Divine Son. Except on the one point of slavery, Old Brown of Pottawatomie was definitely not demented, as those Virginia officials who interrogated him were quick to conclude. Their admiration of his superb behavior during his six-week ordeal after Harpers Ferry was boundless, and from the chief among them, Governor Wise, came this encomium:

"He is a bundle of the best nerves I ever saw, cut and thrust and bleeding and in bonds. He is a man of clear head, of courage, fortitude and simple ingeniousness. He is cool, collected and indomitable, and it is but just to him to say that he was humane to his prisoners."

On October 25, 1859, John Brown's trial began in the courtroom at Charles Town.

9
∎
Brown's Trial and Execution

BROWN HIMSELF admitted that he had been given an eminently fair trial. It was presided over by Judge Richard Parker, a dignified and perceptive jurist. Two capable attorneys were assigned to Brown, and from the beginning to the end of his seven-day trial he had no fewer than five attorneys. One of these, George H. Hoyt, of Athol, Massachusetts, was actually a spy and a plotter, sent south by Brown's terrified Yankee co-conspirators. His real objective was to steal Brown's papers, which might incriminate his true clients. He also tried to arrange a jail rescue, but to Brown's credit he declined. Meanwhile, with the exception of Higginson, who remained loyal to Brown to the end, and the Reverend Parker, who had been careful not to incriminate himself with the written word, and who now, sublime cheerleader that he was, stood bravely in his pulpit offering vocal encouragement, the rest of the indomitable Secret Six broke for cover like frightened rabbits. Smith fled to Canada and thence to the more secure sanctuary of an insane asylum in Utica; Dr. Howe also bolted across the border, dragging a half-reluctant Stearns with him; and Sanborn, who had given Brown a pistol, burned his own papers before flying to Quebec like a distraught Canada goose, twice crossing and recrossing the border in his panic.

There were three charges against Brown: murder, treason and fomenting rebellion. Lying on a cot wrapped in a blanket in the courtroom, the defendant listened impassively to the duel between the prosecutor and his lawyers. Most of the time his eyes were closed, although he would occasionally raise himself to snap out a question or deliver a short speech. He was cool, courteous and civil, never raising his voice in defiance except on a few occasions when he was aroused. He had chosen for himself the role of the victim unjustly accused, and he played the part like the consum-

72

mate actor he could be. After the jury found him guilty on all three counts, Brown addressed the court in what many spectators believed to be the noblest of speeches, one that Emerson would years later compare to Lincoln's Gettysburg Address; after which, aware that he was also speaking to an enormous press corps which would relay his words to a vast unseen audience in the North, he unburdened himself of perhaps the three most egregious lies of his career.

They were (1) that he had intended only to carry slaves off to Canada, (2) that he had not designed any insurrection or caused any bloodshed, and (3) that he had never tried to induce men to join him but had merely accepted them as volunteers. In truth, he had intended to incite slave rebellion throughout the South and had drawn up a constitution for his proposed state of freed black men, he had spread bloodshed throughout Kansas and Missouri and into Virginia, and he had recruited most of his followers, inciting them to commit criminal acts—including murder—from which they would have shrunk without his instigation. But because truth trying to overtake falsehood—especially in those agitated days—is like the sound of the explosion trying to catch up with the flash, many people in the North were convinced that John Brown had been railroaded to his death.

It has also been maintained that, after Judge Parker sentenced Brown to die, Governor Wise had it within his power to defuse the social bomb primed to explode in the North upon execution of that sentence. He could have, say some historians, commuted Brown's punishment to life imprisonment or placed him in a lunatic asylum. Many pleas for leniency fell upon Wise's desk, from the South as well as the North, either on humanitarian grounds or in more subtle warning that to do either would thwart the Abolitionist drive to canonize Brown and thus make his blood the seeds of a new army of antislavery martyrs. Oddly, the Abolitionists were just as fervid in calling for Brown's death as the firebrands of the South. It was a curious if not cynical morality indeed that led the Reverend Henry Ward Beecher to exhort his flock *not* to pray for Brown's deliverance. "Let Virginia make him a martyr," he said. "His soul was noble; his work miserable. But a cord and a gibbet would redeem all that, and round up Brown's failure with a heroic success."

Wise, of course, did have the legal right to reduce the sentence, but not an actual one. Virginia was then in a state of frenzy due in great part to Wise's own frenetic alarums and excursions exploiting to the hilt the myth of a great Northern conspiracy and also undertaken in his fatuous belief that he could yet become president of the United States in 1860. Nay, the entire South was in a ferment, because the fear of a slave insurrection that had terrified the section since the first black African slaves began to arrive there two centuries previously had again come to pass. And this must be understood in any discussion of the Virginia governor's decision to give the South a victim and the North a martyr.

Actually the South, or at least its dominating planter class, had two fears of insurrection: black *and* white. The latter, of course, was the less terrifying and it did not come into the open until as late as 1857, upon publication of Hinton Rowan Helper's book *Impending Crisis.* Helper was born in North Carolina, the son of a poor blacksmith. He had from boyhood learned to detest the pernicious influence of slavery on Southern life. For the blacks themselves he had nothing but contempt, hoping in his program for a new South to have them deported to Africa. He also cared little for the so-called po' white trash, the illiterate, indigent whites, much-maligned "mud-sills" living in shanties on rice and milk, their women working at hand looms at sixteen cents a day; or the wretched starvelings and wild men of the frontier South, dirty, superstitious and idle, wearing the coarsest cloth and feeding on a porridge of cow-peas—to Helper these people were also the victims of slavery, worse off than any Russian serfs, but for them he had no pity. His message was to a Southern middle class which until recently had never been known to exist: a great body of sober, reflective artisans, small farmers, shopkeepers and mechanics from which Helper had himself sprung. These were the nonslaveholders he saw as ruthlessly exploited by the "slaveocrats." Although Helper put the number of slave-owners at 350,000 households, which, when multiplied by five- or six-member families, would raise the total to close to 2,000,000, modern research has shown that there were far fewer. In 1860 there were 1,500,000 heads of families in the entire South, and of these only 46,000 met his rule-of-thumb criteria for planter status: land and twenty or more slaves. Of these only about 2,300 people owned as many as one hundred slaves and extensive acreage. Of all the heads of families only about one-fourth owned any slaves at all, and of these an estimated 60 percent held no more than five.

Actually, Helper's statistics minimized rather than maximized the evil of the Slavocracy, assigning to far too many Southerners a share in the "moonlight and magnolia" existence or a place on the summit of the pyramid of exploitation, while also underestimating the extent of the Southern middle class. Nevertheless, it was this class of whites and no one else with whom he was concerned. His extensive travels in the North had taught him the vast superiority of this section in liberty, wealth, religion, trade, production, libraries, education and literature, while in the South most of the people lived in "deplorable ignorance and squalid poverty." This, he maintained, was the result of freedom in one section and slavery in the other.

"Non-slaveholders of the South!" he cried. "Farmers, mechanics and workingmen, we take this occasion to assure you that the slave holders, the arrant demagogues whom you have elected to offices of honor and profit, have hoodwinked you, trifled with you, and used you as mere tools for the consummation of their wicked designs. They have purposely kept you in ignorance, and have, by moulding your passion and prejudices to suit themselves, induced you to act in direct opposition to your dearest rights and interests." His answer, an insurrection—violent if need be—aimed at depriving the slaveholders of all their privileges and taxing them $60 per slave to bear the cost of shipping them back to Africa. In the North this most impractical plan was hailed with elation and the Republicans had 100,000 abridged copies of the book printed for shipment into Dixie, but it never reached the intended audience. Nevertheless, many Southern leaders dreaded the spread of its arguments, all too aware as they were of the reality of the grievances Helper cited. They wanted nothing of a class war which might also inflame the blacks. Edmund Ruffin was one of these. Scientific planter and agrarian innovator, Ruffin was also one of Virginia's most fervent secessionists. He read Helper's book twice, professing to be amazed that anyone could suggest that there was hostility between slaveowners and slaveless whites. With other writers he neutralized a growing sense of revolt by appealing to racial prejudice.

So far from dividing all whites, they argued, slavery united them. It made them equal while assigning all degrading labor to the inferior blacks. If slaveless whites listened to Helper they would sink to a lower level. The jolly roger of "equality" was waved in their faces. Thus:

> The negro will intrude into [the white man's] presence—insist on being treated as an equal—that he shall go to the white man's table, and the white man to his—that he shall share the white man's bed, and the white man his—that his son shall marry the white man's daughter, and the white man's daughter his son. In short, they shall live on terms of perfect social equality.

There could have been no more compelling vindication of Helper's claim that the Slavocracy molded "the passions and prejudices" of the slaveless whites "to suit themselves" than this appeal to white supremacy. Victims of social injustice that the lower class whites were indeed, they had not yet lost their white skin. This was the saving straw at which they clutched, and it worked. It not only helped to postpone the Southern social revolution for another eight decades, it also helps to explain why so many of these victimized whites rallied with such gallantry and in such great numbers to "the bonny blue flag." Ruffin and his associates had parodied St. Paul: "These three abide: Faith, Hope and Supremacy—but the greatest of these is Supremacy."

To the entire South, of course, a racial war was a far more terrifying tragedy to contemplate than a class struggle, and it is one of the chief pities of the American house dividing that the North did not clearly comprehend this horror. There had been enough slave revolts to justify it: some two hundred of them, albeit mostly minor and local, since the introduction of black slaves into the Americas in the early sixteenth century. At the time of Harpers Ferry there were still Southerners who could remember the awful black insurrections on Haiti and Santo Domingo from 1791 to 1804, when leaders such as Toussaint L'Ouverture and Jean Jacques Dessalines ordered the massacre of the entire white population. Fugitives arriving in New Orleans and Norfolk told terrible tales of whites being buried alive or sawed into living halves or even eaten while their black murderers capered about with their blood smeared on their lips.

Even before then, Gabriel Prosser and his fellow slaves around Richmond planned to destroy the city, their plot being thwarted by the warning of a loyal slave. In 1822 a similar warning prevented a free black in Charleston named Denmark Vesey from leading an insurrection. Vesey had assembled an arsenal of crude arms, calling upon the voodoo man Gullah Jack to convince his followers that the charms he gave them made them bulletproof.

Almost all the adult population of the South could remember Nat Turner's Rebellion in 1831, by far the worst of them all. Turner was a slave preacher whose mind had become unbalanced through reading the bloodthirsty commandments in the Book of Revelation (Apocalypse). Of medium build at five feet seven inches and 150 pounds, coal black with a wispy white beard and burning eyes, Turner had gathered around him seven followers in Southampton County, Virginia—the Black Belt. He had limited his force to guard against the warnings that had thwarted earlier uprisings. "Judgment Day" was to be a Sunday night, when blacks were usually hunting and their masters resting from visiting and drinking, in the "jubilee" month of August, when there was little work for slaves before the harvest. Armed chiefly with razor-sharp axes, drunk on local apple brandy mixed with gunpowder, Turner's band fell on the unsuspecting whites and killed sixty of them—sometimes actually shredding their bodies and drinking their blood—before they were rounded up. Although all were executed, the wave of revulsion engulfing not only Virginia but the entire South provoked a series of punitive laws so grim that even to teach a slave to read and write was a criminal act. Although these laws were gradually eased, the "lynch law" that succeeded Turner's Rebellion grew apace and would not disappear until after World War Two, more than a century later. This, then, was the tenderest of nerves on which the absolutist and probably unwitting Abolitionists were pressing with such reckless fervor. Fear of slave revolt grew along with the slave population itself, that "Malthusian time bomb" which was both an economic threat in falling slave prices and a social one in fear of the chances of racial violence increasing along with the number of blacks. This was one of the reasons why a white population of eight million, fearing the continued growth of the population of four million blacks among them, sought to organize the new lands to slavery: distribution of the blacks would also thin them out.

In this climate, then, it is doubtful that Governor Wise could have raised as much as a corporal's guard to protect John Brown on his way to prison, or could have found a warden or an asylum superintendent willing to answer for his safety. To defuse the Northern social bomb this way would only explode another one in the South; and it would have been only a matter of time before a mob took the law into its own hands. No, no governor of Virginia, from Thomas Jefferson to Henry Wise, "brilliant fool" that he might have been, would have dared or cared to spare John Brown. So Wise signed the death warrant.

December 2, 1859, was a bright warm day in Charles Town. At eleven in the morning John Brown was brought out of jail. Six companies of Virginia infantry and a troop of horse were drawn up on the street, surrounding an open wagon with a pine box containing a heavy oak coffin. Brown scrambled up on the vehicle, seating himself next to his jailer and studying the troops with interest. At a command the wagon creaked off between two files of soldiery, proceeding to a forty-acre field chosen for the execution. More soldiers were massed here, forming a hollow square with cannon commanding the scaffold as a precaution against any rescue attempt.

John Brown could see the lovely, rolling hill country seeming to undulate in the sun. Beyond were the peaks of the distant Blue Ridge, their valleys still wreathed in silvery mist. Around the encircling hills were clusters of spectators, but none but the military were allowed close to the gallows. This disturbed Brown, who said: "I am sorry citizens have been kept out."

He approached the gallows alone, having refused to allow any minister tainted by slavery by his side. Nor was a friend or relative permitted near him. His eye fell on a detachment of cadets from the Virginia Military Institute. Colorful in their gray trousers and red flannel shirts, they were commanded by Professor Thomas J. Jackson, once the intrepid young gunner of Chapultepec. Among the cadets as conspicuous as a tree in a petrified forest stood sixty-five-year-old Edmund Ruffin. His long silvery locks fell to his shoulders, as he stood grim-faced, ramrod straight, clutching his musket with his eyes fixed on the doomed man. With Jackson, Ruffin was impressed by Brown's simple dignity and courage. An actor named John Wilkes Booth was also present, standing at attention with the Richmond militia. Not far from him was Governor Wise's son, a newspaper editor, who would one day give his life for the Stars and Bars.

John Brown climbed the scaffold nimbly, turning to shake hands with the jailer and sheriff who followed him. He stood unflinching while a large white hood with an opening for the hangman's noose was flung over his head. Then the rope was knotted about his neck. When the jailer asked him to step upon the trap, he replied in a muffled voice: "You must lead me—I cannot see." All was ready, but then there was a horrible delay while the last remaining troops marched and countermarched to their position. It took eight minutes, but Brown stood unmoving on the trap, his feet encased in blood-red slippers, his head swathed in white. At last the jailer asked if he were tired. "No, not tired—but don't keep me waiting longer than necessary." At once the jailer swung a hatchet against the rope sustaining the trap. Came a screech of hinges and a rattle of falling planks, and the body of John Brown of Pottawatomie plummeted, jerked—and began to twist slowly on its rope.

10

■

Aftermath: Lincoln's Election

T HROUGHOUT THE NORTH at the hour of John Brown's execution bells tolled mournfully and minute guns were fired. In New York, Philadelphia, Chicago, Cleveland, Boston and many other cities, hysterical crowds were harangued by impassioned Abolitionist ministers or incendiaries such as William Lloyd Garrison and Wendell Phillips, all of them seeming to exult in the gunpowder that they said they smelled. It made no difference that most Northern newspapers, most Northern clergymen and most Northern leaders from Stephen Douglas to Abraham Lincoln denounced Brown as a murderer who deserved to die; the voices that the South heard were those of the firebrands shouting that John Brown had been sacrificed on the altar of slavery. When the South cried in horror, "He wanted to arm the *slaves!*" these Abolitionists could cry in reply, "Yes, and so do *we!*" Famous thinkers and literary men who had sincerely though mistakenly admired Brown as a selfless liberator of the enslaved were so shocked and horrified by his execution that, retreating further from reality, Emerson could now hail him as "that new saint . . . [who] will make the gallows glorious like the cross"; Thoreau could speak of "this Angel of Light" and compare Brown to Jesus Christ; and Longfellow could write in his diary: "The date of a new revolution, quite as much needed as the old one."

But the new Savior left no legacy of love, rather he put hatred in the saddle and sent it at a shrieking gallop across the land. Acrimony in the Thirty-sixth Congress was so bitter that the House seemed more like an arena than a deliberative body. Threats were exchanged, as were speeches dripping with blood. It was a rare congressman who did not carry a weapon, and when a pistol fell accidentally from the pocket of a New York member, Southerners, believing that he intended to shoot one of them, went so wild that a mass shootout was only barely averted. Even the friends of congress-

79

men in the galleries were armed, and Senator James H. Hammond of South Carolina declared: "The only persons who do not have a revolver and a knife are those who have two revolvers." On the floor there were angry harangues and fierce exchanges in language that would have disgraced a barroom, foot stamping, howls and raucous laughter; and from the galleries there came hissing, booing, catcalls and cheers as though some melodrama were being played beneath them. At times the enmity was so great—almost like a living presence—that a single shot or blow might have provoked a bloody battle that not only would have shocked the civilized world but also could have dissolved the very government. Even Washington society was dividing into rival camps. Old friends cut each other dead on the streets while their wives exchanged cold stares at the theater. Guests were invited to balls and cotillions according to their position on the slavery question.

This rising tide of mutual hatred spilled over into Charleston, South Carolina to engulf and divide the dominant Democratic Party convening there in May 1860, to nominate a candidate for president. Senator Douglas arrived in that charming and historic city supremely confident that he would be that nominee. He had no idea of the extent of the Southern extremists' detestation of him as a "traitor" or of their determination to split the party by issuing an unacceptable ultimatum: adoption in the platform of a plank promising "protection" of slavery or withdrawal from the convention.

This was the plan devised by most of the firebrands, chiefly Robert Barnwell Rhett of South Carolina, Edmund Ruffin, Robert Toombs and Alexander Stephens of Georgia, William Lowndes Yancey of Alabama and Jefferson Davis of Mississippi. There were indeed many other Southern firebrands present in Charleston, but these were the arch plotters.

Of all these agitators for secession none was more consistent or fiery than Rhett. As long ago as 1847 he had risen in the Senate to insist that Congress had no power to regulate slavery in the territories, and had joined other Southern senators like him in a passionate warning that if the Union did not protect slavery then it would be better to dissolve the Union. After he left the Senate his impassioned arguments for secession began to appear regularly in the Charleston *Mercury,* edited by his son.

Toombs and Stephens were both apologists for slavery: Toombs in the Senate and Stephens in the House. Known as the Castor and Pollux of Georgia politics, no two men could have been more dissimilar or less likely to be considered twins. Toombs was tall and graceful, handsome, with a merry eye and quick wit and a fondness for a convivial glass. It was he who gave the clearest exposition of the position of the Slavocracy when, speaking in 1856 in Boston—of all places!—he declared: "The white is the superior race, and the black the inferior; and subordination, with or without law, will be the status of the African in this mixed society; and, therefore, it is in the interests of both, and especially of the black race, and of the whole society, that this status should be fixed, controlled and protected by law."

Stephens was a tiny man, probably not more than ninety pounds, known to his colleagues as "Little Aleck." But his mind was sharper and superior to that of his bigger associate. Born into poverty and orphaned at twelve, he aspired to an education, in which determination he was helped by a kindly uncle, being graduated first in his class from the University of Georgia. Feeble and frail, punished by disease, he was driven by a burning ambition which carried him to high honors at the bar and into Congress. He was a man of great charm and high integrity, but on the question of slavery he was as adamant as Toombs. "Our new Government," he said after the Montgomery convention, "is founded . . . upon the great truth that the negro is not equal to the white man; that slavery, subordination to the superior race, is his natural condition. Thus, our new Government, is the first in the history of the world, based upon this great physical, philosophical and moral truth . . ."

The cause of Southern nationalism had no more passionate advocate than William Lowndes Yancey. Of medium height but compact build, with a square, seemingly bland face offset by expressive eyes and eloquent hands, he combined melodious voice with iron logic so effectively that his spellbound audiences were loath to hear him conclude. He had once been an ardent Jacksonian Democrat, but after his marriage into a wealthy planter family he emerged as the South's most eloquent orator in the cause of disunion.

Jefferson Davis, of course, was the beau ideal of the Southern Cavalier, the epitome of the Southern cult of courage. Tall and handsome, a hero of the Mexican War, he seemed not a man of flesh and blood but rather of marble and bronze, one who might be broken but never bent.

Some historians have maintained that Davis was not a fire-eater, but rather a moderate who had no desire to divide the Democratic Party. This might have been true of the Davis prior to John Brown but after Harpers Ferry, like so many less rabid members of the Slavocracy, his position changed. In the Senate he became an outspoken champion of Southern rights, warning that if a Republican were elected in 1860 disunion would be the consequence, and in that event, he thundered, he would tear the star of Mississippi from the American flag "to be set even on the perilous ridge of battle as a sign round which Mississippi's best and bravest should gather to the harvest-home of death."

These, then—Rhett, Ruffin, Toombs, Stephens, Yancey and Davis— were the principal architects of disunion. They derided Douglas's doctrine of popular sovereignty as another name for the containment of slavery which the Republicans sought to achieve through Congress. When their ultimatum was rejected, they led the exodus of secession-minded Southern states from the hall. They were not in the least downcast but rather jubilant, for a divided Democratic Party would guarantee a Republican victory in November and this in turn would ensure secession. So three candidates were eventually selected by the Democrats: Douglas by the Northern wing, John C. Breckinridge of Kentucky by the Southerners and John Bell of Tennessee by a more moderate group called the Constitutional Union Party. Before then the Republicans meeting in Chicago had shown a surprising unity in choosing their own nominee.

When the Republicans convened in the huge tepee-like Wigwam constructed for that purpose the front-running candidate was Senator William H. Seward of New York. He had been governor of that state and as a U.S. senator in 1858 he had said of the slavery issue: "It is an *irrepressible conflict* between opposing and enduring forces, and it means that the United States must and will, sooner or later, become either entirely a slaveholding nation, or entirely a free-labor nation." Although he later tried to soften the provocative phrase "irrepressible conflict," it stuck in Southern throats and made of Seward one of the extremists' chief bêtes noires. Eight years older than Lincoln, of Welsh-Irish stock, Seward was far from striking physically: slim and middle-sized, stooped and white-haired, with a pointed nose and an uninspiring, conversational style of speech, he was also described as having "eyes secret but penetrating, a subtle, quick man rejoicing in power." His manager at Chicago was Albany publisher Thurlow Weed, an adroit politician who well knew how to use all those Eastern dollars at his disposal. Seward, it seemed, in spite of Southern denunciations of him as "monstrous and diabolical," perhaps even because of them, seemed unstoppable. Only Abraham Lincoln of Illinois among the four other men in the running appeared to have any chance of doing so.

When Lincoln came out of retirement in 1854, his goal was not the White House, as is popularly supposed, nor was it his objective during the Lincoln-Douglas debates in 1858. Rather, his eye was on the Senate, where the giants such as Webster, Calhoun and Clay had dwelt. The presidency since Andrew Jackson had been barely more than administrative drudgery, hardly suitable to a man of Lincoln's oratorical skill and breadth of vision, and not the best place to contain slavery. But as Lincoln pressed his relentless attacks on Douglas he became more and more a national figure, especially after his speech at Cooper Union in New York, where he said: "Let us have faith that right makes might, and in that faith, let us, to the end, dare to do our duty as we understand it."

More and more Republicans began to think of Lincoln as their standard-bearer, especially after the state Republican convention in Springfield. Lincoln's cousin John Hanks had come to town carrying two tied fence rails decorated with flags and streamers bearing the inscription ABRAHAM LINCOLN, THE RAIL CANDIDATE FOR PRESIDENT IN 1860. Lincoln's supporters improved upon this and the twin sobriquets of "the Rail-Splitter" and "Honest Old Abe" were born, quickly catching the party's fancy.

Lincoln was also well served in Chicago by his floor managers, especially Judge David Davis, a shrewd mountain of a man, perhaps three hundred pounds of ambition and avarice. When Lincoln in Springfield wired them, "Make no contracts that will bind me," Davis scoffed at the idea that a nomination could be won without deals. "Lincoln ain't here," he sniffed, "and don't know what we have to meet, so we will go ahead as if we hadn't heard from him—and he must ratify it!"

From this exchange has risen a popular misconception that Lincoln's lieutenants won the nomination on their own by making "bargains" with leaders from other states, promising cabinet posts or other offices in exchange for delegations' votes. Doubtless they did give contingent or conditional pledges, as all floor managers do, but they were always acting under Lincoln's instructions. Besides, they had no more political plums to offer than Seward's managers had, and they too were limited by the contingency of victory or defeat. Here, once again, is that mythic Lincoln, "the man of the people," standing above all shady deals done in smoke-filled rooms. Actually, he was still Lincoln the practical politician, and he defeated Seward because most Republicans came to realize that the colorless Seward could not win, and that Lincoln, with his appeal, his record as a loyal party man from a crucial state, his immense popularity in the populous and vital Northeast, could not be defeated. So he was nominated on the third ballot, much to the glee of the Southern extremists, who now proclaimed that election of this "black Republican" would dissolve the Union.

On November 6, 1860, Abraham Lincoln defeated his three leading opponents. He won because his foes were split and because he carried California and Oregon and every Northern state except New Jersey, which divided its vote between him and Douglas. In the electoral college he beat his combined opponents by 180 to 123, but in the popular vote he ran far behind: 1,866,452 votes to a combined total of 2,815,617. Most Americans, then, roughly three out of five, regarded Abraham Lincoln as too radical and dangerous to be president of the United States.

The firebrands of the South thought of him as the incarnation of evil, and the threat of secession was carried out by South Carolina. Moving to Charleston—home of the hotheads—because of the fear of a smallpox epidemic in the capital of Columbia, the state legislature on December 20, 1860, passed the Ordinance of Secession. Within forty-two days the rest of the Lower South—Mississippi, Alabama, Georgia, Florida, Louisiana and Texas—followed her out of the Union, while the Alabama legislature invited them all to attend a convention in Montgomery to form the Confederate States of America and elect a president and vice president.

Secession had come. Had it been inevitable? Probably. Compromise cannot cure every crisis, and some are resolved only by war. For seventy years the new American nation had existed half slave and half free under a Constitution that, except on this very issue of slavery, had become a beacon of liberty for all those oppressed peoples yearning to be free. During those seven decades the institution of bondage hitherto almost universally accepted in the civilized world had withered and died, except in the American South; and even there it had been deplored by many Southerners, not only because it was an evil and a national disgrace but also because, in Jefferson's phrase, "We have a wolf by the ears." Twice the dreaded "firebell in the night" had clanged the discordant note of disunion and neither of the two famous compromises that stifled it had really silenced it. They had been like blinders or a Band-Aid placed over a deep and spouting wound.

Bondage had not only shocked the Northern conscience, it had placed upon the South an intolerable burden of debasing and disciplining a helot population whose productivity was not commensurate with the expense of exploitation; and the costs had been moral as well as economic. Gradually it became apparent to many Americans of good will that the honor, integrity and international influence of the United States now demanded that this pernicious institution be abolished. In the North a powerful new political party led by Abraham Lincoln had risen, insisting that this should be done and that the South should join in discussing and discovering the means by which it could be accomplished.

But the South under the influence of the firebrands who had brought about secession was saying, "No!" or, "Not now." Perhaps some time in the distant future, argued many moderate Southerners, but not in 1860 or even 1870—by which they meant "Not in our lifetime." The South's social and economic fabric had been too closely woven with the thread of slavery to resist such a shock. Even those who abhorred bondage now shrank from a policy that, it seemed to them, would result in racial amalgamation: i.e., "miscegenation," marriage between members of superior and inferior races. Miscegenation was the obverse side of the coin of white supremacy. It was the baleful threat, while supremacy was the sweet lure: the stick complementing the carrot. It was also one way, for it was only used to describe the horror of black men marrying white women. White men bedding black women—forcibly or otherwise—was already an accepted custom in the South, where the mulatto offspring joined the slave population.

So the rupture had come. The passionately righteous North simply could not or would not cease the agitation of the slave question, and the proud and sensitive South could no longer endure the outrageous slings and arrows of the moralizing Abolitionists. Pride versus passion, the unfailing recipe for hatred, had had its way. As Mrs. Mary Chestnut of Charleston was to write in her famous diary: ". . . we are divorced, North from South, because we have hated each other so."

11

.

The South Secedes

O NE OF THE MOST persistent myths that have wreathed the causes of the American Civil War in mists of obfuscation is the mistaken belief that the voters of the seven seceding states of the Lower South were almost unanimous in their desire for secession. In truth, it was only by the narrowest of margins that the extremists with their carpetbags full of hobgoblins were able to bring it off.

Between the secession of South Carolina on December 20, 1860, and January 8, 1861, the voters of six other states of the Lower South chose delegates to conventions that would decide whether or not to leave the Union. There were no party labels during this voting, only an obscure distinction between Secessionists and Cooperationists. Nor was there any antithesis between simple disunionism or unionism, for in fact most of the eligible male voters of the South preferred to remain in the Union if they were given satisfactory guarantees, which, of course, they did not really expect to receive. Conversely, there were few Unionists who publicly preferred loyalty to Washington over "Southern rights." Both parties were committed to Southern rights as well as to the use of secession to obtain them. But the Secessionists were for immediate disunion through the medium of the state conventions, while the Cooperationists were not yet ready to secede and also opposed the means at hand. They wanted a cooling-off period before the entire South could consider it, a position that led the Secessionists to suspect that their demand for delay was a tactic intended to block disunion. Unfortunately the local elections that were held without party labels and thus with no statewide ticket were so poorly organized and patternless that only modern scholarship has determined that secession actually had been "a bit of a near thing." But one fact clearly emerges: the Secessionists, like Lenin and his Bolsheviks in the Russian Revolution, knew exactly what they wanted—and that was dissolution of the Union.

They were also keenly aware of the rising excitement actually approaching hysteria that had gripped the South. John Brown's insurrection was not much more than a year old and the rancor of the presidential campaign remained a lingering bitterness in Southern throats. Hatred of the North and distrust of Lincoln were cleverly stimulated by the Secessionist leaders in endless public meetings, fiery speeches and the organization of military units often called "minutemen." Cooperationists were not only denounced, they were also intimidated, and clergymen in the pulpit joined politicians on the stump in warning of the dangers to Southern rights and urging the people to depart this accursed Union. In this they were assisted by vigilantes organized to defend against supposedly imminent Abolitionist plots to arouse the slaves, or by exuberant youths parading in newly raised military companies with colorful names. Secessionists derided the Cooperationists as old women or abject "submissionists."

Such hostility undoubtedly reduced the number of Cooperationists who voted, and yet, the results were remarkably close. In Mississippi on December 20, with many voters still inflamed by news of the South Carolina secession, some 41,000 votes were cast. Of these about 12,000 were for candidates whose positions were unspecified or are now unknown; and of the remaining 29,000, some 16,800 were for the Secessionists and 12,218 for Cooperationists. In Florida only two days later, the Cooperationists received between 36 and 43 percent of the vote; and in Alabama two days after that, the Secessionist cause received 35,600 ballots and the Cooperationist 28,100.

During January in elections varying between 13 and 20 days after the Charleston declaration, the margin was even narrower. Georgia was only 44,152 to 41,632 at the most generous estimate. Louisiana was 20,214 to 18,451. In Texas, Governor Sam Houston refused to convene the legislature, and an election of convention delegates was called for by an informal group of Secessionists in Austin. Delegates to this assembly of doubtful legality voted 166 to 8 to secede; but then, questioning their own assembly's validity, asked the voters to ratify their action. They did, by 44,317 to 13,020, but it must be remembered that in Texas intimidation of Cooperationists was the most widespread.

Finally, in these most crucial elections in the history of the states conducting them, the voting was extremely light when compared to the presidential election, an indication not of apathy keeping voters away from the polls, for these were exciting days indeed. Rather it suggests something far worse: intimidation. In Georgia the total vote was 82 percent of the presidential turnout, in Alabama it was 70 percent, and in Mississippi only 60 percent. In no state did the Secessionists receive a vote large enough to have been a majority in the November election.

From these facts and figures it may be clearly seen how close the decision to secede had been in the Lower South. If only one or two states, say Georgia and Alabama, had received less resolute and impassioned leadership from the Secessionists, and the Cooperationists had consequently responded less timidly to intimidation, the vote could have gone the other way. And this would have broken the South Carolina spell, for it would have influenced the later-voting states, such as Louisiana and Texas. The Palmetto State would have been left alone as it had been in the Nullification crisis of 1832. But South Carolina had taken the gamble of December 20, and supported by the extremists of other states had acted with a rare speed and decisiveness that had a dizzying effect on the ordinary voter. A South Carolina extremist wrote: "I do not believe that the common people understand it [secession]; but whoever waited for the common people when a great movement was to be made? We must make the move and force them to follow." South Carolina's commissioner to Florida said: "I . . . believe that if . . . South Carolina had stated some distant day for future action, to see if other states would join us, and thus had allowed the public feeling to subside, she herself would have lost the spirit of adventure and would have quailed from the shock of this great controversy." Christopher Memminger, an extremist from the same state, declared, "Our great point is to move the other Southern states before there is any recoil," and so great a fire-eater as Howell Cobb of Georgia cried in alarm: "It looks as if they are afraid the blood of the people will cool down."

Among the states of the Upper South, especially in Tennessee and Virginia, South Carolina was cordially detested as a "pestiferous grumbler" or a "nuisance" or a state seized by "frenzy [that] surpasses in folly and wickedness anything which fancy in her wildest move has been able to conceive." In Wilmington, North Carolina, the *Herald* asked: "Will you suffer yourself to be spit upon in this way? Are you *submissionists* to the dictation of South Carolina . . . are you to be called cowards because you do not follow the crazy lead of that crazy state?" In Charlottesville, Virginia, the *Review* declared that it "hated South Carolina for precipitating secession."

So the Secessionists had triumphed. They had moved swiftly before a solid opposition could be organized, had chosen a period of high excitement and bitter resentment to ask for a decision, and had artfully deceived the people in all the slaveholding states—a majority of whom opposed secession—into believing that they faced an agonizing alternative of either leaving the Union or fighting against the South. Most clever of all they minimized the likelihood of a civil war.

When the firebrands threw down the gauntlet they actually did believe that it would not be picked up, that the soft, effete Yankees would not fight. After all, were not all of America's military heroes Southerners? From George Washington to Andrew Jackson to Winfield Scott to Zachary Taylor, they were all from Dixie. Now, standing behind them stood a new company of glorious Southern knights, commanders such as Jefferson Davis and Robert E. Lee. They would lead the indomitable Southern fighting man in defense of the homeland: those once-despised "Pineys" and "Sandhillers," "Red Necks" and "Peckerwoods," who, for all their ignorance and superstition, had been born and bred to adversity, Napoleon's "school of the good soldier." These hunters and woodsmen inured to the rigors of the outdoor life would surely make the "pasty-faced mechanics" of the North tremble. Would the Yankees dare risk a trial of arms against such leaders and such men? Here was the cult of courage speaking—a bit self-consciously per- haps—and although bravery is indeed the soldier's cardinal virtue, along with élan and esprit, and although these three can surely win battles on their own, they cannot win a war. Certainly not a modern war. What the fire- brands—these sons of an agrarian aristocracy—had ignored or did not appreciate was the North's passionate devotion to the Union, plus the more important fact that the Industrial Revolution had overtaken war.

Splendid troops superbly led still mattered, of course, but only in combat. What now mattered more in waging modern war were railroads and the telegraph, factories and shipyards, together with the technical and organizing skills borrowed from the world of commerce that overcome the vast new problems of logistics—the care, movement and quartering of great bodies of troops—so that men are mobilized more rapidly, armed, clothed and trained, and then sent faster and in superior numbers at the throats of the enemy. In a word, the South might have spiritual power but the North had firepower; the South was not industrialized but the North was.

Few if any of these fiery Secessionists grasped this. Even in the North, with the possible exception of General-in-Chief Winfield Scott, few officers in the tiny regular army of the time could comprehend how much more hideous wheels and turbines, lathes and steam, had made the horrid face of Mars. But William Tecumseh Sherman saw it clearly.

■   ■   ■

Sherman had begun the fourth profession of his checkered career: a soldier, banker and lawyer, he was now an educator, superintendent of the Louisiana State Seminary of Learning and Military Academy (forerunner of modern Louisiana State University). He had accepted the post and come South because he needed employment and thought the warm climate might cure his asthma. He was also very fond of Southerners. But his affection changed to dismay in May of 1860 when the seven cotton states bolted the Democratic convention. He saw the awful specter of disunion and agreed with Alexander Stephens's dire prediction: "Envy, hate, jealousy, spite—these made war in heaven, which made devils out of angels . . . Mark me when I repeat that in less than twelve months we shall be in the midst of a bloody war."

Sherman had hoped that the obvious economic inferiority of a slave society to a free one would make it disappear. He despised the Abolitionists for their naive contention that an ignorant, illiterate slave could instantly step from squalor and bondage into freedom and prosperity, just as they themselves believed that they could destroy the institution with epithets. He also had a fine contempt for disunionist prattle of a great new empire based on bondage when it was just as plain that the cotton states of the Lower South and the tobacco- and corn-growing Upper South would also separate, and that this would be followed by dissolution everywhere. He did not vote in the presidential election, chiefly because he resented suggestions that he show himself at the polls lest he be accused of finding no ticket in Louisiana that suited him. Besides, he believed there would be war no matter who won.

For a prophet of such perception and clarity it is amazing that the actual secession of South Carolina, then, should have come to him as a shocking calamity. It was Christmas Eve at the seminary. The cadets had gone home and Sherman was alone in his room with Professor David French Boyd, a Virginian who was his friend and confidant, when the Charleston *Mercury* arrived with the headline: THE UNION IS DISSOLVED!

The tall, slender Sherman sprang to his feet in anguish. Tears streamed down his cheeks, darkening his red beard. He began to pace the floor, halting occasionally to stand over Boyd and level a finger at him as though he were the people of the South.

"You, you the people of the South, believe there can be such a thing as a peaceable secession. You don't know what you are doing. I know there can be no such thing. . . . If you will have it, the North must fight you for its own preservation. Yes, South Carolina has by this act precipitated war. . . . This country will be drenched in blood. God only knows how it will end.

Perhaps the liberties of the whole country, of every section and every man will be destroyed, and yet you know that within the Union no man's liberty or property in all the South is endangered.

"Oh, it is all folly, madness, a crime against civilization.

"You people speak so lightly of war. You don't know what you are talking about. War is a terrible thing. I know you are a brave, fighting people, but for every day of actual fighting, there are months of marching, exposure and suffering. More men die in war from sickness than are killed in battle. At best war is a frightful loss of life and property, and worse still is the demoralization of the people . . .

"You mistake, too, the people of the North. They are a peaceable people, but an earnest people and will fight too, and they are not going to let the country be destroyed without a mighty effort to save it.

"Besides, where are your men and appliances of war to contend against them? The Northern people not only greatly outnumber the whites of the South, but they are a mechanical people with manufactures of every kind, while you are only agriculturists—a sparse population covering a large extent of territory, and in all history no nation of mere agriculturists ever made successful war against a nation of mechanics . . .

"The North can make a steam engine, locomotive or railway car; hardly a yard of cloth or a pair of shoes can you make. You are rushing into war with one of the most powerful, ingeniously mechanical and determined people on earth—right at your doors. You are bound to fail. Only in spirit and determination are you prepared for war. In all else you are totally unprepared, with a bad cause to start with.

"At first you will make headway, but as your limited resources begin to fail, and shut out from the markets of Europe by blockade as you will be, your cause will begin to wane. . . . If your people would but stop and think, they must see that in the end you will surely fail. . . ."

William Tecumseh paused, his flood of words halted but his tears still flowing. The Union he loved above all else was breaking up. He must draw his sword and fight to preserve it, he said in a voice breaking with anguish: against his friends, "against your people, who I love best."

In February 1861 he resigned his position and hurried north. By then the Confederate States had been formed and given a provisional constitution.

In Montgomery the delegates from the seven seceded states had advanced their own interpretation of the old Constitution: that the Union was not an indissoluble nation of federated states but rather only a league of sovereign and independent states. Reciting their grievances against the North—injury in taxation, tariffs and an unequal distribution of national benefits—they set to work with intelligence and purifying zeal to create a constitution superior to the one that they were repudiating.

They began by invoking "the favor and guidance of Almighty God," an allusion to Providence which the mostly deistic Founding Fathers had studiously avoided, after which they proceeded to make some remarkable innovations. First, the president and vice president were elected for one six-year term only, and the chief executive had budgetary control over expenditures that could be broken only by a two-thirds vote of Congress. Congress was forbidden to pass a protective tariff or to appropriate money for internal improvements, and all outlays were to be subjected to searching scrutiny. There would be no spoils system, no bounties to be paid by the Treasury and no deficit permitted in the postal service. Each law must deal with only one subject, thereby preventing a repetition of Washington's vicious practice of attaching "riders" to bills, and the president had the power of line veto in appropriation bills. Amendments could be ratified by two-thirds rather than three-fourths of the states. Cabinet members were to be seated in Congress for discussion of departmental affairs. Although the new document expressly forbade revival of the slave trade, it spoke openly of "slaves," whereas the old one had used the euphemistic "persons," and in all territory of the Confederacy slavery was to be "protected and recognized" by both the national and state governments. Here indeed was a remarkable attempt to make democratic government more efficient and honorable than the apparatus in Washington, and although it would be another year before this instrument was fully ratified, the provisional government was given all the power of the permanent one-to-be.

A measure of how thoroughly aroused the Lower South had become, and how effectively the voices of reason and moderation had been stilled, was the rapid and unanimous election on February 9 of Jefferson Davis as president and Alexander Stephens as vice president. And when the tall, austere Mississippian arrived in Montgomery on the night of February 16, 1861, it was the fiery and eloquent William Yancey who took him by the hand and introduced him to a wild and tumultuous throng with the clarion cry:

"The man and the hour have met!"

12

■

Jefferson Davis

J EFFERSON DAVIS'S first known ancestor in America migrated to Philadelphia from Wales in the eighteenth century, and his father, Samuel Emory Davis, was a grandson of this Welshman. Samuel left Philadelphia to settle in Georgia, joining the Patriot cause and fighting against the British for four years. While serving in South Carolina he fell in love with Jane Cook, an extremely pretty girl of Scots-Irish stock whom he married after the war. Jane Davis was said to have retained her grace and beauty well into old age, so that at eighty-five an observer could still find her fair to look upon: "Her eyes were bright, her hair was a soft brown and her complexion clear and white as a child's."

For his service in the Revolution the state of Georgia granted Samuel Davis a tract of farming land near Augusta. There his superior education enabled him to secure the position of county clerk, but his restless nature caused him in 1793 to move his wife and five children to the bluegrass region of Kentucky. There he built a double log cabin of four rooms famed locally for its glass windows, and here on June 3, 1808, Jefferson Davis was born. He entered life in surroundings that were luxurious in comparison to the rude one-room cabin in which Abraham Lincoln was born eight months later less than a hundred miles away. Because the new baby was the tenth child and his mother at forty-five could expect no more, Samuel, who named him after his hero, Thomas Jefferson, whimsically added the middle name of "Finis." But Jefferson, who had less humor than his taciturn father, later dropped it.

When Jefferson was two his father moved again, taking the family to Bayou Teche in Louisiana; but a plague of malarial mosquitoes made the area so unhealthy that he later retreated to southwestern Mississippi near a town named Woodville. Here Samuel, who had raised tobacco and horses in Kentucky, became a cotton planter, working in the fields with his few slaves. He prospered, building a fine house with a large veranda which his poetic wife gave the romantic name of Rosemont.

Little is known of Jefferson's childhood, except that as the youngest he was the recipient of much attention and affection from his mother and his siblings, especially from his brother Joseph, twenty-three years older than he, who supplied the paternal fondness sometimes lacking in his austere father. Being the darling of the family quite naturally created in little Jeffie, as he was called, an exaggerated idea of his own worth which would one day emerge as hauteur and often intolerance of others.

Autocrat that Samuel Davis might be—in which he differed not an iota from the standard Southern paterfamilias of his era—he did have the best interests of his children at heart, especially in their education. He also had none of the prejudice against Catholics common to his fellow Baptists, and thus his wife was not really surprised when he announced his intention of sending eight-year-old Jefferson to a Catholic school in Kentucky. Jane's only objection was that he was too young to be sent to school so far from home. But Samuel replied that the Dominican priests at the College of St. Thomas Aquinas were known to be excellent teachers and that was where Jeffie was going. Jefferson was himself elated, finding the trip with a lawyer friend of his brother Joseph a great adventure, especially when passing through the wilderness of the famed Natchez Trace inhabited by Choctaw Indians. But the real high point of the journey came in Tennessee when they stopped for a long visit at the Hermitage, the home of Andrew Jackson and his wife, Rachel. From this experience, Jefferson formed a lasting admiration for Old Hickory, who proved to be as courteous and considerate to his guests as he was known to be tough and formidable to his enemies.

At St. Thomas, Jefferson discovered that he was the only Protestant among the student body. A natural desire to be like his peers led him to ask admission to the Catholic Church, but the fathers, aware of their obligation to the boy's parents, as well as of the transitory nature of such impulsive conversions, gently dissuaded him from this purpose. When Jefferson came home two years later, he was still a Baptist; and also, like his father, totally without prejudice against any sect, a trait that would lead him to oppose the anti-Catholic crusade of the Nativists and Know-Nothings during the Forties and Fifties.

Next Jefferson briefly attended Jefferson College near Natchez, before transferring to the county academy near his home. Although he was highly disdainful of the primitive teaching methods in this typical log-cabin school, he counted himself fortunate in having a brilliant "Boston Yankee" as headmaster. Here there occurred an incident indicative of his high-spirited but willful nature. His teacher gave him a piece to memorize that he considered too long. Next day when the teacher found that he had deliberately not committed it to memory, he threatened to whip him. Jefferson's response was to seize his books and march defiantly out the door. At home his father quietly gave him a choice between returning to school or working in the fields. After two days of picking cotton with the slaves in the hot Mississippi sun, he changed his mind and went back to the academy. Obviously, this imperious son of an autocratic father did not enjoy being crossed or challenged—nor would he ever.

In the spring of 1823—when he was not yet fifteen—Jefferson enrolled in the then-famous Transylvania University in Lexington, Kentucky, and the quality of his education rose dramatically. Here was a distinguished school with an enrollment larger than Harvard's and a reputation rivaling even that doyen of American colleges. Of it Thomas Jefferson, despairing of founding the University of Virginia, could write: "We must send our children for education to Kentucky (Transylvania) or Cambridge (Harvard). The latter will return them to us as fanatics and tories, and the former will keep them to add to their population. If, however, we are to go begging anywhere for education, I would rather it should be in Kentucky . . ."

It was probably at Transylvania that Jefferson Davis began to develop his aristocratic manners and to accept the full set of Southern ideals and values. Granted the aristocratic background of the student body, some of whom came to school attended by slave valets, it could hardly have been otherwise. He was always proud of his association with the school, pleased to find that when he took his seat in the U.S. Senate, six of the other fifty-nine senators were graduates of Transylvania.

In July of 1824, Jefferson was shocked to learn of the death of his father on Independence Day. Jefferson's grief at the loss of the father whose memory he would always revere, if not exactly love, was somewhat assuaged when he learned that the old man and Joseph had secured him an appointment to the United States Military Academy. But then he demurred, hoping to finish at Transylvania or to attend the newly opened University of Virginia. But Joseph persuaded him to go to West Point, and he was accepted there on September 30, 1824.

Jefferson Davis was agreeably surprised by the almost absolute Southern cast of the West Point of 1824. In its ideals, style and religion it was decidedly Dixie and openly patrician. All cadets were required to attend Episcopal services on Sunday, be they Baptist, Methodist, Presbyterian,

Lutheran or whatever other Protestant denomination, and even those rare Catholic birds who alighted on the Plains from time to time found themselves perched in an Episcopal pew.

In its attitude toward government and politics, the Academy was similarly aristocratic. Cadets were encouraged to accept things as they were and not to indulge in any fanciful nonsense about changing the world. It was believed that men of the South, born and bred to rule, were quite properly in charge of the nation. Even the sons of antislavery Yankees came to see the wisdom of this, and were quick to inform their outraged parents that the United States in its history of thirty-five years had spent all of them under presidents of Southern birth or ideals.

Doubtless this disdainfully patrician stance, designed to produce young reactionaries who stood and thought ramrod straight, accounted for the angry resentment of West Point that was at that time common among much of Congress and the nation. In the House the Academy was described as "a hotbed of aristocracy," while in the farm-based West it was openly detested as a school for snobs. Americans who had heard the Indian war whoop or still ate their meals with sharpened sassafras sticks believed that government funds were being used to train the indolent sons of the well-to-do to be "the scions of a nascent nobility." A Western farmer's son had about as much chance of being admitted to the Point as the biblical rich man had of passing through the pearly gates. One result of this attitude was that the West rarely availed itself of its quota of appointees, so that other congressmen—especially those from Dixie with its emphasis on military training—were able to make deals to fill Western vacancies from their own districts. Thus a youth from Georgia who had never been north of the Savannah River would receive an appointment from Ohio. Another consequence of anti-Academy rancor was that West Point was constantly in danger of being abolished.

Founded in 1802 over the objections of the pacifist Thomas Jefferson, the United States Military Academy had not really had the time to graduate officers who would distinguish themselves as generals in a major war. Neither Andrew Jackson nor Winfield Scott—the two heroes of the War of 1812—had attended West Point, and none of the ongoing conflicts with the various Indian tribes could honestly be described as a "war." Nor did the Academy have any means of refuting critics who mocked the "life of luxury" lived on the Plains, except to invite them to inspect the facility.

None accepted, of course. If they had, they would have been shocked by the poor food, spartan discipline and horrendous hours imposed on these supposed aspirants to effete snobbery. Two cadets shared a small room furnished with a table, two chairs and a clothes compartment. There was no bedstead. Instead the cadets slept on mattresses on the floor. They were required to buy their own mirror, washstand and wash basin, and to clean their quarters themselves with their own pails, brooms and scrubbing brushes. Additional furniture or implements were strictly forbidden. So was any literature unrelated to classwork. A cadet could not play a musical instrument on Sunday or profane the Sabbath in any way, and at no time was he allowed to play chess, backgammon, cards or any other games. Cadets also were forbidden to drink or possess intoxicating liquors or to use tobacco. They could not keep a horse, dog or servant.

Discipline was the goddess of West Point and her twin votaries were Drill and Duty. Bugle calls awoke the cadets at dawn and they studied until seven, when they ate a plain and tasteless breakfast, studying or making classroom recitals from eight until one o'clock. They then marched to dinner, returning to their classrooms from two until four. Next came the drilling, marching, and counter-marching to shouted commands or putting their muskets through the manual of arms. It lasted until sunset, when the flag came down with ceremony. After supper, the books came out again to be studied until lights-out was blown at ten o'clock. Between rising and retiring, then, there were roll calls and inspections and for every three hours off duty, one had to be spent walking guard.

A cadet was supposed to be impeccably neat, especially in his uniform, consisting of a gray coat trimmed in black and festooned with brass buttons and topped by a high black leather collar and stiff leather hat. It was uncomfortable, especially the dress uniform with its tight white pants. Sloppy uniforms were the chief cause of demerits given to cadets. Other infractions—all trivial—such as laughing on the parade ground, an unbuttoned coat, walking post in an unsoldierly manner, not properly shaved, late for reveille, etc., could lower a cadet's standing no matter how brilliantly he performed in class. One hundred demerits in any given semester or two hundred in a scholastic year meant expulsion. So did a clandestine visit to Benny Haven's off-limits tavern for a plate of oysters to erase the taste of Academy food or a foaming glass to help forget the rigid regimentation. For first-yearmen or plebes the only real relief came during summer encampment, when they would march from their barracks out to tents pitched on the Plains, living there from late June until late August while learning to ride, shoot or build a bridge.

Academically, West Point stood very low when compared to other American colleges and universities. The law forbade any entrance examination on any subjects other than those taught at rural country schools—in other words, no more than the three R's. Some students had to ask what algebra was. Three years at West Point would put a cadet abreast of a student entering most colleges elsewhere, and four would carry him to the end of the freshman year at Yale, Harvard or Princeton. The scientific and most difficult section of study was two years of mathematics, one in physics and chemistry and one in construction. Then there was a little English, mental philosophy, moral philosophy, elementary law, two years of French and one of Spanish. There was no instruction in strategy or grand tactics, military history or the art of war. There had been a course in Jomini, Napoleon's chief strategist, but this had been dropped. Thus the great military theorist whose works were the bible for the student soldiers of Europe had been ignored, and although rudimentary instruction was given in artillery, infantry and cavalry, there was no attempt to make genuine professionals of these young men, so many of whom were to become the generals of the Civil War.

Cadet Davis was just a shade under six feet tall, slender and graceful, strikingly handsome in a refined and slightly haughty way with his large, deep-set, gray-blue eyes, his thick, wavy blond hair and perfectly proportioned nose and mouth. He was a favorite among his Southern classmates, but not quite so popular among the Northerners, who resented his unconcealed disdain for Yankees, most especially his hilarious contempt for their horsemanship. Davis's willfulness was again evident in his frequent abstentions from chapel—and although he delighted in listening to the soaring periods of Chaplain Charles McIlwaine, he did not drop his critical, skeptical attitude toward revealed religion and become converted, like his friend Leonidas Polk, whose enthusiasm for the Episcopal faith was so great that he eventually became one of its bishops.

Nor was Davis's conduct exemplary. In his plebe year he was arrested and charged with violating the prohibition against drinking or patronizing Benny Haven's tavern. He defended himself with the specious argument that he was accused of an *ex post facto* offense, the ban on the tavern not having been published when he visited it, and also that a heavy rainstorm had driven him there from his tent. The court-martial did not agree, convicting him as charged and sentencing him to expulsion, and then remitting it in consideration of his previous clean record. Two years later—on Christmas Eve, 1826—Davis was caught at an egg-nog party given by Southern students. In a riot against the officers that followed, seventy cadets were arrested and nineteen of them were expelled. Fortunately for Davis, the egg nog had put him to sleep before he could join the protest, and he was merely confined to quarters for drinking.

There were numerous other offenses, so many that it is difficult to understand how this unruly cadet, courteous and charming though he might be in his outward demeanor, could remain at an Academy run by the famous but iron-handed and puritanical Superintendent Sylvanus Thayer. Davis received demerits for sloppy quarters, visiting during study hours, creating disturbances during same, long hair, absent from reveille, absent from class and from evening parade, firing his musket out his dormitory window, disobeying orders, drinking, refusing to march from mess hall, cooking in his quarters after "lights out," candlestick out of place (which sounds like a euphemism for something more serious) and "foul clothes not in clothes bag." Such an accumulation of violations had to have a disastrous effect on Davis's academic standing, and should account in great part for his rank of twenty-third in a class of thirty-two when he was graduated as a brevet second lieutenant on June 30, 1828.

Lieutenant Davis's first assignment was in Fort Winnebago in Michigan Territory. Here he was joined by Jim Pemberton, the faithful young slave given to him by his father. It was Jim who nursed Davis back to health after he came down with pneumonia during the severe northern winter. Though Jefferson was the master and Jim the bondsman, Davis now loved him like a brother. But the illness, the first of many that were to afflict this hard-working man so careless of his health, so gravely emaciated Davis that his deep-set eyes seemed to sink deeper in their sockets and his high cheekbones seemed sharp and chiseled. There now began for Davis a harsh yet tedious routine of life on various frontier forts in Michigan and Arkansas territories. He came to admire the rough frontiersmen he encountered, but developed a contempt for the Indians. "Take them as a mass," he declared years later during a Senate debate, "they are as deceptive, as bloodthirsty, as treacherous, as cowardly a race of men as are to be found on this globe."

In March of 1833 Davis came to a crisis of conscience over the conflict on tariffs between South Carolina and the Federal government. Led by Calhoun, the Palmetto State passed its famous Nullification Act describing the tariff laws of 1828 and 1832 as "null and void" and refusing to collect the imposts. Congress replied by granting President Jackson the authority to use force if necessary to make South Carolina obey the law. Thus Davis as an officer of the U.S. Army might be ordered into action against a state of his beloved South. Of this he later said: "By education, by association and by preference I was a soldier, then regarding that profession as my vocation in life. Yet, looking the issue squarely in the face, I chose the alternative of abandoning my profession rather than be employed in the subjugation or coercion of a State of the Union . . ." At twenty-five Davis was already convinced of the validity of Calhoun's doctrine of states' rights, nor would he, granting his inflexible loyalty to all things Southern, ever deviate from it. Fortunately for him, South Carolina accepted Henry Clay's Compromise Tariff Act and repealed its own law of Nullification.

During his duty on lonely outposts in Michigan and Arkansas territories, where the deadly military routine was only occasionally broken by a horse race or a wolf fight, Davis did not, like so many other young officers, seek to escape boredom by developing a fondness for drink or cards, but rather plunged into a study of the law. Still he was delighted when, in April 1832, while he was at Fort Crawford in Michigan, Colonel Zachary Taylor took command of the post. This was because he almost immediately fell in love with Taylor's eighteen-year-old daughter, Sarah, a pretty and extremely feminine Southern girl with long blond hair, exquisite manners and a will of iron. But Taylor opposed the courtship because he did not want his daughter to embrace the hard dull life of a soldier's wife. So his indomitable daughter arranged to meet her lover secretly at the home of a friend, seeking unsuccessfully, meanwhile, to secure her father's approval of the marriage.

In the meantime, in February 1835, Davis, now a first lieutenant of dragoons, found himself facing a court-martial on charges of conduct "subversive of military discipline." Major R. B. Mason claimed that Davis had failed to answer reveille roll call and, when asked why, had yawned contemptuously, refusing to obey an order to go to his quarters until it was repeated three times. Such accusations, like "silent contempt" or "offensive indolence," usually issue from brains bound in braid and Davis might have laughed his pompous accuser out of court. Instead, his wounded pride led him to spend six days hotly defending his honor and counter-charging the major with having spoken to him disparagingly in the presence of his troops. He concluded with the proud question: "Can it be required of a gentleman, is it part of the character of a soldier, to humble himself beneath the haughty tone or quail before the angry eye of any man?" It was a devotee of the code duello who spoke, and even before he did he had decided to leave the army, and his acquittal only hardened him in that resolve. Granted a leave of absence, he resigned effective June 30, 1835.

Jefferson Davis had spent seven years in uniform and had shown himself to be a courageous, resourceful officer able to command men. He had also revealed an inordinate pride joined to an exalted sense of honor which might find insult in the most honest opposition or criticism and which, shorn of a saving sense of humor, could never be humbled or made harmless. His health had suffered, too, permanently impaired by pneumonia and his eyesight weakened by prolonged exposure to the blinding snows of the frontier. But Jefferson Davis was only twenty-seven, and high-spirited young men are seldom aware of such afflictions. More, he was happy, for by hanging up his sword he had freed himself to marry Sarah Knox Taylor.

The wedding took place on June 17, 1835, at the Louisville home of Sarah's aunt, a sister of Zachary Taylor. No one from either the Davis or Taylor families was present. Sarah later wrote to her mother begging forgiveness for having married without the consent of her parents, and her father sent her large gifts of money, suggesting that he might in time have given his grudging assent.

But there was not to be much time. First the newlyweds visited Davis's brother Joseph and his wife on their great plantation, Hurricane, in Mississippi. Next, for some inexplicable reason, Davis in the late and dangerous summer of the Lower South took his delicate bride into malarial Louisiana to visit his sister Anna. Here both of them sickened of that dreadful fever. They were nursed in separate rooms. Davis, hearing his wife in her delirium singing "Fairy Bells"—a song they both loved—struggled to his feet and went to her side to be with her when she died. That was on September 15. They had been married only three months.

During the following month Davis was himself in danger of dying. But he recovered, and when he was well enough to travel went to his brother's plantation to recuperate. For years afterward he was subject to recurrent attacks of malaria, and his grief at the death of Sarah, easily as deep as his love for her, remained with him even longer. Lonely and bored as well, he sought to revive his spirits by a trip to Havana and thence to Washington. Upon his return to Mississippi, his brother Joseph gave him a plantation which he named Brierfield because of the abundance of briers on the uncultivated land. With the help of Jim Pemberton and a few other slaves he cleared it, planted cotton and built a cottage—and here he lived in seclusion until, at Christmas, 1843, more than eight years after the death of Sarah, he met Varina Howell of Natchez.

Varina was a tall, statuesque brunette with regular features which, though not making for delicate feminine beauty, nevertheless gave her the serene face of a madonna. With her wit, insight and power of expression, she had an attractive personality and was unusually well educated for a Southern girl of that time. For twelve years she had been tutored in the

Greek and Latin classics, and although her family had little in the way of wealth or pedigree she had acquired aristocratic ideas and manners from Natchez society and a certain ancestral pride in a Whig grandfather who had been governor of New Jersey. Varina was only seventeen and Davis was thirty-five when they met, and she was as unlike Sarah as strength differs from the exquisite, yet Davis fell for her.

Varina at first was not exactly overwhelmed by the attentions of this handsome, ardent man. "He impresses me as a remarkable kind of man," she wrote her mother, "but of uncertain temper, and has a way of taking for granted that everybody agrees with him when he expresses his opinions, which offends me." This perceptive and wry young lady could also say: "Yet, he is most agreeable, and has a peculiarly sweet voice and a winning manner of asserting himself. The fact is he is the kind of person I should expect to rescue one from a mad dog at any risk, but to insist upon a stoical indifference to fright afterwards. Would you believe it, he is refined and cultivated and yet he is a Democrat."

He was indeed of that persuasion, and during his courtship he spent many fruitless hours trying to wean his true love away from her Whig allegiance. His assault upon her heart was rather more successful, and in January of 1844, with Varina enjoying the prolonged visit customary among plantation families, they were engaged. Varina returned to Natchez shortly afterward to find her mother adamantly opposed to her marrying a man eighteen years her senior. In the end she relented, probably because Varina's improvident father perceived a good thing in this prospective son-in-law. On February 26, 1845, in a wedding delayed by one of Varina's frequent illnesses, they were married in an Episcopal ceremony at the bride's home in Natchez. None of Davis's relatives attended, especially not Joseph, who had justifiable reservations about his brother's marrying into a large, impecunious family.

The newlyweds took a steamboat down the Mississippi to Louisiana, staying at the home of his sister Anna, where Sarah had died. Jefferson took Varina with him on a visit to her grave, a strange pilgrimage indeed for a man on his honeymoon. Returning with her to Brierfield, he was pleased to see how Varina, who shared his love for roses and shrubs, was delighted with his little cottage. Here they lived for five years until they moved into a more pretentious home which Davis built.

In the meantime, his happiness had ended his seclusion forever and involved him deeper in politics. He had already run for the Mississippi lower house in 1842, only to be defeated by the overwhelming Whig majority in his native Warren County; and in 1844 he spent much of the year campaigning for James Knox Polk. Mississippi voters, and especially his party, were impressed by his dignified calm and melodious voice. His arrant sectionalism, often expressed in frightful purple passages, were the delight of the roaring crowds at all those pig-and-whiskey barbecues. Inevitably his party made him a candidate for the U.S. House of Representatives, and he was elected with the second highest vote, much to the dismay of his wife. She had seen how malaria would succeed his long rides in the sun and how the fever worsened his failing sight and impaired one of his eyes. After he entered politics, Varina wrote: "Then I began to know the bitterness of being a politician's wife, and that it meant long absences, pecuniary depletion from ruinous absenteeism, illness from exposure, misconceptions, defamation of character; everything which darkens the sunlight and contracts the happy sphere of home." Why, then, did this devoted couple endure all this? Not for money certainly, for congressmen were paid next to nothing then. Probably, with Davis at least, it was for prestige and also to defend his beloved South against "the fanatical spirit" of the North. But then in 1846 the wily James Polk provoked the Mexican War, and Jefferson Davis put aside his civilian suit of gray homespun to clothe himself once more in the blue uniform of the United States Army.

Jefferson Davis was made a colonel in command of a regiment of volunteers known as the Mississippi Rifles. It was in great part due to Colonel Davis's discipline and ability to train troops that this formation emerged as one of the finest in the Mexican War. He was strict, holding his troops to his own high code of honor. When they stole corn from a Mexican farmer, he rebuked them and paid for the pilfered grain. No soldier among the Mississippi Rifles dared despoil the Mexican churches gorgeous with silver and jewel-studded statuary. In this they were unlike most volunteers lured into service by recruiters' promises of "roast beef, two dollars a day, plenty of whiskey, golden Jesuses and pretty Mexican girls." These were the wild and green troops who came whooping into the unsanitary camps of the Southwest where they rioted, sickened and died.

Davis was also fortunate in serving under his former father-in-law and old regimental commander, Brigadier General Zachary Taylor. Taylor was the idol of his troops. Unlike Winfield Scott with his fondness for military splendor, he cared little for ceremony. He was short and squat and swarthy, homely and rough-cut, his weather-beaten face lined and furrowed beneath his iron gray hair. One of his men described him as wearing "an old oil cap, a dusty green coat, a frightful pair of trousers and on horseback looks like a toad." But his willingness to share his soldiers' hardships and his courage in battle, calmly issuing orders while seated aboard his horse, Old Whitey, inspired his men. To them he was "Old Rough 'n Ready."

Taylor invaded Mexico from the north after provoking the series of skirmishes that gave Polk the doubtful basis for his call for a declaration of war. Taylor had about 6,600 men, half of them untrained volunteers, the rest regulars of whom 47 percent were foreigners: 24 percent Irish and 10 percent German. He took Monterrey, where Davis and his regiment distinguished themselves, but then was ordered to give Winfield Scott his best officers and most experienced troops for the march on Mexico City. This left him with about 4,800 men, of whom most were raw volunteers and a little more than 500 were regulars. But he still had Davis and his Mississippi Rifles when Santa Anna came against him with about 18,000 troops.

They met at Buena Vista, where Taylor held a fine position in the mountains. Davis, now commanding only 358 rifles, played a crucial role here. After a formation of Indiana volunteers gave way on the left flank, Davis stopped the oncharging Mexicans before they could get into the American rear. When a large force of Mexican Lancers bore down on him, he arranged his troops in a V with the open end toward the enemy. Beautifully massed with pennons waving and the sun glinting on their poised steel lances, the Mexicans swept toward the V. Suddenly, inexplicably, they halted. Wisely so. Had they galloped farther Davis's forward wings could have closed behind them to form a Cannae in miniature. As it was, his frontier marksmen riddled the Lancers with a devastating fire that forced them to flee. This was the turning point at Buena Vista, Taylor's finest victory; and Davis was the hero of that battle.

But he paid for it, suffering a painful foot wound that compelled him to use crutches. He was still using them when he took his seat in the U.S. Senate in 1847, having been appointed by Governor Albert Gallatin Brown to serve the unexpired term of Senator Jesse Speight, who had died in August of that year. In January 1848 the Mississippi legislature unanimously elected him to a full six-year term. With this, Jefferson Davis became one of the leading spokesmen for Southern rights, and then, with the deterioration of Calhoun's health and his death in 1850, its chief champion.

Yet he was no absolutist firebrand like Toombs or Yancey. His views on slavery were surprisingly liberal. He did not believe that slavery was the blacks' permanent condition, although he did insist that it would take several generations before it would be wise and practical to emancipate them. "The slave," he said, "must be made fit for his freedom by education and discipline and thus made unfit for slavery." This time would come, he believed, through the pressure of cheaper free labor. Such convictions were indeed enlightened for the time and section. Yet both Davis and his brother Joseph practiced what he preached. His black overseer, Jim Pemberton, was ready for freedom and so were the Montgomerys on Joseph's plantation.

In May of 1851 the Union Democrats and Whigs jointly nominated Senator Henry S. Foote as their candidate for governor of Mississippi. Foote was a repulsive little man with a big voice reverberating with bombast and belligerence. He was devouring the dull and prosy Democrat, John A. Quitman, the general who had won the race to Mexico City, so that in September of that year Quitman withdrew. At once the Democrats chose Davis to finish the campaign. He accepted, although he had no wish to leave the Senate—still less, with only a few weeks remaining, to enter a rough-and-tumble speaking contest with the slashing, often dishonest Foote. Also he was sick, his eyes so weakened that he could not read or write and needed to wear goggles when he left a darkened room. Nevertheless his high sense of honor and party loyalty caused him to accept. It was a forlorn hope. Strive as he might, he could not persuade the voters of Mississippi to reject the Compromise of 1850. They believed that it represented "the final solution" of the slavery problem and accepted Foote's lying charge that Davis was a disunionist. Nevertheless, he lost by less than a thousand votes.

Varina Davis was secretly pleased by this enforced return to the rose garden at Brierfield. As governor Davis would have been forced to considerable expense and boredom in entertaining, and she would have had to endure the blandishments of fools and favor seekers. But permanent private life—where her happiness lay—was not to last long. Fifteen months after Davis left the Senate he was back in Washington as President Franklin Pierce's secretary of war.

Jefferson Davis was an extremely efficient and hardworking cabinet member. One of his seven clerks said of him: "He was one of the best Secretaries of War that ever served. He was a kind, social man, very considerate, and pleasant to serve under. I never heard a complaint from one of his clerks. Socially he was a most charming man, officially, very pleasant. He was a warm friend and a bitter enemy . . . He was a regular bull-dog when he formed an opinion, for he would never let go." Davis was so scrupulously honest that he would not allow Varina to get employees to do errands for her nor even use the department's stationery. When Admiral Perry's famous expedition to Japan in 1853 brought back exquisite gifts, some of which Pierce offered to Varina, he would not permit her to accept them. Under him, it was said, it was not possible to cheat the government out of a single brass button. Yet, when he formed four new regiments to protect settlers in the far western frontier against hostile Indians, it was charged that they were filled with Southern officers, especially the elite 1st and 2nd Cavalry, and darkly hinted that they would be the cadres for a seceded Southern army. Davis indignantly denied the accusation, but not publicly, which would be beneath his dignity; nor did he defend himself with the truism that more Southerners than Northerners followed army careers. He was most innovative, introducing the Minie ball and experimenting with breech-loading rifles; but his most startling departure was formation of a camel corps to serve the western frontier. Camels traveled twice as fast as horses, ate less and could go three days without water while carrying heavier loads of up to 1,200 pounds. But they were little used after he left office in 1857, and then outmoded by the new railroads.

In that year Davis ran for reelection to the Senate, disdaining, however, to sully his honor with the vain and lowly tactics of "electioneering." If George Washington in 1758 could "swill the planters with Bumbo," i.e., rum punch and whiskey, to the tune of a quart and a half per voter, Jefferson Davis could not. He now despised barbecues, shaking horny hands and kissing babies. One newspaper mocked him for assuming "that he is a great Jupiter and his audiences pigmies." His election by the Democratic-controlled legislature was guaranteed when his friend, R. S. Tarpley, the presiding officer at that party's caucus, broke a tie in Davis's favor. Once again the members of the U.S. Senate heard the musical voice of Jefferson Davis battling for the extreme claims of the South. He was as blind to the evils of slavery as the Northern senators were indifferent to the exploitation of women and children in the sweatshops of their own section. He attacked Douglas with a ferocity that would lead to his eventual defeat in 1860, yet always maintaining that he opposed secession. If he had understood—as no Southern leader ever comprehended—that the Abolitionists were widely despised in the North and that this section was almost as racist though not officially so as the South and that a huge body of Northern public opinion supported the Little Giant, he might not have fired so many damaging slings and arrows at the one Democrat who sought so sincerely to reconcile the extremists of the party's Northern and Southern wings. And so the Democrats were divided, a "black Republican" was elected president and secession followed.

Jefferson Davis was with Varina in the rose garden at Brierfield when a messenger arrived to inform him that he had been elected president of the Confederate States of America. Davis was dismayed. He had neither sought nor wanted that chief office, hoping instead for high command in the Confederate States Army. Varina agreed, writing later: "I thought his genius was military, but as a party manager he would not succeed. He did not know the arts of the politician and would not practice them if understood, and he did know those of war."

This clear-sighted woman, loving her husband, quite understandably omitted to say that he was also fond of glory and prestige. That was why he accepted an office for which he was eminently ill-fitted, rather than wait for the general's stars which he was so superbly qualified to wear.

13

■

The Tension Mounts

O NE OF THE contributing factors—perhaps the decisive one—in the speedy secession of the Lower South was the four-month interregnum between the election and inauguration of President Lincoln.* It also explains the secessionists' obsession with celerity. They wanted disunion to be a fact before any moderating chief executive could enter the White House, and almost two months before that happened they had put in place a new nation guided by a new constitution and a new government headed by a president and vice president, after which, while gladly beginning to accept the proffered swords of 387 of the 1,108 officers in the United States Army, they would choose a Congress and select a Supreme Court.

For the North this was a period of alternating paralysis and feeble or futile attempts to deal with the crisis. Buchanan, now a lame-duck president, had official power but little real power. Lincoln, the president-elect, had no official power and no desire to use his access to real power, if, in fact, the vacillating Democrat Buchanan would have listened to him. Actually, Lincoln was a mere outsider in Washington. He had been in the House only two years and had scarcely set foot in the capital in a decade. Between his nomination in May and the March 4 inaugural he spent ten months in Springfield, his longest sojourn there ever. Before his election campaign he had not met Hannibal Hamlin of Maine, his running mate, or most of the men who were to form his cabinet. He sat quietly in Springfield, badgered by an incredible stream of office seekers, importuned by almost every Republican editor in the country to "do something!" To one in St. Louis he replied: "I could say nothing which I have not already said, and which is in

*March 4 remained the inauguration date until Franklin Roosevelt began his second term on January 10, 1936.

print and accessible to the public. . . . I am not at liberty to shift my ground; that is out of the question. If I thought a repetition would do any good I would make it. But my judgment is it would do positive harm. The secessionists, *per se* believing they had alarmed me, would clamor all the louder." So he sat still while seven states left the Union, Federal forts were seized, along with other military camps, forts, arsenals and mints, vessels and ports, while the Mississippi River was obstructed and even the flag fired upon.

In Washington, Buchanan to his credit did attempt to do something, calling a meeting of his cabinet three days after the election. It was, he said, the most important of his administration; but the officers assembling were so divided along sectional lines that he had to put aside his statesmanlike proposal to issue an immediate proclamation urging Congress to call a constitutional convention to avert secession. Instead he waited until his annual message to Congress three weeks later. But his sympathies were so openly Southern, and his cautious argument that a state could not legitimately secede and the Federal government had no power to prevent it so academic that it earned only scorn from both sides.

The next attempt to forestall disunion came in the Senate where the Committee of Thirteen, led by John J. Crittenden of Kentucky, studied Crittenden's plan to restore the Missouri Compromise line and extend it to the eastern border of California. South of it slavery would exist, recognized in the Constitution for the first time with that very word; north of it, it would be prohibited. But sectionalism also torpedoed this proposal.

One of the chief factors working against compromise of any sort was that the North had become so accustomed to crises provoked by the South—none of them ever actually exploding in disunion—that it was widely believed that Dixie was bluffing once again, and that South Carolina in its secession was merely having another temper tantrum and would shortly be abandoned by its sisters just as in 1832. Another was the absence of huge news-gathering media such as today's print-and-electronics monster that might have informed the nation at large of the gravity of the situation. Congress alone had a national focus but Congress had no leaders willing to address a problem that had become the most urgent in American history. Douglas and Buchanan understood the need for immediate action, but Douglas had been all but broken by his election defeat and would be dead within six months, and Buchanan—who alone understood the depths of Southern fear of slave insurrection—had become so accustomed to following rather than leading his cabinet that in the end he was reduced to wringing his hands and wailing that he had no wish to become "the last president of the United States."

Nevertheless, he did bring himself at that momentous cabinet meeting to address the problem of the two forts still held by Federal troops in Charleston Harbor. They had been built to defend the port against enemy naval attack from the sea, but now they were threatened by land from the rear by aroused South Carolinians already formed into military units. Among them were the Palmetto Guards, with whom Edmund Ruffin marched as a sixty-five-year-old private. Ruffin and others like him sought the forts so that Charleston's splendid harbor could be thrown open to transatlantic trade with Europe by the Confederacy—even by South Carolina alone, should the South once again desert her. The Federal garrison of fewer than a hundred men under Colonel John L. Gardner was on Fort Moultrie, highly vulnerable to assault by land. Sumter, on a small island at the center of the harbor entrance, had just been completed, but was empty. To leave the garrison at Moultrie was to risk losing control of the port, but to transfer it to Sumter might be to provoke war. After some argument, it was decided to replace Gardner with a younger man with a Southern background: Major Robert Anderson of Kentucky.

Hesitant and indecisive though Buchanan was, he was painfully hooked on the horns of a dilemma. If he acted firmly, if there were any hint of the use of force to compel the seven departed sisters to return to the Union, he would lose the states of the Upper South.

Virginia, North Carolina, Tennessee and Arkansas, together with Missouri, Kentucky, Maryland and Delaware were regarded as the Upper South, although Delaware had so few bondsmen it could hardly be considered a slave state and would eventually reject secession. Missouri, Kentucky and Maryland, although condoning slavery, were actually Border States which might go either way, and whichever way they went was indeed vital to either North or South. Yet, after the Confederacy convened in Montgomery, these seven so overwhelmingly refused to leave the Union that it appeared that secession might fizzle. However, for some inexplicable reason the Unionists controlling these states had ignored the fact that in one way or another they had made it plain that if the Federal government should attempt to coerce their brethren of the Lower South they would secede.

It was a strange and delicate situation. Here was the Upper South, stronger and more deliberate than its trigger-happy neighbors to the South, practically guaranteeing their security. What had happened was that the institution of slavery which had provoked disunion had now been superseded by the issue of secession. The South spoke now of "Southern rights" or "states' rights" and the North of "the Union forever!" Bondage, if not forgotten, was at least not a battle cry.

The firebrands of the Lower South well knew that in fact it was they who possessed the initiative. Robert Barnwell Rhett had long ago said that the Upper South "must be made to choose between the North and the South, and then they will redeem themselves, but not before." Another South Carolinian said that if his state seceded by itself "only two courses remain to our enemies. First, they must let us alone; secondly, they must attempt to coerce us; . . . suppose they attempt to coerce us, then the Southern states are compelled to make common cause with us, and we wake up some morning and find the flag of the Southern Confederacy floating over us."

All the high cards, then, were in the hands of the Southern extremists—and the ace was the Charleston forts.

Between the opposition of Southern "fifth columnists" in his cabinet and his own cautious nature, Buchanan in that critical winter of 1860–61 could never come to a clear-cut decision whether or not to reinforce Major Anderson in Fort Moultrie. He sincerely believed that to do so would at the least provoke the secession of the Upper South and might even start a war. Some historians have claimed that his indecisiveness was born of his desire to leave the decision to Lincoln, that he intended to offer the South as little provocation as possible so that by Inauguration Day all blame for starting a war would be born by his Republican successor. If so, and this is doubtful, he was greatly assisted in this intention by Major Anderson.

On December 23 Anderson had received a dispatch from the War Department instructing him to use his "military discretion" in defending himself if attacked, but to make no "useless sacrifice" of lives. If the enemy came at him in overwhelming force, he was to surrender. As a professional, Anderson had no wish to haul down his flag. Nor did he as a Southerner and loyal Unionist desire to provoke a war between South Carolina and the United States. Nevertheless, Moultrie simply could not be held. Sumter guarding the mouth of the harbor could be. Its defenses long a'building were practically completed. To him it was the soul of "military discretion" to transfer his command to Sumter and on the night of December 26, he spiked Moultrie's guns and silently and skillfully moved to Sumter.

In the morning Charlestonians living at the battery a few miles across the water were enraged to see the Stars and Stripes floating over Sumter. In Washington Southern senators led by Jefferson Davis came buzzing around Buchanan like a swarm of angry bees, demanding that Anderson return to Moultrie. For once, Buchanan held firm. Thus, Anderson, an officer of the lowest field-grade rank, had taken the North's only decisive step in that vacillating winter of crisis. He and he alone had determined the place of the final confrontation between North and South. He had also taken Buchanan off the hook. With only eighty-six men and dwindling supplies of food he did not actually believe that he could repulse attack, but rather that Sumter's formidable defenses would discourage it. Thus, if he had not succeeded in intimidating South Carolina, he was at least delaying any assault into the future—possibly as distant as March 4, 1861 (Buchanan certainly must have hoped), Lincoln's Inauguration Day.

Nevertheless, after the last disloyal Southerner had been squeezed out of his cabinet and he felt himself surrounded by staunch Northerners urging reinforcement of Anderson, he finally ordered a relief expedition. The chartered steamer *Star of the West* sailed south with supplies and two hundred soldiers. Reaching Charleston on January 9, it was fired upon by South Carolina batteries and driven back to New York. Now the free states seethed with rage over this humiliation. The flag had been fired upon! In fact, these were the first shots of the Civil War. Many Northerners demanded retaliation. Buchanan might have ended his mediocre term in glory by mounting a massive assault on Charleston. But he wavered—until he was once again lifted off the horns by Anderson. That resourceful officer persuaded South Carolina to join him in referring the matter back to Washington. Nothing came of this if only because the negotiators sent North refrained from serving Buchanan with their demand that Anderson return to Moultrie until the other seceding states agreed to convene in Montgomery.

So the problem of the Charleston forts shifted from the government of South Carolina to the new Confederacy, from Governor Francis Pickens to President Jefferson Davis.

14

■

Davis's Cabinet

PRESIDENT DAVIS left Brierfield on February 11. Because there was no direct railroad between Jackson, Mississippi, and Montgomery, he was compelled to travel by a roundabout route of about 600 rather than 250 miles over rickety, one-track roads. The journey took six days and was an appalling demonstration of the South's decentralized agrarian economy, now teetering upon the brink of war with the centralized, industrial North. No one grasped this more clearly—or with greater dismay—than the former secretary of war. It was because of this that his subsequent speeches would be studded with the phrase, "All we want is to be left alone." Alone for what? To prepare for war, of course. Davis did not deceive himself into believing that Lincoln would adopt a moderating, conciliatory tone, now that the Confederacy had been formed. Even before the seven "secesh" states had convened at Montgomery, they had been seizing all but four of the Federal forts in the South: Sumter at Charleston, and Jefferson, Pickens and Taylor in Florida. In February, General David E. Twiggs of Georgia had deliberately surrendered the nineteen Federal posts in his command to Texan troops, for which shameless act he had been hailed as a hero in the South and dismissed by the Federal government for "treachery to the flag."

However, Davis well knew that the seizures would do little to offset the North's enormous superiority in manpower and industrial strength. By the census of 1860 the South's population was 9,000,000, the North's 20,000,000. In comparative number of males from fifteen to forty eligible for army service, the odds were much worse: 1,140,000 in the South, 4,070,000 in the North, a difference of almost 4 to 1, due mainly to the fact that 4,000,000 people in the South's population were blacks ineligible to serve. They would, of course, be useful in their customary role of slave laborers on the plantations and on the fortifications, but this advantage was

113

more than offset by the fact that the North would be open to recruit immigrants—chiefly from Ireland and Germany—and that even the slaves would be liable to enrollment in the Yankee armies wherever they moved.

Industrially the odds were much worse. The South possessed the modest iron and steel works at Selma, Alabama, plus the sophisticated Tredegar Iron Works in Richmond, which had been making locomotives for domestic and foreign use for a decade, as well as cannon and ammunition for the U.S. Navy. But the North had no fewer than 110,000 manufacturing establishments compared to the South's 18,000, and 1,300,000 factory hands as opposed to 110,000. Massachusetts alone produced 60 percent more manufactured goods than the entire Confederacy, including those still neutral states of Virginia, Tennessee, Arkansas and North Carolina; Pennsylvania turned out nearly twice as much and New York more than twice.

Only in land area did the South have the advantage, albeit a doubtful one. The eleven Confederate states, again presuming the four neutrals would leave the Union, covered an area of 780,000 square miles as opposed to 670,000 in the twenty-two Union states. Even though the South would almost certainly be on the defensive and thus have no small advantage in possession of "interior lines"—with its bases inside its menaced frontiers it could move troops and supplies quicker from point to point than the enemy operating on "exterior lines"—its ability to move rapidly was inhibited by its comparatively smaller and less efficient railroad network: 9,000 miles to 22,000 for the North, which, moving over a smaller area, also had that much less logistical difficulty to overcome.

These were the statistics of modern war, to which a professional soldier and former war secretary such as Davis must pay close attention. But there were other advantages not quite so tangible. First there was the possibility—Davis at this time thought "the likelihood"—that the powerful nations of Europe would come to the Confederacy's side. Hungry for produce for their mills, especially for cotton, they would welcome access to a tariff-free source, and also the chance to cripple a strong competitor in the North. This time, it would be not only France who would cross the ocean to assist a new nation, but also Great Britain and perhaps even czarist Russia. Moreover, President Davis shared the South's unshakable belief in the superiority of its soldiers and in so many officers trained at West Point and seasoned in Mexico and on the frontier, as well as a corps of officers-to-be accustomed to plantation command. In addition to interior lines, a defensive war would give the South a chance to use the improved modern weapons that compelled an attacker to accept losses of two-to-one or even three-to-one. The land that an invader must traverse was crosshatched with rolling hills and mountains made for defense, as well as rivers flowing west to east to block the line of march. Most intangible was the moral force felt by men defending their homeland, and according to Napoleon, the moral to the material in war "is as three to one." Devoted as the North might be to saving the Union, the battle cry of "Home and Hearth" or "Death to the Yankee Invader" was far more inspiring than "The Union Forever!" As Cardinal Newman said: "Most men will die upon a dogma, but few will be martyr to a conclusion." Finally, the South would have its back to the wall. Sheer desperation would compel the region to make a heroic stand. For the South to lose was to accept subjugation by an all-but-foreign foe; for the rank-and-file this could mean loss of privilege and the humiliating accept-ance of the black slave as an equal, and perhaps also the loss of freedom and the right to choose self-government; for the leaders and especially *the* leader—Jefferson Davis—defeat would certainly mean loss of property and perhaps even of life. No such calamitous possibilities confronted the people of the North. The worst that could result from failure in battle was to withdraw from the war and allow the South to go its own way, but there would be no loss of anything: property, liberty or life.

Davis's impression of Montgomery upon his arrival in that somnolent town of 9,000 people, half black, half white, is not known. But it could not have been sanguine. Montgomery was essentially "an overgrown country crossroads" straggling along seven hills beside the Alabama River. Since 1846 it had been limping along as the state capital, so preoccupied with its primary business of servicing politicians and the government that it had allowed the local cotton trade to decline and had attracted no new industry. Inadequate for Alabama—Main Street was not drastically different from the day in 1843 when a team of oxen drowned in one of its many deep mud holes—it was hardly fit to be the cradle of the Confederacy. True enough the state capitol atop a hill a mile inland from the river was an imposing edifice with its neoclassic facade and domed cupola, but this, together with two hotels celebrated for their filth, bedbugs and high prices, was about all there was to Montgomery. There were indeed some splendid houses built on lanes meandering off Main Street, but these were private homes not open to the throng of office seekers and state and national officials crowding into town. Some of these visitors became exasperated at having to pick their way through the mud on poorly built or non-existent streets, or at becoming lost on thoroughfares "laid out before the surveyor's compass was in use."

Still Jefferson Davis was impressed with the torchlight parade that greeted him upon his arrival in Montgomery, and the gaiety, confidence and enthusiasm of the crowd at his inauguration. He was also impressive himself, standing there on the portico of the capitol, tall and slender and boyish-looking in his suit of slate-gray homespun, a wisp of newly grown beard beneath his chin giving his features a saturnine cast, his beautiful musical voice carrying clearly to the throng. Afterwards many of them would say proudly, "Have you seen our President?" Montgomery, it seemed, had fared better than Washington in its choice of chief executives. The crowd was also delighted when the band played "Dixie," then a relatively new tune. Composed by a Northerner, the blackface minstrel Dan Emmett, it would become the South's unofficial anthem.

Davis's inaugural address was not a great oration, although it was studded with references to the Almighty surprising in this religious skeptic. But Davis, aware of the burden being placed upon his shoulders, had been moving steadily toward his wife's Episcopal faith. Thus he concluded:

"Reverently let us invoke the God of our fathers to guide and protect us in our efforts to perpetuate the principles which by his blessing they were able to vindicate, establish and transmit to their posterity. With the continuance of His favor ever gratefully acknowledged, we may hopefully look forward to success, to peace and to prosperity."

Only to his wife did the new president voice the doubts that tormented his soul, writing to her two days later: "The audience was large and brilliant. Upon my weary heart were showered smiles, plaudits and flowers; but beyond them I saw troubles and thorns innumerable. . . . We are without machinery, without means and threatened by a powerful opposition; but I do not despond, and will not shrink from the task imposed upon me . . ."

He did not. Careless as always of his health, he put in a man-killing day: rising early to work until breakfast and then going to his office where he frequently stayed past midnight. Like George Washington, he was putting together a new government, but doing it with the threat of war overhead like a Damoclean sword. His most immediate decision was to choose a cabinet, and he did so with an eye toward rewarding the states most prominent in the secession and states' rights movements. Thus after Robert W. Barnwell of South Carolina declined the offer of secretary of the treasury, recommending Christopher G. Memminger of the same state, Davis selected him. Robert Toombs of Georgia became secretary of state, and Leroy P. Walker, who had led the Alabama delegation from the Democratic convention in 1860, received the most important post: secretary of war. Davis's attorney general was Judah P. Benjamin, the former Louisiana senator, while Stephen Mallory of Florida became secretary of the navy and John H. Reagan, a former Texas congressman, postmaster general.

Surprisingly, these highest posts within the gift of the supposedly aristocratic South went to men of humble origins. Davis, himself the son of a yeoman father, had chosen Reagan, the child of a tanner and himself a slave overseer; Mallory, born a Connecticut Yankee, who had helped his widowed mother run a sailors' boardinghouse in Key West; Benjamin, son of a failed Jewish merchant; Memminger, a German immigrant who grew up in a Charleston orphanage; and among his diplomats, John Slidell, the son of a New York tallow chandler. Nor was it a stable cabinet, changing so often that during its four-year life there were fourteen appointments to six positions.

The fiery Toombs was the first to go. As unfit for the state department as Davis was for the presidency, he chafed at the routine nature of his office and longed for the glory of the battlefield. After five months, he resigned, begging Davis to make him a general. With great reluctance, the president obliged—but Brigadier General Toombs, like so many able politicians, was a failure in uniform. Because his superior officers and the president failed to recommend him for promotion, he turned against Davis and resigned, returning to Georgia so embittered that he rivaled even Vice President Stephens in his opposition to Davis. "Toombs is ready for a revolution," wrote Mrs. Chesnut. "He curses freely everything Confederate from a president to a horse boy."

Memminger entered the cabinet with the reputation of being an able banker and an advocate of sound money. No one suspected, least of all Congress, which quarreled with him over taxation, how harsh his personality could be and how ruinous his financial policy. Yet Davis kept him in office against all opposition. Of him Ordnance Chief Josiah Gorgas wrote: "Mr. Memminger treats others with rudeness, and is, besides, dogmatical, narrow-minded and slow. He places every fresh paper at the bottom of his pile and makes it await its turn patiently without regard to its importance . . ." He was so religious, at least outwardly, that it was said he did not want the army to work on Sunday.

Secretary of War Walker was much like Davis in attending too much to details that should have been left to subordinates. He was described by William Russell Lowell of the London *Times* as "tall, lean, straight-haired, angular, with fiery impulsive eyes and manner—a [chewer] of tobacco and a profuse spitter—a lawyer, I believe, certainly not a soldier; ardently devoted to the cause and confident to the last degree of speedy success." Davis found this Alabama politician unfit to command a war machine and consequently reduced him to the status of a clerk while giving all the military orders himself. Overcome by overwork and failing health, Walker resigned September 16, 1861.

R.M.T. Hunter of Virginia and R.M. ("Constitution") Brown briefly succeeded him, and then the post went to Judah Benjamin. Having found himself an attorney general without a justice department, like Reagan a postmaster general without stamps, he was delighted to take a step higher. Ultimately he would become the ablest man in the cabinet, known as "the brains of the Confederacy." Born in 1811 at St. Croix in the Virgin Islands, he spent his boyhood in Wilmington, North Carolina, and Charleston, where his father struggled as a small merchant. Attending Yale, he left suddenly, charged with dishonesty. Going to New Orleans, he became a successful lawyer and later as a U.S. senator from Louisiana acquired a large sugar plantation with many slaves. Benjamin married a Catholic Creole girl who lived mostly apart from him in Paris. Short, squat, and swarthy, with pronounced Semitic features, he was sneered at by his enemies as "that ever smiling Jew." But he gradually achieved an intimacy with Davis acquired by no other cabinet member. Fond of food and gambling, he was nevertheless a tireless worker. Not particularly touchy about honor himself, he had difficulty dealing with a corps of cavalier generals guided by a chivalrous code. They also resented a civilian chief as "regulation" as Benjamin could become, and so he quarreled with Beauregard and so offended Stonewall Jackson that he offered to resign. President Davis, wearying of patching up these frequent squabbles, was pleased to replace him with George W. Randolph of Virginia, giving him the state department where his subtle mind was of more use.

Randolph, a grandson of Thomas Jefferson, was a true Southern gentleman, by birth, breeding and breadth of intellect. He was decisive, industrious and vigorous, but always tactful and deferential with the president, who never stopped interfering in army affairs. Randolph was also the first cabinet officer to recognize the importance of the West.

Reagan was the most forthright cabinet member, frequently challenging the president and thus confuting the charge that Davis preferred yes-men. He was also one of the three cabinet officers—Benjamin and Mallory were the others—remaining with Davis to the end. An able administrator, he made the post office self-supporting in a monstrously inflated economy, achieving this feat chiefly by inducing postmen to accept lower pay in return for exemption from the draft. He bluntly told Davis that he would have done better to become a general, and was the first to advocate the unpopular policy of conscripting the slaves into the army.

Mallory was another able executive. It was his task to build a brand-new navy, and he sent Southern naval officers into the North, to Canada, and later to Europe to purchase vessels for it. He also had commerce killers built in Britain to prey upon Yankee merchant ships and was an early advocate of ironclads. An innovator, he introduced the use of torpedoes (mines) against enemy warships and also ordered construction of the world's first submarine, the *H. L. Hunley.*

These then, with their chief, Jefferson Davis, were the men upon whom the South depended to create a new nation, as well as the military means to defend the region should civil war with the powerful North erupt. Yet, while frantically preparing to meet this threat, they still hoped at best "to be left alone"; at worst to maneuver Lincoln into firing the first fatal shot that would show the world who the aggressor was.

15

■

Lincoln's Inauguration
and Cabinet

A WEEK BEFORE his departure from Springfield for Washington, President-elect Lincoln visited his beloved stepmother, Sarah Bush Lincoln. When his father had died nine years earlier, he had not attended the funeral, but now he remembered how much his stepmother had meant to him, and he kissed her and held her close. Sarah did not weep, but she had a premonition that she would never see him again.

Back in Springfield on the morning of February 11 Lincoln and his party of fifteen walked slowly through a drizzling rain to the little red-brick depot of the Great Western Railroad. A crowd of about a thousand people had gathered both around and inside the depot. Their mood was somber, and so was Lincoln's as he entered the waiting room. No one smiled or laughed as they came forward to shake his hand. Even the huge Judge Davis wearing a new white silk hat seemed subdued. Like Jefferson Davis, Lincoln had grown a beard, a short black one running from ear to ear. It gave his face dignity, and also accentuated his melancholy expression. Next day, he would be fifty-two, one of the youngest presidents. His look of sadness deepened, and then the locomotive puffing outside in the rain blew its whistle. "All aboard!" Lincoln and his entourage boarded the single passenger car. The crowd following him gathered around its rear platform, the rain thrumming steadily on their upraised umbrellas. Lincoln emerged.

"My friends," he said, standing tall at the rail, "no one not in my situation can appreciate my feeling of sadness at this parting. To this place and the kindness of these people I owe everything. Here I have lived for a quarter of a century and have passed from a young to an old man. Here my children have been born, and one is buried. I now leave, not knowing when, or whether ever, I may return, with a task before me greater than that which rested upon Washington. Without the assistance of that Divine

Being who ever attended him, I cannot succeed. With that assistance I cannot fail. Trusting in Him who can go with me and remain with you and be everywhere for good, let us confidently hope that all will yet be well. To His care commending you, as I hope in your prayers you will commend me, I bid you an affectionate farewell."

The whistle blew again and the crowd backed away. The train lurched forward and slowly chugged into the mist. People waved and shouted.

"Good-bye, Abe."

During the twelve days of his roundabout journey through five states Abraham Lincoln seemed to justify the epithets of "baboon" or "gorilla" or "country bumpkin" hurled at him by hostile newspapers urging him to resign. Determined not to reveal his plans until he had the authority to act upon them, the president-elect sounded like "Mr. Facing-both-ways" during the twenty speeches he made en route. "There is nothing going wrong," he said repeatedly, with a false cheerfulness that fooled no one. Everyone knew that seven states were out of the Union, that the South was arming, that Federal facilities had been seized, that the Mississippi was blocked and that the flag had been fired upon, and yet this clod of an ostrich-man could say, "There is nothing going wrong."

And then the "Bumpkin's Progress," as it might well have been called, took an ugly turn. Baltimore was the last scheduled stop before Washington, and also the first proslavery city he would enter. It had sent him no welcome message as the others had done, and had apparently made no official plans to receive him. In Philadelphia, Lincoln was told that in Baltimore bands of toughs called "Blood Tubs" were plotting his abduction or assassination. They would either kill him or take him to Dixie and hold him as ransom for Southern independence. Lincoln at first scoffed at these lurid rumors, until General-in-Chief Winfield Scott warned him of such possibilities and Senator Seward sent his son to him with so-called documentary evidence. Finally, Allan Pinkerton, the famous railroad detective, informed Lincoln that his operatives had infiltrated these gangs and had witnessed and taken dark and bloody oaths. At last Lincoln was disturbed. But when his friends urged him to cancel his schedule and hurry on to Washington, he refused. Instead, he would speak in Philadelphia and Harrisburg as planned, but if no welcoming message arrived from Baltimore by then, he would either bypass it or slip through undetected.

After he spoke in Harrisburg next day and still did not hear from Baltimore or Maryland, Lincoln returned to his hotel, dining that night with Republican leaders, who now wished him to make quickly and secretly for

Washington. Lincoln protested. "What would the nation think of its President stealing into its capital like a thief in the night?" But he was overruled, and so he put on his overcoat, stuffed a soft wool hat into his pocket, draped a shawl over his arm and made for the railroad station. There he was met by his friend Ward Hill Lamon, known to be a good man in a fight. Lamon not only looked formidable, with his ferocious bulging eyes and drooping frontier mustache, but was armed to the teeth with two pistols, two derringers and two large knives. They boarded an empty, unlighted passenger car, and as it was drawn from the station by a lone darkened locomotive, telegraph linemen cut all wires out of Harrisburg. Arriving safely in Philadelphia, the two men were greeted by Pinkerton. He put them aboard the Baltimore train, on which one of his female operatives had reserved berths for her "invalid brother" and a traveling companion. At half past three in the morning the train rattled through Baltimore's deserted streets. It stopped at the Camden Station, where the sleepless Lincoln heard a drunk bellowing "Dixie" over and over on the platform. At last Lincoln stepped off his train in Washington at six o'clock in the morning. A man approached, crying, "You can't play that on me," and Lamon drew back his fist. Lincoln seized it. "Don't strike him!" he yelled, having recognized Elihu Washburn, an Illinois congressman, and the three men went to Willard's for breakfast.

Up in Baltimore that afternoon the special train from Harrisburg thought to be carrying Lincoln arrived. It was met by Mayor George Brown and a crowd of about ten thousand people. Terrific cheers were raised, but not for Lincoln: three for the Confederacy, three for "the gallant Jeff Davis"—and three loud groans for "the Rail Splitter." It seems doubtless that if Lincoln had been aboard he would have encountered trouble.

Even so, for a chief executive to have entered his capital to take his oath of office in such stealthy style was indeed an embarrassment to his friends, and an occasion for hilarity among his enemies and an elated South. The progress of the bumpkin had now been turned into the flight of the coward, his overcoat became a sinister "long military cloak" and his wool hat—for some inexplicable reason—a Scots plaid cap or tam o'shanter. Soon cartoonists were drawing a quaking Lincoln with his hair on end and surrounded by squiggles suggestive of terror, and the cloak became a woman's dress borrowed from his wife whom he had left to the mercy of the Blood Tubs. Yet, for all this ridicule Abraham Lincoln stubbornly kept his own counsel until Inauguration Day.

March 4, 1861, had dawned cloudy and cold, but a brisk wind had shredded the clouds, revealing the sun as Lincoln and Buchanan rode to the Capitol. Its unfinished dome was still disfigured by scaffolds and the boom of a derrick was flung out from it like a gaunt steel arm. On the grass lay a figure of Freedom, a huge bronze sculpture of a woman grasping a sword in one hand and a wreath in the other, waiting to be fastened aloft on the summit of the dome.

A hush came over the crowd of ten thousand people when Lincoln and Buchanan appeared above them on the East Portico. Lincoln wore a new black suit and a stovepipe hat, and carried a gold-headed ebony cane. Stephen Douglas leaned forward from his seat among the dignitaries to take the hat, while Lincoln put on his spectacles and drew from his pocket the manuscript of his Inaugural Address, which he began to read. Here was no elongated figure of squiggly fear, but once again the calm, confident, straightforward orator of old, speaking at last after four months of frustrating silence, one hundred and twenty days of ridicule and abuse, and his first words were for the South.

"I have no purpose, directly or indirectly, to interfere with the institution of slavery in the states where it exists. I believe I have no lawful right to do so, and I have no inclination to do so." But there could be no constitutional right of secession. "It is safe to assert that no government proper ever had a provision in its organic law for its own termination. . . . No state upon its own mere motion can lawfully get out of the Union . . . I shall take care, as the Constitution itself expressly enjoins upon me, that the laws of the Union be faithfully executed in all the states. Doing this I deem to be only a simple duty on my part; and I shall perform it, so far as practicable, unless my rightful masters, the American people, shall withhold the requisite means, or in some authoritative manner direct the contrary. . . . The power confided in me will be used to hold, occupy and possess the property and places belonging to the government, and to collect the duties and imposts."

Secession "is the essence of anarchy . . . Physically speaking, we cannot separate . . . A husband and wife may be divorced, and go out of the presence and beyond the reach of each other; but the different parts of our country cannot do this. They cannot but remain face to face, and intercourse, either amicable or hostile, must continue between them. Suppose you go to war, you cannot fight always; and when, after much loss on both sides and no gain on either, you cease fighting, the identical old questions as to terms of intercourse are again upon you."

Only the South could choose war. "In your hands, my dissatisfied fellow countrymen, and not in mine, is the momentous issue of civil war. The government will not assail you. You can have no conflict without being yourselves the aggressors. You have no oath registered in heaven to destroy the government, while I shall have the most solemn one to 'preserve, protect and defend' it."

Then came the splendid peroration, rewritten in collaboration with Seward. "I am loath to close. We are not enemies, but friends. We must not be enemies. Though passion may have strained, it must not break our bonds of affection. The mystic chords of memory, stretching from every battlefield and patriot grave to every living heart and hearthstone all over this broad land, will yet swell the chorus of the Union when again touched, as surely they will be, by the better angels of our nature."

Chief Justice Roger Taney stepped forward, clasping his Bible with trembling hands. His tall figure bent and his chest sunken by his years, sepulchral in his flowing black robes, he gave to Lincoln the oath of office he had already given eight times before to eight other men: swearing him in as the sixteenth president of the United States of America.

As might have been expected, Lincoln's address was generally hailed in the North as a masterful expression of the inviolability of the Union. "To twenty millions of people," said the New York *Tribune,* "it will carry tidings, good or not, as the case may be, that the Federal government of the United States is still in existence, with a Man at the head of it." In the South, again as might have been expected, it was excoriated as the rattling of a warmonger's saber. Cried the Charleston *Mercury:* "It is our wisest policy to accept it as a declaration of war."

Such an eventuality, of course, still depended on what happened at Fort Sumter, and in the meantime, on the day after the address was delivered, Congress received and approved the cabinet which the new president had all but completed on the night of his election.

Seward was the new secretary of state. Until the appearance of Lincoln he had been the leader of the Republican Party, and he was still driven by an insatiable thirst for power. As a New York man close to the financial capital, he understood the American economy better than Lincoln. Though an Episcopalian, much of his political strength in New York City had come through his friendship with Archbishop John Hughes, the most influential Catholic prelate in America, and he had launched his political career by joining the anti-Masonic party. Seward was also a bon vivant, a breeder of beautiful Arabian horses and a gourmet: an invitation to one of his elaborate dinners was highly prized in Washington society. Of him his friend Charles Francis Adams wrote: "When it came to drinking, Seward was, for a man of sixty, a free liver; at times his brandy-and-water would excite him, and set his tongue going with dangerous volubility; but I never saw him more affected than that—never anything approaching drunkenness."

The treasury went to Salmon Portland Chase. He had been governor of Ohio and a U.S. senator, as well as one of the early favorites in the convention that nominated Lincoln. His political ambition rivaled Seward's and it was said that Lincoln hoped to isolate him in the treasury so as to neutralize a rival. Indeed, Chase had intended to beg off until his friends persuaded him to accept.

Tall and portly, he was often described as "handsome," although his photographs do not sustain this description. He had been married three times, and over a period of seventeen years had mourned at the graves of three wives and four of his six children.

Chase's grief drew him closer to his daughter, Katherine Jane Chase. This vivacious, lovely woman became his friend and confidante, playing chess with him, walking with him to his office while expounding on the books she'd read or the plays she'd seen, filling her father with pleasant surprise at her insights into politics. Chase was also an idealist and fiery Abolitionist. It was he who had guaranteed half the money to buy the freedom of the beautiful Kentucky slave Eliza; and he took so many cases of fugitive blacks without fee that Kentuckians called him "the attorney general for runaway negroes." Speaking in Cincinnati he had been pelted with a brick and rotten eggs, missiles that to Abolitionists were accolades and brought him forty ballots for the presidential nomination at Chicago. That hunger for power would never abate in Salmon Portland Chase, and it was said of him with delicious malice—and without proof—that he bowed each morning before his mirror, gravely murmuring, *"President* Chase."

No act of Lincoln's prior to his inauguration was as controversial as his appointment of Simon Cameron of Pennsylvania as secretary of war. The uproar of opposition was so widespread and bursting from so many distinguished throats that it threatened to divide and perhaps even destroy the Republican Party. William Cullen Bryant spoke for many when he spoke of "an utter, ancient and deep-seated distrust of his integrity." Thaddeus Stevens pronounced him "a man destitute of honor and honesty." Yet Lincoln was in a bind, for if there were few Republican leaders who supported this prince of corruption there were also not many who could deny his claim to high office. In a deal with Judge Davis unauthorized by Lincoln, it was Cameron who started the stampede to the Rail-Splitter at Chicago by releasing his delegates after the first ballot. Undoubtedly, the "Czar of Pennsylvania" was a man without policy or principle, worshiping before his twin deities of profit and power, the one reinforcing the other, but still, there had been a deal and Lincoln, though supposedly groaning, "How can

I justify my title of Honest Old Abe with the appointment of a man like Cameron," could not repudiate it. What he could really not ignore was the counter-hurricane of endorsement for Cameron that this wily operator had organized, for as often as Simon Cameron was accused of corruption there never materialized any solid proof of specific charge in writing.

Cameron was born March 8, 1799, into a poor family. His mother's father, a German, had fought in the Revolution, but his own Scots father, a country tailor, was a poor provider and it was fortunate for Simon that he was adopted by a physician. At ten he was a printer's devil and before he was twenty-one he was editing the Doylestown *Democrat.* Borrowing money, he bought the Harrisburg *Republican* in 1826, landing a state printing contract that put him on the road to fortune. Next his support of Andrew Jackson for his second term brought him Federal patronage.

Cameron's power was typical of the state "bosses" of those days when, with no truly national organization, presidential campaigns depended on men who could "deliver" their constituencies. Twice he put James Buchanan in the U.S. Senate, and when "Old Buck's" power rivaled his own, he put himself there as a Republican.

Tall, his gray clothes hanging loosely on his slender frame, his thick white hair combed straight back, he was smooth-faced with what might have been called a "noble forehead" but for the cunning eyes and long foxlike nose and slit of a mouth beneath it. People who knew Cameron said he had no face but rather wore a habitual mask to conceal his true intentions. For such a man, Lincoln had nothing but reservations, but to conduct the war that seemed to be impending he needed Pennsylvania's coal and iron and railroads, and so he took him as he was.

No one could have been more unlike Cameron than Gideon Welles, the Connecticut Yankee who was secretary of the navy. Like Cameron, he was an old Jacksonian Democrat; but again unlike him he was a man of abiding principles. Having left the Democrats over the slavery issue, he made an unsuccessful run as a Republican for governor of his state. Fifty-eight years old, short and barrel-chested, he looked like a prophet in a cave with his massive head crowned with a curling wig above a snow-white beard. Lincoln joked that Uncle Gideon didn't know bow from stern, but he was a good administrator who didn't need to be a seagoing old salt. He was an inveterate diarist, given to extreme judgments and an occasional twisted fact—but always delicious.

Edward Bates, the new attorney general, had been born in Belmont, Virginia, September 4, 1793. Having served as a sergeant of volunteers in the war of 1812 he came home to receive his law degree in 1816. After his brother secured for him the post of prosecuting attorney for St. Louis, he went to Missouri, where he became a state senator and a Whig congressman. Beetle-browed with a shock of iron-gray hair and clean-shaven face bottomed off with a wiry white beard, Bates gained a national reputation through speeches and articles pushing the Free-Soil movement. He was a candidate at Chicago, but threw his border state influence behind Lincoln, for which great favor he entered the Rail-Splitter's cabinet. Never known as a wit, he did say: "An Old-Line Whig is one who takes his whiskey regularly, and votes the Democratic ticket occasionally."

Another promissory note written in Chicago by Judge Davis came due for Caleb Blood Smith of Indiana. Boston-born on April 16, 1808, he and his family moved to Ohio, where he passed the bar in 1828. Indiana was his next stop, where he founded a Whig newspaper. Member of both the Indiana and the U.S. House, publisher and promotor of railways and canals, Smith's middle name of Blood indeed belied his cold, calculating temperament. In perhaps the most hirsute era in American military and political history, his clean-shaven face with its big ears, big, bald forehead, big nose and compressed lips stood out as though he were a visitor from another planet. Because he had seconded Lincoln's nomination and stumped for him, and because it seemed Indiana deserved a reward, Smith's interest in internal improvements dictated his appointment as secretary of the interior. Lincoln would regret the choice, for this old-line politician preferred patronage over performance and soon got his benefactor into trouble.

Although Kentucky-born Montgomery Blair was chosen as the new postmaster general, it is safe to say that the post had actually been awarded to the Blair family. Francis Preston Blair was the patriarch of this brood of political animals. Born in Virginia April 12, 1791, he had been graduated from Transylvania, had served in 1812 and had become one of Andrew Jackson's fiercest and most loyal supporters while he edited the Washington *Globe.* It was the Blair family's immense influence among the vital border states—Francis in Kentucky, Montgomery in the Bluegrass and Maryland, and Francis, Jr., in Missouri—that brought those delegates to Lincoln on the third ballot. Their united devotion to the Constitution and opposition to slavery and secession—even though the elder Blair had once owned slaves—greatly impressed Lincoln; and although the chieftain of this clan never held elected office, his sensitivity to political trends and his subtle mind would be of invaluable help to his chief.

His son Montgomery had been born in Franklin in 1813, and had been graduated from West Point, serving briefly in the Seminole War. Resigning to study law at Transylvania, he became successively district attorney for

Missouri, mayor of St. Louis and judge of the court of common pleas. While counsel for Dred Scott he won many friends among antislavery leaders, and when he began to argue before the U.S. Supreme Court his practice became so large that he had to move to Maryland, where he became a Republican leader.

Finally, there was Vice President Hannibal Hamlin, the man who would inherit or alter this cabinet should anything happen to the chief executive. A Maineman and the descendant of Mainemen, where he was born on August 27, 1809, Hamlin was a veteran Democrat who had served twice in the House and once in the Senate, leaving that party on the slavery issue and becoming a Republican. Tall and powerfully built with a rugged face that might have been carved out of New England granite, Hamlin was fond of holding up his ham fists with the remark that he needed no weapons to protect himself. He was also remarkably dark-skinned for a man of pure English stock, and his detractors in the South explained his antislavery views by insisting that he was a mulatto.

Here was a diverse group of Americans indeed, so much so that when Lincoln and his cabinet gave a state dinner later in March, William Russell Lowell of the London *Times* observed that he was "surprised to find a diversity of accent almost as great as if a number of foreigners had been speaking English."

Lincoln could have hoped for a little less diversity among his cabinet members, for when he polled them on the question of the relief or evacuation of Fort Sumter they voted five to two to abandon the fort. The president was dismayed. He was determined to preserve the Union, but he was also aware that whoever fired the first shots into the Charleston powderkeg would be accused of starting a civil war. This stigma he could stand less than Davis, for his problems were more complicated.

The four states of the Upper South, of course, would secede no matter who provoked the war; but Lincoln must still unite the North while holding the border states of Maryland, Kentucky and Missouri. The Northern states were not nearly as united in early March of 1861 as popular history supposes. New Jersey was talking secession, and so was California, which, with Oregon, was considering creation of a Pacific nation. New York City, ever ready to betray since the days of the Revolution, had many Southern sympathizers and would have much to gain economically by becoming a free city. Economic considerations, in fact, were about the only cords binding the North in those days. Eastern manufacturers needed a strong protective tariff lest they lose the lucrative Southern market to tariff-free and better wares from Britain. The Northwest was enraged by Confederate blockade of the Mississippi, for fifty years its outlet to the Gulf of Mexico. Then there were those doves and hawks who wanted disunion for different reasons: the doves cooing, "Let our errant sisters go," the hawks shrieking, "No union with slaveholders! Away with this foul thing!"

Lincoln's problem was to bind these discordant factions into a united whole, and the only way to do it was to maneuver the Confederacy into making the first aggressive move. But he had to do this with all delicacy, for to make a heavy-handed provocation—as James K. Polk had done with Mexico—might justify an armed reaction. Lincoln did not think he had long to wait. He had sent three emissaries to Charleston, among them his friend Lamon—a good fighter but a bumbling diplomat—and had received reports that a conflict was inevitable. Charleston was in a state of feverish excitement. Soldiers seemed to be camping or drilling everywhere, on the squares or at the battery facing Sumter three miles out. Many of them wore gray trousers and jackets with yellow facings and palmetto buttons. The palmetto flag flew everywhere, on ships in the harbor and great storehouses fronting the wharves. The Stars and Stripes was nowhere in sight. More important, all the fire-eaters seemed to have gathered in the Queen City of the South. Among them was Roger Pryor, a smooth-shaven Virginian with long black hair falling to his shoulders. From a balcony in Charleston he told a wildly cheering throng: "I tell you, gentlemen, what will put Virginia in the Southern Confederacy in less than an hour by Shrewsbury clock—strike a blow!" Lincoln was also aware of Governor Francis Pickens's hot temper and of the volatile, glory-seeking nature of the officer President Davis had placed in command of all Southern forces in and around Charleston: he was the Confederacy's first general officer, Brigadier General P.G.T. Beauregard of Louisiana.

16

.

P. G. T. Beauregard

LOUISIANA had been American since 1803, but St. Bernard's Parish south of New Orleans was still Creole country. Its planters—mainly French with a sprinkling of Spaniards—were fiercely proud of their Latin traditions, scorning those bumptious Yankees who had celebrated the Louisiana Purchase by pouring down the Mississippi in an uncouth flood. Jacques Toutant-Beauregard, master of Contreras Plantation in the heart of St. Bernard's, was one of these aristocrats.

Jacques could trace his French and Welsh ancestry back to the thirteenth century. His grandfather was one of those Frenchmen who had settled in America during the reign of Louis XIV, long before the Revolution. His wife was a De Reggio, claiming kinship with an Italian ducal family. When their third child (they would have seven) was born on May 28, 1818, Jacques gave him the sonorous, patrician-sounding name of Pierre Gustave Toutant-Beauregard.

Although it was sugar cane, not cotton, that was nourished by the hot Louisiana sun, the boy grew up in an environment typical of Southern aristocrats. As an infant he was suckled by a black Dominican slave woman, and as a boy he played with black children his own age. The woods in which he hunted and the bayous on which he paddled or fished were no different from the swamp forests of the Cotton Kingdom, with their stands of magnificent live oaks and cypresses, where the sun filtering through bright green leaves made patterns on the water or dappled the rich brown earth.

Culturally and spiritually, the forces shaping young Pierre came not from the American South but from France. The Creoles were Catholic and Gallic. They loved merrymaking and were fond of fine food and wine, of religious splendor and music when high mass would be sung in the Cathedral of St. Louis. Cherishing breeding, exquisite manners, and family tradition, they also prized *l'honneur* to a point that many parvenu Americans found absurd.

Few of these Creoles spoke English, even though many of them were familiar with it. It is doubtful if Pierre tried that language before he was twelve. His education began at a private school near New Orleans in which all instruction was in French. Although little is known of him at this time, he appears to have been studious and reserved. But the violent temper that would characterize his later years became evident at the age of nine, when, teased by a grown man over his skill as a hunter, he seized a stick, chasing his tormentor into an outhouse and keeping him there until he apologized, whereupon he refused to shake hands. Also, at his First Communion in the cathedral, he was walking up the aisle with his class when he heard a rattle of drums behind him. Pausing, hearing another roll, he turned and rushed out of the church. This incident is often cited as suggestive of his early flair for the military, although it is more likely due to the ordinary high-spirited boy's love of drums.

Yet, after his father sent him to "the French School" in New York City conducted by the brothers Peugnet, both of whom had served under Napoleon, Pierre began to develop a deep interest in military history. He was fascinated by the Peugnets' tales of heroism among the French soldiers. He began to study the great Corsican's battles, both during spare time at the school and on vacation at Contreras. Bonaparte became his hero, upon whom he henceforth modeled his life. But Pierre did not neglect his other studies. Working hard, he learned to speak English fluently and to become proficient in mathematics. At the end of four years of study, he shocked his father by asking him to secure him an appointment to West Point.

Jacques protested vigorously. Although he was friendlier toward Americans than most Creoles, he had no desire to see his son serve in the United States Army. But Pierre insisted. He believed himself to be right, and therefore he was inflexible—as always. With reluctance, his father used his political influence, and Pierre Gustave Toutant-Beauregard entered the U.S. Military Academy in March of 1834.

When Pierre arrived at West Point he was sixteen years old, and had all but reached his full height of five feet seven inches. He was slender, but wiry, weighing one hundred and fifty pounds. He wore his uniform well and his carriage was graceful. His complexion was olive, both his hair and eyes were dark, his forehead broad, his cheekbones high and his chin outthrust and bellicose. This last seemed to belie a quiet and reserved manner, but the belligerence was always there, though slumbering. Pierre's most striking feature was his eyes, large and melancholy beneath drooping lids. In later years a curving and carefully groomed mustache completed the portrait of a handsome and extremely confident man.

Beauregard's gravity and studiousness did not invite affection from his classmates. Most thought of him as being French or "foreign." To avoid this stigma, Pierre dropped the hyphen between his two last names, and in a few more years lopped off Pierre, calling himself plain G.T. Beauregard, later restoring the initial P and becoming the P.G.T. Beauregard of history. He also sought to avoid a reputation of singularity and aloofness, but his classmates always remembered him as a cadet who rarely smiled or laughed, was good in sports, rode beautifully and always got high marks. There was also a story—partly plausible, partly romantic—that Pierre had had an unhappy love affair with Winfield Scott's daughter. They were supposed to have become engaged, but General Scott and his wife insisted that they were too young to marry. So Pierre and Virginia parted, writing to each other as promised. But neither one received the other's letters. Mrs. Scott apparently had been intercepting them. Embittered, Pierre eventually married someone else. Mrs. Scott also took Virginia to Europe for five years. While in France the girl became converted to Catholicism, and upon her return to the States entered a convent without her parents' knowledge. She died there in 1845, but before she did she summoned Pierre to her deathbed to tell him that she had only recently learned of her mother's perfidy.

Distraught as Pierre might have been, his unhappy love affair did not affect his studies. In 1838 he was graduated second in a class of forty-five cadets and was assigned to the coveted corps of engineers. His first station was at Fort Adams near Newport, Rhode Island. Second Lieutenant Beauregard was agreeably surprised by the pleasant social life of the old resort town, where a uniform was like a passport to a party. But then a chronic throat ailment that had afflicted him since boyhood became active in the raw Rhode Island winter, and he was transferred south to Pensacola, Florida, to help build coastal defenses. Next he was delighted to be ordered to Barataria Bay on the Louisiana Gulf Coast, to make a topographical and hydrographical survey. Here, so close to New Orleans and his family, Beauregard was a happy man, especially after he met the beautiful Marie Laure Villere, descendant of one of Louisiana's most distinguished Creole families. They were married in September 1841.

But his hair-trigger temper, always slumbering but lightly beneath his Gallic gaiety, exploded shortly afterward in an argument with Lieutenant John Henshaw, temporary commander at Fort Wood. Henshaw refused to send Beauregard the supplies he had requested and ordered his messenger to leave the fort. Beauregard wrote Henshaw an angry letter, calling his action "arbitrary and unjustifiable." Henshaw replied in even more intemperate language that Beauregard said would do "honor to a graduate of Billingsgate." He challenged Henshaw to a duel. After a mutual exchange of insults friends arranged for the pair to meet. They were to fight with shotguns, with only one barrel at a time loaded. The first shot would be fired at thirty yards and if no one was hit, a second at twenty-five. If a third were to be necessary, it would be at the same distance. Fortunately, before the two young hotheads could blow each other apart, a sheriff's deputy arrived and arrested both of them. Beauregard's conduct was typically touchy. *L'honneur* would be like an oriflamme to him all of his life, and as he grew older, if hot lead could not sustain it, he sought satisfaction in scorching language. But then in 1846 his martial spirit was given free rein with eruption of the war with Mexico.

Lieutenant Beauregard was with Winfield Scott during the fighting march from Vera Cruz to Mexico City. It was Beauregard who found a chink in Santa Anna's armor at Cerro Gordo by finding a path around his left flank, and it was he who dissuaded the impetuous but often foolhardy General David Twiggs from making a disastrous frontal assault. When Scott arrived to take command of the turning movement, the Little Creole fell sick of fever and Captain Robert E. Lee continued the reconnaissance leading to the rout of Santa Anna's army. Scott commended all of his engineers but had special praise for Lee, a fondness that Beauregard resented as favoritism. But he was more than satisfied with Scott's remark when he reported the victory at Cerro Gordo to him: "Young man, if I were not on horseback, I would embrace you." He was also cited for his skill and bravery at Churubusco, but it was outside Mexico City that he made his greatest contribution when he persuaded the generals at Scott's council of war to adopt his rather than Lee's approach into the city.

But the Little Creole never forgave the victorious Scott for passing him over for new brevets while Lee and Z.B. Tower received three each. Resentment ached in his soul far more than the Mexican fevers afflicting his body. He spoke deprecatingly of Scott as "our glorious old chief," and whenever he could he held forth on the general's "mistake" in cutting loose from his base at Puebla to go hurrahing off for the Halls of Montezuma. The book-swallowing Beauregard never did develop political acumen and thus he could not understand Scott's real reason for violating one of the cardinal principles of war: do not abandon your base. Scott did so because he feared that at any moment an order might arrive from the jealous and hostile President Polk recalling him to Washington. Although the Little Creole had seen war, books, not experience, remained his guide, and a solution of a situation not arising in print always eluded him.

In March 1850 Beauregard's domestic happiness was shattered when Marie Laure died in delivering their third child, a girl named Laure. A few years later he married again, Caroline Deslonde, a Creole like himself who has been described both as plain and plump and as one of four beautiful sisters. Although Beauregard's ardor had died with Marie Laure, he was devoted to Caroline. From her he gained a powerful brother-in-law, Senator John Slidell of Louisiana. Politics had by then begun to attract the Little Creole. He had rushed to the support of Franklin Pierce, the Democratic candidate for president whom he had known in Mexico, extolling him in New Orleans opposition newspapers in a horrible style which, purple and bloated, studded with solecisms and words abused or misused, must have delighted the hearts of the Whig editors who printed them. Pierce's victory was especially gratifying to Beauregard, inasmuch as it came over his personal bête noire, Winfield Scott. His own campaign for mayor of New Orleans in 1858 was a rowdyish battle between the Know-Nothings on the American side of Canal Street and the Creoles of the French Quarter. The Know-Nothings, better organized, were victorious.

That ended Beauregard's political career, and he devoted all his energies henceforth to his job as superintending engineer of the U.S. Customhouse in New Orleans, a post he held from 1853 to 1860. He showed little interest in the election of 1860 which so divided and inflamed America, except to observe that Lincoln was the South's most dangerous enemy. Yet, it was astonishing that after Lincoln was elected, a man as decidedly Southern in his habits and convictions as Beauregard should have been appointed superintendent of West Point. True, Senator Slidell had been at work, and Secretary of War Floyd yielded to no Southerner in loyalty to men from Dixie. What is even more incredible is that Major Beauregard should have accepted, should have gone there and should have believed that the U.S. government would allow him to stay. Yet he assumed the superintendency on January 23, 1861, three days before his native state seceded from the Union. To a cadet from Louisiana who asked him if he should resign, the Little Creole replied: "Watch me—and when I jump, you jump! What's the use of jumping too soon?"

Beauregard did not jump but was rather pushed, being notified by the War Department that his appointment was revoked. He relinquished command on the twenty-eighth, his five-day tour at the Academy remaining a record for brevity. And of course he protested! With that states' rights legalism which had captured the Southern mind, while he was still in the service of the United States, but planning to join a rebellion against that nation, he actually chided that government for removing him from a post where he could do it great injury. He even demanded $165 from the War Department as expenses for his return trip to New Orleans. The government refused to pay, and yet the Little Creole, after resigning from the U.S. Army on March 1 and joining the Confederate forces, continued to press his claim.

Once he had returned to Louisiana it became apparent that Beauregard's puzzling acceptance of the West Point post might really have been a clever move to fortify his credentials when he applied for a commission in the Confederate Army. All ambition now, the Little Creole thirsted for command of his state's forces, and he was consumed with disgust and dismay when the appointment went instead to cadaverous, sour Braxton Bragg, a North Carolinian but also Jefferson Davis's close friend and favorite. Undaunted, Beauregard put Slidell to work in Montgomery, unaware that circumstances were already marching under his banner.

President Davis had to move speedily and surely if the attempts in Washington to negotiate a settlement of the crisis failed. A demand for the surrender of Sumter would have to be made, and it could be done not by a civilian such as Governor Pickens but rather by a representative of the central government who was also a skilled engineering officer able to conduct a siege. Sumter was far too important as the first military action to be entrusted to a politician. Who else but Beauregard?

So the Little Creole arrived in Montgomery on February 26, conferring with Davis until late that night. When he departed for Charleston he bore the star of the first brigadier general in the history of the Confederate States Army, charged with taking command of all Confederate and South Carolina forces confronting the Union garrison in Fort Sumter.

17

•

Fort Sumter

THERE IS a tradition in American foreign policy that "the other side" must strike the first blow, and that Americans must fight only in defense of their country and their principles. This explains why President James K. Polk worked so hard to goad Mexico into making the attack that gave him his doubtful claim that Mexico "has shed American blood on the American soil."

Such thinking guided the presidents of the United States and the Confederacy and their cabinets, and that is why Jefferson Davis held Beauregard on a leash in Charleston and why Abraham Lincoln hesitated to send an armed relief expedition to Fort Sumter lest it appear to the world an act of aggression and give the South the excuse to strike at the fort. But on the day after Lincoln's inauguration he received word from Major Anderson at Sumter that he had only six weeks' supply of food remaining. That gave Lincoln less than that amount of time to decide among: (1) armed relief of the fort; (2) subtle provocation of the Montgomery government; and (3) letting the fort go. While he pondered this decision, on April 1 he received from Secretary of State Seward a memorandum entitled "Thoughts for the President."

Despite his defeat at Chicago, Seward still thought of himself as the ablest leader in the Republican Party. Lincoln remained to him a well-intentioned incompetent, a prairie lawyer fumbling his way toward disaster. His memorandum opened with the bold if not impudent assertion that the administration was still "without a policy either domestic or foreign" and proposed that Fort Sumter should be evacuated and Fort Pickens in Florida reinforced. This would change the dispute between North and South from one of slavery to one of Union or Disunion. How, Seward did not say; nor did he specify how this would improve the situation. Actually, secession had already superseded slavery as the divisive issue. Next he made the most remarkable and fatuous recommendation in the history of the State Department: go to war with Spain and France over their territorial aspirations in the Caribbean! With one war looming, Lincoln was to provoke two more! Actually this parade of nonsense with its vague circumlocutions was nothing but a mask for Seward's proposal to let him run the government. Lincoln could remain as president—a figurehead—but William Seward would be the premier. To all of this Lincoln responded with customary restraint and dignity, making it firmly plain that if anything was to be done, *he* would do it.

Yet, it is likely that Seward's effrontery may have impelled the president to do *something.* The North was still clamoring for action and decisiveness and on April 5 the Republican *New York Times* in a biting editorial praised the Confederacy for a "degree of vigor, intelligence and success" that was nowhere evident in Washington. "The President must adopt some clear and distinct policy in regard to secession, or the Union will not only be severed, but the country will be disgraced." It was after this that Lincoln began to move toward a policy of subtle provocation of the South to strike the first blow.

Meanwhile, Seward in his campaign against holding Sumter had already been active behind the president's back. Having forgotten his inaccurate prediction that the Confederacy would "fizzle," he still thought that the seven states of the Upper South and the border would remain neutral and that in time the seceded seven would creep penitently back into the Union fold. He was adamantly against holding Sumter, and it was he who had influenced the cabinet to vote five to two against resupplying it. Thus, while Lincoln was embarked on a course of provocation, his chief cabinet officer had decided to adopt one of conciliation.

There were then in Washington three Southern commissioners sent by Davis to arrange for "the speedy adjustment of all questions growing out of separation . . ." The Confederacy having opened the lower Mississippi to the North, Davis thought it only just that the Federal government should turn over Sumter and the Florida forts—and much besides. Lincoln refused to see them. To do so would have been to grant the Confederacy equal status as a legitimate nation rather than to regard it as a "rebellion" by private persons. Seward also could not see them officially. But on March 15, Supreme Court Justice John A. Campbell of Alabama dropped into Seward's office to urge him to receive the Southerners. Seward declined, but he did say, "The evacuation of Sumter is as much as the Administration can bear." Campbell was astounded. Here was Secretary of State Seward actually conceding the chief demand the commissioners had come to make! Campbell said he would write to Davis immediately, and asked: "And what shall I say to him on the subject of Fort Sumter?"

"You may say to him that before that letter reaches him, the telegraph will have informed him that Sumter will have been evacuated."

Thus the Number Two man in the Federal government was giving an unauthorized assurance in direct contradiction to the course being followed by his chief. Seward must have known that Lincoln had sent Captain Gustavus Fox to Sumter to determine if the fort could be relieved. Fox, the brother-in-law of Postmaster General Blair and like him an ardent Union man, was an Annapolis graduate who had organized the expedition to Vera Cruz during the Mexican War. He came back with the report that relief was feasible. Lincoln ordered him to assemble the necessary ships and stand by for sailing orders. At the end of March Lincoln again polled his cabinet, and with one member absent the vote was three to three. Seward now began to see that he might have gone too far in his guarantee to Davis. When Justice Campbell returned on April 1 to demand why the notice of two weeks earlier had not been carried out, Seward blandly replied:

"I am satisfied the government will not undertake to supply Fort Sumter without giving notice to Governor Pickens."

Campbell was again astonished. "What does this mean?" he cried angrily. "Does the President design to supply Sumter?"

"No, I think not," said Seward, still unctuous. "It is a very irksome thing to him to surrender it. His ears are open to everyone, and with schemes for its supply. I do not think he will adopt any of them. There is no design to reinforce it."

Campbell reported this conversation to the Confederate commissioners. They saw it as deliberate deceit, and they wired Davis: "The war wing presses on the President; he vibrates to their side . . . Their form of notice to us may be that of a coward, who gives it when he strikes."

Lincoln had practiced no deception. Rather it was Seward the sophisticate, not the bumbling prairie lawyer, who had misrepresented the situation. Doubtless he was well-meaning; men impressed with their own importance usually are. But he had no business conferring with a man like Campbell, doubtless an agent of the commissioners. And yet he saw him again! After Lincoln on April 6 signed an order dispatching the relieving fleet to Sumter, Campbell came once more to his office to ask if this were true. Seward replied by note: "Faith as to Sumter fully kept. Wait and see." By this Seward meant only to suggest that there would be no action without warning, and the commissioners were outraged to learn that the fleet had in fact sailed. On April 8 there appeared before Governor Pickens a Federal envoy who read him the following message:

"I am directed by the President of the United States to notify you to expect an attempt will be made to supply Fort Sumter with provisions only, and that if such an attempt be not resisted, no effort to throw in men, arms, or ammunition will be made without further notice, or in case of an attack upon the fort."

Pickens could only forward the message to Montgomery, where Davis immediately assembled his cabinet and laid it before them. Their reactions ranged from indignation at Lincoln's "deception," to chagrin at having been maneuvered into choosing between the repugnant alternatives of dropping their demands or firing the first shot—and that to prevent food being brought to hungry men, to a surprisingly ominous and pessimistic warning from the fire-eating Robert Toombs. "The firing on that fort will inaugurate a civil war greater than any the world has yet seen, and I do not feel competent to advise you," he said, pacing the room with his hands clasped beneath his coattails. He turned on Davis. "Mr. President, at this time it is suicide, murder, and you will lose us every friend at the North. You will wantonly strike a hornets' nest which extends from mountains to ocean. Legions now quiet will swarm out and sting us to death. It is unnecessary. It puts us in the wrong. It is fatal."

Davis disagreed. He argued that it was not he who had forced the decision, but Lincoln, and that the world would see this and understand, especially in the light of the Federal chief's base deception. He instructed Secretary of War Walker to send Beauregard this message:

"If you have no doubt as to the authorized character of the agent who communicated to you the intention of the Washington government to supply Fort Sumter by force, you will at once demand its evacuation, and, if this is refused, proceed in such manner as you may determine to reduce it."

Beauregard was overjoyed. His hour of glory had struck! At once he sent two men out to Sumter in a rowboat flying a flag of truce. They handed Anderson a note demanding surrender and stipulating the terms: "All proper facilities will be afforded for the removal of yourself and command, together with company arms and property, and all private property, to any post in the United States which you may select. The flag which you have upheld so long and with so much fortitude, under the most trying circumstances, may be saluted by you on taking it down."

Anderson was a Kentuckian with Virginian ancestry and married to a Georgian, and it was widely believed that Buchanan's Secretary of War

Floyd had given him the Charleston command in hope that he would betray it. Corrupt as Floyd was in his personal financial dealings, he was also one of those cunning men who judge others by themselves. Robert Anderson was a true and honorable man. Handsome, deeply religious and at nearly fifty-six a veteran of thirty-six years in the United States Army, his sense of honor was rivaled by his devotion to the Union. If Kentucky seceded, he had vowed, he would go to Europe "to become a spectator of the contest, and not an actor." His thoughtful eyes were sad as he read the summons. His sorrow was sharpened by the perception that soon the very stones beneath his feet would tremble in the opening blasts of a fierce fratricidal war; that so many brother officers whom he had known would soon be at each other's throats; indeed that this very Pierre Beauregard who was summoning him to the surrender to which he could not in honor agree had once been his artillery student at West Point. In sorrow he wrote, ". . . I regret that my sense of honor, and of my obligations to my government, prevent my compliance," and handed the note to the two emissaries with the wry remark: "Gentlemen, if you do not batter us to pieces, we shall be starved out in a few days."

Excited by this last, Beauregard immediately wired it to Montgomery and was told by Secretary Walker that if Anderson did not state a definite time for surrender he must "reduce the fort." It was now the early morning of April 12, 1861. There could be no delay, for Captain Fox's relief expedition had been sighted off the bar. This time Beauregard sent four men out in the white-flagged rowboat. Anderson told them he could not evacuate the fort until "noon of the fifteenth," unless he received different instructions or supplies. He was unaware that Fox's fleet stood just outside the harbor. But Beauregard's aides were, and they could not accept Anderson's offer lest the Federal warships have time to thicken Sumter's firepower with their own. Anderson was told at 3:20 A.M. that his fort would be bombarded "in one hour from this time." One hour. How many hours had passed since this same Little Creole who now menaced him and his men with death and destruction from forty-seven howitzers and mortars had stood before him in his classroom confidently reeling off his recitations. Ruefully, Anderson shook hands with Beauregard's aides. "If we do not meet again in this world," he said, "I hope that we may meet in the better one."

The emissaries did not return to Beauregard's headquarters in Charleston, but rather rowed directly to Cummings Point on Morris Island and gave the order to open fire. One of the four was Roger Pryor, the fiery Virginian who had counseled "Strike a blow!" just two days ago. He was offered the honor of firing the first shot, but he demurred, shaking his long hair. "I could not fire the first gun of the war," he murmured, his voice husky with emotion. Legend has it that another Virginian, none other than silver-haired Edmund Ruffin—who had vowed to kill himself rather than live again under a Federal government—thereupon volunteered to pull that fatal lanyard. Actually, it was more probably a private named Henry S. Farley who fired the first shot of the American Civil War. Ruffin did, however, fire one of his battery's columbiads.

Arching into the night at 4:30 A.M., the opening shell—a signal shot—described its dreadful red parabola against the night sky, bursting with a yellowish-red glare over the dark pentagonal shape of Sumter. At once Beauregard's massed guns began bombarding the fort. Soon the Charleston battery in full view of Sumter and the waterfront rooftops were thick with cheering citizens, not only from the city, but from surrounding towns, arriving on foot by train or buggy, some with folding chairs and packed lunches as though attending a Fourth of July fireworks display. Every eyeglass was trained on that glowing, shuddering, five-pointed structure now visible in that crimson dawn of April 12, and as the accuracy of the Confederate gunners—who got off a total of 4,000 rounds during the siege—increased with practice, so also rose in volume the delirious cheers of the spectators.

On Sumter Anderson had forty guns, but they were in casemates protecting his gunners and could fire only flat-trajectory cannon using solid shot. They were no match for Beauregard's encircling batteries, whose shells either struck the terreplein or the top of the ramparts, or dug into the earth of the parade, each explosion shaking the fort like a giant hand. Heated shot started fires, threatening the magazine. Smoke filled the casemates, forcing Anderson's soldiers to lie flat, breathing through wet handkerchiefs. It was no contest. There was the fort, visible to the Southern gunners like a fly on a windowpane; there were the Rebel guns, invisible except for muzzle flashes. Anderson had no way of scouting his enemy, and in those days there were no sophisticated devices for locating hostile artillery. Inexorably, Beauregard's gunners reduced Anderson's token defense to a paltry six guns. Yet he fought on. There came a lull in the cannonade and it seemed to the Rebels that the Federals were getting ready to surrender, but then the Yankee guns spoke again and the Confederates cheered.

There was some hope in Sumter and fear in Charleston that the Federal fleet would yet come to the fort's rescue. But the *Baltic, Pawnee* and *Harriet Lane,* though standing off the harbor, wisely decided against running the gantlet* of the enemy's land batteries, and Sumter faced the second day alone. In the morning the last of the rice was cooked and served with pork, and the duel renewed. Rebel fire again set the barracks and officers' quarters ablaze and shot down a flagstaff. It was replaced, but now Sumter was short on cartridges. Suddenly Senator Louis T. Wigfall of Texas appeared inexplicably at the fort and unofficially demanded its surrender. Anderson agreed that he could fight no more and Old Glory was hauled down to be replaced by a white flag. Thunderous cheers arose on the Charleston shore and surrounding islands. First blood to the Confederacy! Bands played "Dixie." Beauregard's aides then arrived, making the unofficial capitulation official.

Surprisingly, there had been no casualties, although Roger Pryor nearly killed himself. Seated at a table in the hospital while the terms were being written, he felt the need of a drink and took a pull at a bottle near his hand without reading the label. It was iodine of potassium. Luckily a Union surgeon was present. He took Pryor outside and drew off the poison with a stomach pump. But then, as Anderson was firing a fifty-gun salute to his flag, an ember fell into a store of powder. The resulting explosion wounded five Federal soldiers and killed Private Daniel Hough, the first man from either side to die in the war.

After the scorched and tattered flag was hauled down, it was given to Anderson, who vowed to be wrapped in it as a winding sheet on his burial day. Then his weary, fought-out gunners marched from the fort to the wharf, colors flying and drums beating. They were taken aboard a steamer from the Federal relief expedition. Marching up the gangplank they could hear the delirious cheers from the Charleston shore. But the Confederate soldiers did not cheer, silently removing their caps in salute.

They knew, better than civilians, what lay ahead.

---

*A "gantlet" is a form of military punishment also used by American Indians in which a man stripped to the waist is forced to run down a lane formed by facing lines of men who strike him with switches or clubs.

18

■

The North United

A S LINCOLN had hoped, Sumter electrified and united the North. That Sunday when the news arrived in Washington that Anderson had surrendered, the White House was besieged with callers anxious to assure the president of their loyalty and support. Among them was Senator Stephen Douglas, who had risen from his sick bed, the pallor of his impending death already on his face, extending his hand with a wan smile and pledging unswerving support in this Civil War now necessary to preserve the Union. Lincoln took the hand with a warm grin, and an inward sigh of relief; the allegiance of the man who remained the idol of the Democrats would remove the danger that the conflict might become partisan.

Across the country the people responded with a wild enthusiasm that astonished and delighted Lincoln. In Washington Senator John Sherman, the brother of William Tecumseh, remarked that the actual advent of war "brings a feeling of relief: the suspense is over." In Boston delirious crowds, ringing church bells and the clatter and clamor of drums and trumpets made one man shout exultantly, "The heather is on fire!" Ralph Waldo Emerson cried: "We have a country again! Sometimes gunpowder smells good."

On that same Sunday a buoyant Lincoln met with his cabinet to issue a proclamation calling on the states for 75,000 ninety-day volunteer militia to be used against "combinations too powerful to be suppressed by the ordinary course of judicial proceedings." Technically this was not a declaration of war, because only Congress could declare war. But Congress was not in session, much to Lincoln's immense relief, for he wanted no hampering congressional committees hung around his neck; and even though he called for a special session beginning July 4, he expected to have the situation in hand by then. If the reaction of the Northern states was any

143

criterion, it appeared that the president had judged correctly: governor after governor wired support and the militia quotas were swiftly oversubscribed.

It was something of a martial picnic in which cheering crowds and waving flags and tootling bands raised the patriotic pulse of scores of thousands of young men to such a heated beat that the recruiters, so far from having to plead for enlistments, found that their most distressing duty was to turn away as many as they accepted. In Iowa alone, twenty times the state's quota of militia rushed to the colors, coming in mostly by farm wagon or on foot. When most of them were rejected, they refused to go home, raising such a clamor that Iowa had to get the Federal government to increase its quota. War was all gaiety to these ardent but naive young men, and a musket seemed to beat a plow or a pencil all hollow. In Wisconsin the boys of one regiment with an unfilled quota rode about in a recruiting wagon accompanied by a fife and drummer shouting "Fourth of July every day of the year!" War meetings were held in towns and villages with songs and speeches, followed by a barbecue. Pretty girls fired with patriotic zeal challenged their sweethearts to join the colors, and at one Wisconsin gathering a girl cried to her boy friend: "John, if you don't enlist, I'll never let you kiss me again as long as I live. Now, you mind, sir, I mean what I say!" Patriotism that swelled hearts to bursting also drew sobs and tears from kneeling officers receiving regimental colors from silver-haired veterans wearing the uniforms of 1812 or from weeping little girls with flowers in their hair and red-white-and-blue sashes across their breasts. Sometimes, when a father in uniform might present a new sword to his son with the injunction to bring it back stained to the hilt, there came a pause in the gaiety, a somber caesura reminding all these naive and tumultuous crowds that these youths whom they were so lustily honoring might soon be facing suffering and death.

So they marched off to the camps surrounding the state capitals, drums rattling, fifes squealing, sergeants growling themselves hoarse in a vain attempt to straighten their spines and dress their ranks. There they displayed a deep distaste for discipline, and in the immemorial way of American militia elected their officers and called them by their first names. "We enlisted to put down the rebellion," said an Indiana private, "and had no patience with the red-tape tom-foolery of the regular service. Furthermore, our boys recognized no superiors except in the line of legitimate duty. Shoulder straps waived, a private was ready at the drop of a hat to thrash his commander; a feat that occurred more than once." Fiercely independent country boys most of them, they simply could not understand that drill and discipline were not meant to humble them or strip them of their democratic rights, but rather were intended to mold them into a single cohesive unit responsive to commands during the fiery crucible of battle. Patriotism, they soon found to their immense disgust, might get them into uniform; but only discipline would hold them steady under bombardment.

No such difficulty inhibited mobilization in Dixie, where Lincoln's call for volunteers provoked a unifying growl of anger from the Southern people, just as Davis's decision to attack Sumter had aroused the North. The Confederacy's all-but-feudal society had no such "leveling" notions that one man was just as good as the next and maybe even a little better. The highborn were accustomed to giving orders, and the lowborn to executing them. The vast defection of trained and seasoned Southern officers from the United States Army, and the much larger reservoir of men of all ages graduated from Dixie's numerous military academies and colleges were other great Confederate advantages.

Even greater was the joyously welcomed parade of the four states of the Upper South into the arms of their sister seven of the Lower. Lincoln's call for volunteers brought angry refusals from the governors of Virginia, North Carolina, Tennessee and Arkansas in a style best expressed by Governor John W. Ellis of North Carolina, who cried that his state would "be no party to this wicked violation of the laws of the country and this war upon the liberties of a free people." But then there was a secession-in-reverse: the non-slaveholders of western Virginia, long resentful of slaveholder domination, loyal to the Union, organized their region into a territory that in 1863 was admitted to the United States as West Virginia. Even so, there were now eleven mobilizing and confident Confederate states arrayed to defend their new homeland in "the War of Northern Invasion."

Scenes identical to those of the North were repeated throughout Dixie, where Davis's call for 100,000 volunteers was just as wildly acclaimed. "Gentlemen privates" everywhere enrolled themselves under the various banners of Dixie—eventually there would be one, the bold red battle flag with its colorful stars and bars, as pretty an emblem as ever was caught in the wind—while a man's capacity to command was measured by the number of bales or hogsheads stacked on his wharf. Dixie, it would seem, had no need for recruiting sergeants, for the Southern woman seemed to have shouldered that duty. Mother, wife, sister, sweetheart, "she was the South's incarnate pride," wrote Stephen Vincent Benet, and "she propped up the South on a swansdown fan." It was her smile the soldier sought, her stony contempt the slacker feared.

War led the South, like the North, to bury even deeper the slavery issue that had made armed enemies of them. "States' Rights!" was still her rallying cry, just as in the North it remained "The Union Forever!" Dixie obviously found it easier to get its men to fight for "ouah rights" than for the institution they instinctively despised, while in Yankeeland, where most of the Abolitionists were cheerleaders at heart, the true fighting men would rather risk their flesh for the sacred Union than for distant blacks whom they mostly loved as little as their Southern opponents. This is not to belittle or mock the motives of the men of the rival Civil War armies. No soldiers were ever more noble or idealistic; but Johnny Reb did not put on Confederate gray or butternut to defend the peculiar institution any more than Billy Yank vested himself in Federal blue to stamp out bondage.

But with what a mixture of high-hearted gaiety and religious fervor did they go off to war! Most of them Protestants of British stock, in the South with a surprisingly large number of Celts—Irish, Scots and Welsh— in the North a generous leavening of both Germans and Irish, they cheered and sang and swore such mild oaths as "dang" and "durn," carrying their Bibles in breast pockets to deflect bullets and attending daily services where they prayed—especially in the South—with an intensity unequaled since the days of Oliver Cromwell and his Roundheads. In them the aristocratic paternalism of the South was meeting the democratic nationalism of the North—an agricultural society arrayed against one of industry—but of these high-flown definitions of their causes they had not the slightest inkling; and if they had, they would have laughed them off with good-natured contempt. Sturdy parochials all, bigots even, with few of them ever having strayed far from the village of their birth, still less from their native county, they would soon shed their naiveté and romantic view of war—without ever losing their wonderful sardonic sense of humor—to become the sturdiest and most durable and ferocious American soldiers ever to march to the squeal of the fife and the tap of the drum.

And as April came closer to May, they, too, came closer to the exhilarating or terrifying sight of the enemy's long, thin bayonets.

Four more seceding slave states had swelled the Confederacy to eleven, while four more still hung in the balance. These were the border states: Delaware, Maryland, Kentucky and Missouri. The first two replied cautiously to Lincoln's call for troops. Although Delaware did not prohibit slavery, it had so few that it could hardly be considered a slave state; and it replied that because it had no militia it could not send troops. Maryland said it would send them only for defense of Washington. But Governor Beriah Magoffin of Kentucky telegraphed: "I say emphatically, Kentucky will furnish no troops for the wicked purpose of subduing her sister Southern states." From Governor Claiborne Jackson of Missouri came this: "Your requisition is illegal, unconstitutional, revolutionary, inhuman, diabolical and cannot be complied with."

Such defiance disturbed Lincoln. Delaware was most unlikely to secede, but the other three border states were vital. His native Kentucky, with its strategic location, rivers and manpower, cattle and horses, was especially important. "I think to lose Kentucky is nearly the same as to lose the whole game," said Lincoln. "Kentucky gone, we cannot hold Missouri, nor, as I think, Maryland. These all against us, and the job on our hands is too large for us. We would as well consent to separation at once, including the surrender of this capital."

Washington was in real danger. Eastern Maryland with its rabid secessionist population encompassed it on three sides, and across the Potomac stood hostile Virginia on the fourth. Rebel campfires were visible on the southern bank. The Confederates had already seized the Norfolk navy yard and Harpers Ferry. They were on fire to capture the Federal capital. "That filthy cage of unclean birds," said the Richmond *Examiner,* "must and will be purified."

Although Washington in 1861 was still the dread of European diplomats accustomed to the splendor, culture and ease of London and Paris, Rome and Madrid, it could no longer be described as "a loathsome community of the debauched, debased and drunken," nor could an assignment there be regarded as "a season in Purgatory." Congressmen had long ago left their raucous—if not rowdy—taverns and boardinghouses and now dwelt in sturdy brick houses or the two leading hotels, the National and Willard's. The main thoroughfare of Pennsylvania Avenue was no longer an obstacle course of rain-filled puddles or drying mud, but was rather paved with cobblestones. Here stood the President's House in the center of twenty-two wooded acres. It had been rebuilt since the British burned it in the War of 1812, and then called the White House after it was smeared with white paint to cover the blackened sections. It was no rival of London's Buckingham Palace or the Tuileries in Paris, and was indeed compared to a rundown Southern plantation. But it was growing in elegance, history and the affection of the American people, until, of course, the South switched from fondness to hatred of the "gorilla tyrant" who dwelt there. It also smelled. Surrounded by noxious flats, a stinking canal and a marsh full of sewerage, suffocating odors drifted regularly into the presidential quarters, exceeded only when the wind shifted to carry a stench off the common, where the city's night soil was dumped daily.

The Capitol, though still domeless, was indeed commanding, and the chambers of the Senate and House truly splendid. Several other government buildings, the Post Office at Seventh and F, the huge brick Patent Office across the street, and the turreted Smithsonian had been completed. But even in 1861 the presence of the Federal government was symbolized by no more than ten buildings, a few statues and the truncated, incomplete obelisk of the Washington Monument. Europeans still teased Americans about the bucolic character of their capital, and one Britisher wrote: "To make a Washington street, take one marble temple, or public office, a dozen good houses of brick and a dozen of wood and fill in with sheds and fields." Yet the roads connecting Washington with the countryside were vastly improved, a fact that did not comfort Abraham Lincoln gazing apprehensively south where Confederate strength was daily augmented by arriving troops, and from which daily Rebel saber-rattling and rumors of impending invasion of the District could be heard.

No doubt about it, Washington was jittery, its chief citizen nearly frantic over the city's feeble defenses. "Why don't they come?" he asked his wife of the 75,000 militiamen as they both stood atop the White House, staring glumly south toward the Confederate flag waving on top of Marshall's Tavern in Alexandria. "Why don't they come?" The Chief Executive might have been even more disturbed if it had occurred to him that the salvation of the nation's capital now depended on a cross-eyed political general from Massachusetts named Benjamin Butler.

Benjamin Franklin Butler was born November 5, 1818, in Deerfield, New Hampshire. He never saw his father, who was away privateering in the Caribbean at the time, dying there of yellow fever. Ben was a puny and sickly child, his features disfigured by a drooping left eyelid and a severe case of strabismus, or crossed eyes. His mother, seeing at once he would need all her care, boarded her older boy with a relative and took the baby with her to her husband's family's farm in nearby Nottingham.

On both sides Ben's parents were Irish Presbyterians. Grandfather Zephaniah Butler had been a schoolmaster who served under Wolfe at Quebec, while his mother could boast of a grandfather who had fought for King William at the Battle of the Boyne.

As a boy, Ben was a good student, blessed with an excellent memory which served him well in an age when learning was chiefly by rote. He also seems to have grown up with a chip on his shoulder, probably because his cross-eyed looks invited a derision which he would not accept. He proved early that he could back up his sharp tongue with his fists. At the age of nine he had impressed his teachers and family so much that he was sent away to Exeter Academy to prepare for college. Thrown in with older boys who seem to have ostracized him, he became even more resentful of slights. Happily for him, he spent only one term there, accompanying his mother when she took a job as manager of a boardinghouse in the boom industrial town of Lowell, Massachusetts.

Ben sought higher education and he wanted to get it at the U.S. Military Academy. But West Point turned him down twice, probably because of his crossed eyes. Typically, he conceived an undying hatred for the Academy. Instead, he went to Waterville (modern Colby) College in Maine, where he was notorious for his aversion to compulsory chapel attendance and his fondness for an argument. Graduated in 1838, he was barely twenty, growing steadily saucier, his eyes still disconcertingly crossed, his red hair rapidly thinning and his heart now set on becoming a lawyer. In those days it was done with comparative ease: three years clerking in an attorney's office, not always preceded by four years in college. Once admitted to the bar, he began practicing in Lowell, although in the beginning he took a teaching position across the Merrimack River in Dracut to supplement his meager earnings. There he met the lovely and stagestruck Sarah Hildreth, daughter of a wealthy and intellectual physician. It was not only Sarah's beauty, with her long braids falling over her shoulders, that appealed to Ben, but also her love of literature, especially Shakespearean drama, and her freedom from the rigid Calvinism characterizing most of the Lowell area girls. They were married in May 1844 at the Episcopal Church of St. Anne's in Lowell.

Ben prospered at the bar, becoming famous if not notorious. His style was flamboyant, and he delighted in baiting judges to ingratiate himself with the ordinary folk of the juries. Many of them were his clients, for Lowell had ceased to be a model of industrial decorum, becoming just another dirty, clanging mill town. The prim Yankee farm girls had been supplanted by a wave of immigrants, most of them Irish, exploited by the lords of the loom through twelve-hour working days and coolie wages. Butler, boasting openly of his Irish blood, forever a friend of labor, became their advocate, doing battle with the staid Whig oligarchy of Massachusetts in the courts, the newspapers and the state legislature. Here was a true Jacksonian Democrat, joyfully tilting at the oppressors of the common man; always careful, meanwhile, to turn a tidy dollar out of his dedication to their cause.

When the Middlesex Mills looked to be failing, Ben acquired a large share of its stock at rock-bottom prices, helping to reorganize the company and taking an immense profit from its rebounding fortunes. He also accumulated extensive real estate, and he had opened a supplemental office in Boston. With his wife and three children he lived in splendor in a fine mansion—Belvedere—above a bend in the river. In 1858 it became the first house in the area to be steam-heated. By then, the future looked bright indeed for Benjamin Franklin Butler. At forty, he was a brigadier general in the Massachusetts militia, although with a corpulence exaggerated by his slight frame and his bald pate shining above a thick growth of hair below it—like the wig of a circus clown—he did not look very martial. But he still had a genius for making powerful friends, numbering among them such Democrats as Buchanan and Douglas in the North and Senator Jefferson Davis in the South. Benjamin Franklin Butler was indeed on his way. He could not, of course, hope for the governor's chair or a seat in the U.S. Senate from the Bay State, which was now solidly Republican. But there was always the House or the cabinet, and after that—who could tell?

In 1860 storm clouds began to gather at the end of Butler's horizon. He had endorsed his friend Douglas's Freeport Doctrine, without quite repudiating the Dred Scott decision, a neat walk on a political tightrope. Yet the Massachusetts Democrats heartily supported Buchanan, who was determined to torpedo the Little Giant. They were making every effort to detach Butler, a delegate to the Charleston convention, from his allegiance to Douglas. Moreover, Butler saw signs of Douglas's impending defeat. Unsure of which way to jump, he nevertheless visited Douglas while en route to Charleston. He promised the Little Giant that he would support him on the first five ballots, which he did; but he then switched to Jefferson Davis, voting for him on fifty straight ballots until the deadlocked convention adjourned. At the second convention in Baltimore, Butler walked out, joining other bolters in backing Breckinridge. Both performances earned him the cordial hatred of the Douglas Democrats and the general scorn of all other parties. His popularity may be measured by the Massachusetts race for governor. Of 169,540 votes cast, Ben Butler as a Breckinridge Democrat received just 6,000, less than 4 percent of the total vote! Ben Butler's political career had flared up and out like a paper blaze, in the light of which all thought of Washington and the White House appeared preposterous. But then he was rescued by the guns of Sumter.

At first it would have seemed that Butler's friendship with Confederates such as Davis and Breckinridge would bury his fortunes even deeper, but Ben the irrepressible had adopted a new creed. It embraced antislavery, branded secession as treason and called upon the nation to prepare for war. It exactly matched the thinking of his erstwhile bitter opponent, John A. Andrew, the Republican governor. Andrew was further delighted when

Butler visited him to present resolutions of support adopted by his brigade. Ben also warned the governor that his troops needed new overcoats, and soon a nice contract for manufacture of the same went to Middlesex Mills. And he knew his days in Limbo were over when, trying a case in Boston, he received orders to muster his troops on the Common. Making a dramatic plea for postponement he strode out of the courtroom like Christ come to cleanse the Temple, emerging outside to the frantic cheers of a crowd gathered there. After this incident, Butler's demand to be made commanding general of all Massachusetts militia in the field was irresistible.

Brigadier General Benjamin Franklin Butler was now ready to move to the relief of beleaguered Washington, and he detached his 6th Massachusetts Regiment to hasten there.

On April 18 about 500 Pennsylvania militia arrived in Washington. Unarmed and untrained, they did not exactly inspire the fearful capital, especially after they told of the cold stares and hostility given them as they passed through Baltimore. They knew that as the major eastern rail center closest to Washington, that rabidly secesh city could cut off the capital from the North. The only good news was that the 6th Massachusetts—about a thousand armed and trained militiamen—would pass through Baltimore next day.

They did, arriving at President Street Station at 10:30 A.M. The regiment was to march to the Calvert Street Station to board a train for Washington. But an angry crowd of secessionists waving Confederate flags and armed with stones and firearms began to gather. Instead, the loaded cars were drawn by horses over the connecting line between stations. The first eight cars passed, but the ninth was stoned with windows broken and some occupants injured. The tenth was blocked by debris on the tracks and forced back. Stranded units now had to join the others by marching through the streets. Stones were thrown at them, then shots fired into their midst. They returned the fire, and men fell on both sides. Casualty reports varied: from four soldiers killed and seventeen to thirty-nine wounded; nine to twelve civilians dead, and an unknown but certainly larger number of wounded than among the soldiers.

Nevertheless, after packing their dead in ice and sending their bodies home and placing their wounded on stretchers, the Massachusetts militiamen arrived in Washington next morning. They were hailed as saviors, while in Baltimore a delegation of enraged secessionist dignitaries entrained for Washington to protest the "pollution" of Maryland soil. Lincoln told them bluntly that he had to have troops to defend the capital. "Our men are not moles, and cannot dig under the earth," he said. "They are not birds, and cannot fly through the air. There is no way but to march across, and that they must do." Angrier then ever at this reply, the delegation returned to Baltimore to order telegraph lines cut, railroad tracks torn up and bridges wrecked. Washington was cut off from the Union.

Worse, Beauregard was reported to be approaching Alexandria with 18,000 men, while Jackson in Harpers Ferry had 8,000 more. Over the weekend of April 20–21, a mass exodus began in Washington. Women and children were sent away. Hotel guests fled the city: at Willard's the guest list shrank from a thousand to fifty. Office seekers scurried home. Trains running irregularly to Baltimore were packed, for even though that city might be held by secesh mobs, it appeared safer than the capital. Frantic refugees paid astronomical prices to hire every means of conveyance to escape Confederate wrath. Up Seventeenth Street there snaked a long, sinuous line of traffic: wagons and carriages, drays and trucks, crammed with little children and household goods. Gleeful secessionists went scurrying across the Potomac in droves, while other, hardier spirits—many of them employees of the U.S. government—openly flaunted Confederate badges and prepared to welcome the Rebel troops.

But for its still inadequate force of defenders, Washington was now a deserted village. Public buildings were barricaded with sandbags and barrels of flour. Armed sentries patrolled the streets and the White House porticoes. Howitzers were mounted on balconies. Pickets watched the roads and bridges. An attack was expected momentarily. And still no sign of more reinforcements. On Tuesday word was received that the 7th New York and a Rhode Island regiment were en route. But next day when some officers and men of the 6th Massachusetts called at the White House, Lincoln told them: "I don't believe there is any North! The 7th Regiment is a myth. Rhode Island is not known in our geography anymore. You are the only Northern realities."

Next day, however, the piercing shriek of a locomotive whistle shattered Washington's noonday quiet. The 7th New York had arrived! Dandies in their tailored gray uniforms, shouldering their new rifles and bringing with them their gourmet cooks, they clambered down the steps to the cheers of a relieved—though sparse—populace. After them came the Rhode Islanders and then the 8th Massachusetts.

Ben Butler had broken the Baltimore blockade. Hearing of the 6th's travail and learning that the capital was cut off, he had seized the railroad steamer *Maryland,* putting his 8th Regiment aboard and heading for Annapolis, the state capital and head of the Elk Ridge Railroad, still open and the last remaining line to Washington forty miles away. There he conferred with Governor Thomas H. Hicks. Though loyal to the Union, Hicks feared the strength of numerous secessionists in the area. He refused to allow Butler's troops to come ashore. Finally, just as the 7th New York arrived in the harbor aboard the steamer *Boston,* Butler persuaded the governor to allow both regiments to debark. At once Butler seized the Elk Ridge line, now seemingly effectively wrecked by the secessionists, who also made the only available locomotive inoperable. But Private Charles Honans had helped to build it in Marblehead, and quickly repaired it. A relief train moved out, preceded by militiamen of both states who straightened the twisted rails, repaired broken bridges and stood guard against ambush.

Next, Butler's troops wrested Baltimore from the grip of the secessionist mobs. With this and his relief of Washington, he was hailed as a hero in the North. But Winfield Scott angrily ordered him to stay put in Annapolis and to issue no more inflammatory proclamations to the people of Maryland. Scott feared that Butler's aggressive style might upset delicate negotiations between Washington and Annapolis. Lincoln shared this apprehension, and approved the order. Neither man wanted General Butler to ride into the nation's capital mounted on a white horse. Yet, to appease both Butler and his admirers—especially the powerful Republican Party in Massachusetts—and to soften Scott's order peremptorily transferring him to Fortress Monroe far from public adulation, Lincoln gave him a second star and his own department with headquarters at Monroe.

By the end of April, Washington had 10,000 troops for its defense with more on the way and with no chance of interference from chastened Baltimore, now held in a grip of iron by the Federal government. Major Robert Anderson, the returned hero of Sumter, was promoted to brigadier general and sent to his native Kentucky to assert the Federal supremacy there. Major General John Charles Frémont, the first Republican candidate for president, was sent on a similar mission to Missouri, home of his father-in-law, the late, great Senator Thomas Hart Benton. With Baltimore held in the grip that would be maintained until the war's end, and Maryland's loyalty thus assured, President Lincoln could now assume the offensive.

Harpers Ferry was recaptured, Arlington Heights and Alexandria occupied. Federal, not Confederate campfires, now winked across the Potomac, and Fortress Monroe at the tip of the York-James peninsula was reinforced. Within another month, Northern despair had been blown away by the friendly winds of victory, and Lincoln's desponding question—"When will they come?"—had been replaced by the more famous wildly optimistic cry:

"On to Richmond!"

19

.

First Bull Run

R ICHMOND HAD BECOME the capital of the Confederacy, as well as of the state of Virginia. Congress and the governmental apparatus had found Montgomery woefully inadequate as to facilities, miserable to live in as to comfort with its overcrowded filthy single hotel and its clouds of mosquitoes. Virginia in seceding was also now the richest, most populous and most powerful state of the Confederacy, with a tradition of leadership not to be matched on either side of the Potomac. Richmond also possessed the valuable Tredegar Iron Works and was a communications and transportation hub.

At first, President Davis opposed the move. He believed that in the all-out war now under way Montgomery, in the heart of the South, where the rebellion had its birth, would be less of a strategic risk than a city on the frontier, close to the arbiter of battle. Capture of Richmond in a single decisive battle could mean collapse of the Confederacy. In this he was probably correct, for George Washington in the Revolution had fought only to preserve his army, not to protect a capital that could hang like a military millstone around his neck. But with hardly a reservation the politicians, chiefly for comfort, insisted on Richmond. Second thought might have suggested to them that, in an essentially defensive war, Richmond, only a hundred miles from the Potomac and accessible by water, was especially vulnerable. Granting the inadequacy of communication and transportation in the huge eleven-state Confederacy, a capital on the fringe rather than at the center of the new nation would have great difficulty in extending its power over this vast hinterland. Locating the government in Virginia might limit its interest in conducting operations west of the Appalachians, the truly decisive area.

In 1861 Richmond was a typical antebellum Southern city, except that

154

it was also by then a center for tobacco and industry. Its flour mills and tobacco factories processed local staples, and its iron industry was the largest in Dixie. Located at the falls of the James River the city traded not only with the countryside but also Europe. Nevertheless, Richmond was Southern. Industrialists and financiers might dominate the city's markets, but the planters and their wives still ruled the drawing rooms—and thus the city.

There were 37,910 inhabitants in Richmond, although this was gradually being augmented by the influx of volunteers and the blossoming of tent camps around its environs. Of these residents, a surprising number were German and Irish immigrants, imported for the industrial labor of which the yeomanry and poor whites were ignorant and at which the slaves could not be trusted.

President Davis, who had graciously acceded to the politicians' insistence on moving the capital, arrived in Richmond on May 29. His two-day trip from Montgomery had been "one continuous ovation," even though he had ruled out ceremony and declined the offer of a special car. Seated in an ordinary seat in the rear coach of a regular train, he was unnoticed by his fellow passengers, until thunderous cries of "Hurray for Jeff Davis" or "the Old Hero" rising from stations along the way directed their own admiring eyes toward him.

In Richmond there was pomp and ceremony: cannon roaring in salute, bands, Governor Letcher to welcome him at the head of a delegation of dignitaries, a carriage drawn by four white horses to take him to his temporary quarters in the Spotswood Hotel. En route one of the bouquets tossed at the carriage fell into the street, and Davis ordered the vehicle halted while he retrieved it and gallantly handed it to a lady companion. It was a gesture appreciated by the Richmond gentry, already impressed by his simple dignity. His poise remained unshaken, even while a group of ladies fanned him at lunch and during a handshaking ordeal at the Fair Grounds, where, in a short speech, he told his listeners that they were "the last best hope of liberty"—thus consciously or unconsciously paraphrasing Lincoln's salute to the United States as "the last best hope of earth"—and added: "The country relies upon you. Upon you rest the hopes of our people; and I have only to say, my friends, that to the last breath of my life I am wholly yours." Like the welcoming throngs in Montgomery, Richmond congratulated itself on possessing such a president. His attendance at the Episcopal Church of St. Paul's elicited their approval, and he was warmly welcomed at balls and parties, where, the matriarchs of the first families of Richmond observed with knowing smiles, he always kissed the young girls upon his arrival, but upon his departure kissed only the pretty ones.

Davis worked long hours, but rode daily to the training camps for inspection tours, sometimes with his staff, more often with a single aide. An observer wrote: "Mr. Davis rode a beautiful gray horse. His worst enemy will allow that he is a consummate rider, graceful and easy in the saddle." Much of Davis's energy went into organizing the Confederate armed forces. He knew those volunteers pouring into the Federal capital were not there for an Independence Day parade, just as he knew Lincoln could not and would not supinely accept secession any more than he himself could or would abolish slavery. Davis also continued to insist that firing the first shot at Sumter had not been a mistake, discrediting the Confederacy in the eyes of Europe. Rather, he pursued the Confederate initiative begun in February for official recognition from Great Britain and France, hoping that their dependence on King Cotton would produce not only this but intervention on the Rebel side as well.

The South fancied itself in the same position as the American colonists fighting for independence, and depending on foreign aid—especially from France—to help make them victorious. Dixie believed that its traditional opposition to high tariffs would make a favorable impression on European exporters, and that Europe would also profit from a transfer of Southern commerce from the North to its own shores. Also, the Southern fight for independence would seem compatible with the spirit of nationalism then flourishing in Europe, while Great Britain would seem particularly pleased with an opportunity to squelch Yankee competition. But most of all the South was convinced that its virtual monopoly of high-grade cotton would be the decisive factor.

Cotton was king and "King Cotton diplomacy" was based on the belief that because three-fourths of the cotton feeding the great textile industries of Britain and France came from the South, those nations would simply have to recognize the Confederate States and support them by breaking the Federal blockade. Consequently there was much enthusiasm for President Davis's policy of placing an embargo on cotton to create a famine in that staple.

But what neither Davis nor the planters realized was that the British mills had accumulated a huge inventory of cotton goods before the outbreak of the American Civil War, and they could now sell these hitherto unsalable products at good profits. Also the South had unwisely sold its bumper crop of 1860 and the British at least had enough raw material to last until the fall of 1862. New sources of cotton had also appeared in Egypt and India.

Another unexpected blow for Dixie was the failure of wheat crops in Britain, with the result that by 1862 Northern wheat seems to have dethroned Southern cotton. In 1859, Britain imported only 90,000 quarters of wheat from Northern granaries, but in 1861 flour and wheat imports rose to 3,500,000 quarters and then more than 5,000,000 in 1862. Wheat might have been obtained on the Continent, but it was costlier there, the North having reaped bigger harvests through the use of machinery invented, ironically, by the Southerner Cyrus McCormick.

Inducing Europe to support Dixie was almost exclusively in the hands of President Davis—who had once described Britain as "the robber nation of the earth"—and Secretary of State Toombs. But Toombs was neither diplomat nor administrator, having once said that he kept Confederate archives "in my hat." It was Davis who sent the first diplomatic agents to Europe. These were William Yancey, as unfit to be a diplomat as Toombs was to be a general; Pierre Rost of Louisiana; and Dudley Mann, a veteran Virginia diplomat. Although they were not officially welcomed by Britain, they did secure an interview with the foreign minister, Lord John Russell, on May 3, 1861. Ten days later, it appeared that the Confederacy was well on its way to achieving its objective: Queen Victoria, annoyed by Lincoln's proclamation of a blockade, granted the South belligerency status. Shortly afterwards Napoleon III did the same.

But the mission got no further; this "triumph" may actually have been due more to Anglo-French pique than Confederate perspicacity. Indeed on June 14 Russell told the American minister, Charles Francis Adams, that he would have no more interviews with Southern agents. Britain still remembered the War of 1812, when it suffered frightful shipping losses, and it is likely that John Bull did not wish to tangle with Brother Jonathan again. Whatever, while Rost went to Spain to make an unsuccessful attempt to persuade that nation to recognize his country, Yancey, enraged by Russell's "truckling" to Adams, returned home full of hatred for Britain and disillusioned with Davis's foreign policy.

"You have no friends in Europe," he told a crowd in New Orleans, repeating his advice to Davis. "The sentiment of Europe is antislavery, and that portion of public opinion which forms, and is represented by, the government of Great Britain, is abolitionist. They will never recognize our independence until our conquering sword hangs dripping over the prostrate heads of the North . . . It is an error to say, 'Cotton is king.' It is not. It is a great and influential factor in commerce, but not its dictator. The nations of Europe will never raise the blockade until it suits their interests."

In its first sally of diplomacy, the Confederacy had been repulsed.

■   ■   ■

Troops continued to pour into Washington and Northern Virginia, so that by mid-July about 60,000 Federals opposed just under 40,000 Confederates. There had already been some fighting. On June 10 down on the York-James Peninsula Major General Ben Butler attacked one of Colonel John B. Magruder's outposts at Big Bethel. Butler had about 7,000 men against Magruder's 1,400, but his poorly trained troops became confused, firing into each other's ranks until they were finally driven back by artillery. Casualties of seventy-six for Butler and about eight for Magruder seemed to confirm the Southern belief that one Rebel was the equal of ten Yankees, but in truth this first land battle proved nothing except to suggest that canny old Winfield Scott knew a political general when he saw one.

The general-in-chief was now seventy-five, no longer the commanding presence he once had been. His great body was swollen with dropsy, and by his fondness for epicurean food and wine. His favorite dish was Maryland terrapin, and he would hold a forkful of it aloft with the pronouncement that it was "the finest food vouchsafed by God to man." Weighing well over three hundred pounds, he could not mount his horse but had to be hoisted into the saddle. Nevertheless, his mind was still sharp and his grasp of military reality sure. By May 3, he had formulated his plan for Union victory, confiding it to Major General George B. McClellan, his protégé. Scott saw the importance of the western theater and realized how much the South depended on the Transmississippi for its produce and meat. He proposed a blockade of the Southern ports while a powerful Union force drove down the Mississippi Valley, leaving behind a string of strong forts. This would "squeeze the South to military death." The phrase led McClellan to call it "Scott's boa-constrictor plan," a description pounced upon by the press and changed to Anaconda Plan, which was widely derided. In truth, a variation of this proposal would have to be adopted after two years of bloody fratricidal strife, but at the time it ran counter to the "On to Richmond!" fever which that consummate cheerleader Horace Greeley and his New York *Tribune* had started burning in the breasts of most Northerners.

Even President Lincoln was not immune to this malady, probably because he realized that many of his ninety-day volunteers were already more than halfway through their enlistments. Lincoln was careworn. A reporter who had known him in Illinois said that he still had that inexhaustible fund of funny stories, but not "the old, free, lingering laugh." He had entered the Gethsemane of his presidency, feeling his mounting sorrow weighing painfully on what he called "the sore spot" of his soul. Sumter had done that to him. Though he had held firm there and had thus unified the

North, it had shown him how wrong he had been in believing that the people of the South shared his great love of the Union and his mystic faith in the American experiment in popular government. He no longer spoke of them as "my friends" but only in the third person or as rebels and traitors. Abraham Lincoln was waging war.

To do so he arrogated to himself powers that no chief executive before or since has ever claimed. In late April he had authorized simultaneous raids on every telegraph office in the North, seizing the originals and copies of all telegrams received or sent during the past year. With this for evidence, and sometimes so little as the word of an informer settling a grudge, men were taken from their homes in the dead of night and thrown into prison without explanation. He took millions from the treasury and handed them to private persons to buy arms at home and abroad. He denied writs of habeas corpus, including those issued by the United States Supreme Court. When Congress finally convened on Independence Day, he explained: "It became necessary for me to choose whether I should let the government fall into ruin, or whether . . . availing myself of the broader powers conferred by the Constitution in cases of insurrection, I would make an effort to save it."

Congress bowed its head and said nothing, probably because the war news was good, especially from the West. A Confederate force of about 4,000 men under Brigadier Robert S. Garnett had invaded western Virginia to reclaim that area for the Old Dominion and to cut the Baltimore and Ohio Railroad linking Washington to the West. Against them came 8,000 Ohio and Indiana volunteers led by General McClellan. Short, stocky, handsome, with red hair and a red mustache, McClellan at thirty-four commanded everything along the Ohio line. Although he would later prove himself to be a masterful military organizer, McClellan's troops were no better trained than Garnett's. They found the country picturesque but difficult: "A land of secession, rattlesnakes, rough mountains and bad whiskey." Still they outnumbered the Rebels two to one. After Garnett divided his forces to hold the passes at Rich Mountain and Laurel Hill, McClellan did the same. Holding Garnett at Laurel Hill, he swung wide to the right with his main body to confront the Confederates at Rich Mountain. Again dividing his forces, he sent a detachment under Brigadier General William S. Rosecrans to strike the enemy flank, sweeping them off the mountain. At a rear-guard action at Carrick's Ford, in which Garnett was killed, the first flag officer to die in a war that claimed more generals than any other in history, he forced them back to Virginia. Never much for modesty, McClellan spoke in his report of "a brief but brilliant campaign," congratulating his soldiers

on having "annihilated two armies, commanded by educated and experienced soldiers, entrenched in mountain fastnesses fortified at their leisure."
Indeed, no one should criticize a commander for praising his men or trying
to lift their hearts, but one may wonder about those "two armies" consisting of separate parts of an ill-trained, ill-equipped force of 4,500 men, and
of an "annihilation" which actually left 3,500 of them still unharmed and
alive. But the order was widely circulated in the North, as well as his
eve-of-battle address to his troops: "Soldiers! I have heard that there was
danger here. I have come to place myself at your head and to share it with
you. I fear now but one thing—that you will not find foemen worthy of your
steel. I know that I can rely on you." Very stirring. Very Napoleonic. Very
McClellanish, as was his telegram to Washington: "Our success is complete, and secession is dead in this country."

But the youthful general was wildly acclaimed, as the North, some-
what sobered by Butler's setback at Big Bethel, found a new hero. So had
Abraham Lincoln, who seized upon McClellan's "complete success" to urge
Irvin McDowell to surpass it by quickly capturing Richmond.

Irvin McDowell was an Ohioan who had been graduated from West Point
in 1838 twenty-third in a class of forty-five. He was six feet tall and plump,
rather than "heavy-set" as some biographies describe him, with dark brown
hair and a grizzled d'Artagnan-like beard he had cultivated in France where
he had attended a military school, spending a year's leave of absence there
studying tactics. From 1841 to 1845 he taught tactics at the Military Academy, and upon the outbreak of the Mexican War served as a staff officer
and was breveted captain. Modest in manner, usually friendly, he had a
tendency to be dogmatic and didactic. He detested alcoholic drink as a
device of the Devil. He was immensely proud of the fact that when a horse
fell on him and knocked him unconscious, a surgeon trying to revive him
with whiskey found his teeth were so firmly clamped together that he could
not pry them apart. Even while senseless, McDowell bragged, he had
rejected the foul fluid. He felt differently about food, possessing a gargan-
tuan appetite that sometimes, like his overbearing conversational manner,
offended other people. On one occasion after a full meal he consumed an
entire watermelon for dessert, pronouncing it "monstrous fine!"

McDowell felt no such fondness for his new assignment. First he had
to reorganize his regiments into brigades and divisions, that is, larger
units—a brigade usually being two regiments and a division two brigades.
Tactics for these larger formations were more intricate, requiring much
more time for drilling, which Irvin McDowell never received. His staff was

inadequate and the War Department was inefficient, thus creating difficulties of supply and equipment. As often as he was importuned to get going, defeat Beauregard's army at Manassas Junction, and then sweep on to Richmond, he replied—quite justifiably—that he needed more time. It did not please him to be told that Beauregard was in no better shape and had a smaller army. Lincoln tried to reassure his hesitant general with the remark: "You are green, it is true, but they are green also. You are all green alike." At last in late June he submitted a plan to General Scott calling on the aging Brigadier General Robert Patterson to hold Brigadier General Joseph E. Johnston's force of 9,000 Rebels fast in the Shenandoah Valley while he would "move against Manassas with a force of thirty thousand men of all arms, organized into three columns, with a reserve of ten thousand." Scott, the only officer in the Union Army who had ever commanded more than 5,000 men, scoffed at the plan as "a little war by piecemeal." He alone was immune to the "On to Richmond!" hysteria, clinging to the solid military wisdom that the enemy's army, not his capital, was the true objective. Thus, he wanted more time to expand and train his forces. But he was overruled and McDowell's plan was approved by Lincoln and his cabinet, fearful as they were that the ninety-day troops would be discharged before ever aiming a musket at a soldier in gray.

On Tuesday, July 21, 1861, McDowell's army, about 35,000 strong, set out for Manassas from Arlington. Fairfax Courthouse, thirteen miles away, was the objective for the first day's march, with Centerville, another nine miles down the road and within striking distance of Manassas, to be reached by Wednesday. It was not a difficult schedule, even in the wilting summer heat, but these were green troops commanded by field and company grade officers—colonels down to second lieutenants—who were only slightly more seasoned if at all. But the five division and eight brigade commanders were regular army men. So the columns undulated like Scott's anaconda, or shrank and expanded like an accordion. Much as the sergeants shouted themselves hoarse, these men simply could not "close up," that is, maintain close marching order to prevent gaps between individual soldiers and then units, a tendency probably the most destructive of marching discipline. Thus when they moved they had to trot to close the gap, often shedding their heavy, rattling, clanking equipment, their breath and sweat coming fast; or else having closed it, they ran into another unit suddenly stationary and had to stand still while the dust settled on them. During such intervals, they either broke ranks to pick berries, or consumed all the rations that were to carry them through the battle. Behind them, sometimes catching up with them, came a gay and carefree procession seemingly including half of official Washington: congressmen with their ladies in bright summer dresses, riding in buggies and gigs packed with picnic lunches, come to watch the show as though on a lark or holiday outing, and infecting much of the soldiery with their festive air.

Thus it was all that McDowell's columns could do to reach Fairfax on Wednesday night, and on Thursday night they were just approaching Centerville. Then it was discovered on Friday that the men had eaten their rations, and by the time this far from small breach of discipline was corrected, it was Saturday, a day spent in scouting and studying maps. Thus Beauregard was given two days' grace to improve his defenses. But the Little Creole, who commanded 20,000 troops at Manassas, was not a bit apprehensive. His efficient intelligence system in Washington had informed him both of McDowell's departure and his strength, and he wired Davis on the seventeenth that he was falling back on Bull Run and might retire farther to Rappahannock, pleading for reinforcements. Davis promptly ordered Johnston "if practicable" to give Patterson the slip and join Beauregard at Bull Run with his 9,000 men. Johnston moved quickly, aware that the sixty-eight-year-old Patterson with 18,000 troops had taken counsel of his fears—believing his enemy superior in numbers and his own supply line inadequate—and fallen back on Charles Town. While Colonel J.E.B. Stuart's cavalry skillfully screened his movements from Patterson, Jackson's brigade entrained first, arriving at the Junction at noon of the twentieth, while the rest of Johnston's force followed as fast as the overworked railroad could move them. Another force of 5,000 men under Brigadier General Theophilus Holmes had arrived from Aquia Creek the preceding day, going into position on Beauregard's right flank. The Little Creole's strength was now roughly equal to McDowell's.

Thus the Southern commanders were already demonstrating superior military skill. First, they had organized an excellent spy system in Washington; second, they had positioned themselves near a railroad to ensure rapid movement between separated forces; third, they had made such excellent use of their mounted force that Patterson did not know that Johnston had moved until the twentieth, much too late to come to McDowell's assistance.

On Sunday morning, Davis in Richmond, aware that the first major battle, perhaps the critical one, of the Civil War was impending, could no longer stand the suspense and boarded a special northbound train. As it neared Manassas the conductor, frightened by the sight of the debris of retreat washing past him, refused to allow it to continue. Davis ordered the engine uncoupled and mounted the cab. At the Junction he obtained a horse and galloped toward the sound of the cannon, and then the irregular rattle of small-arms fire. Suddenly there were men in gray flowing around him: wounded soldiers and skulkers scampering away from the battle. "Go back!" he shouted. "Do your duty and you can save the day!"

But they kept on going.

General McDowell had allowed Beauregard to mass his forces. He had lost one day in slovenly marching, a second in reissuing food, and a third in scouting and probing, only to learn to his dismay that his worst fears had been realized: Patterson had allowed Johnston to join Beauregard, and Holmes had arrived at Bull Run from the south. His former classmate was now his equal in numbers.

Arising Sunday the twenty-first before daylight, McDowell was suffering from stomach cramps. He had eaten his customary mammoth dinner the night before, but this morning his iron stomach seemed not the equal of both giant meal *and* eve-of-battle tension. Still he felt he had prepared an excellent plan. His maps had shown him a hybrid X. One cross stroke was the Warrenton Turnpike running arrow-straight from southwest to northeast; the other was the twisting course of Bull Run meandering northwest to southeast. Steep-banked and dominated by high ground, the stream was difficult to cross except at fords above and below Stone Bridge, carrying the turnpike over the run. At first, McDowell had planned to strike Beauregard's right where that flank offered the best approach to Richmond. But reconnaissance had shown that the fords below the bridge were strongly held by enemy infantry, so he decided to try a turning movement around Beauregard's left. Upstream mounted patrols had found a good crossing at Sudley Springs at the end of the run's western arm and another about halfway out. Both were suitable for wheeled vehicles, meaning that the superior Northern artillery could support the foot troops.

Two of his four divisions of about 8,000 men each would execute the turning movement, while the other two feinted against Stone Bridge and a ford beneath it. Brigadier General Daniel Tyler's division would demonstrate at Stone Bridge, while a brigade from Colonel D.S. Miles's reserve division based at Centerville would do the same at Blackburn's Ford halfway downstream from the bridge. Meanwhile, the divisions of Colonels David Hunter and S.P. Heintzelman, having crossed Bull Run, would sweep down the Confederate bank to unmask both the bridge and the fords, enabling the feinting forces to join them for the main assault. Because it was so complicated—half of McDowell's green army feinting and the other half trying to outflank the enemy, both on a strict timetable—the plan was not as sound as McDowell believed; and it was further inhibited by the inexperience of his troops moving over unfamiliar ground in a coordinated attack. But the Union commander did have the good sense to order an early start to be sure that this feint-and-flank operation began on time. The flankers were to leave camp at 2 A.M. to reach Sudley Springs at seven, the feinters were to depart an hour later.

The approach march began on schedule. With little sleep or none, these weary soldiers in blue stumbled through the black, tripping over roots and logs, whipped by tree branches flung in the face of one man by the passage of the man ahead of him, stopping and going, stopping and going, in duplication of the march from Arlington but now complicated by the darkness. It was not seven o'clock, but half past nine—two and a half hours behind schedule—when the flankers arrived at Sudley Springs. Below them at the bridge and the ford they could hear the guns of the feinters. They had been bellowing for three hours now.

Beauregard at Manassas awoke in good spirits, pleased by the arrival of Holmes and Johnston, even though some of Johnston's men were not due until today. The Little Creole was also delighted when Johnston, who was senior to him, wisely deferred to him rather than conduct a battle on unfamiliar ground. Besides, Beauregard had a plan. It was identical to his classmate's: a turning movement around the enemy left, and this also would be followed by a roll-up movement through Centerville. But this military minuet—for such it might have become—was not to be because Beauregard was later than McDowell. This was chiefly because of the vagueness of his attack order. After an advance across Bull Run, there was to be a second advance on Centerville. Each section of the plan ended, "The order to advance will be given by the commander-in-chief." Thus, his brigade chiefs were uncertain of which advance was meant, and when the order to attack went out, Beauregard heard only a mystifying silence on his right. Worse, there then arrived from Mitchell's Ford, a post two miles below Stone Bridge, a messenger reporting that the enemy had appeared on the left front. Then firing was heard from Stone Bridge. It seemed that an attempted crossing there was either in progress or was imminent, so Beauregard sent his reserve brigades under Jackson and Brigadier General Barnard Bee to strengthen his menaced left flank. Actually all the noise was from McDowell's feinting units.

Nevertheless, at eight o'clock Beauregard moved his headquarters from Manassas Junction to Lookout Hill, just behind Mitchell's Ford. After an hour there, while the roar of the enemy bombardment rose in fury to either side of him, the Little Creole began to suspect that this was a demonstration and that the Union main body was somewhere else—probably on one of his flanks. Just then a message arrived from a signal officer:

> I see a body of troops crossing Bull Run about two miles above the Stone Bridge. The head of the column is in the woods on this side. The rear of the column is in the woods on the other side. About a half-mile of its length is visible in the open ground between. I see both infantry and artillery.

This was it! An ominous silence on his right, where his commanders had still not moved, and a telltale dust cloud floating down from the north confirmed his fear that his own left flank might be crumbling while McDowell's was still firm. At once the Confederate chief sent couriers after Bee and Jackson to divert them to the threatened left, and when Colonel Wade Hampton arrived from Richmond with 600 South Carolinians, he dispatched them there also. When these units joined Colonel N.G. Evans already stationed near the bridge, he would have 6,500 men in place to repel the attack. Not enough for long enough, he thought despairingly; but if his own attack on the enemy left was in progress, it might return the initiative to him! Just then, a message arrived from Brigadier General Richard Ewell on the right flank. He had waited all this time for orders to cross the stream, but now he was going across without them. The Little Creole despaired again. The attack on the right would do no good, but rather would place the troops involved out of his reach. His army was too scattered to meet the challenge from the left, where black powdersmoke now mingled with the widening dust cloud, and from whence the ragged rattle of musketry could be heard. A general engagement! Getting a grip on himself, Beauregard recalled the brigades of Brigadier Generals Ewell and E.E. ("Neighbor") Jones from across Bull Run, hoping to send them upstream toward battle.

For most of this time, Joe Johnston had been standing on Lookout Hill, quietly watching Beauregard move his forces to meet the Union challenge. He refrained from interfering, but as the roar of battle on the left rose to a crescendo, he could no longer remain inactive. "The battle is there," he said, turning to leave. "I am going." Beauregard followed him, after ordering Holmes and Colonel Jubal Early to lead their brigades to the left. He overtook Johnston at about noon, and the two generals with their staffs rode on together, climbing a wooded hill to peer at the conflict raging below them. It was difficult to read that shifting, winking, blinking, thundering panorama unfolding before their eyes. Flashes of musket fire stabbed the drifting smoke: red for the closer Confederates, pink for the distant Feder-

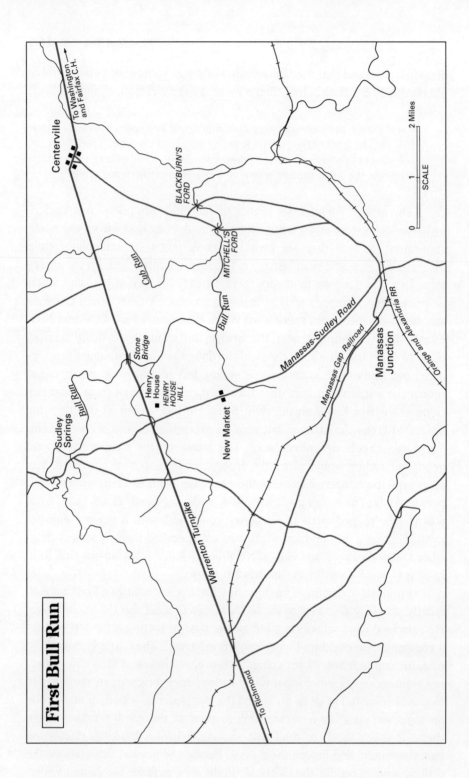

First Bull Run

To Washington
and Fairfax C.H.

Centerville

BLACKBURN'S
FORD

MITCHELL'S
FORD

Cub Run

Bull Run

Manassas-Sudley Road

Stone
Bridge

Sudley
Springs

Bull Run

Henry
House

HENRY
HOUSE
HILL

New Market

Manassas Gap Railroad

Manassas
Junction

Orange and Alexandria RR

Warrenton Turnpike

To Richmond

2 Miles

1

SCALE

0

als. Men in gray were streaming to the rear, suggesting broken units. Men in blue seemed to be coming closer . . . in packed masses . . . It didn't look good.

Once they had rested at Sudley Springs, McDowell's flanking divisions quickly crossed Bull Run, in double columns for speed. Colonel Ambrose Burnside's Rhode Islanders were in the lead. Horse-drawn artillery splashed after them. But as Burnside's men emerged from a wood about a mile downstream they were confronted by a brigade under Colonel Evans. Known as "Shanks" for his skinny legs, Evans had been unhappy to be posted at Stone Bridge far from the Confederate main body. But he soon became convinced that all the noise opposite him was a feint, and when he saw the dust cloud to the northwest, he headed for it on his own initiative. His two regiments were drawn up with six-pounders on their flanks when Burnside appeared.

The collision was sudden, unexpected, what is called "a meeting engagement," and the fight was furious. The Rebels had the advantage of firing the first volley, riddling the Yankees. But they rallied and were about to drive the enemy back when Bee arrived with his brigade. A wild melee ensued, with Bee calling out encouragingly to his troops. Glancing backward he saw Jackson's brigade on a ridge aligned to either side of a battery of six guns, their muskets at the ready.

"There is Jackson standing like a stone wall!" Bee shouted. "Let us determine to die here, and we will conquer."

Jackson had not entered the struggle below his ridge. Rather he had formed his men on the reverse slope to protect them from artillery, calmly preparing to halt the oncharging enemy there. "General, the day is going against us!" a distraught officer cried, and Jackson replied: "If you think so, sir, you had better not say anything about it." Another shouted, "General, they are beating us back," to which the unruffled Virginian retorted: "Sir, we'll give them the bayonet."

Now the blue masses were surging over the crest of Henry Hill as it was called, flowing down toward the Henry House, a small frame building in which the eighty-year-old widow Judith Henry had lain dying. When the battle commenced, her invalid sons had carried her on a mattress to the safety of a ravine. But she pleaded with them so pathetically to die in her own bed that they brought her back, and she was instantly killed by an exploding shell. At last the Federals seized Stone Bridge and General Tyler's division came pouring across as planned. Some 18,000 Union troops were now engaged on the Confederate left. Barnard Bee fell dying, his men breaking as he fell. The blue tide flowed on. Cheering Yankees ascended Jackson's ridge, cresting it and started down—into a terrible volley that shattered them. Another stretched more blue-clad bodies on the ground—motionless, quivering, kicking—and the stunned survivors stumbled back down the hill. There they were rallied by their officers and sent up again, supported by splendidly served rifled cannon. But they could not take Henry Hill.

Beauregard and Johnston came down from the adjoining hill, the Little Creole to reorganize his defenses, Johnston to establish a command post at a road intersection in the rear, there to direct arriving units from the Valley into the battle. Beauregard rode along the line, replacing fallen commanders with members of his staff. Everywhere he shouted encouragement, telling his men that they had held, the crisis had passed, and soon it would be their turn to take the initiative. As reinforcements arrived from Johnston, he directed them to his left, extending it, expecting that McDowell would still try to turn that flank by extending his right. He did, ordering up two batteries of rifled guns supported by a regiment of New York Fire Zouaves, so-called because most of them were New York firemen and they wore the colorful red-and-blue Zouave uniform consisting of baggy trousers, a short jacket and tasseled turban. Both sides had Zouaves, and when J.E.B. Stuart saw the New Yorkers he thought they were from Alabama, facing rear and retreating. "Don't run, boys, we're here!" he shouted, galloping toward them at the head of his mounted regiment. When he saw the Stars and Stripes and realized his mistake, his forward momentum was too great to turn. So he charged, his troopers slashing at the white turbans, panicking and scattering them in gaudy disarray, leaving their gun batteries unprotected. Seeing this, a Virginia regiment ran forward to shoot down every Yankee gunner.

Here was a sight to lift Rebel hearts, and they cheered as they watched from the ridge. But the Federal right still surged forward. Jackson watched them come, riding up and down his line shouting: "Hold your fire until they're on you. Then fire and give them the bayonet. And when you charge, yell like furies!"

Beauregard sensed that the initiative was now his. He had used his reinforcements to build up a solid gray line to either side of Jackson, extending his left so far to the west that he now overlapped McDowell's right. At half past three the long gray line swept forward. The high, shrill, quavering cry of the fox hunter—the famous Rebel yell that Union soldiers would learn to dread almost as much as bullets—broke from thousands of throats; and as it pierced the ears and then the hearts of the startled men in blue, it might have been the culminating factor that shattered their resolve.

They had fought well, these Billy Yanks, fighting as bravely as raw troops ever do. But after their initial successes, after they had chased Johnny Reb from the field and pursued him with lusty shouts, everything seemed to go wrong. They could not know that it was not their fault, nor even the superior fighting prowess of the boys in gray, but rather the surpassing military skill of the Confederate commanders. Beauregard chose to fight near a railroad connecting him with his reserves; the consummate tactician Johnston accepted a subordinate role and kept the reserves flowing into the battle. It was these reinforcements that broke the blue formations. "Where are *our* reserves?" they asked each other in dismay. Then, as most men react in adversity, they began searching for the author of their travail. Unable to believe that they could be so badly led, they concluded that they had been deliberately *mis*led. From their throats broke despairing cries:

"Betrayed!"

"We are betrayed!"

"Sold out!"

Turning in terror from the sunlight dancing on the tips of the long, thin Rebel bayonets, they broke and fled. They ran past mounted officers vainly shouting at them to turn again and stand, slashing the smoke with drawn sabers. "Betrayed!" they yelled back. "Sold out!" Some of them threw away their rifles as they ran, but most of them held onto their weapons, slowing to a sullen walk, pausing to glance fearfully behind them. But they had not panicked—yet.

But then Brigadier General E. Kirby Smith's brigade arrived from the Valley, forming quickly and marching toward the sound of the guns. They had no sooner reached the battlefield than Smith fell wounded. Colonel Arnold Elzey took command, raising his field glasses as a breeze shredded the powder smoke. "Stars and Stripes!" he shouted, pointing ahead. "Stars and Stripes! Give it to them, boys!" Again the falsetto screeching burst from cracked and parched lips, and then Early's brigade joined them, and the furies in gray came sprinting down from Henry Hill to fall upon the demoralized men in blue.

Now the Union forces did panic. They went splashing back through Bull Run, and when again on firm ground made arrow-straight for the Potomac. Irvin McDowell did what he could to regain control of his army. He formed a rally line near Centerville with two brigades from below Stone Bridge, the reserve brigade and a few regiments just arrived from Alexandria. He hoped that his broken, fugitive flankers would turn behind it to confront the pursuing Rebels once more.

But they would not. Panic had at last seized them, and suppressed their sense of shame; panic that plucks at the heart of all losing soldiers, and turns their souls flabby with fear. And there existed in that beaten blue mass no brave commander to inspire them, to seize a flag and dash with it toward the oncoming enemy, crying, "Follow me!" No, their example was taken from the men of a regiment of infantry and a battery of artillery whose enlistment had expired that day, who had faced about and marched back to Washington for discharge, unmindful and uncaring of the jeers and insults that followed them. Slowing to a fast walk, now, they followed the same road—until they blundered into that throng of carefree Washington civilians gathered in a field to picnic on basket lunches and shiver with the vicarious thrill of being a spectator of a battle. "Turn back!" the retreating Yankees cried. "Turn back! We are whipped!"

With a rush the Union capital's social elite piled into their carriages and galloped away north. So many of them clattered over a bridge spanning a little stream called Cub Run that it collapsed. Carriages plunged into each other. Into them rammed caissons and ambulances. Moving into, over and around them came the straggling soldiers, so that this panicked and entangled mass of vehicles, horses, civilians and soldiers stretched for miles in a swath one hundred yards wide. Rebel shells fell upon them, one of them fired by the ubiquitous Edmund Ruffin, and terror was added to panic and confusion as this disgracefully disordered column remained that way until it reached Washington, its parts finally disentangling and going their separate, shamed and silent ways under the pitiless illumination of a full moon. Yet, they had made good time, the militia traveling in one night the distance that had taken three days to cover while they marched boldly on to Richmond.

20

.

Defeat for McDowell
and the Union

NOTHING EXCEPT a battle lost can be half as melancholy as a battle won," said the Duke of Wellington after Waterloo, and nothing could give greater testimony to the truth of this perception than the elated but exhausted Confederate camp after Bull Run, or Manassas as the South called it. Disordered and disarrayed as the beaten North might have been, the Confederates were only slightly less disorganized. They were no more capable of mounting a pursuit than the enemy had been of repulsing one.

On the left where the battle had been lost and won, the gray regiments were halted for realignment. On the right where the troops had forded the stream, the pursuit was abandoned and the men recalled. General Longstreet, who had crossed and recrossed Bull Run five times that day, received his restraining instructions just after he ordered his batteries to fire on the retreating Yankees. Stuart's troopers swinging wide around Sudley Springs might have been able to continue the pursuit, until they became so loaded with prisoners that they were forced to retire. With Stuart was Jefferson Davis, who had ridden to Bull Run in despair and dismounted in delight. Meeting Colonel Elzey, he conferred on him the first battlefield promotion of the war: "General Elzey, you are the Blucher of the day!" Davis later wrote out a full general's commission for Beauregard. He also agreed with Jackson's conviction that he could capture the Federal capital. "Give me ten thousand men," Jackson said while a surgeon dressed his wounded finger, "and I will be in Washington tomorrow."

Hearing this Davis rode back to see Beauregard and Johnston to ask how many troops were available for a pursuit. Both replied that the men were too weary, hungry and confused for any such operation. They required rest. Davis still thought otherwise, but after a steady rain turned the roads

171

of northeastern Virginia into impassable lanes of mud, he became resigned to reality.

The rain increased the agony of the wounded. All night long moans and cries for water or assistance rose from the battlefield. Surgeons also worked through the night attending to the wounded brought to hospital tents. From these pyramids of soaked and dripping canvas there issued the screams of men whose legs or arms were being amputated. A terrible new improvement had been made in the weaponry of war. Formerly, the chief firearm was the musket, smoothbore or rifled, a muzzle-loader firing a relatively small lead bullet dropped down its bore and rammed home. Its range was only a hundred yards. To increase the range and velocity, armorers sought to design a bullet that would expand into the grooves in the bore of a rifle. (The word rifle derives from *rifeln,* the German word for groove.) This was solved by the minié ball, a conical bullet named for the Frenchman who invented it. A rifle's range was now five hundred yards, producing a striking zone five times greater, thus frightfully multiplying casualties; and because the minié was so swift and big at .58 caliber, it possessed a shocking power so great that when it struck a bone it did not merely break or nick it like a musket bullet, but absolutely shattered it. Thus, in the Civil War the minié ball made frequent amputation mandatory. Thus also Bull Run, the first great battle of the American Civil War, was the first great battle of modern arms as well.

Another melancholy phenomenon of this bloody war between brothers appeared with daylight. Like ghouls the Rebels arose to browse among the fallen Yankees, stripping them of the clothing of which they were always in need—especially shoes, for Confederate footwear was usually wretched—and plundering their packs, chiefly for food. They also took souvenirs—a watch, a ring, a pistol, a Bible or a pack of cards—just as the victorious soldiers of every army have done since Hector of Troy vested himself in the armor of slain Patroclus. Meanwhile, armorers were gathering Yankee spoil from firearms to cannon, wagons and caissons, introducing the Confederate custom of living off the enemy that would flourish for the first few glorious Southern years, so much so that a great hairy Rebel soldier, taken captive at Antietam and led through McClellan's enormous artillery park, could scratch his head, spit tobacco and drawl: "You-uns got almost as many of them guns marked U.S. as we-uns."

Federal losses were 481 killed and 1,011 wounded, for total casualties of 1,492, plus 1,216 missing, of whom most were probably prisoners, together with a few deserters or men obliterated by shellfire. Confederate casualties were 387 killed and 1,582 wounded, for a total of 1,969, plus only twelve missing. In losses, the fight had been a standoff; but because the South occupied the field and the North retreated, it was a definite Confederate victory, and might have been decisive had pursuit been possible. Surprisingly, Bull Run—like Pearl Harbor in World War II—may have been more damaging to the victor than the vanquished. It deepened in the Southern mind that fallacious conviction of the invincibility of their fighting men, causing their obviously superior commanders to rely more heavily on willpower against firepower, while ignoring the ineluctable fact that the battle so far from having demoralized the Yankees had actually made them cast aside their vacuous notion of a short, quick war and prepare for a long and terrible conflict, in which, taking stock of their defects and weaknesses, they were even more determined to emerge victorious. The perceptive Brigadier General William Tecumseh Sherman, reorganizing his battered brigade, wrote privately: "Nobody, no man, can save the country. Our men are not good soldiers. They brag, but don't perform, complain sadly if they don't get everything they want, and a march of a few miles uses them up. It will take a long time to overcome these things, and what is in store for us in the future I know not."

Downcast as Sherman was, he did not speak of inevitable defeat of the Union. It was floundering indeed, but its eyes were now open and inquiring. And here is another axiom of war: the victors are content to continue with what succeeded, and thus tend to become moribund; the vanquished investigate the cause of their defeat, tending to become innovative. Probably the best effect of Bull Run on the North was the reaction of Horace Greeley, author of the "On to Richmond!" slogan.

He removed it, and advised Lincoln to sue for a negotiated peace.

On that fateful Sunday afternoon President Lincoln in the White House read telegrams from the battlefield arriving every fifteen minutes. All seemed to be going well. A favorable message was received from General Scott. Confident, Lincoln went for a drive in his carriage, his custom at eventide. In his absence Secretary of State Seward entered the White House, pale and trembling. Lincoln's secretaries jubilantly showed him the telegrams suggestive of victory. "That is not true," Seward said in a hoarse voice. "The battle is lost. Tell no one." A half hour later Lincoln was back in the White House. He listened in silence while his secretaries broke the bad news to him. His face did not change expression, and he arose and walked over to army headquarters.

Next day while the numbed survivors of Bull Run still stumbled in a chill drizzle over the Long Bridge into the capital, thousands of them to be taken into private homes and fed, Lincoln composed a telegram:

General George B. McClellan
Beverly, Virginia

Circumstances make your presence here necessary. Charge Rose-crans or some other general with your present department and come hither without delay.

21

■

The Struggle for Missouri:
John Charles Frémont

WHILE MARYLAND remained firmly in the Union camp—if not actually the Federal fist—the other vital border states of Kentucky and Missouri were still a toss-up. Kentucky had assumed a neutral stance, both the pro-Confederate Governor Beriah Magoffin and the pro-Union legislature announcing that the Bluegrass State would defend its borders against invaders, North or South.

Meanwhile, both sides were arming. Simon Bolivar Buckner, a West Point graduate and a wealthy aristocrat with definitely Southern sympathies, had organized a state militia of about 10,000 men believed to be the best-drilled formation of nonregular troops in the country. Opposing him was the Home Guard, organized by William Nelson, a giant of a man at six feet five inches and over three hundred pounds. Nelson had been a lieutenant in the navy, resigning when the war commenced. En route home he stopped off in Washington to secure a brigadier general's commission and the authority to draw on Federal arsenals for 10,000 stand of arms. A driver and a martinet, this bluff, blustering, profane man was not beloved by his pro-Union recruits. But they did welcome the "Lincoln rifles" he distributed among them. It seemed that the soil of Kentucky—"dark and bloody ground"—might soon be stained with the blood of brothers.

Kentucky was the divided state par excellence. Its sympathies were largely Southern, but its interests lay in the North beyond the Ohio. Moreover, Lincoln had guaranteed Kentucky slaveholders that their "property" would not be endangered. Yet the division was acute: before the war was over, 35,000 men would fight for the South, more than twice that many for the North, including 14,000 blacks.

Senator John J. Crittenden, who had done so much to preserve the peace, typified Kentucky's anguished predicament. Two of his sons became

175

major generals in the opposing armies. Henry Clay had four grandsons who enlisted on the Rebel side, three who fought for the Union.

Into this situation came Brigadier General Robert Anderson. He did not enter his home state, but rather, respecting its neutrality, established his headquarters in Cincinnati, just across the Ohio. Anderson was not well, and he did little. Actually there was little that the hero of Fort Sumter could do. Although both Davis and Lincoln had declared that they would not interfere with Kentucky's neutrality, it was obvious that the people of the state intended to make their divided house fall: one way or the other.

Major General Leonidas Polk of Louisiana wanted it to fall South. Polk had been—and still was—the Episcopal bishop of Louisiana. On a visit to Richmond in June he had conferred with his old West Point classmate Jefferson Davis, leaving the Confederate capital as a major general. The North was scandalized that a man of God should become a man of Mars, but the South was delighted to receive such a heavenly recruit. Polk himself said he felt "like a man who has dropped his business when his house is on fire, to put it out; for as soon as the war is over I will return to my calling."

General Polk's command was over troops in the Mississippi Valley with headquarters in Memphis, Tennessee. He was dismayed by the turn of events across the border in Kentucky. Magoffin was powerless to do anything with the solidly pro-Union legislature, while Buckner, who had refused the offer of a commission in the Union army, fled south in July to escape being arrested as a suspected traitor, receiving a Confederate commission as a brigadier general. Behind him, his militia disbanded, its arms and equipment and some of its members passing into Nelson's Home Guard. Kentucky, it seemed, would very shortly be solidly for the Union. To prevent this, Polk ordered Confederate soldiers to Union City in northwest Tennessee, in position to cross the border and occupy Columbus, Kentucky, whose pro-South citizenry had appealed for Confederate help. Polk would not move, however, until some Yankee act of aggression—real or invented—would give him the excuse of provocation.

Anderson in Cincinnati gave him no such opportunity, but John Charles Frémont in Missouri did. On August 28 Frémont ordered Brigadier General Ulysses S. Grant to prepare to occupy Columbus. Now Polk had his alibi, and he moved quickly to send troops there. They occupied Columbus on September 4, thus forestalling Grant, who, although checked, wisely decided to cross the border anyway and seize Paducah, strategically located at the confluence of the Ohio and the Tennessee. Now both South and North had violated Kentucky's neutrality.

The state's reaction was immediate and against the Southerners, who had been first to enter the Bluegrass. Anderson quickly transferred from Cincinnati to Frankfort, appearing before the legislature there on September 7 to receive an ovation. Four days later that body issued a formal and angry demand that the Confederacy withdraw its troops, sending no such communication to Grant in Paducah. When this was not obeyed, it passed on the eighteenth an act to raise the force necessary to expel them. Kentucky's neutrality had come to an end. Although there was still a star for the Bluegrass in the Confederate flag and there was a secessionist legislature in Russellville, neither represented anything more than the Kentuckians fighting for the South.

Kentucky, the birthplace of both Davis and Lincoln, had chosen the Union. It had done so without bloodshed, a blessing that was not to be bestowed upon Missouri.

From the very outset of the Civil War there was bloody fighting in Missouri, and it would continue throughout the last half of 1861. At the center of it on the Union side was Captain Nathaniel Lyon. A graduate of West Point, where he conceived a deep distaste for higher mathematics, finding that calculus "lies outside the bounds of reason," Lyons had won a brevet captaincy in the Mexican War and was wounded there. Small, red-haired and red-bearded, belligerent and impetuous, he had been a fanatic Democrat until he served a season in "Bleeding Kansas." Disgusted by the excesses of the Border Ruffians, he turned into an ardent Free-Soiler who yearned for a chance to strike a blow at slavery. After Sumter, a transfer to St. Louis seemed to realize that dream, especially after he met Frank P. Blair, Jr., one of *the* Blairs of Maryland, son and namesake of Andrew Jackson's trusted adviser, brother of the powerful Montgomery Blair who sat in Lincoln's cabinet. Both men agreed to stop at nothing to hold Missouri for the Union. Both had their eye on the Federal arsenal in St. Louis. Containing 60,000 muskets, 1,500,000 ball cartridges, cannon and some machinery for making arms, the arsenal was the key to control of Missouri.

Secessionist Governor Claiborne Jackson felt the same. Jackson had tried to persuade a state convention to put Missouri's star in the Confederate flag, but the largely Unionist convention rejected him. He was now waiting for an auspicious moment to seize the arsenal. He also possessed an ace in Brigadier General W. S. Harney, an old Indian fighter and veteran of the Mexican War who was absolutely loyal to the Union, but who also trusted Jackson. Blair sent messages to Washington and, late in April, just after Sumter and Jackson's refusal to provide militia for Lincoln, Harney found himself called to Washington. En route, he was captured by Confederates.

Federal command now fell to Lyon. Still a mere captain, he received from the War Office a set of extraordinary instructions that were at the least irregular. General Scott told him that to maintain order and defend national property he was empowered to enlist up to 10,000 St. Louis citizens in what was nothing less than a private army. These in the main were Blair's German-born loyalists, whom Lyon had been drilling all winter in their turnvereins. Lyon was also authorized to proclaim martial law if necessary.

Governor Jackson's response was to call up 700 troops of the state militia and establish them in a "Camp Jackson" on the edge of St. Louis. Ostensibly they were merely going through routine training; actually, as Lyon and Blair suspected, they were forming to seize the arsenal. Lyon at once began swearing the Germans into the Federal service, unperturbed by the illegal nature of such a procedure. Had not Scott written on his instruction: "It is revolutionary times, and therefore I do not object to the irregularity of this." Next, the eager redhead decided that he had better move quickly before Harney was exchanged and returned to St. Louis.

He needed an excuse, however, and he was sure that he would find it at Camp Jackson. So he disguised himself as a farmer's wife come to bring goodies to her soldier son, putting on a black bombazine dress and matching sunbonnet and heavy veils to hide his red hair and beard, and drove through the camp in a rustic buggy, a basket of eggs on his lap. Under the eggs were half a dozen loaded revolvers. Lyon saw what he hoped to see: streets named after Jefferson Davis, Beauregard and other Rebel heroes, and men drilling with weapons stolen from the Federal arsenal in Baton Rouge, Louisiana.

Lyon hurried back to the arsenal, where he told Blair and his committee of public safety that Camp Jackson must be occupied, the militia imprisoned and all Federal property recovered. A few legalist committee members objected, insisting that his only legal course to recover the property was to go into court for a writ of replevin (recovery). Lyon, Blair and the rest of the committee, quoting Scott, called for immediate action.

On the morning of May 10, 1861, Captain Lyon rode out of the arsenal at the head of a few thousand troops—a few companies of regulars, plus the mostly German home guards—surrounded Camp Jackson, and demanded its surrender. After making a formal protest, D. M. Frost, its commander, meekly complied. Lyon promptly disarmed the seven hundred militiamen, seizing their muskets, cannon, twenty-five kegs of powder and other military equipment, some of it bearing the stamp of the Baton Rouge arsenal. Next he marched his prisoners toward the arsenal, where he intended to place them on parole.

So far things had been almost too easy for Lyon and the Federal government. But then Lyon was knocked unconscious by the kicking and plunging of an unruly horse. He was not badly injured, but while he lay senseless for a few minutes, with no one else to take command, a jeering, howling secessionist mob armed with staves and pistols confronted his troops. They hated the Germans especially, calling them all "damned Dutch blackguards," a very free translation of the regiment name, *Die Schwarze Garde,* or the Black Guard. By the time Lyon regained consciousness and was marching in order toward the arsenal once more, the situation had deteriorated badly. The mob had grown uglier and in size, Lyon's troops were nervously fingering their triggers—and it needed but a spark to cause an explosion. It came when a cursing drunk tried to break through Lyon's columns guarding the prisoners. When he was urgently hurled back, a pistol was fired into the soldiery. They fired back, and soon a melee had been turned into a murderous riot: shots, screams, curses, boots pounding the cobblestones and bodies striking it. Before it ended, twenty-eight civilians were dead and many more wounded. Lyon had accomplished all he had set out to do, but at the expense of an even bloodier riot than the one in Baltimore, and possibly also at the cost of a second, bigger civil war in Missouri.

When the horrified General Harney returned a few days later, he immediately ordered the German militia out of the city and demanded that Blair disband them, until Blair calmly reminded him that, irregularly or not, they were in the Federal service. Still the conciliatory Harney tried to work out a truce with state officials. Still believing that no one in authority could betray his loyalty to his government, he sat down to confer with the commander of the Missouri state troops, General Sterling Price, tall, plump, handsome, a Virginia-born veteran of the Mexican War who had been against secession until the St. Louis riot changed his mind. Between them they worked out a cease-fire guaranteeing the rights of all decent Missourians, while both state and Federal forces were to maintain order and prevent bloodshed.

To the fiery Nathaniel Lyon this was nothing but a false truce arranged with an enemy of his government. Blair felt likewise; he quickly and quietly arranged for Harney to be transferred out of Missouri and obtained for his ally a commission as brigadier general. Now it was General Lyon who contemptuously rejected a secessionist compromise that amounted to making Missouri neutral. He pursued Governor Jackson to the state capital at

Jefferson City, scattering his forces and compelling him to flee to the west and south. Price followed him, and by mid-June Missouri was firmly in Federal hands.

Lyon and Blair had not been precisely legal, acting on the axiom that you become what you fight: with a revolution begun, they became revolutionaries. Although the secessionists had been routed, Abraham Lincoln's problems in Missouri were not at an end. They began anew from a different quarter in July, when Major General John Charles Frémont arrived in St. Louis to take command of the vast Western Department.

John Charles Frémont had become famous in the United States as the legendary "Pathfinder" who, with the help of such guides as Kit Carson, had mapped the Rocky Mountain passes through which settlers moved into the Far West. Some modern historians have argued that since the Indian trails he "discovered" were already there, he should rather be called the "Pathmarker." Be that as it may, Frémont at forty-eight was indeed a man of action, magnetic and also with a mystic cast to his many-sided personality. Under his leadership California was broken loose from Mexico and the grateful citizenry of the Golden Bear State made him one of its first two senators, as well as one of its first millionaires and by extension the Republican Party's first presidential candidate. In physique he was of medium height and seemingly slender, although he was actually one of those wiry and muscular men possessed of surprising strength and great durability. He was also handsome, his thick black hair and beard touched with gray. His glance was piercing, his voice musical, and there was drama in his bearing and eloquence in his hands. Here was a personality truly irresistible, with a consuming ambition exceeded only by the aspirations of his politically intuitive wife, Jessie Benton Frémont, daughter of the illustrious Senator Thomas Hart Benton of Missouri. Before he departed Washington, Lincoln said to him: "I have given you carte blanche. You must use your own judgment, and do the best you can." To Frémont this was like a passport to glory.

Arriving in St. Louis, he immediately invested hundreds of thousands of dollars in fortifying the city, which was not menaced, Cape Girardeau above Cairo, as well as the railheads at Rolla and Ironton and the capital at Jefferson City. These were merely defensive measures, though costlier than usual and undertaken almost as an afterthought to his soaring, shining vision of a descent down the vital Mississippi Valley: first Memphis, then Vicksburg and finally New Orleans, and thus the severed Confederacy would lie gasping at his feet. His plan obsessed him, almost exclusive of all other considerations, while his lofty and mysterious manner alienated his subordinates. Grant described him: "He sat in a room in full uniform with his maps before him. When you went in he would point out one line or another in a mysterious manner, never asking you to take a seat. You left without the least idea of what he meant or what he wanted you to do."

Frémont actually secluded himself from his commanders, working long but inaccessible hours behind a bodyguarding screen of 300 picked soldiers, "the very best material Kentucky could afford; average height 5 feet, 11½ inches, and measuring 40½ inches around the breast." His personal staff made his headquarters in a three-story St. Louis mansion appear like an opera set. Europeans mainly with unpronounceable names, mysterious titles and gorgeous uniforms of plume and braid that the contemptuous locals called "chicken guts," there were so many of them that one of his opponents who read a list of them grunted: "There's too much tail to that kite." There was indeed, but Frémont's greatest defect was his concentration on his grandiose plan so far removed from his capacity while allowing his commanders with their ill-cared-for troops to fall into Rebel traps.

The first of these was the belligerent, red-haired bantam Nathaniel Lyon. In June before Frémont arrived, Lyon had led his force of about 6,000 men, including 1,200 regulars and a few batteries of artillery, into southwestern Missouri, intending to secure that section before moving down into Arkansas, with Little Rock as his objective. By August he had passed Springfield and was near the border. But his army was in wretched shape. Breakdowns in his supply line had left it poorly shod and clothed, short on ammunition. Frémont, obsessed with his master plan, could send no reinforcements. Worse, the Confederate forces to his front were growing stronger daily. Lyon estimated them at 20,000, although they were actually only 12,000, but still twice his number. Most of them were Missouri militia under Sterling Price, and they were more miserable than Lyon's men. Without tents or uniforms, some without arms, others carrying shotguns or 1812-era flintlocks, they were so short of munitions that for projectiles to serve their eight antiquated cannon they laid in a stock of smooth stones, iron rods and rusty chains. The remaining Rebels were Confederate regulars, led by Brigadier General Ben McCulloch, forty years old and a former Texas Ranger. The two generals quarreled briefly over seniority before the two-star Price gave way to the one-star McCulloch so long as he would hasten to fall upon Lyon.

That general had wisely begun to retreat, moving slowly back with the Rebels hanging on his heels. He went into camp along Wilson's Creek, ten miles short of Springfield. Still believing that the Confederates outnumbered him three to one, the Union commander nevertheless chose to launch a daring attack. Lyon believed that the enemy would never expect him to strike in the dark and in the rain. So on the night of August 9–10, he sent a small column under Colonel Franz Sigel on a wide swing to hit the enemy rear while he struck with the main body at his front.

Incredibly enough such a complicated maneuver undertaken in rain and darkness and requiring almost split-second coordination actually seemed to succeed. At dawn Lyon heard and saw gunfire to the Rebel rear. Realizing that Sigel was in action, he launched his own push to the west and east of Wilson's Creek, seemingly closing the upper jaw of his vise. At first the startled Southerners gave way. Many men fled, some to return, others to keep on going. McCulloch soon established a defensive line, while Price, riding up and down with his long silver hair streaming in the growing light, rallied his Missourians.

No struggle could have been less romantic than the Battle of Wilson's Creek. There were no Rebel yells or Yankee cheers. It was cold, merciless slaughter, fought at close quarters because of the short range of the Confederate flintlocks and fowling pieces. Regiments marched up to the firing line to deliver a volley, reload and fire another, keeping up the rhythm and destruction until it was itself fragmented and replaced by another regiment. In such mutual manslaughter weight of numbers had to tell—and it did. Sigel's sally in the south was quickly turned to a rout, his men stampeding, abandoning their colors and all but one of their guns, running all the way back to Springfield. A detachment of regulars which Lyon had sent east of the creek was also shattered. Lyon with the main body west of the stream, seeing that his men were giving way, tried to rally them. A bullet creased his scalp, another pierced his thigh, a third his ankle—and then his horse fell dead beneath him. Limping to the rear, the valiant redhead muttered, "I fear the day is lost." But he soon recovered his spirits, securing a mount and swinging painfully into the saddle. Waving his hat, he rode toward the place where his men were faltering, rallied them and led them forward. Now the Rebels were giving way, but then a bullet struck Lyon in the heart. After he fell, his troops fled and the Battle of Wilson's Creek became another Confederate victory.

Once again, however, the triumphant Southerners were too disorganized to pursue the fleeing Union soldiers. Northern losses were 223 killed, 721 wounded for total casualties of 944, with 291 men missing. Southern were 257 killed, 900 wounded for a total of 1,157, with 28 missing. In one-third the time elapsed at Bull Run and with less than one-third the number of troops involved, more than half as many men had fallen along

Wilson's Creek as during that first battle of the war. Such carnage was a grim portent of a struggle even more horrible than the one predicted by Alexander Stephens.

Yet Wilson's Creek settled nothing in Missouri. President Davis ordered McCulloch to retire into Arkansas, while Price warily followed the retreating Federals, who had been withdrawing before the battle anyway. But the defeat opened Frémont's eyes to reality in Missouri. Without Missouri under control there would be no glorious advance down the Mississippi, and he might even lose his base in St. Louis. Calling upon Washington for reinforcements, Frémont sought to recoup his fortunes by psychological warfare. He issued a proclamation stating that any unauthorized person found north of the line Fort Leavenworth–Cape Girardeau would be court-martialed and if convicted executed. He also announced the confiscation of all property of Missourians who could be "proved to have taken an active part with our enemies in the field," adding: "And their slaves, if they have any, are hereby declared freemen."

There they were—terrorism and emancipation—like twin genies raging out of the bottle to create a storm of approbation and condemnation in both camps. Immediately, Brigadier General M. Jeff Thompson of Missouri issued a counter-pronunciamento of his own: "For every member of the Missouri State Guard or soldier of our allies the Confederate States who shall be put to death in pursuance of said order of General Frémont, I will Hang, Draw and Quarter a minion of said Abraham Lincoln . . . so help me God!" Conversely, in the Northeast antislavery radicals were delighted. But in Kentucky a Unionist volunteer company threw down its arms, and the legislature was having second thoughts about remaining loyal to Washington. Lincoln now was caught between the arrows of the Abolitionists and the slings of the loyal border men, a group of whom wired him: "There is not a day to be lost disavowing emancipation, or Kentucky is gone over the mill dam."

In a circumspect letter, Lincoln explained his predicament to Frémont and requested that he withdraw or modify the edict freeing slaves, while tactfully reminding him that the Confederacy could shoot a Billy Yank for every Johnny Reb he executed. Frémont chose to wait a while before sending his wife to Washington with a letter refusing to "change or shade" his proclamation, declaring: "It is worth a victory in the field." The meeting between Jessie Benton Frémont and Abraham Lincoln was not cordial. She found him "hard" and lectured him on what Europe's reaction would mean, whereupon he interrupted with the remark, "You are quite a female politician." Lifting her chin, Jessie challenged the president to "try titles" with the Pathfinder, and then heatedly declared: "He is a man and I am his wife!" At this point, Lincoln sought to soothe her, but she "left in anger," he said, "flaunting her handkerchief in my face."

Lincoln quickly wrote to Frémont, explaining that although he "perceived in general no objection" to the proclamation, he could not allow Congress's Confiscation Act of 1861 to be overridden. This freed only slaves employed by the Confederates in war work, but did not extend general emancipation. So as commander in chief he *ordered* it modified, while accepting Frémont's promise not to shoot anyone without presidential approval. Thus Lincoln skillfully extricated himself from a potentially dangerous situation. By nullifying the proclamation he mollified the border states, and by stating that his objection was to unlawful interference with the Congress, he placated many of the radical Abolitionists sitting there. Still, he was vilified in the Senate, in the press and from the pulpit. But he rode out the storm, satisfied to have secured the continued loyalty of those vital border states.

But he was thoroughly dissatisfied with his fractious general in St. Louis, especially after a congressional committee investigating why $12,000,000 had been spent in the West found widespread graft and extravagance on the part of "a gang of California robbers and scoundrels" surrounding Frémont. Lincoln now asked Major General David Hunter to take over in St. Louis. Hunter consented, but as he set out for St. Louis, Frémont at last took the field at the head of an army of 38,000 men to oppose between 15,000 and 20,000 well-armed troops advancing on St. Louis under Sterling Price. "My plan is New Orleans straight," he wrote his wife on October 7.

Lincoln was also writing. Encouraged by the rumors of wrongdoing in Frémont's department, and by an assessment of him as unfit for his command by the adjutant general and the secretary of war, as well as Brigadier General Samuel Curtis's judgment of him as lacking "the intelligence, the experience and the sagacity necessary to his command," he sent to Curtis two orders: one relieving Frémont of his command, the other appointing Hunter in his place. Still cautious, remembering Jessie Benton's challenge to "try titles," he told Curtis to deliver them only if Frémont had not won a battle or was not about to fight one. The Rail-Splitter was too political an animal to fire a general on the eve of battle or after a victory.

But Frémont in camp southwest of Springfield was forewarned by news of the orders leaked to the press. Surrounded by his army and his bodyguard he took every precaution against being approached by some strange officer or emissary from the capital. But Curtis had ordered a captain to disguise himself as a farmer and deliver the orders. Reaching Frémont's headquarters, at 5 A.M. November 1, his bucolic pose fooled Frémont's pickets. But at headquarters he was told he must turn over the information he said he had to the general's aides and could not see him personally. He declined, saying he must see Frémont and would wait. After many hours, he was at last ushered into the general's presence. Taking the orders from the lining of his rough coat he gave them to Frémont. The great man frowned.

"Sir," he said, trembling with rage, "how did you get admission into my lines?"

But the Pathfinder still would not accede defeat. A victory would turn the tide! He would fall on Price, rout him and regain all! So he placed the captain under arrest to keep news of his relief secret, and ordered his army to prepare for battle. But Price and his secessionist army were gone, retreating before a superior foe. So was the captain-messenger, who had overheard the password and escaped. Frémont had lost the "try at titles." Next morning he bade his army farewell, while in St. Louis his heartbroken wife cried: "Oh, if my husband had only been more positive. But he never did assert himself enough. That was his greatest fault."

If Abraham Lincoln in Washington had heard this complaint, it is doubtful if he would have seconded it. But John Charles Frémont was gone, and Missouri was still in the Union. But now Abraham Lincoln was beginning to feel uneasy about another American hero, another general whom he had raised to the highest command, and in whom he had placed the highest hopes: George Brinton McClellan.

22

■

McClellan Takes Charge

FOR ALL of the biographies of George Brinton McClellan, very little is known about his childhood or youth except that he was born in Philadelphia on December 3, 1826, the son of a distinguished Pennsylvania family, and reared in an atmosphere of gentility and cultivation.

His father, George McClellan, was graduated from Yale in 1816, and three years later from the medical school of the University of Pennsylvania, one of the best educations available in the America of the early nineteenth century. Although he was not wealthy, he rose to eminence and was one of the founders of the Jefferson Medical College in 1825.

McClellan's mother was Elizabeth S. Brinton, a woman of high character descended from one of the most genteel of Philadelphia families. McClellan was devoted to her, and she seems to have had much to do with his education. He must have been precocious, passing rapidly through a good preparatory school and entering the University of Pennsylvania a few months short of his fourteenth year. His record there was excellent, but he left after two years to enroll at the U.S. Military Academy. It has been said that McClellan yearned to be a soldier, but it is just as likely that he went to West Point to obtain a free education, like so many other American military heroes before and after him. He was not yet sixteen, the minimum age for admission to the Academy, but he had much to recommend an easing of regulations: prep school and two outstanding years at a great college beneath his academic belt; and although he was only five feet eight inches tall, he was a fine physical specimen: muscular, with a deep wide chest and the graceful carriage of a fine athlete. He was also handsome, with thick dark auburn hair and features so regular that cartoonists of the future would have difficulty caricaturing him. His personality was warm and friendly, magnetic even, and he was a great favorite with his classmates.

George did well in his studies, excelling in mathematics and being graduated second in the class of 1846. But he was no bookworm, showing a fondness for social life and the gaiety of formal balls. Soon it became apparent that he preferred the company of Southern youths, of which Dr. William Starr Myers remarked: "It is evident that the culture, refinement and airs of the gallant, so characteristic of the Southern 'aristocrat,' were exceedingly attractive to McClellan and struck a responsive chord in his consciously 'gentle nature.'" One of McClellan's closest friends was his classmate Dabney Maury of Virginia, later a Confederate general, who recalled: "After the Mexican War, while we were both at West Point as instructors, we were, of course, daily associated together for several years, and a happy association it was. A brighter, kindlier, more genial gentleman did not live than he. Sharing freely in all the convivial hospitality of the mess, he was a constant student of his profession. . . . He was an excellent horseman, and one of our most athletic and best swordsmen."

McClellan came out of West Point as a second lieutenant of engineers, just in time for the Mexican War. There he became one of Scott's most valued officers, winning two brevets for gallantry and the offer of a third after Molino del Rey, which he gallantly declined because he had not seen action there. Emerging as a captain he did his tour of duty as an instructor at West Point, before building forts, improving harbors and mapping railroad routes. During this period he met and served under Major Randolph B. Marcy, an explorer only slightly less famous than Frémont. He also met Marcy's beautiful daughter, Ellen, and escorted her to balls and galas. The Marcys were delighted, hoping that their daughter would marry this excellent and capable young man, so obviously headed for great things. But then McClellan, who spoke French, Spanish and German and was studying Russian, was sent as an observer of the Crimean War between Russia and the Anglo-French. He wrote a highly regarded report on cavalry tactics. But while he was away, Ellen, twenty-one, blond, blue-eyed, and vivacious, met another of McClellan's Southern friends from West Point: A.P. Hill of Virginia. They fell in love, and after Hill proposed, Ellen accepted. But the Marcys, aghast at the prospect of losing the eminently eligible McClellan, did all they could to break up the match—succeeding after Mrs. Marcy spitefully spread the story of Hill's contraction of gonorrhea while a West Point plebe. In the end, Ellen married McClellan. Years later, when Hill and McClellan were generals on opposing sides, and Hill launched one of his fierce artillery bombardments, Union soldiers would growl: "God's sakes, Nelly—why didn't you marry him?"

In 1857 McClellan resigned from the army to become chief engineer and then vice-president of the Illinois Central Railroad, and in 1860 president of the Ohio & Mississippi. Upon the outbreak of the Civil War, when he was only thirty-four, he was commissioned a major general of Ohio volunteers, emerging as a national hero after the wildly overblown victories at Rich Mountain and Carrick's Ford, triumphs for which he accepted credit not exactly due him. After Bull Run, of course, he received that fateful telegram from President Lincoln, riding sixty miles on horseback to the nearest railroad station and speeding on to Washington and the White House.

General McClellan arrived in Washington on July 27, 1861, and on the following day Lincoln gave him the command of the Federal Division of the Potomac, including all Union troops in Washington and vicinity, replacing the defeated McDowell. But McClellan now had what McDowell lacked: the time in which to organize and train an army. He had found the capital "almost in condition to be taken by a dash of a regiment of cavalry," and himself hailed as another savior. But he was far more dashing than the first deliverer, Ben Butler—also far more confident of his military ability, writing to Ellen: "I find myself in a new and strange position here. President, Gen. Scott, and all deferring to me. By some strange operation of magic I seem to have become the power of the land." He added: "I see already the main causes of our recent failure. I am sure that I can remedy these, and am confident that I can lead these armies of men to victory."

I, I, I. Not until the appearance of Douglas MacArthur did any American general use the first person singular as frequently as George McClellan. But he did plunge into work at once.

Certainly one of the "causes of the recent failure" was indiscipline, and McClellan employed two regiments of hard-bitten regulars as military police, assigned to clean out the taverns and hotel bars and lobbies then filled with stragglers and shirkers. Officers and men alike were required to show passes authorizing leave from their outfits. The crests of the hills surrounding the capital were fortified, while the slopes became polka-dotted with the white tents of the encampments erected to receive the recruits arriving after Lincoln's call for 300,000 three-year volunteers. Thus, with rapidity and efficiency "Little Mac," as his devoted soldiers now called him, had restored discipline and defensive precautions to the capital in preparation for his great offensive. "I shall carry this thing *en grand,*" he wrote, "and crush the rebels in one campaign."

McClellan was a master of fine and stirring phrases. When campaigning he would carry a portable printing press with him to get his often grandiloquent messages to the troops. All bustle and businesslike energy on the outside, he was inwardly deeply romantic. It was this romanticism, not so much the iron discipline that he installed, that touched the hearts of his soldiers. This was why his bulletins were so blatantly Napoleonic, why the press called him "the Little Napoleon," or spoke of "McClellan's Army." They were his and he was theirs. To those who had survived Bull Run and were still ashamed of the unjust description of them as disgraceful cowards, he gave back their pride and self-respect. To the newcomers he made soldiering seem like the greatest adventure possible.

"The boys are as happy as clams at high water," a Massachusetts recruit wrote to his family. "I never done anything yet that I like as I do soldiering." Of McClellan: "He has got an eye like a hawk. I looked him right in the eye and he done the same by me. I was bound to see what he looked like and I think I would know him if I should see him again . . . The rank and file think he is just the man to lead us on to victory *when he gets ready,* and not when Horace Greeley says to go. For my part I think he is just the man, and the kind of man that can keep a hotel."

When he gets ready! How did a rookie, rear-rank private after his first sight of the general put his finger on the terrible defect in the great man's character? But he was right on the money. Like a historian who will not write his book until he has read every last word on his subject—fearing to be criticized as "incomplete"—and thus writes nothing, George McClellan just *had to be sure* before risking defeat. He did not want to win as much as he feared to lose. No commander so inhibited can ever succeed in battle, but in that frenetic summer of 1861 it was not apparent. What was plain to all was McClellan's remarkable organizing skill and his charm with the troops.

They worshiped him even though he chose not to dwell among them in camp, rather renting a large, comfortable house in downtown Washington not far from the White House. Here he lived in splendor, indulging his fondness for socializing, giving elegant dinner parties for the powerful and influential of the capital, his residence guarded by gorgeously uniformed soldiers, the glittering aides of his considerable staff everywhere in evidence. Frémont's fondness for foreigners was surpassed by the Little Napoleon: he had two real live princes of the blood on his staff. One was the Comte de Paris, pretender to the throne of France, and the other the Duc de Chartres, known respectively to their American comrades as Captain Paree and Captain Chatters. There was also on his staff an American prince, of finance, that is: John Jacob Astor, one of the earlier robber barons, who lived in a style rivaling McClellan's, attended by his own valet, steward, chef and beautiful female companions, whom he took riding regularly in a coach drawn by four white horses, at once the envy of the Washington elite and the disdain of those rustic American soldiers who hooted at his elegance.

It was only at the reviews that the troops saw Little Mac. There were many of these, all following a pattern. Soldiers in blue stood rigidly at attention, their officers in front of them with drawn swords standing stiff as statues. Across the field from them in their carriages were congressmen and diplomats and their wives in starched crinoline. Tense and expectant, all eyes were riveted on the far end of the field where McClellan made his dramatic entrance. Suddenly, there he was! There he was, galloping down the field between soldiers and spectators, mounted on his big black charger Dan Webster, his entourage following in a colorful stream. As he approached with thundering hooves wild and eager shouts broke from the throats of all. And when he acknowledged the soldiers' cheers, they cheered again. And why not cheer this godlike creature who had given them back their self-esteem? One of his officers has described his effect on his men:

"He had a taking way of returning such salutations. He went beyond the formal military salute, and gave his cap a little twirl, which with his bow and smile seemed to carry a little of personal good fellowship even to the humblest private soldier. If the cheer was repeated, he would turn in his saddle and repeat the salute. It was very plain that these little attentions to the troops took well, and had no small influence in establishing a sort of comradeship between him and them."

Thus as summer turned into fall, the training and the drilling continued: brigades and divisions marching and counter-marching on the parade grounds as they learned the intricacies of the maneuvers of large formations; artillerists firing their cannon, watching in awe as the red-hot projectile left the muzzle to become a tiny speck flying through the air before it exploded on target; cavalry recruits accustomed to riding bareback griping bitterly over the strangeness of those stiff government-issue saddles—and everywhere the drummer boys drumming, tapping away in those irregular beats that carried messages to maneuvering soldiers. When a regiment could maneuver all over the parade ground without a spoken command but only the tap of the drum as a guide, it was considered a crack unit. At half past nine it was the drums—not the sad and poignant bugles of today—that sounded lights-out, which is perhaps why the call came to be known as taps. The men fitted words to the beat: "Go to bed, Tom! Go to bed, Tom! Go to bed, go to bed, go to bed, *Tom!*"

General McClellan had no such early bedtime. Alone in his quarters he often took counsel from his fears, reflecting on what had happened to McDowell. Earlier, full of confidence, he had written, "I flatter myself that Beauregard has gained his last victory." But as the leaves began to fall, he wrote: "I have scarcely slept one moment for the last three nights, knowing well that the enemy intend some movement and fully recognizing my own weakness . . . I am here in a terrible place. The enemy have from three to four times my force."

Here was exaggeration at its wildest, but McClellan believed the figures because they came from his chief of intelligence, the railroad detective Allan Pinkerton, who had shepherded Lincoln through Baltimore. Pinkerton had his agents planted inside Confederate lines. In August he told McClellan that Rebel forces around Manassas numbered 100,000 men. His estimates grew steadily, until in October McClellan reported: "The enemy has a force on the Potomac not less than 150,000 strong, well drilled and equipped, ably commanded and strongly intrenched."

It is doubtful that Beauregard and Joe Johnston had half that many, and a suspicion that there might be less arose when a New Jersey colonel led his regiment toward Munson's Hill, the nearest Rebel outpost ten miles outside of Washington. At its crest they could see the silhouette of a cannon. Still, they attacked. A few Jersey boys fell to sharpshooters, but then the hill was strangely silent. The colonel retreated. A month later the Federals found the outpost deserted. Johnston had moved his forces back. Unaware of this, the Yankees went up the hill cautiously, fearing the "artillery piece," until they discovered that it was nothing but a peeled log painted black—a "Quaker gun."

News of how Joe Johnston had bluffed George McClellan aroused widespread indignation and some derision in Washington. Was that all that kept the Little Napoleon from opening his campaign? But then—with the chill hint of winter in the wind—there came proof that the enemy across the Potomac had more than wooden cannon in their arsenal.

McClellan had received word that Johnston was preparing to evacuate Leesburg, up the Potomac about halfway to Harpers Ferry. He decided to reconnoiter the area to determine if the reports were true. One division went up the Virginia shore, stopping at Dranesville, ten miles short of Leesburg. Brigadier General Charles P. Stone with a division on the Maryland shore was ordered to join the reconnaissance. Interpreting this to mean to cross the river, he put his soldiers into boats holding twenty-five men each and shuttled them over the water at Edward's Island and Ball's Bluff farther upstream. Ball's Bluff was a heavily wooded precipice about a hundred feet above the Potomac. Colonel Edward D. Baker was in charge there. "Ned" Baker was perhaps Abraham Lincoln's dearest friend from far back in the prairie days, before he moved to Oregon at the invitation of the people, who made him a U.S. senator. Lincoln's son Eddie, who died in 1850, had been named for him. After Sumter Baker had told a New York audience, "I want sudden, bold, forward, determined war," fitting his action to his words by raising a regiment in Philadelphia and joining that war. When Lincoln offered to make him a major general, he refused because that would mean he must resign from the Senate. At fifty he was still handsome, conspicuously clean-shaven in those hairy days, fond of reciting romantic poetry. "Press where ye see my white plume shine amidst the ranks of war," he declaimed smilingly as he led his troops up the winding cowpath ascending the steep bluff.

Baker was probably so buoyant and confident because as an amateur colonel he did not realize that the situation was not good. A West Point colonel from New York recognized the danger instantly. To the front the Rebels held high ground and were massing for an assault, to the rear was a steep bluff one hundred feet above an unfordable river. True there were boats on the shore, but none could hold more than two dozen men and there were not enough of them to ferry 1,700 men across the stream under fire. But Baker was in command, and the West Pointer said nothing.

Four Union regiments with two cannon had deployed in a ten-acre glade facing thick brush and timber. Rebel snipers in the brush—some in trees—had already begun to pick off Federals. One of the Union cannon fell silent, its gunners either dropped or driven off by snipers. Then the other unwisely placed at the edge of the precipice recoiled and toppled off the bluff. Now Baker realized his predicament. At four in the afternoon he hastened to rally his wavering line, but as he did a bullet pierced his brain. When his body was carried to the rear, troops drawn up to receive the enemy were demoralized. They thought it was the beginning of a retreat, and in panic they started one that swiftly became a rout.

The Rebel brigade opposite them was led by Shanks Evans, who had moved so quickly and decisively to halt the Federal flankers at Bull Run. Why this capable commander did not wear shoulder straps is not exactly known, although it was bruited about that he drank too much. If this is true, then Jefferson Davis was delinquent in not making his brand general issue. Evans was not there that day, but he had trained his men well. Having allowed the Yankees to come close to their Leesburg camp—which was *not* being evacuated—and when the forward edge of the glade was packed with blue uniforms, the high quavering Rebel yell rose from the height above, followed by a crash of musketry—and the onslaught began.

Almost immediately pandemonium broke the Union line. Recalling the limited capacity of the boats, every man seemed to wish to be the first to board one. To do so they did not follow the roundabout cowpath down but took the shorter route: the bluff. Leaping over its edge, some still holding their weapons, they clutched at stones and scrub to break their fall. Soon, as one Rebel witness wrote, "the side of the bluff was worn smooth by the number sliding down."

Sometimes these terrified men came hurtling through the air to land on the backs or bayonets of their comrades. The narrow bank beside the river, where wounded had been arriving all day, waiting to be ferried to the Maryland shore, became a slaughter pen. Rebel bullets struck down Federals with that odd sharp *spat!* of lead striking flesh, or dug up mud spurts on the bank while the water boiled "as white as in a great hail storm." Two boatloads of wounded were shoving off when the panic began. Frantic fugitives from the bluff piled aboard until they were swamped and those wounded who could not swim were drowned. An overloaded flatboat also capsized, drowning many more.

Ball's Bluff was a Union debacle. Federal casualties were 49 killed, 158 wounded and 714 missing, many of them drowned, for a total of 921. Confederate losses were 36 killed, 117 wounded and 2 missing for a total of 155. As battles go, Ball's Bluff was a minor engagement, but because the popular Senator Baker had fallen, and because his death broke the heart of President Lincoln, it had far-reaching consequences in Washington.

Abraham Lincoln was at army headquarters, listening morosely to the telegraph clicking off the bad news of still another Union defeat. Then came the report of Baker's death. The president sat in stunned silence for five minutes, then arose and walked alone through the anteroom, his breast heaving with sobs, tears streaming down his cheeks. Out in the street he stumbled, groping to maintain his balance. Orderlies and newsmen rushed to support him, but he regained his equilibrium and strode silently away.

Congress also experienced an emotional reaction, one of anger at the death of their colleague; at the capture of Paul Joseph Revere, descendant of the legendary rider of the Revolution; and at the wounding of the son of Oliver Wendell Holmes. Among the radical Republicans or Jacobins there arose a thirst for vengeance associated with a desire to change the war for the Union to a war against slavery and to obtain for themselves an equal voice with the president in the conduct of the war. That is what they named their new, witch-hunting agency: the Joint Committee on the Conduct of the War.

Senator Benjamin Franklin Wade of Ohio was the chairman: bluff Ben Wade, short, thick-chested, with sunken jet black eyes, a square shaven face and the upper lip of a bulldog. Wade hated Southerners, slavery and black people themselves with equal fervor. He complained about the "odor" of the blacks, insisting that he had eaten so much food in Washington "cooked by Niggers until I can smell and taste the Nigger." Like many Republicans he thought the solution to the race problem was to ship the blacks back to Africa.

Another member was Senator Zachariah Chandler of Michigan. He had amassed a fortune in real estate and dry goods in Detroit. Profane, hard-drinking and as grim as a gravedigger, he had been one of the founders of the Republican Party. He was unreserved in his hatred of slavery and Southerners, and when some of them brandished pistols and bowie knives in the Senate itself, he embarked on a program of bodybuilding and marksmanship. To Chandler the Confederacy was a body of "armed traitors" who should be destroyed.

Wade's committee was nothing less than a Star-Chamber proceeding among the Union generals. Just like a secretive Star Chamber, its members met alone in the basement of the capital, imperiously summoning generals before them to answer accusations without being faced by their accusers or even being told who they were. General Stone was the first victim. It was he who had ordered Baker to take charge of the reconnaissance. Baker, of course, escaped all blame, although he was wholly responsible for the debacle on Ball's Bluff, having escalated a scouting mission into an assault with his back to a cliff and a deep river, with his line of communications all but cut and an entrenched enemy on a height above him. Even if the members of the Joint Committee had understood this—which they definitely did not—they would have ignored it. Stone was guilty because Stone was suspected of proslavery sympathies.

It mattered not that this capable commander was the trusted friend of Lincoln and the confidant of McClellan, or that he had done an excellent job making the capital secure during Lincoln's inauguration. What mattered was that in September he had ordered his men "not to incite and encourage insurbordination among the colored servants in the neighborhood of the camps." From this it was easy to suggest that this traitor had deliberately sent Baker on a mission doomed to disaster. There were no formal charges against Stone, only this cloud of vague accusations and rumors, settling on him like a shroud in which he was wrapped and buried in prison for months.

Eventually he was released—not exactly cleared, because he had not been charged with anything—and he emerged from jail a ruined soldier.

George McClellan understood what was going on. This well-named committee actually did desire to conduct the war, and they would sacrifice any man who stood in their way: even Lincoln. "I have to deal with a set of men unscrupulous and false," McClellan told his wife. "If possible they will throw whatever blame there is on my shoulders, and I do not intend to be sacrificed by such people."

McClellan was by then engaged in a running battle with General Scott. Little Mac had come to Washington full of veneration for the man who had been his mentor, but when Old Fuss 'N Feathers repeatedly torpedoed his plans for reorganizing his army, this feeling turned to exasperated resentment. It is hard to blame McClellan. Scott was by then in what art critics call "his late bad manner," and the old man thought the war should be fought as he had fought his war in Mexico. He objected to creation of divisions, insisting that brigades should remain the army's largest unit. He openly scoffed at Pinkerton's reports, much to McClellan's mortification, refusing to believe that Little Mac's army was outnumbered. On August 9 McClellan wrote his wife: "Gen. Scott is the great obstacle. He will not comprehend the danger, I have to fight my way against him."

So Little Mac counterattacked, striking the old man in his weak spot: his pride. He snubbed him in public, contradicted him in councils, goading him into such fits of fury that at last in October, Scott turned upon him with the remark: "You were called here by my advice. The times require vigilance and activity. I am not active and never shall be again. When I proposed that you should come here to aid, not supersede me, you had my friendship and confidence. You still have my confidence."

No rebuke could have been gentler or more poignant and civilized, and it is possible that the striking phrase, "to aid, not supersede me," suggested a final remedy in the mind of Abraham Lincoln. On November 1, 1861, the president accepted Scott's standing application for retirement, and on the same day appointed McClellan to take his place while remaining in command of the Washington army. Scott departed with the noble promise: "Wherever I may spend my little remainder of life, my frequent and latest prayer will be, 'God save the Union.' "

McClellan to his credit saw the old warrior off. At four in the morning he and his staff arose to escort him to the station with a squadron of cavalry. It was rainy and dark. Gaslight gleamed on the black rain suits of the general's escort. The old man was touched, inquiring after the health of

McClellan's wife and baby. Then he mounted the car and rode out of American history.

McClellan was now completely in charge, confident and buoyant. Only the day before an apprehensive Abraham Lincoln had come to his headquarters, wondering aloud if the double burden he had placed upon Little Mac was too much for one man to bear.

"It is a great relief, sir!" McClellan replied. "I feel as if several tons were taken from my shoulders today."

Still uncertain, the president mused, "In addition to your present command, the supreme command of the Army will entail a vast labor on you."

"I can do it all," said McClellan.

During that momentous November of 1861, while changes and promotions were common on both sides, and while the war seemed to be heating up, at last shedding its improvised character, the provisional government of the Confederacy became permanent, with the election on the first Wednesday of the month of Jefferson Davis and Alexander H. Stephens. Davis was positive that the Confederacy *was* a permanent entity, and so he told the Provisional Congress at its last session. He also used the occasion to excoriate Lincoln for his repeated reference to the war as a "rebellion," declaring:

"If instead of being a dissolution of a league, it were indeed a rebellion in which we are engaged, we might find ample vindication for the course we have adopted in the scenes which are now being enacted in the United States. Our people now look with contemptuous astonishment on those with whom they had been so recently associated. They shrink with aversion from the bare idea of renewing such a connection. When they see a President making war without the assent of Congress; when they behold judges threatened because they maintain the writ of habeas corpus so sacred to freedom; when they see justice and law trampled under the armed heel of military authority, and upright men and innocent women dragged to distant dungeons upon the mere edict of a despot; when they find all this tolerated and applauded by a people who had been in the full enjoyment of freedom but a few months ago—they believe that there must be some radical incompatibility between such a people and themselves. With such a people we may be content to live at peace, but the separation is final, and for the independence we have asserted we will accept no alternative."

But even as Davis denounced the "tyrant" of the North, he found himself facing the same agonizing choice between winning a war and preserving freedom that had confronted Lincoln. When Julius Caesar said, "War doesn't permit free speech," he was speaking a profound truth, as Davis now learned with the explosion of an insurrection in the Unionist region of east Tennessee. Bridges were burned and men armed themselves in anticipation of the arrival of a Union force through Cumberland Gap. The area was vital: it not only provided the Confederacy with grain and meat, it was strategically important because the Virginia & Tennessee Railroad ran through it to Chattanooga and Memphis and the Transmississippi. Davis reacted swiftly and sternly, sending troops from Memphis and Pensacola to the uprising, suppressing it and arresting many Unionists. Habeas corpus "so sacred to freedom" died a quick death. Davis ordered that those not known to be actual bridge-burners were to be held as prisoners of war, while the others were "to be tried summarily by a drumhead court martial, and, if found guilty, executed on the spot by hanging."

Five men were hanged, and others held captive, including William G. Brownlow, a former Methodist parson and editor of the Knoxville *Whig,* who had vowed to fight secession "until Hell freezes over, and then fight on the ice." But nothing could be proved against Brownlow, and because his continued incarceration seemed to imitate what was happening in those "distant dungeons" of the North he was released into Union lines. "Glory to God in the highest," Brownlow exulted, "and on earth peace, good will toward men—except a few hell-born and hell-bound rebels in Knoxville."

A rising clamor of criticism in that November 1861 was another duplicate of Lincoln's problems. Fire-eaters urged Davis to drop his defensive stance and concentrate on a bold invasion of the North. This would bring quick victory, they argued, while Davis replied it might also bring quick defeat. The South's war was preeminently defensive, and it could never sustain a war of conquest. Its policy must be to watch and wait—for what Davis considered to be the inevitable foreign intervention on the side of the South.

Apparently Yancey's advice to Davis had gone unheeded, for on August 24 Davis launched another diplomatic offensive by naming two former U.S. senators as his new emissaries to Britain and France. These were John Slidell of Louisiana and James M. Mason of Virginia. Mason was the more prominent of the two, being a grandson of George Mason, the framer of the Bill of Rights, and generally considered an able statesman. His looks, dress, habits and manners, however, suggest an unpredictable eccentric. Mason's face was large, pale and clean-shaven, with a broad fleshy nose, deep-set, dark, "burning" eyes and a slit of a mouth. At sixty-three his thinning brown hair shot with gray had receded far back from his forehead and was worn long. He had served ten years on the Senate Foreign Relations Committee, but was probably best known—and hated in the North—as the author of the Fugitive Slave Act. Of this arrogant and domineering aristocrat, Mrs. Chesnut has written: "My wildest imagination will not picture Mr. Mason as a diplomat. He will say 'chaw' for chew, and call himself 'Jeems,' and he will wear a dress coat to breakfast. He is above law."

Slidell, the brother-in-law of Beauregard, was well named. He looked and was sly, with his carrot of a nose and twisted little mouth. A British journalist wrote of him as "a man of iron will and strong passions, who loves the excitement of combinations and who in his dungeon, or whatever else it may be, would conspire with the mice against the cat rather than not conspire at all." Born in New York, he migrated to New Orleans to escape debt and prosecution for a duel with a theater manager over the affections of an actress. In the Crescent City he amassed a fortune in sugar, took a Creole wife and served one term in the House and two in the Senate. Like Mason, Slidell did not seem to be an especially happy choice for diplomacy. He was probably chosen because he spoke French, although it is doubtful if the sophisticates who served Emperor Napoleon III so described his Creole dialect.

In early October both men were in Charleston, Slidell's wife and daughter with them, waiting for the chance to run the blockade. Booking passage on a small private steamer, *Gordon,* they slipped out of the harbor during a driving rain in the early morning of October 12, making for Nassau. Finding no transatlantic packets there, they put to sea again, eventually reaching Havana, where on November 7 they boarded the British mail steamer *Trent.* With the Union Jack whipping in the wind it seemed to them that they were safe at last.

But at noon of the following day the United States Navy sloop *San Jacinto* commanded by Captain Charles Wilkes approached and put two shots across the *Trent*'s bow. Her skipper was furious, and when armed American sailors and Marines came aboard demanding the surrender of Slidell and Mason, he screamed at them, "Pirates! Villains!" But he had no choice, and Slidell and Mason were transferred to *San Jacinto* and taken as prisoners to Fort Warren in Boston Harbor. Captain Wilkes became an instant hero in the North, while in the South the fury of the British reaction delighted Jefferson Davis and his people. War between the United States and Britain appeared imminent, especially after the British ominously sent 8,000 troops to Canada, and Prime Minister Lord Palmerston composed an arrogant letter to Lincoln. Fortunately, Prince Albert was able to modify it, and both Lincoln and Seward were wise enough to disavow Wilkes's act and the two emissaries were set free.

Upon their arrival in their respective assignments, they followed their instructions to abandon King Cotton diplomacy, and to appeal for recognition instead on their fight for self-government. More, they informed their hosts that the North could never conquer the Confederacy, and that the South would never rejoin the Union. They also promised to pursue a low-tariff policy. But they soon discovered that only the ruling classes of Britain, France and Spain favored the South. The middle and lower classes, detesting slavery, were solidly for the North. This was especially true in Britain, where the English aristocracy as well as the lower classes were firmly opposed to the institution. All that Mason in London could find as favorable to his cause was the English aristocracy's naive belief that the South was pure English, while the North was a mongrel conglomeration of races. True as this might have been of the North, it was not so of the South. There were in Dixie quite a few French—usually Huguenots—many Germans and many, many Scots, Scots-Irish, Welsh and Irish: in a word, Celts. And they were native-born. Long before the Civil War the Catholic Church in America had coined the word "leakage" to describe the vast number of Celts and Germans who had left their homelands Catholic only to become Protestants in the southern United States.

Mason certainly did not help the Confederate cause. His ridiculously fancy dress detracted from his dignity, and when he was a guest in the House of Commons and lustily cheered a pro-South speech by a shipbuilder scenting profits, this breach of decorum "damaged him terribly." So did his habit of chewing tobacco furiously during the debates, covering the carpet in front of him with brown tobacco spit.

Finally, the most Davis's agents were able to do was to persuade the ruling classes of Europe to believe that the North could not defeat the South. In turn, they received the unhappy impression that Yancey had been exactly right, that only the South's "conquering sword dripping" with the lifeblood of the North would induce them to intervene.

23

■

The Anaconda Plan:
Ambrose Burnside

PART OF Winfield Scott's Anaconda Plan had called for a naval invest-ment of Southern ports, and although the proposal had been derided and rejected, Abraham Lincoln on April 19—five days after Sumter fell—had proclaimed that very blockade.

At the time, the South hardly felt threatened: the Union navy scat-tered over the seven seas consisted of only 42 ships, 555 guns and 7,600 sailors. By the end of the year this would show a spectacular increase to 264 ships, 2,557 guns and 22,000 seamen, but in that April of 1861 it appeared to Southerners that Lincoln with his handful of ships patrolling 5,000 miles of Confederate coastline was pointing a popgun at them. Even more difficult, this enormous distance was multiplied by the numerous barrier islands, rivers, lagoons and creeks that could receive blockade-runners putting out from the neutral islands of Cuba and Bermuda, which, in turn, could receive the return traffic. It was also comical that, after Jefferson Davis placed an embargo on shipment of cotton to Europe in order to create a cotton famine, Abraham Lincoln was now proclaiming a blockade that would help enforce it. At this time also, the South had no navy. Few sailors and no ships had turned Confederate in the way of all those West Pointers. Nevertheless, Jefferson Davis decided to float an irregular one to function while a regular sea force was being built. Under the Declaration of Paris in 1856, the European powers had condemned privateering as piracy, but the United States had refused to sign it. In the War of 1812 American privateers had been incredibly successful against the British merchant marine, and Washington did not wish to abandon a naval weapon it might need again. Mindful of this, the Confederate Congress authorized the issue of letters of marque, authorizations by a government for one of its citizens to seize the property of an enemy. Soon about twenty of these certified seawolves were operating against the American merchant marine.

Lincoln immediately branded them as pirates, promising that upon capture they would be tried as such and if convicted hung by their necks. Davis quickly responded in this escalating duel between presidents, declaring that for every Confederate sailor so executed he would do the same to a Union soldier of corresponding rank chosen by lot among the thousands of prisoners-of-war in the Richmond tobacco warehouse.

In June the battle of executive wills was joined when the privateer *Savannah* was taken, with its captain and crew jailed awaiting trial for piracy. Throughout the North the cry of "Hang 'em!" could be heard, but the crisis passed when a New York jury could not agree on a verdict. Later in the year, however, the sailors of the captured *Jeff Davis* were tried in Philadelphia, convicted and sentenced to the rope. When Lincoln seemed ready to execute the sentence, Davis ordered the fatal lots to be drawn in Richmond. One of the short-straw unfortunates was the nephew of Paul Revere captured at Ball's Bluff, who was placed in a condemned cell with other candidates for the noose. It was a tense moment, with not only the North and South watching with narrowed eyes but also most of the civilized world. Lincoln backed away, for which humane and brave act he was condemned as a coward on both sides of the Mason-Dixon line. Thus the atmosphere of mutual hatred had so thickened by the end of 1861, that many normally reasonable people had wanted to see the American presidents engage in a hanging match. Such a macabre contest would not have made a very pretty page in the history of the New World. Once again the exigencies of war had shrunk the area of justice and reason in Lincoln's "last best hope of earth" and in Davis's "last best hope of freedom." War, they were learning, not only inhibits free speech, as Caesar said, but also breaks "the cake of custom," thereby freeing those dreadful passions which the leash of civilization can at best restrain but never quite subdue.

Meanwhile, the small but growing Federal navy had made an outstanding contribution to the Anaconda Plan.

It had not begun well; in fact, even before it got started, the Confederates had seized the naval base at Norfolk, Virginia, capturing enough big guns to arm forts all over the South, while raising the sunken U.S. *Merrimac,* one of the Union's first-line warships. If there was any blockade anywhere, it had been the Confederate batteries on the Potomac denying Washington access to the sea.

But then in late August, a lean, irascible flag officer named Silas Stringham joined Ben Butler in preparing for an amphibious strike against

Fort Hatteras in North Carolina. Not much had been heard from Butler since Winfield Scott had practically exiled him in Fortress Monroe. Militarily, there was not much he could do there. But then his hair-splitting lawyer's mind fastened on the problem of what was to be done with runaway slaves entering Union lines. Federal commanders everywhere were harassed by this problem, and they had seen that if the fugitive slaves were returned to their owners, as Stone had ordered, they could land in jail; if they declared them freed like Frémont, they could lose their job. So cross-eyed, clever Ben Butler decided that they were "contraband of war." Contraband in its widest definition is anything that can assist a nation in its war effort, and thus a neutral ship carrying arms or supplies to a belligerent could be seized by another belligerent and its cargo confiscated. So Ben determined that the fugitive black was bona fide contraband, a species of property owned by a man in rebellion, one which was of direct military use to the Confederacy at war but which, by the act of rebellion, could be seized. This legal refinement committed no one to either side of the slavery issue, and while it outraged the South, it pleased the Northern commanders, who for the rest of the war treated runaway slaves and displaced black people in general as contraband.

Delighted to find himself basking once more in the warmth of public admiration, Butler was also elated to be chosen to lead the troops in the expedition against Forts Clarke and Hatteras, positions that the Rebels had built to either side of Hatteras Inlet leading into Pamlico and Albemarle sounds in North Carolina. Enclosed by a barrier of islands and reefs, these waters were ideal havens for raiders and blockade-runners. On August 26 fourteen ships and 860 men under Stringham and Butler dropped down from Hampton Roads to invest both ports. Actually, Stringham and his superior naval guns did all the Union fighting. Standing out of range of the Confederate guns, he battered both forts at will, suffering no harm himself. Although 300 of Butler's men were landed above the enemy, they saw no action, arriving at Hatteras in time for Butler to join Stringham in accepting that fort's surrender. Clarke had pulled down its colors the day before.

Next on the Union navy's schedule was Ship Island off the coast of Mississippi, an even bigger piece of cake. Possession of it could seal off the great port of New Orleans from the Gulf of Mexico and thus also deny this sanctuary to seawolves and blockade-runners. It was taken on September 17, after its Rebel garrison evacuated their incomplete fortifications without firing a shot.

Far more ambitious was the third and final naval operation of 1861: an attempt to seize Port Royal Sound in South Carolina, the waters lying between the vital Rebel ports of Savannah and Charleston. An invasion fleet of no fewer than seventy-four ships sailed under Captain Samuel F. Du Pont, with 12,000 soldiers under Brigadier General Thomas W. Sherman— not to be confused with William Tecumseh, as sometimes happened, or, worse, to be called "the other" General Sherman. This irascible officer had another distinction: walking 400 miles from his home in Newport, Rhode Island, to obtain an appointment to West Point from President Andrew Jackson. On November 7, Du Pont and Sherman appeared off the entrance to Port Royal Sound. Two forts blocked their passage, Beauregard on Bay Point to the north, Walker on Hilton Head Island to the south. To reduce them both, Du Pont evolved a novel and intricate plan of action.

He formed his main force into nine of his heaviest sloops and frigates ranged in line ahead, a squadron of five flanked by gunboats. They were to enter the sound in parallel columns, the gunboats on the north or starboard side, to receive and return the fire of both positions. Two miles inside the sound, Du Pont with the main force would round and strike at Walker in the south, turning to bombard Beauregard. Meanwhile, the lighter squadron would engage any Rebel gunboats.

It worked. Du Pont had completed two passes at each of the forts, when he learned aboard his flagship *Wabash* that Walker had been abandoned. At 2:20 P.M. a landing party raised the Stars and Stripes above its ramparts. At sunset Beauregard hauled down its flag, and Union troops took possession of it in the morning. Meanwhile, the Confederate flotilla under Du Pont's old messmate from U. S. Navy days, Commodore Josiah Tattnall, had been chased up Skull Creek, three times dipping his pennant in jaunty salute to his friend-turned-enemy before putting about.

Although there had been a great roar of battle, much smoke and flames, casualties were light. For the Federals there were eight men killed, six badly wounded, and seventeen slightly wounded. Rebel losses were eleven dead, forty-eight wounded, three captured and four missing. Soon Sherman's soldiers were ashore occupying Hilton Head Island. The Union now had driven a wedge between Savannah and Charleston, but neglected to exploit it on land. Still, possession of Hilton Head and thereby the sound remained a menace to the Confederates throughout the war, as well as a valuable base for the coaling and supply of Union blockaders. Later it also became a sanctuary for runaway slaves.

Scorned and rejected, old Winfield Scott's Anaconda Plan had taken root. As early as the fall of 1861, the strategy to destroy the Confederacy was in place: seal off the Southern coast, descend the Mississippi to sever the South, then move east from the West to destroy secession, Rebel state by Rebel state. Meanwhile, one more leapfrogging expedition along the Confederate coast was proposed, and this was to take Roanoke Island, the key to Albemarle Sound north of Pamlico. If the Federals held Albemarle they could invest the Confederacy's vital Norfolk navy yard from the rear. Lying just north of the four barrier inlets, Roanoke—famous in history as the site of Sir Walter Raleigh's "lost colony," and the birthplace of Virginia Dare, the first English child born in the New World—was like the cork in the Albemarle bottle. McClellan liked Roanoke very much and was glad to give command of the operation to the man who proposed it, his old West Point classmate Ambrose Burnside.

Ambrose Everts Burnside was the great-grandson of Robert Burnside, a native of Scotland who, with his brother William, followed the fortunes of Bonnie Prince Charlie until the Duke of Cumberland crushed the Young Pretender in the bloody Battle of Culloden in 1746. Thereafter Robert sought sanctuary in South Carolina. He became a successful planter and sided with King George III against the colonies, although two of his sons served in the Revolutionary Army. His grandson Edghill Burnside, disturbed by the growth of slavery in the Palmetto State, journeyed to Indiana, where he selected a home site in the newly staked-out town of Liberty. Returning to South Carolina, he married Pamelia Brown, the daughter of an Irish immigrant, on July 14, 1814. She was eighteen, he was twenty-four.

Edghill brought his young bride back to Liberty, where he built a log cabin on the quarter section of land he owned and began to farm. On May 23, 1824, his fourth child—a strapping boy—was born.

At first glance the child appeared still-born. But then Dr. Sylvanus Everts saw that the baby was having difficulty breathing. He tickled his nostrils with a chicken feather, thus provoking a spasm that set the lungs in motion. Pamelia Burnside was so grateful to Dr. Everts that she named the boy Ambrose Everts Burnside.

Ambrose grew to be tall, handsome in a florid way, strongly built and lithe. His complexion was fair, his eyes were hazel and he had begun to grow a singular facial adornment of thick brown whiskers which started beneath both ears, looping beneath his cheeks to pass his clean-shaven chin and end under his nose. It was as though his face had been garlanded on either side.

He was a good-natured young man, never witty or especially perceptive, but diligent and determined. He had hoped to attend Miami University in nearby Ohio, but after the death of his mother a few days before his seventeenth birthday, his father discovered that his family was too large and his income too small to bear such expense. He also needed financial help. So Ambrose was indentured to a tailor at Centreville fifteen miles away.

Ambrose accepted this comedown without complaint, carrying out his duties as shop errand boy with such good cheer and dispatch that he was soon promoted to a place on the sewing board as an apprentice. But he had no intention of remaining a tailor, even as a journeyman. He read constantly, his appetite for knowledge eventually surpassing his capacity for fun. Military history especially enchanted him. He loved to listen to stories from veterans of Jackson's campaigns or of Harrison's fights with the Indians.

His interest in war led to his appointment to West Point. Congressman Caleb Smith had come into his shop seeking repair of a torn coat. As Ambrose began to sew it, pausing frequently to study a tome on tactics, Smith cried, "You should be a cadet at West Point." Smith did not immediately wave the wand of the good fairy over Ambrose, but he did excite his ambition to be appointed to the Academy and when his father—now in the Indiana senate—learned that the education there was free he used all his influence to gain an appointment. It came in March of 1843.

Cadet Burnside became friendly with second-classman George McClellan. He was only a mediocre student himself and his fondness for fun and practical jokes earned him 198 demerits, only two shy of the expulsion level. In his second year, determined to improve, he was distinguished enough in drill to become a cadet-corporal.

In his final year it appeared that Burnside had sobered somewhat. He advanced to twelfth rank and was made a cadet captain. But then he was found to be AWOL—probably to Benny Haven's popular tavern on the Hudson, or else to court a young lady in town—and he was busted back to private. His rank declined again, and he was eighteenth when the Class of 1847 was graduated, singing:

> Doff the cadet and don the brevet
> And change the gray for the blue.

Ambrose Burnside was delighted to be assigned to the Second Artillery in Mexico City. But before he could get there the war was over. However, he did see action after being ordered in December of 1849 to join Braxton Bragg's battery at Las Vegas, New Mexico. After a party of Apaches and Eutaws ambushed a mail detail, killing ten Americans, Lieutenant Burnside's detachment was sent to the scene to bury the dead and bring in what mail he could recover. Later a group of about sixty Apaches appeared in Las Vegas hoping to exchange furs for ammunition. They were refused and rode away in anger. The fort's commandant sent Burnside after them with twenty-nine men on orders to arrest the chiefs. Riding through the rolling, broken countryside, the Americans overtook the Indians. Burnside was about to call upon them to surrender when they preempted his decision with a volley of arrows and musket balls. Burnside's bugler blew a charge and the Americans closed at a hand-gallop. Using their sabers only in the ensuing hand-to-hand fight, they killed about twenty braves and took three prisoners. American casualties were slight, with no one killed. Burnside, among those wounded by arrows, was commended for bravery.

In 1851 Burnside became absorbed in developing a new shoulder weapon. He had long been aware that the firearms used by the soldiers of Taylor and Scott were essentially no different from the arms fired at Yorktown and New Orleans, except that they were lighter. They were atrociously inaccurate, and it was a common army saying that to kill a single enemy other than by accident his weight in ammunition must be fired. Burnside's experiments produced a breechloader capable of rapid fire without overheating which was just as watertight as a muzzle-loader. At that point—December 16, 1851—he was promoted to first lieutenant and given a furlough. He immediately returned to Indiana, there meeting *the* woman.

She was from Kentucky, beautiful, well-bred, well-educated and charming. Burnside fell for her and asked her to marry him. She accepted. A wedding date was set and they soon stood together before a preacher. The critical question was put to Burnside, and he said: "I do." Then it was the lady's turn and she said, "I do *not.*" Unable to believe what he had heard, Burnside made every effort to change her mind, but she was adamant. So the handsome lieutenant retired from the scene, wounded again by an arrow, this time from the cruel bow of Cupid. (A few years later the same lady rode toward the church on her wedding day, accompanied by a prominent Ohio attorney, her bridegroom. He produced a pistol and told her that she would leave the church either as his wife or as a corpse. She married him.)

Lieutenant Burnside was more fortunate in romance after his assignment to Fort Adams in March 1852. There he met Mary Richmond Bishop of Providence, a tall, stately, quiet woman and the daughter of an army major. They were married April 27, 1852. Mary Burnside seems to have had some influence in calming Burnside's boisterous style and in smoothing the coarseness of his barracks-room tongue. He swore off profanity—at least in her presence—after she heard him curse out a delivery boy who broke a demijohn of wine he had planned to offer guests.

Now happily married, Burnside returned with zest to improving the breech-loading rifle he had invented. Congress was preparing to appropriate $100,000 for a breechloader, and among ordnance experts it was conceded that Burnside's was far superior to all others. It was probably because of this that he resigned from the army November 1, 1852, and turned, with capital provided by friends, to establishing a factory for the manufacture of the weapon in the quaint old town of Bristol, Rhode Island. Although he spent long hours at the Bristol Rifle Works, or in studying all available material on development in his field, he did not lose his love of soldiering, becoming a major general in command of the Rhode Island militia.

In 1857 he entered a competitive test of breech-loading rifles sponsored by the Ordnance Department. Actually the weapon was a carbine—a short-barreled shoulder weapon issued to mounted troops. Eighteen inventors submitted their carbines, but Burnside's was easily the best. He received an award of $10,000. Elated, he confidently expected the remaining $90,000 of the appropriation to be paid to him for making carbines. But only three hundred were ordered. He protested. A second test was held, and he won this one even more convincingly. Certain that this second endorsement would persuade Secretary of War John Floyd to release the money to him, he went to Washington. There friends broadly hinted that he would get the contract if he crossed certain palms with silver. Burnside was shaken. He had trained himself too long in rectitude to become an instant cheat. One day he told a West Point friend with whom he was sharing a hotel room that he would know his fate that night.

The friend recalled: "After midnight he came in, awoke me and said 'I am a ruined man! I met a man tonight, by appointment, and he informed me that if I would pay $5,000 I could get the award, otherwise not. I at once indignantly refused,'—and after a moment he added, 'there is but one thing that I regret, and that is, that I did not fell him to the ground!'"

It had not occurred to Ambrose Burnside that he might compromise his honor, but he was indeed a ruined man. Refusing all offers of financial help from friends, he went to New York, where he assigned everything he possessed—including letters-patent for his invention—to the creditors of the Bristol Rifle Works. Next, he walked into a Bowery secondhand clothing store and sold his uniform, sword and epaulets for thirty dollars. He added half of this to the twenty dollars in his pocket and sent it to his wife in Bristol. Then he wrote a letter to George McClellan, vice-president of the Illinois Central Railroad, explaining his predicament—and headed westward in search of a job.

Stopping at Liberty, he received an answer from McClellan inviting him to take the vacant position of cashier for the Railroad Land Office in Chicago. He accepted, soon sending to Bristol for Mrs. Burnside. To help reduce expenses, the couple lived with McClellan. Burnside also remitted the remainder of his salary to Rhode Island for payment of his debts, eventually meeting every obligation.

That was in April 1858. By June 1860 he had so impressed his employers that he was sent to New York City as corporation treasurer. There he met old friends, many of them Southerners who shocked him by their open—and sometimes venomous—threats of secession. "There will be no war," they said, in effect. "Northern men will not fight."

"You entirely mistake the character of the Northern people," Burnside replied. "They will fight. They never will allow the Union to be broken, and a free government to be thus destroyed without a contest."

On the fifteenth of April, 1861, with the cannon shots of Sumter reverberating all over the United States, Ambrose Burnside in New York received this message from Governor William Sprague of Rhode Island: "A regiment of Rhode Island troops will go to Washington this week. How soon can you come on and take command?"

"At once!" Burnside replied, and left that night for Providence to take command of those Rhode Islanders who formed the spearhead for McDowell's roundhouse right at Bull Run. By early January of 1862, now with a brigadier's star on his shoulders, he had assembled an invasion force of 13,000 troops and eighty ships. Twenty of these were light-draft gunboats armed with antiquated cannon salvaged from various navy yards. Sixty others dignified with the names of "transports" and "supply ships" were actually unseaworthy tugboats, converted barges, ferries and flat-bottomed river steamers collected from Northern rivers and harbors. Many of Burnside's soldiers were veteran New England seafarers who looked askance upon this conglomeration of wretched hulks, shaking their heads in dismay. What they did not realize was that these vessels had been chosen for the very reason of their light draft in order to enter the shallow waters of Hatteras Inlet. Burnside sought to reassure them by choosing the dinkiest of them all for his headquarters ship, which gesture of conciliation, after all, was only to promise them that he would be the first to drown. Actually, Burnside came very close to achieving that distinction. Clearing Hampton Roads on January 11, the fleet ran into a gale off Cape Hatteras the following night, and the rickety little headquarters boat nearly vanished in the trough of mast-high waves. But she rode out the storm to arrive off Hatteras Inlet the next morning.

There Burnside received another shock: the inlet was not eight feet deep at high tide but only six feet, meaning that many of his ships could not enter the lower sound to turn north for Albemarle. Fortunately, these same balky seafarers knew exactly what to do. They ran the larger ships full speed ahead until they were aground on the bar, and there, with the vessels secured by tugs and anchors, the racing current washed away the sand from beneath their bottoms. It was a time-consuming process, bumping them forward length by length, and while it continued, the Confederate commander at Roanoke sought desperately to improve the island's defenses.

The commander was Brigadier General Henry A. Wise, the same "brilliant fool" who as governor of Virginia had signed John Brown's death warrant. He was not now quite so foolish in his estimate that the 2,500 men holding Roanoke were insufficient and their defenses inadequate. He drove piles and sank hulks in the channel, calling on the district commander at Norfolk for more pile drivers, arms and soldiers. He was told to keep cool and work hard "with the troops you have," after which the naval commander seized all his work boats except one tug, turning them into a force of one-gun gunboats that Wise derided as "a mosquito fleet." Rushing to Richmond, he appealed to Secretary of War Judah Benjamin, then in deep trouble for having interfered in the Shenandoah Valley command of Thomas J. Jackson—now and forever known as "Stonewall." At that very moment Stonewall was composing his letter of resignation, which President Davis discreetly refused to accept. Thus, when Wise complained that there were 13,000 idle soldiers in Norfolk, the suave and rotund Benjamin replied with his customary bland smile and a polite suggestion that perhaps the district commander knew best. When word was received that the Federal fleet was poised outside the channel, he quickly got rid of Wise by ordering him back to his post. Returning to his headquarters at Nag's Head on the coast opposite Roanoke, Wise took to his bed with a severe attack of pleurisy, and he was still there when, on March 7, the Federal fleet began passing through the broad, eight-foot channel cut through the Hatteras Inlet bar.

To stop them, the mosquito fleet took station behind Wise's pilings, but as soon as the Federal warships bore down on them with nine-inch guns and 100-pounder rifles roaring, they scampered out of range, leaving the water batteries to maintain the island's defense. There were two of them, at the northern end of the island, and while they dueled the gunboats in a noisy, smoky, bloodless battle, the transports unloaded their troops midway up the ten-mile island's length. By midnight all the troops were ashore and the undefended southern half of the island was secured without firing a shot.

At dawn the defended northern half looked like serious business. Up its center ran a causeway flanked by "impenetrable" quicksand. Here the Rebels had placed a three-gun battery with infantry on either side. Burnside saw no alternative but to attack up the middle, while sending probing forces into the marshes. Immediately a murderous fire hammered his center force to the ground. But then there were heard Yankee whoops to either flank: the probers had successfully penetrated what was merely knee-deep ooze, and were even then assaulting Confederate gunners unable to turn their cannon against them. When the men of the center force arose, also whooping, to join the attack, the Rebel battery was overrun, and with that the Battle of Roanoke Island came to an end.

Casualties were light: for the Federals about 264 killed and wounded, for the Confederates 143. But the benefits for the Union were enormous. Not only had 2,675 Graybacks and 32 cannon been captured, but the blockade of the Southern coast had been screwed one thread tighter. Through skillful combination of land-sea forces the Union had armed itself with a truly fearsome amphibious whip: it not only opened a second front in Virginia's rear, while striking fear into the hearts of all the Confederate coastal commands, it had made it possible to sail right up to the back door of Norfolk, where the captured Federal navy yard was still busily engaged in building Rebel ironclads.

In the summer of August 1861 a Swedish inventor named John Ericsson wrote to President Lincoln offering to design and build an ironclad warship capable of wrecking the Rebel fleet in Norfolk.

In time, Ericsson's offer was accepted, although some naval officers scoffed at his plan for a ship with but two guns mounted in a revolving turret and a water line so low that it seemed any passing wave might sink her. One officer said that to worship Ericsson's model of his *Monitor* could not possibly be idolatry "because it was in the image of nothing in the heaven above or in the earth beneath or in the waters under the earth." Lincoln himself held the model in his hand and said: "All I have to say is what the girl said when she put her foot into the stocking. It strikes me there's something in it."

Before Ericsson went to work on the *Monitor,* however, the Confederate Navy had raised the sunken forty-gun U.S. frigate *Merrimac,** cov-

---

*The ship was renamed *Virginia,* but, perhaps because of the alliteration and rhythm in the phrase, "the *Monitor* and the *Merrimac,*" that is how she entered history.

ered her with four-inch iron plates, and fitted her prow with a formidable cast-iron ram. It did not seem that Ericsson's bizarre little toy could possibly oppose this big ironclad, and even as a tugboat began towing *Monitor* south from New York, *Merrimac* on March 8, the day after the fall of Roanoke Island, moved out of Norfolk against the wooden Union warships *Congress* and *Cumberland,* blasting and battering them into floating wrecks. *Minnesota,* also wooden, was forced aground. Next day she too would be smashed and the Rebel ironclad would be free to move on Washington.

Terrified Federal authorities nearly panicked, and no one was more frightened than Secretary of War Cameron. Now everyone in authority lamented the time and money wasted in the crackbrained *Monitor* experiment. Moreover, they asked, where is the *Monitor?*

She was limping south, storm-tossed. One fierce blow had sent black waves breaking over her low decks. Water tumbled down her blowers to swamp the engines, and Lieutenant John Worden and his crew hurriedly rigged hand pumps. Then a second storm threatened to part her towline. But at last *Monitor* made Hampton Roads and came to the side of stranded *Minnesota.* At dawn of March 9, 1862, *Merrimac* came out to finish *Minnesota,* and tiny *Monitor* sailed straight toward her.

Federal troops at Newport News cheered when the little raftlike Union vessel came at the big roof-shaped Confederate. Rebel sailors in the harbor laughed in astonishment at this upstart "cheesebox on a raft," this "tin can on a shingle," this David challenging Goliath two guns to eleven. Lieutenant Catesby Jones, acting captain of *Merrimac,* ordered broadside after broadside hurled at the little Yankee—but most of the Rebel shot screamed harmlessly over her low silhouette, or rattled off her turret like pebbles.

Inside that turret the Union sailors heard a monster metallic clanging, and some were stunned by the impact of the enemy shells. But they kept on firing their brace of 11-inchers. Each time the guns were withdrawn into the turret for recharging, metal stoppers were swung into place to seal the gun ports. Each time the turret began to revolve, the guns were fired "on the fly" for it was not possible to stop or reverse the turret once started.

Although the battle began at a mile range, the two ironclads gradually closed the distance until they were 100 yards apart, sometimes scraping up against each other. Once the *Merrimac* tried to ram. But her iron beak had been twisted off the day before, and she struck only a glancing blow which started a leak in her own armor. Next the audacious little *Monitor* tried to ram *Merrimac*! But she missed.

After four hours of inconclusive thundering, the two ships drew away. History's first contest between ironclad battleships had ended in a draw, although both sides claimed a victory. In a sense, the Union cause had been better served, for the menace of the *Merrimac* had been ended for good and the Union navy now had the time in which to build a fleet of ironclads.

24

■

Halleck and Buell

WHILE CONTINUING to build his Washington forces at his own deliberate speed—despite charges of vacillation from his critics and Horace Greeley's recovery of his nerve and renewal of his "On to Richmond!" cry—McClellan had also been busy reorganizing the war in the West, where there had also been little activity.

Frémont's old Department of the West, to which that part of Kentucky west of the Cumberland River had been added, was given to Henry W. Halleck to command, while the Department of the Ohio, including the remainder of Kentucky and all of Tennessee, was under Don Carlos Buell. They were responsible to McClellan, but not accountable to each other. Here would be the cause of much mischief, for both, being ambitious soldiers, would intrigue for the chief command, neither hesitating to impugn the other.

Three years older than Buell at forty-six, and with two stars his senior, Henry Wager Halleck was known in the United States Army as a fussy, intellectual sort of officer, nicknamed "Old Brains." He was born on January 16, 1815, the first of thirteen children on his father's farm in New York's Mohawk Valley. His father, Joseph, was a descendant of Peter Halleck, who migrated from Britain in 1640; his mother, Catherine Wager, was of German descent.

Henry lived on his father's farm for sixteen years, working hard during most of the time, but in 1831 he rebelled against the plow and ran away to live with Grandfather Wager. Wager sent him to Fairfield Academy in Hudson, and later to Union College in Schenectady. When Henry was twenty, his grandfather secured him an appointment to West Point. At the Academy he came under the spell of Dennis Hart Mahan, a disciple of Baron Henri Jomini, the Swiss military thinker who had served Napoleon. Jomini, horrified at the dreadful casualties of the Napoleonic Wars, and disgusted by the Corsican's costly frontal assaults, advocated what was by contrast careful, cautious "scientific" war. His ideal was an interior line of communications issuing from a strong base and lying between two wings of the enemy. Jomini also believed that occupation of strategic points was more decisive than destruction of the enemy's army, a radical reversal of objectives. To Halleck idolizing Mahan as he did, all this was gospel.

Graduated from West Point third in the class of 1839, he spent a year teaching French at the Academy, before being transferred to New York City to work on fortifications. There he wrote a paper for the Senate that caught the eye of Winfield Scott, who sent Halleck to France to study military history. One result of this sojourn was Halleck's *Elements of Military Art and Science,* largely a translation of Jomini's writings. But it was accepted as a textbook at West Point and had an immense influence among American army officers. During the Mexican War, Halleck was assigned to California, out of range of combat. In 1849, having studied international law, he helped form a firm that became one of the most successful in California. Five years later, he resigned from the army a wealthy man. In the following year he married Elizabeth Hamilton, the granddaughter of Alexander Hamilton. In August 1861 Winfield Scott recommended him for appointment as a major general in the regular army and he returned to service.

No one was less soldierly looking than Henry Wager Halleck. Balding, he wore heavy mutton-chop whiskers, and had a double chin. His complexion was olive and his skin hung so loosely on his face that it seemed to quiver when he talked. When excited or irritated, he crossed his arms to scratch his elbows. He was harsh and impatient with subordinates, when in conversation with them staring fish-eyed past them with his head held sideways. In essence, Halleck was an intellectual who preferred theory to action. His was a classroom mind bound by the book, incapable of innovation or improvisation, disdainful of the practical, never one "to get in there and fight." It was well said of him that he was "a vast emptiness surrounded by an education."

Buell was an unpleasant commander of a different order. Methodical, careful of detail, an excellent organizer, he seemed the very model of a professional soldier. Precise, he was also prim. Thirteen years in the adjutant general's office had done him no good, for he reveled in being "regulation," conforming to "the book," and doing things "by the numbers." Thus he detested the untidy. If a man was slovenly in his dress but could shoot and was brave, he saw only that he was out of uniform. He also had little use for volunteers and their officers, which was unfortunate since such troops made up all but a tiny portion of his command. Buell was no scholar like Halleck. Born in Lowell, Ohio, in 1818, he was graduated thirty-second in his West Point class of 1841. But he fought like a hero in Mexico, gradually earning a reputation as a good strategist and a brave soldier. Dark complexioned with an iron-gray mustache and pointed beard, his face was grim and his glance piercing. His icy reserve and contempt for volunteers did not endear him to his men. He was also humorless, although he did possess a peculiar parlor trick. At home with guests, this muscular general was fond of taking his wife by the elbows to place her on the mantelpiece—no mean feat when it is realized that the lady weighed 140 pounds.

Oddly enough, Buell had evolved a theory of war that was very close to the Jomini war that Halleck had learned at Mahan's feet. He believed an important campaign might be won by maneuver without a single major engagement. Battles should be fought only when success seemed certain. "War," he said, "has a higher object than bloodshed." This is pompous nonsense masquerading as insight. The purpose of war is to compel the enemy by force of arms to submit to your will, or to defend the homeland, or to exact vengeance. Bloodshed is no more an object than broken bones in football; it is a cost and consequence of war. Buell, then, seemed to be another of those Union generals who believed so earnestly in bloodless victories, war by maneuver, what Clausewitz called "rosewater war." Victory is won in battle, and battle can no more be bloodless than an omelet can be made without breaking eggs.

Instruction for both these commanders in the West were simple. Both were told to hold firmly all that had been gained in Missouri and Kentucky, and to make plain to the people that their purpose was to preserve the Union and not to abolish slavery. Halleck was directed to gather his troops "on or near the Mississippi, prepared for such ulterior operations as the public interests may demand," meaning Frémont's and Scott's dreams of descending the valley of the Father of Waters. Buell was ordered to mass for an invasion of East Tennessee, the dreamland of Abraham Lincoln with its numerous Union loyalists and the South's vital east-west railroad to the Transmississippi, their "hogs and hominy," as Lincoln called the Southwest. "My distress," wrote Lincoln, "is that our friends in East Tennessee are being hanged and driven to despair . . ."

Buell had at first been enthusiastic for this campaign, until he realized that to capture Knoxville he would have no railroads to haul supplies, but rather would have to depend on wagon trains moving over wretched roads and vulnerable to raiders. He rather preferred to move against Nashville in the center of the state because it was closer, the capital and a manufacturing and transportation center. It would also outflank the Confederate troops in East Tennessee, compelling them to withdraw so that Knoxville could be occupied unopposed.

McClellan was dismayed by this proposal, even though he saw that it was strategically sound and even brilliant. The president's desire to do something for the people of East Tennessee could not be easily ignored, nor could the chance to sever one of Virginia's supply arteries. Mulling it over, at the end of November he suggested to Buell that he attack both cities: with 15,000 men at Knoxville and 50,000 at Nashville. This meant a movement through western Kentucky by Halleck, to which Old Brains firmly replied: "I assure you, General, this cannot be done with safety at present."

In truth Halleck was busy cleaning up the mess bequeathed to him by Frémont: restoring order and discipline and putting an end to waste and corruption. His first inspection of his new command had convinced him that he did not have an army "but rather a military rabble."

He telegraphed McClellan: "Affairs in complete chaos. Troops unpaid; without clothing or arms. Many never properly mustered into service and some utterly demoralized. Hospitals overflowing with sick." It is also likely that Halleck was not enchanted with the prospect of assisting in an operation from which, if successful, Buell would gain most of the glory.

Buell meanwhile was facing much the same problems that tormented Halleck. He saw no chance of attacking in either direction, either at Knoxville or Nashville, much as McClellan and Lincoln kept urging him to move. Both generals promised action once their commands were reorganized. Halleck, meanwhile, was having difficulty with two of his subordinates: William Tecumseh Sherman and Ulysses S. Grant.

Sherman had succeeded Anderson when the Sumter hero's health failed. But then Sherman began to act strangely, given to melancholy broken by alternating fits of rage and fright. When it was remembered that he had told the secretary of war that at least 200,000 men would be needed to crush the Rebels in the Mississippi Valley, this "evidence of insanity" helped lead to his being superseded by Buell. Sent to serve under Halleck, his frantic warnings of approaching Confederate armies began to strum like a banjo pick on Old Brains's nerves. Halleck told McClellan that Sherman was "stampeded," but the general-in-chief put it plainer: "Sherman's gone in the head." So Halleck gave the frenetic redhead an indefinite leave of absence in hopes that a rest would calm him, and his wife took him back home to Ohio.

Grant was a different problem. He seemed to like a fight, a trait that the fussy Halleck—unlike his commander in chief—did not greatly appreciate. Twelve days before Halleck took command of his department, Grant had shown the kind of decisiveness that Halleck would regard as "chancy" or "impulsive."

Frémont had ordered him to make a demonstration against Polk in Columbus. Accordingly, on the sixth he put about 3,000 men, including a six-gun battery and cavalry, aboard four transports and steamed down the Mississippi protected by two gunboats. Nine miles below Cairo he tied into the eastern bank for the night. At two o'clock in the morning he was informed that Polk had ordered a strong force to destroy the column that he had sent to do the same to M. Jeff Thompson down near the Missouri boot heel. Within an hour Grant decided not to demonstrate opposite Columbus but to attack Belmont across the river, where the enemy force was reported to be assembling.

It was a bold decision, but based on faulty intelligence. Polk was not sending a column south but was still in Columbus in strength, and Belmont was not a staging area but only an observation post held by one regiment of infantry, half of whom were sick. At eight o'clock in the morning of the seventh, Grant's men came ashore three miles above Belmont while the gunboats slipped downriver to duel Polk's guns on the Columbus bluff. Forming battle lines, Grant's men began marching south.

By the time they reached Belmont they were under fire, and there was much more than a half-sick regiment to oppose them. Polk, learning of the attack, had sent four regiments under Brigadier General Gideon Pillow across the river as reinforcements. Nevertheless the Federals attacked with great élan, urged forward by Grant, riding from point to point of the forefront. Earlier in the war, Grant had learned a lesson in timidity. As a colonel commanding a regiment he had been ordered to move against Colonel Thomas Harris at a little Missouri town named Florida. As he neared Harris's camp on the brow of a hill, he recalled, "my heart kept getting higher and higher until it felt to me like it was in my throat. I would have given anything then to be back in Illinois; but I had not the moral courage to halt and consider what to do. I kept right on." Ascending the hill he found Harris gone. "My heart resumed its place. It occurred to me at once that Harris had been as much afraid of me as I of him. This was a view of the question I had never taken before; but it was one I never forgot afterwards."

He was still mindful of it at Belmont, leading his troops straight ahead, all six of his guns blasting away. There ensued a stiff, stand-up battle lasting two hours, when the Confederates finally broke in a panic, taking refuge on a narrow strip of mud beneath a steep low bank. To their surprise, the victorious Federals ignored them, gleefully plundering the Rebel camp while their officers on horseback delivered eulogies on the Union and encomiums on their bravery. But the battle was far from over. Polk, informed of Pillow's repulse, sent three more regiments across the Big Muddy, following to oversee the struggle himself. When these men arrived on the Belmont shore, the terrified men on the mud bank called out to them: "Don't land! Don't land! We are whipped! Go back!" Unfortunately for the Union cause, they were ignored. Meanwhile, Polk's artillery on the Columbus bluff had been pounding the looters in a camp now empty of Graycoats. Also, Polk's reinforcements under Brigadier General B. F. Cheatham had formed line of battle and were advancing. Grant with 3,000 men now faced Polk with 5,000. In disgust, Grant ordered the camp set afire and did what he could to reform his abashed plunderers and orators. When an aide rode up crying, "General, we are surrounded!," Grant replied calmly: "Well, we must cut our way out as we cut our way in." This was a little more difficult—as it usually is—but Grant managed to hold his command intact. He was the last man to board the last of the departing Union transports. When the skipper saw him sitting his horse on the riverbank, he put out a gangplank for him. Polk also saw him, telling his staff: "There is a Yankee. You may try your marksmanship on him if you wish." No one did, and Grant's horse—"seeming to take in the situation"—put its forefeet over the edge of the bank, tucked its hind legs under its rump, and slid down the bank to go trotting up the gangplank to the lusty cheers of the "Bluebellies."

Since Bull Run that had been the Rebel soldier's contemptuous word for Union cowards. But these men now used it like an accolade. They had fought and beaten the Graybacks, and though Belmont meant nothing strategically, psychologically it loomed large in the mind of the men of the West; and also to the nation and its commander in chief, both elated at giving the Confederates more than they got, and both delighted to read of the calm battle presence of a fighting commander with the captivating name of U. S. Grant.

25

■

U. S. Grant

OF ALL THE TOP COMMANDERS in the Civil War, U. S. Grant's American pedigree was certainly the longest, stretching back to Matthew and Priscilla Grant, a Puritan couple who arrived in Boston Harbor aboard the *Mary and John* in 1630. Matthew, whose diaries suggest a devout and perceptive man, was also industrious and ambitious, helping to stake out the town of Dorchester and later founding the town of Windsor, Connecticut, on the river of that name. He became both town clerk and surveyor, key positions which brought him influence and affluence, assuring his descendants of comfort and prestige in colonial society.

It lasted for more than a century, until his grandson Noah, the second Grant of that name, was killed fighting at Crown Point during the French and Indian Wars. From then onward the family fortunes declined, especially when the third Noah Grant turned out to be a wastrel, fond of a glass and a lass. Jailed for debt, he sold his farm to get out, migrating to Pennsylvania, where he met and married Rachel Kelly. She bore him five children and was pregnant with a sixth when the family moved farther west to East Liverpool, Ohio. There two more were born, one of them named Jesse, who became a prosperous tanner at Point Pleasant on the Ohio River. Jesse married Hannah Simpson, a girl of Irish descent, like his own mother. On April 27, 1821, their first child was born, a boy with reddish-brown hair, sunken blue eyes, pink-and-white complexion and weighing 10¾ pounds.

A Grant-Simpson family conference was held to name the child. There were many suggestions, but the outstanding ones came from Grandfather Simpson, who thought "Hiram" was a manly sounding name, and Grandmother Simpson, like Jesse an avid reader, who had read her son-in-law's copy of Fenelon's *Telemachus* and was fond of Ulysses, its hero. After a vote, Jesse announced that his son would be named Hiram Ulysses, although in practice everyone called him Ulysses or "Lyss."

Although Lyss had shown promise of growing into brawny manhood like his father, he turned out to be short and fat. At the age of two he was small and plump with dainty hands and feet. As he grew older he came to abhor the tannery his father had built in the neighboring town of George- town, drawn there by the rolling forests of oaks with their bark full of that tannic acid which turns animal skin into leather. The stench of the bloody hides lying in the lime vats filled with oak-bark liquor appalled Lyss, along with the buzzing of clouds of black flies. When he accompanied his father to the farms on hide-buying expeditions he put his fingers in his ears to shut out the horrible bellowing of terrified livestock being herded to the slaugh- ter. Crude though Jesse was, he did not regard his son's scruples as effemi- nate or fastidious. Actually, he doted on Ulysses, astonished as he was by the boy's two remarkable qualities: an incredible composure that he proba- bly received from his mother and an amazing understanding of horses.

Lyss's mystical communion with horses sometimes horrified neigh- boring mothers, who could not bear to look at the little fellow crawling among the feet of strange teams standing outside the tannery gate, stamp- ing their feet at the flies. Frequently he would hang on their tails, laughing, undaunted by their iron-shod hooves. When the housewives brought their fears to Hannah Grant, she nodded calmly and said: "Horses seem to understand Ulysses." Hannah was like that, quiet and composed, trusting unequivocally in God, unshakably convinced that everything would turn out all right. It seemed to her to be foreordained that her tiny son should stand there in the road, barefoot and in petticoats, gazing up rapturously into the faces of horses while ignoring the cries of his playmates beseeching him to join their games. As he grew older, Ulysses not only rode bareback but barefoot, standing grinning on the swaying back of a horse like any circus daredevil.

When Lyss was nine his father granted him his fondest wish, absolv- ing him from work in the tannery and giving him the regular job of wagon driver. This made him seem godlike among boys his own age. As wagon driver Lyss could use the team for bobsled rides, and his popularity soared with the girls as he sat among them with the whispering of the runners on the snow mingling with their shrieks and the tinkling of the sleigh bells. Girls liked Ulysses because he never smoked or "used bad words." One of them said later, "He was a real nice boy who never had anything to say, and when he said anything he said it short." Usually, Ulysses went with boys older than himself. He was shy in crowds, only talkative among his few intimates. Team sports he did not like, although he was well coordinated and known to be an expert swimmer able to outswim older and bigger boys.

Jesse's endless bragging about his precocious son often bored and annoyed his listeners, so much so that they cherished stories that would make Lyss look like a mean or dull boy. It was said that he hated grinding oak bark at the tannery so much that he would cajole other boys—and even girls—into doing it for twelve or fifteen cents a day while he was being paid a dollar or a dollar and a half for the job. When Jesse spoke glowingly of his prowess at arithmetic and especially mental arithmetic, it was said that besides horses that was all that he knew. His silence in crowds and his tongue-tied failures at public speaking were cited as signs of his stupidity, while his horror of bloodshed and refusal, as Lyss himself said later, "to eat anything that goes on two legs," were regarded either as "queer" or "squeamish."

In 1837 the resourceful Jesse was elected mayor of Georgetown and had begun to exert an influence on Whig Party politics reaching into Washington. His election coincided with a religious revival in the village, part of the evangelical fire that was then roaring and crackling across Ohio. For weeks the little Methodist church across the street from the Grant home resounded to stentorian voices breathing fire and brimstone, followed by the wild cries and ecstatic singing of as many as one hundred and fifty sinners in the Mourner's Bench. Such frenzies merely disgusted the hard-headed Jesse, but they appalled and embarrassed his devout and decorous wife. Hannah turned away from the sight of young men and women rolling and pitching in each other's arms while they "wrestled with the Devil," or the rows of mature women twitching and jerking in "the Penitent's Pen," struggling to free Satan's scorching fingers from their souls and howling like wolves in the famous "holy laugh" when they at last escaped his clutch. Fifteen-year-old Ulysses heard all this while lying quivering in his bed, repelled not so much by the tumult and the wailing as by the singing and the sound of music. As he grew up, music affected him adversely more and more. He never could tell tunes apart and once said that he knew of but two: "One was 'Yankee Doodle,' and the other wasn't." He had a peculiar nervous revulsion to all music, reacting toward it as a cultivated ear might be outraged by cacophony, and even at this stage of his life he "would go a mile out of his way rather than listen to the playing of a band." And yet, in two more years he would be living in a place where such sounds would violate his hearing daily and for hours at a time.

Jesse Grant first thought of sending his oldest child to the United States Military Academy during the Panic of 1836. With his finances shrinking and his family expanding, he was attracted by the free education there. In the spring of 1837, as the panic peaked, West Point seemed even more desirable; and then when Dr. George Bailey, Jesse's rival for prestige in Georgetown, sent his son Bart to the Academy it became irresistible. Jesse simply could not let Bart Bailey outshine Lyss Grant. So he began to use his political influence to get his own son appointed to the Military Academy as well. Then came great news: Bart Bailey had flunked out of West Point! He left the Plains at about the same time that Jesse received notice of his own son's appointment. Overjoyed, he told Lyss, only to be dismayed when a stubborn glint came into the boy's blue eyes and he said:

"But I won't go!"

Well, Jesse Grant allowed that he thought he would go, and as Ulysses recalled later, "I thought so, too, if he did."

He went, but with great reluctance. He was seventeen years old, stood one inch above the minimum requirement of five feet and weighed 117 pounds.

When Ulysses arrived at West Point he went to the adjutant's office to write "Ulysses Hiram Grant" in the register. He was immediately told there was no appointment for a cadet of that name. There was an Elihu Grant from New York and a Ulysses Simpson Grant of Ohio. Unaware that the congressman who made the appointment had forgotten his full name but had remembered his mother's maiden name, Ulysses patiently explained that he was the Ohio Grant. He asked to have the name corrected and was tartly told that only the War Office could change it. Having already juggled his name, being patient, Ulysses sighed and said: "The change of an initial makes no particular difference to me. My object is to enter the Academy as a cadet." When his classmates learned of the incident they gleefully pounced on the initials "U.S." and began calling him "United States Grant" or "Uncle Sam Grant" or "Uncle Sam" until finally he was just plain "Sam." Much derision also fell upon this diminutive country lad who had spent so much of his life on horseback that he walked with the heavy, slow-footed gait of a veteran horseman. Before he received his uniform, his rustic clothes and big-toed shoes so contrasted with the stylish dress of the Eastern and Southern boys that he became known as "Country Sam." Having no ear for music or rhythm whatsoever, the constant daylong drumming only upset him and he could not keep in step. Yet he was liked by his fellow plebes, who found him "entirely unselfish" and quiet but not reticent. They were impressed by his confidence and courage the day he knocked down big Jack Lindsay—a colonel's son who was the darling of the Academy staff—for shoving him out of line during drill. But the day that little Sam first mounted a horse he had the entire Academy at his feet. It was as though the horse and the rider were one, like the legendary centaur, half man and half horse. In his later years at the Academy the plebes would go to the riding hall just to watch Grant ride. "It was as good as any circus," one boy wrote. "There was a dark bay horse that was so fractious that it was about to be condemned . . . Grant selected it for his horse. He bridled, mounted and rode it every day at parade, and how he did ride! He handled the refractory creature as a giant would a child."

As a student Sam was mediocre, although he excelled in mathematics. He would be graduated twenty-first in a class of thirty-nine. But he did become president of the cadet literary society and by his senior year had thoroughly overcome his fear of public speaking. Actually, he was lazy, detesting classrooms and spending as much time reading romantic novels as in studying. Whenever a resolution to abolish West Point was introduced in Congress, he prayed fervently that it would pass so that he could go back home with honor. "A military life had no charm for me," he said, "and I had not the faintest idea of staying in the army even if I should be graduated, which I did not expect."

But he was, after one last triumph on horseback. The riding hall was thronged with spectators when the senior class held its graduation exercises there. Swords flashed and horses neighed and wheeled or leaped over the bar and then the seniors drew their mounts into line down the long tanbark floor, waiting . . . waiting for something special. . . . The sergeant riding-master walked onto the floor and fixed the bar over his head. There came a gasp from the crowd. The top of the hurdle!

"Cadet Grant," the sergeant called.

A slender cadet—now five feet seven but still only 117 pounds—rode from the ranks on a big, powerful, long-legged sorrel, galloping to the far end of the hall.

"He's on *York*," cadets whispered to their guests. *York,* the great horse of the stables, which only Sam Grant and one other cadet could ride. Now man and horse came thundering toward the hurdle, gaining speed. Sam could feel the muscles of the great beast gathering beneath him, and then they were into the air, up, up, up and over and across the breathless silence came the voice of the old sergeant: "Very well done, sir! Class dismissed!"

The top of the hurdle—five and a half feet or more than six feet, it is not now known which—but it stood as a record for twenty-five years, a momentous quarter century beginning with glory and greed in Mexico, gold and greed in California and ending with blood and tears from coast to coast.

■   ■   ■

At his first station in Jefferson Barracks, Brevet Second Lieutenant Grant became conspicuous for abstaining from the gay life in nearby St. Louis and for adopting studious, abstemious habits. He had been assured that he would be called back to West Point as a mathematics instructor as soon as a vacancy occurred. Forgetting his original intention to resign from the army, he buried himself in books, while friends such as James Longstreet were already planning to marry. One day he rode out to White Haven, the home of his roommate, Frederick Dent, to introduce himself to Dent's parents. Grant was now heavier, close to 140 pounds, and extremely hand-some. Little Emmy Dent was smitten, thinking: "He's as pretty as a doll." Mrs. Dent was charmed by this quiet, perceptive young man who "explains politics so clearly I can understand the situation perfectly," while Grant had the tact not to cross political swords with "Colonel" Dent, as this garrulous, slaveholding hater of Whigs and Abolitionists was called.

Eventually Grant met Fred's sister Julia, "as dainty a little creature as one would care to see, plump, neither tall nor short, with beautifully rounded arms, brown hair and brown eyes, and blonde and rosy complexion. She had a beautiful figure." She also had a slight squint in one of her eyes, a defect that Grant never seemed to notice for he became immediately attracted to her. They went on long rides and Grant frequently came back to barracks late for dinner, earning the enmity of the president of the mess, Captain Robert Buchanan, a crusty old Indian fighter and a martinet with his brains bound in braid. When "Old Buck" fined him a bottle of wine for the third time, Grant bristled and said if he were fined again he would refuse to pay. Infuriated, Buchanan cried: "Grant, young people should be seen and not heard, sir!" Thereafter the two men became enemies.

During the spring of 1844 the nation was sharply divided over the proposed annexation of Texas. Grant was opposed to it and was dismayed when he was ordered to join Zachary Taylor's Army of Observation waiting in Louisiana to enter the Lone Star State once it was admitted to the Union. He might have resigned, except that he thought that this would be akin to "showing the white feather." Before he left, he proposed to Julia. She was only nineteen and she knew that her Yankee-hating father would disapprove of marriage on this ground. So she cautioned her lover not to ask for her hand, while accepting his class ring as the symbol of their "secret" engagement. Grant rode back to camp overjoyed.

Life with Taylor's Army of Observation was a typically dull peacetime routine. Grant spent much of his time writing to Julia. After Congress voted to annex Texas on March 1, 1845, the observing army became an Army of Occupation, ready to enter the Lone Star State the moment Texas ratified the act on the Fourth of July. Grant was not at all deceived when the movement to Corpus Christi by Taylor's little army did not provoke the Mexicans to attack, nor was he surprised when President Polk ordered Taylor to move 150 miles deeper south to a point on the Rio Grande opposite the Mexican town of Matamoros. "We were sent to provoke a fight," he wrote later, "but it was essential that Mexico should commence it." And that was exactly what happened and the war that resulted was to the clear-eyed young lieutenant "one of the most unjust ever waged by a stronger against a weaker nation." Nevertheless, he remained a loyal soldier, obeying every order, even the distasteful one making him regimental quartermaster.

Yet at Palo Alto, Resaca de la Palma and Monterrey he left his safe position in the rear to take part in fighting at the front, where he was splattered with the blood and brains of slain comrades. After having fought in the northern wing of the American invasion, he became one of the few officers so blooded to march on Mexico City with Winfield Scott in the south. Once again the little quartermaster fought like any lion of the line, earning a shower of promotion and brevets that raised him to brevet captain with the permanent rank of first lieutenant. There was also praise from on high, but the sweetest came from his friend Longstreet, who remembered him as "always cool, swift and unhurried in battle . . . as unconcerned as if it were a hailstorm instead of a storm of bullets."

After the war, Grant on August 22, 1848, married Julia at a "sweet, old-fashioned wedding" held in the Dent winter home in St. Louis. Captain Longstreet was in the wedding party. Grant was sent to Detroit where he again became regimental quartermaster. Bored by this clerkly life, he observed: "I was no clerk, nor had I any capacity to become one." But the social life in this gay city of 20,000 souls pleased Julia until she became pregnant with their first child, born in 1850 and named Frederick Dent Grant.

There was much camaraderie in this tiny American army of 8,000 men, where everyone seemed to know each other, and as a consequence there was also much convivial drinking, in which Grant joined only modestly. No one was surprised when he entered the Sons of Temperance and swore off drink; and then, into this idyll came the shrill blast of the bugle again: the 4th Infantry was ordered to California. In the enlisted barracks there was much elation, with soldiers planning to desert for lucrative employment in the gold mines. Captain Grant was uneasily aware of this, as he was of the exploding cost of living on the West Coast. He could never afford to support his little family there, nor could Julia, pregnant once more, travel. So he left her and Fred behind in June of 1852, reporting to Governor's Island. There he found to his dismay that the 4th's commanding officer was Lieutenant Colonel Benjamin Bonneville, a crotchety, vain and choleric little man who disliked him because of "something that happened in Mexico" and that the regiment's senior captain was Old Buck Buchanan, him of the braid-bound brain. With this pair as superior officers, Grant's task as quartermaster, charged with supervising the movement of eight companies of men with their wives and children across vast and foreign seas and then through Panama's malarial swamps infested with vagabonds and epidemic with quick-killing cholera, would not be easy.

It was not. First, the War Office had at the last moment booked passage on the paddle wheeler *Ohio,* whose cabins and steerage were already filled with civilians. Quartermaster Grant was compelled to construct berths on deck for his charges, and also to assuage the friction between the irascible Bonneville and the *Ohio*'s skipper. His skill at smoothing over officers' quarrels earned him the sobriquet of "long-headed Sam."

Then as the soldiers debarked to begin the trek across the Isthmus of Panama it was found that the treaty with Panama forbade American troops to carry arms there. So Grant had to bring up all the regiment's weapons and ammunition, as well as all its other equipment and personal and official baggage. Paddled across the Chagres River by half-naked, cigar-smoking natives who made the nights hideous with their howling, drunken knife fighting, he next had to move overland through the monsoon and mud so deep that men stricken by cholera simply vanished. Along the way Grant buried his dead. Once at night, playing euchre, his friend Major John Gore coughed, dropped his hand and gasped: "My God, I've got the cholera!" Grant replied reassuringly, "No, Major, you've only eaten something that doesn't agree with you." A few hours later Gore was dead.

At last the horror seemed to have ended on the shores of the Pacific at Panama City, where the San Francisco steamer *Golden Gate* awaited them—but under quarantine. The insensitive Bonneville had put all the women and children and his infected regiment aboard. Grant leased an old hulk as a hospital ship, bringing to it the sick from the *Golden Gate.* Regimental surgeon Tripler denounced Bonneville for his "inhumanity" and was in turn threatened with a court-martial. Here long-headed Sam intervened. With Tripler, he persuaded Bonneville to move his men into a fresh-air camp while *Golden Gate* was fumigated. At last, on August 5, the regiment sailed.

Though emaciated and drawn, Sam Grant was strangely elated. He had not written an official word of what he had endured and done, but he knew in his heart that—come crisis, come catastrophe—he was fit to command.

Grant did not tarry long in San Francisco—where he was appalled at the prices, finding that even a cook could not be hired on a captain's pay—but moved on to the lonely splendors of Fort Vancouver in Washington Territory. He began to despair of ever bringing Julia west and thought of resigning to farm Julia's sixty acres; he also forsook his oath as a Son of Temperance and began to drink. As a friend said, "he was not by any means a drunkard," but rather given to two- or three-day sprees two or three times a year, and when friends pleaded with him to stop he would do so. His spirits were somewhat revived when in mid-September of 1853 he was promoted to captain and ordered to take command of Company F at Fort Humboldt in northern California.

Unfortunately, his old enemy Buchanan was now a colonel commanding the regiment. When he saw Grant tipsy at the paymaster's table he gave him the option of resigning or facing a court-martial. Grant quit—on the very day that his captain's commission finally arrived from Washington— "to go farming."

Leaving the army did not end Grant's ordeals and failures. Without money to buy seeds and equipment to plant Julia's sixty acres, he sold firewood in St. Louis instead. He soon became a familiar figure in the city, sitting on his wagon in his faded overcoat of army blue. He was not the least ashamed of his predicament, chatting easily with those officers who could not conceal their embarrassment to see him, as they thought, so destitute.

He built himself a house from logs he cut and squared himself, and called his place "Hardscrabble Farm," a sly dig at the high-falutin names which the wealthier families in the area had given to their homes. It was indeed a hardscrabble, a bare subsistence existence that Grant was tugging out of the soil. He appealed to his father for financial help, but Jesse wasn't listening, concerned as he was by the panic of 1857. In that year, Grant realized that his wheat planting, so far from yielding an anticipated four or five hundred bushels, would produce only seventy-five; and his corn and oats, while good, were not worth hauling to town because the panic had so depressed prices. At Christmas he pawned his gold watch and chain to buy presents for his family. In the following February a fourth child—a son—was born, and in the following spring he rented Hardscrabble to another farmer and leased White Haven from his father-in-law, who, now a widower, went to live in the city. But here also he failed, and the excuse of cold weather and poor prices could not sustain his sinking self-esteem.

White Haven had to be sold, and Hardscrabble would have followed, except that Grant traded it for a house and lot in St. Louis where he tried his hand at real estate—and failed again. When the job of engineer for St. Louis County at $1,800 a year opened up, his friends sought to secure it for him—but it went to someone else. Sam Grant's coat of army blue was now almost bleached white, his slouch hat was formless, its brim pulled down low over his eyes as though he were shutting out the world. Actually, he was shutting himself *in*. He was anguished by the open talk of disunion he heard from his Southern friends, appalled to hear Northern ministers calling for rivers of blood to avenge the execution of John Brown. He was a man without a job, without an income, without a party even—and without a future.

Sadly, but with gratitude, he accepted his father's offer to join his brothers in the Galena retail store in which his father was a partner. It could have been worse, he thought, boarding ship for the trip upriver—it could have been the tannery.

Ulysses was not an employee of J. R. Grant being paid a fixed salary. He was an equal with his younger brothers, Simpson and Orvil, and their cousin, W. T. Burke. His job was with the ledgers, keeping the store supplied and billing customers.

Few of the customers at J. R. Grant knew that he was around, while for the people of Galena he might have been an invisible man. All that was remembered of him was that once, before his family joined him, he quietly entered a tavern favored by lawyers, listening to them discuss a current case. One of them noticed him and they began to exchange guying small talk.

Finally, the lawyer said, "Looks as though you might have been through hell," to which Grant replied, "I have."

"Well, how did you find things down there?"

Grant grinned. "Oh, much the same as in Galena—lawyers nearest the fire."

After Sumter Grant said to Orvil, "I think I ought to go into the service," but he turned down a militia command as beneath a former captain in the

Regular Army. He did, however, help train the Jo Daviess Guards from Galena, accompanying them to Springfield. While there his friends sought to influence Governor Richard Yates to make him a colonel. But Yates was unimpressed by the quiet, modest little professional in civilian clothes, not at all like the crowd of boastful command-seeking politicos in gorgeous uniforms who besieged him daily. Eventually, however, his military aides made him aware of Grant's abilities, and he gave him command of Camp Yates, outside the capital. There Grant could scarcely conceal his contempt for the undisciplined volunteers and their unmilitary custom of electing their own commanders. He repeatedly refused to "run" for colonel of regiments that promised to elect him. This puzzled Yates at first, but when he became aware of the professional pride that motivated it he offered Grant command of the Seventh District Regiment. Grant accepted, even though he was aware that this formation, known as "Yates's Hellions," was the worst in Illinois. Barefoot farm boys who were both undrilled and un-uniformed, these so-called soldiers mutinied over bad bread, burned their guardhouse and insulted their officers, while robbing surrounding farms by day and drinking themselves inebriate by night. They told the governor they would not reenlist for three-year hitches on June 15 unless he fired their idiot colonel. Yates obliged, and gave them Grant.

"What a colonel!" they cried in derision when Grant came among them dressed in an old coat worn out at the elbows and a dingy plug hat. "Look at the little 'un! Damn such a colonel!"

To humiliate him, some of them began to shadowbox behind him. By accident Grant received a powerful blow on his back that knocked off his hat. He retrieved it amid a shocked silence, dusted it off and put it back on his head. Then he turned on these so-called soldiers with that silent stare which had such astonishing power to intimidate. They became uneasy. Some of them rushed up to apologize. Grant said nothing, but his later actions—getting them fed and clothed and drilled—were far more eloquent than words.

At last reenlistment day arrived. Accompanied by Generals John A. McClernand and John A. Logan, both political generals from the Democratic Party, Grant confronted his men. He was not happy. He had planned to appear in a handsome new uniform and his war horse, Rondy, both of which he had bought with borrowed money. The uniform had arrived in time, but not Rondy; and it was only at the last moment that a hare-brained cousin had arrived with a showy livery horse. Despising his mount, aware that he would have to pay for it, as well as the cousin's trip from Galena and back,

Grant was fuming while McClernand and Logan exhorted his men to reenlist.

"Speech!" the men cried as their disgruntled colonel trotted before them. "Speech!"

Grant was in no mood for exhortation, but his eyes did narrow in that steady stare, and he snapped: "Men, go to your quarters!"

His men blinked and exchanged glances. What a speech! Here were no honeyed words of blandishment or golden promises. Here was no ring-tailed roarer spouting death and destruction on Dixie like a dragon spitting flame. Yet, the Little 'Un did speak "as one having authority," and they marched back to their camp to reenlist "almost to a man."

· 26

■

Movement in the West:
The Capture of Fort Henry

I N WASHINGTON in that fall of 1861 George McClellan was still busying
himself with reviews. On the twentieth he put on the grandest of all at
Bailey's Crossroads. It was vintage McClellan: seven full divisions with
cavalry and cannon, a force 75,000 strong, marching in fine array behind
bands playing stirring martial airs, before the customary throng of important
spectators, ladies waving their handkerchiefs, politicians reverently placing
their hats over their hearts as Old Glory went waving by.

But this time it had a reverse effect. Congressmen still ashamed of
Bull Run and Ball's Bluff—perhaps even more so by the travesty of the
Quaker gun at Munson's Hill—were beginning to wonder aloud if such a
fine body of men as the Army of the Potomac could not at last put off
parading and begin to fight. When Lincoln discovered that McClellan had
no plans to move south as he hoped before the onset of winter, he devised
a plan of his own: a simultaneous frontal and flanking attack. McClellan put
it on ice for ten days and then returned it with the polite objection that it
would not work. Besides, he informed the president, he was beginning to
evolve a plan of his own. Buell's refusal to move against Knoxville to put
himself on Joe Johnston's flank had prompted McClellan to abandon any idea
of a direct march south. Instead he decided to make an amphibious move
down the Potomac to Chesapeake Bay and thence south to the mouth of
the Rappahannock, sailing up that river to a landing at Urbanna on the south
bank. This would cut his marching time in half and put him in Johnston's
rear only fifty air miles from Richmond.

It was a beautifully simple plan which took advantage of the superiority of the U.S. Navy. Best of all it was bloodless. "I have no intention of
putting the army into winter quarters," Little Mac declared confidently. "I
mean the campaign will be short, sharp and decisive." Soon, however, the

231

enormous logistic problems of moving 150,000 men by water—especially the difficulty of assembling transports secretly so that Johnston would not suspect such a movement—overcame even McClellan's organizing skills. "I am doing all I can to get ready to move before winter sets in," he wrote his wife, "but it now begins to look as if we were condemned to a winter of inactivity." With that, the rains came, making the roads axle deep in mud, turning the fields into quagmires and drowning the Urbanna Plan. And then McClellan fell ill of typhoid fever and his chief of staff, Brigadier General Randolph B. Marcy, who was also his father-in-law, was sick as well.

Lincoln despaired. On the last day of 1861 he asked Buell and Halleck if they were cooperating. When they replied in the negative, Lincoln wrote on the back of Halleck's letter: "It is exceedingly discouraging. As everywhere else, nothing can be done." Wiring both generals to meet immediately, he went to the office of Quartermaster General M. C. Meigs, complaining: "General, what shall I do? The people are impatient; Chase has no money, and tells me he can raise no more; the General of the Army has typhoid fever. The bottom is out of the tub. What shall I do?"

There was no answer, and indeed none was expected. Lincoln knew that the bottom was not really out of the tub, and he also knew what to do. Since his inauguration he had spent many midnight hours reading military history and theory, poring over maps, and this together with his conversations with professionals had finally given him a grasp of what was necessary. In a letter to Buell he explained that the Union had superior numbers and superior facilities for moving them, and that therefore the objective should be to strike the enemy at different points at the same time. If the enemy weakened one point to strengthen the other, then it was the weaker of the two that should be attacked. In essence this was the basis of Scott's Anaconda Plan, and the president had grasped it. He also sensed, after suffering so many snubs from McClellan, and then being denied admission to his sick room when so many others were admitted, that Little Mac was definitely not the man. He would say this in so many ways: "He has got the slows." "If McClellan does not wish to use the army, I would like to borrow it." What was needed was a dedicated, dogged killer, a general willing to take risks and to accept casualties if, in so doing, he was whittling his inferior foe.

But where?

In the West there was such a general, but he wore gray. He was Albert Sidney Johnston, the ranking Confederate officer in the field. Born in Washington, Kentucky, February 2, 1803, Johnston had been graduated from

West Point eighth in the class of 1826. While there, he had renewed his friendship with Jefferson Davis, two classes below him, whom he had known earlier at Transylvania and who would always admire him with a fervor bordering on hero worship. Johnston was a big man, over six feet tall, broad-shouldered, and slightly under two hundred pounds. He was also handsome, with a noble brow, thick wavy brown hair touched with gray, wide-set dark eyes and a shaven bold jaw beneath a heavy guardsman's mustache. For all of his commanding presence, Johnston was a man of gentle manners and great personal charm, blessed with a sense of humor rare among generals. It was he who said there was "too much tail" to Frémont's kite.

Johnston had had an amazingly varied and colorful career: veteran of the Black Hawk War, revolutionary fighter in Texas and Sam Houston's first secretary of war, gentleman farmer like Davis, Mexican War colonel, U.S. Army paymaster and commander of the famed 2nd Cavalry Regiment. Zachary Taylor said that he was the finest soldier he ever commanded, and Winfield Scott called him "a Godsend to the Army and to his country." In 1861 Johnston was a brevet brigadier general in command of the Pacific Coast, but with the secession of Texas—his adopted state—he declined an offer of high rank in the Federal service and led a group of thirty like-minded Southern officers on horseback across the desert to Galveston. Arriving by ship in New Orleans, he was hailed like a savior and his trip to Richmond by train was a triumphal progress. Davis was waiting at the end of the line, handing him his lofty commission as commander of the Western Department.

"I hoped and expected that I had others who would prove generals," Davis said later, "but I knew I had *one,* and that was Sidney Johnston." Still later he called him "the greatest soldier, the ablest man, civil or military, Confederate or Federal, then living."

Johnston needed all these qualities to maintain a line stretching five hundred miles from eastern Kentucky across the Big Muddy into Arkansas, trailing off somewhere in Indian Territory. It was menaced by two Union armies—Halleck's and Buell's—each larger than his own, and penetrated by navigable rivers, chief among them the Mississippi, Tennessee and Cumberland, over which the superior enemy navy could rapidly move troops from point to point.

To defend this line Johnston had scarcely 50,000 men, but he was fortunate in being served by some very fine subordinates. In the Transmississippi, his left or western flank, the rivalry between Price and McCulloch was settled by placing Major General Earl Van Dorn, a West Pointer from

Mississippi and a man of considerable fire and dash, over both of them. On his right or eastern flank he positioned Brigadier General Felix Zollicoffer, a former Tennessee newspaper editor and congressman, with his little army of recruits to guard the vital Virginia-Tennessee Railroad and the passes leading down to Nashville. In Nashville itself he found Simon Bolivar Buckner offering his services, and he gave him two regiments and a star and sent him to Bowling Green, where he was joined and superseded by another West Pointer, Georgia-born Major General William J. Hardee, forty-six, once the commandant of cadets at the Academy. Gideon Pillow, who had crossed swords with Grant at Belmont, became second in command of Hardee's Army of the Center.

Johnston had three outstanding Kentuckians to help him gain control of his native state. The oldest was George B. Crittenden, forty-nine, a West Pointer and the son of that Senator Crittenden who had struggled so earnestly to avert the war. He was dispatched to the Cumberlands with headquarters in Knoxville. The other was John C. Breckinridge, only forty but already one of the most distinguished men of the Confederacy. He had been Buchanan's vice-president, had been the runner-up to Lincoln in the Electoral College, and presided over the joint session of Congress that proclaimed Lincoln the president. Afterward elected to the Senate, his opposition to the war brought a warrant for his arrest. Breckinridge arrived inside Buckner's lines as a fugitive, informing his fellow Kentuckians: "I exchange with proud satisfaction a term of six years in the Senate of the United States for the musket of a soldier." Instead, Johnston gave him a brigade, even though he was without military experience.

Johnston's line east of the Mississippi had Polk on the left at Columbus with 16,000 opposing Grant around Cairo with 20,000; Hardee in the center at Bowling Green commanding 22,000 confronting Buell below Louisville with 45,000; and Zollicoffer on the right had 4,000 in front of Cumberland Gap arrayed against Brigadier General George Thomas with 8,000. Although Halleck's army now numbered 91,000, most of them were in St. Louis out of striking range except for Grant's 20,000. Perhaps even worse than being outnumbered, Johnston had to contend with the Tennessee and Cumberland rivers flowing parallel to pierce the center of his line like highways. His predecessors had moved to block this threat by building Fort Henry on the right bank of the Tennessee and Fort Donelson on the left bank of the Cumberland. The forts, begun during Kentucky's period of "neutrality," had necessarily been chosen south of the Bluegrass border, just twelve miles apart. Work on these positions had been fitful, due to much argument among the engineers. Johnston tried to improve them by sending Brigadier General Lloyd Tilghman, another West Pointer who had gone into civilian life to become a highly successful engineer. Meanwhile Johnston appealed to Alabama and Georgia for reinforcements. "Our own coast is threatened," Alabama replied, while the long-white-bearded Governor Joe Brown of the Peach State, who took the theory of states' rights a little too seriously to suit Jefferson Davis, was more emphatic. "It is utterly impossible for me to comply with your request." Turning to his friend in Richmond, Johnston sent a messenger to Davis with an urgent request for help. "My God!" Davis cried in consternation. "Why did General Johnston send you to me for arms and reinforcements? . . . Where am I to get arms or men?"

Johnston was dismayed at Davis's reply that he must rely on his own resources. He knew how slim they were, and he knew also that he had been openly boasting of his strength in an effort to bluff the Yankees. It had worked with the high-strung Sherman, but not with the phlegmatic Buell. Now, Johnston realized, with reverses coming down the road, his critics would wonder how he could do so little with so much.

Crittenden in Knoxville had ordered Zollicoffer with about 4,000 men to move seventy miles north to Mill Springs on the south bank of the Cumberland. He did, but then, to Crittenden's dismay, he moved across the river to Beech Grove on the north bank and set up camp there. Crittenden immediately ordered him to return to the south bank. But he stayed where he was and when Crittenden arrived to question him, he explained that Beech Grove afforded a better campsite. He added that the Yankees were approaching and to fall back would seem cowardly. Crittenden was horrified. To put a broad river between yourself and your enemy was not cowardly but wise; while to put yourself in front of the same stream was not bravery but stupidity. When he heard that George Thomas was leading the oncoming Bluebellies his horror mounted.

Thomas was a Virginian who had remained loyal to the Union, and although Southerners might denounce him as a traitor, they could not deny the ability of a man who had been a major in Johnston's 2nd Cavalry and was widely respected as a solid unshakable soldier. Crittenden now assumed command. Realizing that he dared not be caught retreating across the Cumberland, he did what he could to prepare Zollicoffer's troops for the imminent shock.

But what came was not battle but a week of steady, pelting rain. Even though it broadened the river to the Rebel rear, it also made the roads to their front impassable and the creeks and brooks swollen and overflowing.

On January 17, finding his men bogged down in "a continuous quagmire," Thomas went into camp at Logan's Crossroads, nine miles above Beech Grove. Thomas's position was on both sides of Fishing Creek. This seemed to Crittenden a highly vulnerable arrangement, and he decided to make a surprise dawn attack on the Union left, and then, having destroyed or routed it, turn to vanquish Thomas's right. On the night of the eighteenth the Confederates moved out, a driving rain wind-blown in their faces, jagged streaks of lightning fleetingly illuminating the ghostly, water-soaked woods around them and the ubiquitous mud clutching at their feet and sometimes sucking off their shoes.

At dawn of the eighteenth Thomas sent out a cavalry patrol. They came riding back shouting that they had run into skirmishers of a large enemy column. Then the Union pickets came tumbling back, firing as they did—after which the Graybacks became visible through the rain, their soaked uniforms heavy with mud.

Although Crittenden had not surprised his enemy, he pressed forward with Zollicoffer leading the attack. At first, the Federals recoiled from the Confederate rush. But the Rebels had entered battle weary from that miserable night march, and that last burst of energy had exhausted them. Worse, wet flintlocks would not fire and those units armed with them had to be sent to the rear. Meanwhile the unruffled Thomas had brought reinforcements from his right across a creek not nearly as high as Crittenden had imagined. At this point, Zollicoffer, conspicuous in a white rubber raincoat, was shot dead by a Union colonel he had mistaken for one of his own officers. News of his death brought a keening wail from the throats of his hard-pressed men. They had been fond of him, in spite of his rashness, perhaps even because of it. Then, like the Bluebellies at Bull Run, they raised the cry: "Betrayed!"—breaking and running in a panic that infected Crittenden's entire command.

Thomas prepared to give chase, but the Rebels were so far down the road that he could not overtake them before night fell. Under cover of darkness they crossed the Cumberland on a dilapidated stern-wheeler which they burned against the southern bank. In the battle known variously as Mill Springs, Logan's Crossroads or Fishing Creek, the Confederates lost 125 killed, 309 wounded, and 90 missing for a total of 534. Thomas's casualties were 39 killed, 209 wounded and 15 captured or missing for a total of 263. The Federals also captured twelve guns, 1,000 horses and mules, 150 wagons and half a dozen regimental colors.

Mill Springs was only a minor battle when compared to the dreadful struggles that would ensue with the growing strength and skill of the adversaries, but it was still the first Confederate defeat. A scapegoat was sought to soothe Southern pride, and the logical victim was Crittenden. It was remembered that his brother was a Union general and charged that he was drunk throughout the battle. Although the South had no Joint Committee to throw him into jail as the North had done to Stone, a court of inquiry found him guilty of intoxication, reducing him to colonel and sending him into the Limbo of the Transmississippi.

That was much later. At the moment, Albert Sidney Johnston was disturbed to learn that his fear of reverses had been so quickly realized. His right flank was broken. Where would the Yankees strike next?

After being bedridden with the measles for four days, Henry Wager Halleck was back at his desk, his restless brain turning again, his fingers gently scratching his elbows. When the news of Mill Springs arrived the scratching turned agitated. Halleck instantly remembered what Rosecrans had done for McClellan in western Virginia, how Little Mac's star shot up like a rocket afterward. Had Thomas done the same for Buell, his rival? Mill Springs was far more significant than Rich Mountain and Laurel Hill. It had opened the way into east Tennessee, Abraham Lincoln's land of heart's desire. Buell might get the West! What to do to send his own star soaring?

The answer came that same day when U. S. Grant reported his return to Cairo after demonstrating opposite Polk in Columbus. Halleck immediately ordered Grant to come to St. Louis. The interview fell flat. While Grant outlined a general forward movement, Old Brains stared at him cold and fish-eyed in obvious distaste. It was not that Halleck disliked Grant, he merely distrusted him. He was rash, like Nathaniel Lyon—yes, like Zollicoffer even. Grant returned to Cairo "very much crestfallen." He felt like a small boy trying to remember what he might have done to displease his father.

At Cairo he found a report from Brigadier General Charles F. Smith, who had demonstrated up the Tennessee while Grant pretended to strike Columbus. Grant was fond of old "C.F." He had been commandant of cadets when Grant was at West Point. A veteran of thirty-five years service, he was the epitome of the pre-war regular army officer. Tall, slender and ramrod-straight, with pink cheeks and clear blue eyes, great white mustachios dropping down either side of his chin, he was a strict disciplinarian and a terror of volunteer officers. Grant, who outranked him, always felt that "it does not seem quite right for me to give General Smith orders." But this never bothered Smith, and he was frankly proud of his former pupil.

Now, in his report, he told Grant: "I think two ironclad gunboats would make short work of Fort Henry."

Grant was electrified. Here was something specific, the sort of solid objective that Halleck might have been looking for. At once he wired St. Louis: "With permission, I will take Fort Henry on the Tennessee, and establish and hold a large camp there." Halleck was delighted. While sick he had been contemplating an advance up the Cumberland and Tennessee, and had told McClellan it should be undertaken by no less than 60,000 men. Grant had barely a third that number, but Halleck liked the terse, confident tone of his telegram and quickly granted him permission to move. Fort Henry being in Tennessee, he did not neglect to wire McClellan: "I respectfully suggest that that state be added to this department." Finally, he curtly informed Buell of his decision, so shaking him that he at once informed McClellan: "I protest against such prompt proceedings." With the last round in this high-level game of one-up-manship going to Halleck, Grant on February 3 with twenty-three regiments began moving up the Tennessee.

The Union commander in St. Louis would have been even happier if he had read Lloyd Tilghman's reports to Johnston on conditions at Forts Henry and Donelson. In a splendid understatement he said "(I) do not admire the aspect of things," asking for more troops, muskets for his unarmed men and heavy guns. Neither of the forts was actually completed, and Henry situated on low ground on one side of the river was dominated by a height across it and subject to flooding when the river rose. Said Tilghman: "The history of military engineering records no parallel to this case."

Johnston did what he could so that Tilghman eventually had 5,700 men: 3,400 at Henry and 2,300 at Donelson. He also sent Pillow to Clarksville within supporting distance of the forts, while Floyd and Buckner were dispatched to Russellville midway between Pillow and himself. Finally he wired Tilghman: "Occupy and intrench the heights opposite Fort Henry. Do not lose a moment. Work all night."

Grant's invasion force was led by four spanking new ironclad gunboats. They were built by James B. Eads of Indiana at his own expense, and designed by him especially for river fighting. They were 175 feet long and 50 feet in the beam. Overlapping plates of armor two and one-half inches thick were bolted to the bows for protection from head-on fire and the sides were sloped at thirty-five degrees to deflect shells. Their own armament was of thirteen guns: three at the bow, two at the stern and four on each side. In spite of all this weight of metal they were extremely maneuverable.

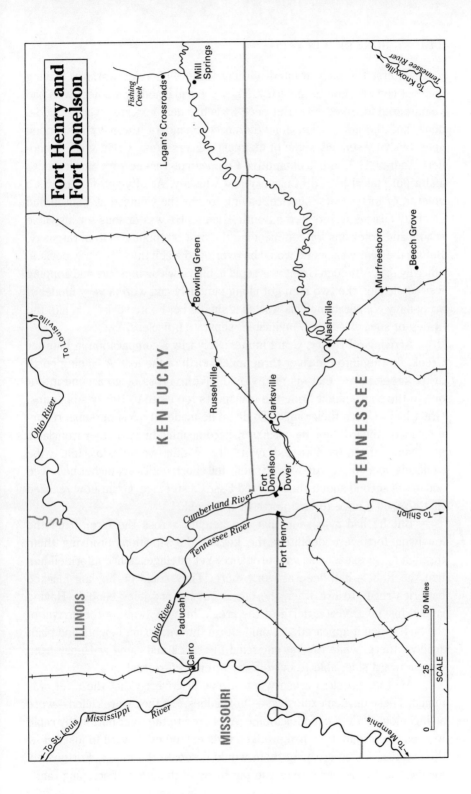

Fort Henry and Fort Donelson

At first the navy wanted nothing to do with river warfare, leaving gunboat construction to the army. They were manned by soldiers who had volunteered for river duty. But once Eads had demonstrated what could be done, and the army asked for veteran commanders, the navy responded generously by sending some of its finest officers West. Grant got Commodore Andrew H. Foote, a diminutive Connecticut Yankee with burning eyes and a puritanical hatred of slavery and whiskey. At fifty-six, Foote was a veteran of forty years' service, having fought the Chinese at Canton and gleefully chased slavers in the South Atlantic. He was famous for his Bible school and notorious for commanding the first teetotaling ship in the navy. Before the year was out he would be overjoyed when the U.S. Navy became officially dry. Although Grant was tepid in his views on bondage and sopping wet on alcohol, the two men got along famously and were a very model of army-navy cooperation. This was as it should be, Foote said: " . . . like the blades of shears—united, invincible; separated, useless."

Arriving off Henry, Grant immediately saw a complication in Panther Creek, flowing into the river three miles north of the fort. A landing north of the creek meant that his men would have to cross or go around it, but one to the south might bring the transports too close to Henry's big guns. Grant had to learn their range. To do so he made a typical personal reconnaissance. Aboard the gunboat *Essex,* accompanied by two other ironclads, he steamed up to the fort to draw its fire. Within two miles of Henry, the ironclads opened fire. Answering shells fell short, until a six-incher bellowed and on its second shot a shell pierced Essex's steerage. Grant now realized that he would have to land north of the creek.

But he had also seen that the heights across the river from the low-lying fort were definitely the key to the situation. Studying them through his glasses, he saw no ordnance. Yet intelligence had informed him that the Rebels had been at work there. They could be holding masked batteries ready to fire when the target got big and juicy enough. Having landed his 1st Division north of the creek, he was awaiting the arrival of the 2nd. When it appeared, it would storm the west-bank heights and plant artillery there, while the 1st encircled the creek and came at Henry from the landward side, able to cut off any attempted retreat.

Another problem arose when it was discovered that the river was mined. These unseen explosives—"torpedoes," as they were called—were an ingenious variety of contact mine. Anchored to the river bottom by cable to keep them rigid, they had pronged rods extending upward to just below the surface. A ship scraping them would detonate the mines. Fortunately for the Union, the rising river had put many of them out of scraping range

and torn others loose from their cables. One of these had been fished out
of the water by a gunboat crew and the curious Grant and Foote came
aboard to inspect it. Five feet long and a foot and a half in diameter, its rod
extending from its head like the horn of a unicorn, it looked dangerous
enough. Grant asked how it worked, and the ship's armorer got to work
with his tools. Suddenly an ominous hissing sound issued from the device.
At once the spectators exploded in every direction, some hitting the deck,
some running for dear life. Foote and Grant headed for the ship's ladder,
Foote in the lead. At the top, just as the hissing stopped, Foote turned with
a sly smile.

"General, why this haste?"

"That the navy may not get ahead of us."

Lloyd Tilghman was a well-born Marylander who had been graduated as far
down as forty-sixth in the West Point class of 1836. His low rank may have
led him to decide against becoming a professional soldier; instead he entered civilian life to begin a successful career as an engineer, returning to
service as a volunteer general's aide during the Mexican War and again
when he put on Confederate gray as a brigadier general. Slim and dark-
skinned, with a carefully groomed black mustache and narrow beard that
effectively hid his mouth and chin, his piercing black eyes suggested a
decisive and resolute personality. But as he watched the enemy buildup
across the river and on land to his left flank, his resolution could not quite
overcome his misgivings over his predicament.

His 3,400 men were armed with miserable weapons: hunting rifles,
shotguns and antiquated flintlocks. His guns were no better, two of them
having burst in target practice, and others condemned as more dangerous
to their crews than the enemy. Torrential rains that had begun in mid-
January had caused the Tennessee to rise fourteen feet, demonstrating the
folly of building the fort on a low bank of the river, while submerging six
of Henry's fifteen guns. Still, Tilghman did not despair, wiring Polk in
Columbus for reinforcements and telling Johnston: "If you can reinforce
strongly and quickly we have a glorious chance to overwhelm the enemy."
But then the arrival of Grant's 2nd Division made those brave words seem
a little foolish. At a council of war on the night of February 5, 1862,
Tilghman announced his decision to save what he could of his troops,
sending them as reinforcements to the stronger Fort Donelson on the
Cumberland, while a sacrifice garrison dueled the enemy to give them time
to escape. Next morning—the seventh—while a company of Tennessee
artillery of 54 men and 2 officers manned the remaining serviceable guns,

about 3,650 infantry filed out of the fort heading for Donelson. Tilghman accompanied them part of the way, returning to the fort to direct the battle of his forlorn hope. He arrived at noon to the sound of gunfire.

At eleven o'clock, right on schedule, Grant's three-pronged attack began with a simultaneous advance of his two divisions moving along either bank. Foote was to have furnished the third prong with his gunboats, but he deliberately held off until just before noon to give the foot soldiers a head start. When he opened fire, the Battle of Fort Henry became an artillery duel, ultimately overturning the old military adage: "A ship is a fool to fight a fort."

Not that Tilghman and his gallant forlorn hope did not fight bravely and well. They struck Foote's flotilla with fifty-nine shots, some of them causing death and damage. One shell pierced the boiler of the luckless *Essex,* scalding twenty-eight men, some of whom died of burns. But it was only the heavy shells of the six-inch rifle and a giant columbiad firing a monster 128-pound projectile that hurt the Federals. The others, low-sited with their muzzles just above the water, could do no more than bounce their 32- and 42-pound shells off the sloped sides of the ironclads. When the rifle burst while firing, putting both its crew and flanking pieces out of action, and the columbiad was spiked by a broken priming wire, Tilghman saw that it was now time to haul down his flag. He had wanted an hour's grace for his fleeing garrison, and had been given two. Shortly before 2 P.M. he pulled down his colors. The Rebels had lost 5 killed, 6 wounded, 5 disabled and 5 missing. Union losses were 11 dead, 31 wounded and 5 missing. A jubilant Grant wired Halleck:

"Fort Henry is ours. I shall take and destroy Fort Donelson on the 8th and return to Fort Henry."

27

.

Fall of Fort Donelson

L IKE THE LOOSE THREAD that unravels a sweater, the loss of Fort
Henry had undone Johnston's Kentucky line. His right had already been
smashed at Mill Springs, and now his center had been penetrated at Henry,
outflanking Columbus on his left and Bowling Green on his right center.
Both would have to be abandoned. Buell, meanwhile, was slowly moving
south. When Donelson fell, as Johnston expected shortly, those fearsome
Federal ironclads could go rampaging up the Cumberland, as they had done
on the Tennessee, forcing the fall of Nashville, his main supply depot,
cutting off the Army of Central Kentucky from the southern bank.

Johnston had two choices, both unpleasant. He could stand and fight
against two converging armies, each larger than his, or retreat south of the
Cumberland to save his own, ready to strike north again when the opportunity arose. Calling a council of war he conferred with his two top generals,
Hardee and Beauregard, who had recently arrived, but with a mere handful
of staff officers and no regiments. Davis had meant it when he said he could
send no more troops. The Little Creole had expected that Johnston was
going on the offensive with 70,000 effectives, and was badly shaken when
he learned the true predicament of the West. Nevertheless, his spirits
recovered, he recommended that Johnston concentrate at Donelson, defeat
Grant there, and then drive Buell back to the Ohio. Johnston disagreed. To
concentrate on Grant would be to abandon Nashville to Buell, thus surrendering his army's subsistence. Even if Grant were defeated, that would
leave Buell astride the army's communications, possessing its base and
fresh for battle. No, Johnston said, there is no alternative: we must retreat
into Tennessee behind the Cumberland. Regretfully, Beauregard ac-
quiesced. For the present, Kentucky must be abandoned.

■ ■ ■

Grant meant what he had told Halleck—that he would "take and destroy" Donelson on the eighth—until he scouted the fort himself, coming within a mile of the outlying rifle pits the Rebels were digging. What he saw convinced him that he must wait until he was stronger, until the river stopped rising and the gunboats were repaired and at his service once more. Meanwhile, Halleck, eager for that supreme command of the West for which in his dispatches to McClellan he had recommended himself, actually was sending Grant "everything I can rake and scrape together from Missouri." By February 12—Lincoln's birthday—with 25,000 men now at his command, the ironclads available, the weather clear and sunny for the first time since leaving Paducah nine days earlier, he began his movement on Donelson.

Brigadier General John Buchanan Floyd was in command at Fort Donelson, having only just arrived with his brigade, thus raising the fort's strength to about 17,500 men. Floyd, born in Montgomery City, Virginia, June 1, 1806, was a lawyer and planter who had had a brilliant career as a politician. Elected to the Virginia House of Delegates and then to be governor of that state, he became Buchanan's secretary of war in 1857. During his service Floyd came under suspicion of using his office for personal profit and was indicted for malfeasance, although the charge was dropped; after he resigned under a cloud in December 1860, he was also suspected by the North of having surreptitiously supplied the South with arms from Federal arsenals.

Floyd's position at Donelson was considerably stronger than Tilghman's had been at Henry. He had twelve excellent and well-protected cannon in place, chief among them a rifled 128-pounder and two 32-pounder carronades emplaced on top of the bluff overlooking the river, plus six light batteries able to bear on the landward side. Here on a ridge below or south of the fort the Confederates had dug a line of rifle pits, shoveling the yellow clay onto logs to form barricades. Here he had Buckner on the right and Pillow on the left, with his own brigade in reserve. Floyd was optimistic about holding Donelson, wiring Johnston: "Our field defenses are good. I think we can sustain ourselves against the land force."

Grant arrived off Donelson's landward side about noon, pleased that the enemy had made no attempt to strike at his columns while making a vulnerable 10-mile march through broken country. He was also elated to hear the sound of cannon booming on the river, supposing that Foote was already at work. But he wasn't. There was only one ironclad off Donelson: the *Carondolet*. The three others were downriver with Foote and the transports bringing up Grant's 3rd Division. Actually, the gunboat's first shots were only signals to Grant that the ship was active. But there was no answering fire from the fort and the bluff, and the *Carondolet* retired to anchor downstream for the night.

Next morning, at the request of Grant, who still did not know that only one ironclad was present, the *Carondolet* went forward in support of a Union attack. During a two-hour bombardment she got off 139 rounds, receiving only two hits in return. This was very poor gunnery, except that by luck a 128-pound solid shot crashed through a broadside casemate into the engine room, bowling over a dozen men and bounding after others "like a wild beast pursuing its prey." It also tore out steam pipes and beams, filling the air with fine steel needles and thin slivers of wood as though it were a deadly porcupine. *Carondolet* at once withdrew to transfer wounded and make emergency repairs, but she returned to fire 45 more rounds at the enemy.

Grant, meanwhile, had put his two divisions in line opposite the Confederate ridge. Silver-haired C. F. Smith was on the left, Brigadier General John A. McClernand's brigade on the right. McClernand was a political general Grant had known at Camp Yates, and he was a bit skeptical about him, as he was of all politicians turned soldier. Born near Hardinburg, Kentucky, on May 30, 1812, McClernand moved with his mother to Illinois after his father's death, becoming a lawyer and settling in Springfield, where he befriended Lincoln. Every bit as ambitious as Honest Abe, he was also selfish and pompous, though an accomplished orator. His popularity with Illinois Democrats gained him five terms in Congress, and also was productive of his rank. Thin as a straw, with a glistening jet black beard and mustache, hawkish nose, and sunken dark eyes, he gave the impression of being tall when he was actually only just a shade taller than Grant. On the following morning—the thirteenth—McClernand gave notice of how difficult he could be by attacking on his own to silence a troublesome enemy battery. Twice his brave but green boys from Illinois went forward at the run, and twice they were repulsed with heavy casualties. On the left a brigade sent into action by Smith took its objective, but then came under such intense sniper fire from the ridge that it had to be withdrawn. Grant now realized that Donelson was not just tougher than Henry: it was much, much tougher, but he was happy to retire that night in a big feather bed set up in a warm farmhouse kitchen. The sound of rain on the roof and then sleet put him to sleep.

Outside the sleet had changed to snow and the temperature was plummeting to 12 degrees. Confederates in their hilltop rifle pits shivered in the biting cold, but the Yankees below them were even more miserable, so many of them having shed their coats and blankets during the approach march the day before. Some of the wounded between the lines froze to death, and when the men of both sides awoke the following morning they saw with amazement a soft white landscape on which the snow had made mounds of the corpses and the ice-clad trees in the woods around them glittered like crystal chandeliers.

Grant had been wondering why the bombardment of Donelson did not seem as furious as the fusillade that had humbled Henry. He soon found out that there was only one ironclad on the river, and immediately called up 2,500 troops left behind at Henry, assigning them to Smith. When Foote and his other units began arriving that day—the fourteenth—he formed them into a third division under the youthful Brigadier General Lew Wallace and put them into line between Smith and McClernand. Only thirty-four, Wallace was an Indiana lawyer with literary aspirations whose political influence put a star on his shoulder. His thick black beard and mustache, probably grown to conceal his youth, and straight nose made him resemble McClernand, although he was taller.

Grant now had about 27,500 men opposing Floyd's 17,500, superior numbers, of course, but nothing approaching the three-to-one ratio considered necessary for frontal assault on a fixed position. But now he did have Foote and his ironclads, which should more than compensate for this lack—and he requested the commodore to commence firing.

Foote had been planning to make a personal reconnaissance, but Grant's request was for an immediate attack, so he promptly sallied forth with four ironclads. They were his flagship *St. Louis, Carondolet, Pittsburg* and *Louisville. Essex* had been so badly damaged that it was still being repaired, and *Cincinnati* was at Henry. On they came four abreast, with the wooden gunboats *Tyler* and *Conestoga* about a thousand yards astern. At about a mile and a half the Confederate batteries opened up, churning the water in front of the Union flotilla. Foote did not reply until he had closed the range to a mile. Onward they steamed, black smoke boiling out of their funnels, muzzles spitting flame—their missiles falling on the fort in a steady, thundering rain. Although the Rebels stood to their guns, it appeared that nothing could withstand this dreadful two-hour bombardment, a fusillade so fierce that the soon-to-be-famous cavalry leader Nathan Bedford Forrest shouted to an aide who had been a minister: "Parson, for God's sake pray! Nothing but God Almighty can save the fort!" Floyd doubted even this, amending his earlier wire to Johnston with: "The fort cannot hold out twenty minutes!"

Unknown to them they need not have despaired, for Commodore Foote had made a grave miscalculation. Evidently he had not grasped the significance of the shot that had staggered *Carondolet,* for his order to close until the enemy batteries were silenced canceled out the superiority of his armament in number, size, velocity and range. Moreover, the closer he came to the bluff, the more the foe's rounds ceased to be long-range arching shots and became close-range plunging fire. This in turn canceled out his armor, even the five-inch-thick overlapping bow plates, while the sloped sides designed to deflect a flat trajectory could not withstand the terrible velocity of plunging shells. Even though the service of the big 128-pound rifle that shook *Carondolet* was lost when it was spiked by its own priming wire—the second such mishap—the remaining Confederate guns now raked and ruined the oncoming Yankees.

At 500 yards side armor was being skinned away "as lightning tears the bark from the tree." And yet the Federal ships steamed closer in a foolhardy, perverse, boomeranging attempt to storm what might have been taken almost at leisure, if Foote had stood out of the fort's range and blasted away with his long-range guns. Just as the commodore aboard *St. Louis* thought that he saw signs of panic among the Rebels, a solid shot crashed through the flagship's superstructure, carrying away the wheel, killing the pilot and wounding everyone else in the pilot house including Foote. Having no helm, *St. Louis* drifted helplessly away with the current. *Louisville* followed, sinking like a sieve and kept afloat only by her compartments. *Pittsburg*'s tiller ropes were shot away, and she too swung helplessly off with the current. Only *Carondolet* remained, gamely but foolishly facing the enemy batteries alone at 200 yards, but then she too retired, furiously firing her cannon to escape under cover of her own gunsmoke.

Confederate gunners cheered and threw their caps in the air, jubilant to have routed the Yankees' dreadful flame-spitting steel dragons, while their commander recovered his spirits to wire Johnston: "The fort holds out."

Grant was dismayed by the repulse of Foote's ironclads. This, together with the double setback of the preceding day, led him to wire Halleck: "Appearances indicate now that we will have a protracted siege here." But he was not discouraged, assuring his chief: "I feel great confidence . . . in ultimately reducing the place."

In contrast, Floyd was highly elated, especially because he thought he had accomplished the first half of his assignment by keeping Grant off Hardee's flank while his center force retired south from Bowling Green. Soon he would safely join Johnston, already in Nashville with the van of his army. The second half of Floyd's mission was to escape from Donelson to Nashville. He had already begun planning for it during a council of war that morning. It had been decided that Pillow would try to break through near the hamlet of Dover, where a road led south, then East to Nashville seventy miles away. Buckner's division would cover his withdrawal before following. The breakout had been scheduled for that day—the fourteenth—but then the ironclads had appeared and by the time they were driven off, it was too late to move.

Another council of war was held that night. Pillow enthusiastically insisted on going forward with the breakout. Buckner was pessimistic. Floyd swung back and forth between them, like the amateurish, indecisive soldier that he was. Also, between the professional Buckner and the political Pillow there was bad blood. During the Mexican War Buckner had joined the general derision of Pillow when he was found digging a trench on the wrong side of a parapet. Eventually, probably to avoid a nervous breakdown, the vacillating Floyd ordered the breakout to begin at dawn on the fifteenth.

That night another fierce storm flayed the soldiers of both sides, shrieking winds flogging them with icy whips. Yet the howl of the storm muffled the sound of the Confederates moving off the ridge, especially the sound of steel-shod gunwheels on frozen earth. At dawn Pillow ordered his regiments forward. With Forrest's cavalry riding flank guard on his left, the Graybacks surged forward against McClernand's division on the Union right.

They encountered fierce resistance. For three hours the battle raged back and forth until McClernand's Bluebellies, waving empty cartridge boxes to show that they had fought until they ran out of ammunition, turned and fled. As they drifted left, they exposed Wallace's right flank. The road to Nashville lay open. And Pillow refused to follow it! He feared a counterattack against his right flank while moving south. Now it was Buckner who urged speed and daring. His soldiers could hold the door open, he said, but Pillow would not listen, ordering him to take his men back to the ridge. Now Floyd appeared, standing indecisively between them once more. At first he sided with Buckner, but then, after Pillow took him aside, his timorous logic appealing to his own faint heart, he ordered both divisions back to the ridge.

The bold breakout had been abandoned.

■   ■   ■

Grant had not been present when the battle began. The wounded Foote, planning to go downriver for repairs, had requested a meeting before he left. Grant received his message before daylight, riding off after leaving orders for his division commanders to hold to their present positions. Thus when the reeling McClernand asked for help, his colleagues were bound not to send it—although Wallace finally sent him a brigade which helped defend his own exposed right. But Grant, strangely confident that the enemy would not do what he had the need and the capacity to do—break out—learned nothing of what was happening until noon as he was returning from his conference with Foote. A distraught staff officer told him that McClernand's men had been routed.

Superb horseman that he was, even Grant dared not spur his mount over that icy road, and so it was not until one o'clock that he reached Smith's lines on the far left. Reassured to find the troops there calm, he rode over to McClernand's. There the shamefaced, sullen Federals again brandished their empty cartridge boxes. Grant was told that the Rebels had three days' cooked rations in their packs, meaning that they expected three days of battle. But Grant said, no, three days' marching—they're trying to escape, and he told his staff: "The one who attacks first will be victorious, and the enemy will have to be in a hurry if he gets ahead of me." To McClernand's men, he said: "Fill your cartridge boxes, quick, and get into line. The enemy is trying to escape and he must not be permitted to do so." They obeyed, calmed by Grant's cool confidence. Returning to Smith he spoke of his belief that in order to make their breakout assault, the enemy must have stripped the ridge almost bare. Ordering him to attack, he assured him of "a very thin line to contend with."

Thin or thick, the sixty-year-old Smith was overjoyed at the chance he had dreamed of all of his military life: to be a general leading his troops in battle. He rode ahead of them, his sword pointed at the enemy. When some of them faltered, he turned in the saddle and yelled: "Damn you, gentlemen, I see skulkers. I'll have none here. Come on, you volunteers, come on! This is your chance. You volunteered to be killed for the love of country, and now you can be. You damned volunteers—I'm only a soldier and I don't want to be killed, but you came to be killed and now you can be!" So taunted, they went forward with a yell, although one of them later recalled: "I was nearly scared to death, but I saw the old man's mustache over his right shoulder and went on." So did they all, stumbling through the fallen timbers of an enemy abatis to drive back Buckner's rear-guard regiment. They might have stormed the fort itself, except for the return of Buckner's division. Still, they had entrenched themselves on the enemy's right, while McClernand's men assisted by Wallace's had pushed back his left. What might have been a Confederate victory had been aborted by the Pillow-Buckner rivalry and Floyd's timidity, and then was turned around by Grant's calm demeanor and the valor of his men. On the following morning there was Union artillery on the ridge seized by Smith's soldiers. Meanwhile, McClernand had recovered most of the ground he had lost earlier in the day. Donelson's defenses had been penetrated, and it seemed to a jubilant Grant that there would be no long siege after all.

Floyd had called another council of war, this time inside the little frame two-story Dover Inn. For the second time Buckner and Pillow reversed moods, Buckner becoming sour and silent, Pillow recovering his courage. He was all in favor of trying again, but Buckner wisely pointed out that Grant's forces had improved their position and the men were too downcast to attempt another assault. Floyd was once again in the middle, although this time he leaned toward Buckner, who also predicted that Smith's artillery would be firing at dawn. Colonel Forrest, who was also present, suggested escape by a riverside road open to the south. But when he reported that the water was waist-deep where it crossed a creek, the army surgeon advised against it as an ordeal that would kill the troops. There was also a report that Grant had received another 10,000 men. In the end, it was agreed to surrender.

But both Floyd and Pillow refused to give themselves up, Floyd remembering that nol-prossed indictment for misfeasance which could easily be reopened, Pillow insisting that he intended to keep his vow never to surrender. Buckner had no such reservations, probably counting on his friend Grant, to whom he had loaned money when Grant was down-and-out, to give him lenient terms. So the change in commanders was carried out.

Floyd said to Pillow, "I turn the command over, sir."

"I pass it," Pillow replied.

"I assume it," said Buckner. "Give me pen, ink and paper, and send for a bugler."

Forrest arose in indignation. "I did not come here to surrender my command!" he cried in a wrathful voice, and stamped out into the night, ordering his troopers to saddle up and then leading them through the flooded road to freedom. Floyd made his escape later, commandeering a steamboat that arrived during the night to land 400 reinforcements, who, of course, were included in the surrender. Floyd put himself and his own brigade aboard the ship and shoved off into the darkness. Pillow was not so fortunate. An abandoned scow fit to hold only himself and his chief of staff was all he could find to take him upriver.

Buckner's offer to surrender was taken by Smith to Grant, asleep in his cozy farmhouse kitchen. When Grant asked Smith what he thought of the request for terms, the old soldier snapped: "I think, no terms with the traitors, by God!" Grant nodded, climbed out of bed and dressed before taking a tablet of paper and writing rapidly on it. He gave it to Smith, who snorted: "By God, it couldn't be better!" Grant had written:

> . . . No terms except an unconditional and immediate surrender can be accepted.
> I propose to move immediately upon your works.

Buckner was crushed and then resentful when he read this message, but there was nothing that he could do—and he capitulated without terms. But Grant laid no harsh hand upon the captive Confederates, indeed allowing many of them to stroll through his lines to freedom, observing: "It is a much less job to take them than to keep them." When Buckner reproached him with the remark that it would not have been so easy for him to take Donelson if he had been in command, Grant replied that in that case, "I should not have tried it the way I did." He also told his friend—if such he still was—that he was glad Pillow had escaped. "If I had captured him, I would have turned him loose. I would rather have him in command of you fellows than as a prisoner."

And so with more than 12,000 prisoners, most of them the cream of Confederate volunteers, Ulysses S. Grant had erased the shame of Bull Run and Ball's Bluff. In the North church bells rang jubilantly while men embraced on the streets or recited to each other Grant's message to Buckner. It would become immortal, and so would the new hero's nickname fitted to his initials that had gotten that way by accident. "U. S. Grant" became "Unconditional Surrender Grant" and the fame begun at Belmont now soared with the twin victories of Henry and Donelson as the Union placed the laurels of a hero on the brow of the little general who had actually fought and won two battles. And here was an unanticipated boomerang that had Henry Wager Halleck furiously scratching his elbows: when Grant, now a major general commanding with 30,000 men, offered to march on Nashville, Old Brains responded with thunderous silence.

But Buell was already moving—though cautiously—against Johnston's headquarters, and after Hardee arrived there with only two-thirds of the 14,000 he had led out of Bowling Green, Albert Sidney Johnston decided to evacuate the city. That left the people in a panic, believing the retreating

Graybacks' stories of Buell's bloodthirsty Bluebellies. Only the offer of free food that could not be removed by Johnston's retreating troops calmed them. Even so, many left the city. Meanwhile with Nathan Bedford Forrest and his cavalry acting as a rear guard, Johnston fell back toward Murfrees-boro, forty miles southeast at the head of what remained of the vanquished Army of Central Kentucky. On February 24, 1862, Buell's spearheads entered Nashville. The capital of Tennessee, C.S.A., had once again become the capital of Tennessee, U.S.A., and would remain so throughout the war. Next day Buell's forces began pouring into the city, finding the streets deserted, very little loot—Forrest had done his customary thorough job in shipping Rebel supplies south—the statehouse deserted with the Confeder-ate government fleeing to Memphis, most of the better homes and shops empty and hotels boarded up. A war correspondent seeking shelter knocked on the locked door of a luxury hotel. It was swung open by a black man, who stood on the threshold grinning broadly, ivory flashing in his dark face as he announced:

"Massa done gone souf."

28

■

Battle of Pea Ridge

WHEN PRESIDENT DAVIS solved the problem of the Price-McCulloch rivalry in the Transmississippi by placing Earl Van Dorn over both of them, he chose a bold commander of fire and dash who yearned more for battle than most officers hunger for rank. Born near Port Gibson, Mississippi, on September 17, 1820, Van Dorn was appointed to West Point by his great-uncle, President Andrew Jackson. There this slender, five-foot five-inch gamecock earned himself a reputation for gallantry, and notoriety as a poor student finishing fifty-fourth in the class of 1842. Having won two brevets in Mexico, and been wounded five times there and while fighting Comanches, he received a coveted captaincy in the 2nd Cavalry Regiment. Handsome, with jet black hair, thick mustache and pointed beard, impeccably polite, almost as fond of the ladies as of action, he was the Beau Sabreur of Southern legend. When he arrived at his headquarters in Pocahontas, Arkansas, in mid-January of 1862, he was still limping from a bad fall from horseback suffered attempting an impossible jump, but he was nevertheless buoyant and eager to execute a grandiose plan he had conceived which was nothing less than a glorious ascent of the Big Muddy, whipping Yankee armies as he went—a Frémont in reverse. "I must have St. Louis—huzza!" he wrote his wife.

But there was not very much to huzza about in Transmississippi Department Number Two. Between them, Price and McCulloch could muster only 14,000 men, but with these and sixty guns Van Dorn on March 4 moved north determined to defeat in detail the 12,000-man Federal army that had cleared Missouri of Confederates. His was a strange column, what with 2,000 pro-South Indians—Cherokees, Chickasaws and Choctaws, Creeks and Seminoles—led by gray-bearded, colorful Brigadier General Albert Pike, a giant of three hundred pounds, and also something of a mental prodigy: poet and orator, scholar and duelist. Much too heavy to be carried any distance by horse, Pike rode in a carriage dressed like a Sioux in his buckskin shirt, fringed leggings and beaded moccasins. His braves all wore feathers in their hair, scalping knives stuck in their waistbands, and some carried a musket in one hand and a tomahawk in the other.

Van Dorn also was horse-drawn, stretched out straight in an ambulance still suffering from his fall and afflicted as well by chills and a fever resulting from swimming his horse across an icy river in his haste to reach his command. His mount was hitched alongside. As the Confederates clattered and shuffled north, a brisk wind blew snow in their faces.

Brigadier General Samuel Ryan Curtis was the officer so helpful to Lincoln in ridding himself of Frémont. He had reported that the Pathfinder "lacked the intelligence, the experience, and the sagacity necessary to his command"—three qualities that Curtis admired most and which he firmly believed he himself possessed in rare abundance. An Ohio-born West Pointer who had been graduated twenty-seventh in the class of 1831, Curtis had been a colonel of Buckeye volunteers in the Mexican War, as well as a general's aide, after which he left the army for an engineering career. For three years he was chief engineer for the city of St. Louis, eventually moving to Keokuk, Iowa, where he had opened a law office. Elected mayor, he was also named to three terms in Congress, cutting short the third one to become a soldier again. Long-headed, with a bulging, balding, belligerent forehead, he was conspicuously clean-shaven except for a pair of fluffy gray side-whiskers.

On the afternoon of March 3 Curtis sat in his headquarters tent at Cross Hollows, Arkansas, about a dozen miles above Van Dorn at Pocahontas. As was his custom he wore his dress uniform, sword and epaulets, braid and buttons, even though he was merely writing a letter to his wife. From the south he heard the hollow boom of distant cannon. He counted the reports: forty, a major general's salute. A two-star Confederate now west of the Mississippi, and obviously on the lookout for him—Curtis. And his command divided! Of his four divisions, two were with him and the other pair thrown forward under Franz Sigel, the German immigrant who had been a mathematics instructor in civilian life, and now notorious for his swift rear-march at Wilson's Creek. Next day when his scouts—including a young Wild Bill Hickok—reported a strong enemy column marching toward him, Curtis notified Sigel to join him at Sugar Creek up near the Missouri border. Both men knew it to be a defensible position, having passed through it while pursuing Sterling Price.

Thus as Curtis fell back north, Sigel disengaged from the Rebels and also hurried in that direction, the enemy harassing him all the way. At sundown on March 6 he arrived at Sugar Creek. He was a small red-haired man, given to quick professorial gestures, with watery eyes behind tiny spectacles. He told Curtis he had lost two regiments en route, and also announced, more petulantly, that he was hungry. Curtis fed him and told him to put his two divisions in line on the right. Because of Sigel's losses, Curtis was now down to 10,500 men opposing Van Dorn's 14,000. They occupied a two-mile-long shelf overlooking Sugar Creek, fortifying and entrenching it. A mile to their rear was tiny Leetown, a dozen cabins clustered around a blacksmith shop and a store. Another mile back and Pea Ridge reared abruptly into the sky. It let down into a defile through which ran the Wire Road, so called because the telegraph had its southern terminus there in Elkhorn Tavern, where the telegrapher lived. From the tavern in Curtis's left rear the road passed through his far right flank and across Sugar Creek to the point where Van Dorn's army had arrived shortly after Sigel. Their campfires below the creek were clearly visible on the Federal height. Snow was falling, and the men of both sides built their fires higher.

March 7 dawned bleak and gray but warmer, with no snow. Curtis's men blinking awake blinked again when they looked down at Sugar Creek and saw an empty Rebel camp. Van Dorn, though impetuous, was not foolhardy. He would not hurl his hungry, bone-tired men against that fortified height above him. Instead, he chose to send one column on a night flank march around and behind Pea Ridge to follow the Wire Road into the Federal rear. Another column would move along another road on Curtis's right flank, then wheel to come into the Union rear around Leetown. Price with his Missourians would make the longer flanking march; Pike and McCulloch with their Indians, Texans, Arkansans and Louisianians would make the secondary thrust around Leetown. Van Dorn accompanied Price. After dark the night of March 6, the Rebel columns filed silently away to their left, leaving their campfires burning so that at dawn of March 7 the Federals saw nothing but gray ashes.

Curtis was puzzled by Van Dorn's disappearance, until his scouts came riding in to report that they were behind Pea Ridge, about to debouch into the Wire Road and Curtis's rear. Curtis faced difficult alternatives. He could turn about and meet the Rebels somewhere around Elkhorn Tavern, or retreat southward across Sugar Creek into enemy country, leaving Van

Dorn astride his communications. The second choice invited disaster, and the first only difficulty, so he chose to about face and confront the foe. Of his own two divisions he sent one under Colonel Eugene Carr to hold the road above Elkhorn Tavern, and the other under an Indiana-born colonel with the improbable name of Jefferson Davis to a position north of Leetown. Of Sigel's divisions one under Colonel Peter Osterhaus went into line south of Leetown, and the other under Colonel Alexander Asboth was held in reserve. All these commanders were veteran soldiers, especially Carr, who had fought Indians, and been wounded by an arrow, and at Wilson's Creek, where he distinguished himself. Davis had been fighting since Sumter, Osterhaus—a German—had also been at Wilson's Creek, while Asboth—a Hungarian—had been a freedom fighter under Louis Kossuth in Hungary.

Van Dorn fumed at the delay caused by road obstructions behind Pea Ridge. He was three hours behind schedule, when—at 10:30 A.M.—Price's soldiers attacked. They came on yelling, moving through the brush on both sides of the road, their guns firing from both flanks and the rear. Carr had prepared a defense in depth with gun batteries staggered at intervals, a strong force of infantry posted in support of the forward battery while three others fired over their heads. But a Rebel salvo knocked out three of the first battery's four guns, blowing up two caissons and killing all the cannon cockers. At this, the foremost infantry fell back upon the second battery, just north of Elkhorn Tavern. There they stopped two Rebel assaults, but with Price re-forming for a third, Carr sent a messenger back to Curtis calling for reinforcements.

Curtis had his headquarters on a little knoll midway between the tavern and Leetown. As usual he was in dress uniform and his staff was also dressed more for a ball than for battle. They were startled by the sudden eruption of musketry on their left front, followed by a hellish howling and screeching. Pike's Indians had attacked Osterhaus, so unnerving his men that they broke and ran, abandoning guns and equipment. Davis had moved over to close the gap, but he too needed help. His messenger came galloping up on the knoll just after the arrival of Carr's. Curtis remained calm. Though his commanders right and left were in trouble, he didn't think the situation serious enough to commit his reserve, and sent word for both to hold with what they had.

Now as the rising sun burned off the mist and melted the snow, Van Dorn began to be concerned. He seemed to be winning the battle but he wondered how much energy his weary, hungry men had left. Price's third assault had pushed Carr back, forcing him to re-form below and to the left of the tavern, but his Graybacks had moved like zombies. Worse, the secondary sector under Pike and McCulloch was silent—and Price discovered why all too soon.

Pike's Indians had begun a victory celebration, prancing around the "wagon guns," as they called the Federal cannon. Then they took the collars off the slaughtered horses and draped them around their necks, their trace chains jingling against the frozen ground as though in tune to the chant: "Me big Injun, big as horse!" Pike tried desperately to reorganize them so as to help McCulloch fighting furiously on his left. But they balked at fighting "white-man's war," preferring, as always, the tactics of the ambuscade or pounce-and-withdraw.

McCulloch's advance was blocked by an Illinois regiment and when he tried to break through with an Arkansas regiment he fell, shot through the heart. Word of his death spread quickly among his devoted soldiers and the despairing cries arose: "McCulloch's dead! They killed McCulloch!" Just like Zollicoffer's men, without McCulloch they would not fight. Dazed and grieving they wandered off the field, and Davis and Osterhaus, who had driven the Indians off, were content to let them go.

News of the right wing's failure reached Van Dorn just as he and Price were preparing for the fourth and—they hoped—final assault on Carr's third line. Price, his wounded arm in a sling, calculated that his Missourians had just enough left for this final fling, and if enough daylight and ammunition remained, it could be done. It seemed that way as Confederate artillery—superior to the Federals for one of the few times in the war—knocked out Carr's guns and sent his men reeling backward. Just before leaving a wrecked battery, an Iowa cannoneer tossed a smoldering blanket on top of a caisson loaded with ammunition. Sprinting to the rear, while the victorious Rebels capered around the captured battery, he heard a tremendous explosion behind him, turning in time to see Confederate limbs, heads and headless torsos flying through the air, while a huge ball of fire followed by a pluming cloud of black smoke climbed into the air. Thus ended Price's fourth fruitless assault, and thus by the capricious winds of war—defection of a feckless ally, death of a beloved commander and a decisive accident at the critical moment—do the tides of battle ebb and flow.

From his headquarters knoll, Curtis could see the column of smoke against the setting sun, and he decided that the time had come to send in his reserve. At seven o'clock Asboth's fresh division relieved Carr's battered but unbowed warriors. Van Dorn had gained some ground on them, but they had held firm at Carr's third position below the tavern. That night, Curtis called a council of war. All of his commanders but the usually silent

Davis were for retreat. But Curtis, certain that Van Dorn had shot his bolt, overruled them—ordering them to reform on Carr's line.

In the morning when Curtis saw the long concave line that Van Dorn had formed, with defense obviously in mind, he realized that he had been right. When the Confederate artillery began a desultory bombardment, Curtis sensed at once that it was merely a probing or testing fire, delivered in hopes that it might just bowl over an exhausted enemy. It suggested also that Van Dorn was low on ammunition. So he ordered Sigel on the left to attack. He did, commanding his infantry to lie down in muddy fields while he moved his batteries 250 yards closer to the foe before they opened fire. It was a devastating cannonade. One by one the Rebel batteries were shredded. Sigel rode ramrod-straight among his bellowing guns, sometimes dismounting to sight a piece himself. His men cheered him, and they were still cheering when he pointed his saber at the enemy position and ordered them forward. He stood in his stirrups watching ecstatically while his blue-clad Germans went surging forward. "Oh, dot vas lofely," he cried.

On the right Davis's men joined the assault. Curtis was with them, riding from point to point, checking his watch to see that the units went into the line with split-second timing. Two of Curtis's orderlies were killed with him as he galloped among the bursting shells. When the Federal wings converged with a shout past Elkhorn Tavern, driving the Rebels and their careening guns and neighing horses up the Wire Road in pell-mell confusion, through the defile and past Carr's original position, the Battle of Pea Ridge or Elkhorn Tavern had ended in a smashing Union victory. Van Dorn's units were scattered far and wide, and it would be a week before they returned to the Boston Mountains, where they regrouped near Van Buren.

Pea Ridge was the Civil War's fiercest battle fought west of the Mississippi, and though the Union was victorious, Curtis's Army of the Southwest suffered higher casualties: 203 killed, 980 wounded for a total of 1,183, with 201 missing. Confederate losses were 600 killed and wounded with 200 missing.

29

■

The Union Generals Bicker

F OR THE UNION the year 1862 had begun auspiciously on land and sea: Mill Springs, Forts Henry and Donelson, Pea Ridge, Roanoke Island and the conquest of the *Merrimac*. Before any of these military victories occurred, Abraham Lincoln on January 15 had achieved a political triumph that was to have far-reaching effects on the war itself.

For months there had been steadily increasing reports of graft and waste in the War Department: contracts going to the highest bidder; rotten meat, shoddy cloth, weevily flour and guns that would not shoot, or worse, exploded upon being fired. As one jubilant jobber remarked in the bar at Willard's: "You can sell anything to the government at almost any price you've got the guts to ask." Always, this corruption and inefficiency seemed to be traceable to the desk of Secretary of War Simon Cameron. Even with Lincoln hot on his trail, Cameron seemed safe. To the Jacobins he was "one of us," he was "right" on slavery. Had he not in his annual report included a long passage advocating freedom for Southern slaves and their induction into the Union army? When Lincoln recalled this pamphlet and expunged the passage, the Republican radicals accused him of being "soft on slavery." Thus Cameron was astonished and shocked when Lincoln on January 11 sent him a curt note declaring: "I . . . propose nominating you to the Senate next Monday as Minister to Russia." The power broker from Pennsylvania was being banished, and after the nomination was approved—chiefly because of the loyalty of the radicals—one senator who knew Cameron well remarked: "Send word to the czar to bring in his things at night."

Cameron was replaced by Edwin McMasters Stanton, a singular and happy though not always popular choice. Stanton was born in Steubenville, Ohio, son of a New England father and a Virginia mother. That unlikely union might have been productive of his personality: a welter of contradictions. When his father died in 1827, Stanton at thirteen had to leave school and work in a bookstore. Still, he saved enough to spend two years at Kenyon College, and in Columbus completed his law studies in the office of his guardian. His rise as a corporation as well as a trial lawyer was meteoric and he soon had a national reputation. He delighted in taking criminal cases, and his fees were as high as his client's guilt was deep. When one of them complained, he asked: "Do you think I would argue the wrong side for less?" When another tried to persuade Stanton not to force him to sell the house he lived in to pay Stanton's fee, saying that it would ruin him, he was told: "You deserve to be ruined, for you were guilty." It would not occur to a man as self-righteous as Stanton that, even if he felt no shame about arguing to thwart justice, he might at least feel a little gratitude for the guilt that was enriching him; but then, he never doubted the probity of his motives, even when he was defending scoundrels.

Stanton was just as overbearing and rude with his generals, many of whom walked in terror of being fixed by Stanton's little, near-sighted black eyes behind their thick-lensed spectacles and subjected to a furious tongue-lashing. Stanton was short, thick-set, with quick stubby legs. His hair was thinning, so he wore it long on the sides and back, with sideburns joining at his chin from which sprouted a long, narrow black beard—like the tail of a squirrel—streaked with gray. Asthmatic, slightly hysterical, full of self-pity and subject to fits of weeping, he was nevertheless a driver. Shortly after he took over the War Department on January 16, he received from Harpers Ferry an urgent request for guns. He ordered them sent at once. Finding that evening that they had not been shipped, he ordered the gates of the locked arsenal broken and helped workmen tow the guns outside and load them on a train. Next morning the arsenal officer told him that he had been unable to send the guns the day before but would do it now, to which Stanton replied, his usually deep voice rising to a piercing shrillness: "The guns are now at Harpers Ferry, and you, sir, are no longer in the service of the United States government!"

Stanton made no secret deals. Any contract seeker coming to him was compelled to make his proposal in the presence of his staff. Stanton's answer—Yes or No—was given on the spot. He was determined to make the War Department honest and efficient, declaring: "As soon as I can get the machinery of the office working, the rats cleared out, and rat holes stopped—we shall *move!*" Stanton was not above public criticism of Lincoln. Long ago when he, the bigtime lawyer, came to Springfield to argue a case, he saw Honest Abe approaching to join him as an associate, and asked, "Who is that long-armed gorilla?" Now he spoke of him as "the original gorilla" or "that giraffe." Asked when he took office what he would do, he replied: "Do? I will make Abe Lincoln president of the United States."

Lincoln was undisturbed by Stanton's barbs and posturing. "I guess we'll let him jump a while," he drawled. But the showdown came sooner. As Lincoln was busy with a roomful of people, Stanton came rushing in waving a sheet of paper and crying: "Mr. President, this order cannot be signed. I refuse to sign it." There was a hush and their eyes met. "Mr. Secretary," Lincoln replied calmly, "I guess that order will have to be signed." Stanton returned to his office and signed the order.

Like so much of official Washington, and especially among the radical Republicans who admired Stanton to a man, the new secretary was obsessed with suspicions of treason. He kept a little bell on his desk to summon guards to arrest anyone he suspected of disloyalty. When a man asked him to release a friend jailed on such suspicion, Stanton pointed to the bell and shouted in shrill rage: "If I tap that little bell, I can send you where you will never hear the dogs bark. And by heaven, I'll do it if you say another word!" On this point, Horace Greeley wrote that Stanton would know how to deal with "the greatest danger now facing the country— treason in Washington, treason in the army itself, especially the treason which wears the garb of Unionism."

Treason. The word was heard everywhere in Washington during early 1862, so that a visitor from another planet counting its numerical incidence in comparison to other words in the English dictionary would have concluded that this little two-syllable word was surely what the Union was fighting for. Treason was the watchword of the Joint Committee on the Conduct of the War. Not everyone was suspected of it, just everyone who was not "right" on slavery, that is, for immediate emancipation. Not even George McClellan escaped suspicion, and because his plan for an amphibious operation against Richmond seemed to leave the capital defenseless against a sudden Confederate sally, he was called before the Joint Committee for questioning. Wade and Chandler made most of the queries. Chandler began by asking why McClellan's army, after five full months of training, was not marching against the enemy. McClellan answered that there were only two bridges across the Potomac into Alexandria, and this was not enough to maintain an orderly retreat should his forces be repulsed.

"General McClellan," Chandler interrupted, "if I understand you correctly, before you strike at the Rebels you want to be sure of plenty of room so you can run in case they strike back."

"Or in case you get scared," Wade snapped scornfully.

Struggling to conceal his exasperation at Chandler's oversimplification of military problems, as well as his resentment of their open hostility, McClellan again embarked upon a lengthy explanation of the necessity of lines of retirement. This time Wade interrupted.

"General, you have all the troops you have called for, and if you haven't enough, you shall have more. They are well organized and equipped, and the loyal people of the country expect that you will make a short and decisive campaign. Is it really necessary for you to have more bridges over the Potomac before you move?"

"Not that. Not that exactly. But we must bear in mind the necessity of having everything ready in case of a defeat, and keep our lines of retreat open."

Obviously disgusted, the committee dismissed Little Mac. After he left, Chandler said to Wade: "I don't know much about war, but it seems to me that this is infernal, unmitigated cowardice." Wade agreed. As committee chairman he went to Lincoln and said that McClellan must go. When the president asked who should replace him, Wade snapped: "Anybody!" Lincoln shook his head sadly. "Wade, anybody will do for you, but I must have *somebody.*"

Even the Lincolns were objects of suspicion. Their grief at the death from "bilious fever" of their son Willy at the age of twelve on February 20 was cruelly sharpened by a whispering campaign accusing Mary Todd Lincoln of disloyalty. It was said that this daughter of the Bluegrass was "two thirds slavery and the other third secesh." It was observed that while one of Mary's brothers and a half-sister stayed with the Union, another brother and three half-brothers were Confederates, and three half-sisters were married to Rebels. Accusations became so persistent that the matter was taken under consideration by a congressional investigating committee. Lincoln himself had to appear at one of its secret sessions to declare: "I, Abraham Lincoln, President of the United States, appear of my own volition before this committee of the Senate to say that I, of my own knowledge, know that it is untrue that any of my family hold treasonable communication with the enemy."

That ended the campaign of calumniation but it did not terminate Mary's unbearable sorrow to have lost a second—and her favorite—son. She wept constantly and became hysterical frequently, coming so close to insanity that Lincoln, with a rare bluntness, took her by the hand to lead her to a window and point to a lunatic asylum and say: "Mother, do you see that large white building on the hill yonder? Try and control your grief, or it will drive you mad and we may have to send you there."

■　■　■

Out West, the struggle for possession of the vital Mississippi Valley had begun in earnest.

P. G. T. Beauregard commanded the left flank of Johnston's line. After the fall of Henry and Donelson and the evacuation of Nashville he had found himself alone and on his own as well. "The separation of our armies is for the present complete," Johnston had told him. At first the Little Creole dreamed of a grand offensive aimed at St. Louis, assisted by Van Dorn across the Mississippi, but when he learned of Van Dorn's defeat at Elkhorn Tavern he shelved that plan and began to think defensively. Columbus, Missouri, with its 17,000 men, heavy equipment and guns must be evacuated, he realized, and although Polk, proud of having constructed "the Gibraltar of the West," protested vehemently, he was overruled. Seven thousand of his men and his heaviest cannon were to be sent to New Madrid, Missouri, while the remaining 10,000 would take station farther south in Humboldt, Tennessee.

Beauregard had chosen to make his defense of the Big Muddy at a point where the river makes two great bends. At the first as it flowed south from Missouri into Tennessee was Island Number Ten with thirty-nine guns, including a floating sixteen-gun battery, commanding the straight approach to it. At the second bend, as the river turned north again to flow back into Missouri was New Madrid, with three forts mounting seven guns each. Beauregard told Polk that this position must be held "at all costs," for its fall would mean "the loss of the whole Mississippi Valley to the mouth of the Mississippi River."

Brigadier General John Pope commanded the expedition Halleck sent against Island Number Ten and New Madrid. A big, handsome, robust man, Pope was born in Louisville, Kentucky, on March 16, 1822, but he was raised in Illinois. At sixteen he entered West Point, where he became famous one term for wearing a new-fangled pair of pants which buttoned down the front rather than at the sides as was then customary. The superintendent, a practical man, at once decreed that all cadets must have "flies" on their trousers. Many of West Point's leading hostesses were outraged by this lewd focus on the male genitalia, vowing, in the prudish spirit of an era that called a cock a rooster, that no one wearing this immodest garment would ever darken their doorsteps. Such an innovation was typical of the flamboyant Pope, whose brash, boastful manner never endeared him to his fellow officers, many of whom agreed with Major General Samuel Sturgis's remark: "I don't care for John Pope one pinch of owl dung." But Pope was brave and aggressive, having been breveted captain for gallantry during the Mexican War.

He showed these qualities as he brought his four divisions overland down the right bank of the river, arriving outside New Madrid and Point Pleasant eleven miles below on March 3. He at once laid siege to both places, capturing them within ten days, along with twenty-five heavy guns and large stores of equipment and supplies. The garrison, however, escaped to Island Number Ten.

This formidable position was a truly tough nut. Confederate batteries commanded the long straight river approach and would make matchwood of Pope's transports. Pope—with two stars on his shoulder after New Madrid—chafed at the delay, and repeatedly urged Commodore Andrew Foote to run the batteries with his ironclads. Foote, having recovered from his wound at Donelson, had arrived March 17 with seven gunboats. But he preferred to reduce Island Ten by standing upriver in Missouri and bombarding the position. This brought howls of protest and then derision from Pope and his officers, who had been expecting the navy to take the lead, as at Henry and Donelson. One of them, when asked what Foote's flotilla was doing, replied contemptuously: "Oh, it is still bombarding Tennessee at long range."

Pope angrily insisted that one gunboat running past the Rebel batteries would solve his problem, but Foote said that to run this bristling gantlet would be to sacrifice both ship and men, "which sacrifice I would not be justified in making." Then Commander Henry Walke of the *Carondolet* volunteered to make the attempt. Walke was a proud sailor who had been in every river battle from Belmont on. At Donelson he had taken his gunboat closest to the fort and was still smarting from having had to flee under cover of his own gunsmoke. Foote approved his request, and Walke began to make elaborate preparations for his daring venture.

He chose to slip past Island Number Ten the night of April 5 when a new moon would set at 10 P.M. To protect his ship against plunging shot, he covered his decks with planks from a wrecked barge, while coiling anchor chain in vulnerable spots and wrapping the pilot house up to its windows with an 11-inch hawser. His boilers were enclosed in cordwood barriers and a barge loaded with bales of hay was lashed to the port side. Silence was ensured by piping the steam through the paddle wheel rather than the smokestacks, and the only light he carried was a single lantern in the engine room. Fearing capture because his ship alone might be a match for her six sisters, he armed his crew, took aboard a dozen sharpshooters and hooked up hoses to the boilers to repel boarders by scalding. If all this failed, Walke himself would sink his ship.

Shortly after ten o'clock, *Carondolet* slipped her moorings, sliding silently downstream under a starless sky. Just as she cleared a line of mortar rafts, a violent storm broke overhead. Thunder crashed and lightning flashed and now *Carondolet* was sailing down the glittering obsidian surface of an illuminated river. Yet to Walke's amazement no enemy guns roared and he safely passed the first battery. Moving toward the second still undetected, flames leaped from his smokestacks. Dry soot gathered in her chimneys normally kept wet by steam had taken fire to shoot torches five feet into the air and light up the ship like an excursion steamer. Now Island Number Ten came to bellowing life. Shells screeched over the Union gunboat, or plunged into the water—but only two came near the ironclad: one hit the side of the portside barge, another struck the hay. Safely downstream, Walke moored his ship at the New Madrid landing. Two nights later *Pittsburg* joined her and a delighted Pope took his transports downriver under cover of the gunboats' cannon. After a two-day siege, Island Number Ten surrendered. Brigadier General W. W. Mackall with 7,000 men, twenty-five guns and much ammunition and other supplies were captured—and the North had a new hero.

Halleck was jubilant. Pope might be the very man he sought as a replacement for Grant, and he wired him: "I congratulate you and your command on your splendid achievement. It excels in boldness and brilliancy all other operations of the war. It will be memorable in military history and will be admired by future generations. You deserve well of your country."

This was vintage Halleck at his effusive worst, almost every word calculated to undermine the man whom at the moment he was so slyly smearing: Ulysses Simpson Grant.

During the month between the fall of Donelson and the surrender of Island Number Ten, Henry Halleck had been beseeching McClellan to make him supreme commander in the West. "Give me command of the West," he wired him. "I ask this in return for Forts Henry and Donelson." Next he became obsessed with the fear that Grant's victories might provoke the Confederates into a desperation attack on him in St. Louis. He pleaded with Buell to join him, but Buell said he had problems of his own. Stung, he demanded that Buell be placed under his command, but McClellan said no. Next he went over McClellan's head and appealed directly to Stanton, who also said no. Still frantic in his fear of a sudden sally by Beauregard, he suddenly realized that he had not heard from Grant for some time. Where was he? Better still, where were his 30,000 men, so vital to any defense of St. Louis?

Halleck began to wonder about two possibilities: one, had Grant's great glory led him to celebrate with drink again?; two, had it gone to his head so that he no longer felt subordinate to his chief, Halleck? Worse, there was a third: had it led him to covet Halleck's job? On March 3 he wired McClellan: "I have had no communication with General Grant for more than a week. He left his command without my authority and went to Nashville. His army seems to be as much demoralized by the victory of Fort Donelson as was that of the Potomac by the defeat of Bull Run. It is hard to censure a successful general immediately after a victory, but I think he richly deserves it. I can get no returns, no reports, no information of any kind from him. Satisfied with his victory, he sits down and enjoys it without any regard to the future . . ." McClellan, who could scent a rival just as quickly as Halleck, promptly replied: "Generals must observe discipline as well as private soldiers. Do not hesitate to arrest him at once if the good of the service requires it . . ."

Halleck was not quite willing to go that far, but he did order Grant to turn his command over to Smith and remain at Fort Henry, asking: "Why do you not obey my orders to report strength and positions of your command?" Next he wired McClellan: "A rumor has just reached me that since the taking of Fort Donelson, General Grant has resumed his former bad habits." As Halleck well knew, Grant's drinking was common knowledge among U.S. Army officers. McClellan would get the point.

But then a telegram arrived from Grant after he had turned his command over to Smith as ordered. It read: "I am not aware of ever having disobeyed any order from headquarters—certainly never intended such a thing." What had happened was that a telegraph operator had defected to the Confederacy, taking all of Grant's reports with him. But this did not satisfy Halleck, who still complained about Grant's silence. Annoyed, Grant asked to be relieved from further duty in the department. Halleck refused, yet he did forward an anonymous letter suggesting that Grant had improperly handled property captured at Henry. Now the Little 'Un lost his temper and wired: "There is such a disposition to find fault with me that I again ask to be relieved from further duty until I can be placed right in the estimate of higher authority."

To Grant's amazement the next telegram from Halleck might have been sent by his father. "You cannot be relieved from your command," it said. "There is no good reason for it. . . . Instead of relieving you, I wish you as soon as your new army is in the field to assume command and lead it on to new victories."

What had changed Halleck's mind was an alternating train of good-bad-then-good-again events. First, the evacuation of Columbus had relieved him of his fears of a Rebel attack, while there had been good news at Elkhorn Tavern and New Madrid. Then there came a peremptory order from the adjutant general telling him that Lincoln and Stanton desired him to forward specific charges against Grant. This shook Halleck, if only because he had nothing specific on Grant, only rumors and his own enmity. But then he was overjoyed: *he got the West!* In the same General Order that relieved McClellan as general-in-chief, Lincoln created the Department of the Mississippi, stretching five hundred miles from Knoxville to Kansas, with Halleck in command. So now Old Brains had become quite fond of U. S. Grant, the fightingest general in his department, just the man to discomfit Beauregard concentrating around Corinth with 20,000 men. "The power is in your hands," he wired Grant. "Use it and you will be sustained by all above you."

Vindicated, Grant rejoined his army at Pittsburg Landing on the Tennessee.

Grant was delighted when he found his old friend William Tecumseh Sherman at Pittsburg Landing. He had brought an untrained new division there from Paducah, taking command of the army when old C. F. Smith skinned his leg jumping from a steamboat to a rowboat, this seemingly slight injury becoming infected so that he had had to take to his bed. Sherman's ebullient nature had returned. For once Halleck had been right: rest was the one thing that the jittery Sherman had needed. His nerves had been unable to withstand the shock that secession had delivered to his mystic devotion to the Union, but now he was calm again, perhaps too calm, scorning to entrench his men at his position near Shiloh meeting house, fewer than twenty miles away from the main Confederate force. Grant had told him that he didn't need to entrench. Buell would soon be there and then Halleck himself, and they would all go down together to Corinth and finish the Rebels off.

William Tecumseh Sherman was overjoyed.

30

·

William T. Sherman

TWO FRONTIER FAMILIES of the Northwest Territory* combined to shape the mind and character of William Tecumseh Sherman. The first, of course, was his own family, the Shermans of Connecticut, descendants of Samuel Sherman, an Anglo-Irish Puritan preacher who had immigrated to the Nutmeg colony in 1634. Samuel helped to found the town of Woodbury, becoming both a judge and a legislator. Four generations of Shermans following him also sat on the bench or in the legislature, or practiced law.

Charles Sherman was the last of these. A graduate of Dartmouth College, he read law in his father's office, being admitted to the bar in 1810. In the summer of that year he married Mary Hoyt, a Norwalk neighbor, and set out for the Northwest Territory to claim a tract of land owned by his father. But the Northwest was then being ravaged by the followers of Tecumseh, the great Shawnee chieftain who sought to unite the Indian tribes against the advance of white men. Instead Charles went to Lancaster, Ohio, where he opened a law office and began to prosper. On February 8, 1820, a red-haired son, their sixth child, was born to Charles and Mary, and the father named him Tecumseh in honor of the Indian chief whom he admired for the humane way in which he tried to restrain his Indians. Unable to pronounce their baby brother's unusual name, his siblings called him Cump.

Thomas Ewing's family was the second force molding William Tecumseh Sherman. His forebears had come to America from Ireland in 1718, settling in Greenwich, New Jersey. His father, George, had been a lieutenant in Washington's army. Financial failure had sent George migrating west of the

*Modern Mid-West.

268

Alleghenies and north of the Ohio River. Thomas had grown up in a log cabin with windows of oiled paper and tables made of split logs, beds upheld by poles and bedclothes of deerskin and bearskin. Meat and vegetables were dried on the rafters. On the table stood pots of venison, bear meat, raccoon or wild turkey, which was eaten with sharpened sassafras sticks. A strange vegetable was added to the menu when little Apphia Brown ate a "love apple" and did not die of poison as everyone expected, but lived to be celebrated as the first person to eat a tomato in the Hockhocking Valley.

At maturity, Thomas Ewing was a mountain of a man: well over six feet tall, 260 pounds and a head so massive that it was said that his hat would fall down to an ordinary man's shoulders. In his boyhood and youth he had educated himself with books bought with skins of the animals he had trapped or shot. Eager for formal education, he spent his summers boiling salt at the Kanawha Salines in Virginia, earning from this grueling work enough money to put himself through Ohio University. Settling in Lancaster, he befriended Charles Sherman. Just before Tecumseh was born, Ewing married Maria Boyle, the beautiful and cultivated daughter of Hugh Boyle, an Irish immigrant who had fled County Donegal because of "some troubles" with the British and had become Fairfield County clerk. Maria's Catholicism was no more an impediment to Ewing's intent to marry her than Charles Sherman's Masonry was a barrier to their friendship, much as Ewing disapproved of secret societies. Nor did Hugh Boyle try to block the marriage of his daughter to a Presbyterian. Life on the frontier was too hard, too intimate, too much a shared experience to allow prejudice to poison the lives of decent people.

So the Ewings—eventually eight of them—and the Shermans—thirteen strong—lived in warm and affectionate friendship only a few doors apart on the hill rising in the center of Lancaster. And then, in June of 1829, Charles Sherman died of what was diagnosed as typhoid fever. Mary Sherman was left with eleven children, saddled with debts and an expectation of only $400 a year, a legacy from her father. Ewing organized a fund to retire the mortgage on Mary's home. But he knew that the widow still would not have enough to feed and clothe all those children. So he decided to take one of them off her hands.

"I want one of them," he said to seventeen-year-old Elizabeth Sherman. "You must give me the brightest of the lot, and I will make a man of him."

"Take Cump, the red-haired one," Elizabeth said. "He's the smartest."

Thomas Ewing took nine-year-old Cump by the hand and led him up the street to his own fine brick mansion. It was a short walk, but it led the boy deep into Ewing's heart and the bosom of his family.

Dominican priests came regularly to the Ewing home, staying for a week to instruct the children. One day one of the Ewings remarked that Cump had never really been baptized. Maria Ewing immediately ran down the street to the Widow Sherman, an Episcopalian, who said she had no objection to her son's being baptized by a priest. But when the white-robed son of St. Dominic heard that the boy's name was Tecumseh, he was scandalized. "He must be named for a saint," he said, opening *The Lives of the Saints.* "Today is the feast of St. William, June 25," he said. "I shall name him William." So Cump became William Tecumseh Sherman, although no Ewing ever called him Bill. Nor did Cump show any more enthusiasm for his new faith than he had shown for the mainline Protestant sects in which most residents of Lancaster were enrolled. Throughout his life he would follow the faith of his foster father: devotion to the Union and tolerance of religion. The great questions—deism or atheism, accident or design— never seemed to appeal to his otherwise speculative, lucid, perceptive and penetrating intelligence.

Cump Sherman was extremely happy with the Ewings. His best friend was Philemon Ewing, a lighthearted boy of his own age, and he idolized his foster father, who kept a careful eye upon his upbringing. Ewing had a great affection for the boy, referring to him as "Cumpy" in his letters home from Washington, after he had become one of the most powerful men in America, a U.S. senator from Ohio and a cabinet officer under two presidents. "There was nothing especially remarkable about him," Ewing wrote later, "except that I never knew so young a boy who would do an errand so correctly and promptly as he did. He was transparently honest, faithful and reliable, studious and correct in habits. His progress in education was steady and substantial."

Cump's education became one of Thomas and Maria Ewing's main concerns as the red-haired boy entered his teens, growing tall and muscular for his age. Ewing could make appointments to the Military Academy. One of these was offered to Phil, who is said to have disdained it as the son of a wealthy man who did not wish to be educated at public expense. So it was given to Cump, who, already sensitive to the Ewings' generosity and determined to sponge off them as little as possible, accepted it because it freed him of that embarrassment.

Cump impressed his West Point instructors as a brilliant scholar, but his dress and decorum brought him so many demerits that he was dragged down in the standings. He had the westerner's indifference to elegance of either clothes or manner, judging a man by what he said and did. "I was not considered a good soldier," he wrote later. "I was not a Sunday-school cadet. I ranked 124 in the whole student body [of 211] for good behavior. My average demerits, per annum, were about 150 [50 below the maximum], which reduced my final class standing from Number 4 to Number 6."

Throughout his years on the Plains, Cump maintained a continuous correspondence with Ellen Ewing, "my best Lancaster correspondent." There was something more than sister and brother between these two, although at the time neither was aware of it.

West Point's haughty and aristocratic attitudes were also developing in Cump a deep distrust of democracy, or at least of the leveling principle which he thought he perceived in it; and for politicians he had an even deeper contempt, confirmed by the scurrilous, drunken and vulgar presidential campaigns waged by Martin van Buren and William Henry Harrison in 1840, the year of his graduation. By then William Tecumseh Sherman was "Cump" no more, for his classmates had begun to call him Bill.

Because Sherman was only sixth in his class, he missed assignment to the engineers, then the elite corps. But this did not disappoint him, since he sought service in the Seminole War, and when he was ordered to join the 3rd Artillery there he was delighted. He smelled no gunpowder, however, although he did see slavery at work for the first time, the spectacle of slave-owners from Georgia and South Carolina recovering runaway bondsmen captured by the U.S. Army. Since colonial days slaves had sought refuge—and sometimes marriage—among the swamp-dwelling Seminoles of Florida. It was to recover these runaways as much as to crush the Indians and drive them west of the Mississippi that the U. S. government had sent troops into the peninsula. To Sherman, then, slavery had governmental sanction and was an institution to defend.

He also saw that the army's tactics against the Seminoles were succeeding. Constant raids on their villages in which homes and crops were destroyed and Indians taken captive were whittling their spirit of resistance. From this his sharp mind drew a military lesson he never forgot: strike at the enemy's people and productive capacity and you will weaken their morale and starve his armies.

On November 30, 1841, only eighteen months after being graduated, Sherman was commissioned a first lieutenant, a promotion rarely achieved in less than five years. It also brought him a transfer to Picolata, and thus there began a love affair with the South that was to last many years. The bond grew stronger in Charleston, where he spent five years, charmed by his gracious hosts, but dismayed by their open, fire-eating talk of secession. This struck at the heart of his religion of Unionism. Returning to Lancaster, he found Ellen at nineteen beautiful and desirable, and the two came to an agreement that they would marry. Maria Ewing was at first opposed, but then, realizing that the children were not actually related, she withdrew her objections. Nevertheless, the Ewing family was shocked. Six-year-old Sissie spoke for all of them when she cried: "Why, they *can't!*" But wedding bells would not ring soon for the brother-and-sister turned lovers. Sherman could not support a wife and family on $70 a month and Ellen was so fond of Lancaster it was not likely that she would embrace too eagerly the post-to-post boredom and privation that was the lot of a lieutenant's wife.

So he resumed his other love affair—with the South—charmed once again by Charleston, to which he returned via St. Louis, fascinated by the mighty Mississippi's incredible ship traffic and, when he sailed downriver to New Orleans, enchanted by roses blooming in winter there. Infatuated as he was with Southern aristocracy, he ignored the hideous economic base upon which all this grace and elegance rested. Army duties also took him into Georgia and Alabama, where he rode over terrain that he would put to the torch two decades hence. On long and lonely horseback rides he learned the lay of the land from Rome, Georgia, to Bellefonte, Alabama, from Kenesaw Mountain to Augusta, studying its slopes and curves, peaks and valleys with a thoroughness springing from his passion for the earth.

Sherman by the time he was twenty-six had become so completely Southern that he could applaud the annexation of Texas—the root cause of the Mexican War—while his detestation of Abolitionists as meddlers grew apace. When the war with Mexico did come he never heard the sound of cannon but found himself aboard ship bound for California.

California prepared Sherman for business, not for war. He became quartermaster for Major General Stephen Kearny's command, showing extraordinary organizing skill in making the post self-supporting. He built sawmills and gristmills, buying horses and beef at rock-bottom prices and keeping the commissary supplied with deer, elk and wild fowl. Kearny was impressed with the young officer's executive ability, and so was his successor, Colonel K. B. Mason. Nevertheless, Sherman was bored with California. He felt worse after the war ended in 1848 and he read of the promotions awarded the men he had known at West Point or served with elsewhere.

He thought of resigning, but then Colonel Mason called him into his office and pointed to some yellow rocks on a table, asking: "What is that?"

Sherman called for a hammer and beat the rocks flat. "It is pure gold," he replied, his eyes gleaming. Mason nodded, and told him that Captain Sutter had found the nuggets while digging a race for a new sawmill on the Sacramento River. Sherman immediately grasped the significance of the discovery, riding out to Sutter's mill to find four thousand prospectors eagerly panning yellow sand. He packed $3,000 worth of gold nuggets into a tea caddy, wrote a report, and sent both post haste to Washington. When President Polk shook the world with his announcement of the California discovery, he quoted Sherman's report.

But the Gold Rush brought nothing but misery to the lieutenant and his brother officers. Private soldiers, laughing at their "pay" of seven dollars a month, deserted in droves to work in the mines at twenty-five dollars a day. Sherman decided to resign, but was dissuaded by his commanding officer, and then he was liberated from Limbo by an order summoning him to Washington as a bearer of special dispatches. His foster father, now secretary of the interior in President Taylor's cabinet, had been pulling strings.

It was now a happy Cump who came home to Ewing's mansion near the White House in the winter of 1850. At last he could marry Ellen. She was twenty-seven, already an old maid by the standards of the day, and he was thirty. She had waited eight years for her lover, but now, on May Day, with the capital bursting into blossom, they were married in the family home. President Taylor and the entire cabinet was there, as well as Daniel Webster and the aging lion of Kentucky, Henry Clay. There were, of course, many handsome presents, but the best was Thomas Ewing's assurance that four new captaincies were to be created and Sherman would get one of them. That would be enough to keep the newlyweds financially independent.

Captain Sherman was delighted to find that his new assignment was St. Louis, the booming city on his beloved Mississippi. He leased a home, but Ellen was soon gone, back in Lancaster to prepare for the baby that arrived nine months to the day after their wedding. This would be a pattern in their marriage, for Ellen preferred Lancaster to any other place in the world. Seeing no war on the horizon, Sherman resigned from the army on September 6, 1853, to manage a branch bank in San Francisco for the St. Louis financiers, Lucas & Symonds. He was to be paid the handsome salary of $5,000 a year, and receive a one-eighth interest in the bank.

Sherman was an immediate success, raising his bank's deposits from $300,000 to half a million within a year and erecting a new bank building. Correctly diagnosing a decline in real estate sales amid booming prosperity as a sign of approaching financial collapse, he retrenched and his bank remained solvent during the San Francisco crash of 1854–55 while banks around him were going under. His grateful employers added $4,000 to his annual income. They added another $4,000 when he turned down a city offer to become its treasurer with the remark "I am not eligible because I have not been graduated from the penitentiary."

In this there was more truth than wit, for San Francisco by then was an almost totally lawless city. Yet he refused to join the vigilantes forming to fight crime and corruption. They met secretly, not scrupling to hang known criminals without benefit of trial, and although they did clean up San Francisco, Sherman wrote that they had "given stimulus to a dangerous principle, that would at any time justify the mob in seizing the powers of government."

From financial success Sherman soon sank to financial ruin after both state and city repudiated their debts. He became penniless after he assumed responsibility for a $13,000 loss suffered by old army friends who had asked him to invest money for them. This he certainly did not need to do, granting the risks of investment, but William Tecumseh Sherman's moral code was a bit higher than a stockbroker's.

Ewing tried to interest Sherman in managing his investments, or in running his salt mill near Lancaster, but his red-haired son-in-law was so proud, so sensitive to being patronized, that he resisted every attempt to rescue him from ruin. At last, he agreed to go to Leavenworth in Kansas, a little village of four thousand souls near the fort of that name and where young Tom Ewing was busy in politics and the law. He would look after his father-in-law's interests there.

In Leavenworth without Ellen and the children, Sherman became interested in the law and was admitted to the bar "on the grounds of general intelligence." The year was 1858, and Sherman, at thirty-eight, was described in a local paper as tall, lean and muscular, with a "long, keen head, bluish-gray eyes that smouldered with fire, a sharp, well-cut mouth; complexion fair, hair and beard sandy-red, straight, short and strong." In his eyes there were "gleams of saturnine humor and kindness around the mouth." He was extremely opinionated and an incredible conversationalist.

Opinionated he was indeed, and when he began to sound forth on the profession he had once detested he annoyed his new partners, Tom Ewing and Daniel McCook. They decided to let him try a case alone. When his opposing counsel denounced him as a robber and exploiter of the poor, Sherman fell for this ancient shyster trick, flying into a rage and threatening to thrash his critic. Of course, the jury found against him, and Sherman stomped back to his office vowing to have nothing more to do with the law.

Unemployed, Sherman next put his restless mind and his powers of prophecy to work on a plan for a coast-to-coast railroad. At first he answered his brother John's objection that his road would pass through hostile Indian territory with the observation: "So large a number of Irish workmen distributed along the road will introduce enough whisky to kill off all the Indians within 300 miles of the road." With incredible accuracy Sherman predicted exactly what route the road should follow, its cost of $200 million taking ten years to build, and every other detail down to where deposits of coal and wood could be found and the revenue to be received. With typical modesty he did not mention his own railroad experience or the exploring parties he had sent into the Sierra Madre. As he proposed, the road was finished in 1869 despite the ravages of the Civil War.

With remarkable clairvoyance Sherman also prophesized in another letter to John: "I think in the next ten years we will have plenty to do in the war line—Mormon war, civil broils and strife, contests growing out of slavery and other exciting topics." Within a year the U.S. Army would be sent to Mormon Utah to restore order, and within another "civil broils" with all their bloodshed and agony would torment the land. For himself, the gloomy Sherman's powers of prophecy failed him, writing to Ellen:

"I look upon myself as a dead cock in the pit, not worthy of further notice . . ."

Sherman was now determined to leave Kansas. He had handled his father-in-law's investments with meticulous care, but had done little for himself. He wrote to his friend Don Carlos Buell, then assistant adjutant general and close adviser to Secretary of War Floyd, asking if there were any vacancies in the army. Buell replied that there were none but told him that Louisiana was planning a state military college. General George Mason Graham, half-brother of that Colonel Mason who had been Sherman's friend in California, was advertising for a superintendent. At once Sherman sent him his application, which Graham enthusiastically supported. So did his sister, a nun who remembered Ellen as one of her favorite pupils. Sherman's terse and straightforward application of less than a hundred words also helped.

After it was read, a member of the Board of Supervisors named Sam Henarie cried: "By God, he's my man. He's a man of sense. I'm ready for the vote."

"But we have a number more applications," Graham protested.

"Well, you can read them," Henarie snorted, "but let me out of here. When you get through, call me and I'll come back and vote for Sherman."

Richard and J. P. Taylor, son and brother of the late President Zachary Taylor, also urged Sherman's appointment, and Graham, secretly pleased, consented. Late in October, William Tecumseh Sherman set out for Alexandria to take up his fourth profession.

On January 2, 1860, Sherman opened the doors of the academy to some fifty-six cadets. At once he told them and their parents: "There can be but one master." Those who rebelled against this dictum were summarily expelled, and a plot against him conceived by their influential parents thwarted by his own powerful friends. But then came the division of the Democratic Party, the election of Lincoln and South Carolina's secession. Resigning in anguish, Sherman headed north to take charge of a St. Louis streetcar company. Sumter put him back in uniform and Bull Run gave him his first experience of combat. Then came the Kentucky jitters, but now, at Shiloh with his old friend Grant—the "dead cock in the pit" rejoining the down-and-outer from Hardscrabble Farm—William Tecumseh Sherman was once again a soldier's soldier.

31

·

Shiloh

ALTHOUGH DISMAYED by the loss of New Madrid and the investment of Island Number Ten, Beauregard at Corinth had not given up on his dream of moving on St. Louis and recovering the initiative in the West. His thinking was based on this conviction: "We must defeat the enemy *somewhere,* to give confidence to our friends. . . . We must give up some minor points, and concentrate our forces, to save the most important ones, or we will lose all of them in succession." His belief in the Napoleonic concept of concentration led him to persuade Van Dorn to join him and to encourage Johnston to hurry to Corinth from Murfreesboro. Full of dramatic Napoleonic messages to his soldiers, he even appealed to the planters of the Mississippi Valley to give him their bells to melt down for sorely needed cannon. This provoked much mirth in Kentucky, where the Louisville *Courier* declared: "The Rebels can afford to give up all their church bells, cow bells and dinner bells to Beauregard, for they never go to church now, their cows have all been taken by foraging parties and they have no dinner to be summoned to."

In late March Beauregard thought he saw a golden opportunity for quick offensive action. Grant's army of 35,000 was twenty-odd miles above him while Buell with 50,000 had not yet left Nashville to join him. On March 24, after Albert Sidney Johnston arrived in Corinth, the Confederate army with Beauregard's, Polk's and Van Dorn's formations numbered about 40,000 men. This was just larger than Grant and smaller than Buell. Beauregard reasoned that if they could pounce on Grant to destroy him before Buell arrived, they could then turn on Buell, and thus the way to St. Louis and Louisville would lie open. It was a good plan, and after Johnston took command he promised to follow it.

■　　■　　■

There might have been something to Halleck's belief that Grant's great glory and fame had gone to his head. He knew that across the North he was Unconditional Surrender Grant now, and his picture had been on the cover of *Harper's* magazine. His fame had even led him to change his style of smoking. So many admirers had sent him so many boxes of cigars that he had put away his trusty meerschaum pipe and begun to appear everywhere with a cheroot in his mouth. He had developed the habit when a march or battle was in progress of sitting on a log by the roadside, chewing or smoking his cigar while whittling on a stick. It was a significant habit, and his troops did not like to see him thus because "it always means hard fightin'." Grant had also trimmed his long beard so that it was just a short brown wreath from ear to ear. Most noticeable to those who knew him was his dilatoriness. He did not bother to fortify his position at Pittsburg Landing. His six divisions were encamped inside two creeks wherever they found a suitable open field, and there were no provisions for their defense. In this Grant may have been another of those Mexican War veterans who had little faith in fixed positions, having stormed so many of them so successfully. "By God," old C. F. Smith cried from his sickbed, "I ask nothing better than to have the Rebels to come out and attack us! We can whip them to hell. Our men suppose we have come here to fight, and if we begin to spade it will make them think we fear the enemy." Security, meanwhile, was sketchy at best. Only Sherman was alarmed. "We are in danger here," he told reporters, and when he was asked why he did not warn Grant, he shrugged and said: "Oh, they'd call me crazy again." Gradually, however, Sherman also became complacent, assuring Grant that he did not expect "anything like an attack." Grant meanwhile had set up his headquarters nine miles downriver at Savannah. He explained this almost fatal separation of the army's brains from its body by saying he had been ordered to meet Buell there. And yet on the night of April 5 the Confederate army was only two miles away from Sherman south of Shiloh Church.

If Grant's men were unprepared, Johnston's were untrained and unseasoned. Except for Forrest's troopers, and a handful of Polk's who had fought at Belmont, the rest had never heard a shot fired in anger. Nor had they done much marching. Braxton Bragg, that tall, gangly, stern-eyed West Pointer from North Carolina, a bushy-browed disciplinarian with the face of a hangman, spoke contemptuously of "this mob we have, miscalled soldiers." By comparison, two-thirds of Grant's men had been in battle— victorious battle. Johnston had wanted to give the Army of the Mississippi more training, but when on April 2 Beauregard received a telegram suggesting a Federal move on Memphis, he notified Johnston: "Now is the moment to advance, and strike the enemy at Pittsburg Landing." This meant marching without Van Dorn, and Johnston wanted to wait for him. At last he agreed to move and the orders were drawn up. It was to begin April 3, with the attack scheduled for April 4.

Two parallel roads formed like a bow and string led to the assembly area at Mickey's, twenty miles north, and two divisions were to march along each one of them to prevent confusion and traffic jams. But sloppy marching discipline—especially in Bragg's division—and the onset of thunderstorms caused a two-day delay. Worse, the men had consumed their three-day cooked ration, believing, as the Rebels always did, that rations were easier to carry in the stomach than the haversack, and during the numerous delays they had taken to pot-shooting rabbits and birds and practicing Rebel yells. On April 5 an infuriated Beauregard at a roadside conference, convinced that the vital element of surprise had been lost, counseled an immediate return to Corinth. "There is no chance for surprise," he said angrily. "Now they will be entrenched to the eyes."

Johnston was shocked and disagreed. So did the division commanders—Bragg, Polk, Breckinridge and Hardee—and Johnston said: "Gentlemen, we will attack tomorrow." When Beauregard protested that Buell most likely had joined Grant and the Federals now numbered about 70,000, Johnston paid no heed to this objection but rather ordered his four commanders to deploy in line of battle. Hardee with 7,000 would be in the lead, followed by Bragg with 16,000, Polk with 10,000 next and Breckinridge with 7,000 in the rear. If Van Dorn with his 15,000 arrived in time for the fight, the Rebels would outnumber the Federals. Johnston also ordered the men to sleep on their arms in battle formation. As he left the conference, he said to an aide: "I would fight them if they were a million. They can present no greater front between two creeks than we can, and the more men they crowd in there, the worse we can make it for them."

Both sides slept fitfully that night under a sickle moon.

Beauregard had been partially right: some of Buell's troops had joined Grant. One division was outside Savannah. The remainder of his force would arrive next day and the following—the sixth and seventh. He would confer with Grant on the sixth.

Meanwhile, Grant on the sixth was reading reports, unable to take his steamboat ride south. His horse had slipped and fallen on his leg. His ankle had swelled so much that his boot had had to be cut away, and he was compelled to hobble about on a crutch. Still he was delighted that Buell had arrived. The attack on Corinth could now be launched without delay, with the Union possessing a superiority in numbers. One of the messages that Grant read was from Sherman, reporting the presence of enemy cavalry, infantry and artillery to his front, and promising to send him ten prisoners taken in a skirmish the night of the fifth.

Grant did not bother to question the prisoners. Besides, the officer most adept at interrogation was at Hamburg, inspecting the campsite for Buell's army. There was nothing for Grant to do but go to sleep in the fine big mansion on the bluff at Savannah where the bedridden Smith also lay. Before he did he wired Halleck that he had not "the faintest idea" of being attacked.

In the morning at breakfast he heard the boom of guns to the south.

Shiloh Church was a Methodist meeting-house of logs named for an Israelite town in Ephraim, where the Tabernacle and the Ark of the Covenant had once stood, and where the prophet Samuel had seen great visions. It meant "place of peace." By air it was about four miles from Pittsburg Landing, by the winding road that ran past the church about six. Of Grant's six divisions, one under Lew Wallace was five miles north of Pittsburg Landing at Crump's Landing, while the other five were in various camps between the two creeks with Sherman and Benjamin Prentiss forward at Shiloh, Sherman on the right, Prentiss on the left. None of these formations was in battle array nor was there any line between them.

Before the battle was joined Beauregard again attempted to persuade Johnston to return to Corinth, but the commander, drinking coffee from a cup, made no reply. From the front there came a ragged ripple of musketry, like the sound of cloth tearing. At once Johnston handed his half-empty cup to an orderly. "The battle has begun, gentlemen," he said. "It is too late to change our dispositions." Mounting his big bay horse, he sat silently in the saddle, sunk in thought. Then he twitched the reins and his mount began walking toward the front. Turning, Johnston said to his staff: "Tonight we will water our horses in the Tennessee River."

The battle had begun ahead of schedule because Union patrols had collided with Confederate skirmishers. Mistaking them for a scouting party, the Yankees attacked, driving them back only to be repulsed themselves by a volley from Hardee's main body. They went scampering to the rear, one of them yelling, "The Johnnies are there thicker than Spanish needles in a fence corner!" Thus the alarm was given to Sherman, but he ignored it because it came from a jittery Ohio colonel who had been crying wolf all

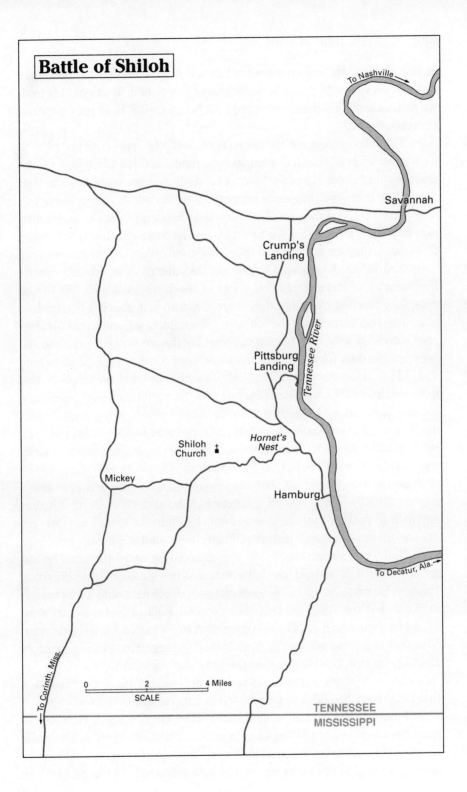

Battle of Shiloh

To Nashville

Savannah

Crump's
Landing

Tennessee River

Pittsburg
Landing

Hornet's
Nest

Shiloh
Church

Mickey

Hamburg

To Decatur, Ala.

0   2   4 Miles
SCALE

To Corinth, Miss.

TENNESSEE
MISSISSIPPI

night long. But when Sherman went forward with an orderly to investigate and a Rebel volley dropped the orderly dead beside him, he cried, "My God, we're attacked!" To the men around him, he shouted: "Hold your position, I'll support you."

They did, except for the nervous colonel who quickly departed with his troops, while Sherman formed his men along the ridge where their white tents were pitched. Hardee's Graybacks could see the tents and the blue dots of the enemy as they came surging out of the wood. Yelling like fiends they came up the slope, but the Federals of Sherman's mostly green division held their ground. Four times they repulsed the gray lines, but on the fifth assault they gave way, retiring in fairly good order to form another line. They had inflicted ferocious losses on the enemy. The 6th Mississippi Regiment alone had entered that valley of death with 425 men, but by the time they reached the ridge they were down to just above a hundred.

Prentiss's troops on the left were also fighting gallantly, and McClernand's division, marching toward the sound of the guns, moved into the gap between the two forward divisions to present a solid three-division blue line. Most astonishing in this steady reaction to what was only a few minutes short of a complete surprise, was the performance of Sherman's troops—and this was chiefly due to their commander, who moved confidently among them shouting orders. The redhead had been hit twice already: a bullet through the hand and another one clipping his shoulder strap and merely creasing his skin. A headquarters aide riding into the battle to appraise the situation found Sherman leaning against a tree. His eyes never moving from the scene unfolding before him, he said: "Tell Grant if he has any men to spare I can use them. If not, I will do the best I can. We are holding them pretty well just now. Pretty well—but it's hot as hell!"

Grant was already at Shiloh. The moment he heard the guns he had gathered his staff and ridden down to board the steamboat for Pittsburg Landing. En route he wrote two orders: one to Buell canceling the Savannah meeting, and the other to Brigadier General William Nelson—the man-mountain former naval officer—directing him to march his brigade from Savannah to a point across the river from Pittsburg. Approaching Crump's Landing, he saw Lew Wallace on the jetty and shouted to him to put his men on the alert for a possible attack in that sector. Wallace yelled back that he already had, and Grant nodded in satisfaction.

Pittsburg was already under attack when Grant landed. He rode toward the uproar around Shiloh Church with his crutch strapped to his saddle like a carbine. After he saw wounded men stumbling to the rear, and mixed among them skulkers hurrying for the safety beneath Pittsburg bluff, he immediately ordered a straggler's line across the road leading out of the battle. Military police crying "Show blood!" to soldiers leaving the battle were backed up by a battery of artillery. Grant next rode forward to where Stephen A. Hurlbut and W.H.L. Wallace had begun to feed reinforcements to Sherman, and was again satisfied. Now, it seemed to him, was the time to call upon his reserve, and he sent a summons to Lew Wallace to join the right flank. This meant leaving Crump's Landing exposed to a turning movement, but the way the battle boomed and roared like nothing he had ever heard before convinced him that the enemy was making an all-out frontal assault.

What Grant saw at the front was also satisfying, even though Sherman told him that one of his brigades had simply vanished, that the other two were resisting under heavy pressure at their second position. Sherman feared that they might run out of ammunition, but Grant assured him that more was on the way. Next he visited McClernand, who was fighting furiously behind Shiloh Church, but hanging on. Prentiss's division had been driven from its first position by Hardee's opening onslaught, but in retreating his men had found a sunken wagon road from which they were now taking a terrible toll among the oncharging Johnnies.

Returning to Pittsburg Landing Grant was shocked to see the thickening flood of fugitives streaming to the rear. The threats of the military police and their officers at the straggler line failed to intimidate them, and once they had found the sanctuary under the bluff they were impossible to move. Also, word awaited Grant of the retirement of Sherman and McClernand still farther to the rear. W.H.L. Wallace and Hurlbut had committed all their troops and nothing had been heard of Lew Wallace. At any moment the continuing—nay, mounting—fury of the Confederates might burst his front, and he had no reserve with which to contain a breakthrough. At once he dispatched two staff officers to hasten Lew Wallace and got off a message to Nelson: "If you will get upon the field, leaving all your baggage on the east bank of the river, it will be a move to our advantage." And then, in a gross exaggeration perhaps calculated to induce speed: "The Rebel force is estimated at over 100,000 men."

Albert Sidney Johnston had ridden toward the forefront of the battle. Standing tall in the saddle on his splendid mount, the Texan brought cheers from his admiring men. He had left Beauregard in Shiloh Church to do for him what Joe Johnston had done for the Little Creole at Bull Run: forward arriving units to him and stop the rearward flow of skulkers and only slightly wounded men. Johnston was pleased to hear the shrill fox hunter's cries breaking from the mouths of his troops as they drove the Yankees out of their second position. But just like Grant, he had problems with stragglers. One wrathful Arkansas major told him a fleeing Tennessee regiment crying, "Retreat! Retreat!" had led his men to believe that this was an order so that they, too, retired. The Tennesseeans were in such a fright, he said, "that they ran over and trampled in the mud our brave color-bearer." Also the Orleans Guard Battalion, proudly bearing Beauregard's name on its roster, had unwisely entered battle wearing dress blue uniforms and were immediately fired upon by their comrades in gray. They fired back, and when told they were firing on friends, their colonel cried: "I know it. But, dammit, sir, we fire on everybody that fires on us!"

Such confusion is common to the battlefield and hardly disturbed Johnston. What dismayed him was the spectacle of many of his hungry soldiers, who had long ago consumed their rations, sitting down to finish the uneaten Sunday morning breakfasts of the surprised Yankees. They also foraged in their tents for loot, or opened their haversacks for souvenirs, gleefully reading aloud the love letters of the Federals' sweethearts. Thus hundreds of men—perhaps even a few thousand—were lost in the attack which was beginning to slow down in confusion.

Beauregard's plan—based on Waterloo, of all Napoleon's battles!—which had looked so neat and sure on paper was beginning to be shredded by the uneven terrain of the Shiloh plateau, by gullies and bushes and the bullets of the stubborn men in blue. It had called for an assault by three corps in line ahead, each behind the other, and each feeding units into the one ahead. But these formations had become so intermingled that commanders found themselves bellowing orders to strange battalions or companies. Much valuable time was lost until coordination could be restored by dividing the front into four sectors: Bragg and Breckinridge on the right, Hardee and Polk on the left. Even this was not sufficient as this great clanging, smoking, roaring battle—the first pitched struggle in the history of modern arms—split off into perhaps a hundred furious little conflicts, a hideous, cacophonic symphony in powder and iron, two hundred cannon thundering like giant drums counterpointing the timpani of the musketry, the whistling of the minié balls and the screams of the stricken.

Johnston had hoped to turn Grant's left and thus cut off any attempted escape to the Tennessee, but Prentiss's stubborn Bluebellies in their sunken road thwarted every attempt to outflank him. "It's a hornet's nest in there!" a Rebel soldier cried, and so the Federal position came to be called the Hornet's Nest. As it continued to hold out, the Confederate left drove deeper than the right, thus presenting a most dangerous opportunity for the Union to strike at this wing's exposed right flank and achieve a penetration. Johnston himself rode to the stalled far right. He had rebuked a young officer for looting a Union tent, but in his right hand he carried his own souvenir: a captured cup which he held like a baton, his index finger crooked inside the handle. On the right of the Hornet's Nest was a ten-acre peach orchard held by Hurlbut's men supported by artillery. Its branches were bright with pink blossoms. Johnston arrived there just after the Federals had repulsed a charge by one of Breckinridge's brigades. Petals clipped free by bullets were still fluttering to the ground like a rain of pink confetti. Johnston rode among the shaken Graybacks, shouting: "Men, they are stubborn! We must use the bayonet!" To make his point he touched the tips of their blades with his cup. "These must do the work." Riding front and center he rose in his stirrups, waving his hat. "I will lead you!" Cheering wildly, the Graybacks swept forward and drove the Yankees out of the orchard. Johnston came riding back smiling in exaltation, his uniform ripped and torn by bullets, a boot sole cut in half. He shook it so that the dangling leather flapped, laughing. "They didn't trip me up this time." Suddenly he reeled in the saddle. Governor Isham Harris of Tennessee, one of his aides, rushed to his side.

"General, are you hurt?"

"Yes," Johnston gasped. "And I fear seriously."

Harris led Johnston's horse to a ravine where he helped the stricken general to the ground. He began to undo his clothes, searching for a bullet hole. He saw nothing until he noticed that Johnston's right boot was full of blood. In the hollow of his knee he found the hole. A bullet had severed the femoral artery. If Harris had known anything about tourniquets he might have stopped the flow of blood. But he did not. Johnston's staff physician had been ordered to care for a group of wounded prisoners. When he protested, Johnston said: "These men were our enemies a moment ago. They are our prisoners now. Take care of them." Thus, by his own compassion, Johnston had deprived himself of the one man who might have saved him. Harris knelt in front of him, crying: "Johnston, do you know me? Johnston, do you know me?"

There was no answer, for the gallant Albert Sidney Johnston was dead.

After Beauregard took command he made the wise decision to keep the news of Johnston's death from the army. He saw clearly that the general attack could not be renewed until the Hornet's Nest was overrun. Accordingly, he massed sixty-two guns to bombard it into submission. Prentiss's position literally exploded under this weight of metal. Bodies, uprooted trees, and great clods of earth flew through the air. Prentiss still held out. On his flanks the divisions of Hurlbut and W.H.L. Wallace began withdrawing, Wallace's men turning to flee after their commander was killed. Hurlbut's followed. Alone, Prentiss was still defiant, still obedient to Grant's order to "maintain that position at all hazards." But then, from being outflanked he became surrounded. Rebels pursuing Hurlbut's and Wallace's fugitives flowed around him and then sealed him off. Only then did this brave and loyal officer surrender himself and 2,200 survivors, much less than half of the number that began the battle, a good two hours after the Confederate batteries had begun to bay.

Two whole hours lost on a battlefield can be decisive, and Beauregard soon learned that "the unforgiving minute" was now his enemy. When he attempted to renew the assault with the sunken road now in his rear and his line shortened, he saw that his men were exhausted. Though green, they had fought valiantly, but now, after twelve hours of unremitting combat, they had nothing left. As they withdrew rain began to fall. Thunder crashed and lightning flashed above this bloodiest battlefield since the Civil War had begun eight days short of a year ago this day—and the rain came down harder. It drummed upon the white Federal tents in which many of the fought-out Graybacks now slept, and it fell coldly on the upturned faces of the quick and the dead.

Prentiss and his men by their valiant stand had probably saved the Union army. By it Sherman and McClernand on the right and to a lesser degree Hurlbut on their left, and still less, Wallace's division, had been saved. So Ulysses S. Grant thought as he sat his horse surrounded by his staff just to the rear of the massed batteries that had helped shatter Beauregard's final assault. When an aide said the situation was dark, Grant replied: "Not at all. They can't force our lines around these batteries tonight. It is too late. Delay counts everything with us. Tomorrow we shall attack them with fresh troops and drive them, of course."

Even as he spoke, Buell's troops were filing up the bluff, glaring contemptuously at the thousands of skulkers huddling there, their souls gone flabby with fear. Others were trying to hitch rides on the ferries, or paddled logs to the greater safety of the eastern shore. "We are whipped!" they called out to the men of Nelson's leading brigade. "Cut to pieces! You'll catch it! You'll see!" Nelson himself was so incensed at his failure to shame them, either by insult or entreaty, that "I asked permission to fire on the knaves." It was refused, of course, and Grant was content to let the skulkers stay where they were, lest they infect the arriving troops with their defeatism. At dusk, Lew Wallace's division came marching in, five hours behind schedule, sheepish beneath the catcalls of the men who had fought. It was not their fault or Wallace's. He had moved to join Grant's right flank, but then had been forced to counter-march when he learned it had been driven back. Grant now had about 25,000 fresh troops, and would renew the battle on the morning of the seventh with more than he had had at dawn of the sixth. Of these about half would be unwearied by battle. Though supremely confident, Grant did not return to Savannah but sought shelter from the rain in a little cabin on a bluff, until he realized that he had stumbled into a makeshift hospital where the screams of the amputees and the sound of the bone saws, like Macbeth, did murder sleep. Instead he wrapped himself in a poncho and lay down beneath a dripping oak tree.

Beauregard slept much more comfortably—and just as confidently—in Sherman's bed inside the Shiloh Church. He had received an inaccurate telegram reporting that Buell had changed direction and was marching toward Decatur, and was convinced that he could complete destruction of Grant's battered army in the morning. Nathan Bedford Forrest had no such delusions. On a scouting ride he had seen Buell's men climbing the bluff, but upon his return to the Confederate camp he could neither find Beauregard nor convince anyone in authority to heed his warning. Hardee told him the battle orders could not be changed, and Forrest stamped away, swearing: "If the enemy comes on us in the morning, we'll be whipped like hell."

They did come, at seven o'clock of the morning of April 7, 1862, and P.G.T. Beauregard was shocked to learn that Don Carlos Buell was in the field, his three divisions advancing on the left of Grant's four behind a shattering artillery bombardment. But the Little Creole quickly recovered his élan, organizing his army to receive rather than deliver an attack. He had some difficulty, his men being scattered all over "the place of peace." Polk had misunderstood the retirement order and gone back as far as the original attack line. Upon his return Beauregard faced Buell and Grant's seven divisions with four: Hardee on the right, Breckinridge and Polk in the center, and Bragg on the left. Like Johnston, Beauregard twice attempted to rally his weary, faltering troops by seizing regimental colors and dashing forward. Rebuked for rashness by a friend, he replied: "The order now must be 'Follow!' not 'Go!'"

But it was not enough. His bone-weary troops simply could not overcome the dejection that engulfed them when they learned that the Yankees had received massive reinforcements. The thought of imminent victory had buoyed them, but now the specter of unavoidable defeat drained away their ardor. Governor Harris, still on the battlefield, sensed this feeling of futility and spoke of it to the chief of staff. He agreed and went to Beauregard with the famous question: "General, do you not think our troops are very much in the condition of a lump of sugar thoroughly soaked in water—preserving its original shape but ready to dissolve? Would it not be judicious to get away with what we have?" Beauregard nodded unhappily. "I intend to withdraw in a few moments," he said.

By four o'clock the retrograde movement was complete, Hardee, Bragg and Polk retiring, while Breckinridge in rear guard covered their retreat with booming guns. He need not have worried, for Grant was content with recovery of the Union camps. That night the soldiers of the departed divisions camped where they had slept on their arms two nights previously. A pounding rain fell, and after the wind veered to north, it turned to sleet. Hailstones as big as bird's eggs came whistling down, increasing the misery of the wounded piled in the wagons like "bags of grain." Beauregard rode up and down the toiling column to offer commiseration to the stricken. Coming up to a youth with a bandaged head, he extended his hand and said: "My brave friend, were you wounded? Never mind. I trust you will be well, soon. Before long, we will make the Yankees pay up, interest and all. The day of our glory is near." The young soldier was enchanted, writing home: "It is strange Pa how we love that little black Frenchman."

Thus ended the Battle of Shiloh, the first great conflict of the Civil War with more than 100,000 men engaged. Nearly two thousand bodies were strewn over the muddy, bloody ground of the place of peace. They had begun to swell and turn black in the April sun and many of them would burst after the rain stopped and the sun returned. Union casualties were 1,754 killed, 8,408 wounded, and 2,885 missing (mostly captured), for a total of 13,047; Confederate 1,723 dead, 8,012 wounded, and 959 missing, for a total of 10,694. Tactically, it had been a standoff, although in possessing the field the Federals may be said to have won a victory. Beauregard, of course, reported a great triumph, and the South went wild with joy. Actually, Davis—grief-stricken to learn of Johnston's death—and his military adviser Robert E. Lee knew better. Lee wired eastern commanders to send reinforcements West, for, as he said: "If Mississippi Valley is lost, Atlantic States would be ruined." Actually, Shiloh was a decisive victory for the North. The Confederacy simply *had* to win at Shiloh if it hoped to recover Kentucky and Missouri, or even to hold Tennessee. Because the South did not triumph, the way to Union conquest of the Mississippi Valley was open. Shiloh was indeed a turning point, a decisive battle, but it was not considered so then; just as the First Battle of the Marne was not at the time understood in World War One or Guadalcanal in World War Two. Shiloh had other portents. It made clear that for the most part the soldiers of both sides were hardy and valiant warriors ready to risk their lives, and that this first of modern wars—made so much more hideous by the telegraph, trains and improved weaponry, so that men might be martialed more efficiently and in greater numbers and set more rapidly at each other's throats with better weapons—was going to be the bloodiest in human history up to this point in time. It also made clear that neither side was anywhere near ready to quit the war, as both felt the other would do. Thus, with his customary lucidity, U. S. Grant could say that after Shiloh:

"I gave up all hope of saving the Union except by complete conquest."

32

■

Billy Yank and Johnny Reb

S HILOH, the first of the bloodbaths of the American Civil War, was also
the dividing line between the improvised war of 1861–62 and the organized war to come. At the beginning of these twelve months of conflict,
Americans both North and South had been individualist in temperament and
inclined to meet each successive crisis by improvising. But nothing changes
a society like war. In America this first of modern struggles eventually
substituted discipline, conformity and planning for what had been individualist, singular and ad hoc. This transformation was especially true of the
North, because the Union had embarked on the more difficult course of
invasion and conquest. Still, both sides had huge bodies of men to be
organized, armed, clothed, fed, trained, cared for and transported from place
to place, all of which required not only an unprecedented increase in production as well as in the raising of moneys needed to finance it, but also an
enormous concentration on planning and control. And when Americans
became a single nation again, this change in the national character would
be, after the preservation of the Union and the destruction of slavery, the
most outstanding single result of the war. Yet, to paraphrase a French
proverb, the more the national character changed, the more its Graybacks
and Bluebellies remained the same old Johnny Reb and Billy Yank.

Except for differences in accent and the color of their uniforms it was hard
to tell these Yankees and Rebels apart. Because the chief commanders of
both sides were almost all West Pointers, there was no difference in training
methods, just as there was an identical lack of experience among the junior
officers. At the outset of war, most of these were elected by the men, and
because companies were raised by town or county, everyone knew everyone else and the election of officers was nothing more than a popularity

contest. Enforcing orders was not easy, especially if the officer issuing them had once been a clerk in the store owned by the man he was putting on a latrine detail. Drilling made for comedy. If a hare happened by the drill field men ran off in whooping pursuit, or wandered into the woods to relieve themselves. At dusk or dawn those very woods might be filled with officers practicing shouting commands for the maneuvers learned in General Silas Casey's three-volume *Infantry Tactics,* the military bible for both sides.

But if the officers eventually learned the intricate drill of the day, the men didn't. A Rebel major leading his command single file up a hill was distressed by the straggling that was fragmenting his formation, so he shouted: "Tell the men that the order is 'double-quick!' " But it came out, "The order is to 'double-quick' *back there,"* and the men turned and raced downhill. The major was so upset, said his chaplain, that "flat on his back with his heels in the air he poured forth benedictions of an unusual kind for a Presbyterian elder." Grand reviews were often a travesty. When the soldiers of the 118th Pennsylvania stepped out for their first, immaculately dressed with the sun gleaming on their bayonets, they strode smartly through clusters of hornets' nests and were promptly routed by clouds of stinging yellowjackets. At the first dress parade of the 36th New York—a predominantly Irish outfit with a reputation for fighting—the officers gathered in front of the men to receive the colonel's instructions. Thinking that a fight was in progress, the men together with the camp sentinels and off-duty soldiers all rushed forward to "see the show"—whereupon the outraged colonel dismissed them all. A Texas major, similarly enraged by the insouciance of his men, quit the army, telling them before he left, one of them said, "that if he had to associate with devils he would wait until he went to hell, where he could select his own company."

During weapons training accidents were commonplace. Cavalrymen drilling with bared sabers often pinked their horses, starting stampedes. A Massachusetts artillery battery zeroed in on a big tree standing on a hilltop 1,000 yards away, but the gunners set the sights at 1,600 yards. Only a blessed accident saved a village on the other side of the hill from destruction.

There were musket shortages on both sides, and many a new unit was armed with hunting weapons. When the 27th Alabama marched off to war it was said the men carried a thousand double-barreled shotguns and a thousand homemade bowie knives. John McDonald of the 6th Tennessee was a walking arsenal. "His idea," a comrade explained, "was to use the minié [musket] at long range, then his shotgun, then his pistols; and then, with sword in one hand and a big knife in another, to wade in and dispatch the ten traditional Yankees" any decent Rebel was expected to kill.

Weapons issued by both sides early in the war were hardly an improvement. Besides many European models which were of universally poor quality, some more dangerous to the shooter than the enemy soldier to be shot, there was the old smoothbore musket: the legendary "buck and ball" shoulder weapon of the U.S. Army. It was so named because it fired a round ball and sometimes a cartridge containing one round ball and three buckshot. It was supposed to have a range of 250 yards, although this is doubtful, and it could not have been more inaccurate even in the hands of an excellent marksman. A hunter from Wisconsin said it took a real fine rifleman to hit a barn door at fifty yards. Up close, of course, its scatter-gun effect made it dangerous. By the fall of 1862 it was being replaced on both sides by a rifled musket firing the dreadful minié ball.

This increased the killing range by five times to about a half mile and was also more accurate. But even a good soldier could get off only two rounds a minute because of the time it took to load and fire. To do so a soldier had to bite off the end of a paper cartridge, pour the powder down the barrel, ram the bullet down it with his ramrod, cock the hammer with his thumb, place a percussion cap on its nipple to ignite the powder and then aim and pull the trigger. Because this weapon was a muzzle-loader it was safer for the soldier to load and fire it from entrenchments where he would not be visible to the oncharging enemy. If he were in the open or attacking—moving forward in short rushes—he would either load in the prone position or seek the cover of a boulder or bush. Early in the war surgeons realized that the preponderance of wounds in the right hand or arm were the result of loading in the prone position.

The rifled musket conferred a great advantage on the defense, bringing an end to the shock tactics of the eighteenth century and the Napoleonic Wars, when the musket was actually a noise-and-smoke-making machine with little killing effect and actually intended to frighten the enemy and conceal the grand bayonet charge bursting out of the smoke. Bayonet charges in the Civil War were rare. Of some 245,000 wounds treated by surgeons in Federal hospitals, fewer than a thousand were from bayonets. Actually this wicked-looking narrow stabbing instrument eighteen inches long with its triangular ridges intended to allow the passage of blood was useful only as a candlestick: thrust into the ground, its socket, which fit around the musket muzzle, was exactly right to receive a candle.

Artillery firepower had also been improved with rifled cannon beginning to appear. But the standard fieldpiece was still the twelve-pounder brass smoothbore, the legendary Napoleon.* Until the end of the war it was popular in both armies, especially for close work. The Napoleon fired a round ball about four and a half inches in diameter and was supposed to have a range of one mile. It might travel that far but it seldom hit the target except by accident, being woefully inaccurate at any range over a half mile. When it fired case shot or canister at close range it was murderous, like a huge sawed-off shotgun. Case shot was a thin-walled shell filled with a bursting charge and about fifty lead slugs. Canister was a metal cylinder filled with a powder charge and about two or three hundred bullets.

The new rifled artillery had twice the Napoleon's range and was extremely accurate. Most common were the Parrot guns designed by West Pointer Robert Parker Parrot. They were of iron, with a single reinforcing band on the breech. Made for the Union army, many fell into Confederate hands during the seizure of Southern forts just before the war or were captured on the battlefield. The most common was the three-inch iron rifle and the ten- and twenty-pounders. Some Parrots ranged all the way up to three hundred pounds but the bigger they were, the more likely they were to explode. Although some artillerists complained of their inaccuracy they were cheap to manufacture and immensely practical. All were muzzle-loaders. Breechloaders appeared only when the South bought some from Britain, but these were impractical, firing a twisted projectile designed to fit the spiraled, hexagonal tubes. At sea there was the Dahlgren gun designed by Admiral John Adolf Dahlgren. These were bronze boat howitzers and rifles and iron 9- and 11-inch rifles. All were smoothbores. Thus rifling of both infantry and artillery weapons improved the defense, but if improved range and accuracy enabled cannon to mow down infantry, foot soldiers could pick off gunners.

In this foot soldier's war par excellence rivalries between the infantry, artillery and cavalry of both sides were intense. In the Union army some 80 percent of the men were foot soldiers, 14 percent were mounted and the remaining 6 percent were cannon cockers. Confederate strength was 75 percent infantry, 20 percent cavalry and 5 percent artillery. Whether Yankee or Rebel, the footsloggers detested both troopers and gunners. An officer of the 123rd Illinois said of the cavalry: "They won't fight, and whenever they are around they are always in the way of those who will fight." D. H. Hill offered "a reward of Five Dollars to anybody who could

---

*Modern ordnance land and sea is now measured by the diameter of the missile rather than the weight. Naval guns are measured in inches, land cannon by millimeters, with twenty-five millimeters roughly the equivalent of one inch. However, it is just not possible to give an equivalence of pounds to either millimeters or inches.

find a dead man with spurs on," and Jubal Early vowed that "if the cavalry did not do better, he would put them *in the army.*" Even the gunners, derided by the infantry as pampered rear-echelon dandies firing their guns from far behind the front, distrusted the mounted troops as light-fingered swashbucklers who would steal a red-hot stove "if they could pick up a mule to carry it along." Between the Western and Eastern armies of both sides the rivalry was a bit more good-natured, each—in the way of all troops since Agamemnon led his soldiers against Troy—proclaiming themselves the other's superior in battle and least favored by the quartermaster. A Louisiana soldier in the Army of Tennessee complained with some justification: "The Western army got only what was left . . . after the requisitions of the Army of (Northern) Virginia was honored. Instances occurred when six-foot men were issued clothing designed for boys, and No. 6 shoes were gravely provided for No. 10 feet." Good-natured ribbing between men of the various states was also common. A man in a Virginia regiment passing a unit of Tarheels from North Carolina shouted:

"Any more tar down in the Old North State, boys?"

"No, not a bit. Old Jeff's bought it all up."

"That so? What's he gonna do with it?"

"Go'n to put it on you'uns heels to make you stick better in the next fight."

These were men of the infantry company, the basic fighting formation of both sides. Ten companies composed a regiment, which, on the Federal side, consisted of 39 officers and 986 enlisted men; on the Confederate, 49 officers and 1,340 men. This, of course, was the supposed strength; in actuality casualties, sickness, desertion and furloughs reduced the Civil War regiment to about half these numbers. Three to five regiments made up a brigade, of roughly 2,000 or more men, the smallest unit in which all arms were joined: infantry, artillery, sometimes but not always cavalry, signal detachments, medical teams, quartermaster, commissary and ammunition trains. A brigade was also the largest unit within range of the voice of its commander, a brigadier general who led at the front. Up until the Civil War this had been the largest formation in the United States Army, but in 1861 was superseded by a division of two to three brigades under a major general. Two or more divisions made a corps, also led by a major general, and two or more corps comprised an army, usually led by a lieutenant general.

The Johnny Rebs and Billy Yanks marching in these units were men of diverse callings and backgrounds. Southern rolls listed a hundred different vocations. Of the 749 members of the typical 19th Virginia, there were

302 farmers, 80 laborers, 56 machinists, 10 lawyers, 14 teachers, 24 students, 3 blacksmiths, 2 artists, a distiller, a well digger, a dentist and 4 men who described themselves as "gentlemen." Northern regiments were even more diverse, listing more than three hundred different occupations, so that any emergency suddenly arising could be quickly overcome by some skilled Billy Yank, such as the mechanic in Ben Butler's 6th Massachusetts who repaired a sabotaged locomotive he had once helped to make.

A typical Civil War soldier was white, native-born, usually a farmer, and a Protestant between eighteen and twenty-nine years of age. There were, of course, many under or over that age. Some underage boys would write "over 18" on a slip of paper to be inserted in one of their shoes; so that when the recruiter asked such a boy his age, he could answer truthfully: "I'm over eighteen." Men in their fifties and sixties who "jined up" fooled no one but were enrolled by unscrupulous recruiters. The youngest soldier was nine-year-old Edward Black of the 21st Indiana, who served as a musician in 1861 but was mustered out the following year. The granddaddy of them all was Curtis King, who enlisted in the 37th Iowa at the age of eighty but was discharged a few months later for disability.

Billy Yank and Johnny Reb were not nearly as tall as modern American men, the average being between five feet five and five feet nine inches. They were also of slight build, not having today's balanced diets and enriched foods, but they were as tough as squirrels. Supposedly the shortest Federal on record was an unnamed Ohioan standing three feet four inches. Two of him would not have matched Captain David Van Buskirt of the 27th Indiana, who stood six feet eleven inches tall and weighed 380 pounds. Van Buskirt was captured in 1862 and gleefully put on exhibition as "the biggest Yankee in the world." He seemed to enjoy his notoriety, telling those who gawked at him that when he went to war each of his six sisters "leaned down and kissed me on top of my head."

By 1860 almost a third of America's male population was foreign-born, driven to these shores either by the potato famine in Ireland or as fugitives from the failed Central European revolutions of 1848. Some 200,000 Germans wore Union blue. They were not very popular, unfairly considered to be thick-headed and slow, when actually they were just careful and sober. They were also extremely capable craftsmen whose technical skills were a great boon to the Federal army. And they were absolutely devoted to the Union. As unlike them as gaiety differs from sobriety were the 150,000 Irish who became Billy Yanks. Welcomed for their sparkling wit and dry humor, as well as their fighting spirit, their fondness for drinking and fighting made them difficult to discipline. During drill in New York's Irish Brigade an angry sergeant was heard to shout: "Kape your heels together, Tim Mullaney in the rear rank, and don't be standing wid wan fut in Bull Run and the other in the Sixth Ward." Missouri's Irish Brigade began its first day in camp with only 800 men, but there were still 900 fistfights, and when the Illinois Irish Regiment—the 90th—began setting up camp a quarrel led to a free-for-all with tent poles and pickax handles, quelled only when the infuriated Colonel O'Meara came rushing out of his tent swinging the flat of his ancestral broadsword.

About 45,000 Englishmen and 15,000 Canadians were in the Federal army, while the French residents of New York City raised and equipped the 55th New York: "La Garde Lafayette." The 15th Wisconsin was all-Scandinavian, mostly Norwegian—with five men named Ole Olsen—and the 12th and 65th Illinois were all-Scots. So was the kilted 79th New York, which switched to Cameron tartan trousers to silence all those wisecracks. The 27th Pennsylvania, according to a Bay State soldier, was composed of "Germans, French, Italians and everything else," while its colonel learned to give commands in seven different languages. American Indians also served in the Civil War, mostly in the Confederate army—Cherokees, Choctaws, Chickasaws and Seminoles—with one brigade of Creeks on the Union side.

Only 9 percent of the Rebel army was foreign-born, mostly from the Emerald Isle, but a surprisingly high percentage of the South's population—never accurately calculated, of course—was of Celtic descent, as the biographies of its leading commanders clearly suggest. Scots-Irish, German and Irish companies came from every state, while Louisiana raised a mixed European battalion under the command of Count Camille Armand Jules Marie, Prince de Polignac, a sonorous name which the Texans in his next command quickly shortened to "Polecat."

When the war began there were 3,500,000 slaves and 135,000 free blacks living in Dixie. A handful of these went to war with their masters as "body servants," but the problem of whether or not to put eligible black males in uniform agitated the South in bitter debate for years. Most planters believed that to arm slaves was to invite insurrection, or at least challenge the white supremacy theory. As Howell Cobb put it: "The day you make soldiers of them is the beginning of the end of the revolution. If slaves will make good soldiers, our whole theory of slavery is wrong." It was not until a month before the war ended—in March of 1865—that the Confederate Congress by the narrowest of margins authorized enlisting blacks as soldiers. But when the first contingent of blacks raised in Richmond marched proudly down the street in gray, whites on the sidewalks threw mud at them.

Blacks in blue suffered hardly less indignity after the Federal Enrollment Act of March 1863 made blacks eligible for conscription. Many Billy Yanks looked upon them as the cause of the war that they hated with such passion. An Illinois soldier wrote: "If the Negro was thought of at all, it was only as the firebrand that had caused the conflagration—the accursed that had created enmity and bitterness between the sections . . ." Union soldiers who welcomed the blacks usually did so out of a sense of self-preservation: "Better him than me." This sentiment was wryly put to the lilting music of an old Irish ditty by "Private Miles O'Reilly," the synonym for Charles G. Halpine of New York:

> Some tell us 'tis a burnin' shame
>   To make the naygers fight;
> An' that the trade of bein' kilt
>   Belongs but to the white;
> But as for me, upon my soul!
>   So liberal are we here,
> I'll let Sambo be murthered instid of meself
> On every day of the year.
> On every day of the year, boys
> An' every hour of day
> The right to be kilt I'll divide with him
> An' divil a word I'll say.

Like gasoline and alcohol blacks and whites in uniform did not mix very well. Fights were frequent whenever they met, and sometimes there were murders. Worse, in combat blacks occasionally had to fear their friends as much as their foes. At Ship Island, Mississippi, Federal naval gunners detailed to support three assaulting black regiments deliberately fired on them. Of a minor battle in Olustee, Florida, in February 1864, a Virginia soldier wrote: "The negroes saw a hard time; those who stood were shot by our men, those who ran by the Yankees."

The food on which Johnny Reb and Billy Yank subsisted in the Civil War can only be described as from the bland and tasteless down to the horrid and nauseating—and almost always in short supply when the armies were on the move. Both sides believed that if the men were issued sufficient supplies they could feed themselves. This worked fairly well during long encampments when regular issues could be maintained, but failed completely during campaigning seasons. A system of company cooks also was abandoned, chiefly because few true cooks were in either army and those chosen for the job were usually misfits and trouble-makers shanghaied into the kitchen. Eventually, both Graybacks and Bluebellies cooked their own messes in groups of three or four buddies. Unfortunately, they believed in frying everything in a sea of grease, from which unhealthy practice many of them sickened and sometimes died. One Union surgeon said his chief problem was to save soldiers from "death from the frying pan."

"Coffee was the mainstay," a Massachusetts private wrote. "Without it was misery indeed." Another Federal surgeon, A. G. Swartwelder, wrote that the bean "is furnished to the soldier in the crude state—that is, just from the sack. The first thing, therefore, he has to do is to 'toast' it. Such was done in a camp kettle for 10–15 minutes or longer. The result was often that instead of 'toasted' coffee, the soldier had charcoal." To reduce the beans to powder soldiers used rifle butts or flat stones, or jabbed at them in the kettle with their bayonets. Coffee and sugar were kept mixed in a cloth bag, and whenever there was a marching break, soldiers were quick to empty two tablespoons of the mixture into a pint cup of water and boil it over a tiny fire. If it was mealtime, the coffee would be used to wash down a meal consisting of a strip of bacon roasted on a stick and an army biscuit or two.

This biscuit was "hardtack," the standard bread ration in the Union army. It was a cracker three inches square and a half-inch thick, so stale that it was almost unbreakable and as often as not populated by worms. Said an Illinois private: "We live on crackers so hard that if we loaded our guns with them we could of killed seceshs in a hurry." One Bluebelly said he soaked a hardtack cracker in coffee for six weeks and when he ate it it still loosened his teeth. The letters B.C. stamped on the side of hardtack crates stood for "Brigade Commissary," but the troops insisted that it was the date of the year they were baked. One squad of artillerists used them as pavingstones through the mud outside their tents, and the classic quip of the Civil War came from the Bluebelly who, when his company commander angrily demanded to know why he was chewing hardtack in ranks, replied with a straight face: "For the juice, sir. I'm very fond of the juice."

Cornbread was the Confederate staple, washed down by coffee whenever that precious but rare liquid was available, or by a substitute made from peanuts, peas, corn or rye. Cornbread was baked with unsifted meal, was coarse, panfried and cooked to such an amazing consistency that Private Ted Barclay of Virginia compared it to India rubber. "It could be stretched into ropes and pressed into balls."

Civil War meat rations were appalling. Issued fresh or pickled, it was barely more chewable than hardtack. A private in the 34th Louisiana wrote: "It was thrown down in the butcher pen and was covered with mud and dung and a decent dog would have turned up his nose at it, but a hungry man will eat almost anything." Often an army on the march would be accompanied by herds of thousands of lowing cows to be slaughtered on the eve of battle for cooked rations. Sometimes it was not too well done, "eaten, in many cases, raw and quivering," wrote William Lincoln of the 34th Massachusetts. Pickled beef was usually so foul-smelling that it would stunt the appetite. "The boys call it 'salt horse,'" said Millett Thompson of the 13th New Hampshire. This was because horseshoes and muleshoes were often found in the bottom of the barrel, it was said, but never a cow or ox hoof. A Jersey private swore: "The salt junk as we called our pork was sometimes alive with worms . . ."

Much of the scurvy—a disease marked by swollen and bleeding gums—in both armies was due to the lack of fresh vegetables. Federal quartermasters sought to prevent it with an issue of "dessicated compressed mixed vegetables," which the troops promptly christened "desecrated vegetables." It was, in a word, a dried cake of four or five vegetables which when soaked expanded with water like a balloon with air. It was not popular and many Bluebellies who had sickened on it refused to eat it.

For these often hungry and sometimes starving soldiers there were three sources other than the daily ration. One way to obtain decent food was in packages from home. Soldiers of both sides constantly wrote home begging for food, but when the packages arrived they were usually so badly damaged or had taken so long in coming that the contents were inedible or could be made edible only by pounding them with a musket butt. A second source was the sutler or civilian vendor allowed to peddle his wares in camp. His prices were supposed to be regulated by military panels, but in practice this rarely happened. All soldiers hated sutlers for their outrageous prices. "He would skin a louse for its hide and tallow," an Illinois soldier wrote, while a Grayback from North Carolina complained "a common size chicken sold in camp the other day for $6.00." When it is considered that a Yankee private earned $16 a month and a Rebel $14, this one meal out of ninety would cost 13 percent or more of his wages. Obviously the sutler was no friend of the soldier, and upon the cry of "Rally! Rally!" a cloud of men in blue or gray would descend upon his tent or cart and plunder its contents, occasionally caressing the jaw of the hated vendor with their hands—closed, that is.

The third way to supplement the rations was simple "foraging," a euphemism for plundering farms of their vegetables and livestock. Usually, the troops preferred obtaining such provender from the farms of the enemy, but if they happened to be marching through friendly territory their reluctance to do the same there was reduced in exact proportion to the growth of their hunger. Thus John Casler of the 33rd Virginia could excuse his "foraging" of the home folks by saying: "We would not allow any man's chicken to run out on the road and bite us as we marched along." In Mississippi, the excuse offered by Henry Schafer of the 103rd Illinois was the farmers' refusal to take the oath of allegiance to the Union.

Such supplements were sporadic at best and did little to improve a steadily unhealthy diet. As a result more Civil War soldiers died in hospital cots than on the battlefield. Statistics on these hospital deaths are not exact—and those from Dixie are incomplete—but it is safe to say that twice as many were from disease as from gunshot wounds. Union figures alone show 6,454,834 *recorded* cases of wounds and disease. Not all sickness could be attributed to defective diet: the poor health of many of the men enlisting in the early stages of the war was another cause. Those who examined the men of the 5th Massachusetts were not even physicians, while in Chicago a contract surgeon "expanded" a regiment by having 1,000 men parade before him in the rain. A New Jersey soldier wrote of a surgeon who "inspected" candidates by asking them questions rather than examining them. Eventually a few months of camp life weeded out these unhealthy recruits, but many died before they could be discharged.

Unfortunately for Johnny Reb and Billy Yank they had been swept into war at the wrong time: improvements in the technique of killing coincided with a period of backward medical science. A surgeon knew enough to amputate a limb or heal a wound, but half the time when his patient was merely sick he did not know what ailed him. Usually it was the so-called "childhood diseases": chicken pox, mumps, measles and whooping cough. Most of these soldiers from farmhouses and wood cabins had never been exposed to these maladies before, and the combination of poor food and imperfect medical care aggravated them so that many of the afflicted perished of what would be routinely cured a generation later. Measles was the greatest killer. A soldier of the 1st Maine recalled: "Though we enlisted to fight and die, nothing happened to us so serious as the measles." Surgeon Legrand Wilson of the 42nd Mississippi declared that the onset of this illness "astonished everyone, even the surgeons." They could not do much to treat a disease about which they knew so little that some of them said it was caused by the straw used in bunks. Of malaria—with typhoid fever another dreadful killer—they believed it originated from the vapors of nearby ponds.

Yet almost all of these surgeons—no more ignorant than their counterparts elsewhere in the civilized world—were paragons of compassion, working on the wounded in hospital tents sometimes for days on end, without sleep, sustained only by a cup of coffee or a swig of medicinal brandy, until at last they could no longer stand and sank into sleep among the stricken soldiers. Dr. J. B. Weist of an Ohio regiment has described the horrible scenes within the field hospitals:

> There are a few tents and improvised tables. . . . Wounded men are lying everywhere. What a horrible sight they present! Here the bones of a leg or an arm have been shattered like glass by a minié ball. Here a great hole has been torn into an abdomen by a grape shot. Nearby see that blood and froth covering the chest of one choking with blood from a wound of the lungs. By his side lies this beardless boy with his right leg remaining attached to his body only by a few shreds of blackened flesh. This one's lower jaw has been carried entirely away; fragments of shell have done this cruel work. Over yonder lies an old man, oblivious to all his surroundings, his grizzly hair matted with brain and blood slowly oozing from a great gaping wound in the head. Here is a bayonet wound; there a slash from a saber. Here is one bruised and mangled until the semblance of humanity is almost lost. . . . This one has been crushed by the wheel of a passing cannon. Here is one dead, and over yonder another; they died while waiting for help that never came. Here are others whose quivering flesh contains balls, jagged fragments of shell, pieces of iron, and splinters of wood, from a gun blown to pieces by an exploding shell, and even pieces of bone from the head of a comrade who was torn to pieces by the explosion of a caisson. The faces of some are black with powder; others are blanched from loss of blood, or covered with the sweat of death. All are parched with thirst, and many suffer horrible pain; yet there are few groans or complaints.

Probably the most grisly sight of the war was the piles of bloody limbs lying outside the amputation tents, and even worse sometimes the horrible spectacle of pigs from nearby farms gobbling their flesh. On such occasions the beasts were driven off and the legs and arms hastily buried. And yet, with their unfailing gallows humor, Johnny Reb and Billy Yank could joke about such horrors. They loved to recount stories such as the one about the Grayback who had lost his leg at Seven Pines. Hobbling on crutches he stopped at one of these piles, flailing with one of the crutches to drive off the clouds of buzzing black flies, and then went rooting with it among the limbs. A passing Rebel asked him, "Whut the damn hell yawl doin'?" Came the reply: "Lookin' fo' mah leg. See! Theah it is—the one with the bunion on the heel." Glancing skeptically at the limb, and then back to the Grayback, the Rebel drawled: "Yawl had two left legs?"

But all was not agony in the life of Billy Yank and Johnny Reb, else they could not have endured it. High-hearted youths that they were, they loved to play sports, especially the new game of baseball said to have been devised by General Abner Doubleday. Pranks and practical jokes relieved the tedium of drill—the boring opposite twin to terror. Hiding a buddy's musket was considered great fun, or else covering a log-hut chimney with a board to smoke out the occupants, or even lowering a bag of bullets down the chimney into the fire to flush them out like a covey of quail. When they could, they liked to guy some pompous visitor to the camp. Thus when an elderly minister rode into the bivouac of the 7th Virginia, his long white beard flowing in the wind, a Rebel wag cried: "Boys, here's Father Abraham!"

"Young man, you are mistaken," the cleric replied. "I am Saul, the son of Kish, looking for his father's asses—and I have found them!"

Civil War soldiers were for the most part profane—although their sulfurous language shocked many a righteous comrade who maintained that he would not have under his feet what they had in their mouth—and they were also great gamblers. They bet on everything: cockfights, boxing and wrestling matches, horse races—even lice races among those ubiquitous insects which they carefully hunted and plucked from their tormented bodies every morning. Dice games were also popular—especially craps—but card playing was the favorite. Alexander Hunter of Virginia claimed that five of every six Rebels played cards, especially draw poker. When they were broke, some of them played on with "O.P.'s"—orders on the paymaster.

But the onset of battle could halt all gambling and card playing. Men would throw away all cards and dice so that if they were wounded or killed these "tools of the Devil" would not be found on their person.

They also finished all their whiskey. Here was one of the great solaces of most soldiers. Nothing could cure a fit of homesickness or depression or the fear of impending battle better than "a noggin of old rye." "Red eye," it was usually called, for the dreadful hangovers it produced. It must have been horrid stuff, full of fusil oil, for it was often boiled before it was drunk in the belief that this would improve its flavor and reduce the aftereffects. George McClellan considered drunkenness to be his army's greatest evil, demonstrating once again that if he could charm his troops he could not understand them. Total abstinence, he said, "would be worth 50,000 men."

But no officer—not even the commander in chief in Washington—could suppress drinking in the Federal armies, in which the officers drank even more than the men. Further, because Billy Yank received regular rations of rye and was closer to the big cities he drank more than Johnny Reb.

Proximity to urban centers also inclined Billy Yank to partake more often of the charms of ladies of pleasure, although prostitution was only less rampant among the Johnny Rebs. The restraints of home life having been removed, and individual inhibitions reduced by group morality, or rather the lack of it, many soldiers flocked to the bawdy houses that always spring up in the train of Mars. Washington, the seat of Federal government and the focal point of military activity, was also the sex capital of the North. There were 450 known houses of ill repute and, according to the Washington *Star,* some 7,000 prostitutes at work. If the long lines of sheepish, giggling soldiers in front of these centers did not suggest the nature of the business inside, then their unabashed signs made it plain: "The Haystack," "Hooker's Headquarters" or "Mother Russell's Bake Oven." Because there was nothing criminal about this recreation, however immoral it might have been, and because sexual assault was so rare in the Civil War as to be almost unknown, both armies made no attempt to curb it.

Because only punishment or the fear of it can maintain an army's discipline, neither side hesitated to use it. Much of it was corporal and cautionary, intended to "let the punishment fit the crime" and thus impress the guilty soldier's comrades. Thus a Federal trooper who was caught stealing a saddle had to parade for hours with the saddle on his back. Six soldiers stole a rowboat, and four of them were ordered to carry the craft around camp while the other two sat inside it rowing in the empty air. Men found guilty of cowardice in battle stood atop barrels wearing wooden placards saying "I am a coward" or "I'm a deserter"—and sometimes a commander would order his soldiers to parade past them and spit upon them—or a man caught stealing from his buddies wore one marked simply "Thief." Another punishment for these offenses was "riding the horse." Two uprights eight or ten feet high held a pole between them. Wearing such placards, the guilty man was placed on the pole, his ankles were bound and he struggled to maintain his balance amid the jeers and hoots of his comrades. For medium-to-serious offenses a soldier was hung by his thumbs just high enough so that he could prevent their being torn from his hands by standing on tiptoe. "Bucking and gagging" was the most painful. A bayonet or stick was forced into a man's mouth and held in place by a string tied behind his ears. Next he was seated on the ground and ordered to bring his knees up to his body so that a stick could be passed under them. His arms were then placed under the stick and tied to it. The cramps and thirst produced by this fixed position were excruciatingly painful and they lasted for hours.

In the beginning of the war both armies treated the chief military crime of desertion as a delinquency. At the most a deserter would be branded on the hip with a "D" and then dismissed from service. Besides exempting the guilty man from the horrors of war, such leniency did nothing to deter other likely deserters—frequently for the honorable reason that their wives and families had no one to support them. As the tide of desertions rose, execution was at last introduced. Chaplain Thomas H. Davenport of the 3rd Tennessee, after seeing fourteen deserters shot, wrote: "I think they are objects of pity, they were ignorant, poor, and had families dependent upon them. War is a cruel thing, it heeds not the widow's tear, the orphan's moan or the lover's anguish." Yet the executions continued, some five hundred of them in both armies, almost two-thirds of these for desertion.

It was usually done by a firing squad. Two parties of a dozen men each were chosen by lot. In each of them was an unloaded musket so that no man knew for certain if his shot had killed the doomed man. The first squad was to carry out the sentence, but if the men missed, the second squad would replace it. The man's brigade would form a three-sided square with a freshly dug grave at the open end. From perhaps a half mile off the low dolorous notes of a funeral dirge would be heard, counter-pointed by muffled drums. Moving in a slow march the band approached, followed by the firing squads, provost guards and two white horses drawing a cart bearing a coffin on which the condemned man sat with a chaplain beside him. The coffin was laid beside the grave while the prisoner and chaplain knelt beside it to pray. Then the guards bound the man's arms and placed him in a kneeling position on the coffin, wrapping a white handkerchief around his eyes. Quickly the firing squad walked to within a few paces of the prisoner. Came the orders: "Ready! Aim! Fire!" Came the explosions and the man pitched forward. If he were not yet dead, the officer fired the *coup de grace* into his head. Placed face downward in the coffin, he was buried without a headboard or even a mound to mark his grave.

Strangely enough, though the soldiers of both armies made no protest about being compelled to punish or even kill their own soldiers, they were uncommonly kind to their enemy. No soldiers in history fraternized like Billy Yank and Johnny Reb. Often they would make a "bargain" with each other not to snipe at one another, or if they were drawn up on either side of a river

Johnny Reb would float over tobacco on a little makeshift raft that Billy Yank returned with a sack of coffee. A Pennsylvania soldier at the siege of Petersburg wrote: "Although intercourse with the enemy was strictly forbidden, the men were on the most friendly terms, amicably conversing and exchanging such commodities as coffee, sugar, tobacco, corn meal and newspapers." They would gravely salute enemy officers and even play cards together. If ordered to fire at the foe, they would shout "Look out, Johnny!" or "Hunt your holes, Billy!" Once when Federal General Samuel W. Crawford climbed atop a parapet to study the enemy position through field glasses, a rock bounded into a Union rifle pit. A paper wrapped around it said: "Tell the fellow with the spy glass to clear out or we shall have to shoot him."

They even sang together, these men of the Civil War who were also perhaps the singingest soldiers ever. Because they knew each other's songs they could harmonize. The greatest favorites were "Home, Sweet Home," "The Girl I Left Behind Me" and "When This Cruel War Is Over," perhaps the best-selling song ever sung in America. It sold one million copies, roughly the equivalent of ten million today.

> Weeping sad and lonely,
> Hopes and fears in vain!
> Yet praying, when this cruel war is over,
> Praying that we meet again.

One night at Fredericksburg in December 1862, when the Army of the Potomac and the Army of Northern Virginia confronted each other across the Rappahannock, a Rebel band marched down to the riverbank and played "Dixie." A Union band "retaliated" with "The Battle Hymn of the Republic." Back came "The Bonnie Blue Flag" followed by "The Star-Spangled Banner." There was a silence and in it a Union bugler blew the sweet-sad notes of "Home, Sweet Home"—the universal favorite among these sentimental, homesick soldiers. Silence again. Not a sound. Men sat in the dark with their eyes squeezed shut against the tears trickling out under the eyelids. Then, still silent, they returned to their billets. Tonight, friendship and brotherhood, but next day Johnny Reb and Billy Yank would fall upon each other in one of the most wrathful bloodbaths of this sad, sad war between brothers.

33

■

The Fall of the South's Main Ports

FOR THE UNION one of the unforeseen dividends of Shiloh was that the Confederacy had stripped many of its coastal commands of troops to send to Beauregard and Johnston. One of these was New Orleans, probably the most vital seaport in the South. The Crescent City itself was the largest city in the Confederacy, bigger than any other four combined. But it was the great port with its shipyards one hundred miles above the mouths of the Mississippi that was of most value. New Orleans was counted upon to ship out the cotton to buy the guns that she would take in. And so, while the Confederacy was concerned with defending the upper reaches of the Father of Waters, it seemed not to notice that the Union also had designs upon its mouths.

Major General Mansfield Lovell commanded at the Crescent City. A West Pointer who had fought in Mexico, he resigned to go into business in New York City, where he became deputy streets commissioner. Through political influence he rose quickly in the Confederate Army. If he was distinguished for anything, it was for the longest mustache on both sides, stretching from ear to ear. Otherwise he was an incompetent braggart who thought his defenses were impregnable. For this reason he scoffed at the capture of Ship Island by troops under Ben Butler near the mouths of the Mississippi as being an indication of Federal plans to seize New Orleans, declaring: "A black Republican dynasty will never give an old Breckinridge Democrat like Butler command of any expedition which they had any idea would result in such a glorious victory as the capture of New Orleans."

Perhaps so, but a much more solid reason for his confidence was the presence of a pair of star-shaped masonry forts on opposite banks of the river about seventy-five miles downstream from the city. Fort Jackson on the right bank was the larger with seventy-four guns, while Fort St. Philip a bit farther upriver mounted fifty-two. The combined garrison was 1,100 men, enough to fire its formidable armament. Such positions were the basis of the old naval adage: "A ship is a fool to fight a fort." By this was meant that vessels with wooden hulls and limited supplies of ammunition, food and water could not hope to overcome fixed ground positions made of masonry and stone with unlimited supplies. More than this, these two forts had been built in almost impassable swamps. They could be approached only by water in full view of the garrison and ships would be compelled to slow down by a treacherous stretch of water and a sharp turn. Moreover, the forts were supported by gunboats, fire rafts and river obstructions. Finally, the New Orleans shipyards were even then busy building two monster ironclads— *Louisiana* and *Mississippi*—which when completed could make matchwood of any Federal fleet. So Lovell's boast was based not on political sagacity but rather on knowledge of solid defenses which would become invincible when the ironclads were afloat.

So it seemed to Union Secretary of the Navy Welles during the winter of 1861–62, until Commander David Dixon Porter came to him with a plan to reduce the forts. Welles had always thought the Porter family addicted to what he called "cliquism." Porter's father, also named David, was a distinguished naval officer and diplomat, his brother was Commodore William D. Porter, his adopted brother was Commodore David Glasgow Farragut and his cousin was General Fitz-John Porter. Still Welles listened when Porter insisted that the two positions could be battered into submission by proper shelling, and he authorized Porter to gather a fleet of vessels armed with huge mortars capable of hurling 13-inch shells into the air. Here two of those enormous military assets possessed by the industrial North and ignored by the agricultural South made themselves felt: the forges and foundries of Pittsburgh and the great iron-ore ranges of the Great Lakes, the two firmly linked by water. From these Porter got his monster mortars mounted on twenty ships. And then he was delighted to find himself under the command of his adopted elderly brother: David Glasgow Farragut.

Born at Campbell's Station, Tennessee, on July 5, 1801, Farragut had been adopted by the senior Porter and commissioned a midshipman when he was nine years old. At twelve he served in the War of 1812 as a prize master, eventually rising to captain in 1855. Retired, he became a resident of Norfolk, and after Sumter, warning his secessionist neighbors, "You fellows will catch the Devil before you're through with this business," he closed his house and went North to return to the United States Navy. Although he was sixty, he was still spry and active, still keeping to the habit of turning a handspring on every birthday just to prove it. He turned another one after Welles made him a commodore in charge of the fleet assigned to capture New Orleans.

By late January 1862, Farragut had assembled his fleet consisting of eighteen warships: two steam frigates, seven screw sloops and nine wooden gunboats, all mounting a total of 243 guns, most of them heavy. To this were added Porter's twenty mortar ships with 30,000 shells. By mid-April the expedition, collected in greatest secrecy, was complete with 18,000 men under Butler. There was some difficulty working upstream because of the deposits of silt at the great river's mouths, and Farragut was forced to leave his heaviest warships back in the Gulf. But on April 18, only three miles downriver from the forts he signaled his adopted brother to open fire.

There was consternation in New Orleans. The two great iron dreadnoughts designed not only to clear the Mississippi but also to lay the Northern coastal ports under levy were far from finished. *Mississippi,* weighing over 4,000 tons, 270 feet long and 58 in the beam, had been launched, but she still had to be armored and her great drive shaft could only be made at the Tredegar in Richmond. It would be weeks, perhaps months, before the shaft could be installed. *Louisiana* had also been launched, armored and armed, but her power plant would not function. Worse, Richmond had denied Lovell's request that eight gunboats upriver be brought back down to the Crescent City. All Lovell could do was to have *Louisiana* towed downstream to be secured to the east bank above Fort St. Philip. Here, at least, her sixteen heavy rifles could be of use.

Porter's two-hundred-pound shells were more spectacular than effective. For ninety-six hours, most of them non-stop, 13,000 of the great projectiles swooshed into the sky—glowing red at night—to burst with a roar inside and around the forts, and by the end of this period only four Rebel gunners were killed, fourteen wounded and seven guns disabled. Much of the levee had been cut away, sending floodwaters onto the parade grounds, but the forts still maintained an answering fire. It was the Federal gunners who seemed most shaken. Concussion had numbed them. They had spent these days as though living inside a huge tolling bell. Porter resumed the assault, firing 3,800 more rounds into the positions—and still they returned the fire. At last Farragut, who had not placed much faith in the mortars anyway, decided that he would make the perilous run upriver at midnight of the twenty-fourth.

To protect engine rooms and magazines, anchor chains were looped over the sides of the ships. Jacob's ladders were hung around so carpenters could descend to make quick repairs on holed hulls. Tubs of water were spotted about the decks and fire brigades armed with grapnels to drag off fire rafts, while the hulks were smeared with Mississippi mud to darken them and reduce visibility. At last two red lanterns—the signal to get underway—were hung from the masthead of Farragut's flagship, the wooden screw sloop *Hartford,* and the fleet sailed straight between the two still formidable forts. Immediately Confederate gunboats entered the battle, steaming downstream behind the smoking, blazing fire rafts drifting down the glittering black current. Guns were booming everywhere, flame gushing from the forts' casemates and from the ships firing broadsides. Billowing gunsmoke drifted low over the water, creating pockets through which Farragut's ships sailed blind, their crews gagging. Passing Fort Jackson, *Hartford* ran aground near Fort St. Philip. A tugboat quickly jammed a blazing fire raft against the ship's side. She caught fire and red spirals of flame went snaking up her rigging. Her gunners flinched fearfully away from the licking tongues of flame, and old Farragut shouted down at them from the poop: "Don't flinch from that fire, boys! Give that rascally little tug a shot!" They did. Two quick shots holed and sank her, and suddenly the worst was over. *Hartford*'s engines roared, driving her out of the mud, and the fleet was safely above the forts, the Rebel gunboats either sunk or driven off while the dreadnought *Louisiana* sat silent throughout the battle.

At daybreak Farragut anchored his ships halfway between the forts and the city to bury his dead and make repairs. He had no fear of the forts still in his rear, for they were completely cut off with their exhausted garrisons on the edge of mutiny. They would soon surrender and the positions would fall to Union troops. So would New Orleans, defenseless now that it had been shorn of forts, dreadnoughts and gunboats. Rain was falling when Farragut's ships approached the levee, jammed with thousands of angry civilians, jeering, cursing and breathing impotent defiance. Soon the Stars and Stripes was waving over the city's public buildings and Ben Butler's soldiers came marching in on the heels of the fleeing general who had sneered at "the Breckinridge Democrat." Destruction of *Louisiana* and *Mississippi* completed the victory, and by the end of April all that the Confederacy possessed along the Father of Waters was the stretch between Baton Rouge and Vicksburg.

New Orleans was the high point of the tide of Federal naval victories rolling along the Atlantic and Gulf coasts that momentous spring of 1862. By mid-March the conquest of Roanoke Island had been extended to New

Bern and other important stations on the North Carolina sounds, while the railroad funneling supplies and troops into Virginia had been seized. Fernandina on the north Florida coast had been taken at the same time, while Jacksonville and St. Augustine, undefended since the dispatch of troops to the West, were occupied without a fight. Charleston and Savannah were still menaced from Port Royal, and the Georgia city was neutralized with the smashing of Fort Pulaski at the mouth of the Savannah River.

Only Wilmington, North Carolina, remained a Confederate port, soon becoming the only available sanctuary for blockade-runners of any size. In and out of this holdout haven slipped the sleek, ghost-gray shapes, usually at the dark of the moon, burning smokeless coal and feathering their paddle wheels to reduce noise. In the beginning the risks were slight, but now the ever-warier blockaders had brought the odds down to the loss of one in eight. Still, the profits exceeded the risks: two trips paid for the ship, after which any successful run was all profit, less expenses. The showcase voyage remained the arrival in Savannah in the fall of 1861 of a blockade-runner carrying 10,000 Enfield rifles, 1 million cartridges, 2 million percussion caps and a store of cutlasses, sabers and revolvers. Passage of more than a year with nothing to match this spectacular success was an ominous sign that the Confederacy was losing badly on the water. Its oversea supply lines were shrinking. In Richmond there were other ominous signs.

"Jefferson Davis now treats all men as if they were idiotic insects," R. B. Rhett wrote in his Charleston *Mercury.* "It seems that things are coming to this pass," a former member of the Confederate Congress told his wife, "to be a patriot you must hate Davis." And from the inverately invidious Yancey, still smarting from his diplomatic defeat, came the complaint that Virginia had twenty-nine generals and his native Alabama only four. Meanwhile some congressmen were secretly debating the deposition of Davis, until they glumly realized that this would leave them with Alexander Stephens, whom they trusted less.

Thus the Confederate government in that doleful spring. Stung by a string of defeats, Congress tried to supplant Benjamin with Lee, but Davis blocked the move on the grounds that only a civilian could head the War Department. He also vetoed a scheme to create a commanding general able to take command wherever he wished as a violation of his rights as commander in chief. Worse than all these squabbles and enmities was the general realization that the Southern fighting man's ardor had waned and that the one-year enlistments so popular after Sumter were not only due to expire in April, but also were not likely to be renewed. Faced with the possibility that the already outnumbered Rebel armies might melt away, the president bit the bullet and in late March recommended conscription for all able males between eighteen and forty-five. Congress debated the bill bitterly, but on April 24, aware that they were staring defeat in the face, its members, after lowering the age limit to thirty-five, passed the first national conscription act in American history.

Reaction among the states-righters and fire-eaters was immediate and blistering. Davis-hating Governor Joe Brown of Georgia expressed the minds of all of them when he declared that no "act of the Government of the United States prior to the secession of Georgia struck a blow at constitutional liberty as fell as has been struck by the conscription act." Criticism of Davis spread and his critics multiplied. He was openly compared to Napoleon—whose glory was based on conscription—Cromwell and Richard III. Most sinister of all these rebukes and threats was the black coffin found near the Executive Mansion with a hangman's rope coiled on its lid.

Even the diplomatic front had been battered. Slidell had lost patience with the French and their courteous indifference, while Mason informed Benjamin that he was going to give Lord Palmerston an ultimatum, and if it were ignored he would "remain no longer in England." Unsmiling for once, Benjamin, now the secretary of state, persuaded him to stay.

Thus within a year Confederate confidence was ebbing fast away. It had sunk from the peak of exaltation and euphoria following Sumter and Bull Run, to the nadir of Forts Henry and Donelson, Pea Ridge and Shiloh. The screws of the Federal coastal blockade were twisting tighter and all of the Confederacy's major ports were either gone or neutralized, while on the mighty Mississippi only that small stretch from Baton Rouge to Vicksburg remained. These were indeed despairing days.

34

■

Joe Johnston:
Start of the Peninsula Campaign

A FTER BEAUREGARD was transferred to the West, command of what
was now called the Army of Northern Virginia passed to Joseph Eggleston Johnston. Joe, as he was always called, was born into one of the most
distinguished families of Virginia. It was founded by Peter Johnston, who
migrated from Scotland in 1727 to become a successful merchant. One of
his sons, also named Peter, at seventeen joined the legion of Light-Horse
Harry Lee, serving in it with such distinction during the Revolutionary War
that he became a favorite of his commander.

In 1788 Peter married Mary Wood, a niece of the fiery patriot Patrick
Henry. Active in politics, Peter served thirteen terms in the House of
Delegates, twice being elected its speaker. In 1811 he became a judge of
the Virginia General Court.

Mary's eighth son, born February 3, 1807, at Cherry Grove, was
named Joseph Eggleston after the captain under whom his father had
served. When Joe was four, the family moved to their new home—Panicel-
lo—near Abingdon, to be closer to the southwest Virginia circuit. Joe was
an active youngster, taking part in all the local games with his friends,
fishing and hunting and becoming an excellent horseman and marksman.
From his mother, an extremely cultivated woman, he developed a deep love
of literature, especially the classics. His father also noticed that he was
enchanted by the war stories of the numerous veterans of the Battle of
King's Mountain who lived in the area. Upon entering Abingdon Academy
he distinguished himself as a student, displaying an interest in military
history so intense that his father gave him the sword that he had carried
in battle. It was almost inevitable then that Judge Johnston should secure
an appointment to West Point for his son.

■ ■ ■

Joe was eighteen when he arrived on the Plains, immediately renewing his friendship with Robert Edward Lee. For a time, an eye affliction hampered Joe in his studies, but he persevered and was graduated thirteenth in a class of forty-six cadets. He was now nearing maturity and would stand about five feet seven inches of wiry, well-proportioned build and weighing about 150 pounds. His most distinctive feature was a high forehead, which a receding hairline seemed to make higher, above wide-set calm gray eyes. In time, he would cultivate a well-groomed mustache and sharply pointed imperial. Although Johnston was now out of the classroom as a brevet second lieutenant of artillery, he never lost his love for reading and would one day be regarded as the best-read officer in the United States Army.

Johnston's first assignment was at Fort Columbus, New York, but his next two were at potential trouble spots: Fort Monroe at the time of Nat Turner's rebellion, and Charleston Harbor during the Nullification crisis. Unlike Jefferson Davis, Johnston did not believe that his service under Scott against a sister Southern state raised any crisis of conscience, although he was pleased when South Carolina backed off.

He was still with Scott when Old Fuss 'N Feathers was sent to Florida to suppress the Seminoles, and here he did see action. On January 15, 1838, he was with a small engineering detachment in South Florida when it was ambushed by a band of Seminoles. When the commander fell, Johnston took charge, showing "coolness, courage and judgment" in routing the attackers. He was slightly wounded when a bullet struck his forehead, leaving a lifelong scar.

Shortly after this, again assigned to coastal survey work, he met Lydia McLane, daughter of a prominent Delaware family. They were married July 10, 1845, in Baltimore, to which her family had moved. Although Lydia was not a great beauty, she was a woman of charm and grace who shared her husband's intellectual interests. Because they were childless, they drew ever closer—although in later years they became like fond parents to Preston Johnston, a nephew who also had been graduated from West Point.

Upon the eruption of the War with Mexico, Johnston was again reunited with his friend Lee as they sailed south with Scott for the march from Vera Cruz on Mexico City. They were with Scott aboard a small wooden scout ship when the Fortress of San Juan d'Ullua took them under fire. Also aboard were Beauregard, G. W. Smith, McClellan and George Gordon Meade, the highly intelligent and trained engineers of Scott's cherished "little cabinet." If that ship had been sunk, it is possible that the U.S. Army might not have recovered from the loss of such talented soldiers, or at least not have conquered Mexico so easily. Without the Mexican land acquisition, then, there might not have been an American Civil War.

After the march began, Lieutenant Colonel Johnston was given command of a regiment of skirmishers. He led them on a reconnaissance far in advance of Scott's army, and was wounded twice by musket fire. After recuperating Johnston led his skirmishers into battle twice more—at Molino del Rey and Chapultepec—and was wounded three more times, leading Scott to remark: "Johnston is a great soldier, but he has an unfortunate knack for getting himself shot in nearly every engagement."

After the Mexican War Johnston and Lee drew different assignments, and though they corresponded, their letters had a slightly formal tone. Johnston filled the void by befriending a group of younger West Pointers, among them McClellan, nineteen years his junior. When McClellan went to Russia to observe the Crimean War, Johnston asked him to obtain for him a "good sword for fighting" and the latest cavalry manuals in English. In 1858 Johnston and his wife were delighted to be assigned to Washington. Mary Johnston was pleased to be near the family home in Baltimore, and to resume her friendship with the wives of Senator Jefferson Davis, Lee and Lieutenant Colonel William H. Emory. Of these three, Mrs. Chesnut wrote: "In Washington, before I knew any of them, except by sight, Mrs. Davis, Mrs. Emory and Mrs. Johnston were always together, inseparable friends, and the trio were pointed out as the cleverest women in the United States."

But they were separated after Sumter, when Lee and Johnston chose their "country," i.e., Virginia, and Emory remained with the Union. General Scott, after his unsuccessful attempt to get Lee to remain in the U.S. Army, made the same sally with Johnston, but through his wife.

"Get him to stay with us," he told Mary Johnston. "We will never disturb him in any way."

"My husband cannot stay in an army which is about to invade his country."

"Then let him leave our army, but do not let him join theirs."

"This is all very well," Mary said firmly, "but how is Joe Johnston to live? He has no private fortune, or no profession but that of arms."

So Joe Johnston resigned from the U.S. Army and went to Richmond, where Lee prevailed upon Davis to make him a major general. After his distinguished action at Bull Run, he was made a full general, but not the senior one, as he complained, but only fourth in line. Because he had been the senior brigadier in the Union army, he believed himself entitled to four-star seniority as a Confederate. His dissatisfaction irked the president, and Davis, never a man to forget a friend or forgive a foe, who could never say like Lincoln, "I will hold McClellan's horse, if he will bring me victories," gradually became estranged from him, if not actually his enemy. Thus General Joseph Eggleston Johnston at fifty-four: calm and deliberate, with a fine mind and retentive memory, an excellent planner and strategist, extremely courteous—like most Southern patricians—a man who, in Lord Chesterfield's famous definition of a gentleman, "was never rude except on purpose"; he was also "critical, controversial and sometimes irritable," while to some associates and quite a few subordinates his natural reticence seemed more like a cold and aloof reserve. And now across the Potomac his old friend McClellan—his "Beloved Mac"—was now also his enemy.

It had not been a pleasant winter for George McClellan. True, there had been the pleasure of seeing the entire Union army expand and improve under his own hand. But he had also been harried by a revival of the cry, "On to Richmond!" as well as by radical Republicans who did not scruple to suggest that Little Mac deliberately dragged his feet to serve the South.

More by accident than design (at least at this time), McClellan had become identified with those Northern Democrats who wanted the war won only to restore the Union. But among Republicans there was a growing conviction that the secession could only be crushed by stamping out slavery. To the Democrats, this was a harsh position; to the Republicans anything less than this was soft. Thus the Republicans distrusted the Democrats, if not as outright traitors at least as fainthearted patriots or Southern sympathizers, and each new delay on the part of McClellan was looked upon as another proof of doubtful loyalty. Thus, also, the Republican government was not in harmony with its Democratic general-in-chief.

On March 11, in fact, McClellan was relieved of over-all command, ostensibly so that he would have more freedom for action in the field. The real reason was McClellan's refusal to move until he was ready, capped by his failure to move against Joe Johnston's army while it was concentrated around the old Bull Run battlefield. On March 9 the wily Johnston pulled his 40,000-man force back behind the Rappahannock River. Union soldiers entering his abandoned trenches and log-hut encampments found evidence that McClellan's army had been more than twice as big as Johnston's, and the cautious Little Mac had been bluffed by dozens of Quaker guns. Lincoln, who had resumed his complaint, "He has got the slows," was now exasperated. Unfortunately, no new general-in-chief was appointed for four months, and the military reins remained firmly in the hands of the president.

One result of this was a clumsy command setup. Between them, two political generals, Nathaniel Banks and John Charles Frémont, had about 28,000 troops in the Shenandoah Valley and West Virginia. Both men were coequal to McClellan and any coordination of their movements had to come from Washington. This was to work to McClellan's disadvantage, as was the fact that Lincoln and Secretary of War Stanton, being politicians first and military men second, were both unduly concerned with the defense of Washington. Stanton, a fierce man outwardly who was constantly threatening generals with dismissal, was inwardly timid. The slightest Confederate gesture toward Washington brought him close to panic.

Thus Stonewall Jackson was able to do McClellan a great disservice when he tangled with a Union force under James Shields at Kernstown in the Shenandoah Valley. Jackson was defeated, but his presence in the valley so upset Lincoln and Stanton that when McClellan finally did begin moving south, they withheld 35,000 troops under Irwin McDowell to stand guard in upper Virginia.

McClellan, disappointed in his hopes to drive overland against the Confederate capital, had decided to steam down to Fortress Monroe on the tip of the York Peninsula. Landing not far from the site of Washington's victory at Yorktown, he would march quickly up the peninsula between the York and the James rivers and so take Richmond from the side door. The Union navy, meanwhile, would guard his flanks.

It was a pretty plan, except that the *Merrimac* still barred the James, and Rebel batteries inside the York were too strong to pass. The navy could offer McClellan only token support, and it could not get around Yorktown, the anchor for a line of fortifications stretching across the peninsula to the James. McClellan would have to breach this line, and on April 4, 1862, he ordered an advance. Next day, he changed his mind.

There were only 15,000 men in the Rebel line, opposing 53,000 under McClellan, but they were commanded by that consummate actor, John Bankhead Magruder. McClellan might well have remembered "Prince John's" penchant for theatricals, and might have regarded the constant marching and countermarching of the Rebel army as a stage production. Instead, he was deceived into thinking Magruder led a large force, and he at once settled down to siege warfare. No fewer than 150 huge mortars, among other big guns, were mounted in the Union lines opposite Magruder; and no less than a solid month was lost, during which Johnston gathered his forces and placed them between Richmond and the Army of the Potomac. In joyous amazement, Johnston told Lee, "No one but McClellan could have hesitated to attack." On May 4, when Little Mac finally did give the order to bombard the line he considered "one of the most extensive known to modern times," his shells fell into empty trenches. Johnston had waited until the last moment, and then, on the preceding night, had quietly fallen back on Richmond.

McClellan now ordered a pursuit, while collecting an amphibious force to sail up the York and cut off Johnston's retreat. But he was too slow in getting his enveloping movement water-borne, and Johnston, anticipating him, defeated his forces when they attempted to land at West Point. There now ensued the Battle of Williamsburg, which was to be the first engagement between former friends—all veterans of the Mexican War—one of the most poignant characteristics of the Civil War. Confederate Brigadier General James Longstreet, wounded fifteen years before at Molino del Rey, was attacked by a division led by Union Brigadier General Joe Hooker, who had earned a brevet at Pueblo. Longstreet hurled Hooker back, and then, counterpuncher that he was, attacked himself—and that was when a third hero of the Mexican War came galloping up the muddy road.

Fiery Phil Kearny had fought for the French in Africa and Italy since he lost his left arm at the San Antonio Gate. Fierce as ever, sword in hand and reins in his teeth, he led his division to Hooker's rescue—and found the road blocked by wagons mired in the mud. "Tip those wagons out of my way!" he roared, and when an officer tried to explain that the wagons were stuck, he bellowed: "Move them, I say—or I'll put the torch to them!" The wagons were dragged aside, and Kearny's men sloshed forward to see their general go dashing across the Confederate line like a flame in the saddle and deliberately draw the fire that gave away the enemy positions. At that juncture, the Yankee-hating D. H. Hill—who had helped storm the heights of Chapultepec—brought his division to Longstreet's side. The battle raged on inconclusively, until Winfield Scott Hancock—who had been with Hill at Chapultepec—took his Union division wide to the right and found an opening on Longstreet's flank and rear. Under cover of darkness, the Confederates withdrew.

Tactically, the battle had been a Confederate victory, for Longstreet had held off the Federals long enough to cover the withdrawal of Johnston's precious supply trains. Measured by Civil War standards, however, Williamsburg had not been a major battle. Yet in miniature it possessed all those elements that were to be characteristic of the dreadful, three-year struggle between the Army of the Potomac and the force that Lee named the Army of Northern Virginia. Bull Run had shown what the war was not to be like, Williamsburg showed what it would be. At Williamsburg men who had fought together in Mexico as lieutenants and captains now fought each other as generals, and they commanded troops whose fighting qualities probably have never been surpassed. Because both sides now realized that

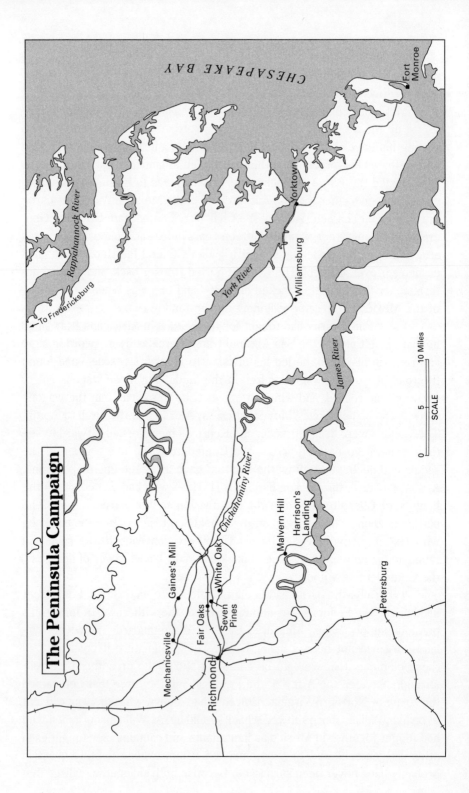

The Peninsula Campaign

CHESAPEAKE BAY

Fort Monroe

Rappahannock River

To Fredericksburg

York River

Yorktown

Williamsburg

James River

Chickahominy River

Malvern Hill

Harrison's Landing

Gaines's Mill

White Oak

Fair Oaks

Seven Pines

Mechanicsville

Richmond

Petersburg

SCALE

0   5   10 Miles

the enemy was in earnest, because both had a supply of trained commanders who wanted passionately to win and a reservoir of men who wanted
fiercely to kill, the battles in the East—like those already fought in the
West—were to be to the finish. Very few commanders were going to be
bluffed or maneuvered off the field. Most of them were going to stay until
beaten. And that, of course, meant a bloodbath of three years' duration.

Williamsburg, a delaying action, was therefore only a smaller bloodbath. But the Federals occupying the field that night were nevertheless
horrified by the black and bloated dead, as well as the cries of the wounded
and the sound of surgeons sawing off limbs whose bones had been shattered
beyond repair by the huge bullets of .58 caliber and more fired by both sides.
There was also the customary horror of battlefield theft. In the morning the
pockets of friend and foe alike had been turned inside out, and even the
buttons cut from their uniforms. Such ghouls and scavengers have marched
with every army since Agamemnon's, and the men of the Army of the
Potomac were only being introduced to another of the ancient horrors of
war when they heard a swag-stuffed Union soldier simper: "I wish there
was a battle every week."

McClellan now had another chance. He had broken through the defenses
of Yorktown and forced the evacuation of Norfolk, which opened the James
River to him. With Norfolk gone, *Merrimac* had no home. The big ironclad's
draught was too deep for her to flee up the James, and so, at the end of
an eventful two-month career, she had to be blown up. But then the Union
navy was dealt one of its rare reverses. Attempting to reduce the Rebel
forts at Drewry's Bluff seven miles below Richmond, its ships were driven
off. For nearly three years the river approach to Richmond was to remain
in Rebel hands, and McClellan was thus denied that convenient avenue to
the capital.

Yet McClellan had 105,000 men against Johnston's 60,000, and he still
did not move until another month elapsed. Depending on intelligence reports supplied by the woefully inept railroad detective, Allan Pinkerton, he
believed that Johnston's strength was double his own. Perhaps he unconsciously wanted to believe Pinkerton. He certainly accepted the detective's
incredible calculations without a murmur of surprise, and he failed to question methods that may have been fine for catching bank robbers but which
were dreadful for counting enemy heads. Throughout the Civil War there
was never a time when any single army in the field numbered as many as
150,000 men; in fact, the peak strength of the entire Confederate Army,
reached in June 1863, was only 261,000 men. Yet in May of 1862 McClellan

believed or preferred to believe that Johnston alone commanded from 250,000 to 300,000 soldiers.

McClellan did have some excuses. First, the weather was wretched, making movement difficult and his men miserable. Second, he was thwarted in his desire to have McDowell's force of 40,000 sent south to join him in front of Richmond. In this the villain was again General Stonewall Jackson.

35

■

Thomas Jonathan "Stonewall" Jackson

T HOMAS JONATHAN JACKSON's oldest known ancestor was John Jackson, a giant of an Irishman who migrated to Maryland in 1748 and thence westward into what is now West Virginia. During the Revolution he and his two sons took sweet revenge on King George III, and after the war he helped evict Indian tribes from his area. On his death he left his heirs huge tracts of land.

Jackson men prospered, becoming congressmen, judges, state legislators and tax collectors. But Edward Jackson, John's grandson, was a struggling young lawyer in Clarksburg when he married Julia Neale. They had four children: Elizabeth, Warren, Thomas and Laura. Thomas was born January 21, 1824.

When he was three his sister Elizabeth died of a mysterious fever. Two weeks later her father, who had tended her, was dead of the same affliction. Widow Jackson sought to keep her family together by operating a little school and sewing for her neighbors. Two years of poverty and her growing ill health induced her to accept a proposal of marriage from Captain Blake Woodson, a lawyer even less successful than her former husband. But Woodson managed to become court clerk of Fayette County to the west, moving there with his wife.

Julia's children were farmed out to relatives. Thomas and Laura were to go to the farm of their grandmother near the village of Jane Lew, where John Jackson had once fought Indians and buffalo. But when an uncle arrived to fetch them, five-year-old Tom ran into the woods and spent the night there. Only after two days of bribery and promises did he agree to leave his mother. He was to find life with his grandmother, maiden aunts and high-spirited, godless uncles an idyll of unbridled freedom and limited schooling.

But then the grandmother died in 1835 and the family decided that the farm, with the maiden aunts married and the bachelor uncles still gleefully stomping on the Ten Commandments, was no place for an eleven-year-old boy. He was sent to William Brake, a cousin living near Clarksburg. Tom did not like his new home, running away with the calm announcement, "I have disagreed with Uncle Brake. I have left him, and I'm not going back." Upon his return to the farm, he got a riotous reception from the bachelor Jacksons, especially Uncle Cummins, the chief of this whiskey-drinking, fox-hunting horse-racing clan.

Resuming his idyll, Tom divided his time between racing horses on the farm's four-mile track, directing crews of black lumbermen, fishing and hunting, tending sheep, milling flour in the family grist mill, flailing flax— and, of course, erratic attendance at the schoolhouse. Eventually, Tom reversed his attitude toward learning, becoming so devoted to study that he would lie on the floor reading while a slave held a burning pine cone over his book. It had been agreed that Tom would pass on his learning to the slave, who, it is said, soon became educated enough to escape on the Underground Railway.

At fourteen Tom also reacted against the farm's godless environment and began to walk three miles every Sunday to listen to a minister preach. Three years later, through the offices of Uncle Cummins and numerous Jackson kin, he was appointed country constable. About this time—1841— he showed the first symptoms of lifelong hypochondria as well as his highly notional means of correcting these afflictions, some real, most imagined. Believing himself suffering from chronic indigestion, he thought riding horseback would improve his condition and thus welcomed the opportunity to ride through the hills serving legal papers.

Such employment, however, was far from satisfying the deep but formless ambition beginning to burn within him, and he was accordingly delighted to know that a boy from his district, having been accepted at West Point, had withdrawn and left a vacancy for western Virginia. Uncle Cummins came through again, prevailing upon a congressman friend to obtain the appointment for his nephew. Tom at that time had no known desire to become a soldier, but he did have a dogged determination to succeed somewhere. That characteristic was apparent to all who saw him upon his arrival on the Plains July 1, 1842. Dabney Maury, who was himself to become a Confederate general, remembered the occasion.

"A cadet sergeant came by us conducting a newly-arrived cadet to his quarters. . . . His figure was angular and clumsy; his gait was awkward. He was clad in old-fashioned Virginia homespun woolen cloth; he bore across his shoulders a pair of weather-stained saddle bags, and his hat was one of those heavy, low-crowned, broad-brimmed wool hats usually worn in those days by overseers, county constables, wagoners, etc. He tramped along by the side of the sergeant, with an air of resolution, and his stolid look added to the inflexible determination of his whole aspect, so that one of us remarked, 'That fellow has come here to stay.' "

He had indeed, even though he was keenly aware of the deficiencies in his education, especially in mathematics. He studied long after lights-out, banking coals on his fire and lying huddled before it to cram knowledge into his brain. In class he was so ill at ease, squirming at the blackboard in mental agony, his hands, face and uniform smeared with chalk, sweating profusely, that his peers mocked him as "the General," but his instructors came to respect his diligence and forthright admission of his own ignorance. Drill and horseback riding were no easier. Though trained as a jockey, he was a clumsy figure aboard a cavalry horse; and his tramping stride, like a farmer treading through asparagus muckland, was the laughingstock of the Academy. He also stood at the bottom of The Immortals, the sarcastic name given the lowest group in a class, and it appeared that one morning at roll call his name would be called and there would be no response. But he persevered, steadily, but not easily, rising in rank while gaining a reputation for rectitude when he refused to accept the offer of his roommate—acting as orderly-sergeant—to grant him immunity from answering roll calls in the chilly dawn. On July 1, 1846, Thomas Jonathan Jackson was graduated seventeenth in a class of fifty-nine with a reputation as a reticent but sound soldier—"but not quick." He had reached his full height of five feet, nine and three-quarter inches. He was slender, with small, deep-set blue eyes, beautiful dark brown hair, a small firm mouth and long aquiline nose set in an oval face of dark complexion. Breveted a second lieutenant of artillery, Tom left West Point just in time for the Mexican War.

Second Lieutenant Tom Jackson was with Winfield Scott when he landed at Vera Cruz. His light battery had distinguished itself in the bombardment of Fort San Juan d'Ullua, and Jackson's rank was made permanent. Cited for gallantry at San Antonio, he was again in the foremost fighting when the Americans stormed Chapultepec, for which he received a brevet major's rank. His senior officers were amazed by his calmness under fire. Battle seemed to exalt him, and he himself explained: "I seem to have a more perfect command of my faculties in the midst of fighting."

He seemed also to enjoy peace, especially dancing with beautiful Mexican senoritas. He was also fascinated by the beauty of the Catholic churches he visited. The reverence of the worshipers awakened in him a deep religious feeling which he was later to express not in the ritual and music and splendor of the ancient church, but in the grim Presbyterianism of his forebears. It is also possible that Jackson fell in love with a senorita during his sojourn south of the border: his letters to his sister Laura hinted at it, and his cryptic remark "Mexico is for lovers" before his return to the states suggests that he might have been disappointed.

Assigned to Fort Hamilton on Long Island and committed to a dull routine, his interest in religion grew to the extent that he had himself baptized in a nearby chapel, which, by chance and not by choice as he observed, was Episcopal. He prayed constantly while his inner life quickened, and it is possible that he was becoming something of a mystic.

Transferred to Fort Meade, Florida, he wrote with enthusiasm of the peninsula's wild beauty and his devotion to the military life, and then, in a stunning about-face, shocked his sister by announcing that he had applied for the vacant chair of Natural and Experimental Philosophy at Virginia Military Institute in Lexington. He had formidable competition—George B. McClellan and William S. Rosecrans among them—but D. H. Hill, another Mexico veteran who now taught mathematics at Washington College also in Lexington, campaigned so enthusiastically on Jackson's behalf that "the Major"—as he was to be called for the next decade of his life—received the appointment on March 28, 1851.

Just before Jackson went to Lexington he encountered Dabney Maury, his old West Point classmate, who wrote: "He had then become hypochondriacal. He had queer ideas about his health; he thought one side of him was heavier than the other, and sometimes he would raise one hand up to the arm's length to let the blood flow downward and lighten that arm." He had also developed the habit of sitting bolt upright to preserve the natural alignment of his internal organs. The Major's latest panacea for all those afflictions—headaches, failing eyesight, indigestion, chilblains, inflammations of the ear and throat, neuralgia—was now hydropathy, or the water cure, consisting of copious use of the liquid both externally and internally. He spent the summer of 1851 visiting the spas and springs along Lake Ontario, and did the same in Virginia after he took command of the VMI cadet corps in its summer encampment.

Jackson's belief in God had become such a powerful force in his life that he could scarcely separate his apologetics from his artillery courses. Many of his students found him dull and narrow-minded, calling him Tom Fool. He would allow them to reach conclusions only through his orthodox approach. Any piece of brilliant intuition or a beautiful solution achieved by an original approach was disallowed.

His eccentricities were legion. He was so punctual that, like the neighbors of the German philosopher Immanuel Kant, the people of sleepy little Lexington could set their watches by his movements. VMI's superintendent, at first astounded to see Jackson pacing outside his office in pouring rain, waiting for the exact moment to make his weekly report, soon became accustomed to the Major's passion for precision. And to his legendary obedience as well, characterized when the superintendent called Jackson into his presence and asked him to wait in an anteroom until he could attend to another matter, and then, forgetting him entirely, went to his home for the night with the Major still seated in the foyer. Finding him there the next morning, he received the typical explanation: "It never occurred to me to leave the spot of duty, where my superior told me to stay."

Thus Tom Fool Jackson, eccentric, inflexible, abstemious, bound by a rigid code excluding all but a few small pleasures, extremely polite to women while rarely seeking their company, and so religious that he opened a Sunday school for slaves—it was no wonder that the people of Lexington were incredulous when in April 1853 he announced his engagement to Eleanor Junkin, the daughter of Dr. George Junkin, a Northerner and a Presbyterian minister, and also president of Washington College. The courtship had been a secret, kept not only by the lovers but by Eleanor's twin sister Margaret as well. They were so close that Margaret accompanied the newlyweds on their honeymoon to Niagara Falls and Canada. It was Margaret who remembered her brother-in-law's awe when he stood on the Plains of Abraham to quote the victorious James Wolfe's dying words: "Now, God be praised, I will die in peace," and to stand before his monument on tiptoe, his nostrils quivering with emotion while sweeping his arm in an encompassing movement around the Plains, and cry:

"To die as he died, who would not die content!"

Jackson was extremely happy with his "intellectual, pure and lovely lady." They led a quiet, normal life, but the marriage ended in tragedy. Though pregnant, in November 1854 Eleanor took a jolting stagecoach ride to visit Jackson's relatives in western Virginia. Upon her return she went immediately to bed. She died in childbirth and the baby was still-born. "She has now gone on a glorious visit, though through a gloomy portal," Jackson announced to his family. "I look forward with delight to the day when I shall join her."

Jackson seemed to be interested in real estate at this time, but then, after a trip to Europe, he remarried. The bride was Mary Anna Morrison, also the daughter of a Presbyterian minister and college president. She lived in Lincoln County, North Carolina, where her father presided over David-son College, which he had founded. They were married at her family's home in July 1857.

In the spring of 1858, Anna gave birth to a baby girl who died a few weeks later. Once again Jackson's consolation was that this second tragedy was also the will of God, writing to a niece: "My little daughter was called from this world of sin to enjoy the heavenly happiness of Paradise."

The Major was genuinely fond of his plump little brown-eyed wife. He delighted in teasing her. Once he returned home in full regimentals, drawing his sword and brandishing it fiercely over her head, but the moment the timid little lady showed fright he threw it down and embraced her in glee. Many times he would hide behind a door when he heard her approaching, springing out to greet her "with a startling caress." No one in the village or at the Institute could imagine that this fierce Christian soldier—the reincarnation of Gideon or Joshua or both—could be so coy and uxurious. Jackson actually did have two faces: an austere one for the world, and a happy and smiling one for his home and hearth. As the war came closer, he shrank from joining the arguments dividing villages and towns North and South, although he did make his sympathies known when he said: "If I know myself, all I am and have is at the service of my country."

He showed this spirit in the spring of 1861 when, before Virginia seceded, the VMI cadets ripped down the United States flag and replaced it with a state banner. Lexington militia drove off the cadets and hoisted the national colors once more. Instantly, the Institute drums beat the alarm and the cadets poured out the gates en masse. Fortunately, the superintendent ordered them back inside, whereupon they began calling for Jackson. Shed-ding his customary reserve, Jackson told them:

"I admire the spirit you have shown in rushing to the defense of your comrades; and I commend the way in which you obeyed the commands of your superior officer. The time may come, young gentlemen, when your state will need your services, and if that time comes, draw your swords and throw away your scabbards."

Roaring like the guns of Sumter, the cadets were ready after Virginia seceded and Jackson led the upper classmen to Richmond. There he was all but ignored, until Major General Robert E. Lee intervened in his behalf and he was made a colonel and sent to Harpers Ferry to defend that captured Federal outpost and hasten its precious munitions and rolling stock toward Richmond. He carried out his mission so well that he received a general's star and command of a Virginia brigade. Before Joe Johnston abandoned the post, Jackson seized a couple of Union horses. One of them was Little Sorrel, the stout mount that was to become famous along with its master. Thomas Jonathan Jackson was riding Little Sorrel when he led his brigade toward Piedmont and the trains waiting to take them to Beauregard's main body at Manassas—where he first set foot on the path to immortality and received his undying nickname.

36

■

Fair Oaks

O N APRIL 21, 1862, the Federal forces faced their finest opportunity to date in Virginia: nothing less than the opportunity to crush Johnston and win the war. North, west and northwest of Richmond they possessed a numerical advantage of 65,000 to 24,000 men. If Banks and Frémont in the Shenandoah Valley could keep Jackson and Ewell occupied, then McDowell driving south to join McClellan could brush aside C. W. Field's little brigade at Fredericksburg, cross the Rappahannock, and drive on Richmond, lying open only sixty miles away. He would also be astride Johnston's communications before Johnston could get back to the Confederate capital. If McClellan struck Johnston suddenly, he might destroy him before he could fall back on Richmond. Even if the Federal forces were not capable of all these operations, it was certain that McDowell and McClellan would unite before Richmond, forcing Johnston to retire into North Carolina—the beginning of the end.

Johnston and Lee were very much alive to this danger, and each had a plan to meet it. Johnston wanted to meet concentration with concentration, to allow the Federals to advance far from their bases and then strike them with all Confederate forces from the Rapidan to the Savannah. Lee's plan, characteristically, was bolder, much more economical in manpower, and likely to pay dividends equally as great as Johnston's. He envisioned an offensive-defensive, that is, to order Stonewall Jackson to overwhelm Frémont and Banks in the Shenandoah Valley and feint toward Washington to frighten the Federal government into recalling McDowell and his 40,000 for defense of the capital.

On April 21 Lee sent to Jackson one of the most momentous dispatches of his career. He outlined the situation and suggested three possibilities. If Jackson believed that he could drive Banks northward down the

Valley by combining with Ewell, he should do so. If Banks were too strong, then Jackson should put Ewell between Fredericksburg and Richmond so that he could support Jackson, Field or even Johnston. If Jackson thought that he could handle Banks on his own, then he should do so and have Ewell reinforce Field. Lee himself favored an attack on Banks by Jackson and Ewell, with Stonewall in command. "The blow, wherever struck, must, to be successful, be sudden and heavy." In any event, McDowell must not be allowed to advance south to reinforce McClellan.

Jackson answered that he could not strike Banks with Ewell unless he had 5,000 more men. After Lee replied that he could not provide them, Jackson said he would combine with Brigadier General Edward Johnson, then being pressed back on Staunton by Frémont. This led Lee to doubt the wisdom of striking Banks, and on May 1, instead authorized Jackson for joint operations with Johnston west of Staunton.

Lee, a born gambler, was taking a great chance on Jackson. Stonewall's reputation then was not so great; indeed, it had been tarnished at Kernstown. Many Confederate commanders believed him a madman or at least eccentric. He was too pious, always on his knees praying, refusing to do so much on the Sabbath as write a letter, still less launch an attack. In his soft, gentle voice he could call a colonel "a wicked fellow" for swearing at his men, yet murmur to an officer regretful at having to kill brave Federals: "No, shoot them all. I do not wish them to be brave." Jackson's men knew his qualities, calling him "Old Blue Light" for the way his eyes blazed in battle, dubbing themselves "Jackson's foot cavalry." They laughed at his eccentricities, his habit of sucking lemons for his indigestion, swearing that he always called for artillery because that was where he kept those yellow fruits.

The foot cavalry moved with customary celerity toward Frémont, and with the usual silence. Jackson always said, "If my hat knew my plans, I would burn it," and he gave the anxious Lee no hint—either by mail or by telegraph—of what he intended to do.

What he did do was to move rapidly west and jump the unsuspecting Frémont's advance guard in one of the passes of the Alleghenies. It was not an especially important battle, but it upset Frémont in his plans to invade eastern Tennessee. Frémont had changed not at all since his Missouri days. He was still surrounded by his retinue of foreign aides-de-camp "dazzling in gold lace," and still full of grandiose plans never really formulated clearly. It took him two weeks to recover from Jackson's attack and to prepare to receive another, by which time Stonewall was long gone, hurrying back to the Valley with his strength now up to 15,000 men.

Banks was his target, Banks the prince of all the political generals who abounded on the Yankee side. Born in poverty, he rose to become a leader of the Democratic Party in Massachusetts, until his hatred of slavery led him to join the Republican Party, becoming governor of the Bay State in 1858, and then, in 1861, a Union general. Banks confidently expected Jackson at Strasburg, which he had fortified, until the wily Stonewall fell upon his rear guard at Front Royal and destroyed it. Banks quickly retired to Winchester, and here, on May 25, in a savage early-morning fight, Jackson turned Banks's right flank and drove him pell-mell back across the Potomac.

Once again, Washington was in a state of near panic. It was rumored that Jackson was bent on invading the North. Frantic telegrams alerted Northern governors to the danger. McDowell's orders to join McClellan were canceled, and he was told to combine with Frémont and Banks to converge on Jackson. But the fast-moving Stonewall was by then heading home, at last informing the near-frantic Lee on May 26 that he had accomplished his mission.

McClellan, denied his vital reinforcement, was now caught on both sides of the flooding Chickahominy River.

Little Mac had sent one part of his army south of the Chickahominy to hold a bridgehead, while keeping the larger part on the north bank to protect his base. After McDowell arrived, he would move the entire army across the river. That was all right. But then McDowell was diverted to the Valley, and McClellan still clung to this vulnerable position. So General Johnston decided to try to wipe out the small Union force south of the river before the larger force north of it could come to the rescue.

Heavy spring rains worked to Johnston's advantage. They turned the Chickahominy into a raging torrent that threatened to sweep away the bridges built by McClellan's engineers. Confederate staff work, however, redounded to Johnston's disadvantage. Longstreet, in charge of the main attack, took the wrong road and fed in his units piecemeal.

The battle began on May 31, 1862, and ended the next day. It was fought over and around a railroad station known as Fair Oaks and a farm called Seven Pines, and bears both those names. In the end, the Rebels got so thoroughly in each other's way that they were too late to stop Union reinforcements from rushing over bridges that did hold, despite the flood. Fair Oaks–Seven Pines was as bloody as it was confused and inconclusive: some 5,700 Rebels dead or wounded, some 4,400 Union casualties.

Among the Confederate casualties was Joe Johnston himself, his bad luck with enemy bullets still holding. He had received two more wounds— his seventh and eighth—so painful and so serious that he would need months to recuperate. That was indeed a great calamity for the North, for command of the Army of Northern Virginia now passed to Robert E. Lee.

37

■

Robert E. Lee

A MONG ALL THE GENERALS of the Civil War none had a pedigree
approaching the ancestry of Robert Edward Lee, just as none could
boast of a family more distinguished in its devotion to the Union than the
Lees of Virginia. Two of Lee's ancestors—Richard Henry and Francis
Lightfoot Lee—were signers of the Declaration of Independence, and his
own father—Henry—was the celebrated Light-Horse Harry Lee of Revolutionary War fame, so trusted by Washington that he reported to no one else.
It was Henry Lee who celebrated the Father of His Country in the famous
phrase: "First in war, first in peace, first in the hearts of his countrymen."
After the war he appeared to be embarked on an illustrious career of his
own. He married his cousin, Matilda Lee, who had been left mistress of
Stratford, the great estate on the Potomac, and promptly entered politics.
Elected to the House of Delegates in 1785, he was chosen to sit in the
Continental Congress, and was a leader in the Virginia convention of 1788
in supporting the new Constitution, matching his own eloquence against the
thunders of Patrick Henry, who opposed it. In 1791 he was elected governor of Virginia, serving three terms of one year each. And yet, for all of this
glory and honor, there was a huge hole in Henry Lee.

He had a passion for speculation, unmatched by any grasp of the harsh
realities of profit and loss. All of his projects were grandiose, all would make
millions—all failed miserably. His own father had seen this defect, passing
him over in selecting an executor, while leaving him great parcels of land.
His wife, Matilda, to protect her family against her husband's numerous
creditors, deeded Stratford to their son, Henry, one of two children of the
four born to her who survived. Shortly afterward she died.

Grief-stricken and desperate, Lee attempted to return to the army but
was passed over for unknown reasons. Next he thought of resigning as

332

governor and going to France to join the revolutionaries! Fortunately, his friend Washington wisely advised him against it. It was then that he visited Shirley, the home of Charles Carter, the richest man in the Old Dominion next to Washington, and fell in love with his twenty-one-year-old daughter, Anne. Though seventeen years younger, she returned his affection and they were married.

Remarriage seemed to have steadied Lee—but only temporarily, for soon his old passion for speculation seized him so completely that he was eventually compelled to sell off his remaining land to pay his numerous debts. He was approaching pauperhood, and the pinch of poverty was plain in the fading cheeks of his wife. A month after her father died, on January 19, 1807, she gave birth to her fourth child: a robust baby boy whom she named Robert Edward after two of her brothers.

When this child was sixteen months old, his half-brother Henry took possession of Stratford. Lee and his family were now the guests of his son by his first marriage, and after he was jailed for about a year for non-payment of a debt, the family moved to a small house in Alexandria. A trust left to Anne by her father could not be touched by her husband, and it was just enough to sustain her family—but no more. And then Light-Horse Harry Lee sank from financial ruin into physical debility.

As a Federalist Lee had opposed the War of 1812. So had a young Baltimore editor. After Lee and other sympathizers joined the editor at his home, a wrathful mob of idlers gathered outside. Police were compelled to escort him and his friends to the safety of a jail. The mob followed and broke in. One man was killed and eleven fearfully beaten. Lee was one of these. Drunken fiends poured candle grease into his eyes and pierced his body with pen knives, waiting with sadistic pleasure for signs of pain. One of them tried to cut off his nose. Finally, he was rescued and taken to a hospital. His death was reported in Washington. Because of his splendid physique, he survived: but as a hulk of a man condemned to invalidism for the remaining six years of his life. Henry Lee now sought nothing so much as to leave the country he had loved and served so faithfully, and in which he had been so tragically overwhelmed by failure. President James Monroe arranged for him to go to Barbados, and in the summer of 1813 he bade his beloved family farewell and sailed downriver forever out of their sight.

Robert was eleven when word was received that his father had died on March 25, 1818, while sailing home from Barbados. Soon responsibility for the family fell upon him, his three older brothers being either away at school, practicing law in Washington or at sea as a midshipman. His mother was now an invalid and his young sister Anne hardly better. It was Robert's duty to attend to both of them, a responsibility he accepted without hesitation.

After his graduation from Eastern View Academy in 1820, the question now in the Lee family was what should Robert do, what career should he follow? He had neither the money nor the land to embrace a Southern patrician's life as a planter, he detested both politics and the law and because he was not especially religious he never thought of presenting himself for the ministry. But he had shown an aptitude for mathematics and a fondness for military glory. It was decided that he should try for West Point, and his family name was still of such influence that he was granted a personal interview with Secretary of War Calhoun. On March 11, 1824, he was appointed to the United States Military Academy effective July 1, 1825.

Robert had been pleased to learn that Joe Johnston of Virginia would be in his class. There had always been a bond between the Lee and Johnston families because of the service of Joe's father in the regiment commanded by Robert's father. Now at West Point, the two young men were drawn closer together. Joe was a good student, but not the equal of Robert, who would be graduated second in his class, as corps adjutant—the highest rank for a cadet—and without a single demerit. This last might suggest a prissy character, but Robert E. Lee was in fact one of the most popular cadets in the corps. He was warm-hearted and good-humored, though not exactly witty, able to win friends easily and keep them. His dignity was natural, and his gravity probably the product of the misfortune that had overwhelmed his father and the responsibility of caring for his mother and sister during his boyhood. He was almost incredibly handsome, called the Marble Model by his classmates. He stood five feet eleven inches tall, weighing 170 pounds, with a powerful torso and lean, athletic hips, big hands and surprisingly small feet. Upon a horse which he sat with easy grace his torso made him look bigger. Lee's wide-set eyes beneath narrow brows were dark brown, which sometimes seemed black in dim light, his hair thick, black and wavy, his mouth beautifully formed, and his entire countenance manly and appealing, beaming as though illuminated from within by the glow of friendship. As a brevet second lieutenant of engineers he quickly grew a pair of narrow black sideburns.

Lee returned home to Alexandria and was at his mother's bedside when she died on July 10. Soon thereafter he visited Arlington, the home of George Washington Parke Custis, Martha Washington's grandson and

George's adopted son. Custis had lived with the Washingtons for ten years, and he still delighted in being known as "the child of Mount Vernon." Lee was drawn there by the presence of Custis's only surviving child, twenty-one-year-old Mary Anne Randolph Custis. They were distantly related and had become fond of each other. Mary Custis was a frail blond girl, and no beauty, with her too-sharp nose and oval masculine face, but she had an engaging personality, and perhaps just as important to Robert Edward Lee, a direct family connection with George Washington. To join that most illustrious name to those of the Carters and Lees was to incarnate in him the very soul of Virginia and the Federal Union. They were married June 30, 1831, at Arlington, and on September 16 of the following year Mary bore a fine baby boy named George Washington Custis Lee, called Custis by his family. During the next nine years Lee was occupied in engineering and survey work rising to captain, while Mary presented him with five more children: William Henry Fitzhugh ("Rooney"), Robert Edward, Jr., Anne, Mary and Mildred. The last five of these years were spent at the Narrows in New York, and he was there when the Mexican War erupted.

Captain Lee's first service was with Brigadier General John E. Wool, who commanded a brigade in Zachary Taylor's army. Although he saw no action, he distinguished himself as a tireless, courageous and perceptive scout. He was delighted when he was transferred to Winfield Scott's army preparing to invade Mexico at Vera Cruz. Scott had already formed a high opinion of Lee and had made a special request for him. After Vera Cruz surrendered to the Americans on March 27, 1847, Scott decided that his next objective should be the new army organized by General Santa Anna after his rough experiences at the hands of Zachary Taylor. To do this, Scott must march on Mexico City, following the 150-mile route traversed by Cortés nearly three and a half centuries before. Lee performed great service for Scott at the Battle of Cerro Gordo, finding a path around the Mexican left. His greatest achievement was at Chapultepec when he discovered a path through the Pedregal, a great gray field of broken lava looking like a storm-tossed sea of stone, which blocked Scott's approach to the fortress. Lee was wounded during the storming of Chapultepec, and was breveted to the rank of colonel.

Robert Edward Lee had learned much about the conduct of high command during that series of battles from Cerro Gordo to Mexico City. Scott's daring had led Lee to cherish audacity; his careful planning and delegation of authority taught him that the supreme commander need not personally fight the battle in detail; his reliance on a trained staff inspired

Lee's own emphasis on efficient staff work; Lee's own frequent scouting expeditions opened his eyes to the importance of reconnaissance and how this in turn could lead to turning movements; and, finally, his experience siting and emplacing artillery impressed upon him the necessity for strong fortifications. For Lee, then, twenty months in Mexico had given invaluable instruction in the art of war as it actually is fought: on earth, not on blackboards; by flesh-and-blood soldiers crossing mountains and deserts, fording streams, fighting and dying, not by pen-and-ink creatures marching over maps. He had actually enjoyed it, and was not especially enchanted to return to his new assignment: building Fort Carroll in Baltimore. But then, on May 28 Lee learned with mixed emotions that he had been appointed to be the ninth superintendent of the United States Military Academy.

He was honored to be the recipient of this, one of the few prized posts in the overworked engineer service, but also with characteristic modesty doubted that he was qualified to be an educator. In this he was overruled, and on September 1 began his tour at the Plains.

Lee's family was happy with the new life, especially his wife, after the horses were brought up from Arlington and some of the furniture to make the pleasant superintendent's quarters even more comfortable. Custis was at the Point as a third-year man and could visit Saturday afternoon with friends, while Fitzhugh Lee, the superintendent's nephew, arrived as a plebe the following year. "Fitz" was a high-spirited youth fond of after-hours excursions to Benny Haven's and was twice caught red-handed. Lee avoided embarrassment by recommending that Fitz and his fellow culprits be court-martialed. On the first count his nephew was severely punished, but not expelled, and on the second he went scot-free after Secretary of War Jefferson Davis accepted his class's unanimous pledge not to commit any offenses during the academic year.

As superintendent Lee was like that: eminently fair while adhering strictly to regulations, but also, in his genuine affection for the young men of the cadet corps and concern for their well-being, watching over them like a guardian so that he might not even have to consider tempering justice with mercy. Punishment might be painful to mete out, but he believed that "true kindness required it should be applied with a firm hand and not converted into a reward."

On April 12, 1855, Lee received orders to take command of the 2nd Cavalry at Louisville. For the first time in his career he was in direct command of troops, and he was delighted to lead his troopers to their new station at

Jefferson Barracks. Here he learned for the first time that he was expected to sit regularly on court-martials, to him a most frustrating and boring experience. Intermittently for the next five years he would ride hundreds of miles and spend hundreds of monotonous hours listening to the droning testimony of witnesses and the dull arguments of the advocates.

It was about this time that Lee put down on paper his attitude toward the institution of slavery that was then dividing his country. He had been at Fort Leavenworth on court-martial duty and had seen at first hand—and deplored—the passions aroused in "bleeding Kansas." He had experienced slavery all of his life and had owned six slaves given to him by his father-in-law, but he believed in gradual emancipation and had sent to Liberia those who wished to go. Having in July 1853 presented himself for confirmation in the Episcopal church, along with his daughters Mary and Annie, Lee had begun to develop a simple faith in "a wise Merciful Providence." In a long letter on the subject of slavery, which he condemned as "a moral and political evil" more harmful to white than black men, he spoke in essence of his belief that emancipation would come to the blacks—"immeasurably better off here than in Africa"—only "from the mild and melting influence of Christianity, [rather] than from the storms and tempests of fiery Controversy." These of course were the views of the patricians of the Upper South, who had seen slavery in its least injustice, even known educated black men, but had never ventured into the misery and degradation of the cotton and sugar plantations of the Lower South.

In October of 1857 Lee received word that his father-in-law had died, and he applied and obtained leave to return to Virginia. His service in Texas had not been as unproductive as he thought. For the first time he had commanded the mostly ignorant and even illiterate private soldiers of the day, and had learned to understand them. That tedious duty on court-martials had also taught him to be a bit more distrusting of his fellow man: prone to deceit, venality and selfishness. Finally, he had for the first time become adjusted to the privations of life on the line. Without his suspecting it, of course, duty in Texas—like war in Mexico—had trained Robert Edward Lee for high command.

Upon his return to Arlington Lee found two pressing problems: his wife was now a chronic invalid and his father-in-law's will was so vague and full of excessive legacies to his own daughter that it would be some time before it could be executed. In the meantime, as he had done with his mother in his boyhood and youth, he accepted the role of nurse for Mary. To solve the second problem required his presence at Arlington and part of his salary, so Lee obtained two months' leave and devoted himself to the duties of a planter. It was not quite as idyllic as he had envisioned when he thought of life after retirement, but he stuck to it doggedly, his repeated leaves punctuated by duty on courts-martial or courts of inquiry.

On October 17, 1859, he was startled to see Lieutenant Jeb Stuart on his doorstep. Stuart had been one of his favorite cadets in his first year at the Academy. The lieutenant bore a sealed note from the War Department informing him of John Brown's seizure of Harpers Ferry and summoning him to Washington. After Lee had captured John Brown and been sent to command troops at Harpers Ferry to guard against a rumored Abolitionist attempt to seize it again, he returned to Arlington. The furor that succeeded Brown's execution had little effect on Lee. He believed Brown to be a "fanatic or madman" and was quite satisfied that the slaves would never rally to anyone like him.

On February 10, 1860, Lieutenant Colonel Lee said good-bye to his family once more and returned to active duty as temporary commander of the Department of Texas. There the approaching dissolution of his beloved Union produced in him a striking change in personality. More than any other officer from Dixie, he had spent much time at home or near home, and had come to share the conviction of his numerous cousins that belief in the rectitude of the Old Dominion was akin to faith in God. Being a planter had also given him a deeper sense of union with the spirit of Virginia. It was this upon which his soul fed as his anguish upon the forthcoming shipwreck of the Union caused him to withdraw more and more into himself. The gay, lighthearted officer of early manhood and middle age was now at fifty-four an aloof, cold patriarch, looking like an unapproachable God of Battles with his full white beard and mustache. Of him then an associate wrote: "I knew him well, perhaps I might say, intimately, though his grave, cold dignity of bearing and the prudential reserve of his manner rather chilled over-early, or over-much intimacy."

After the Lower South seceded, Lee was ordered by General Scott to report to him in Washington. Scott had never hidden his admiration for Lee, and had spoken openly of his hopes that he would one day succeed him. The two officers talked for three hours in Scott's office, but not a word of the conversation has ever been revealed. Obviously, Scott could have desired nothing less than for Lee to command the army assembling after Sumter. An actual offer to that effect had been authorized by Secretary of War Cameron and made to Lee by Montgomery Blair. It was tempting—the rank of major general commanding an army of from 75,000 to 100,000 men, full support of the government, a chance for military glory rivaling even

Washington's—but not to a man of Lee's character and convictions. He refused, explaining later: "I declined the offer he made me to take command of the army that was to be brought into the field, stating as candidly and as courteously as I could, that though opposed to secession and deprecating war, I could take no part in an invasion of the Southern States." Instead, he said: "If the Union is dissolved and the government disrupted, I shall return to my native state and share the miseries of my people and save in defense will draw my sword on no one."

Lee was true to his word. After Virginia seceded he resigned from the United States Army on April 20 and returned to Arlington. Two days later he accepted command of the Old Dominion's defenses and on August 31 he was promoted to full general as military adviser to President Davis. Sent to western Virginia in an attempt to regain that area for the Confederacy, on September 11 he tried to overcome the separated Federal forces at Cheat Mountain Summit and Elkwater, but he was defeated by stubborn Union resistance, difficult mountain terrain and incessant rains. Next, he ably directed strengthening of Rebel fortifications in South Carolina and Georgia, returning to Richmond in March 1862, to resume his post as Davis's aide. Some critics derided this position as degrading him to the rank of "military clerk." Actually, Davis did depend on him heavily, and there was really no place to send him. Albert Sidney Johnston was in command in the West seconded by Beauregard, and Joe Johnston seemed to have taken firm charge of the Rebel forces around Manassas. But then Old Joe's bad luck with bullets had held.

38

∎

Mechanicsville, Gaines's Mill, Malvern Hill

NEVER BEFORE nor since has one man transformed an army by the sheer force of his presence and personality in the way that Robert Edward Lee inspired the Army of Northern Virginia. He was almost worshiped by those gaunt and dauntless scarecrows whom he now commanded, this flower of Southern chivalry, the last White Knight of the Battlefield, whom they called "Marse Robert." When he rode among them on his great gray stallion Traveller they did not whoop and cheer, but rather stood in awe or removed their slouch hats while gazing reverently at this powerfully built, white-bearded patriarch of a soldier. "I've heard of God," one Southern lady remarked, "but I've *seen* General Lee."

The comparison was apt, for not since the Middle Ages, when allusion to the Almighty was as perfunctory as a genuflection, have the orders of a chief been so full of supplication to God. They are like a litany: the Almighty sends sun to warm the Army of Northern Virginia, or rain to enmire the Army of the Potomac; God gives victory or defeat, and if it is success then He is to be praised; if failure, then the Army of Northern Virginia must search its soul for the sin that has caused the Heavenly Father to avert his face. In this, there exist a submission and fatalism that are perhaps not helpful for a commander of armies. So also is a strange gentleness and compassion alien to the battlefield. Jackson might mutter, "Kill the brave ones!"—as he did—but Lee, the warrior of the New, could take the hand of a wounded and defiant Union soldier, and say: "My son, I hope you will soon be well." Lee was instinctively combative, of course, but some of Jackson's ferocity might have made him a better commander.

In his very real humility, he deferred almost without deviation to Jefferson Davis. In his gentleness, he could not be severe, and therefore found it difficult to dismiss incompetent officers or to settle disputes over authority or to discipline those magnificent scarecrows whom he loved to the depths of his being. And in his simplicity, in his very desire to live no better than any private soldier, he was sometimes unapproachable. Too many Confederates thought of Robert E. Lee as a saint, and because human beings, prone to mistake goodness for saintliness, are also afraid of sanctity, they kept away from him.

Such were the virtues that sometimes tended to become defects when mounted in the saddle of the commander in chief, and they are detailed here only because the personality of Robert E. Lee seems to be buried beneath an avalanche of bronze statues, Lee memorial days and the uncritical adulation of worshipful biographers. Lee the man is frozen inside a marble myth. Great soldier that he was, he was not matchless; and he might have been even greater had his idealism been tempered with an understanding of the holes in human nature. Nevertheless, his nobility of character made him the soul of his army. No commander ever possessed a greater capacity for inspiring troops, for electrifying them by his very presence on the field of battle. Nor was any commander more masterful in defense, in devising fortification—or more audacious in attack.

McClellan, still convinced that he was outnumbered, made no offensive moves after Fair Oaks. He seems to have been preparing to take Richmond by siege operations. But Lee was busy, building fortifications with that energy and skill that caused his men to call him the "King of Spades," and drawing up a plan to strike McClellan. First he needed to know McClellan's exact position, and for this information he called upon Jeb Stuart.

Five feet nine and a half, but of powerful build, Stuart's West Point classmates had called him Beauty in joking reference to his homely face and big bold nose. Jeb Stuart was a Southern Cavalier par excellence; for all his homeliness and huge cinnamon-colored beard curling down below his breastbone, he was the darling of the Southern ladies, whose delight it was to garland his bridle with roses or to make some contribution to a costume that made the hussar getup of the flamboyant Federal cavalryman, George Custer, seem funereal garb indeed. Beneath a broad gray hat looped with a gold star and adorned with a plume, Stuart wore a short gray jacket bright with buttons and braid. A gray red-lined cavalry cape trailed from his shoulder, around his waist was an ornate and tasseled yellow sash from which a light French saber hung, great leather gauntlets reached almost to his elbows, on his legs were enormous jack boots with gold spurs, while his saddle held a pistol and a bright red blanket. When Stuart gave commands, it was in a voice that carried like a bugle call, and on June 12 he was singing "Kathleen Mavourneen" as he led some 1,200 horsemen on a spectacular 150-mile ride around McClellan's army.

Lee had an anxious three days before this dashing young trooper whom he loved so well at last appeared back in headquarters on June 15. His ride had been much more than a daring feat of mounted reconnaissance, for he was able to tell his chief that the roads in the Union rear were worse than on the Confederate front. The Army of the Potomac was being supplied by wagon trains from the town of White House as well as by railroad, and it did not appear that McClellan intended to change his base to the James. All this indicated that if Lee could turn McClellan's right, he might get on his line of communications. Stuart also told him there were no Federals on the long ridge beyond the headwaters of Beaver Dam Creek, suggesting a turning movement there to fall upon White House. Stuart had done all that Lee had asked—and more—thus whetting his appetite for more of the sensational same.

Nevertheless, Lee now knew that McClellan had moved most of his army south of the Chickahominy but had left one corps under Fitz-John Porter on the north bank at Mechanicsville. Lee decided to have 25,000 men under the actor John Magruder hold down McClellan's main body of 60,000, while hurling 65,000 men against Porter's 30,000. To do this he ordered Jackson to march down from the valley and hit Porter's right flank. As he did, A. P. Hill would cross the river at Mechanicsville to clear the town. After this, Longstreet and D. H. Hill, across the river above the town, were to come in behind Jackson and A. P. Hill in support. Together, the four commanders would roll Porter down the river bank before McClellan could come to his rescue.

It was a fine plan, but as had happened to Johnston, it went awry. Jackson was slow in arriving and did not get his men into action. A. P. Hill, despairing of Jackson's arrival, went rushing across the river without orders and charged smack into the formidable Union line. The result was miniature disaster. The Battle of Mechanicsville ended in 1,500 Confederate casualties against 250 for the Union.

Lee was annoyed but not dismayed. Magruder had succeeded in deceiving McClellan again, and the bulk of the Rebel army was north of the river in position to crush Porter. Next day, June 27, 1862, at Gaines's Mill, the attack was renewed. Again and again the Confederates charged the Union line, only to be repulsed each time. Artillery thundered throughout the day, and Union guns south of the Chickahominy reversed aim to hurl shells into the onrushing Rebels. Rifle fire was so thick that the brush and saplings were cut down as though scythed.

Just before sunset there was a lull. Weary Union soldiers thought the battle had ended in a Rebel defeat. But Lee, across the river, had assembled every available man for a general assault. Behind a sudden crash of artillery, screeching the Rebel yell, they came running forward—and this time the Federals broke and ran.

Gaines's Mill was a victory for Lee, but it had cost another 8,750 casualties against 4,000 for the Union. Yet, if Porter had not been crushed, as expected, then McClellan had been cowed. South of the river that night, where he had held his main body inactive all day, McClellan ordered a retreat to the James River.

Once again Magruder had fooled him with one of his typical productions—marching men in full view, sending out patrols and skirmishers, firing off cannon—but he had not beguiled Hooker or Kearny, who knew Prince John too well. These two division commanders had the audacity to burst into McClellan's headquarters, and when Little Mac curtly demanded the reason for such behavior, Kearny burst out: "The enemy lines around Richmond are thin. They can and must be broken. An order to retreat is wrong! Wrong, sir! I ask permission to attack Magruder at once."

"Denied," McClellan snapped, and after Kearny renewed his arguments, he said: "Nothing has changed, General. The retreat will be made on schedule." With that, according to General Hiram Berry, who was present: "Phil unloosed a broadside. He pitched into McClellan with language so strong that all who heard it expected he would be placed under arrest until a general court-martial could be held."

McClellan, however, merely allowed Kearny to calm down, and let him go without a word. That night, the supply trains of the Army of the Potomac began the retreat.

One of Robert E. Lee's favorite maneuvers was to strike the flanks of a moving enemy, and he tried it repeatedly against the retiring Federals. Once, at Frayser's Farm, there was an opportunity to gain a splendid victory. But for the fourth time since Lee began his campaign, Stonewall Jackson was slow in moving. Throughout June 29, he stayed in his camp and wrote a letter to his wife telling her how much to contribute to their church. That night he fell asleep while eating, and when he did move out the following day the opportunity was lost. Either because he thought the enemy's position too strong, or because he had lost too much of the sleep his frail physique required, Stonewall had failed the leader whom he idolized as "the only man whom I would follow blindfold."

Lee never got over the missed opportunity at Frayser's Farm, and when Jubal Early expressed concern that McClellan was escaping, he lost his habitual self-control and snapped: "Yes, he will get away because I cannot have my orders carried out."

McClellan did make it safely to Harrison's Landing on the James. Here his supply line was safely in the hands of the Union navy, and his front was guarded by Malvern Hill, blocking the road to the James.

Malvern Hill was a natural fortress. With his fine engineer's eye, Lee saw this at once as he rode forward to sweep the position with his glasses. Still, he thought so little of McClellan that he believed one more blow might crumple the enemy. He became more confident after Longstreet reported that a Confederate crossfire could silence the Union artillery so that the Butternuts could charge the Federals off their 150-foot hilltop. D. H. Hill disagreed saying, "If General McClellan is there in strength, we had better let him alone."

He was there in strength. Massed infantry held every strongpoint, and there were divisions in reserve. Artillery was abundant, with some hundred fieldpieces parked hub to hub to blast any Confederate assault. Still, on July 1, 1862, Lee attacked—and it was the Confederate artillery, not the Union, that was knocked out. Throughout the war, Union artillery was to dominate the Confederate, and Malvern Hill was probably its finest hour. One by one, the Southern fieldpieces were silenced. And when the gallant gray lines surged forward, the Union guns shredded them, maimed them, pulped them—and then a storm of rifle fire broke them in blood. Some 5,500 Rebels fell in those dreadful wasting attacks, and next day a horrified Federal officer looked down the slopes and saw: "A third of them were dead or dying, but enough of them were alive and moving to give the field a singular crawling effect." Long afterward, D. H. Hill wrote of Malvern Hill: "It was not war, it was murder."

39

.

Withdrawal from the Peninsula: Union Squabbles in the West

G ENERAL HILL was right, but the great tragedy of the Civil War was that neither he nor General Lee nor U. S. Grant nor any other high commander ever came to realize why it was that war had become "murder," or, in the phrase of William Tecumseh Sherman, "all hell."

The rifle bullet was the reason. The bullet had given the advantage to the defense. It had dethroned the bayonet, the shock weapon of the assault, and together with its handmaidens, the ax and the spade, had made the defense just about invincible.

The point that had been missed was that the rifle bullet ended the era of headlong assault. In the days of edged or pointed weapons—the sword, the battle-ax and the lance—the assault was the ultimate tactic because all fighting was hand to hand. An attacker had little difficulty in approaching his enemy. This situation might have been ended by the bow and arrow, except that the invention of gunpowder came so close upon perfection of the English longbow that the possibilities of this silent missile were not fully realized. When smoothbore muskets appeared the bullet was subordinated to the bayonet.

What was needed were new weapons and tactics whereby the defense could be pinned down in its entrenchments while its flanks were turned, or so that the attack might advance to within assault range at a minimum risk. These were not developed, and it would be far from fair to fault either Lee or Grant for failing to understand the revolution worked by the rifle bullet. It was not understood in the West as late as World War I and beyond, when automatic weapons and barbed wire made the power of defense even greater, and the famous "banzai" charges of the Japanese during World War II were even bloodier repetitions of the shock tactics that reddened the slopes of Malvern Hill.

Lee's explanation for these assaults was that he believed the enemy to be demoralized. Granting him the universal failure to grasp the limitations now imposed upon the attack, his judgment must be upheld. During the Seven Days' Battles begun at Mechanicsville and ended at Malvern, Lee had suffered 20,000 casualties against 16,000 Union losses, and yet it was McClellan, not Lee, who was backing off.

McClellan ordered a general retreat to Harrison's Landing on the James about fifteen miles below Richmond. His decision enraged many of his officers, none more than Phil Kearny, who slammed his famous kepi into the mud, and roared: "I, Philip Kearny, an old soldier, protest this order for retreat. We ought, instead of retreating, to follow up the enemy and take Richmond. And in full view of all the responsibility of such a declaration, I say to you all, such an order can only be prompted by cowardice or treason."

Neither accusation, of course, was true. Phil Kearny was one of those fighting generals who walk in a two-tone world and whose contempt for politics often conceals an inability or reluctance to swim in those conflicting currents. McClellan missed his great chance because he was still adding up the disadvantages and therefore submitting to the moral mastery of Robert E. Lee. Besides, he was playing politics.

Not long after the withdrawal, President Lincoln came down to Harrison's Landing and McClellan gave him a letter that was nothing less than a blueprint for running the war. In effect, he advocated those very policies that the Republicans detested as "soft" and intimated that his army, McClellan's army, the fighting force molded by McClellan in McClellan's image, would not fight to destroy slavery. Lincoln, who was already coming to the conclusion that some form of emancipation was necessary, read the letter in McClellan's presence and put it in his pocket without a word. He never replied to it, masterpiece of self-important insolence that it was, and a few days later he lifted Henry Halleck out of the West and brought him to Washington as general-in-chief. Halleck assumed command of all the armies on July 11, 1862. In Virginia he confronted this situation:

On June 26, because of failures in the Shenandoah and command complications there, Lincoln had created the Army of Virginia under General John Pope. Pope had a threefold mission: to protect Washington, to guarantee the safety of the Valley, and, by threatening Lee's rail communications, to draw troops off from Richmond and thus make McClellan's task easier. McClellan, however, continued to mark time at Harrison's Landing, and so Halleck went down to see him.

Once again, Little Mac wildly overestimated his enemy's strength, claiming that Lee had 200,000 men when he actually had fewer than McClellan's own 90,000. He asked for 30,000 more men, but Halleck told him he could have only 20,000 and would that be enough to take Richmond. McClellan answered modestly that there was a "chance." Halleck at once concluded that if Lee's army was so big it would be madness to allow him to sit between McClellan's and Pope's divided forces. So he ordered McClellan to return to his Washington base and then unite with Pope.

That, of course, meant an ignominious end to George McClellan's Peninsular Campaign, and a victory for Robert E. Lee. As the Army of the Potomac began its ponderous slow movement north, George McClellan was shocked to read in the newspaper that his old post as general-in-chief had gone to his subordinate Halleck. His meteoric rise to become "the power in this land," had flared and faded out like a shooting star.

There was now a whole host of luminaries in the Federal firmament: Farragut, Burnside, Pope, Ben Butler, Curtis—all of them stars in the ascendant. A few others, like McClellan's, were on the descent—especially U. S. Grant's. Shiloh did to Grant what the Peninsula did to Little Mac. Cashiered officers like the Ohio colonel who had told his men, "Retreat! Save yourselves!" were back home spreading vicious rumors about Grant. War correspondents arriving late for the battle, who got most of their information from the rear—"not the best place from which to judge what is going on in front," Grant dryly observed—filed stories claiming "complete surprise." Grant was lazy, they wrote, incompetent, a drunk and a butcher who heartlessly fed men into the sausage machine of battle. His heavy casualties hit the Northwest hardest, and politicians from that region rose in Congress to denounce the man they had idolized after Donelson. Ohio disclaimed him, insisting that he came from Illinois. Everyone in authority, it seemed, had turned against old Unconditional Surrender Grant—except Abraham Lincoln.

Late one night at the White House, A. K. McClure, the influential Republican leader and publisher from Pennsylvania, came to see the president. He spoke for almost two hours on how "the tide of popular sentiment" had turned against Grant. Lincoln listened in silence. At last he came erect in his chair, and said: "I can't spare this man—he fights!"

True enough, but at that moment—April 1862—Grant was not only not fighting but was wondering if his fighting days were over. That was because Henry Halleck—months before Lincoln brought him to Washington as general-in-chief, and before John Pope was given command of the Army of

Virginia—had boldly cut himself loose from his desk in St. Louis and come down to Pittsburg Landing to take command of all his forces. Immediately reorganizing them, he consolidated Buell's Army of the Ohio with Pope's Army of the Mississippi with Pope in command. Grant's Army of the Tennessee was merged with the division commanded by George Thomas, now a major general, and given to Thomas. McClernand received command of a reserve of three divisions, and Grant was named second to Halleck, thus keeping him where he wanted him—under his fish-eyed stare. Halleck now had fifteen divisions numbering 120,000 men with two hundred guns. With these, he planned to crush Beauregard at Corinth.

Pope and Thomas were pleased with the new arrangement, Buell and McClernand outraged. Grant was not enchanted, either, and when he complained to Old Brains, Halleck charged him with ingratitude, actually replying, like Iago reproaching Othello: "For the past three months I have done everything in my power to ward off the attacks that were made upon you." Old C. F. Smith got nothing because he was still bedridden, his infection worsening—and soon he would be dead of blood poisoning.

On April 28, 1862, Halleck's grand army surged forward: Thomas on the right, Buell in the center, Pope on the left and McClernand in reserve. Halleck remained in Pittsburg, pacing by the hour in front of his headquarters, his thumbs hooked into the armpits of his vest, glancing quickly to right and left, like a flustered goose. He was already worried about Beauregard with his 70,000 entrenched troops twenty miles away. Two days later he set out after his slow-moving army, and when he reached it its pace was reduced from a walk to a crawl. It was a mole's march. Every night the men dug for four hours, took six hours sleep, and then were up at dawn to repel any surprise attack. This was "scientific war," à la Baron Jomini. As Halleck inched forward, he alternated between listening in dismay to Rebel deserters' reports of huge reinforcements at Corinth, and distress at Pope's fondness for brisk movement. "Don't let Pope get too far ahead," he warned Grant. When Grant suggested that he shift Pope from the swampy left to a ridge on the right and send him rapidly along the high ground into Corinth, Old Brains replied with the fish-eyed stare. This was not—repeat not—Jomini. Grant made no more suggestions.

Now the rate of advance dwindled from a mile a day to a half-mile or less. Sweating under the hot Mississippi sun in their winter uniforms of wool, the men dug and cursed, cursed and dug, and on May 28—a month after they left Pittsburg Landing—they had marched fifteen miles. Halleck now believed that the Little Creole had 200,000 men in his command.

■　■　■

Actually, Halleck's first estimate of enemy strength had been correct. Beauregard had then exactly 70,000 men, but a crushing number of deaths due to wounds received at Shiloh—eight of ten amputees died of wounds—and the outbreaks of measles, dysentery and typhoid fever in near epidemic proportions had left him with 52,000, even with the addition of Van Dorn's 16,000—less than half the number Halleck had cautiously brought before him.

Beauregard had played on Old Brains's jangled nerves, carefully coaching his "deserters" in what to say once they reached Yankee lines and were taken to see the commanding officer. He also tried to whittle Halleck's forces by creating diversions in his rear to draw off troops. But Halleck remained calm, although he was definitely upset when he saw Corinth's entrenchments. Beauregard's men had been digging and cursing just as vigorously as Halleck's, but in the same place and for a longer period of time. Corinth ridge was a natural obstacle, but Halleck was appalled when he saw its frowning fortifications of close-packed red earth. A siege seemed more advisable than an assault.

Unknown to Old Brains, a siege was exactly what the Little Creole could not survive. To his water shortage and growing sick list was now added a scarcity of food. On May 25 he called a council of war. Hardee's recommendation to evacuate while it could be done unmolested was agreed upon, and speeded up after Halleck ordered a dawn-to-dusk bombardment on the twenty-eighth. Beauregard's preparations for withdrawal were superb. Wounded and sick, along with heavy baggage and camp equipment, left by rail. Three days' cooked rations were issued to the troops, indicating an attack; and, as the Little Creole expected, some of them went over to the enemy with the news. All the generals were ordered to memorize the retreat details and recite them by rote. Even the area's signposts and direction pointers were removed to confuse a pursuing enemy.

In the afternoon preceding the night of departure, the troops were let in on the secret. They responded with great glee, playing their parts like experienced troupers. Before they slipped out of their trenches, they left dummy guns behind them, manned by dummy artillerists made of ragged uniforms stuffed with straw. Some of them had mocking grins painted on their "faces." A band moved up and down the lines, stopping regularly to play retreat, tattoo and taps. Campfires were left burning, stoked by drummer boys ordered to sound reveille at dawn before skedaddling. A train of empty cars rolled up and down the Corinth tracks, stopping to blow its whistle to the lusty cheers of leather-lunged Johnny Rebs.

The Federals were completely fooled. At 1:20 A.M., Pope notified

Halleck: "The enemy is reinforcing heavily . . . I have no doubt . . . that I shall be attacked in heavy force at daylight." Dawn displayed thick black clouds of smoke uncoiling in the sky, but no Confederates. Corinth was not only wrecked, but deserted—only two Rebel families remaining behind. Nevertheless, Halleck in his dispatch to Washington reported a great victory, with Pope capturing 10,000 prisoners and 15,000 stand of arms. "Your glorious dispatch has just been received," Stanton replied, "and I have sent it into every State."

In time, however, the true nature of the March of the Moles was revealed, the Chicago *Tribune* reporting: "General Halleck . . . has achieved one of the most barren triumphs of the war." Nevertheless, evacuation of Corinth, whether a "victory" or no, was productive of other successes along the Mississippi. Fort Pillow, outflanked, was abandoned on June 4, along with supporting Fort Randolph fifteen miles below. Memphis was now menaced by the Federal gunboat flotilla commanded by Captain Charles H. Davis.

Surprisingly, the citizens of Memphis were not in the least alarmed. On May 10 they had rejoiced in the news from the Battle of Plum Run Bend just above Fort Pillow. The puny Confederate River Defense Force had sunk two of Davis's ironclads, and although driven back to Fort Pillow, the Rebels had considered themselves victorious. By June 6 they had eight gunboats on the river. On that day, tens of thousands of civilians from Memphis and environs gathered on the bluffs above the Mississippi. They were in a holiday mood, eager to watch a repetition of Plum Run Bend. They watched quietly when four Federal gunboats in line abreast became visible around a bend, cheering wildly as their own warships advanced to meet them. Suddenly their cheers died in their throats when nine of the strangest-looking craft ever seen on the Big Muddy came knifing between the ironclads bearing swiftly down upon the Confederate vessels.

They were rams. Colonel Charles Ellet, Jr., had designed them especially for riverine warfare where narrow waters made maneuver difficult. Ellet was an elderly engineer who believed that velocity plus mass would sink anything on the Mississippi. To achieve the first, converted steamboats were equipped with powerful engines which could drive them at fifteen knots—fastest speed on the river—and the hulls packed with weight to achieve the mass and the shocking power to sink any ship they rammed. Ellet's vessels made short work of the Rebels. Only one of them survived, and although Ellet died of an infected wound—the only Union casualty—his victory at the naval Battle of Memphis forced the evacuation of that city. Downriver, Baton Rouge and Natchez had already fallen to Admiral Farragut, so that after Pope's troops occupied Memphis, only Vicksburg along the Father of Waters remained in Confederate hands.

Meanwhile, Beauregard had arrived in Tupelo fifty-two miles south of Corinth. He was infuriated at Halleck's boast of "victory," and rightly so, for he had carried out the most difficult of military operations: an evacuation and successful retreat in the face of a vastly superior foe. However, Jefferson Davis in Richmond was far from pleased with the Little Creole. He had sent him west to recover lost territory, and now he had lost more. While Beauregard on his doctor's advice had gone to Bladon Springs in Alabama in an effort to recuperate from a throat operation that had never really healed, Davis replaced him with Braxton Bragg. The Little Creole was incensed, and denounced Davis as "a man who is either demented or a traitor." He did not speed his recuperation by thinking up other vituperative phrases, such as: "That living specimen of gall and hatred—that Individual."

40

·

Second Bull Run:
The End of Pope

WHEN JOHN POPE took command of the Army of Virginia he was still the blustering, boastful officer who had alienated so many of his colleagues, and he immediately angered his troops with his first general order: "I have come to you from the West, where we have always seen the backs of our enemies." Conversely, he convulsed the Confederate troops with his bulletins dated: "Headquarters in the saddle." Even the consummately courteous Robert E. Lee permitted himself a witticism with the remark: "General Pope has his headquarters where his hindquarters ought to be."

But Lee found nothing comic about Pope's harsh orders regulating Confederate civilians within Union lines, and he tartly observed that Pope would have to be "suppressed." Such suppression was to be the mission of one of military history's finest exponents of that peculiar art: Stonewall Jackson.

Jackson began the business on August 9, 1862, at Cedar Mountain. Here he met Pope's advance guard under Nathaniel Banks and was rocked back on his heels by a fierce Federal rush against his left flank. The Confederates were on the verge of being routed when A. P. Hill's division arrived, after which Jackson mounted a counterattack to drive off the outnumbered Banks. Next day Pope's main body came up and Jackson drew off to await the arrival of Lee.

Lee was quick in coming. As soon as McClellan's withdrawal from Harrison's Landing began, leaving only two brigades behind, he hurried to join Stonewall with the rest of his army in hopes of carrying out the "suppression" before Pope could be joined by McClellan.

Lee, however, was surprised to find Pope countering all his own maneuvering skill with an equal mastery. Marching and countermarching was wearying Lee's troops and would soon wear down their fighting edge. Something had to be done, and that something was triggered in Lee's mind by one of Jeb Stuart's typical exploits.

Lee had sent his cavalry leader to ride into Pope's rear at Rappahannock Station, and there to wreck a railroad bridge. On August 17 Stuart found the Federal army northwest of Clark's Mountain, apparently preparing to march. It was too late to ride to Rappahannock Station, so he rode back to a village named Verdiersville accompanied by Colonel John Mosby, the famous irregular leader. There they stopped at a house, entering the yard where Stuart tied his horse Skylark to a fence, leaving him saddled. Then he spread his gorgeous red-lined cloak on the porch floor, removed his plumed hat and gloves and lay down to sleep. Mosby stretched himself out beside him. He was the first to hear approaching hoofbeats. Federals! At once he roused Stuart, who ran for his horse. Skylark lived up to his name by sailing over the picket fence. Both Stuart and Mosby got away, but the Knight of the Golden Spurs had lost his brilliant raiment—both cloak and hat.

Jeb was so piqued that in retaliation he raided Pope's headquarters and there found not only the Union general's dress coat but also many of his papers and a dispatch book. From these Lee learned that overpowering reinforcements were en route to Pope, who even then outnumbered Lee 75,000 to 55,000. If Lee was to move, it must be quickly. So he called Stonewall Jackson to his headquarters and ordered him to take 25,000 men on a wide sweep around Pope's right flank to get in his rear, and to cut his communications to Washington.

No more daring move could have been devised. Even today there are critics who say it was foolhardy to violate the sacred canon of concentration of forces by committing the cardinal sin of dividing them in the face of a superior foe. But the audacious Lee was a gambler. Throughout his leadership of the Army of Northern Virginia he was guided by the principle that he must take long chances to offset an enemy superior in men and munitions. He was not, however, contemptuous of Pope, as has also been said. He was merely trying to make him retreat by getting on his line of communications in his rear. He did not then intend to give battle. Only after the grasp of the situation slipped suddenly from Pope's fingers did he move to strike.

Jackson worked that change. After a two-day march his "foot cavalry" came out of the Bull Run mountains to fall upon Pope's supply base at Manassas Junction. With glad yells and shouts of famished glee, they gorged and looted, and then they filled their wagon trains with ammunition and rations, put the torch to the rest, cut the railroad—and vanished. Pope

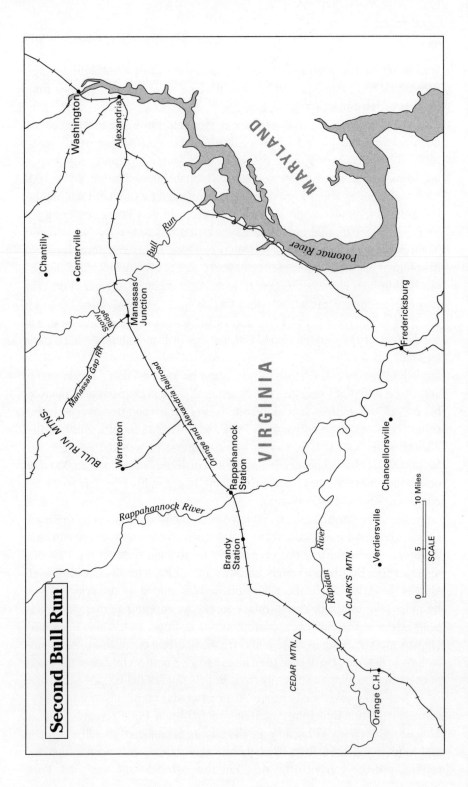

Second Bull Run

sought them frantically. In the interval Jackson took a strong position on Stony Ridge overlooking the old Bull Run battleground, while Lee hurried to his side with Longstreet and 30,000 veterans.

On August 29 Pope found Jackson and began battering him with steady, heavy attacks. He also finally began to think about the rest of Lee's army and sent a force to hold them off while he disposed of Jackson. But he had not sent enough, and before the first day of battle had ended, Longstreet was in position on Jackson's right. That was the moment for Lee to swing hard at Pope's unsuspecting left. Three times Lee declared to Longstreet that the magic moment had come, and three times the solid but slow "Old Pete" declared against it. Because the gentle Lee could not bring himself to order Longstreet forward, the moment passed—and Jackson spent the day fighting for his life against determined Federal attacks.

That night Pope became convinced that the Confederates were withdrawing. He jubilantly telegraphed Washington that the Rebels were in retreat, and next day he ordered a pursuit. But when the "pursuing" Federals came up against Jackson's right wing, Longstreet's artillery came plunging among them and broke them. Lee, seeing his opportunity reappear, did not delay this time. He at once ordered Longstreet forward, and the gray lines smashed Pope's left flank so thoroughly that his entire army was broken and sent reeling back on Henry House Hill, the place where Stonewall Jackson had won his nickname the previous year.

This time there was no Federal panic, and next day Pope began an orderly withdrawal. Hoping to strike at his rear again, Lee sent Jackson on another sweep. But the Federals were prepared, and on September 1, 1862, a savage battle was fought at Chantilly mansion. As a storm-tossed night closed in, Confederate riflemen under A. P. Hill heard a horse galloping toward them. A flash of lightning illuminated a Union officer. The Rebels opened fire, the horseman turned—and then fell with a bullet in his spine. Hill ran to the fallen man and peered at him by the light of a lantern.

"You've killed Phil Kearny," he gasped. "He deserved a better fate than to die in the mud."

Second Bull Run (Manassas) had been a Union defeat indeed, with 1,724 killed, 8,272 wounded and 5,958 missing (probably mostly captured), for a total of 15,954 casualties. Confederate losses were 1,481 killed, 7,627 wounded and 89 missing, for a total of 9,197.

On the afternoon of September 2, Pope's army was moving north toward Washington when the sun came out, illuminating a long powdery cloud of dust raised by the marching men. Pope and McDowell rode in the lead, their uniforms and their beards gray with dust. Ahead of them they saw a little band of horsemen trotting toward them. In the lead was a short, broad-shouldered officer with a bright yellow general's sash around his waist. Coming up to the two puzzled generals his hand flew to his cap in a quick, snappy salute that could be delivered by only one man. In the rear, Major General John Hatch stiffened. *McClellan!* Hatch rode forward just in time to hear George McClellan inform Pope and McDowell that President Lincoln had ordered him to take command of their troops. Hatch smiled maliciously. A few days ago John Pope had given him a tongue-lashing for failing to carry out his own imprecise orders, relieving him of his command. Now it was Hatch's turn. Cantering back toward his troops, in a voice easily heard by Pope and McDowell, he bellowed:

"Boys, McClellan is in command of the army again! Three cheers!"

They came—after a brief, stunned silence—and there were more— many, many more—than just three of them. Men broke ranks, capered, pounded each other on the back, threw their caps in the air, rolled on the ground, howled, danced, laughed and wept. Down the line went the tumult as the word spread rapidly throughout the entire army. One witness wrote: "Shout upon shout went out into the stillness of the night; and as it was taken up along the road and repeated by regiment, brigade, division and corps, we could hear the roar dying away in the darkness. The effect of this man's presence upon the Army of the Potomac—in sunshine or rain, in darkness or in daylight, in victory or defeat—was electrical, and too wonderful to make it worth while attempting to give a reason for it."

Indeed, none was needed, for all that mattered was that Little Mac was back.

During that summer of 1862, when the sun of military success that had shone so warmly on the North swung South—Confederate recovery of most of Virginia, Braxton Bragg's invasion of east Tennessee and Kentucky—there came a subtle shift in the attitude of many Northerners toward the institution of slavery. Up until then Union soldiers generally had no crusading attitude toward bondage. As free men they could do no other than detest it, but not enough to fight for its destruction. The Union was their cause, and except among soldiers from southern New England— especially Boston—it was rare to find a Yankee who had shouldered a musket to free the slaves. But some of their more perceptive commanders such as Ulysses S. Grant began to realize how much the South depended on its slaves. Of the long lines of camp-following contrabands trailing Union armies, Grant said: "I don't know what is to become of these people, but it weakens the enemy to take them from them."

Something of the same was stirring in the mind of Abraham Lincoln, perhaps planted there by the repeated urgings of the Jacobins: Sumner, Wade and Chandler from the Senate, Thaddeus Stevens of Pennsylvania from the House. No one was more vitriolic in his condemnation of slavery than this tall, tousle-haired, grim, sardonic, dark-complexioned bachelor with the club foot and the cutting wit. His wisecracks were often so risqué or obscene that they had to be deleted from the Congressional *Globe,* and his fondness for gambling so obsessive that it relieved him of much of the wealth he accumulated as an iron-master. Stevens lived with his mulatto housekeeper, Lydia Smith, who was also his mistress—a liaison that probably kept him out of the Senate and redoubled his hatred of slavery.

With the other radicals, Stevens rammed through Congress a program of antislavery legislation. One measure forbade return of fugitive slaves to the Rebels; another outlawed slavery in Washington, compensating owners for their loss; still another outlawed all human bondage in Federal territory. Lincoln signed all these bills into law, joining Congress in recognizing Haiti and Liberia. This last was intended to facilitate resettlement of slaves in those black republics.

Lincoln still clung to his cherished colonization program. He had hoped that the border states would abolish slavery in return for Federal compensation, and that the freed slaves would resettle voluntarily in amenable black nations. Both houses of Congress—now overwhelmingly Republican since the departure of the Southern Democrats—approved the plan. But not the border states. "I utterly spit at it and despise it," said one Kentucky congressman.

Gradually through the summer of 1862 the Jacobins began urging Lincoln to proclaim emancipation as a *war measure.* To deprive the South of its work force would cripple the Confederacy and help hasten destruction of the rebellion. Sumner, now very friendly with Lincoln, and also one of his chief advisers on foreign policy, joined emancipation to American problems abroad. Britain then seemed on the verge of recognizing Richmond, a step that, if not disastrous to the Union, would at least prolong the war. Lincoln was so impressed that on July 22 he assembled his cabinet and read his preliminary Emancipation Proclamation.

Come January 1, 1863, as commander in chief of the armed forces in time of war, he would free all the slaves everywhere in the Rebel states.

Reactions were varied. Some members approved, others wanted it strengthened, some weakened. Only Seward opposed it, but only because he believed that it would be considered a sign of weakness by the European powers, coming on the heels of Union military reverses. "It will be considered our last *shriek* on the retreat," he said, suggesting that Lincoln postpone it until Union arms were crowned with a great success. On reflection, Lincoln agreed. "I put the draft of the proclamation aside," he later told an artist friend, "as you do your sketch of a picture, waiting for a victory."

It would come, sooner than the Rail-Splitter thought, and not where he thought: not in Virginia or the West but right in his own back yard.

41

■

Longstreet, D. H. Hill, A. P. Hill

A FTER HIS GREAT VICTORY at Second Bull Run, Robert E. Lee began to think about invading the North. Although he had cleared most of Virginia of Federals, he did not believe he should remain on the defensive and thus surrender the initiative to McClellan. If he did, an even larger Army of the Potomac might move south again. So he decided to go on the offensive.

His reasons were cogent. First, by entering Maryland and Pennsylvania he would draw the enemy away from his Washington defenses. With Maryland held by the Confederacy, no Union army based on Washington would dare march south again and Virginia would be free, with Richmond safe. Lee also was convinced that most Marylanders were pro-South and that they would flock to his colors once he crossed the Potomac. Invasion of the North would also widen the gulf between the Peace Democrats and the Republicans, and most desirable of all, bring about the friendly intervention of France and Britain.

So far King Cotton diplomacy had utterly failed to budge both countries from their neutral stance. But after Second Bull Run they began to consider a proposal calling for a peace based on an independent Confederacy. Even Jefferson Davis had not dreamed of such a dramatic about-face, and Lee reasoned that the psychological impact of carrying the war to the enemy and scoring another resounding victory would make the Confederate cause irresistible in London and Paris. That is why the defense-minded Davis approved Lee's plan.

Marse Robert was well aware of the risks involved. For one thing, if he had inflicted 16,000 casualties on the Army of the Potomac, the Army of Northern Virginia had lost more than 9,000. He knew that many of his soldiers—especially the Virginians—sworn to defend the South, would not follow him into the North, but rather return to Dixie to await another call to defend the sacred homeland. Such military subtleties as an offensive-defensive—to free the South of the enemy by invading the North—would be lost upon them. Lee was also short of rations, thousands of his men were shoeless and would find the hard Maryland roads painful while many of his horses were worn out. Marse Robert was himself incapacitated, having severely injured his hands the day after Second Bull Run. He was standing by Traveller with the reins on the horse's neck when someone shouted, "Yankee cavalry!" The cry startled Traveller, and Lee stepped forward to seize the bridle. He tripped and fell heavily on his outstretched hands. A surgeon coming up found a small bone broken in one hand and the other badly sprained. Nevertheless, on September 5, only four days after Chantilly, confined to his dismay in an ambulance, Lee watched the vanguard of his 40,000 sunburned, tobacco-chewing scarecrows begin splashing across the Potomac singing, "Maryland, My Maryland".

They received a frosty reception. Secessionist sentiment had had seventeen months to subside in Maryland, and even those still sympathetic to the South were repelled by the sight of these ragged, ravenous "liberators." In Frederick City Dame Barbara Fritchie, approaching one hundred years, is supposed to have shaken the Stars and Stripes defiantly at Stonewall Jackson. Whittier immortalized her with the lines, " 'Shoot if you must this old gray head, but spare your country's flag,' she said." As Carl Sandburg has observed, no Rebel poet lifted his pen to do the same for the woman who stood on her doorstep, crying: "The Lord bless your dirty ragged souls!"

But there were not many like her, and Lee was disappointed. Nevertheless, he pressed on, full of contempt for George McClellan and confidence in himself, in his men, and above all in commanders such as Jackson, and after him both the Hills and James Longstreet.

So little is known about the childhood and youth of James Longstreet, the third person of that Confederate trinity of Lee, Jackson and Longstreet, that this superb soldier and corps commander has entered history without a middle name. Even his family origins are obscure. It is not definitely known from which country in Europe the Longstreets derived, although it is believed that some of his ancestors were from New Jersey and were Dutch in blood, the family name being Langestraat.

Longstreet himself left few records. His existing antebellum private letters can be counted on the fingers of one hand, and his massive autobiography, while saying perhaps a little too much in defense of his military career, says next to nothing about his father's family or his own wife and children; least of all of his character and convictions, his fears and foibles. What personal records he did possess were destroyed in a fire.

Even the record of his birth on January 8, 1821, at his grandparents' cotton plantation in Edgefield District, South Carolina, does not state clearly whether these were the parents of his father or mother. But he did spend the first eight years of his life on his father's farm outside Gainesville, a rural village in the hill country of north Georgia. His father was also named James and his grandfather was William Longstreet, an inventor who built one of the first steamboats and ran it on the Savannah River. But he had not the means to perfect it, and when the Georgia authorities refused to grant him funds, he withdrew from the inventors' race eventually won by Robert Fulton.

North Georgia in the 1820s was actually part of the frontier South, where men still wore buckskin and carried long rifles, regaling each other with tales of Indian fighting heard at their fathers' hearths. Even though the Longstreets could claim connections with such seignorial families as the Randolphs and Marshalls of Virginia, the rough customs common to their surroundings were as alien to the genteel Tidewater as those of the town-hall towns of New England. In these wooded hills, James lived the happy, carefree outdoor life of the rural Southern lads of the period. He loved to swim, hunt and fish, becoming an excellent horseman and marksman. He was also self-reliant, giving early signs of the immense strength that would be his at maturity. But for his desire to follow a military career (there was a family fiction of descent from William the Conqueror), James might have grown into a typical country bumpkin. Instead he moved to Augusta to attend a local preparatory school in hopes of going on to West Point. Here he lived at Westover, a large cotton plantation owned by his uncle, Augustus Baldwin Longstreet, one of the most famous men in the South. Lawyer, judge, Methodist minister, president of Emory College, South Carolina College and the University of Mississippi, editor and publisher, writer and humorist—this extremely talented and charming man polished off his bucolic nephew's rough edges, giving him, if not the poise of a patrician, at least the ability to move easily among the most aristocratic of Southern families.

James's stay at Westover became permanent after his father died in 1833 and his mother moved to northern Alabama, probably to live with relatives. Augustus and his wife, Frances, thus became his de facto parents. At sixteen he applied for an appointment to West Point from Georgia, and was dismayed to learn there were no vacancies. But then, in the trade-offs then common in Congress, an Alabama cousin who was also a congressman obtained him an appointment from that state, and he arrived at West Point in June of 1838.

Longstreet was only sixteen years old, yet he was almost fully mature physically. Six feet two inches tall, powerfully built, with blue eyes and thick wavy brown hair, he was voted the handsomest cadet at the Academy. His good looks became but a memory with those who knew him then, for he eventually grew perhaps the longest, thickest and most luxuriant beard in North America. He would always remain a striking figure, a big man poised gracefully on a powerful war horse. Like his friend Sam Grant, Longstreet was a poor student and an indifferent soldier. Preferring pranks and good times to spit-and-polish, he was graduated fifty-fourth in the 1842 class of sixty-two.

Assigned to Jefferson Barracks, he was transferred in 1844 to Zachary Taylor's "Army of Observation" in Louisiana, and was with him at Palo Alto, the first engagement of the Mexican War, although he saw no action there. But he did smell gun powder when he joined Winfield Scott as the 8th Infantry's regimental adjutant and fought in most of the battles during the march on Mexico City. Although a staff officer not required to enter combat, he always volunteered for it as a color-bearer, and it was in this capacity that he was wounded at Chapultepec. When the war ended he was a brevet major.

While recovering, Longstreet began to reflect on the losses suffered in the numerous frontal attacks ordered by Scott and Taylor. Although he admired and respected both, and would never be disposed to question victory, he wondered if the costs in human life of these offensive charges were not too high. His own 8th Infantry had suffered grievously. Casualties at Resaca de la Palma were so high that four riddled companies had to be disbanded and the survivors transferred to other units. At Molino del Rey half of the regiment's officers were casualties. At Churubusco so many men fell he was just barely able to maintain his attack. Although Longstreet typically left no record of these meditations, it is possible that here was the beginning of his reluctance to attack fixed positions, of his preference for maneuvering the enemy into making the frontal assault.

Upon his return to the States, Longstreet on March 8, 1848, married Marie Louise Garland, whom he had met at Jefferson Barracks while serving under her father, Colonel John Garland. Marie was a relative of Grant's wife, which led the two friends to think of each other as kinsmen. It was a happy and fruitful marriage, ten children being born of it, of whom two died. The size of his family led Longstreet in 1855 to transfer from the infantry to the paymaster department, where the pay was higher and life more settled. He was stationed at Albuquerque, New Mexico, when the newspapers arrived bearing the news of Sumter, and he resigned almost immediately from the U.S. Army. When some of his friends attempted to dissuade him, he replied: "What would you do if your state seceded?" There was no answer, and Longstreet went ahead with submitting his resignation. Then he left Albuquerque, heading for Texas. En route he stopped at Fort Fillmore, where he was asked, "How long will the war last?" His reply was quick. "At least three years, and if it holds out for five years you may begin to look for a dictator." In those days, when everyone measured the war in days, his estimate seemed preposterous. Longstreet remembered his excitement when he entered Virginia by train. "At every station old men, women and children assembled, clapping hands and waving handkerchiefs to cheer the passengers on to Richmond." Arriving in the new Confederate capital, he went immediately to the War Department where he modestly applied for a commission in the paymaster department. Bugle calls and the acrid smell of powder still seemed far behind him.

But then, to the surprise and delight of the commander whom Robert E. Lee would rely upon as "my old war horse," he was given a commission as a brigadier general in the Confederate Army and ordered to report to Beauregard at Manassas Station. His skill in deployment during that first battle earned him another star and a full division, which he led with distinction on the Peninsula and at Second Bull Run, and which he still commanded in Maryland. As steady and reliable as ever, a favorite with his men, Old Pete nevertheless remained slow to carry out orders calling for one of those costly frontal assaults he distrusted so much. In this he was the exact opposite of the officer known as "Davis's maverick general"—Daniel Harvey Hill.

D. H. Hill, as he was known in manhood, received that sobriquet for his bitter criticisms of the president's two favorite generals: Robert E. Lee and Braxton Bragg. Faultfinding seemed to come naturally to this sour soldier, perhaps because of the pain and poverty that were the constant companions of his childhood and youth, the early death of his father and the grim Presbyterianism of his mother. Born on July 21, 1821, in the York District of South Carolina, Harvey was the youngest of eleven children. Four years later his father, Solomon, died, leaving his mother, Nancy, with debts that reduced her to dependence on a small tract of barren soil. Though the family was thus introduced to poverty, it was of a genteel order, for Harvey's

Scots ancestors had served with distinction in the Revolution, the War of 1812 and against the Indians. Nothing however could alleviate the pain produced by what might have been that dreadful childhood disease: poliomyelitis. Of this he wrote: "I had a spell of sickness in my boyhood, which left me with a weak and suffering spine." And again: "I have a very feeble frame and have been a great sufferer from boyhood."

Although Nancy Hill was a loving mother, she was moody, possessed of "many of the dark traits" that Harvey saw in his own character. The Sabbath was kept in her household with such stern devotion that Harvey's older brother John—the "wild son"—"took the blues on Thursday morning because Sunday was coming."

Next to Harvey's belief in God was his conviction that Southerners were superior Americans. Southerners led by Washington had won the Revolutionary War and Southerners led by Andrew Jackson had conquered Wellington's finest at New Orleans. He was proud also of his family's traditional loyalty to the doctrine of states' rights, and of Grandfather Hill's friendship with Calhoun. Because of the family's military tradition, and also because West Point offered a free education, he applied for admission to the Academy and was admitted on June 1, 1838. He was graduated twenty-eighth in a class of fifty-six cadets.

After a few years service as a brevet second lieutenant of artillery, Hill joined Zachary Taylor's command at Corpus Christi, Texas, in August 1845, and was with him at the outbreak of the Mexican War. His bent for criticism was exercised after he returned to Fort Monroe, Virginia, and there wrote a scathing indictment of "the ignorance and imbecility of the War Department" as the cause of the widespread misery among Taylor's poorly supplied and equipped troops. It was published under a pseudonym in the Southern *Quarterly Review* and provoked such a sensation that had his identity been known he would surely have been court-martialed and cashiered. Back in Mexico, he was twice breveted for gallantry.

On November 2, 1848, Hill married Isabella Morrison, the oldest daughter of Robert Hall Morrison, a prominent Presbyterian minister from Lincoln County, North Carolina. Shortly afterward he resigned from the army because of boredom, low pay and his unwillingness to subject his young wife to the rigors of army life. He became a professor of mathematics, first at Washington College in Lexington, Virginia, and then at Davidson in North Carolina. At Washington he helped Stonewall Jackson obtain his teaching post at Virginia Military Institute, and after Jackson's first wife died and Stonewall married the younger sister of Hill's wife, the two friends became brothers-in-law. Hill also guided the God-seeking Jackson into the bosom of the Presbyterian church.

A virulent Yankee-hater and also a master mathematician, Hill published *Elements of Algebra* in which he gave expression to both traits in such "problems" as: "Buena Vista is 6½ miles from Saltillo. Two Indiana volunteers ran away from the field of battle at the same time; one ran half a mile per hour faster than the other, and reached Saltillo 5 minutes and 54⁶⁄₁₁ seconds sooner than the other. Required: their respective rates of travel." Again: "A Yankee mixes a certain quantity of wooden nutmegs which cost him one-fourth cent apiece with a quantity of real nutmegs worth four cents apiece . . ." When a friend suggested to him that this clever rancor might surely reduce his Northern sales, he replied that he didn't care because it was such fun peeling Yankees. After Sumter, of course, it was much greater sport shooting them, and he did it so well that he rose rapidly from the rank of colonel of North Carolina volunteers to a major general commanding a division in Lee's army then marching merrily through Maryland.

The other Hill—Ambrose Powell—was not related to D. H. Hill, and had no youthful torments of pain and poverty to sour his disposition. Indeed Powell was to the manor born, entering life at eight o'clock in the morning of November 9, 1826, as the eighth and last child of Thomas and Fannie Baptist Hill—one of the oldest families in Virginia. The first Hill—William—arrived in the Old Dominion in 1630, barely twenty years after the first English settlement at Jamestown. Indeed, the Hulls (as the family name was first spelled) might even trace their origins back to the twelfth century and lay claim to royal blood. There is some evidence suggesting that the family was descended from Hamlet Plantagenet, a son of King Henry II. However that may be, the Hills of Culpeper County were at the least considered members of the landed gentry of north-central Virginia: wealthy planters, merchants, soldiers and law-makers for almost two centuries.

Powell's father was a highly esteemed farmer, merchant, and politician. He was called "Major" out of respect, and has been described as "a splendid looking man, tall, taciturn, noted for his courage, famed for his hospitality and beloved for his character." His mother, who had come to her husband's estate as a nineteen-year-old bride, was something of a hypochondriac. It was said that she spent much of her married life suffering from "ills real or imaginary" and that she was "much petted by her husband and children." Powell, being the youngest and possessed of a loving nature indulged her the most.

At fifteen, Powell had begun to think about a military career. He had listened enraptured to family tales of the exploits of ancestors Henry Hill and Ambrose Powell. His father encouraged his ambition but his mother thought him too young and loving to forsake home and endure the harsh discipline of the U.S. Military Academy. Eventually, Powell persuaded her to give her reluctant consent. On April 26, 1842, he wrote to Secretary of War John C. Spencer to thank him for his appointment as a cadet. As he prepared for his journey north, his father gave him a Bible inscribed: "Ambrose Powell Hill: Peruse this every day." His mother gave him a small ham bone as a good-luck charm, while schoolmaster Albert Simms, with Baptist fire-and-brimstone glinting in his eyes, solemnly shook his hand and intoned: *"Dulce et decorum est pro patria mori."* Hill never forgot that grim farewell:

"It is pleasant and proper to die for one's country."

Hill was just a half year shy of seventeen when he arrived at West Point. He was tall, thin, with a high forehead and hazel eyes that could dance with mirth or go cold with fury. He wore his beautiful chestnut hair long and swept to one side. Hill quickly made friends with other Virginia cadets, but there was one Virginian who coldly rebuffed him. His name was Thomas J. Jackson.

Hill's roommate was George McClellan, who was of great assistance to him in his first semester, especially in mathematics. But Powell improved in the next term and was overjoyed when he was given a second-classman's furlough of two months. It was an exhilarated and happy young man who returned to the Plains in that fall of 1844, only to be shocked to discover that he had contracted venereal disease.

It was gonorrhea, probably the result of a stopover in New York City and a visit to the "harems of pleasure in Church and Mercer streets." Although gonorrhea then usually ran its course, leaving no lasting debility, Powell Hill was not so fortunate. His affliction led to attacks of painful prostatitis which would increase through the years. Hill had to go home on convalescent furlough, and his recuperation was so slow that he was told that he had been away from classes so long that he must repeat his second year. He did, and upon graduation in 1847, Hill stood fifteenth in his class. Assigned to the artillery he was ordered to proceed immediately to Mexico City to relieve Second Lieutenant Thomas J. Jackson. But when he got there the war was effectually over. In 1855 he was ordered to Washington and assigned to the U.S. Coast Survey, a naval agency.

It was there that he met Ellen Mary Marcy, the girl his old friend

McClellan hoped to wed upon his return from Russia. Ellen accepted his proposal of marriage, only to break off the engagement after her mother circulated the story of his venereal illness.

Hill's sorrow was deep and lasting until, in 1859, he met and married Dolly Morgan McClung, a captivating widow of twenty-three and daughter of a wealthy Kentucky family. Although he detested slavery, he loved Virginia and did not wait until Sumter to leave the U.S. Army, submitting his resignation on February 26, 1861.

When war came, Hill hoped to receive a general's star, but accepted a colonel's commission and distinguished himself: first as a trainer of troops, next as a commander in battle. By May of 1862 he had won his second star and was given the largest division in the army, six brigades strong. He called it the "Light Division," and it did gain a reputation for fast marching and hard fighting. It was an ideal formation for Stonewall Jackson's style of battle, and Hill was pleased to be transferred to his corps, even though he was aware of Old Blue Light's dislike of blue bloods such as himself, but not quite as conscious of his own disdain for back-country mudsills.

Probably it was inevitable that they should clash. In the early morning of September 4, Jackson found that Hill's men were not ready to begin the march to Maryland at 4 A.M. as he had ordered. He chided Hill, gently enough, but in the presence of one of his brigade commanders. Hill's face flushed with anger, but he said nothing. Then it was Jackson who became infuriated by the poor march discipline of Hill's soldiers. He halted Edward Thomas's brigade. Hill came riding back to Thomas in a fury, demanding: "Why did you halt your command without my orders?" Thomas pointed to Jackson standing dismounted nearby, and said: "I halted because General Jackson told me to do so." To Hill this was the final outrage. He had been driven almost to distraction by Jackson's secretive habits, and now Stonewall was interfering in his division! Dismounting, he strode up to Jackson, drew his sword and handed it to him hilt first.

"If you take command of my troops in my presence, take my sword also."

"Put up your sword and consider yourself under arrest," Jackson replied, and rode away. Then he relieved Hill of his command.

As the Army of Northern Virginia approached the southern shore of the Potomac River, Ambrose Powell Hill, probably its most brilliant division commander, marched on foot at the rear of his troops.

42

■

Antietam Begins

FOR ALL OF HIS SHORTCOMINGS, George Brinton McClellan had no peer at motivating the common soldier. Lee might instill in his men feelings of awe and reverence, but Little Mac inspired affection, infusing confidence. In the beginning he had made soldiers of men of straw and now he had done the same when they were straws of shame. McClellan understood their fondness, and he returned it when he told them: "We are wedded and should not be separated." Twice, then, he had saved the Union's major army from despair, and now, in September 1862, he was leading it north from Washington searching for General Lee.

Entering western Maryland, these 88,000 Billy Yanks received a warm and even tumultuous reception in sharp contrast to the cold shoulder given the Johnny Rebs of Robert E. Lee. It seemed that at almost every gate there stood a pretty girl with a bucket of cool spring water for thirsty Union marchers. In Frederick, where only a single lady invoked the Lord's blessing on those scarecrows in gray, the boys in blue were hailed as liberators: ". . . hundreds of Union banners floated from the roofs and windows, and in many a threshold stood the ladies and children of the family, offering food and water to the passing troops . . ." The 3rd Wisconsin found that "so sumptuous was the fare of cakes, pies, fruits, milk, dainty biscuit and loaves" they could forgo their army rations. All this joy and generosity, as well as the beautiful countryside, was in sharp contrast to the understandable but still unpleasant hostility of the people of Virginia's flat, dank, wooded peninsula. As one exuberant private cried: "Colonel, we're in God's country again!"

But where was Lee? Try as he might McClellan could not find him. But two of his soldiers—Corporal Barton Mitchell and First Sergeant John Bloss—made a find of their own in the sleepy town of Frederick. It was a prize, three cigars wrapped in a paper, and that meant a smoke apiece with perhaps a flip for the odd one. Then Corporal Mitchell noticed the paper, smoothed it out and began to read:

SPECIAL ORDERS NO. 191
Headquarters, Army of Northern Virginia,
September 9, 1862

The army will resume its march tomorrow, taking the Hagerstown road. General Jackson's command will . . .

There were other generals mentioned—Longstreet, Stuart, D. H. Hill—and the two soldiers jumped to their feet in excitement and ran for the captain. The captain dashed for the colonel, the colonel jumped on his horse and clattered away for the general, and thus, with a speed not always characteristic of the Army of the Potomac, the deployment ordered by Robert E. Lee was very shortly known to George Brinton McClellan.

Lee had again divided his forces. Confident that McClellan was still marking time around Washington, and anxious to protect his line of communications to Virginia, Lee had ordered Stonewall Jackson to capture Harpers Ferry and then rejoin him at Hagerstown before McClellan could move. McClellan, at Frederick, read of this deployment with rising jubilation. Here was a heaven-sent opportunity to destroy Lee's army in detail. Lee was not only fragmented, but the fragments were closer to McClellan than they were to each other! Waving the captured order, McClellan cried: "Here is a paper with which, if I cannot whip Bobbie Lee, I will be willing to go home."

All was now plain to George McClellan. Jackson was at Harpers Ferry to his left, Longstreet and D. H. Hill at Boonsboro to his right. With Jackson was Lafayette McLaws, whose division held the key at Harpers Ferry, blocking the escape route for the 12,000 Yankees surrounded there. McClellan himself held the Catoctins, but beyond them rose South Mountain, a towering extension of the Blue Ridge. This range was penetrated by two passes: on McClellan's right Turner's Gap leading to Boonsboro, and Crampton's Gap six miles south on his left opening on the road to Harpers Ferry. McClellan planned to send William Franklin on his left through Crampton's with 18,000 Federals, while he would take the remaining 70,000 men of his center and right through Turner's on the right to destroy Longstreet and Hill. Little Mac's orders to Franklin were, "You will move at daybreak in the morning" and "your duty will be first to cut off, destroy, or capture McLaws's command and relieve Harper's Ferry. My general idea is to cut the enemy in two and beat him in detail," he said, concluding: "I ask of you, at this important moment, all your intellect and the utmost activity that a general can exercise."

There stood George McClellan once again, the Prince of Hesitance, pointing with one finger at the enemy he is about to destroy, and with the other ticking off the difficulties that will defeat the attempt. *Franklin should have moved at once!* The speed with which McClellan's left wing could converge on Harpers Ferry was vital to the entire operation. Franklin's men were well rested, not having fought since the Seven Days. The weather was clear, the roads were good and the distance was not great. And the stakes were enormous: nothing less than destruction of Lee and a probable end to the war. Instead, McClellan tells him to march "at daybreak," saying nothing of speed or urgency, thereby losing sixteen valuable hours in which Lee might learn of the lost order and begin to concentrate.

And he did learn. A Maryland civilian with pro-South sympathies was at McClellan's headquarters when the lost order arrived, becoming such common knowledge that this gentleman, for all of his known disloyalty, was allowed to learn of it and ride promptly west to warn Jeb Stuart, who immediately notified Lee. Meanwhile, McClellan wasted that lucky afternoon of September 13 tidying up his operation as though no counter-stroke of fortune could happen, and therefore that speed was not of the essence. He had even telegraphed Lincoln that he possessed "all the plans of the rebels," thereby risking revelation of the lost order from another source, while predicting that he would destroy them "if my men are equal to the emergency." "If." In that last phrase McClellan shows that he is still beset by all those sinister shadows at the back of his brain: his wildly exaggerated estimate of Lee's strength at 200,000, his fear of what another disastrous Union defeat would do to him and his country, of how the Jacobin wolves would howl again, how Halleck would slyly hang all blame around his neck, how Lincoln would again raise the ax. *"If."* It was McClellan's middle name.

Next day the Union forces did move. Franklin passed through Crampton's but was stopped by McLaws short of Harpers Ferry. Believing himself outnumbered, having no sense of urgency or suspicion of splendid opportunity, he dug in, and Harpers Ferry with its 12,000 men fell to Jackson. On the right, McClellan's main body did force Turner's Gap in the fierce and bloody battle of South Mountain, but the forewarned Lee had already made his plans for concentrating at Sharpsburg on the Maryland side of the Potomac, there to be rejoined by Jackson. The lost order had enabled McClellan to wreck Lee's invasion of the North, but his faulty security and sixteen-hour delay had ruined all chances of destroying Marse Robert's divided army by defeating it in detail and probably ending the war.

Nevertheless, McClellan with 70,000 men did follow Lee to Sharpsburg. There he found him with 39,000 soldiers and across his front a sluggish creek called the Antietam.

As at Shiloh, there was a little church at Antietam. It was a Dunker church, built by members of that German sect of pacifists who, abhorring war, were now horrified to find Mars on their doorstep devouring their crops and cattle. The church stood white and peaceful along the Hagerstown Pike with a wood to its front and across the pike to its rear a cornfield and another wood. These were to be known in history—front to rear—as the West Wood, the Cornfield and the East Wood. Here on the morning of September 17, 1862—the bloodiest single day in the long history of American arms—Mars began to consume men as well.

The day came in dank and dark. Mist lay on the ground, thick in the hollows. The men of both sides were thankful for the small favor of fighting on a sunless day. But in another hour the sun burned off the mist and the day turned scorching, banishing the shadows in the groves and valleys. Those who could cooked and ate breakfast or boiled coffee. But many a rookie with a butterfly stomach could neither eat nor drink. In blue or in butternut they knew that there would be a terrible battle that day. They did not welcome it. Many Civil War historians have written of men eager for battle. But this is not so. Men in ranks are almost never eager for battle; only their commanders, and these usually the professionals yearning for glory and promotion. A Union soldier who fought at Antietam has described how he and his comrades felt that misty morning: "We heard all through the war that the army 'was eager to be led against the enemy.' It must have been so, for truthful correspondents said so, and editors confirmed it. But when you came to hunt for this particular itch, it was always the next regiment that had it. The truth is, when bullets are whacking against tree trunks and solid shot are cracking skulls like eggshells, the consuming passion in the breast of the average man is to get out of the way." In brief it is not so much fearlessness or iron discipline that impels soldiers forward into enemy fire, but rather the urge to be known as a brave man coupled with the fear of being called a coward. And the so-called "killing frenzy" that seizes men almost never occurs anywhere but in the pursuit: more men are bayoneted in the back than the chest. Finally, there were much too many skulkers in the Civil War to justify the paeans of praise poured out upon the men in blue and gray. And yet on this dreadful day in September in Maryland there was much heroism and even the killing frenzy seizing men

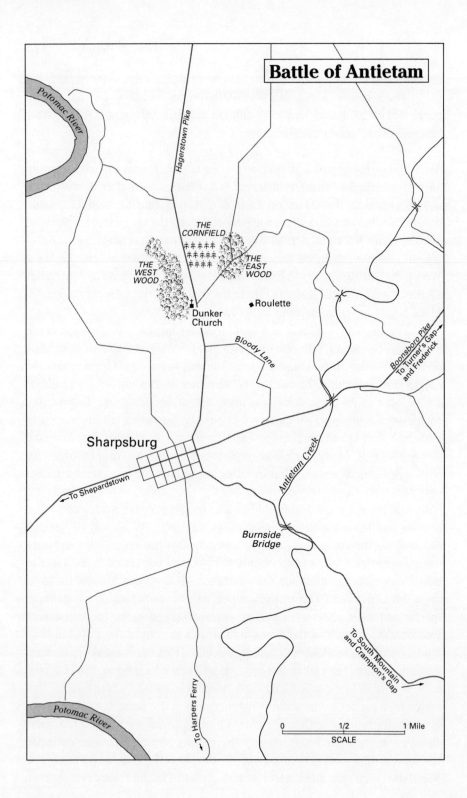

Battle of Antietam

Potomac River

Hagerstown Pike

THE
CORNFIELD

THE
WEST
WOOD

THE
EAST
WOOD

Dunker
Church

Roulette

Bloody Lane

Boonsboro Pike
To Turner's Gap
and Frederick

Sharpsburg

To Shepardstown

Antietam Creek

Burnside
Bridge

To South Mountain
and Crampton's Gap

Potomac River

To Harpers Ferry

0   1/2   1 Mile
SCALE

in trenches. As one Yankee officer wrote: "The men are loading and firing with demoniacal fury and laughing and shouting hysterically."

The battle began when Fighting Joe Hooker attacked Stonewall Jackson holding Lee's left by the Dunker church. Mounted on his milk-white steed, the flamboyant Hooker held his glass to his eye to study both woods and Cornfield. Jackson's men and his artillery were in the Cornfield. Jeb Stuart's guns were on a wooded hill. They opened up. So did Yankee gunners to the north and east. By six o'clock an artillery duel had begun and men on both sides were falling. Then beyond the Antietam McClellan's big guns began baying. They plowed up the Cornfield so that Hooker could say that much of it was cut down as though "with a knife." Many Rebels died or were maimed under that cannonade, while the Yankees hugging the ground felt the concussion waves undulating over them. Then the guns fell silent and the Bluebellies flowed forward.

They charged the Rebel outposts concealed in the home and outbuildings of a farmer named Miller or behind a fence there. A withering fire thinned their ranks but they kept moving forward. Black powder smoke drifted over the sweating combatants, smudging their faces and hands and giving them a ghoulish look. Wild shouts and even hysterical laughter rose above the clamor of combat, while the struggle gradually centered around the fence. Bluebellies crowded forward, jostling each other, the men in the rear handing loaded rifles forward to the forefront men. Doggedly, the Rebels held on. But then, their ranks riddled, they suddenly broke and ran—and with a single mighty shout the Yankees swept over the fence and chased them toward the Cornfield.

It was then that the Billy Yanks heard that dreadful high cry of Johnny Reb. Lee had fed in reinforcements from D. H. Hill's division and John Bell Hood's famous division of Texans and Mississippians, both from Longstreet's I Corps. They had been eating their first solid meal in a week when the order came to form and march forward. In dismay, they stuffed their mouths, seized their rifles, and came running north at the double—smashing into Hooker's Bluebellies and driving them back at the run. Still screaming, Hood's men pursued, supported now by three of Hill's brigades coming in from the East Wood.

The Federal retreat was bordering upon a rout when Brigadier General John Gibbon brought up a battery of artillery from his famous "Iron Brigade," the black-hatted boys from one Indiana and three Wisconsin regiments. The battery served as a landmark around and behind which the fleeing Federals could halt and rally. Four of Marsena Patrick's New York regiments came up as reinforcements. On came the Rebels, charging straight toward it. Gibbon on horseback noticed that his missiles were flying over the enemy's heads. An accomplished artillerist, he saw at once that the elevating screws were run down so that the gun muzzles pointed high in the air. His shouts unheard by the gunners, he jumped down from his horse, knelt and spun the screws upward so that the muzzles came down aimed point-blank at the Graybacks. Gibbon stepped aside and the gunner pulled the lanyard, smashing the fence and sending pieces flying in the face of the enemy. Other gunners quickly corrected their elevation and soon were firing double-shotted canister at a deadly range of fifty feet, and the onrushing Confederate columns were blown clean away. Fittingly it was Bluebellies from Indiana who had helped repulse the men of Yankee-hating D. H. Hill, whose first mathematical "problem" had derisively begun: "At Buena Vista . . . two Indiana volunteers ran away from the battle . . ."

During two hours of close-up fighting in that blood-drenched forty-acre stubble some 2,500 Yankees had been lost, while just as many had fled. Hood and D. H. Hill's men had suffered just as grievously, even though they now held the East Wood and the Cornfield. There were so many bodies strewn about living and dead—in one sector lay 146 bodies of Graybacks, lying in a neat, soldierly line—that Hood was constantly afraid that his horse would step on a wounded Rebel. Those formations that had been in the field at the start had lost 50 percent of their men. Yet, they must hold on in the face of a renewed Yankee attack.

It came from Joseph Mansfield's XII Corps, which McClellan had placed at Hooker's disposal. Nearing sixty, with his mane of thick white hair, hoary long beard and mustache, Mansfield led his men toward the battle-ground looking like a martial Santa Claus. Seeing him, the men of the Iron Brigade sprang to their feet cheering. "That's right, boys, cheer!" Mansfield cried, waving his hat. "We're going to whip them today!"

Mansfield rode toward the East Wood at the head of his first brigade. Hooker cantered up, shouting: "The enemy are breaking through my lines—you must hold them!" Mansfield nodded, though he was puzzled. Rebel fire came whistling from the wood, which was nearly as ghastly a sight as the Cornfield. The Yankees could not tell whether it was friendly or enemy fire. In the battle smoke the light was dim, and the Confederates, now fighting Indian-fashion from behind the trees, could not be seen. Mansfield had received from Hooker the impression that there were Pennsylvanians in the wood. Telling his men to cease firing, he jumped the fence and rode forward to investigate. A soldier warned, "Those are Rebels, General," and as Mansfield replied, "Yes, you're right," a volley burst from the Cornfield. A bullet hit Mansfield. He dismounted heavily to clamber over the fence. Some Pennsylvania rookies made a litter of their muskets to carry him back into the East Wood and lay him down. Three Maine veterans, seeing an excuse to go to the rear, picked him up to lug him to an aid station. But Mansfield was heavy, and so, encountering a black cook hunting for a prized frying pan, they forced him to help them. At the aid station a shot of whiskey did little to help, and between the bullet in his belly and the rough handling of his rescuers, the old man died.

While he lay dying his leading brigade had penetrated Rebel lines around the church, but then a fierce counter-attack by Hill's Graybacks forced them back. More of Mansfield's Bluebellies flowed past the Miller farm and the human wreckage where Gibbon's battery had made its stand and into the Cornfield, where a bitter battle ensued. Here Hood's men tried to hold, but as their commander had feared, they were forced to withdraw with half their number shot down. Here also Hooker was wounded in the foot and compelled to ride to the rear dripping blood. Command passed to Alpheus Williams, Mansfield's senior division commander, known affectionately as Pop to his troops. Riding up and down his line waving his sword, an unlighted cigar gripped in his teeth, Williams rallied the Yankees to drive the Rebels out of the East Wood and across the turnpike into the West Wood. The East Wood and Cornfield were now firmly in Union hands. Still the Confederates held the West Wood in strength, and so it was that McClellan sent the II Corps under Edwin Vose Sumner into the battle.

43

■

Antietam Ends: Lee Repulsed: Slaves Freed: McClellan Fired

SIXTY-FOUR YEARS OLD when the war began, "Bull" Sumner was by then a veteran of forty-two years' service in the regular army. He had been breveted twice in Mexico and was famous for his great, roaring voice and his pure white hair and whiskers. A simple, straightforward soldier, his credo was devotion to duty, discipline and country. Like so many regular generals, he could never quite trust volunteers, and would shake his head in amazement and mutter under his breath when he saw a stripling with dark hair wearing major's shoulder straps. In Bull Sumner's army, a man never made field grade until his hair was hoary.

Sumner rode with John Sedgwick's leading division. He knew little of what had happened on the Federal right, but had the impression that Hooker had gained a victory and his assignment was to go in and nail it down. But when he reached the East Wood he saw omens not of triumph but of disaster. Not so many Bluebellies lying still and sprawling, but so many of the able-bodied wandering around when they should have been on the firing line. To his right Sumner could see gunsmoke and hear firing in the vicinity of the Miller farm. Entering the Cornfield and facing west the scene was even more ghastly—as many Rebels as Yankees strewn about and the stubble black and smoking. From various reports coming to him, Sumner finally realized that two whole Union corps had been devastated and that he had not a battle to complete but one to begin.

His plan was simple. Because he was beyond the Federal right flank, he reasoned, he must also be beyond the Confederate left. So he would advance straight ahead—directly west—into the West Wood until he was well in the rear of Lee's line, and then swing left to sweep down the ridge to roll up the Army of Northern Virginia. There was nothing wrong with this plan except the false premise upon which it reposed. He was not

376

beyond the Rebel left, for Lee had sent reinforcements there: two fresh divisions under the redoubtable John George Walker and Lafayette McLaws, Jubal Early's brigade from Jackson's corps and all other stray formations at hand. Lee now had more men on his left than Sumner had on the right.

Still Sumner came on confidently, Sedgwick's brigades in three lines numbering 5,000 men, veterans all. Behind him were two more divisions, supposedly following close-up. But they were not. The second division under William French had already gone astray, swinging to the southeast to attack the high ground around the Dunker church, and the third had not even started because of wretched staff work. Sumner as corps commander should have known this, should not have been in the forefront like the Indian-fighting, hell-for-leather cavalry colonel of old, but riding along his line-of-march to make certain that his orders had been carried out or at least sending aides riding rearward to do so.

Sedgwick's veterans were not as confident as their corps command-ers. What they had seen in the East Wood and the Cornfield had unnerved many of them. Too many friendly dead, too many ambulances some of them filled with amputees holding their truncated limbs aloft to ease the pain—too many counsels of defeatism from the numerous skulkers. Moreover these three brigades were too closely packed together for maneuver should they be attacked, too perfectly aligned as they crossed the turnpike and entered the West Wood—a thrilling sight to staffers at McClellan's head-quarters peering through their telescopes and assuring each other that this should finish Bobby Lee.

Sumner on his horse studied the ridge to his front from which came Rebel fire, and then from the wood on his left came a terrible storm of musketry, the rising weird yelling of thousands of Rebels, the shriek of enemy shells and the screams of his own stricken. Whoever had given the order to strike first at the Yankee rear brigade had embraced a dreadfully effective tactic.

Here were four Philadelphia regiments forming the Philadelphia Bri-gade under one-armed O. O. Howard. Standing at ease in the wood they found themselves ripped from behind. Pandemonium ensued. No enemy was to be seen, but bullets still came whistling among them along with exploding shells from a new formation of Rebels going into line on the ridge above—followed by artillery. Soon Sumner realized that his lead division was being shot at from three sides—front, flank and rear. Fear-crazed men were running this way and that just like chickens with their head cut off (there is no other image), officers were cursing and bellowing orders, beating the fearful with the flat of their swords, trying desperately to get them to face toward a foe unseen but for those on the ridge—and this they could not do. Sumner came galloping up to Howard shouting, "My God, Howard! You must get us out of here!" It was a notion shared already by Howard and every man in his brigade, but there was no way out except a mad dash by an undisciplined mob breaking for the turnpike and dashing north along it for sanctuary and safety. Howard's brigade had disappeared, leaving more than 500 of its soldiers fallen, having fired hardly a shot.

Up front the first rank fared barely better. A fierce Rebel charge came in from the front, exchanging volleys with the 15th Massachusetts at the unbelievable range of fifteen yards. When the 34th New York sought to help it was caught between two enemy lines and was so scourged front and rear that it lost half of its men within a few minutes. Sedgwick attempted to rally his second rank to provide flank protection for the first. But it was not possible in that close-packed mass of blue-clad men into which the Rebels poured shot and shell without remorse. Sedgwick received a bullet in the arm, refusing to go to the rear for aid, and then another which lifted him from the saddle and sent him into hospital for five months.

Now with Howard's brigade gone, the middle brigade began to go to pieces. From its rear came a Confederate brigade moving over ground vacated by Howard's men, firing into the rear of the 59th New York and 15th Massachusetts. Among those who fell was Captain Oliver Wendell Holmes, Jr., down with his second wound of the war.

In just fifteen minutes Sedgwick's division ceased to function as a military entity. As its demoralized soldiers flowed out of the West Wood either across the turnpike to re-form or running madly north along it— although some of its regiments actually retreated proudly at a walk—some 2,100 men were left behind in the West Wood. Confederate losses, though not exactly known, were negligible. Indeed, it appeared that the virtually unscathed commands of McLaws, Walker and Early would continue east to retake the Cornfield. They charged into it—only to be met by a murderous fire from the remnants of Sumner's corps lined up to receive them, together with a brigade from Mansfield's corps, as well as showers of shells from massed Union artillery on a slope north of the Cornfield. This slowed them down, halted them—and drove them back to the sanctuary of the West Wood.

In just five hours of dreadful but inconclusive battle some 12,000 Americans lay dead or wounded on Robert E. Lee's left flank. Now the focus of battle shifted to a sunken farm lane southeast of the Dunker church.

■   ■   ■

Just as at Shiloh, there was a sunken farm road at Antietam. It was at the center of Lee's line, zigzagging for about a half mile from the Hagerstown Turnpike to the Boonsboro Road. It would shortly enter history as Bloody Lane. D. H. Hill's Graybacks held Bloody Lane and its environs. Against them came the Bluebellies in the division commanded by Brigadier General William French, known as "Old Winkey" or "Old Blinky" for his disconcerting habit of opening and shutting his eyes as he talked. It was French's division—the second in Sumner's corps—which had gone astray under its commander's mistaken impression that he was to attack the high ground around the Dunker church. Having crossed the Antietam, French brought his men up the western hills, passing on their right a blazing farmhouse belonging to one Mumma, which Hill had ordered set afire so that it could not be occupied by Yankee sharpshooters. Pausing briefly to realign their ranks once more, the men stepped out under bright sunlight in perfect parade-ground formation climbing the hill toward the Roulette farm. At this point regimental surgeons and medical orderlies saw a big barn in which they set up operating tables while the orderlies covered the ground with straw for the wounded to lie on.

Now rifle fire from the crest of a rise to their front began to riddle French's men. Hill had cleverly stationed his men on that rise, ordering them to lie down for concealment. Still the puzzled Yankees came on, until suddenly the air was full of not only singing bullets but also the angry buzzing of thousands of bees. Rebel fire had infiladed a long row of beehives and clouds of infuriated insects emerged from the holes like so many tiny tornadoes. Their stinging attacks nearly broke the Yankee lines, but the Federals outdistanced the bees and ascended the hill which the Rebel sharpshooters had just abandoned. Below them was Bloody Lane, stuffed with Graybacks who had dismantled a rail fence for use as a barricade, making them close to three feet below the ground and out of sight. Behind them was more Rebel infantry in another cornfield and above and beyond that on the high ground across the Hagerstown Pike batteries of artillery. Down marched the Bluebellies four ranks deep. "Their gleaming bayonets flashed like burnished silver in the sunlight," a Rebel colonel wrote. From Bloody Lane came a flickering flash of flame followed by curling black smoke and a ragged rattle of musketry. Now those serried blue lines were broken into clots and bunches of dazed men reeling among the dying quivering on the slope or the stricken clutching their wounds. The first rank was literally torn apart. Pausing, trying to re-form, the Yankee brigade received another shattering volley, and the Federals turned and ran back up the hill. Re-forming again, they marched downward once more, precise

as the tap of the drum. Again the crashing volley, and this time the Bluebellies halted halfway down to throw themselves on the ground and return the
fire from the prone position. But then, with no one actually to aim at and
the Rebel fire becoming heavier, they faded back up the hill for good—and
French sent in another brigade.

As he did the Union artillery across the Antietam entered the battle,
firing counter-battery on the Rebel guns on the high ground behind Bloody
Lane. It was a one-way fight, for the Grayback gunners had been ordered
not to fire counter-battery but to concentrate on the enemy infantry. The
Union cannon cockers, growing more and more confident with each minute
of unanswered fire, began to deliver a massed fire on one battery at a time.
Thirty or forty guns simultaneously bombarded a single Rebel unit, and
began to take them out one after another. Their shells smashed into guns
firing low at the approaching Yankees, splintering wheels, killing and maiming gunners, as well as screaming horses. One shot hit a caisson which
exploded with a mighty roar heard all over the battlefield. Atop the hill to
the front of Bloody Lane the Roulette barn was packed with wounded lying
on the straw. It was a ghastly place, like a foretaste of hell: surgeons
spattered and streaked with blood working bare-armed with scalpels and
bone saws among the stricken soldiers on the operating tables, the piles of
severed limbs with their frayed edges leaking blood upon the straw, the
groans of the wounded mixing with the curses and prayerful cries of others
begging for assistance. Many men choked in the black smoke drifting inside
while the sound of battle outside mounted to a steady roar.

Under cover of the smoke, and with no enemy artillery to scourge
them, French's second brigade drove in closer and began to give as well
as take. Here and there crazed Rebel formations jumped out of Bloody Lane
to charge them, always riddled and sometimes annihilated with the help of
horse-drawn artillery. Gradually, however, these Bluebellies fought themselves out, using up all their ammunition and leaving half their men behind
as they withdrew. But there were fresh troops to take their place, for
Franklin's corps had arrived on the field to protect French's threatened
right. So had Bull Sumner's third division under Israel Richardson. Known
either as "Fighting Dick" for his valor or "Greasy Dick" for his complexion,
Richardson was a descendant of Israel Putnam of Revolutionary War fame,
and a veteran of both the Seminole and Mexican wars, winning two brevets
in the latter. His favorite formation was the famous Irish Brigade of New
York City. This was because one of his aides, Irish-born Captain Jack
Gosson, had told the Irishmen that his chief was sending over three barrels
of whiskey—one to a regiment—before coming over to inspect them. When

Richardson did arrive—sans whiskey—the Irishmen threw their caps in the air and gave him such a resounding cheer that his dark face flushed with pleasure. Forever afterward, they were his pet brigade, and now he was sending them into battle to save French's crumbling left flank.

They were led by Thomas Francis Meagher, born in Waterford, Ireland, from boyhood a thorn in the side of Erin's British oppressors until he was exiled to Australia; he escaped to California, thence on to New York, where he became a power among his countrymen. Irish to a man, they formed under their beautiful colors: emerald green emblazoned with a golden harp and angel figurehead and underneath the inscription: *"Erin Go Bragh!"*

"Erin go bragh!" the Irish cried, charging into French's menaced flank. "Ireland forever!" They collided with a Confederate line marching to meet them and both sides fired punishing volleys. Then Meagher ordered his men forward. "Boys!" he cried, rising in the stirrups, "raise the colors and follow me!" Up went the green flags with a wild cheer and the Graybacks slowly retired into the safety of the sunken lane. There they turned and delivered a devastating fire into their tormentors. That first volley felled half of the 63rd New York. Green flags fell to be snatched aloft only to go down again. Still the Irish drove to within one hundred yards of Bloody Lane, when a bullet killed Meagher's horse in full gallop, making it fall so heavily that Meagher was knocked unconscious and had to be carried to the rear. His men stayed where they were until their ammunition ran out, and Richardson sent another brigade advancing through them while they went to the rear for more cartridges.

Now the Bluebellies were within thirty yards of Bloody Lane, and now D. H. Hill found a gap between French and Richardson and sent troops charging toward it, while another force of North Carolinians slipped south and east to get around Richardson. The first attempt was brushed aside, but the second came within a few minutes of succeeding until Fighting Dick spotted it and ordered the 5th New Hampshire under Colonel E. E. Cross to stop it. Cross's men met the Butternuts in a fierce firefight amid the burned-out stalks of the second cornfield. Now Cross, romantic-looking with a blood-stained bandage around his head, massed his men facing Bloody Lane. "Put on the war paint!" he shouted, and his men seized their grimy cartridge papers to smear their faces. "Now give them the war whoops!" Yelling like any Rebel, the New Hampshire boys went forward supported by the fire of Colonel Francis Barlow's two New York regiments on high ground. It enfiladed Bloody Lane and the startled, fought-out Graybacks at last gave way.

The sunken road was abandoned. Still yelling, the Federals clambered over the fence-rail barricade and down into it, firing at the backs of the enemy. Crisis had come for the Confederacy—except that D. H. Hill seemed not to be aware of it. Forming a scratch formation from whatever remnants of former commands he could scrape together, he seized a musket himself and led a counter-attack. Yet the Federals broke it up. Crisis returned. Hill held but a thin gray line behind Bloody Lane. As Longstreet said later, ten thousand fresh Yankees could then and there have crushed Lee's army and ended the war.

They might have come, for when Richardson fell with a fatal wound and Barlow went down badly hurt, McClellan at his headquarters detached Winfield Scott Hancock from his own brigade to take command of Richardson's division. The valiant Hancock wanted to attack, and so did Franklin with his fresh corps, but both were overruled by Bull Sumner. Although the crusty old Indian-fighter had seen much action on the frontier, he had known no such carnage as he had witnessed on this bloody seventeenth of September. He was certain that the entire Union Army was fragmented and scattered, and he told Franklin that if another attack failed it would be the end.

At that point a staff officer from headquarters arrived with McClellan's suggestion that an attack be launched. "Go back, young man," Sumner cried in a rage, "and tell General McClellan I have no command! Tell him my command, Mansfield's command and Hooker's command are all cut up and disorganized. Tell him General Franklin has the only organized command on this part of the field!"

It was done, and the fears of an old man bred to frontier pig-sticking and badly shaken by his first experience of the horrors of modern war were transmitted to his chief—who upheld him. Lee's thin and ragged line—if it was even that—had held, and the Battle of Antietam shifted to the Federal left.

Ambrose Burnside's IX Corps was on the Federal left east of the Antietam. McClellan had planned to have the attack here coincide with the strikes on his right and center. But for some reason, probably because he did not have complete control of the battle, it did not begin then—and when it did come, about three hours or more after Hooker's assault began, it was not a knockout blow as planned but hardly more than a timid—or tentative—shove.

Opposite Burnside's position the Antietam twisted into loops and curves. It was crossed by a narrow little bridge that Burnside believed ideal to cross and turn Lee's exposed right flank. Inventor of ordnance that

Burnside might be, he did not have an explorative or original mind. If he had cared to examine the Antietam he would have found a slow-moving stream never deeper than the average man's belt buckle, and in some places easily fordable by men and horses drawing wagons and guns. He would also have seen that the ground on the other side fronting Sharpsburg rose from steep banks into low hills on which enemy infantry—and especially sharp-shooters—could easily be concealed. But Ambrose Burnside's plan was fixed: his brigades were to cross the creek by that bridge.

The first to attempt it was Colonel George Crook, with three Ohio regiments. Crook would become perhaps the most famous of all frontier fighters after the war, but on this day he was as lethargic as his superiors. He missed the bridge entirely, emerging upstream on a plateau beneath zeroed-in Rebel guns. Advancing to the bank the Ohioans were sighted by the Grayback gunners and immediately subjected to a punishing fire forcing them to take cover behind fences and in the underbrush. Fizzle No. 1.

Next to march west against the Confederates was the division led by Samuel Sturgis, he who cared for John Pope "not one pinch of owl dung." His spearheading 2nd Maryland and 6th New Hampshire marched straight to the bridge without mishap, unaware that there were indeed sharpshoot-ers on the heights above it—two regiments of them—as well as field pieces sighted in on it. Commanding the snipers was none other than Brigadier General Robert Toombs. At the height of his glory twenty months ago he had held Jefferson Davis's hand aloft in Montgomery to cry, "The man and the hour have met!" Today he was still an unhappy one-star general so disgruntled at having been repeatedly passed over for promotion that he had become, with Alexander Stephens, the co-commander of that legion of Davis-haters now growing in the South. Today he was as inept as ever, but it really didn't matter because his Georgian marksmen didn't need a general to tell them what to do. Along with the artillery they struck the Bluebellies with such a deadly fire before they reached the bridge that they broke them up and sent them sprinting for the shelter of the woods. Federal artillery with its customary skill delivered a stunning bombardment that silenced the Rebel fire, but it was obvious that once the cannonade lifted the Graybacks would be ready for any renewed assault. There was none, but now Burnside came alive to the possibilities of finding a ford, sending Isaac Rodman's division downstream to seek one. He was not heard of for some time, and in the meantime Toombs's sharpshooters and the Rebel guns kept the IX Corps immobilized across the creek for two hours.

McClellan was by then beside himself. Although his left flank had erupted in much sound and fury it seemed to signify nothing, and he had repeatedly sent messengers to Burnside urging him to move. Finally he dispatched a staff colonel with a peremptory order to attack at once. This miffed Burnside, but he nevertheless ordered Sturgis to resume his attack across the bridge. The assignment went to Colonel Edward Ferrero, a trim, black-haired, dapper little man who commanded Sturgis's second brigade. Ferrero broke out the 51st Pennsylvania and 51st New York and told them: "It is Burnside's especial request that the two 51sts take that bridge. Will you do it?" There was a silence suggesting that they were not on fire to try that narrow avenue of death. Actually the hard-drinking Pennsylvanians were not then too fond of Ferrero, who had withdrawn their whiskey ration. A corporal among them cried: "Will you give us our whiskey, if we make it?"

"Yes, by God!"

The regiments cheered and fell into line side by side, each in columns of twos. They were to dash straight downhill to the bridge rather than to take the line of approach beside the creek that their predecessors had unwisely chosen. Connecticut riflemen were to cover them from behind a stone wall along the creek while Crook upstream emplaced a battery for more support and the massed Union field artillery began to punish the Rebel guns again. Thus as the two 51sts went forward with a rush the sound and the fury of battle was renewed, but this time signifying success. Though struck fiercely by enemy shot and shell, the Bluebelly columns reached the bridge. A murderous fire plunged among them from the Rebels only twenty-five yards away, but then it began to weaken perceptibly, and as it became apparent that the Federal supporting barrage was driving the enemy off, the two regiments poured across, fanning out to left and right as they reached the opposite bank, and then, as the tail of the columns cleared the bridge, turning to face west against the enemy.

Lee's right flank was now in deep danger.

It was even more imperiled when General Rodman finally realized that the local farmer he had dragooned as a scout was actually leading them on a labyrinth to nowhere. Suspecting him of being a secesh sympathizer, he dropped him and sent his own troops searching for a crossing. They found one quickly, but it was by then noon. As they waded across, they heard the eruption of battle around the bridge once more. But there was no one to oppose their crossing, and after they reached the opposite bank Rodman tried to form them into line of battle. He was certain that he had gotten around Lee's right flank and eager to exploit the advantage. But many of the men in his small 3,000-man division were untrained, three-week soldiers. They weren't able to execute their commanders' orders either promptly or exactly. There then ensued that confusion that destroys armies. Rodman's brigades became separated and gaps yawned between them. Then the general found to his dismay that there were Rebels on *his* flank. He was not around Lee, Lee was around *him!* And many of the Graybacks coming yelling through a cornfield firing as they came were dressed in Union blue!

Robert E. Lee had been alive to his danger from the moment that Bloody Lane had fallen to the Federals and D. H. Hill had drawn his thin gray line behind it. Although his left and center were holding, it was a miracle that McClellan had not seized the opportunity to smash them. He had no reserves remaining to strengthen his right, now under Union attack. He had lost so many men on his left, especially in the Cornfield, where it was possible to walk from end to end without touching the ground. Wounded who had crawled from the battle to take refuge in haystacks were burned alive when the hay caught fire. Losses had also been great in Bloody Lane in his center, where a single Rebel's body draped over a fence contained fifty-seven bullets. At three o'clock, after the Bluebellies had stormed the bridge and waded the Antietam below it, Lee faced disaster. He could only hope that A. P. Hill, who had been restored to command of his division, might arrive in time from Harpers Ferry, seventeen miles away. Then, at two thirty, a courier galloped up breathless with the news that Hill's men were only an hour off. Could the Butternuts hold?

Standing in the high echoing streets of Sharpsburg, Lee could see the Federal columns plunging forward under a pall of smoke. He pointed to a distant column and asked a lieutenant named John Ramsay, "What troops are those?" Ramsay focused his telescope and replied: "They are flying the United States flag." Lee pointed to another column on his right and repeated the question. Ramsey started, as though puzzled. He could not be sure, but many of these marching men appeared to be dressed in blue. Then his face cleared, and he cried: "They are flying the Virginia and Confederate flags." Lee's breast swelled with a vast thanksgiving and he said quietly: "It is A. P. Hill from Harpers Ferry."

It was only half of Hill's division, for the other half was strewn along the roadside half-dead from the killing pace of the march. Hill had driven his men mercilessly, so alive to the danger that he had sent that courier galloping ahead to advise his chief of his approach, and it had indeed encouraged Marse Robert to hang on. Another general might have advanced more deliberately, arriving on the battlefield with all his men but too late to be of use. And as these valiant fighters arrived they flowed immediately into action, striking Rodman's surprised left flank. Many of them were indeed in blue, for Union uniforms were part of the loot from Harpers Ferry. This contributed immensely to the confusion of the troops on Rodman's left. When the barely trained 16th Connecticut fell apart under the onslaught of Hill's veterans, he ordered in the 4th Rhode Island. These men, seeing men in blue running from other men in blue, were so puzzled that they held their fire—just long enough to encourage the oncoming Rebels. And then Rodman was killed and the Rhode Islanders joined the rout.

A. P. Hill had saved the day, and Burnside was compelled to halt his assault, withdraw and call for reinforcements. But they did not come. There is a story that as McClellan received this message he still had Fitz-John Porter's V Corps available in reserve, enough to join Burnside's stalled right to overwhelm Hill's marched-out, fought-out division and turn the tide of battle again. For a moment, McClellan seemed inclined to approve the request, but then Porter said to him, "Remember, General, I command the last reserve of the last army of the republic," and Little Mac changed his mind. The story may be spurious, and Porter himself later denied saying any such thing, but there is still a basis of truth to it, however fictitious or embellished: McClellan's wildly exaggerated fears of Lee's strength. He simply would not risk his last reserve against a foe he considered so superior to him in numbers.

But Robert Edward Lee's superiority was moral, not material. Next day he remained in battle array as though daring Little Mac to try again, but even though he had been reinforced by two more divisions, McClellan did not strike. That night the weary men in blue heard on their front a great, flowing sound like the passage of a mighty river. It was the steady tramping of Lee's army marching back to Virginia. In the morning the Bluebellies saw that they possessed the field: but what a field! What a mass of swelling corpses blackened by the sun! All day burial parties were at work, and great fires lighted to consume the carcasses of hundreds of horses. A cloud of greasy black smoke rose above the Antietam, while a huge trench was dug to receive the bodies of slain Rebels, and little white crosses were planted above the individual graves of their Federal comrades.

Confederate casualties were 2,700 killed, 9,024 wounded, and about 2,000 missing for a total of 13,724; while the Union lost 2,108 killed, 9,549 wounded, and 753 missing for a total of 12,410. In a single day, then, the losses at the Battle of Antietam (Sharpsburg) totaled more than 26,000 men, more than the total casualties of the War of 1812, the Mexican War, and the Spanish-American War *combined*. Examined from the standpoint of casualties only it was a standoff. Strategically, however, it is best described as a resounding Rebel defeat, for Antietam repulsed Lee in his invasion of the North and sent him back to Virginia. Also, it is significant that this was the first time Robert E. Lee was on the offensive, and although the lost order quickly compelled him to resume a defensive stance—at which he had no peer—he was still denied in his attempt to carry the war to the enemy.

In its effects Antietam was probably the most important battle of the war, a true turning point. First, it caused Britain and France to postpone a decision on intervention. Second, and more important, it gave Lincoln the opportunity to make public the preliminary Emancipation Proclamation he had shelved in July.

Throughout that gloomy summer, when the Federal government found it necessary to call for 300,000 more recruits, Abraham Lincoln had been beset by Americans singly or in groups coming to the White House to beseech him to free the slaves. When a Quaker woman arrived, Lincoln, who had no love for pacifists, said curtly: "I will hear the Friend." She told him God had told her to inform him that he had been chosen for this great work. Lincoln replied that it was strange the Lord had told her but not him. When a delegation of ministers from Chicago made the same appeal, Lincoln replied that in the present situation such a course would be about as effective as "the Pope's bull against the comet." Also, he said, it would cause "fifty thousand bayonets" in the border states to be lost to the South. One of the ministers, however, gave him the same message as the Quaker lady, and the Rail-Splitter murmured that it was strange that "your Divine Master" would send this message by "the roundabout route of that awful city of Chicago." His patience was exhausted, however, when on August 20 Horace Greeley published an open letter entitled "The Prayer of Twenty Millions," accusing Lincoln of being "strangely and disastrously remiss" in not announcing that the war was being fought to abolish slavery. Two days later, the President replied:

> I would save the Union. I would save it the shortest way under the Constitu-
> tion. The sooner the National authority can be restored, the nearer the Union
> will be "the Union as it was." If there be those who would not save the Union
> unless they could at the same time *save* Slavery, I do not agree with them.
> If there be those who would not save the Union unless they could at the same
> time *destroy* Slavery, I do not agree with them. My paramount object in this
> struggle *is* to save the Union, and is *not* either to save or destroy Slavery.
> If I could save the Union without freeing *any* slave, I would do it; and if I
> could save it by freeing *all* the slaves, I would do it; and if I could do it by

freeing some and leaving others alone, I would also do that. What I do about Slavery and the colored race, I do because I believe it helps to save this Union; and what I forbear, I forbear because I do *not* believe it would help to save the Union. I shall do *less* whenever I shall believe what I am doing hurts the cause, and I shall do *more* whenever I shall believe doing more will help the cause. I shall try to correct errors when shown to be errors; and I shall adopt new views so fast as they shall appear to be true views. I have here stated my purpose according to my view of *official* duty, and I intend no modification of my oft-expressed *personal* wish that all men, everywhere, could be free.

But now, after Antietam, Lincoln on September 22 was free to announce that effective New Year's Day, 1863, slaves in the Rebel states "shall be then, thenceforward and forever free." By this momentous document he probably did more to change the Anglo-French mind than the battle itself. As Henry Adams, son and secretary of U.S. Minister to Britain Charles Francis Adams, wrote to his brother: "The Emancipation Proclamation has done more for us here than all our former victories and all our diplomacy."

The proclamation did not free a single slave, simply because they were all in Rebel hands; it was of doubtful legality under the president's vague "war powers"; and if Abolitionists thought it was not strong enough, the loyal slave states and the Northern Democrats thought it went too far. Yet the Emancipation Proclamation is among the most profound and revolutionary events in history. It opened the worldwide struggle for racial equality, and it opened it within the one country that, possessing in miniature all those colors and creeds, prejudices and fears that divide humanity, had it therefore in its power to produce the model solution.

In its immediate effects, the proclamation isolated the Confederacy. No foreign power responsible to public opinion dared enter the war against a nation now dedicated to the destruction of slavery, and henceforth all the South received from abroad was sympathy. Henceforth, also, the Civil War was a war to the death.

In the South, Emancipation Proclamation was spelled *Unconditional Surrender.* A wave of fury swept the Confederacy. Lincoln was accused of violating the sacred rights of property, of encouraging Negroes to rise in murder and rapine. Members of the Confederate Congress talked wildly of running up the black flag and killing all enemy wounded and prisoners. In effect, the Southern spine was stiffened to fight to the end.

So was the North's. Abraham Lincoln had lifted the North's purpose from the cause of Union to the high call of the crusade to crush slavery. Soldiers in blue now marched to a nobler end than the cry of "Home and Rights," which drew the Butternuts into the field. And they also sang a nobler marching song. It had been "John Brown's Body" until Julia Ward Howe replaced that monotonous litany to a murderer with her magnificent "Battle Hymn of the Republic."

Julia Ward Howe was the daughter of a New York banker and the wife of Dr. Samuel Gridley Howe, the Boston reformer who had been such an outspoken admirer of John Brown. One day in Washington she was returning from a military review over roads thronged with singing soldiers. In the carriage with Mrs. Howe were her minister and other friends and they, too, began to sing. After they sang "John Brown's Body", the soldiers around them shouted, "Good for you!" and her minister said, "Mrs. Howe, why do you not write some good words for that stirring tune?" She replied that she had often thought of doing just that, but the words never came.

Next morning she awoke in the gray of twilight and as she lay waiting for the dawn, the words began to form in her mind. Lest she fall asleep again and forget them, she sprang erect and wrote them down. Finished, she returned to her bed and fell asleep again, thinking: "I like this better than most things that I have written." Indeed she should have, for she had composed the verses to what was not only the greatest song to come out of the Civil War, but to one that transcends any particular conflict and can be sung to celebrate all great moral crusades.

Mine eyes have seen the glory of the coming of the Lord:
He is trampling out the vintage where the grapes of wrath are
    stored;
He hath loosed the fateful lightning of his terrible swift sword:
    His truth is marching on.

I have seen Him in the watch fires of a hundred circling camps;
They have builded Him an altar in the evening dews and damps;
I can read His righteous sentence by the dim and flaring lamps.
    His day is marching on.

I have read a fiery gospel writ in burnished rows of steel:
"As ye deal with my contemners, so with you my grace shall
    deal;
Let the Hero, born of woman, crush the serpent with his heel,
    Since God is marching on."

He has sounded forth the trumpet that shall never call retreat;
He is sifting out the hearts of men before his judgment seat:
Oh! be swift, my soul, to answer Him! be jubilant, my feet!
　Our God is marching on.

In the beauty of the lilies Christ was born across the sea,
With a glory in His bosom that transfigures you and me:
As He died to make men holy, let us die to make men free,
　While God is marching on.

Only the soldiers of the Civil War could have sung such a song. Only the sons of a nation just shedding its innocence could have been exalted, rather than embarrassed to cry aloud: "Oh! be swift, my soul, to answer Him! be jubilant, my feet!" or to attest in song that they were where Abraham Lincoln always said he wanted to be: on the side of the Lord. The first time Lincoln heard "The Battle Hymn" he cried aloud: "Sing it again!" It told him that he himself had strummed a mystic chord within the nation's soul. He had truly "sounded forth the trumpet that shall never call retreat."

Unfortunately, Lincoln possessed no trumpet that could call George McClellan into battle again. Having permitted Marse Robert to depart Sharpsburg unmolested, he now allowed six weeks of splendid autumn marching weather to elapse before crossing the Potomac in pursuit. Even then, he was annoyed by Lincoln's frequent messages importuning him to get going. "I feel that I have done all that can be asked in twice saving the country," he wrote somewhat petulantly to his wife.

McClellan's disposition was not improved when Jeb Stuart with 1,800 horsemen and four guns crossed the Potomac above Martinsburg at dawn October 10 under orders from Lee to scout McClellan's army, and also, if possible, to destroy the railroad bridge over the Conococheague and thus cut Little Mac's supply line. Stuart reached Chambersburg, Pennsylvania, that night, capturing the town and bivouacking in its streets.

In the morning he encountered two disappointments: a bank official had fled with all the cash in the vault and the Conococheague bridge, being built of iron, was indestructible. Nevertheless Jeb and his high-spirited boys had a great time spending near-worthless Confederate money in the town's well-stocked stores, while imprisoning and paroling 280 Union soldiers. They also "appropriated" a thousand excellent huge dray horses of Norman and Belgian stock, fully equipped with the great collars that no Southern quartermasters could have furnished.

When the column formed next morning, Jeb led it due east rather than back the way he had come, and the Grayback troopers whooped in delight to realize that they were going to do another "Ride Around McClellan." Late in the afternoon they crossed into Maryland at Emmitsburg, beyond which they forded the Monocacy in darkness. Many of them had dismounted to stay awake while others actually fell asleep in their saddles, snoring and spluttering away.

Word of the raid reached Washington and an infuriated Halleck wired Little Mac, "Not a man should be permitted to return to Virginia," to which the Young Napoleon replied that he would "teach them a lesson they will not soon forget." Jeb's boys guffawed when they heard the threat, and their whoops of derision rose louder as they splashed through the Potomac again, reaching the safety of Confederate lines with only a few men wounded and two others missing, believed to be casualties of Yankee whiskey. The "lesson" was not lost on Abraham Lincoln, and when he was asked aboard a steamer what he thought of it, he drew a circle on the deck with the ferrule of his umbrella. "When I was a boy we used to play a game, 'Three times round—and out.' Stuart has been around him twice. If he goes around him once more, gentlemen, McClellan will be out."

Actually, the president had earlier drawn a deadline for McClellan in his own mind. If he should permit Lee to cross the Blue Ridge and again interpose his army between Richmond and the Army of the Potomac, McClellan would be through. This did happen, but just before the November 4 elections, so that Lincoln waited until the returns were in. They came in a shocking setback for the Republicans. Although the Republicans remained in power, the Democrats raised their congressional delegation from 44 to 75, and all the blame was placed on Lincoln's shoulders. Three days later— the night of November 7, 1862—two generals stumbled through a driving snowstorm to reach McClellan's headquarters tent near Rectortown in northern Virginia. One of them was Ambrose Burnside and the other Adjutant General C. P. Buckingham. Snow had gathered on the crowns and brims of their hats, sifting into the folds of their uniforms. Burnside's huge whiskers were powdered with it. "Dear Burn," as Little Mac always addressed him in his letters, seemed embarrassed and upset. His companion was uneasy.

McClellan looked up from the letter he was writing to his wife and cordially invited them to enter and sit down. He could sense from his visitors' manner what was in the envelopes Buckingham carried, but

George McClellan was, above all else, a gentleman. After an exchange of pleasantries, Buckingham handed him the two messages—one from Halleck, the other from the War Department—and Little Mac read that he was relieved of his command. He looked up with a smile, and said in a pleasant voice: "Well, Burnside, I turn the command over to you."

Burnside was now close to tears. He had twice refused the appointment, and once again that very evening, on the grounds that he was not competent, but after Buckingham told him that if he persisted in his refusal the job would go to Joe Hooker, whom he did not like, he accepted. Now he begged McClellan to stay with him a few days to familiarize himself with the command. McClellan agreed, and the two generals went out into the snowstorm again.

Alone at his desk once more, McClellan resumed writing, telling his wife what had happened, crying: "Alas, for my poor country! I know in my inmost heart she never had a truer servant." His men—the soldiers of the force Little Mac always called "my army," and Lincoln described as "McClellan's bodyguard"—shared that conviction. Their rage and sorrow knew no bounds when they heard of his dismissal. Next day when drawn up to exchange salutes, the men broke ranks and crowded around him, shouting and sobbing, touching his boots and stroking the flanks of Dan Webster. "Send him back!" they cried in their fury. "Send him back!" The Irish brigade threw their colors at his feet, calling upon him to ride over them, but he ordered them to retrieve them. One general cried that "he wished to God that McClellan would put himself at the head of the army and throw the infernal scoundrels at Washington into the Potomac!" Burnside beside him was so overcome, so close to tears again, that when Major General Darius Couch offered him his congratulations he implored him in a choking voice: "Couch, don't say a word about it."

On November 11 as McClellan rode down to Warrenton Junction to board a waiting train for Washington, the 2,000-man detachment standing there to give the farewell salute broke ranks and surrounded the train, uncoupling McClellan's car and pushing it back, shouting threats against the administration and begging him not to leave. Another soldier might have thought the time had come to cross the Rubicon, but McClellan, sincerely devoted to constitutional government, calmed his men and reminded them of their duty. Then—in his ears the melancholy roar of "one long and mournful huzza"—he rode out of their sight but never out of their hearts, bound for a return to civilian life and a new career in politics that would lead him to the Democratic nomination for president opposing the very man who had finally given up on him.

So ended the military career of George Brinton McClellan: intelligent, proud, sensitive, alternating in the extremes of self-praise, self-pity and self-excuse, a superb organizer, but because he was hesitant in battle and had no killer instinct, he was a man who should never have been a general.

44

■

Battle of Corinth: Philip Sheridan: Battle of Perryville

THE FEDERAL CAMPAIGN to clear the Mississippi Valley, on hold since May 30 when Halleck's farcical March of the Moles burrowed into Corinth, was renewed by Grant in mid-September with an assault on Iuka, Mississippi, twenty-odd miles down the Memphis & Charleston Railroad from Corinth.

Sterling Price was in Iuka with about 14,000 men. Price was spoiling for a fight, eager to recover Kentucky and his native Missouri, where editors had pinned the derisive nickname of "Old Skedad" on this 290-pound giant. Price was also angered by reports that he was a West Pointer, and he sought to correct this vile calumny by taking an advertisement declaring that he owed "his success to practical good sense and hard fighting. He never attended a military school in his life." Price's hopes to recover the two western border states were based upon Van Dorn's joining him in Iuka with 8,000 Graybacks.

Grant, however, forestalled that union by sending Rosecrans against Price. In a short, sharp fight on September 19, Rosecrans drove Price out of Iuka. Union losses were 141 killed, 613 wounded, and 36 missing, for a total of 790 out of about 17,000 men; Confederate casualties were 263 killed, 692 wounded and 561 captured for a total of 1,516 out of 14,000. Price and Van Dorn joined each other at Ripley, from which they marched north toward Corinth, now held again by Rosecrans under Grant.

What the Rebels saw when they bore down upon Corinth after feinting at Bolivar above it was Beauregard's (and Van Dorn's) old entrenchments intended to receive Halleck, but now crammed with Bluebellies. Neither Price nor Van Dorn liked what he saw. They had thought they possessed superior numbers, 22,000 to 15,000. Actually, Rosecrans had 23,000 in his command, most of them occupying that formidable ridge, its fortifications now beaten brown by nearly four months of exposure to the weather. What had happened was that Van Dorn's feint at Bolivar had convinced Rosecrans—as Van Dorn desired—that he was going to strike there. Accordingly, he had recalled two divisions and was planning to march to Bolivar when Van Dorn appeared north of Corinth.

Typically, the bellicose little Mississippi terrier attacked in force, and one of the most violent battles of the war ensued. Yelling, the Butternuts swept up the ridge, scythed by Union cannon and muskets, falling, but driving steadily upward to penetrate the first of Rosecrans's double line of entrenchments. But the Federals fought stubbornly, taking up no fewer than four different positions between the two fortified lines. At sundown, the Rebels had driven to within musket range of the town itself, but by then they were exhausted. Van Dorn recalled them, and while they drew heavenly buckets of water from captured Yankee wells, he resolved to crush his old classmate "Rosy" Rosecrans in the morning.

Rosecrans, meanwhile, was thinking that if he had had one more hour of sunlight he would have done the same to Buck Van Dorn, and he wired Grant, "If they fight us tomorrow, I think we shall whip them." Then reflecting on Van Dorn's fondness for surprise moves and abrupt changes of direction, he added: "If they go to attack you we shall advance upon them."

But Van Dorn was done with feinting and jabbing. On October 4, with the temperature at 94° in the shade, he came at Rosecrans with all that he had: guns and guts. Just before dawn his artillery opened up, which was a mistake as it often was when the gray gunners dueled those in blue. Immediately, the Federals answered. "It was grand," a Yankee brigadier recalled. "The different calibers, metals, shapes and distances of the guns caused the sounds to resemble the chimes of old Rome when all her bells rang out." After sunrise the roar of the cannon ceased, followed by a long lull which puzzled Rosecrans. Was Buck up to his old tricks? "Feel them," he told a colonel ordered to probe the front, "but don't get into their fingers." Unfortunately that was just what this rash fire-eater did, shot in the neck himself and captured, his regiment shredded by those merciless steel fingers. Rosy now knew that Buck was still there.

Shortly after ten o'clock Van Dorn ordered an all-out assault by Price's two divisions of Texans and Arkansans. On the left they suffered a bloody repulse, but they broke through in the middle, routing Union gunners there, sweeping into the streets of Corinth itself. But there the Federals held, and the Butternuts were compelled to fight their way out—always much more difficult than battling the way in. That was the deepest

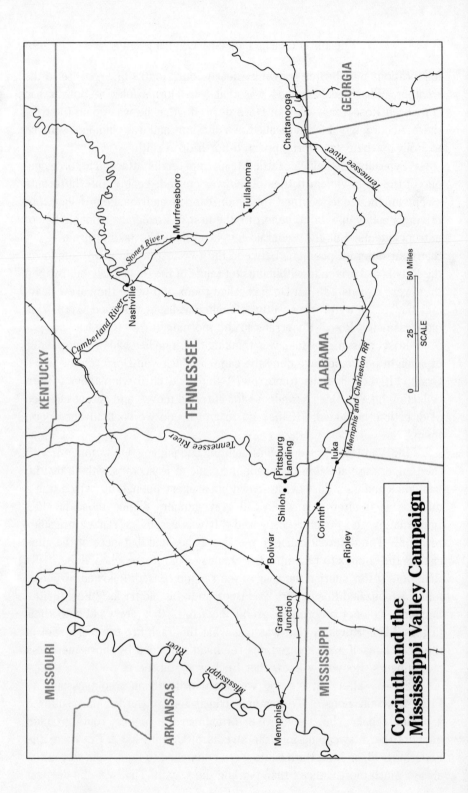

**Corinth and the
Mississippi Valley Campaign**

penetration, and as one heat-exhausted Graycoat said: "Our lines melted under their fire like snow in a thaw." By noon Van Dorn knew that his gamble had failed, and he began to withdraw, eventually reporting: "Exhausted from loss of sleep, wearied from hard marching and fighting, companies and regiments without officers, our troops—let no one censure them—gave way. The day was lost."

How utterly he did not realize until he counted his men. The figures: Union, 355 killed, 1,841 wounded and 324 missing, for a total of 2,520; Confederates, 473 killed, 1,997 wounded and 1,763 missing, for a total of 4,233. And if anyone was to be censured it was Van Dorn himself. If his men were wearied from loss of sleep and hard marching, it was he, a general on horseback, who sent them into battle so exhausted. If they suffered almost 80 percent higher casualties than the enemy, it was Van Dorn who ordered them against an equal number of entrenched troops possessing superior artillery, a situation usually requiring an advantage of three to one with at least comparable ordnance. Except that he had prevented Grant from sending reinforcements to Buell menaced by Bragg in Kentucky, he had failed to destroy Rosecrans and thus derail the Union campaign in Mississippi.

Price wept as he watched the remnants of his command march by him with sullen faces, while on the ridge above him Rosecrans rode among his men to doff his hat with the remark: "I stand in the presence of brave men, and I take my hat off to you."

The vastly underrated Battle of Corinth was not only bloody in relation to the number of men involved, but significant strategically; for it opened the way to the move on Vicksburg, the last Confederate stronghold on the Mississippi River. Meanwhile, the left wing of the two-pronged Rebel invasion of the border states having been crushed, the right wing under Bragg was still advancing in Kentucky. Following him—but timidly—was the Army of the Ohio under Don Carlos Buell.

It had been an unpleasant fall for General Buell. The best that could be said for it was that, while Bragg and E. Kirby Smith wasted precious time by setting up a Confederate government of Kentucky in Frankfort, he had been able to win the race to Louisville. But then on September 29 two hammer blows fell upon him.

In the first, one of his most trusted subordinates, the huge, three-hundred-pound General William Nelson, who had done so much to keep Kentucky in the Union and had brought his fresh brigade to Grant at Shiloh, had entered into a running argument with that Indiana brigadier who was also called Jefferson Davis. Nelson was an overbearing man, Davis a touchy one. Nelson thought he had solved their dispute over the defense of Louisville by ordering him out of the department. But Davis returned. He accosted Nelson just after breakfast in the lobby of the Galt House. Davis demanded satisfaction for Nelson's "rudeness," Nelson called him "an insolent puppy," for which Davis flung a balled-up calling card in Nelson's face. At once Nelson back-handed him on the jaw, sending Davis staggering backward. Turning, Nelson ascended the stairs toward Buell's room, muttering to a man coming down: "Did you hear that damned insolent scoundrel insult me, sir? I suppose he don't know me, sir. I'll teach him a lesson, sir." Behind him, Davis borrowed a pistol and followed. Nelson's hand was on Buell's doorknob when he heard someone call his name. It was Davis, leveling his pistol and crying: "Not another step farther!" At eight feet he shot Nelson in the chest. The big man fell, murmuring: "Send for a clergyman. I wish to be baptized." Before one could arrive, he gasped, "I have been basely murdered," and died.

An outraged Buell placed Davis under arrest, but before he could try him—indeed before he could launch an investigation or even digest his breakfast—the second blow fell: an order from Halleck, insisted upon by Lincoln, relieving him of his command, to be succeeded by General George Thomas. "Old Pap," as the troops now called Thomas, was dismayed. He wired Halleck: "General Buell's preparations have been completed to move against the enemy, and I therefore respectfully ask that he may be retained in command." Halleck, who had received word that Buell had beaten Bragg to Louisville, Lincoln's condition that he retain his command, replied: "You may consider the order as suspended until I can lay your dispatch before the Government and get instructions."

Buell was saved by Thomas's generosity, and he was so relieved that he forgot about Davis, who was never court-martialed and eventually returned to duty. On October 1, Buell left Louisville seeking battle with Bragg and E. Kirby Smith, still in Frankfort. Buell's Army of the Ohio now numbered about 75,000 men, about three times as many as the enemy, and was divided into ten divisions.

One of these was commanded by a brand new brigadier named Philip Henry Sheridan.

Phil Sheridan was born March 6, 1831, the third of the six children of John and Mary Sheridan, an Irish immigrant couple. Where is not exactly known. It might have been in County Cavan, or aboard ship as John and Mary sailed for the New World, or in Albany, New York, or Somerset, Ohio, the little town to which the Sheridans eventually moved. Somerset stood on a high ridge dividing the Hocking and Muskingum rivers. People living on the Hocking side were known as the Pig Foots and those on the Muskingum side the Turkey Foots. Between the boys of either side there raged a bitter rivalry. The Pig Foots were Irish—and among this bellicose race none is more pugnacious than the smaller specimens. Thus, Little Phil earned a reputation as a scrapper early in life, and because he had a deep sense of justice he was always ready to lift his fists in defense of weaker or smaller boys.

There were not many his age smaller, and he was also quite unbeautiful. He had a bump on his round head so large that he had difficulty keeping his hat on. His bandy legs were short and his arms were long and he was so quick and agile that it was difficult not to compare him to a monkey, although such an observation was certain to produce a fistfight. One of his friends recalled: "He had arched, heavy eyebrows, from underneath which large, piercing black eyes looked out at you. One could tell from his eyes in a moment whether he was fiercely angry or only indignant; whether he was serious, sad or humorous, without noticing another feature of his face. I never saw eyes which showed so many shades of feeling as those of Phil Sheridan." Phil's eyes were actually dark blue—Irish eyes "put in with a sooty finger"—turning black only when enraged. Yet he was indeed different and might have been a fierce Mongolian lad washed up on the shores of the Hocking River. There is no place in the world where an ugly shrimp is not fair game, who can silence taunts and insults only with his fists, and Little Phil Sheridan was a prince among such pugilists. By the time he was ready for West Point he could lick any boy in Somerset.

Phil detested school, chafing at the boredom of the classroom when he might be swimming bare-behind in the Hocking, or devouring books on military history. His hero was William Tecumseh Sherman, the tall redheaded West Point cadet who came often to Somerset to visit Ellen Ewing, a student at St. Mary's Female Academy on the hill. Phil dreamed of going to West Point, and was overjoyed to be appointed to the Academy. His parents were not so happy. They had heard that West Point was under the influence of the Episcopal church and feared that Phil might lose his faith there. They went to the same Dominican fathers who had baptized Cump Sherman. One of them suggested that if they really believed this, the appointment should be rejected. Sheridan, aware of how Phil's heart was set on the Academy, cried out in anguish: "But what shall I do with the boy?"

"Rather than send him to West Point," Father Joshua replied with heavy humor, "take him out in the back yard behind the chicken coop and cut his throat."

Shocked, the Sheridans went home and Phil went to West Point, arriving there in July of 1848. He was seventeen, having reached his full height of five feet five inches, and weighing 115 pounds. Homely and rough, he was an ugly duckling among all those cultivated Easterners and smooth Southerners. He felt the difference keenly, and was especially aware that his race and his faith did not place him very high on the social ladder. He knew that many of the Easterners, especially those from New England, were the sons of Nativists and Know-Nothings or of members of the American Protective Association, three organizations sworn to protect "native Americans," by which was meant what is now called a WASP: white Anglo-Saxon Protestant. They were particularly virulent against the Catholic Irish, then coming to America in a vast flood in flight from the dreadful Potato Famine. It was maintained that the Irish would turn America into a Papal colony, and signs such as "Help Wanted—No Irish Need Apply" or "No dogs or Irishmen" were posted everywhere in the Northeast.

But it was the Southerners with their aristocratic airs whom the unhappy Sheridan particularly detested. He was, like his hero Napoleon, full of cold contempt for people who considered themselves superior because they had emerged from a pedigreed womb, and their imperiousness no more reduced him to a servile sense of inferiority than did the frigid hostility of the Easterners. It seemed to him that social grace did not make a soldier, but rather audacity and the ability to withstand adversity—qualities he possessed in abundance. Life at West Point for Phil Sheridan might have been even unhappier and his stay there of short duration, had it not been for his roommate, Henry W. Slocum, of Delphi, New York. Phil was struggling in his studies, but the kindly Slocum, who had once taught school, tutored him each night after taps with a blanket hung over their only window. Because of Slocum, Phil gained a classroom confidence that he never lost, amazing his instructors with his quick grasp of tactics in all arms.

But as he began his third year in September 1851, his short fuse nearly ruined his career. He had long been exposed to the haughty eye and caustic tongue of Cadet Sergeant William R. Terrill, a Virginian. One day on the parade ground Terrill rapped out what Phil thought was an unnecessary order given in an insulting tone, and he lunged at him with his bayonet, catching himself just in time to avoid stabbing his tormentor. That was bad enough, whatever the provocation, but then, later on, Phil attacked Terrill with his fists. Surprisingly enough, Phil was not expelled, but only suspended for a year, and upon his return he showed himself a changed youth.

No more public brawls for Phil Sheridan, only "private" fistfights with cadets twice his size, and it was not an uncommon sight to see him being carried back to barracks on a shutter.

In 1853 Phil was graduated thirty-fourth in a class of fifty-two cadets, spending the next eight years on lonely outpost duty in Texas and the Pacific Northwest, where he was cited for gallantry by Winfield Scott for his relief of a blockhouse in Yamhill County, Oregon, besieged by local Indians. He was still at the Yamhill post after Sumter. When Captain James J. Archer of known Rebel sympathies arrived there to relieve him, he refused to relinquish command. Archer departed for the South, where he joined the Texas Brigade under Sheridan's old friend and classmate, John Bell Hood. After Bull Run Sheridan was ordered to St. Louis. Henry Halleck, in one of his few decisions entitling him to his country's gratitude, made him a full colonel. After Beauregard evacuated Corinth Sheridan at the head of a cavalry regiment pursued him with such dash that he won his first star.

He was with Buell advancing against Bragg at Perryville, Kentucky, when, before sunrise of October 8, he led one of his brigades in a furious assault upon Doctor's Creek, hoping to obtain water for the thirsty Federals. He not only succeeded, but then, waving his little black porkpie hat that was to become famous, this thirty-one-year-old general seized the dominant heights beyond, driving the Rebel snipers off it and posting his men there to prevent their return. This was the first action in the Battle of Perryville. It upset his corps commander, who warned him against provoking an engagement, which Buell did not desire. Sheridan replied that he expected to be attacked with daylight, and he was—repulsing the Confederates in a short, sharp fight.

But the Rebels under Hardee and Polk were gradually massing behind a screen of woods on the Federal left. They had chosen well to fight there. The ground had been only recently reconnoitered by Alexander McDowell McCook, and his two green divisions were only filing into position when their blue uniforms were spotted through the trees. McCook, meanwhile, had ridden off to report to Buell at his army headquarters, where for most of the day he would be isolated from the sound of battle by an atmospheric freak, and thus would be unable to get most of his army into action.

One of McCook's brigade commanders was Brigadier General William Terrill, a Union-loyal Virginian and the same man whom Sheridan had nearly bayoneted in their cadet days. They had met, shaken hands and become friends—which was well and made Sheridan happy, because Terrill was one of the first to fall when that mass of Graybacks came flowing out of the woods yelling like madmen. Volleys of Confederate musketry and that high-pitched, piercing yell turned the hearts of most of McCook's raw soldiery flabby with fear—and they broke and ran. McCook returning to his front found both his divisions in a state of panic, and called for help from the corps on his right. There was no appealing to Buell, for the Union commander still did not know he had been attacked.

What help that came to McCook was not infantry, but Sheridan's guns firing at the gray columns in enfilade, or like a battleship crossing the T. Rebels fell like tenpins, among them the gallant Irish-born Pat Cleburne of Arkansas, who had only recovered from one wound to receive another in the leg as his horse was shot from under him. All over the field, now, blue was mixed with gray, friend fired upon friend, and men mistaking the enemy for their own were taken captive. Bishop-General Leonidas Polk in his dark-gray uniform was thus approached by an incautious Union brigadier who shouted to him above the uproar: "I have come to your assistance with my brigade!" To which Polk blandly replied: "You are my prisoner."

As dusk began to fall Polk saw what he believed to be a unit of Confederates firing into the flank of one of his own brigades, and he hurried forward to correct this tragic but common error. When he ordered their colonel to cease firing at friends, he replied:

"I am sure they are the enemy."

"Enemy!" Polk exclaimed angrily. "Why, I have only just left them myself. Cease firing, sir! What is your name, sir?"

"Colonel Shryock, of the 8th Indiana. And pray, sir, who are you?"

Polk felt quite conspicuous back there, all alone behind a Yankee regiment, and he hoped the twilight would make his dark-gray uniform a little darker. But he rode brazenly toward the Yankee, shaking his fist and shouting: "I'll soon show you who I am, sir! Cease firing, sir, at once!" Turning, he rode slowly back toward his own lines, unable to keep from screwing up his shoulders to receive a shower of bullets.

It was by then almost night, and it was too late for the Confederates to continue to exploit the breakthrough begun four hours earlier. Yet, the night was clear and a moon just past the full was shining so brightly on the battlefield that some Federal commanders were urging Buell—at the front at last—to launch a counter-attack. Buell himself had earlier tried to organize such a movement, but the messenger carrying Thomas's verbal order to Crittenden on the right to move forward got lost along Doctor's Creek and did not find him until after sunset. So Thomas ordered Crittenden: "Have your different divisions ready to attack at daylight."

In the morning, Buell waited impatiently for the sound of battle on his right. None came. At eight o'clock, three hours after dawn, he asked Crittenden: "What delays your attack?" Crittenden replied that he had been ordered to be "ready to attack," which was what he had done. Exasperated, Buell told him to get going at once—and he did.

But Bragg was gone.

Thus the Battle of Perryville, the last major engagement on the soil of Kentucky, which was now and forevermore a Federal state. Casualties had been high: Confederates, 519 killed, 2,635 wounded and 251 missing, for a total of 3,405; Federal, 845 killed, 2,851 wounded, 515 missing, for a total of 4,211. Don Carlos Buell had fought his first battle and had not done well. True, that freak silence had prevented him from even knowing that he had been struck until four o'clock in the afternoon, but he had still been roughly handled by a force not one third as large as his own. He also could have made a night assault in that bright moonlight with all those fresh troops at his disposal. Bragg had not done well, either. "For God's sake, General," Kirby Smith had urged him that night, "let us fight Buell here." Bragg responded, "I will do it, sir," but he did not. Fierce on the outside, he was timorous on the inside—and he pulled out at midnight heading for Tennessee. The last of the three Confederate invasions in that melancholy fall of 1862 had foundered: Van Dorn and Price at Corinth, Lee in Maryland and now Bragg in Kentucky.

Don Carlos Buell had also fought his last battle. He had let Braxton Bragg get clean away with his battered army, and his failure to pursue or to seize the opportunity to liberate east Tennessee—Lincoln's "land of heart's desire"—had so disgusted the president that Buell was relieved on October 24, never to command troops again. William Rosecrans replaced him, and Buell's Army of the Ohio became again the Army of the Cumberland.

45

■

Burnside and Fredericksburg

A BRAHAM LINCOLN's reasons for selecting Burnside to replace
McClellan, other than his natural combativeness, the one virtue the
president admired most in a commander, was that he had done well at
Roanoke Island and Antietam, had been Little Mac's friend before and
during the war and thus was not one of those numerous critics who might
receive a hostile reception from the Army of the Potomac and, finally, that
he was not interested in politics. This last would put the Jacobin wolves at
bay, Lincoln thought, although he must have known that the radicals really
did not care what a man's politics were so long as they were Republican
and Abolitionist. Thus, what really impressed them—in the negative—was
Burnside's well-known friendship with the man they had just helped to
destroy.

Burnside was not so naive as not to suspect this; and yet, there was
always something pitiful, even pathetic, about this big, burly, friendly man.
His continued insistence that the job was too big for him had already led
to much head shaking among his generals, one of them asking rhetorically
how could they "have confidence in the fitness of our leader if he had no
such confidence in himself?" Burnside, again not so starry-eyed as he
frequently appears in history, was quite aware that the chief cause of
McClellan's dismissal was his chronic case of the slows. So he quickly
prepared and submitted to the president a plan for immediate action.

Lee's army had been reorganized into two corps commanded by
Jackson and Longstreet, both new lieutenant generals. Jackson was north
at the foot of the Valley with 40,000 men, Longstreet south around Culpeper with 45,000. Lee's strength had risen to this figure of 85,000 through
the return of stragglers from Second Bull Run and those who had refused

to join the invasion of the North. Burnside, however, was still vastly superior with 120,000 men.

He proposed to convert the concentration at Warrenton above Longstreet into a feint under cover of which he would "accumulate a four- or five-days' supply for the men and animals; then make a rapid movement of the whole force to Fredericksburg, with a view to a movement upon Richmond from that point." This was the "covering approach" that Lincoln always favored because it protected Washington, but the president now showed that he had profited from those long nights spent poring over military history by objecting that Lee's army, not the Confederate capital, should be Burnside's true objective. In this he was absolutely correct. Only very rarely does an enemy's chief city take precedence over his army. But the "On to Richmond!" virus was still strong in the North, and Richmond itself was like a dreadful magnet drawing Union armies to their destruction. Lincoln, however, pleased by the prospect of fast action in the East, swallowed his reservations, so that on November 14 Halleck could wire Burnside: "The President has just assented to your plan. He thinks that it will succeed, if you move very rapidly; otherwise not."

Burnside did move swiftly, for he was, like McClellan, a superb organizer. On the day he received Halleck's wire, he reorganized his army into three "grand divisions," right, center, and left. Old Bull Sumner commanded the right. The left was led by Major General William B. Franklin, a slow-moving, methodical soldier whose rate of speed was not quite what was required at Antietam. Apart from this defect, he was a solid, capable soldier in whom Burnside had great confidence, as he did in Fighting Joe Hooker, who had the center grand division. Each of these formations was composed of two corps each, while a seventh corps under Franz Sigel comprised the reserve.

Burnside's reason for this reorganization was that it would enable him to handle his army more deftly, and the speed with which these seven corps with their cavalry and artillery moved down the Rappahannock to Fredericksburg seemed to bear him out. Sumner arrived on the seventeenth, two days after setting out, and the others came in on schedule. Burnside himself was in Falmouth just to the north on the nineteenth, jubilantly wiring Halleck that there were few Confederates in Fredericksburg and that, "As soon as the pontoon trains arrive, the bridge will be built and the command moved over."

So much depended on the pontoons that Burnside had carefully left their shipment in the hands of Halleck, and he probably would have been horrified to learn that Old Brains—master paper-shuffler that he was—had assigned this vital requisition to an unknown subordinate. Whoever was responsible, the bridges did not arrive until eight days later, by which time a three-day rain had raised the level of the fords making them impassable, the roads had been turned into sloughs of mud and the formidable James Longstreet had arrived in Fredericksburg with 45,000 men. Burnside's vexation at having lost the advantage which his speedy movement to the target city had gained him was understandably great, and he flatly informed Halleck that now "I cannot make the promise of probable success" given in his belief that his plans would be followed. Lincoln was dismayed by this massive hedge and hurried by water down to Aquia Creek to confer with his new army chief. What he heard disturbed him even further, and he returned to Washington suspecting that Burnside, now in possession of a scapegoat should he fail, seemed nevertheless determined to order his men to storm the Rappahannock. So the president drew up a substitute plan of his own based on two amphibious assaults. He showed it to Halleck and Burnside, both of whom said it would take too long to prepare. His own condition of urgency was thus turned against him, and he had to be content with telling Burnside to do what he could. Thus, in the melancholy rhythm of "For want of a nail, a shoe was lost, For want of a shoe, a horse was lost, For want of a horse, a kingdom was lost," had an administrative breakdown in what should have been a routine supply of an abundant if vital military item—to wit, bridging pontoons—prepared that incarnadine road to Richmond for still another Northern bloodbath.

There was a stubborn streak in Ambrose Burnside. He had said he would take Fredericksburg, and, by God!, he would. Gradually, as November became December, his depression at the loss of surprise vanished, and he became optimistic. Unlike McClellan with his penchant for exaggerating the enemy's strength, he had correctly estimated Lee to be in Fredericksburg with about 80,000 men. His own immediate force of about 121,000 effectives, he reasoned, should be sufficient to cross the river and crush Lee's left held by Longstreet before his right under Jackson about twenty miles downstream could rally to the rescue. Moreover the intelligence supplied by his newfangled observation balloons suggested that Lee did not expect him to attempt a massive river crossing on his front. Burnside knew that Lee was not in the town in force, but had occupied a long, low, wooded ridge above the plain to its rear. From a distance it did not look like much; indeed, Burnside's reliance upon his balloons, badly hampered by bad weather, rather than basic reconnaissance was to prove almost as great a handicap as the loss of surprise, for Lee's position was perhaps the strongest held by either side during the course of the entire war.

Graybacks were entrenched in successive lines beginning with a sunken road at the foot of Marye's Heights and protected by a stone wall facing the town all the way to the top of the ridge. Guns were sited everywhere to rake the plain approaching this position.

Burnside's plan was that in the predawn darkness of December 11, 1862, his engineers would throw across the river six pontoon bridges for the double crossing of infantry and cavalry, immediately to be followed by artillery positioned close up to support the assault. Franklin would be on the left, Sumner on the right, each grand division reinforced by formations taken from Hooker's grand division, so that each numbered about 60,000 men. Franklin on the left would assault the lower end of the Confederate ridge, then wheel to its right or north to roll up the enemy held in place by Sumner's assaults on the right. There would also be a demonstration downstream at Skinker's Neck to convince the Confederates that a crossing would be attempted there. It seemed to Burnside that his was a good plan, and he wired Washington: "We hope to succeed."

Success in battle depends more on unknown factors than the known. What Ambrose Burnside did not know was the strength of Lee's defensive position and his decision to leave in Fredericksburg a brigade of Mississippi sharpshooters under William Barksdale, a former congressman with long silver locks and a thirst for glory that his men had come to believe was unquenchable. They and he had been in every Eastern big-shoot since First Bull Run, but now it seemed the glory hound was at last to drink his fill.

Lee, unwilling to draw upon the town the wrath of those Union guns on the opposing Stafford Heights, so superior in number and service, had decided not to contest the crossing except with Barksdale's marksmen. Most of them were posted in sturdy brick houses whose rear walls looked out upon the river. In these Barksdale's men knocked openings providing firing loopholes behind which they sat silently chewing tobacco, waiting for the sight of dawn and the noise of the enemy building his bridges. The first sound they heard, to their amazed delight, was the voice of an old woman calling from the opposite bank that the Yankees had drawn a large issue of cooked rations—a sure sign of impending battle. Then they heard the clatter of lumber and low-voiced commands, followed by the loud cracking of half-inch skim ice covering the Rappahannock's 400-foot width of water. The sounds drew closer as the bridges that were being built of six-foot pontoons drew nearer. Finally, guessing that the Yankee engineers were

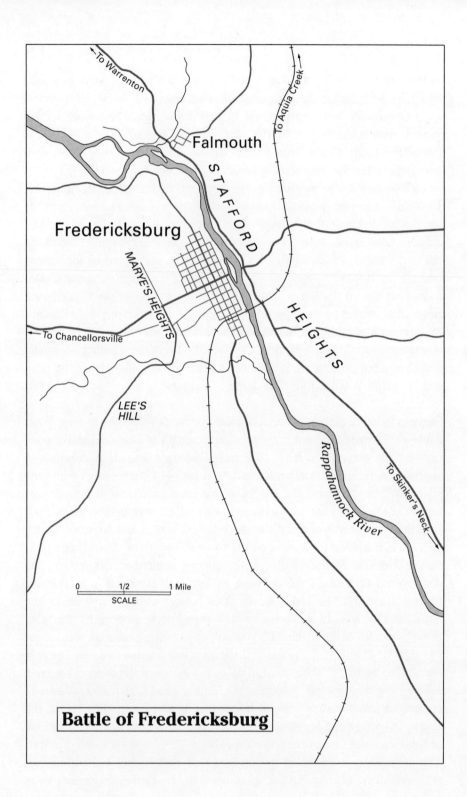

Battle of Fredericksburg

at midstream, they began firing by ear. Screams followed by the pounding of feet on planking told them that they had not missed. Again and again, the brave Yankee engineers crept out on their swaying bridges, commanded to silence, but always undone by a cough or the squeak of a bolt bringing a hail of Deep South bullets down upon them. When the sun rose to burn off the river mists that concealed them, their Gethsemane began. Rushing out on the bridges visible to marksmen to whom a range of 200 feet was not even shooting, they were sent splashing into water that soon was red with their blood. The carnage continued for hours, with the Mississippians hooting and shooting, and the Yankees running a double gantlet: out to the ends of the bridges until they could endure the scything no more, back again to the safety of the Union shore.

Meanwhile, Burnside waited for his snipers to take out the hidden Rebel marksmen, but by ten o'clock his patience was exhausted and he ordered his chief of artillery, Brigadier General Henry Hunt, to smash the enemy hornets' nests. Hunt had 147 heavy guns posted on Stafford Heights. They began to roar in a deep-throated chorus that lasted more than an hour, hurling 5,000 shells into the old town in a shattering cannonade that infuriated Robert E. Lee. "Those people delight to destroy the weak and those who can make no defense!" he cried indignantly. "It just suits them!" However, Marse Robert's fury was a bit illogical. As he well knew, in war military necessity takes precedence over all rights and privileges, as his own marksmen understood when they knocked firing holes in the homes of their countrymen; and as Longstreet comprehended when, asked by Barksdale if he should have his men put out all the fires in Rebel homes, he replied: "You have enough to do to watch the Yankees."

They continued to do that with great skill, but then General Hunt, aware that his guns could never dislodge the enemy sharpshooters, suggested that the pontoons be converted into assault boats to take infantry across the river to pry the sharpshooters out of their rubble with bayonets. It was done. With a Michigan regiment in the lead supported by two from Massachusetts, the Federals seized a bridgehead behind which the bridges were securely laid and protected by more infantry. Barksdale withdrew at dark, and the entire incident, though costing Burnside a day's delay, and the lives of many brave engineers, was significant only historically: it showed in this first of modern wars that the destruction of a city is always a mistake, for it turns it into an eminently defensible warren of twisted steel and mortar. Burnside was not only undaunted by the delay but also pleased by his balloons' reports that Lee had not yet called for Jackson to join him, becoming so confident that he decided to wait another day before launching the assault so that he might safely assemble his army across the Rappahan-nock. It was done in the morning under cover of a fog that also prevented Burnside's balloons from reporting that Jackson, recalled by Lee late the previous night, was moving north with half his command. At noon, the fog lifted so that Lee standing on the ridge that was to bear his name, seeing the thousands upon thousands of neatly dressed Bluebellies assembling on the plain below him, immediately realized that this was no feint but the main effort, and quickly summoned Jackson's two other divisions to the ridge.

Behind the plain in Fredericksburg, meanwhile, the Federal soldiery went wild in an orgy of looting and destruction. Cavalrymen ripped the lids and strings from beautiful old grand pianos to make feed troughs for their horses, mirrors were smashed with musket butts, and family portraits slashed with bayonets, while Yankees tipsy with rare old Madeira found in the cellars, dressed themselves in women's fine underthings or crinoline gowns snatched from closets and drawers to go dancing and cavorting on precious rugs now sticky with a mixture of flour and molasses. Eventually, some of the more sober-minded became uneasy at the absence of Confeder-ate shells exploding in the town. One of them—a barracks-room lawyer—opined that Lee had lured them into this rampage so that he could show the world what beasts the Yankees were. But a hardheaded veteran scoffed at this starry-eyed speculation. "Shit," he snorted. "They *want* us to get in. Getting out won't be quite so smart and easy. You'll see."

Action at Fredericksburg began on the Federal left under Franklin, oppos-ing Jackson in full strength on the Confederate right. Here the fog rolled rapidly away and the entrenched Rebels gasped to see 60,000 Yankees advancing toward them in long lines so neatly dressed that they could count the regiments and brigades. Here also two horse-drawn Rebel guns came racing toward the Union host; Marse Robert standing on Lee's Hill with his eyes fastened to his binoculars gasped in amazement at the audacity of this lone sally—toy-sized in the distance. It was made by Major John Pelham of Alabama, at twenty-four already a legend in the Confederate army for his daring feats. Hurling shells at the startled Federals he brought upon himself the wrath of four full Union batteries, which put one of his beloved Napole-ons out of action. Helping to serve the other one, he refused Stuart's order to retire, doing so only after his caissons were empty. Lee on his hill put down his glasses with a smile. "It is glorious to see such courage in one so young."

Uncommon courage was common that dreadful blood-red day of De-cember 13, 1862—especially among Hooker's troops assaulting Longstreet's corps on Lee's left. Marse Robert had expected Burnside to concentrate against Jackson on his right flank, never dreaming that the Union commander would dare to test Longstreet entrenched in ascending lines on Marye's Heights. Here was a death trap, here was another sunken road, even deeper than those at Shiloh and Antietam. The side facing the Federals was lined with a stone wall four feet high forming a perfect parapet for the Rebel riflemen. Behind the road rose Marye's Heights, crowned by Longstreet's artillery. To approach this position the Federals had to cross open, uphill country. It was no wonder one of Longstreet's artillerists said to him: "General, we cover that ground now so well that we comb it as with a fine-tooth comb. A chicken could not live in that field when we open on it!"

Longstreet laughed, just as he had chuckled when Stonewall Jackson appeared that day wearing a handsome new gold-braided dress coat. "Old Jack's" men whooped and hollered at the sight: "Come here, boys! Stonewall has drawed his bounty and has bought himself some new clothes." Watching the midmorning sun burn off the mists above Fredericksburg, seeing the steeples appear and the streets filled with marching Federals, Longstreet jokingly asked Jackson if he was not afraid of all those Yankees. No man for a joke, Jackson growled: "Wait till they come a little nearer, and they shall either scare me or I'll scare them." One of Stonewall's aides thought the general was allowing the enemy to get too close, but Jackson said: "Major, my men have sometimes failed to *take* a position, but to *defend* one—never!"

Recovering quickly from Pelham's daring attack, Franklin's artillery began supporting his skirmishers in blue, but then Jackson's guns broke up the Federals. It was then that Hooker's divisions swept toward Longstreet, holding the sunken road and Marye's Heights. From the stone parapet came a crash and a flash of flame, from the hill behind it a roar of artillery—and the carnage was begun. Again and again these gallant Union soldiers obeyed those remorseless, heartless, mindless orders to conquer a very hell of flame and steel. They were like lead soldiers storming a stove. They had only their blouses between their hearts and the bullets of the entrenched Rebels, yet onward they came, flesh flowing against lead, brigade after blue brigade, and the Rebels standing four deep behind the stone wall loaded and fired, loaded and fired, shattering the blue lines into fragments, scattering them across the frozen mud.

Such was the charge at Marye's Heights, a tragedy of high courage at the abuse of high incapacity. Even the Rebels were thrilled by the bravery of their enemy, and George Pickett later wrote his wife: "The brilliant assault . . . of their Irish brigade was beyond description. Why, my darling, we forgot they were fighting us, and cheer after cheer at their fearlessness went up all along the line." Fearlessness, however, cannot conquer entrenched rifles, and some 7,000 Federals fell before Marye's Heights.

On Lee's right, more Yankees were falling as Franklin renewed his assault on Jackson. Here a Confederate counter-attack was launched, and Lee, standing on a hill, heard the weird high cry of the Rebel yell and saw a line of ragged Butternuts come running out of a wood in pursuit of a body of fleeing Federals. Lee's eyes flashed, but then the gentler, truer side of his nature came uppermost and he murmured: "It is well that war is so terrible—we should grow too fond of it!"

By late afternoon the Army of the Potomac was so stunned that Lee might have destroyed it with a counter-attack. Jackson, his countenance glowing as though on fire, urged him to approve an assault on Franklin. He feared that once again Marse Robert "would gain no fruits" from his victory and argued for a counter-stroke preceded by a heavy bombardment that would scatter the Yankees so that they could be pinned to their destruction against the river. It should begin at sundown, he said, so that he could withdraw under cover of darkness if he failed. Lee agreed, and Jackson's four divisions remained concealed in the woods while his batteries moved forward to pound the Union left. But the mere sight of these luscious targets visible to Stafford Heights for the first time seemed to make that eminence jump and flash with sound and flame. Shaken, Jackson at once recalled his battered gunners and canceled the assault, and that was the end of the Battle of Fredericksburg.

Early next morning Burnside arose still convinced that he could conquer Lee with the same battering-ram tactics. To his surprise, old Bull Sumner, who had been five years a soldier before Burnside was born, and whom he had ordered not to leave his headquarters lest he be killed leading a charge, was shocked by the proposal. "General," he said, "I hope you will desist from this attack. I do not know of any general officer who approves of it, and I think it will prove disastrous to the army." Hooker and Franklin were of the same opinion, and it was a surprised and shaken Burnside who retired to his tent. "Those men over there," he cried, his voice breaking, pointing to the plain now carpeted in blue. "Those men over there!" It is possible that Ambrose Burnside had hoped to lead the assault in person, to die a hero's death in expiation for his terrible defeat.

That night as though to sharpen his anguish, the aurora borealis appeared—a rare phenomenon so far south—to illuminate the battlefield. Few of the Confederates gazing in amazement at these bright white lights had ever seen them before, and they thought "that the heavens were hanging out banners and streamers and setting off fireworks in honor of our great victory." But once these freezing Rebels in their scanty clothing recovered from the ecstasy inspired by this celestial benediction, they crept down from their ridge to strip the warm clothing from the bodies of Yankees who now had no need for anything save salvation. A Southern soldier on burial detail has described the scene which the more familiar phenomenon of the sun revealed next day.

> Eleven hundred dead bodies—perfectly naked—swollen to twice the natural size—black as Negroes in most cases—lying in every conceivable posture— some on their backs with gaping jaws—some with eyes large as walnuts, protruding with glassy stare—some doubled up like a contortionist—here one without a head—there one without legs—yonder a head and legs, without a trunk—everywhere horrible expressions—fear, rage, agony, madness, torture—lying in pools of blood—lying with heads half buried in sand—with fragments of the shell sticking in the oozing brain—with bullet holes all over the puffed limbs.

There were more than 1,100 dead Federals buried during the truce granted by Lee for the purpose of burial. In all, Union casualties were 1,284 killed, 9,600 wounded and 1,769 missing, for a total of 12,653; Confederate, 595 killed, 4,061 wounded and 654 missing, for a total of 5,310. No one has explained Fredericksburg's enormous eight to one ratio of wounded to killed compared to the normal three to one ratio of modern war, although it is true that the bloody frontal assaults characteristic of the Civil War did produce much higher ratios.

And there might have been still another bloodbath along the Rappahannock if Burnside had had his way. Becoming suddenly bold, he tried to get around Lee's left by moving farther upriver. On January 20, 1863, his army began its march, just as three days of ice-cold, pouring rain commenced. Wagons, horses, guns and soldiers sank deep into the bottomless roads of northern Virginia. The impossibility of movement was best described by the officer who requested "50 men, 25 feet high to work in mud 18 feet deep."

Drenched and dispirited, the Army of the Potomac slogged back into camp to conclude what both sides derided as "the Mud March," and with this ludicrous maneuver to cap the holocaust of Fredericksburg, Ambrose Burnside was relieved of his command.

46

■

Stones River/Murfreesboro

F OUR COMMANDERS of Union armies in the East—McDowell, McClellan, Pope and now Burnside—had found that the magnet of Richmond was actually the blade of a guillotine, and as the year 1862 ended with the disaster at Fredericksburg it seemed to the North that the sun was still shining South. Since the Republican election setback in November the Peace Democrats had been steadily gaining strength, and in the Northwest war weariness had become so widespread that Lincoln was told he must open the Mississippi or face a demand for a negotiated peace.

It was to the West, then, that the eyes of the Union turned. There, Grant with his Army of the Tennessee was poised to move against Vicksburg in the campaign that would make a Federal stream of the Father of Waters and cut the Confederacy in two. Just below Nashville, Tennessee, was William Rosecrans with his Army of the Cumberland.

Old Rosy, as he was called by his troops, was a tall, heavy-set man with a red face and a big baroque, even redder nose. He was actually fond of his men, regularly inspecting their mess shacks or talking to them as they stood in line for chow. At reviews, he would rein in his horse to give them advice on how best to kill Johnny Rebs. "It's not the number of bullets you shoot but the accuracy of aim that kills men in battle. . . . When you meet the enemy, fire low. . . . Never turn your backs to the foe—cowards are sure to get shot."

He had a habit of strolling through camp after lights-out, and if he saw a light burning he would whack the tent canvas with the flat of his sword. Sometimes the men inside would shout profanities in reply, feigning surprise when Rosecrans's red face and bulbous nose came poking through the tent flap, pretending that they thought it was a sutler or a drunken wagoneer who had pounded the tent canvas, and apologizing profusely. Old Rosy was not taken in by such burlesque, especially not after he heard the muffled laughter after the light went out, but he would walk away chuckling. His refusal to be furious endeared him to his men. His officers also found him friendly and approachable, although some of them dreaded those late-night sessions around the mess table when Rosecrans, a heavy drinker but a devout Catholic withal, carrying a crucifix on his watch chain, would expound upon such theological distinctions as the difference between profanity, which he considered harmless, and blasphemy, which horrified him; or else, more subtly, discuss the Principle of the Excluded Middle: between mutually contradictory opposites there can be no middle ground. Rosecrans had studied his profession seriously—having been graduated from West Point fifth in his class of 1838—and possessed a vast store of theoretical knowledge of war. Like Beauregard, he was inclined to view actual combat with a classroom mind. In battle he became restless, his voice rising so in excitement that he could hardly be understood.

He was aware that his predecessor Buell had fallen from grace because he did not share Lincoln's passion to possess east Tennessee, but after a few weeks of reading Halleck's importunate demands to get going in that direction he began to sympathize with Don Carlos's complaint that such a campaign was much easier to plan in Washington than to execute in the Volunteer State. So he concentrated at Nashville, about thirty miles above Bragg at Murfreesboro, reaching a strength of about 82,000 men; and on the day after Christmas, 1862, he began marching in that direction with about 44,000 men comprising three corps under Crittenden, McCook and Thomas.*

This was about half his real strength, but because he was moving over enemy terrain infested by such skillful cavalry leaders as Nathan Bedford Forrest and John Morgan, he was compelled to detach units to hold bridges in his rear and guard his supply line and wagon trains. To do so he drew upon all three corps commanders, but most heavily on Thomas, much to Old Pap's dismay. Thomas had not forgotten that but for his generosity to Buell his relationship with Old Rosy might have been reversed: Thomas commanding the Army of the Cumberland, Rosecrans leading a corps.

Braxton Bragg, the martinet commanding the Army of the Tennessee in Murfreesboro, had also been graduated fifth in his West Point class, but there the resemblance between himself and cheerful Old Rosy came to an end, for this sixth four-star general in the Confederate army was far and

*For a map of central Tennessee and Murfreesboro, see page 396.

away the most dour, disputatious, dyspeptic, and devoted executioner of wayward soldiers ever to wear the Rebel gray. Superstition might suggest that all these doleful qualities were due to the circumstances of Bragg's birth. His mother, Margaret Crosland Bragg, while pregnant with Braxton had killed a freed black who had acted "biggity" toward her, and although she was jailed in Warrenton, North Carolina, on a charge of murder she was never brought to trial, being released from prison just in time to give birth to a baby boy on March 21, 1817. More likely, Bragg's grim personality—a match for his scowling, iron-gray visage—might have derived from the constant ill health which had afflicted him since youth, most of which was probably psychosomatic, for his illnesses only appeared when he was depressed or frustrated. These moods, in turn, derived from his passion for perfection: when he failed to achieve it, despondency followed. Authoritarian himself, he was forever challenging his superiors, often dipping his pen in acid to criticize them in literary or military journals.

As a young lieutenant commanding a company he was also the post quartermaster. As company commander he submitted a requisition for supplies which, as quartermaster, he rejected. Resubmitting it with additional reasons for his needs, he changed hats again to deny it. Finally he took the dispute to the post commander, who needed but a glance at the correspondence to cry aloud: "My God, Mr. Bragg, you have quarreled with every officer in the army, and now you are quarreling with yourself!" While commanding an artillery battery with Taylor at Buena Vista history books of the time credited him with turning the tide after Old Rough 'n Ready said: "A little more grape, Mr. Bragg." Taylor himself later is supposed to have insisted that he said something more like, "Whither the haste, Mr. Bragg?" It was also said that in Mexico one of his men exploded a twelve-pound shell under his cot, blowing the bed to bits but not even scratching Bragg.

In 1856 Bragg resigned from the army to become a sugar planter in Louisiana. In March 1861 he was appointed a Confederate brigadier general. Before Shiloh he established his reputation as a disciplinarian, and during it earned another one as a fighter. But both such abilities combined were certainly not enough to put three more gold stars on his shoulders. Rather what was needed was his close friendship with his great benefactor, Jefferson Davis. Bragg was delighted when Davis came to Murfreesboro during his first western tour, his arrival coinciding with the good news from Fredericksburg, which he regarded as vindication of his strategy of a defensive stance. The Confederate president enjoyed the Christmas festivities at Murfreesboro, a red-hot Rebel town where gallant soldiers and pretty girls in crinoline sang such stirring songs as "The Bonny Blue Flag" or danced to the sentimental strains of "Lorena". The high point of the season was the wedding of thirty-seven-year-old John Morgan, the fabled cavalry leader, to young Martha Ready, daughter of a Tennessee member of the Confederate Congress, who had resolved to marry Morgan before even setting eyes on him. They were married by Leonidas Polk, turning bishop again for the occasion, after which Bragg permitted Morgan to gallop off on another of those flamboyant but often useless raids characteristic of both sides. This deprived Bragg of the services of about 4,000 hard fighters. Then to his dismay friend Davis decided that John Pemberton in Vicksburg needed more troops—which could come only from Bragg. With surprising grace Bragg agreed to send a division to the Mississippi, but Joe Johnston, recovered from his Seven Pines wound and now in Chattanooga to coordinate the movements of Pemberton and Bragg, protested that it was like robbing Peter to pay Paul. But Davis was adamant, although the transfer would not be made before the end of the year.

Bragg had other difficulties. Hardee and Price were the only experienced major generals left to him in direct charge of troops, and he had to train and toughen raw troops to flesh out formations bled white at Shiloh or weakened by pestilence at Corinth. Besides this there was an upsurge of desertion, probably in good part due to his harsh discipline. Bragg always believed that the best warning for deserters should come from the twelve little round mouths of a firing squad, and accordingly one of his soldiers could write: "Almost every day we would hear a discharge of musketry, and knew that some poor trembling wretch had bid farewell to mortal things here below." Another said of Bragg: "He loved to crush the spirit of his men. The more of a hangdog look they had about them the better was General Bragg pleased. Not a single soldier in the whole army ever loved or respected him." With 38,000 of these unloving soldiers, then, Braxton Bragg decided to attack Rosecrans's 44,000 at Stones River a few miles outside of Murfreesboro.

On December 30 Rosecrans's scouts sighted Bragg's army drawn up outside town. Hardee was on the left and Polk on the right, both west of icy Stones River. Breckinridge's division detached from Hardee was on the other side of the stream, an awkward arrangement explicable only in that Bragg planned to use it strictly as a reserve. Rosecrans at once deployed: McCook on the right, Thomas in the center and Crittenden on the left. A brigade crossed the river to watch Breckinridge. Both generals planned to strike with their left at the enemy's right, which meant that the first to move might hold the advantage.

Night came down cold and miserable. The ground was wet and the shivering soldiers of both sides lighted fires to stay warm. Rosecrans decided to deceive Bragg into thinking his right was very strong by lighting campfires two miles beyond McCook's men. Bragg fell for the ruse, but in a way that backfired upon Rosecrans. He made his left immensely strong. When dawn broke cold and sullen, McCook's men farthest right came blinking awake to behold a great gray mass approaching from the south. Four columns of a brigade each supported by a big reserve barely visible in the dim gray light behind them burst upon the Bluebellies with a great roar of artillery, a rattle of musketry and the yipping high cry of the Rebel yell. The effect was so sudden and devastating that a Federal battery limbering up to withdraw to higher ground was swept by an incredible volley that killed seventy-five horses, leaving the cannoneers unable to move a single gun and so terrified that they promptly fled. McCook's reserve a mile to the rear barely heard the sounds of battle before the front-line fugitives were in their midst spreading their infectious fear. Only the stubborn resistance of Phil Sheridan's division prevented Rosecrans's entire right from collapsing.

Now it was up to George Thomas. Old Pap had his two divisions posted on higher ground on what was once the center but now because of the rout of McCook was the Union right. As usual he was unshakable. Getting reinforcements from Crittenden, he not only held his ground but had his men pour out a fire on the Confederates so loud that Graybacks moving through cotton fields stopped to pluck the white balls and stuff them in their ears.

Rosecrans was everywhere, shouting commands. Beside him his chief of staff was beheaded by a cannon ball, his blood and brains splattering over Old Rosy's uniform. But he formed a new line chiefly from McCook's fugitive regiments so that ultimately the Federal front was like an arrow-head: right and left packed close together in a tight inverted V. There they held.

That night Rosecrans held a council of war. Thomas tilted back his chair and fell sound asleep, while the other chief commanders debated the next decision. The word "retreat" filtered into Old Pap's consciousness and he awoke to mutter, "This army can't retreat," before falling asleep once more. His word held. That night the men of both armies, forbidden to light fires, crouched chattering and shivering in the cold dark, morosely listening to the cries and groans of the wounded, preparing for the renewal of battle and perhaps the end of their young lives. But there was no fighting. Bragg, informed by scouts that the road to Nashville was noisy with the rattle of

Federal wagons, mistook the transfer of Rosecrans's wounded to carefully prepared hospitals in that city to be the sound of a Federal retreat, and had not prepared for battle. New Year's Day of 1863 was quiet. Next day Bragg ordered Breckinridge with four brigades to drive the Union far left back across the river. Although the former vice president protested that the assault would be suicidal, he obeyed—and Federal artillery massed on the other side of the stream shredded his formations. Seventy minutes and 1,700 casualties later, his gallant Bluegrassmen were back in their entrenchments. "My poor orphans!" Breckinridge sobbed. "My poor orphans!" That night Bragg ordered a full retreat to Tullahoma.

It is difficult to determine what was gained by the slaughter at Stones River/Murfreesboro. Federal losses were 1,677 killed, 7,543 wounded and 3,686 missing, for a total of 12,906; Confederate, 1,294 killed, 7,945 wounded and about 2,500 missing, for a total of 11,739—or a staggering 30 percent of the 82,000 men engaged. Because he possessed the field, Rosecrans properly claimed a victory, even though his casualties were greater, declaring: "Bragg's a good dog, but Hold Fast is better." Otherwise nothing substantial was gained. Both armies went into winter quarters and Bragg's forces still blocked Rosecrans's objective at Chattanooga.

47

■

Joe Hooker

O N JANUARY 23, 1863, President Abraham Lincoln made Joe Hooker the fifth choice in his search for the general who would lay the prize of Richmond at his feet—and in so doing placed the Army of the Potomac under the most colorful, controversial and contradictory commander in its history.

Hooker was a descendant of an old Massachusetts family, and the fifth in a row to be baptized Joseph. The first Joseph migrated from England in 1689, settling in Wenham, just north of Salem, where he prospered. The second moved on to Westford to become a wealthy farmer and landowner. The third served in the French and Indian Wars and chose to live in Greenwich, from which village he led a party of Minutemen to Cambridge in April of '75, later rising to captain in George Washington's army. He amassed a considerable fortune in real estate, but the fourth Joseph Hooker was not so fortunate in holding on to his share. After his first wife died, he moved to Hadley on the Connecticut River, hoping to recoup his losses with a fresh start in the west. He married Mary Seymour of Hadley, who bore him three daughters. Her fourth child, a healthy, handsome baby with blond ringlets, born November 13, 1814, was the fifth Joseph Hooker.

Joe, as he was always called, never knew anything of the Hooker family's luxurious life-style. By the time he was three the War of 1812 had devastated his father's dry-goods business and the family had to move from a comfortable, roomy house to a rented dwelling. Only the determination of Mary Hooker, and her children's willingness to work at odd jobs, kept the family together.

Mary Hooker was determined that her children should have a good education, and she sent them all to Hopkins Academy in Hadley, even though the tuition was $12 a year. Joe paid his own way from the money earned pressing hairpin-shaped wires into thin hardwood boards to be used in home wool-spinning. He had a quick mind but no love of study, although it developed that he had a resonant speaking voice. It seems his mother had hoped that he would enter the ministry. For himself, however, he appears to have chosen law.

But there was no money for such an education and it seemed that Joe would not go to college, until a teacher named Giles C. Kellogg suggested that he might get a free education at West Point. Kellogg persuaded Congressman George Grinnell from the Hadley district to secure an appointment for Joe, and then helped the youth to pass the examination. In June of 1833, at the age of eighteen, Joe Hooker arrived on the Plains.

It is probable that never before or since—and this includes Robert E. Lee and Douglas MacArthur—has a handsomer cadet than Joe Hooker appeared at West Point. "What a handsome fellow he was!" an officer who saw him after his graduation exclaimed. "Tall, straight, wavy light hair, blue eyes and a complexion a woman would envy, polished in manner, the perfection of grace in every movement, and with all, the courtesy of manner we attribute to an old-time gentleman. He was somewhat effeminate in freshness of complexion and color perhaps, but his figure was robust, and of good muscular development. He was simply elegant, . . ."

In the adjoining town of Highland Park Joe was called "the beautiful cadet," and yet for all of his seeming girlishness and exquisite manners— which might have derived from growing up under the direction of four women—there was no one at the academy more masculine than he. Nor more outspoken, as he demonstrated in frequent "discussions" of the slavery question between cadets of the South and North. His arguments usually prevailed, although his style—one part logic and one part invective—did not widen his circle of friends. In fact, although he was an excellent student at West Point, his belligerence and quickness to take offense earned him so many demerits that he was only twenty-ninth in a class of fifty when he was graduated in 1837.

Serving briefly in the Seminole War, he also was with General Winfield Scott in the so-called Timber War on the Canadian border. Because the boundary between Maine and New Brunswick was still poorly defined, lumberjacks of both sides frequently crossed axes in a dispute over timber. Scott's mission was to cool the hotheads while a commission successfully drew a line satisfactory to both parties.

For the next four years Hooker inspected 1st Artillery posts throughout New England, which brought him often to Fort Adams and fashionable Newport, a town full of beautiful, wealthy and unwed young ladies. It was also a natural for handsome Joe, but Hooker, always a free lance with the fairer sex, made no attempt to make the customary match between impecunious military glamor and well-bred wealth, refusing to surrender his cherished freedom.

In Mexico with both Taylor and Scott, he earned three brevets, raising his rank to lieutenant colonel. He became the de facto commander of the division officially commanded by Gideon Pillow, President Polk's friend and former law partner. Among the boldest and bravest, he almost lost this command at Churubusco when an enraged bull attacked him as he crossed a field on foot. Hooker fought him off with his saber, but even so the bull might have been the victor had not a soldier shot him dead.

Hooker became one of Scott's favorite young officers, but after the war he testified at a court of inquiry on behalf of General Pillow, who had conspired with Polk to relieve Scott of his command. Hooker did not criticize Scott, but his testimony helped to clear Pillow—a fact which the vindictive Old Fuss 'n Feathers never forgot.

Hooker was delighted to be transferred to California, which he believed to be the land of golden opportunity. But boredom soon led him to seek relief in poker, drink and the company of ladies of easy virtue, all to be found at the Blue Wing Tavern in Sonoma. He usually won at cards, but Phil Kearny and George Stoneman noticed his tendency to choke when the stakes were high. "He could play the best game of poker I ever saw," Stoneman recalled, "until it came to the point where he should go a thousand better, and then he would funk." Eventually, Hooker did tire of army life and his request for a two-year leave of absence was granted on November 24, 1851.

The Colonel, as he was frequently called, acquired title to 550 fertile acres near what is now Agua Caliente a few miles north and west of Sonoma. He built a small four-room house on the property and planted ten acres with wine grapes, dreaming, meanwhile, of becoming a wealthy rancher. But he knew nothing of viticulture and his wines were abominable, while the potatoes he planted next were only slightly better. So he secured an army contract to provide cordwood for posts in San Francisco, leaving the actual logging to his lumberjacks while alternating between the pleasures of the Blue Wing and hunting in the woods. One day he was attacked by a ferocious bear. He got off a hurried shot, but either missed or failed to stop the bear's charge. Man and beast grappled, rolling down the side of a canyon. Badly mauled, Hooker managed to break free and take refuge in the limbs of a huge redwood tree. Why the bear, a better climber, did not pursue is not known, but it is possible that he was wounded and wanted no more of Joe Hooker. That worthy, meanwhile, was also taking no chances, remaining in his perch until a rescue party arrived.

The Colonel had other predicaments: gambling debts and frequent lawsuits, neither adding to his reputation for honorable dealing or business acumen. He is supposed to have borrowed money from Halleck and Sherman, both then prospering in San Francisco, which he did not repay. True or not, both disliked him. Next he tried politics, but lost by thirteen votes as a Democratic candidate for the state assembly. Then from Oregon came a political plum as superintendent of military roads. He was back in California when war came, trying desperately to get back into uniform. But all of his requests were directed to Old Brains, whose thunderous silence was understood only too well by his former favorite. Out of funds as usual, he had no way to get to Washington to press his cause in person. Despondent, he drifted into Chapman's, a popular San Francisco restaurant, walking to the table Billy Chapman reserved for his friends. He slumped into a chair, sunk in dejection. Chapman came up to him.

"What's the matter, Colonel?"

"I was wishing that I was in the East," Hooker replied. "I'm a West Pointer, as you know, a trained soldier. I could be of use in this struggle, but here I am tied down to a ranch in California, merely because I lack funds to clear off some little debts and pay my expenses to Washington."

"How much would you need?"

After a moment's thought, Hooker said $700 would be enough. Chapman went to his office and returned holding a roll of bills.

"Here's a thousand, Colonel. Take it and go to the front. I wish I could go with you—but I am not quite willing to be a private, and they wouldn't give a commission to a faro dealer. The steamer sails day after tomorrow. I'll be at the wharf to see you off, and you needn't buy any liquor or cigars to keep you cheerful on the way. There will be a few necessaries of that sort in your stateroom."

Whether or not the money was a gift or a loan is not known, but Hooker took it with great joy. When the steamer sailed, he was aboard.

Upon arrival in the East, Hooker sought out Oregon's two senators, James W. Nesmith and Edward Dickinson Baker, Lincoln's dear friend who was killed at Ball's Bluff. Baker wrote to the president extolling Hooker's ability, and Lincoln forwarded the letter to General Scott's office. The end of the line. Next Hooker sought out Senator Sumner of his native state, seeking his support, which was forthcoming but also was stymied by Scott. After watching the debacle at Bull Run it was a morose Joe Hooker who accompanied George Cadwallader, on whose staff he had served in Mexico, to the White House. He was introduced to the president as "Captain" Hooker. Lincoln acknowledged the introduction and turned to move away. Hooker called after him.

"Mr. President, I was introduced to you as Captain Hooker. I am, or was, Lieutenant Colonel Hooker of the regular army. When this war broke out, I was at home in California, and hastened to make a tender of my services to the government. But my relation to General Scott, or some other impediment, stands in the way, and I now see no chance of making my military knowledge and experience useful. I am about to return, but before going, I was anxious to pay my respects to you, sir, and to express my wish for your personal welfare, and for your success in putting down the rebellion. And while I am about it, Mr. President, I want to say one thing more, and that is, that I was at the battle of Bull Run the other day, and it is neither vanity or boasting in me to declare that I am a damned sight better general than you, sir, had on that field."

Lincoln stared at Hooker searchingly. He seized his hand and told him to sit down, beginning to question him. Rising, Lincoln placed a hand on Hooker's shoulder, gazing down on him from his great height.

"Colonel—not lieutenant colonel—Hooker, stay. I have use for you and a regiment for you to command."

It was not a colonel's silver eagle but the gold star of a brigadier general of volunteers that Joe Hooker wore as a result of that fortuitous meeting. His political friends were also still active and soon Hooker rose from brigadier to a major general commanding a division. His bravery during the Peninsular Campaign earned him the nickname of "Fighting Joe" Hooker, although it has also been maintained that the nickname was the result of a New York printer's error. When a late dispatch arrived from the front, a copy editor quickly keyed it to a running story slugged "Fighting" and then added "—Joe Hooker." The printer dropped the dash and thus it became headed "Fighting Joe Hooker." Hooker himself detested the sobriquet, saying: "Don't call me Fighting Joe. [It] makes the public think that I am a hot-headed, furious young fellow, accustomed to making furious and needless dashes at the enemy." Lincoln may have detected something of this quality in his latest Potomac chief when he wrote perhaps the most extraordinary letter of promotion ever composed by a commander in chief:

> I have placed you at the head of the Army of the Potomac. Of course I have done this upon what appears to me to be sufficient reasons, and yet I think it best for you to know that there are some things in regard to which I am

not quite satisfied with you. I believe you to be a brave and skillful soldier, which, of course, I like. I also believe you do not mix politics with your profession, in which you are right. You have confidence in yourself, which is a valuable, if not an indispensable, quality. You are ambitious, which, within reasonable bounds, does good rather than harm; but I think that during General Burnside's command of the army you have taken counsel of your ambition, and thwarted him as much as you could, in which you did a great wrong to the country and to a most meritorious and honorable brother officer. I have heard, in such a way as to believe it, of your recently saying that both the Army and the Government needed a dictator. Of course, it was not for this, but in spite of it, that I have given you the command. Only those generals who gain successes can set up dictators. What I now ask of you is military success, and I will risk the dictatorship. The Government will support you to the utmost of its ability, which is neither more nor less than it has done or will do for all commanders. I much fear that the spirit which you have aided to infuse into the army, of criticizing their commander and withholding confidence from him, will now turn upon you. I shall assist you as far as I can to put it down. Neither you nor Napoleon, if he were alive again, could get any good out of an army while such a spirit prevails in it. And now beware of rashness. Beware of rashness, but with energy and sleepless vigilance go forward and give us victories.

To Lincoln's gratified surprise, Hooker proved himself a superb organizer and a great favorite with the men. The president, satisfied that Hooker was a fighter, had added a reservation: "But whether he can 'keep tavern' for a large army is not so sure." Joe Hooker could indeed keep tavern. Within a single week after taking command he had ordered his army's rations expanded to include fresh vegetables and soft bread, had decreased sickness and depression by cleaning up the unsanitary camps, and by instituting a generous furlough system and tightening security had reduced desertion. "Ah! the furloughs and vegetables he gave us!" one veteran later recalled. "How he did understand the road to a soldier's heart!" He even brought army paymasters with bulging money bags into his camp near Falmouth to surprise his men with six months' back pay, and that alone sufficed to end all grumbling and discontent. Ennui, that stifler of the soldier's soul, was displaced by esprit after Hooker revived McClellan's policy of grand reviews. Unit pride rose even higher with his introduction of the so-called Kearny shoulder patch—a device the late Phil Kearny had used to identify and inspirit his division—for the entire army. Corps insignia of various shapes, cut from red, white or blue cloth to indicate first, second, or third division, were sewn to the crown of forage caps. Thus the regiments swinging by the reviewing stand where their handsome, pink-cheeked, clean-shaven commander stood, could earn his praise or scorn for the smart or sloppy way they executed the command "Eyes right!" or their precision or lack of it in shifting gleaming, bayoneted rifles from shoulder to shoulder. No mistake about it, these Union soldiers loved Fighting Joe Hooker, even for his complexion "as delicate and silken as a woman's," and they hooted down those caustic critics who said Hooker shaved because he thought it made him look like Alexander, and when his roseate glow was traced to the bottle, they took it as a compliment, singing:

> "Joe Hooker is our leader—
> He takes his whiskey strong!"

Actually, it may have been that Hooker swore off drink the day he took command of the Army of the Potomac. At least a close friend who was with him almost daily contended that even if Fighting Joe's headquarters might resemble a barroom, as was often charged, Hooker himself did not imbibe. But he still liked the ladies, or at least that was what one of his cavalry officers—Charles Francis Adams, Jr., son of the minister to England, grandson and great-grandson of presidents—maintained with the priggishness of a typical Yankee Puritan. Adams excoriated Hooker as "a noisy, low-toned intriguer" whose headquarters was "a place to which no self-respecting man liked to go, and no decent women could go. It was a combination barroom and brothel." Perhaps. Even probably. Certainly Hooker's name has entered the dictionary as a synonym for a whore or woman of easy virtue, as well as a shot of whiskey, and one could well blink in surprise at his choices for chief of staff and commander of a corps:

Dan Butterfield and Dan Sickles.

48

■

The Two Dans:
Butterfield and Sickles

HOOKER AT FIRST had asked the War Department to assign Brigadier General Charles P. Stone to him as chief of staff. Stanton was aghast at this attempt to resuscitate the ruined career of this first martyr to the venomous hatred of the Joint Committee to Conduct the War. Actually, it is surprising that Hooker had the moral courage even to suggest it, but once he learned how offensive this choice would be to the radical Republicans, he shook the wind out of his sails and settled for Brigadier General Daniel Butterfield, a stocky little ex-militia officer from New York who was politically safe. He was also a breezy, self-indulgent bon vivant of the Blue Wing Tavern cast, who had no particular qualifications for such a decisive post, except that Hooker liked him. He also had an unsuspected musical streak.

Butterfield had early noticed that brigade calls played too close to other brigades sometimes created confusion, so he composed his own recognition call: two whole notes followed by a triplet. The troops, as always put words to it: "Dan—Dan—Butterfield!" Butterfield also disliked the lights-out drum call, finding it unmusical and preferring a poignant, bitter-sweet bugle call signifying the end of the cares of day. Calling a bugler into his tent he whistled a little tune to him and asked him to play it on his horn. The bugler, a bit startled by such an order from a general, nevertheless obeyed. Unsatisfied, Butterfield did more whistling until he finally struck the right notes, whereupon the bugler wrote them down upon the back of an envelope—and thus was born "Taps," that sad, keening, unforgettable bugle call that ends a soldier's day. Whether the name came from the "taps" of the original drum beat, or from the "tap-to" bugle call closing the taverns each night in a little town in the Pyrenees, as is also maintained, or even if it was original with Butterfield, is not known; but "Taps" is now known the world over as the call that puts American servicemen to sleep

427

each night, or eternally in their graves.

Thus Dan Butterfield's contribution—quite different from that of Dan Sickles.

Daniel Edgar Sickles was the only child of George Everett Sickles, a clever New York patent lawyer, politician and up-and-down financial entrepreneur who traced his ancestry back six generations to a Dutch immigrant to New Amsterdam named van Sicklen. His wife, Susan Marsh Sickles, was a devout Episcopalian and a woman of uncommon gentleness and warmth. A few years after Dan appeared on October 20, 1819—that is, as soon as he was able to speak and make his wishes known—the Sickles realized with dismay that he was an incredibly willful child.

Dan was what today is called "a fresh kid" who wanted his own way come what may and so resented corporal punishment that he would run away to escape it. As he grew into a handsome though smallish boy with bright blue eyes and beautiful thick chestnut hair he drove his parents to distraction as he alternated between furious insubordination—probably because as an overindulged only child he knew he could get away with it—and a warm amiability spiced by wit. He was also audacious and bright enough to convince them that if he could learn to control himself he would go very far in life. So at fifteen they sent him to an academy in Glens Falls specializing in the burring and polishing of such rough diamonds, except that when this one was rebuked by the master he lashed out at him in a rage and quit school.

Dan did not return home but took a job as a printer's devil, thus beginning his on-again, off-again affair with the Fourth Estate as it either provided him with his livelihood or condemned his style of life. Although Dan's propensity for sampling the fleshpots of New York and Philadelphia was his father's daily despair, he at last consented to return home to pursue a college education at New York University. With characteristic impulsiveness he soon left college, and in 1840 he entered the law office of a prominent New York firm and was admitted to the bar in 1843. In one of his early cases—heard in Washington by a board headed by Daniel Webster—he was praised by Webster for his presentation.

But his reputation for rectitude did not equal his renown as a pleader. He was an unabashed womanizer and had been indicted three times on accusations relating to the misuse of clients' funds, and although he was never prosecuted it was rumored that his father's money or his political influence had squelched the charges.

About this time Dan entered politics, which meant, of course, the

Democratic Party and Tammany Hall, and in 1847 he was elected to the state assembly in spite of having been prosecuted on charges of stealing a mortgage. A directed verdict of acquittal based on a technicality seems not to have damaged him too severely. But when he brought his mistress, a beautiful prostitute named Fanny White, to Albany with him he scandalized many friends, and then lost a few more by introducing her at the hotel table and escorting her into the assembly chamber.

Although Dan seemed to have straightened out in 1852 after he married the beautiful sixteen-year-old Teresa Bagioli—seventeen years his junior—Fanny was with him again when he sailed to England as secretary to James Buchanan, the U.S. minister to Great Britain. He brought her along at one of Queen Victoria's receptions, introducing her as "Miss Bennett of New York City" and thus taking a satisfying revenge on his bitter enemy, James Gordon Bennett, publisher of the New York *Herald*. But he also so impressed Ambassador Buchanan with his ability that when "Old Buck" ran for president of the United States Dan was on the same ticket as a candidate for the House.

After Buchanan entered the White House, Representative Sickles became his Grand Almoner. Among those whom he favored was Philip Barton Key, U.S. attorney for the District of Columbia. A word from him to Buchanan saved Key's job. Tall, handsome, socially prominent as the son of Francis Scott Key, composer of "The Star-Spangled Banner" and nephew of Supreme Court Chief Justice Roger Taney, Key was also perhaps a more successful seducer of women than Sickles. His boast was that he needed only thirty-six hours with any woman to have his way with her. It was soon validated after Key volunteered to lead the lonely Teresa (Dan was again busy with other ladies) through the Washington social whirl. From being her escort he became her lover.

Sickles eventually learned of the affair. Confronting his hysterical wife, he compelled her to sign a written, detailed confession, after which he took from her his wedding ring. Then he prepared to deal with Key. His opportunity came when he saw Key outside his mansion focusing a small opera glass on Teresa's window and waving a white handkerchief. A maniacal scream burst from his throat and he ran outside clutching a pistol. Overtaking Key outside the National Club on Lafayette Square, he shouted:

"Key, you scoundrel, you have dishonored my bed—you must die!"

His first shot missed, and Key ducked behind a tree, crying, "Don't shoot!" Sickles steadied his aim and Key drew his opera glass from his pocket and hurled it at him. It struck Sickles harmlessly and fell to the ground. Dan's next shot staggered Key. He screamed and pitched forward into the gutter, still begging for mercy. Sickles fired again, perhaps twice more—and then walked up to the quivering Key to aim point-blank at his head and pull the trigger. But the gun misfired. By then horrified passersby hastened to restrain Sickles. Key was carried unconscious into the National Club nearby and a few minutes later he was dead.

The murder trial of Daniel Sickles was probably the most sensational in the history of American jurisprudence, and also came the closest to becoming a travesty. Old Buck Buchanan quickly came to the side of his friend, first frightening a page boy who could have been an important government witness into hurrying home to North Carolina, then elevating the slain man's assistant, Robert Ould, to be U.S. attorney charged with prosecuting the case. Against this plump, mild, courtroom clod, a man obviously convinced that to win was to lose his job, came eight of Washington's best lawyers, headed by Edwin McMasters Stanton. True, a second lawyer to help Ould was hired by friends of Key, but the trial was still an egregious legal mismatch, especially after it became apparent that Stanton el al intended to put Key on trial for adultery, rather than Sickles for murder. They also contended that their client was so overcome by grief and rage that he could not be held accountable for his actions: the first such insanity defense in American legal annals. Finally, they repeatedly spoke of the "unwritten law" justifying the killing of "the defiler of the marriage bed."

Ould might have countered with a searching inquiry into Sickles's own background, to argue that he had killed a man for doing to him what he had done to other men. But he did not, making it pathetically patent that the prosecutor's heart was not in his work and that the verdict was almost foreordained: not guilty.

And then Dan Sickles took Teresa back.

Incredible as it sounded to America, and especially to New York and Washington, Dan had forgiven his wife and restored her to his bed. The wedding ring he had once returned to her broken as a symbol of rejection was once again on her finger rejoined. Dan had done this knowing full well that it meant the end of his political career, but he had never anticipated the storm of denunciation that would swirl around his head, or the verdict of ostracism that was now pronounced against him. He sat silently and alone in the House like a carrier of the plague bacillus, a pariah and a moral leper. He made no attempt to run for reelection in 1860; and then, the shots fired at Sumter saved him from oblivion.

■   ■   ■

At the outbreak of the war Dan Sickles was working in his father's law office. He was unhappy. To be just another successful lawyer, no matter how lucrative, did not satisfy this one-of-a-kind human being in his search for singularity. Moreover, the reunion with Teresa had been a failure. Despairing at having ruined her husband's career, she had become addicted to opiates. One day at Delmonico's Dan was discussing the war with Tammany cronies when Captain William Wiley offered to raise a regiment if Dan would lead it. Sickles agreed and soon he had a brigade and a star on his shoulder put there by the Republican governor, Edwin Morgan. In May 1861 they quarreled, and Morgan, seeking the star for a loyal Republican, ordered Sickles to disband his formation. He refused and went to Washington to ask Lincoln to accept his men as volunteers. Lincoln liked the idea, but said: "What will the governors say if I raise regiments without their having a hand in it?" Nevertheless, Lincoln was anxious to get able men of all persuasions behind the war effort and he told the Democrat Sickles to keep his men together until they could be accepted.

Returning to New York, Sickles found his creditors and official Albany arrayed against him. Demands for immediate payment of the debts incurred in feeding and clothing his Excelsior Brigade mingled with complaints from the police that his men were unruly and from the Board of Health that they were filthy and verminous. Forced out of the city, he found quarters on Staten Island, where he began to lose men to malaria and desertion. But then came Bull Run, compelling Lincoln and his cabinet to accept the reality of a prolonged war. From Secretary of War Cameron came a call to Washington, and on July 22, 1861, Sickles and his Excelsior Brigade entrained for the capital.

There it was assigned to Hooker's division, and Sickles began his friendship with Fighting Joe. Eventually he won another star and a division, fighting bravely in the Peninsular Campaign. When Hooker scrapped Burnside's unwieldy grand divisions and reorganized his army into seven infantry and one cavalry corps, he gave the III Infantry Corps to his crony, Sickles. In his blue uniform with his immaculate big white gauntlets, his full chestnut mustache, trim Van Dyke and his braided little forage cap, Dan Sickles cut a fine military figure. But what he really knew about the military art would not be known until Fighting Joe Hooker, moving his army south toward Richmond, collided with Robert E. Lee.

49

■

Kelly's Ford:
The Funk of Fighting Joe

M Y PLANS are perfect," Fighting Joe Hooker boasted with a ballooning self-confidence that dismayed Abraham Lincoln. "And when I carry them out, may God have mercy on Bobby Lee—for I shall have none."

To do this he would strike him with what he had already called "the finest army on this planet" and "the finest body of soldiers the sun ever shone on." Such braggadocio, the chief executive knew from sorrowful experience, might as likely camouflage a lack of confidence as spring from an excess of it; and yet, Hooker's plan was indeed, when compared to the bloody, bull-like charges of his predecessor Burnside, a model of maneuver. He had very quickly decided against the obvious tactic of crossing the Rappahannock well below Fredericksburg, because this (1) would uncover Washington and upset Lincoln; (2) would by the necessary laying of pontoons announce his intention in advance; and thus (3) by sending his troops up against a prepared and well-entrenched enemy once again soak that fatal Fredericksburg ridge incarnadine with Yankee blood. And Lee was more than just well entrenched. On a front stretching twenty-five miles from Port Royal to Banks's Ford, even though outnumbered about 120,000 to 60,000, he was nothing less than impregnable. Along the lower slopes of the hills ran zigzag lines of shortened, squad-size rifle trenches which were made mutually supporting by traverses and designed to guard against flank attacks and all but a direct hit by that matchless Union artillery. Sited above them were Confederate guns commanding all approaches. Where the line ran over open plain it was linked by formidable redoubts. So strong was this bristling crescent covering Fredericksburg and all the nearby river crossings that one young student of the Napoleonic Wars could murmur: "The famous lines at Torres Vedras could not compare to them."

Even to get at Lee, Hooker must first cross the broad Rappahannock, now running swift and swollen with the spring rains. Upstream, however, the river narrowed and there were shallow fords there: Banks's Ford five miles above the town and United States Ford seven miles farther west. Hooker reasoned that if he could march to these crossings undetected, he might overwhelm the light detachments holding them and force Lee to swing about to face him without the advantage of his fortifications, plus the disadvantage of maneuvering against a foe twice his strength. Also, Hooker hoped to move against the Confederate commander's communications by sending a huge force of cavalry into his rear.

In this he demonstrated a warranted confidence in his own reorganization of his mounted arm. "Hooker *made* the Federal cavalry," an admiring trooper said, and it was true. Up until Fighting Joe took them in hand, the Union horsemen could not compare to their hardy opponents, trained in the saddle since childhood. The Rebel riders' scathing contempt for these "white-faced clerks and counter-jumpers" was indeed justified, and the bungling way they were handled by the Union regimental commanders to whom they were assigned piecemeal beggars description. At first these Yankee riders had been mounted on crow-bait nags supplied by crooked contractors. Scarcely knowing the on- from the off-side of their horses, they had controlled them with clucking or cries of "Whoa!" or "Git up!" or "Go-long, there!" rather than with bit and spurs like those true troopers from Dixie. But after Stanton cleansed the Yankee stables of the equine refuse collected there and chased or jailed the dishonest traders who had so stocked them, while putting the fear of his little bell in the hearts of venal purchasing agents; and after the ungainly Yankee horsemen had gradually evolved into trained riders, Hooker was able to field a single force of about 11,500 troopers mounted on 13,000 well-fed, strong-limbed, and sound-winded beasts.

Oddly enough, quite the opposite had happened to Lee's famous mounted arm under the redoubtable Jeb Stuart. By the spring of 1863 there was a critical shortage of horses in the Army of Northern Virginia. Worse, there was also a lack of fodder, so that those beasts that had survived the campaigning and attrition of winter were in danger of dying. So calamitous were these twin erosions that four hundred artillery horses procured in Georgia that winter had to be kept in North Carolina, far from the critical northern battleground, because there was so little forage available in Virginia. An exchanged Union officer has described these animals: "Their artillery horses are poor, starved frames of beasts, tied to their carriages and caissons with odds and ends of rope and strips of raw hide . . ."

On March 17 the deteriorated state of the Confederate cavalry, and the improvement of the Federal horse, was made evident in the St. Patrick's Day battle between mounted Bluebellies under William Wood Averell, who had crossed the Rappahannock at Kelly's Ford, and a detachment of Graybacks which Fitzhugh Lee, Marse Robert's fiercely combative nephew, had led north to intercept them. Once again old West Point friends were meeting in combat, and this time it was the Federals who gave more than they got: 133 Confederate casualties to their own 78. They also killed Major John Pelham, the gallant and handsome young hero of Fredericksburg, bringing grief to Robert E. Lee and causing many a Southern belle to put on mourning. Actually, this first triumph of Union cavalry might have been a Confederate rout had Averell been the aggressive commander whom Hooker thought he had in Brigadier General George Stoneman.

Stoneman was a West Pointer who at forty had spent most of his army career as a leader of mounted troops. His brief service with the infantry had won him a brevet for bravery at Fredericksburg, but now he commanded Hooker's cavalry corps, three divisions strong. He had one less star than Fighting Joe's seven other corps commanders because the army chief was withholding promotion until Stoneman could prove himself capable of carrying out his assignment in the attack upon Lee. This was to cross Rappahannock Bridge and Beverly Ford about thirty miles above Fredericksburg on the morning of April 13, 1863, with his entire corps less one brigade and all of his twenty-two guns "for the purpose of turning the enemy's position on his left, throwing the cavalry between him and Richmond, isolating him from his supplies, checking his retreat, and inflicting on him every possible injury which will tend to his discomfort and defeat." Stoneman was also told: "If you cannot cut off from [the enemy's] column large slices, the general desires that you will not fail to take small ones. Let your watchword be fight, fight, fight, bearing in mind that time is as valuable to the general as rebel carcasses."

Stoneman took no slices and did no fighting. At the ford he found the opposite bank strongly held, but by no means firmly enough to deter his 10,000 troopers. Yet he hesitated, and while he did, the rains came drumming down and the river rose black and writhing, and now Stoneman thanked God that he had not crossed, because that would put an impassable torrent at his rear with an equally torrential Rapidan to his front.

Chagrined and outraged, Hooker told Stoneman to stay where he was until the rains stopped, and then drive south. But the rains did not stop, persisting for nearly two weeks. During that period, Hooker swallowed his disappointment like a true commanding general and came up with an even better plan. Banks's Ford and U.S. Ford, the crossings closest to Lee, were too heavily defended for a turning movement against Marse Robert's left. But Averell had found that Kelly's Ford fifteen miles above the junction of the Rappahannock and the Rapidan—which occurred one mile above U.S. Ford—was unfortified and comparatively shallow. Once the Rappahannock subsided it could be forded by men on foot and horses drawing wagons and guns. It was also far enough away from Lee's left flank to encourage Hooker to hope that half his army could reach it undetected. While the other half massed around Banks's and U.S. fords to give Lee the impression that it was the main body preparing for the major assault, this flanking force—after making another crossing at the Rapidan—could debouch into a heavily wooded area known as the Wilderness and move under cover of the trees into Lee's rear. As the flankers marched they would uncover both U.S. and Banks's fords, thus shortening Hooker's lines of communication and putting the two halves of the Army of the Potomac within reinforcing range of each other should some emergency arise. Also, the high ground at Banks's dominated Lee's position behind Fredericksburg. Should all go well, Lee would be compelled to do what by his skillful generalship he had so far avoided: come out and fight on open ground against a superior foe.

No more daring—even dazzling—plan had ever been devised in the American Civil War, before or since. Hooker realized that he was dividing his army—one of the cardinal sins of military doctrine—but Robert Edward Lee had shown so often that the profits of this transgression could outweigh the risks; and besides, each of the halves of Hooker's divided army was superior to Lee's 54,000 scarecrows. Moreover, one of Lee's two best corps commanders—Longstreet, with two divisions—was on temporarily independent command in southern Virginia and North Carolina.

On April 26 Fighting Joe ordered the corps of Henry W. Slocum, O. O. Howard and George Meade, with Slocum in overall command, to march for Kelly's Ford the following day, and to be ready to cross the Rappahannock by 4 P.M. on the twenty-eighth. Then the flankers would move south to the Rapidan, crossing at Ely's and Germanna fords to pass through the Wilderness, debouching into the open at Chancellorsville, ten miles west of Lee's left flank. Meanwhile, Darius Couch's corps—minus Gibbon's division, which, in plain view of the Rebels on Marye's Heights, dared not move and thus alert the enemy—would move out at dawn of the twenty-ninth to a position behind Banks's Ford, standing ready to cross via pontoon bridge once Slocum's flankers had flushed Lee out of his position. Opposite Lee another 60,000 Federals in the corps of John Sedgwick, John Reynolds and Dan Sickles—with Sedgwick commanding—would move down to the riverbank opposite Fredericksburg where Franklin had crossed in December and establish a west-bank bridgehead in full view of Lee. This demonstration was intended to distract Marse Robert from his vulnerable rear and perplex him as to where the major blow would fall. Stoneman was to multiply his doubts by striking first at the Virginia Central Railroad and then following the Richmond, Fredericksburg & Potomac eastward to interpose his cavalry between Lee's army and Richmond should the Confederate commander attempt to escape the closing jaws of Hooker's vise by falling back on his capital.

Thus Hooker's plan in detail, thorough and even brilliant, except for one vital defect not immediately apparent. This was that in assigning Stoneman with the bulk of the cavalry to strike at Lee's communications, he was leaving himself almost blind to enemy movements. Otherwise it not only looked great on paper—as most plans do—but actually worked on earth. Slocum's blue-coated soldiers were in high spirits as they stepped out from their camps around Falmouth, singing while their bands played "The Girl I Left Behind Me". Even so acerbic a man as George Meade, given more to criticism than compliment, was as high-hearted as a twelve-year-old on the last day of school when he rode into the hundred-acre clearing in the Wilderness and saw the brick-and-timber, porticoed Chancellor House standing alone among its out-buildings to give this tiny, no-count crossroads hamlet its grandiloquent name of Chancellorsville. When his chief arrived at 2 P.M. on the thirtieth Meade cried: "This is splendid, Slocum! Hurrah for old Joe! We are on Lee's flank and he doesn't know it!" It was true. Hooker's meticulous attention to detail, his strict secrecy, his marching discipline and his demonstration opposite Lee had all contributed to one of the finest maneuvers in military history. Meade was so enthusiastic that he wanted to plunge back eastward into the Wilderness so as to be out of that tangle of trees and vines and underbrush by nightfall and halve the distance between the flankers in Lee's rear and Sedgwick on his front. Slocum agreed, but as they talked a courier rode up with a dispatch signed by Butterfield declaring: "The general directs that no advance be made from Chancellorsville until the columns are concentrated. He expects to be at Chancellorsville tonight."

Crestfallen, Meade, along with Slocum and Howard, began putting his troops into bivouac. A few hours later, lusty cheers rippling along the turnpike into the clearing signaled the arrival of General Hooker, radiant and jubilant astride a big, milk-white horse. At once he explained his restraining order to his corps commanders. Their eastern advance had succeeded in flushing the Rebel defenders out of U.S. Ford, enabling Couch to move upstream to cross the river there. He was now on the march for

Chancellorsville, with Gibbon following in his tracks. That would put four entire corps in Lee's rear, and a fifth would be added when Sickles in reserve also made for Chancellorsville. With cavalry and other arms, Hooker would now have 80,000 men in back of the unsuspecting Army of Northern Virginia, with Sedgwick and 60,000 more to its front. Next day— May Day—would see the destruction of that army front and rear in a great victory that could end the war. That night Hooker's eve-of-battle order was read to his troops:

"It is with heartfelt satisfaction that the commanding general announces to the army that the operations of the last three days have determined that our enemy must either ingloriously fly, or come out from behind his defenses and give us battle on our own ground, where certain destruction awaits him."

The dire alternatives of "Mr. F. J. Hooker," as Lee called his Yankee opponent, had not exactly occurred to Marse Robert on that momentous morning of April 29, when a courier from Stonewall Jackson awoke him with the news that the Bluebellies massed at Franklin's Crossing were putting pontoon bridges over the Rappahannock. Instead, as he peered through the rifts of the early morning fog, watching Sedgwick's men expanding their bridgehead, he felt an almost irresistible urge to attack them before they could complete their buildup. But then, mindful of those long-range Union guns positioned on Stafford Heights, and of the folly of coming out of such an impregnable position to challenge them, he decided instead to remain on the defensive as he had done in December, hoping that the Yankees had not lost their fatal penchant for perishing under his guns. So he told Jackson to bring up the rest of his corps from below and notified Richmond to alert Longstreet with his two divisions for movement north from Suffolk. Shortly before noon he received word from Jeb Stuart that an enemy force of about 14,000 men with artillery had crossed Kelly's Ford and appeared to be headed for Gordonsville to the southwest. A few hours later Stuart reported that the enemy column was headed for Ely's and Germanna fords. Realizing that the Federals were between him and his cavalry, Lee immediately ordered Stuart to come eastward to join him. Although this would leave the enemy horse free to operate against his lines of supply, Lee did not want to be fighting blind against a hostile force appearing to be moving toward his rear. This supposition was confirmed just before sundown with the arrival of a third courier reporting the Federals over the Rapidan and still marching eastward.

Lee at once concluded that part of the Federal army was attempting to get around his left flank. He had no idea of its strength, but he could not ignore such a threat—and he didn't. Fortunately, Major General Richard ("Fighting Dick") Anderson had two of his brigades at U.S. Ford and he ordered him to send them west toward Chancellorsville and to meet them there with the rest of his division. Anderson, among Lee's most trusted commanders, moved out at nine o'clock, marching for three hours through driving rain, informing Lee at midnight that he was concentrated east of Chancellorsville. Anderson might not be strong enough to stop the Federals, but he could delay them—which was all that Lee needed. Relieved, he went to sleep.

Daylight of the thirtieth revealed five bridges across the river below Fredericksburg and a greatly expanded Federal bridgehead. On Lee's Height, the gray-bearded Rebel chief again studied the enemy through his glasses. It seemed to him that they were more disposed to receive an attack than to launch one. Stonewall Jackson disagreed. Throughout the preceding three months—the most pleasant period of his life, spent in a cozy little cottage at Guiney Station with his wife, Anna, and the baby girl he had never seen—he had been preaching his gospel of attack. "We must make this [spring] campaign an exceedingly active one," he warned his brother officers. "Only thus can a weaker country cope with a stronger. It must make up in activity what it lacks in strength." Then, his eyes glowing with the old blue fire, he would cry: "I wish they would come!"

Now they had, and he yearned to assault the blue masses below. Lee told him: "If you think you can effect anything, I will give orders for the attack." His eyes aglow again, Stonewall strode off to scout the enemy. When he returned the glow was gone. The Federals were too strong, he admitted reluctantly. Lee nodded, still studying the bluecoats below, receiving and evaluating reports. Anderson sent word he was in good position in the woods four miles east of Chancellorsville. Lee, who had alerted Lafayette McLaws to prepare to join Anderson with his division if needed, told Anderson to provide defenses for McLaws as well as himself. "Set all your spades to work as vigorously as possible," the King of Spades replied. His binoculars still to his eyes, Lee listened to his staff officers debating whether Hooker would strike from upstream into their rear, or downstream on their front. He settled it by returning his glasses to their case, shutting it with a decisive snap, and declaring: "The main attack will come from above."

Lee saw that if Hooker's flanking column drove any deeper into his rear it would be between him and Richmond, forcing him to retreat. Rather than give ground, he decided to strike at the Federals behind him with most of his badly outnumbered army, leaving a skeleton force to hold his ridge. This mission went to Jubal Early's division, one of McLaws's brigades and the artillery reserve. McLaws with three brigades left at midnight to join Anderson. Jackson's corps would follow in the morning, accompanied by Stuart's cavalry and Lee himself. Thus Marse Robert had about 45,000 men to hurl against Hooker with about 80,000, and Early a mere 10,000 to hold off Sedgwick with 60,000.

Both armies started out at about eleven o'clock of a fine May Day morning. They would collide in the Wilderness midway between Chancellorsville and Tabernacle Church in what military historians call a "meeting engagement." Hooker had Slocum on the right advancing along the plank road supported by Howard, and Meade on the left following the turnpike supported by Couch. Sickles was in reserve behind them. Hooker also ordered Sedgwick to search for a weakness on the ridge above him, and if he found one to attack. At one o'clock he was to threaten an attack "in full force" and to maintain that attitude "until further orders." Slocum and Meade were in high spirits because it appeared that Hooker had the situation in hand, even designating Tabernacle Church as his headquarters. That would bring them out of the woods and converging on each other for the final blow.

In the beginning their paths diverged and they were soon out of touch with each other. Couch and Meade also became separated. The men of Couch's leading division under the capable Major General George Sykes—two-thirds regulars and one-third battle-seasoned New York volunteers—had penetrated the Wilderness two miles and were climbing a long slope whose crest overlooked open country when they ran into Rebel skirmishers. Driving them back they encountered the enemy main body. Confederate artillery roared and shells exploded among them. The long gray lines started forward, threatening to overlap Sykes's flanks. He withdrew. Couch came up immediately to stabilize his force by throwing in Major General Winfield Scott Hancock's division. Just as he did, a message arrived from Hooker. "Withdraw both divisions to Chancellorsville."

Couch—a born fighter, slight and frail but peppery—was thunderstruck. Here he was, he said, with "open country in front and in a commanding position." On his right he heard gunfire and saw smoke and guessed that Slocum was also engaged. But he, too, was holding his own, while Meade's two divisions on his left had encountered no opposition. And Hooker had ordered him to retreat! Conferring with Sykes and Hancock, who were equally amazed, he sent a courier to Hooker to tell him that the situation was under control and that he was ready to resume his eastward advance. Half an hour later the messenger returned with a peremptory repeat of the order: retire to Chancellorsville without delay. Angered, Couch thought of disobeying. Brigadier General Gouverneur K. Warren, chief engineer of the army, rode up to urge him to do just that while he rode back to explain things to Hooker. He galloped off, but Couch, a West Point professional, then decided to obey. Just as he completed a skillful disengagement, a third message arrived: "Hold on until 5 o'clock." Couch guessed that Warren had presented a persuasive argument, but by then he was so disgusted with Hooker that he snapped at the courier: "Tell General Hooker he is too late. The enemy are already on my right and rear. I am in full retreat."

Actually, the outlook was not quite as rosy as Couch had thought. Slocum on his right, engaged by Anderson, had already begun Hooker's order to retire and was falling back down the plank road. But on his left Meade was even more outraged to receive Hooker's order, for he had encountered nothing and was within reach of Banks's Ford, capture of which would vastly shorten the lines of communication between the Army of the Potomac's separated wings. He obeyed, crying angrily: "If he thinks he can't hold the top of a hill, how does he expect to hold the bottom of it?" Thus ended the first phase of the Battle of Chancellorsville. Hooker had outmaneuvered Lee, and though he outnumbered Marse Robert better than two to one, Hooker had allowed Lee to outmenace him.

Fighting Joe was standing in front of the Chancellor House, an easy smile on his rosy face as he greeted each of his three infuriated corps commanders upon their return. Couch said nothing when Hooker cried airily: "It's all right, Couch. I've got Lee just where I want him. He must fight me on my own ground." Years later, Couch wrote: "The retrograde movement had prepared me for something of the kind, but to hear from his own lips that the advantages gained by the successive marches of his lieutenants were to culminate in fighting a defensive battle in that nest of thickets was too much . . . I retired from his presence with the belief that my commanding general was a whipped man."

Joe Hooker, the poker player par excellence until the stakes became too high—when he would funk—had once again folded a high hand.

There can be no other explanation of Hooker's surrendering the initiative to Robert E. Lee, when he had him badly outnumbered and almost exactly where he wanted him. This is not to suggest that Hooker was a coward. Indeed, no officer in the Union army was braver. His coolness in combat was legendary. But there is a vast difference between physical courage and moral force. Moral force is the supreme requirement in a supreme commander, and this is what Napoleon meant when he said, "The general is the head, the whole of the army." There are, of course, other explanations of his conduct. Perhaps he missed the stimulus of the whiskey which he swore off when he took command of the Army of the Potomac. Or else the ease with which he had flanked Marse Robert suggested to him that Lee—not Hooker—had his enemy just where he wanted him. He might even have believed those wildly exaggerated reports by captured Confederates that the Army of Northern Virginia had been heavily reinforced, although he certainly was aware that the Rebels frequently sent out bogus "deserters" to spread false information, while he also knew that Longstreet was still in Suffolk with two divisions and that Lee's strength could not exceed 60,000 and was more likely less. Would Lee dare to divide his forces, leaving a scratch force to hold the Fredericksburg ridge while attacking with barely more than half of Hooker's strength? Of course he would, if the record of the last eleven months was any indication! Yet Hooker preferred to believe that reports coming from his observation balloons indicated a strong force moving toward him, and thus he wired Butterfield at two o'clock: "From character of information have suspended attack. The enemy may attack me—I will try it. Tell Sedgwick to keep a sharp lookout and attack if he can succeed." "Character of information" indeed! Rather lack of character in the supreme commander, as his downcast generals well knew when he gathered them around him and sought to cheer them up with such remarks as "The Rebel army is now the property of the Army of the Potomac," or "The enemy is in my power, and God Almighty cannot deprive me of him." He even wired Washington, "I think the enemy in his desperation will be compelled to attack me on my own ground."

Unfortunately for Mr. F. J. Hooker, that was exactly what the "helpless" enemy was at the moment contemplating, although not exactly out of desperation.

50

■

Chancellorsville:
The Death of Jackson

LEE AND JACKSON met at sundown on the plank road about a mile
southeast of Chancellorsville. They sat on a log together, Lee as usual
immaculate in his neat gray uniform devoid of decoration except for three
stars on each turned-down collar, gray-bearded and grave like a biblical
patriarch; Jackson in the rather gaudy uniform Stuart had given him and
which had so amused his men at Fredericksburg, trembling with excitement, his pale blue eyes aglow. It might have been Moses and Joshua
conferring outside Jericho. Both were eager to attack the enemy, and they
talked of ways of doing it as the night deepened and the moon rose. Jackson
believed that the ease with which he had repulsed Hooker's spearheads that
day suggested a general withdrawal. "By tomorrow morning there will not
be any of them this side of the river," he said. Lee disagreed. Although he
was puzzled by Hooker's about-face, he still believed that the Union commander had been planning to strike him in the rear with his main body. Even
if he wasn't there tomorrow, they still should plan as though he would be.
The question was where. Jackson had already told him that the terrain was
too difficult and Hooker's defenses too strong to make a frontal assault.

At that moment Jeb Stuart rode up, his gold spurs jingling and silver
moonlight falling on his great cinnamon beard and his floating red-lined cape.
He brought the exciting news that Fitzhugh Lee had found Hooker's right
flank hanging "in the air" on the Orange Turnpike. A holy light shone in
Jackson's eyes, and Lee, visibly excited, glanced up at Stuart to ask if he
knew of passable roads running west and suitable for a covered approach
to the turnpike. Stuart replied that he didn't, but would try to find some and
swung jingling aboard his horse to vanish down the road. Now Lee and
Jackson together peered anxiously at the map on Lee's knee—searching,
searching, searching for those vital roads. "How can we get at these peo-

ple," Lee mused aloud, half to himself, half to Jackson. "You know best," Stonewall said. "Show me what to do, and we will do it." Lee stretched out a hand, tracing with his fingertip a route running about two miles west to Catharine Furnace, then turning south a little farther before veering northwest four miles to the Orange Plank Road. Jackson shot erect with an angelic smile, saluting. "My troops will move at four o'clock," he said.

Unwittingly, Robert E. Lee had placed his fingertip on the one chink in Fighting Joe Hooker's armor. It was not a physical or visible defect, for Lee's engineers had been correct in describing the Yankee defenses as too formidable to assault. So had Hooker in his optimistic flank-to-flank inspection tour begun in the early morning of May 2. "How strong! How strong!" he murmured as he rode on his big white horse among his wildly cheering troops, his rosy cheeks flushed with pride, his mood still expansive. He had reason to be confident. A spy in Richmond had assured him that Lee was receiving barely 59,000 rations daily and that Longstreet with two divisions was still in Suffolk. That meant the enemy force east of Chancellorsville probably did not number 50,000, for Lee would certainly leave at least 10,000 or 12,000 men behind to hold his ridge. Even so, just before two o'clock that morning he had directed Sedgwick to send Reynolds's corps to Chancellorsville, thus raising Union strength to better than 90,000 men.

From Meade on the left to Slocum and Couch in the center and Howard on the right, Hooker found that his lines could not be improved upon. He was particularly pleased with the right flank, where Howard's Germans had shown the customary Teutonic efficiency with pick and shovel. Unknown to him, as well as to Marse Robert, here was the chink; not a gap or a path or even that flank "hanging in the air"—but rather a hole in the human heart.

In Howard's Germans.

Fifteen of the twenty-six regiments in the XI Corps commanded by Major General Oliver Otis Howard were listed as being composed of German immigrants. There were, of course, many non-Germans in some of these, but it is still safe to say that about half the men in the XI Corps were German. Many of them were veterans of the Revolution of 1848, when the oppressed men of about a dozen German states rose in rebellion against royal despotism. Crushed in blood and proscription lists, many of these freedom-fighters migrated to the United States, storied land of the free. To them such ideals as freedom and justice were sacred values not to be taken for granted, as so many native-born Americans did in fact do. They settled in free-soil lands, these sober, decent men, and loving liberty as they did they quite naturally hated slavery. Thus when war came they flocked to the Union standards. A division of them under the celebrated revolutionary Louis Blenker served under Frémont in a mountain campaign and fared very badly. Then Franz Sigel, another hero of 1848, succeeded Frémont and the phrase "I fights mit Sigel" became a proud boast among the Germans, especially after Sigel's command became the XI Corps of the Army of the Potomac. Actually, the XI was not beloved of the rest of the army. Under Frémont it had done poorly and hardly better under Sigel, and had arrived at Falmouth too late to fight at Fredericksburg. Moreover, the native-born Americans of the day were deep-dyed—if unconscious—xenophobes. They distrusted all foreigners, especially those who spoke a broken English that was considered comic. This did not apply to the numerous Irish in the Federal army. Except among men from the Nativist and Know-Nothing strongholds of southern New England—especially Massachusetts—where the Irish were despised as "R.C.'s," the sons of Erin were generally accepted as worthy comrades, not only because they spoke the language with a charming brogue, but also because of their courage, wit and stirring songs. Not so the "Dutchmen" or "Dutchies" as the entire XI Corps came to be called because of its many Germans, and "I fights mit Sigel" became a mocking taunt.

In the spring of 1863 Sigel resigned in a huff. After Hooker, he had been the army's ranking general, but led its smallest corps. He told Halleck that in justice it should be enlarged, and Old Brains, also afflicted with the anti-foreign virus, refused. When Sigel asked to be relieved, Halleck promptly obliged him, thus satisfying his prejudice; and by replacing him with Howard he placated a fellow West Pointer who complained that he was senior to Sickles who had a corps while he still led a division.

Oliver Otis Howard was not the man to command a body of troops as unhappy as those of the XI Corps. Indeed, he seems not to have been very much aware of the discontent of "my men," as he always addressed them, and by his obtuse crusading zeal against drink and gambling he not only alienated them but also showed how little he understood the alternating rhythm of terror and tedium that was the common soldier's hard lot. Most of his Germans were free-thinkers, and he was a devoutly religious man who wore his faith on his sleeve. Preachy and prissy, he had arrived at West Point wearing the top hat and carrying the cane symbolic of his graduation from Bowdoin College in Maine, and by combining this air of superiority with an abrasive Abolitionist stance, he bored many of his Northern classmates while offending the Southerners. Of him Sherman said, "he ought to have been born in petticoats and ought to wear them." Yet he was a brave and professional soldier who lost his right arm at Seven Pines. (It is said that Phil Kearny, who lost his left arm at Mexico City, in visiting Howard in the hospital, said to him: "General, let us buy our gloves together.") Just a little warmth or the slightest spark of human understanding would have made O. O. Howard a better leader than the textbook commander he was, and if he had expressed his Christian faith through care and concern for his troops, rather than admonition and prohibition, they would not have despised him as a creeping Jesus. And it was against him and his disgruntled corps that Stonewall Jackson was marching with 31,000 men.

Robert E. Lee awoke early on the morning of May 2, 1863, to see Stonewall Jackson bending over a small fire built by a courier. It was already past four o'clock but Stonewall explained that he was awaiting a report from a cartographer sent to explore the local roads. The two men sat on hardtack boxes abandoned by the Federals, warming their hands at the tiny fire. At dawn the cartographer appeared. He was delighted. He had found a covered approach! He showed it to Jackson on the map. Stonewall's eyes gleamed. He would take his entire corps west. This left Lee with about 15,000 men to repulse the huge Union force opposite him should Hooker attack. With Early on the ridge outnumbered almost as badly, Lee was taking the greatest risk of his career. But he merely nodded. "Well, go on," he said, and Jackson strode off while the sun broke red and fiery over Fredericksburg behind him.

It was not until eight o'clock that Jackson's corps moved out. But the four-hour delay did not seem to disturb him. There was still plenty of time to make the ten-mile march to the plank road. Mounting ox-eyed Little Sorrel he met Lee astride tall gray Traveller at the turnoff to Catharine Furnace. Both men gazed silently at each other. Jackson pointed to the west, Lee nodded—and Stonewall rode off into the woods.

Hooker was still buoyant when he returned to the Chancellor House at nine o'clock that morning. A courier from Sickles was waiting to tell him that a division Sickles had sent out to high ground at Hazel Grove to see what the enemy was doing had reported sighting a huge Rebel column moving south of Catharine Furnace before vanishing into the woods. It included infantry, artillery, wagons and ambulances. Hooker at once consulted his map, finding that the road in question veered west under a screen of trees. Lee was retreating! Probably to Gordonsville. Hooker was exultant. But then, re-

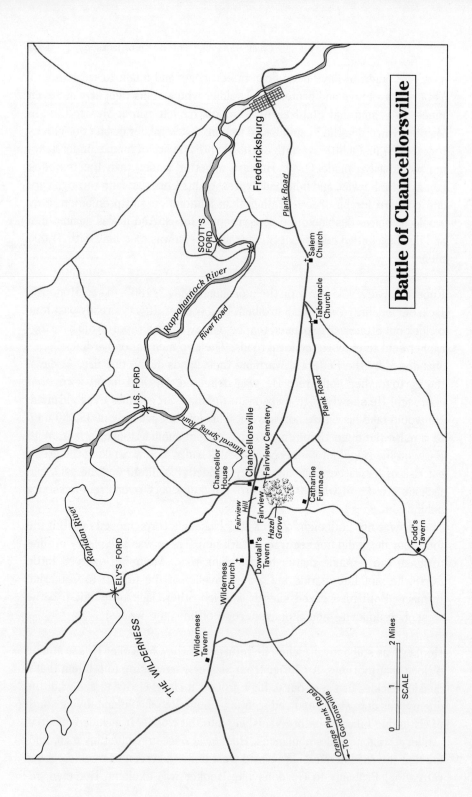

Battle of Chancellorsville

Fredericksburg

SCOTT'S FORD

Rappahannock River

River Road

Salem Church

Tabernacle Church

Plank Road

Plank Road

U.S. FORD

Mineral Spring Run

Chancellor House

Chancellorsville

Fairview Cemetery

Catharine Furnace

Fairview Hill

Fairview

Hazel Grove

Todd's Tavern

Rapidan River

ELY'S FORD

Dowdall's Tavern

Wilderness Church

THE WILDERNESS

Wilderness Tavern

Orange Plank Road

To Gordonsville

SCALE

0   1   2 Miles

membering that his opponent was the wily Marse Robert, he decided it would be wise to alert Howard on the western flank. "We have good reason to suppose that the enemy is moving to our right," he warned. "Please advance your pickets for purposes of observation as far as may be safe to obtain timely information of their approach." There does not seem to be much doubt that Fighting Joe should have ridden west himself to be certain that his right flank was secure. However, he did receive a message from Howard, arriving before his own could have been received, reporting that he had also seen the column, and declaring: "I am taking measures to resist an attack from the west." Even so, some member of his staff could have been sent to inspect Howard's position; and here, Hooker's mistake in sending away his cavalry left him without enough horse to patrol the numerous roads and trails winding through the Wilderness. Howard's message allayed Hooker's concern, and his next step was to direct Sedgwick to attack the Rebel ridge if there was a "reasonable expectation of success." Some time after three o'clock Sickles, who had gone forward to Hazel Grove with two divisions, reported capturing enemy soldiers and wagons at Catharine Furnace but had lost sight of the main body. *This was it!* Lee was unquestionably on the retrograde, waiting with the main body to follow the column moving west. Jubilant, at half-past four Hooker ordered Sedgwick to throw all that he had across the river and attack. All that was needed was for Hooker's staff to finish writing the orders intended to put his entire force in pursuit of Lee next morning. He would strike him when an army is most vulnerable: on the march!

Unknown to Fighting Joe, many of his couriers and even unit commanders did not share his confident conviction that Lee was retreating. They came riding frantically up to the Chancellor House with wild warnings that the enemy was massing for an attack on the right flank. However, staff officers, always adept at shooing such hysterical people away from their chief, gently explained that Hooker was aware of the danger and had taken steps to meet it. They also pooh-poohed what Sickles's captured Johnnies were supposed to have said. Georgians, healthy-looking men in neat butternut, they had been angered when one Yankee snarled, "We'll have every mother's son of you before we go away." One of them snapped, "You'll catch hell tonight," and another: "You think you've done a big thing now, but wait till Jackson gets on your flank." Bunk, said the staff officers. Typical Rebel moonshine. Lee is in retreat. The chief has given orders for the pursuit. Go back to your units.

Howard also received warnings which he ignored. One major on outpost duty sent back the frantic message: "A large body of the enemy is massing in my front. For God's sake make dispositions to receive him!" Hysteria, Howard thought. Lee was in retreat. And besides, hadn't he already "taken measures" to resist any surprise attack?

As Stonewall Jackson approached the Federal right flank he began to realize that he would not have much daylight in which to complete the destruction of the enemy. At first he had not been upset by the four-hour delay in moving out, believing that a ten-mile march over roads that were narrow but firm, "just wet enough to be easy on the feet and free from dust," would not take long. Yet his progress was slow, for he was conducting a flank march—that is, a progress across the front of the enemy—one of the most difficult and dangerous of military maneuvers, especially with a force as large as the 31,000 men Jackson commanded, with all those horses, wagons and ambulances mixed in. He had to be careful. If Hooker suspected his strength and purpose, he could overwhelm him, and then destroy Lee and Early at his leisure. Thus the very nature of what he was attempting counseled caution, and caution consumes time. "Press forward!" Stonewall continued to cry. "Press forward!" At one point he remarked: "I hear it said that General Hooker has more men than he can handle. I should like to have half as many more as I have today, and I should hurl him into the river." That was at two o'clock, with the sun on the descent and a sense of urgency coming over Stonewall Jackson. Just then, Fitzhugh Lee rode down the plank road toward him from the west, offering to show Jackson the Federal right.

The column halted and Stonewall and Fitz Lee climbed a small hill before dismounting. Parting the leaves, Lee showed Jackson a panorama that set the blue light glowing in his eyes. "What a sight presented itself before me," Fitz Lee wrote later. "Below, and but a few hundred yards distant, ran the Federal line of battle . . . with abatis (felled trees) in front and long lines of stacked arms in the rear. Two cannon were visible in the part of the line seen. The soldiers were in groups in the rear, laughing, smoking, probably engaged, here and there, in games of cards and other amusements indulged in while feeling safe and comfortable, awaiting orders. In rear of them were other parties driving up and butchering beeves."

Jackson was all a'tremble, but then he realized that an attack up the plank road would strike the enemy at an angle in the middle, rather than end-to as he desired. He would have to march another two miles west until he got beyond Howard's reach and until he found a dense wood thick with underbrush screening him from the enemy a bare half mile away. This took more than an hour, and another two hours were spent massing his troops in three assault lines two miles wide. At 5:15, with only ninety minutes of sunlight remaining, and his third line only half formed, Stonewall looked up impatiently from his watch to ask Brigadier General Robert Emmett Rodes, commanding the first line, if he were ready.

"Yes, sir."

"You can go forward then."

The positions Jackson and Fitz Lee had studied were those of Howard. The two small cannon they had seen were his "measures" to repulse attack, and the lounging, laughing men two regiments of Germans numbering about 900 men. All Howard had done was to "refuse" his flank a bit, that is, bend it back and fortify it, but with these puny defenses. Nearly as bad was a half-mile gap between Howard's left and Slocum's right caused when Slocum's reserve brigade had been detached to guard the flank of Sickles's force as he moved against the Georgians. This unit, unknown to Howard, had not returned; and if he were struck on his right and forced to fall back on this gap for support, he would, in Shelby Foote's graphic phrase, be like a man sitting on a chair that has been yanked from under him. Due west of Howard's dangling flank was the dense wood screening Jackson. Howard considered it impenetrable. So did Brigadier General Charles Devens, who commanded this western edge of Howard's position. A soldier more familiar with military history than Devens, aware that it abounds in impregnable forts that fall, impassable swamps that are pierced and impenetrable forests that are penetrated, might have done something about this question mark on Howard's flank: at the least, cut it down to turn a covered approach into a field of fire. But the official word was that Lee was retreating, and General Devens of Boston, disdainful of this Dutch corps he had only latterly joined, quite properly shared this assessment of the situation. He laughed at the three Ohio colonels who came to him with reports of Rebels massing on the right, told them that western officers were scaredy-cats and ordered them back to their regiments. His men, of course, heard nothing of danger. Their weapons were still stacked behind them, while they continued in their light-hearted "grab-assing," sometimes pausing to sniff hungrily at the aroma of roasting beef.

"Deer!" a soldier cried, pointing toward the wood. "Look at the deer!"

Their white tails held high, their velvety brown eyes rolling in terror, scores of deer burst from the woods to go galloping east down the plank road, followed by scurrying rabbits and lumbering raccoon. Whooping and waving their hats, the soldiers watched them as they peeled off into the underbrush, and then a higher, keening, weirder yelling erupted from the woods and the cries of the Germans froze in their throats to see a broad gray-and-butternut mass of Rebels bearing down on them. Their ragged uniforms were torn or covered with prickles and burs, their faces scratched or bleeding from contact with brambles and branches, and the dying sun glinted weakly on their bayonets as they came screaming forward to unleash great, rolling volleys of musketry. Bluebellies began falling on the ground, where they lay still, or writhed or beat the earth with drumming feet. Artillery was roaring in the distance and shells—solid and explosive— thickened the Confederate fire. Some of the Germans had their weapons and got off a few rifle shots, but most turned to sprint toward their stacked rifles, some never pausing to seize them but dashing right by them in their fright. Now the screaming Confederates fell upon the two abandoned cannon and turned them to fire down the plank road packed with fleeing Bluebellies.

One of the colonels Devens had rebuked galloped up to him to plead with him to change front to the west before all was lost. "Not yet," the confused Devens replied, glancing to his right as though looking for reassuring word from corps headquarters. *Not yet!* It was already too late, except for another Ohio colonel named Reilly who rallied his regiment and fought furiously for ten minutes until he was killed and his men joined the panic-stricken rout. Within minutes, Devens's division had disappeared.

Howard's extreme right flank had vanished, and the men who had held it were now a confused, terrified, yelling mass struggling down the turnpike—into which the plank road had flowed—shoulder to shoulder. Again and again some lone Union units attempted to make a stand in the forest, but always the shrieking demons in gray and butternut simply beat them back or flowed so inexorably around their flanks that they had to withdraw. Most of these fleeing Federals still held their rifles, but almost all of them drew their knives as they ran to cut the straps of their haversacks rather than lose precious time by halting to unbuckle them. At Wilderness Church Major General Carl Schurz put two of his regiments into a line facing west. With them was Captain Hubert Dilger, another freedom-fighter from Germany and a consummate and daring artillerist who was known as "Leatherbreeches" for the doeskin pants he wore. Leatherbreeches quickly wheeled his guns into line and swept the Rebels off the turnpike. But they came on again to outflank the Federal riflemen and drive them back. Leatherbreeches was all alone. Still he fought on, firing double-shotted canister, until the yelling Confederates neared his guns—when he limbered up to leave. A Rebel volley dropped three of six horses drawing Dilger's gun.

They fell screaming and kicking, their mouths working hideously over their great teeth. Leatherbreeches tried to drive the gun away, dragging the three dead beasts still in harness. Finding it impossible, he mounted the driver's seat of another gun and clattered off to join the brigade of Colonel Adolphus Buschbeck, who had put his men into abandoned rifle pits. Here Dilger helped Buschbeck check the gray tide once again just as the smoke-shrouded sun disappeared behind the western treetops. But the Rebels came on once more, pausing only to tidy up their lines, for they were nearly as fragmented and confused as the retreating Yankees. Once again Leather-breeches held them off, firing a few shots, limbering up to retreat a hundred yards, firing again. . . . But Buschbeck's men had had enough and joined the swelling, jostling blue throng hurrying east.

Oliver Howard came riding frantically toward them, bareheaded and weeping, abandoned colors tucked under the stump of his right arm, his reins in his left. He pleaded with his men to turn and form to receive the enemy. But they paid no attention to him, hurrying into that wide gap left in the Union line between Howard and Slocum, driven into higher speed by the demonic yelling behind them. Once they had cleared that point in their flight to Chancellorsville, the Union right flank ceased to exist.

Fighting Joe Hooker knew nothing of this. For almost an hour after Jackson struck he had been sitting in the gallery of the Chancellor House chatting with his staff. An acoustic freak of the sort that had immobilized Don Carlos Buell at Perryville, and the insulating effect of the forest, had smothered the roar of battle and re-directed it so that it came to Hooker faintly as the sound of what he assumed to be Sickles down at Catharine Furnace chewing up the Rebels. At sundown an aide went out on the road to determine the source of the sound, just in time to perceive a horde of riderless horses, bouncing wagons and swaying guns mixed in with wild-eyed Federals in huge undisciplined masses come sweeping down on him. His yell—"My God—here they come!"—was drowned in the uproar of their passage as they flowed frantically past headquarters bound for anywhere but the front.

Hooker had heard and seen them, and he ran for his white horse, vaulting into the saddle to go galloping away west. Fortunately, Sickles's third division which Fighting Joe had once commanded himself was available. He ordered it to wheel to its right and halt the rout. "Receive them on your bayonets!" he yelled. "Receive them on your bayonets!" Not sure whether their commander meant the demoralized Dutchmen flowing around them or the pursuing Graybacks, the startled Yankees nevertheless maintained good order and marched rapidly toward the last rays of sunset.

Stonewall Jackson was among the pursuers, shouting to his men, "Push right ahead!" When an exulting young officer yelled, "They are running too fast for us! We can't keep up with them," Stonewall replied sternly, "They never run too fast for me, sir. Press them! Press them!" Presently night began to fall, and shortly afterward the moon rose, blood red behind the smoke, but then, rising above it, glowing gold. Stonewall realized with only fleeting dismay that those seven lost hours—four in getting started, three in marching those extra two miles and in massing— might have cost him the complete destruction of the blue host. But then, wasting no time on useless regrets, he glanced at the glowing moon and began to think of a night attack. Although most of his spearheads were approaching exhaustion, four of A. P. Hill's brigades were still available in reserve. A moonlight march deep into Hooker's rear at U.S. Ford could block any escape attempt across the river. Just before sundown he had heard Lee's guns thundering against the Yankee left and was sure that his chief could prevent any intervention from that quarter. Although there had been a meeting engagement between Union cavalry and Confederate infantry on his right, just south of the turnpike, and enemy artillery had been roaring on Fairview Hill to his front, he was convinced the Yankees were firing blindly to discourage pursuit and that there was really very little or even nothing between him and Chancellorsville.

Stonewall Jackson went searching for A. P. Hill. Finding him, he gave him direct oral orders: "Press them! Cut them off from U.S. Ford, Hill. Press them!" Then he rode off with his staff to search for a road into Hooker's rear.

Darkness brought no end to the fight. Down at Catharine Furnace, Dan Sickles with 15,000 men knew nothing of the battle that had broken the Federal right until he heard the roaring of Union batteries to his rear: thirty-four guns at Fairview Cemetery, twenty-two at Hazel Grove. These were the guns Jackson had heard, and Sickles, upon learning of the enemy breakthrough and the direness of his own predicament between Jackson on his right and Lee on his left, decided to pull back to Hazel Grove as quickly as possible. There was a trail leading north that he could follow, and he put one of his divisions on its left and another on its right and at some time after nine o'clock went hurrying for the safety of friendly guns and the turnpike.

As so often happens in night marches, especially those conducted in battle, there is a tendency to drift. Usually, it is to the right; but if a unit is on the left in rear march it may veer in that direction. This is what happened to Sickles's divisions: the one on the left drifted west toward the enemy, the one on the right east toward friendly troops. They blundered into and fought both of them. There was hand-to-hand fighting on the left where flashing gun muzzles identified the Confederate lines and bayonets gleamed in the moonlight. On the right amid the screams and yells of the dying and stricken, and the crying on both sides of "Friendly troops! Friendly troops!" there began to fall a scourging fire from Yankee gunners in the cemetery, followed by showers of shells from Rebel guns to the west.

Finally it was the Yankee artillery that stabilized the battle. Its shells broke up the Confederates trying to form for an assault. Most of Sickles's two divisions got safely inside the Union lines while a smaller group bivouacked on Hazel Grove. An eerie silence began to settle around and upon Chancellorsville.

When Stonewall Jackson and his staff rode past the Confederate pickets in search of a route into Hooker's rear, they heard the ring of axes to the east where the Federals were trimming and notching logs to build a new barricade. "General," an aide asked, "General, don't you think this is the wrong place for you?" Jackson shook his head. "The danger is all over. The enemy is routed. Go back and tell A. P. Hill to press forward." Then Jackson sat silently on Little Sorrel to listen to the sound of the axes. They sounded closer, and he turned to ride back the way he had come, apparently satisfied that whatever the Yankees were doing, it would not be enough to stop Hill. Coming upon Hill, he paused to confer with him. Both men were surrounded by their staffs so that about twenty horsemen were gathered in a clearing in sight of the North Carolina pickets, who had only recently collided with saber-swinging Federal cavalrymen. This group also looked like Yanks, and they opened fire on them.

"Cease firing!" Hill shouted. "Cease firing! You are firing into your own men."

Fortunately, no one had been hit. But the Tarheel commander thought the order was a Yankee trick and he shouted to his men: "Who gave that order? It's a lie! Pour it into them, boys!" They did—not only the pickets but the whole battalion blasted away at twenty paces with such a torrent of bullets that fourteen empty saddles were counted later.

Little Sorrel was not among them, having panicked and fled toward the Federal lines at the first outburst of fire. With difficulty Stonewall calmed him and turned him back toward the pickets, riding slowly west again with his right hand upraised to guard against low-hanging branches. It was then that that second, devastating fusillade came whistling through the wood. Once again Jackson's mount whirled and went galloping toward the enemy, completely uncontrollable this time because Stonewall was limp in the saddle with two bullets through his left arm and one through his right hand. In exquisite pain, he nevertheless wheeled the terrified beast once more and rode slowly back to the clearing. All around him in the darkness he could hear groans and screams. A dismounted officer seized Little Sorrel's bridle and stopped him. Another steadied the stricken general in the saddle. "Wild fire, sir," Stonewall muttered. "Wild fire." One of the officers asked, "How do you feel, General?" Jackson replied: "You had better take me down. My arm is broken." They did, alarmed to find him already so weakened from loss of blood and shock that they had to free his feet from the stirrups. At once Little Sorrel turned and galloped toward the enemy lines for a third time, finally making them while the officers laid Jackson under a tree. One of them went off in search of a surgeon. "My own men," Jackson murmured in a dazed voice.

A regimental surgeon was found who administered first aid and ordered Stonewall carried to the rear on a stretcher. Now a two-hour ordeal ensued as the bearers staggered through intense Federal artillery fire, repeatedly halting to lay the general down and fall flat themselves. Once they dropped him hard on the wounded arm, forcing from him his only groan. Finally they found an ambulance that took him to the aid station at Wilderness Tavern, where his medical director, Dr. Hunter McGuire, examined the arm and immediately ordered Jackson prepared for amputation. When the chloroform pad came down over Stonewall's nose and mouth the surgeon could hear his muffled voice murmuring: "What an infinite blessing . . . blessing . . . bless—" McGuire removed the shattered arm but for a two-inch stump. A half hour later—at about three o'clock in the morning—Jackson began to recover from the anesthetic. He spoke of hearing "the most delightful music," which might have been the whining of the bone saw.

But then he was shocked when a courier arrived with the news that A. P. Hill had been wounded in both legs by shell fragments and that Jeb Stuart, now in command, wanted Stonewall's advice. For a moment the holy fire seemed to burn again in Jackson's pain-clouded eyes. He knit his eyebrows as though concentrating, but then he sighed as though the effort were too much. "I can't tell," he muttered in confusion. "Say to General Stuart he must do what he thinks best."

But there was nothing more to be done that night. Robert E. Lee, stunned by the report of Jackson's wound but still not aware of how serious it was, ordered Stuart to "dispossess" the Yankees of Chancellorsville in the morning. Gradually, the fires burning everywhere had begun to subside. There were no high winds to fan them, to gather them together into one great, consuming holocaust that would destroy both gray and blue coat alike, especially the wounded lying unconscious or groaning inside the thickets or beside the trails. Soon the smoke cleared and the moon glowed gold again, bathing the dozing Rebels and Yanks in silvery light. Suddenly these weary soldiers came awake, startled: above them they heard the strident, shrill song of the whippoorwills serenading the moon.

In his attempt to dispossess the Yankees of Chancellorsville on May 3 Jeb Stuart had a great ally in Fighting Joe Hooker. Hooker was still thinking defensively, even though the arrival of Reynolds's I Corps had given him a two to one superiority over the enemy. Moreover, the Confederate army could not be more vulnerable, split completely in two as it was with each half at least a day's march from the other. Yet Hooker made no effort to regain the initiative but rather ordered a secondary line of defense to be prepared north of Chancellorsville. Worse, he ordered Sickles to abandon the high ground at Hazel Grove. This height also commanded Fairview, to which Sickles had retired with most of his men during that costly night withdrawal, but there was still a good-sized detachment of his occupying that vital height. Rather than order Sickles forward to organize it and so arm it that it could command the Confederate approach, he ordered him to abandon it—and this was his most distinguished blunder of the battle. It would not take Stuart long to recognize Hazel Grove's value, for Rebel artillery on that eminence could pound and shatter the point of the formidable V-shaped line that Hooker, with that customary organizing skill which can never be denied him, had put into place. No fewer than six corps were deployed in it: Slocum at the tip of the V with Sickles and Couch behind him right and left, then Meade and Reynolds in the longer arm of the V on the right and Howard on the shorter leftward arm. The end of the right arm was anchored on the Rapidan just above its confluence with the Rappahannock and of the left on the Rappahannock below the juncture. Meade was planted squarely where Jeb Stuart would have to strike if he sought to continue Jackson's advance to the north to cut off Hooker from U.S. Ford. This Stuart did not attempt to do. Instead he hammered at the point of the V, especially at Sickles.

Charge after Grayback charge was hurled at Sickles, and to a lesser degree at Slocum at the tip and Couch behind him on his left. Eventually it became clear that the Rebel infantry was never going to penetrate the well-entrenched Yankee line, covered by their blazing cannon on Fairview Hill. At this point the Confederate artillery, only recently reorganized by Lee, demonstrated a new-found proficiency in close-up support. First,

Stuart's efficient artillery chief, Colonel E. P. Alexander, had begun to wheel battery after battery atop Hazel Grove. By midmorning they were thundering away at the Federals in Chancellorsville and environs, shattering the blue infantry, devastating the Union cannon at Fairview. Soon they were joined by more Rebel guns at Dowdall's Tavern and inside Stuart's lines to the east. In all, eighty-four Confederate cannon scourged the Bluebellies of Slocum and Couch as never before. Beneath this fiery rain the Federal lines were in danger of dissolving. The woods were full of blue coats flitting furtively to the rear. They were also on fire seemingly everywhere. While the air grew stiflingly hot, a mixture of wood and powder smoke threatened to suffocate the dismayed Federals. The narrow roads were choked with skulkers, wagons, artillery, ambulances, cavalry and droves of cattle lowing pathetically and pawing the ground in terror. Chancellor House, converted into a hospital with doors torn from their hinges to be used as operating tables, had so far been safe from the bombardment. But shortly after nine o'clock the rain of fire began to fall there as well. Among its victims was Hooker himself, standing on the veranda leaning against one of the pillars supporting the balcony. A solid shot struck it, splitting it lengthwise and driving Hooker to the floor. Stunned, he was revived by aides who poured brandy down his throat, his first drink in weeks. Stumbling toward his horse, he mounted it slowly, his left side numb, and rode toward the rear, where he lay down on a cot inside a tent, behind Meade's lines. From there he called for Couch to join him.

Couch, second in command, knew nothing of Hooker's injury until he was told of it by Meade. Neither man said anything, but Meade's face was alive with anticipation best expressed by one of his colonels: "By God, we'll have some fighting now!" Inside the tent, Hooker said: "Couch, I turn the command of the army over to you." But it was only on a string, as his next sentence indicated. "You will withdraw it and place it in the position designated on the map," pointing to a second, shallower V drawn behind Mineral Spring Run a few miles north. Although Couch was a fierce fighter, it is possible that he was relieved, and did not want to take command of a demoralized army in such a fix. When he learned Hooker was hurt, he had asked himself: "If he is killed, what shall I do with this disjointed army?" Thus, when he emerged from the tent and met the imploring eyes of his friend Meade, he merely shook his head grimly and relayed Hooker's order for a withdrawal.

Actually, fighter that Couch was, there was not much else that he could do. Hooker's great blunder of neglecting to fortify Hazel Grove and to stuff it with guns had not only enabled Stuart to seize that vital height, but had also allowed him to take and fortify Fairview Hill, which was already pounding the troops of Sickles, Slocum and Couch streaming across open fields to seek sanctuary in the new fortifications to the north. Counter-attack here could be suicidal, just as Stuart's assaults would have been broken in blood had the Federals held Hazel Grove.

Couch also knew from the moment he obeyed the order to halt his advance and retreat to Chancellorsville that Fighting Joe Hooker was a beaten man. Everything that he did was defensive, calculated to save his army—and perhaps his own reputation—rather than destroy the enemy's. And thus, by retiring, he effected the "dispossession" of Chancellorsville and the reunion of the divided Army of Northern Virginia. And what a scene ensued when Lee the Lord of Battles rode forward on Traveller from Hazel Grove to the Chancellor House clearing. His arrival symbolized the reunion of the divided Army of Northern Virginia, and he was greeted by one long unbroken cry of exaltation. The wounded and the well, all with smoke-blackened faces, raised their voices—feeble or strong—in a wild, tumultuous screeching and cheering that brought a flush of pleasure to the face of the Rebel patriarch and led him to lean forward to calm his mount. Around him surged his victorious scarecrows, removing their hats, touching his legs, stroking Traveller's withers. It was a reception so voluntary and unprecedented that one of Lee's staff officers wrote: "I thought that it must have been from such a scene that men in ancient times rose to the dignity of Gods."

And of course even then, at the height of his glory, Lee the aggressive, Lee the audacious, Lee the relentless, thought of nothing but pursuit: of rounding up the remaining Yankees loose in the woods, of pausing momentarily to regroup and reorganize his own scattered and exhausted command—and of going forward again this very day to pin Hooker against the Rappahannock and there destroy him or compel his surrender. At once orders were issued for that purpose, but then, just as he was about to order the attack a courier on a lathered horse galloped into Chancellorsville with tidings of disaster in the east.

"Uncle" John Sedgwick, a bachelor from the Nutmeg State, beloved of his troops, broad-shouldered and big-boned, beefy, too, as unmilitary-looking as Zach Taylor with his boots either mud-coated or mud-stained, a worn black slouch hat on his head and his heavy featured face kindly above his tangled brown beard—here was perhaps the most unruffled and steadiest, if not the slowest, Union commander in the Civil War.

At nine o'clock on the night of May 2—the evening of Jackson's flank attack—Hooker had sent Sedgwick the desperate instruction to "cross the Rappahannock at Fredericksburg on the receipt of this order" and to "attack and destroy any force he may fall in with on the road." This meant to overwhelm Early on the ridge and to come in on Lee's rear where "between us we will use him up . . ."

Sedgwick obeyed. At dawn his Bluebellies swarmed over pontoon bridges, feinting at Early's thin lines on the far left and again on the right before assaulting the middle on those very same Marye's Heights and the sunken road where so many of Burnside's bluecoats died. They were twice repulsed. Then Colonel Allen of the 5th Wisconsin—one of those Badger State regiments that Sherman said was worth a whole brigade—told his men: "When the signal *forward* is given you will advance at double-quick. You will not fire a gun, and you will not stop until you get the order to halt." He paused. "You will never get that order." Cheering, the Wisconsin boys went in at the run. Just as in December, they took a withering fire from the wall until the right flank overran the Rebels there and put down a devastating enfilading fire that carried the day.

As ordered, Early abandoned his guns and retreated south to protect Lee's trains at Guiney Station. Sedgwick probably would have enjoyed pursuing his old West Point classmate, but his orders from Hooker, another classmate, were to attack Lee's exposed right flank on the Orange Plank Road "at once." Leaving Gibbon behind to hold the ridge, he moved out along the turnpike with about 22,000 men.

Lee saw instantly that he could not allow this grave threat to his rear to pass unchallenged. Postponing his plan to strike hard at Hooker, he sent McLaws east along the pike with four brigades and Anderson with a division in the same direction along the River Road to block any union between the two Federal forces. He also ordered Raleigh Colston to take his division north on the Ely's Ford Road to watch for any attempt by Hooker to sally out of his defenses. Thus with 37,000 Lee would hold Hooker with 80,000 in place while McLaws-Anderson with 22,000 would stop Sedgwick. Once again Marse Robert was improvising and dividing his army in a daring attempt to stabilize the situation. When this occurred, he would decide which of the Union forces he would leap upon, probably the first one to make a mistake.

McLaws met Sedgwick just east of Salem Church, two and a half miles east of Chancellorsville. Uncle John, quite understandably believing that Hooker would go over to the assault once he heard his guns, also mistakenly assuming that his was the superior force, immediately attacked. At first, he seemed to be succeeding, until his men ran into the Rebels' main line and were driven back. The Confederates thereupon counter-attacked, but were also repulsed and both sides bivouacked for the night.

In the morning of May 4, Lee saw that Hooker had greatly strengthened his already strong position, and this led him to make the accurate deduction that his opponent was still thinking defensively. Whereupon he resolved to leave Stuart in front of Hooker with 25,000 while he personally sought to destroy Sedgwick's corps—now down to 19,000—with the 21,-000 remaining Rebels still concentrated at Salem Church. But during the night Uncle John had wisely put himself in reach of the north bank of the Rappahannock by means of a pontoon bridge laid at Scott's Ford. However, during the day Early had returned to Fredericksburg, forcing Gibbon to withdraw. Then Early joined Lee. The situation at Salem Church seemed to favor Lee, but Sedgwick, by skillfully deploying his deep horseshoe defense across the Orange Plank Road, thus denying the Rebels a communications artery, had delayed Marse Robert's own deployment so greatly that it was not until 5:30 P.M. that he could attack. Like Jackson massing on Howard's flank, this left Lee even a quarter hour less daylight in which to crush Sedgwick—and it was not enough. After darkness fell, Uncle John artfully disengaged and retired to the north side of the river, taking up the pontoon bridge after him. Gibbon also crossed the river at Fredericksburg, and all bridges from U.S. Ford down to that city were removed. There were now no Bluebellies south of the Rappahannock except those in Hooker's huge and heavily fortified V, and this Lee intended to strike on the morning of May 6.

It is tempting to speculate on what might have happened if Robert Edward Lee had indeed hurled himself upon Mr. F. J. Hooker on that May morning, even though he was outnumbered more than two to one and striking at a most formidable fixed position. Moreover, the men he brought back from Salem Church were exhausted. Nevertheless, he fully intended to strike, impelled by that irrepressible combativeness that was both his great virtue and the defect of that virtue, as witness Malvern Hill. But during the night of May 5–6, Hooker had called a council of war, so often the device of commanders unwilling to take responsibility for a risky decision. Couch, Reynolds, Meade, Howard and Sickles reported promptly to their chief's tent, but Slocum, who had the farthest to go, did not arrive until after the meeting had broken up. Hooker put the question of retreat to the five generals present, observing that covering Washington was paramount in his instructions. Then he retired to allow them to vote.

Reynolds, who was weary, gave Meade his proxy—providing he

voted for attack—and then lay down to sleep. Both Howard and Meade were for attacking. Couch was surprisingly for retreat, but for the understandable reason that he no longer wished to serve under Hooker. Sickles, modestly describing himself as an amateur soldier, certainly aware that Hooker—the man who had made him—was for withdrawal, also voted to retire. When Hooker returned to receive the three-to-two decision to take the offensive, he immediately announced that he was withdrawing. As the generals departed, Reynolds in a voice deliberately raised so that Hooker could hear, angrily inquired: "What was the use of calling us together at this time of night when he intended to retreat anyhow?"

The answer should have been clear to all of them. Hooker had indeed made up his mind, but he also wanted certification from his corps commanders, so that if the vote had been for retreat, he could shift blame by maintaining that he had bowed to the wisdom of his generals.

That night Fighting Joe Hooker crossed the Rappahannock with his artillery, and at five o'clock the following morning in a heavy rain, with Meade's V Corps in place as a rear guard, his infantry began to cross. There was a difficult moment when the rising river threatened to break the pontoon bridges, which became too short as the stream widened. But after two bridges were made into one, the crossing continued. For a moment it seemed that Couch in command on the south bank was about to give the order for an attack, until Hooker sent him an emphatic order to withdraw.

Thus ended the Battle of Chancellorsville, Robert E. Lee's greatest victory. He had inflicted losses of 17,000 on the enemy while suffering about 13,000 of his own. In truth the triumph was perhaps Pyrrhic, for the Army of the Potomac could stand such attrition far more than the Army of Northern Virginia. And once again Marse Robert had been denied in his fierce resolve either to annihilate this northern host or capture it, as his dismay and anger suggested when he was told in the morning that the foe had vanished. "That is the way you young men always do," he snapped at the officer who made the report. "I tell you what to do, but you won't do it!"

Chancellorsville appeared even more Pyrrhic four days later when Lee learned that Stonewall Jackson—of whom he had said, "He has lost his left arm, but I have lost my right"—had gone to his reward.

At first Dr. McGuire thought his patient would recover. So did Jackson. "I am wounded, but not depressed," he said. He was in especially good spirits when he was moved by ambulance to a comfortable cottage near Guiney Station, where he had spent that idyllic interlude with his wife and daughter. Country people crowding to the roadside to offer him gifts of buttermilk, fried chicken and hot biscuits brought tears to his eyes. He even chatted with his aides about his turning movement, saying that Hooker's plan had been a good one, "But he should not have sent away his cavalry. That was his great blunder. It was that which enabled me to turn him, without his being aware of it, and take him by the rear."

McGuire was supremely confident that Jackson would soon return to duty, until the morning of May 7 when he found his patient restless and in pain. Examining him, McGuire sorrowfully diagnosed his new affliction as pneumonia. His wife, Anna, was summoned and taken to the sick room. She was shocked when she saw the change in the husband she had left only eight days previously. He scarcely knew her. But then, in a lucid moment, he saw her at his bedside and murmured: "My darling, you are very much loved. You are one of the most precious little wives in the world."

Jackson's condition became the concern of the entire South. Newspapers insisted that the Almighty would not deprive the Confederacy of such a "great soul." General Lee felt the same. "God will not take him from us now that we need him so much." But Stonewall grew steadily worse. Sometimes in moments of clarity, when the pain eased, he and Anna would discuss the hereafter. Stonewall said that he would submit to the Lord's will. "But I do not believe I shall die at this time." Soon he was in delirium, back on the battlefield crying out orders.

On Sunday May 10 McGuire told Anna that her husband would not last the day. Stonewall seemed not to understand when she again spoke to him of salvation, and said his time was come. The third time she did, he said: "I may yet get well." Anna burst into tears and told him that the doctor had said there was no hope. Stonewall summoned McGuire to ask if this were so, and when the doctor said it was, he fell silent. Then he said, "Very good, very good, it is all right. It is the Lord's day. My wish is fulfilled. I have always desired to die on Sunday."

In the afternoon he was delirious again, his breathing fast and faint, his mind back on the battlefield. "Order A. P. Hill to prepare for action! Pass the infantry to the front. . . . Tell Major Hawks—" Suddenly he smiled, and said in a calm voice: "Let us cross the river, and rest in the shade of the trees."

He did cross, and Lee, the Jove of war, had lost his thunderbolt.

51

.

The Northern Draft Riots

CHANCELLORSVILLE HORRIFIED the North. Hooker's boasts and glowing forecasts of a great victory impending had prepared the country for a victory celebration, but the news that the Army of the Potomac was retreating had the effect of a bridegroom falling to the floor among his reveling guests writhing in the throes of the Black Death. "My God, it is horrible," Horace Greeley croaked, his face pale and lips trembling. "Lost, lost!" Senator Sumner groaned, bursting into the office of Navy Secretary Welles with outflung arms. "All is lost!" Abraham Lincoln was shocked as never before. After the Emancipation Proclamation he had been so confident, confiding in a friend: "We are like whalers who have been on a long chase. We have at last got the harpoon into the monster, but we must now look how we steer, or with one flop of his tail he will send us all into eternity." Then Fredericksburg had come, and he said: "If there is a worse place than Hell, I am in it." Now Chancellorsville, and the monster's flailing tail had all but knocked him out. A visitor to the White House saw him with the report from Chancellorsville in his hands. His face "was ashen in hue," much like the gray wallpaper behind him. "My God, my God!" he cried, pacing the room with hands clasped behind his back. "What will the country say? What will the country say?"

It was a question that an agonized president well past the midway point of his administration well might ask. Since Burnside's dreadful bloodbath there had been, with the possible exception of the standoff "victory" at Murfreesboro, a funereal procession of military defeat and political crisis, beginning in April with the attempt to capture Charleston.

Charleston was not especially important, not since the blockade had effectively sealed it off. But Charleston, the home of the hotheads, the place where the war had begun, was a symbol. If taken and made to feel the whip of war it would not only chastise people such as the firebrand Rhetts and their kind all over Dixie, but also humble the seat of the rebellion and lend encouragement to the hunger for peace growing in some disenchanted Confederate hearts. "My prayer is for a tidal wave of peace," Mary Chesnut wrote.

At first it was believed that Charleston could be taken by naval force alone, and a fleet of seven ironclads, an armored gunboat and the flagship *New Ironsides* was assembled under the command of Rear Admiral Samuel Francis Du Pont, commander of the South Atlantic Blockading Squadron that had done so much to seal off the Confederacy from the sea. P.G.T. Beauregard was again in command in Charleston. On the afternoon of April 7 the Federal fleet steamed into the harbor to begin bombarding Fort Sumter, which, with Moultrie, returned the fire. Du Pont's doubts that naval vessels alone could destroy these formidable positions were justified, while his "shotproof" monitors proved to be something less than invulnerable. Within forty minutes Rebel guns fired 2,209 shells, compared to 154 from the Federals, plastering Du Pont's ships with hits ranging from thirty-five to fifty-one. Five of them were disabled and one sunk, and at darkness Du Pont retired—going into personal retirement after Navy Secretary Welles refused to publish his charge that the ironclads were unfit.

Chagrined by the repulse, Welles decided to try again, this time with a joint army-navy assault force. Rear Admiral John A. Dahlgren, the ordnance expert who had invented a bottle-shaped gun that contributed much to Union victories on the water, was given command of a bombardment fleet. A 15,000-man landing force was to be led by Brigadier General Quincy Gillmore, a thirty-eight-year-old fortifications and siege expert who had been top man in his class at West Point. Gillmore saw that Sumter was the key to Charleston, but agreed with Du Pont that ships could not reduce it. His plan was to mount heavy guns on the tip of Morris Island, a few miles south of Sumter in the middle of the harbor mouth, and batter the fort to pieces. But Morris was held by a Confederate force in entrenched batteries, so that Gillmore's troops would have to make an amphibious assault and evict them.

The Yankees were in high spirits, especially the 54th Massachusetts, an all-black regiment with white officers led by Colonel Robert Gould Shaw. A wealthy Boston blue blood like many of his white officers, Shaw had left Harvard in his third year to join the New York National Guard. When war came, he transferred to the 2nd Massachusetts as a second lieutenant, rising to captain. Like his mother, he was an ardent Abolitionist, and he believed that black troops could fight as well as white soldiers. When the

War Department in January 1863 approved Governor John Andrew's request to raise a regiment of black soldiers, command and the rank of colonel was given to this handsome twenty-five-year-old. After he paraded the regiment in Boston, his mother wept for joy, exclaiming: "What have I done that God has been so good to me?" Much of the excitement over the Charleston operation derived from the belief—or hope—that the soldiers of this first black regiment in the history of American arms would exact a fearsome vengeance on their hated oppressors.

In July Gillmore's spearheads landed unopposed at the southern end of Morris and began driving north toward Battery Wagner and Battery Gregg. Casualties had been light, and Gillmore ordered an all-out assault on Wagner next morning. The first wave made it to the parapet, but was shredded by the fort's heavy volleys of grape and musketry, while Gregg in support devastated the following units. Undaunted, Gillmore brought 3,500 more men ashore and began plastering both positions with his own guns. On July 18 the attack was renewed—and so was the carnage. The 54th Massachusetts suffered grievously. Shaw was killed and so were many of his black soldiers. Against only 174 defenders killed or wounded, the attackers lost 1,515. Battery Wagner may have been the Civil War's most hideous battlefield, limited in area though it was: the exact result to be expected when flesh-and-blood men attempt to storm a fixed position in the face of point-blank artillery fire. Dead and wounded men lay in piles, their bodies horribly mangled, limbs, torsos, and heads scattered among and around them. In that intense, moist heat of a Lowcountry summer, the bodies began decomposing fast, and eventually, to prevent the spread of pestilence, had to be buried in a common grave.

So Charleston was not taken, and indeed would not be taken until February 1865, by which time the doom of the Confederacy was apparent to most Southerners.

Yet the bravery of the black troops at Battery Wagner—where Sergeant William Carney became the first black man to win the Medal of Honor—had a profound effect upon the use of black soldiers in the Federal service. For one thing it shattered the prejudice against them as being unfit for combat, and for another it helped to bring almost 200,000 black recruits into the Union army and navy. Half of these were from Southern areas occupied by Federal forces and the other half were Northern freedmen. They fought in 449 engagements and suffered 35 percent more casualties than their white comrades, in good part because Rebel commanders refused to take black prisoners.

Although freed blacks and former slaves were proud to wear the

Union Blue, and some of them were able to obtain an elementary education, there was still much discrimination against them. Few blacks rose to the rank of officer in the U.S. Colored Troops, where the pay was less than in the all-white Union army, and most of the soldiers were assigned to heavy labor or guarding rear-echelon facilities. In 1865, however, they received the same pay as white soldiers, and provided nearly two-thirds of the troops in the Mississippi valley. Their presence in the Union army, said Abraham Lincoln, had been decisive in the ultimate victory.

"War," said Edmund Burke, "never leaves a nation where it found it." And thus in that spring of 1863, which witnessed the twin Union defeats of Charleston and Chancellorsville, the Lincoln Administration was being buffeted by winds of war that were blowing away some of the most sacred misconceptions of the American people. One of these, the persistent notion that America was a nation of small farmers, was yoked to the other unfounded belief that there was no oppressed or exploited class in the country, as there was in Europe, or Asia or Africa. But there was: the miners of the anthracite coal mining counties of northeastern Pennsylvania. They were mostly Irish immigrants, and they were beginning to give violent expression to their hatred of the war and the military draft.

Because of the population explosion, coal mining had rocketed from a scant million tons a year in 1840 to eight and one half million in 1860. The character of mining had also changed. Where it had once been personal and human, small mines run by an owner who knew his handful of workers by name and was kind to them, it had been consolidated into the hands of a few immensely wealthy and usually absentee owners caring only for profits. Competition for labor was stifled by importation of hordes of impoverished immigrants—again usually Irish, probably because they could speak the language—who lived in squalor in dreadful company housing and bought what they needed at the company stores, paying for their purchases with company scrip—their wages—which could be used nowhere else. Indeed, it was not until ten years after the war that the owners were compelled by law to pay in American currency. Of protective legislation and safety regulations there was none.

Added to these privations and indignities was social and religious prejudice. All the miners were Irish and Catholic, while all the bosses were English, Scots and Welsh—and Protestant. They shared the contempt of the foreign-born—especially if they were Catholic—which was still nurtured both North and South by the Know-Nothings and Nativists. They despised the Irish miners as a lawless race given to fighting and drunken-

ness. Just as the Southern ruling class advanced the ignorance and squalor
in which they kept their black slaves as the reason for doing it, so their
Northern counterparts insisted that the similar destitution of the Irish was
a racial characteristic, rather than the result of pay so low that they could
barely meet the rents and prices of company house and company store.
Thus the Irish, by no means a docile race, countered the contempt of the
bosses with implacable hatred, which could and did grow violent with
passage of the draft act.

Although the South passed the first American conscription law on
April 16, 1862, the North did not enact its own until March 3, 1863. In the
coal regions the miners were compelled to register for the draft against
their will. Soon it became clear that "troublesome" miners were called up
first, while the mine bosses either never were conscripted or else bought
a "substitute" for three hundred dollars. Some protesting miners were
literally dragged into service, tied to the stirrups of a cavalry horse. Thus
onto social indignity, religious prejudice and economic exploitation was
piled this final injustice of a discriminating draft. Moreover, since the Emancipation Proclamation had made the war a crusade against slavery, the
miners, like all factory hands and mechanics all over the North, came to hate
it as a conflict that would end with blacks flooding the country with cheap
labor. So the quick-tempered Irish rebelled and there was bloodshed.

Mine bosses were beaten up or murdered. In one town a group of two
hundred infuriated miners raided a colliery, beat up the office staff, seized
the hated company store which, they said, firing shots into the air, if it ever
were reopened would provoke "real trouble." Other mobs visited the
homes of men believed to be pro-company and pro-draft, pulled them out
of bed and killed them. Such organized bands eventually appeared to have
gained complete control of the anthracite region, and soon it became known
that the uprising was the work of a mysterious secret organization known
as the Molly Maguires.

Actually what was happening was that here, in blood—and indeed
revolutions against social injustice are often written in no other medium—
was the first faint stirring of the American labor movement. The miners
were trying to organize, clumsily, of course, and in the face of economic and
political power that they could never hope to conquer, still less persuade.
All the powers-that-were condemned them as Copperheads and traitors. It
was said that the Molly Maguires dominated Schuylkill County, the center
of unrest. When Governor Curtin of Pennsylvania refused to use militia to
crush the "uprising," Secretary Stanton—a simplicist who saw all problems
in black and white, good and bad—in effect reached for his little bell and

sent the 10th New Jersey in to restore "law and order." But the soldiers of this regiment sympathized so openly with the miners that their colonel begged to have them withdrawn before they did something embarrassing, or something serious happened. He did not specify, but he might have feared that they would join the miners.

The dispute reached the crisis stage when the county's draft commission composed a long list of draftees, most of whom were miners. They were supposed to entrain for Harrisburg where they would be enrolled in the Federal service. They announced that they would not go. Not go: period. On departure day a huge mob of miners surrounded the train and turned the draftees loose. Now an infuriated Stanton vowed that they would go "at the point of the bayonet." Governor Curtin and Lincoln's friend A. K. McClure, the Republican leader of Pennsylvania, begged Stanton to calm down, but he would not, and the next day the enforcing regiments appeared in the county. With this, McClure dumped the problem in the lap of his White House friend. Lincoln's reply was a model of double-talk which the diplomatic McClure understood at once. The president, of course, was bound to see the law executed, but if it *appeared* to be executed, that would be satisfactory, too. So McClure had the county draft commissioner collect a huge number of affidavits proving that a great number of Schuylkill residents had joined the army in places such as Harrisburg or Philadelphia or wherever, and that this satisfied the Schuylkill County quota. It also satisfied Lincoln, who was perhaps more than satisfied later when a similar situation arose in Philadelphia and McClure waved his magic wand in reverse.

The City of Brotherly Love was then a Republican stronghold, but the War Department that spring declared that it was also short of its quota by 3,000 men. To enforce the unpopular draft there might well be to lose the city to the Democrats. Studying the figures, McClure saw that many out-of-towners who had enlisted in Philadelphia had been properly credited to their own districts, and so, lifting Aaron's rod—presto, chango!—he transformed 3,000 of them into bona fide Philadelphians.

Thus riots and bloodshed over the draft had been avoided in Pennsylvania, but in New York City widespread resentment of a policy of discrimination simply could not be contained.

In July of that year a mob infuriated by the inequities of the draft terrorized New York. Howling, "To hell with the draft and the war," they burned homes, public buildings, churches, police stations, stores, factories, saloons, even an orphanage, murdering blacks; and battling police and soldiers hand-to-hand in the streets or from behind barricades, driving draft officials from their offices and wrecking draft apparatus, the rioters exploded in a fury of resentment against "a rich man's war and a poor man's fight." In the end, the draft was suspended in New York and regiments from the Army of the Potomac marched into the city to quell the mob. But not before 400 persons had been killed or wounded and $5 million lost in property damage.

In truth the rioters, incited by antiadministration newspapers as well as by such personages as Franklin Pierce and Governor Horatio Seymour, had much to resent in a draft law that permitted anyone to buy an exemption for $300 or to hire a substitute to go in his place. Obviously the law was designed for well-heeled lip-servers of the Union cause, most notable among them being Grover Cleveland, who hired a substitute to fight his fight for the nation which he was twice to lead as president. In New York City some $5 million was siphoned from the city treasury for draft-evasion purposes, the money going to politicians, lawyers, examining physicians, fixers and other patriotic types who would thus see to it that the "right people" would be deferred. Thus, of 292,441 men called in New York, 39,877 failed to report, 164,394 were exempted, 52,288 bought exemption for $300 apiece and 26,002 hired substitutes. Only 9,880 men—about one out of 30—who either lacked political pull or possessed true patriotism went off to fight. No wonder the mob rose in fury! No wonder there were similar though not nearly so violent protests throughout the North, especially in New England, where sanctimonious bluenoses often bought exemption and then, once the war was over, piously prevailed upon local legislatures to repay them for this patriotic outlay. The humorist Artemus Ward ridiculed such coat-holders with the remark: "I have already given two cousins to the war, & I stand reddy to sacrifiss my wife's brother, ruthurn'n not see the rebellion krusht. And if wuss comes to wuss, I'll shed every drop of blood my able-bodied relations has got to prosekoot the war." So it was the farmers, the wage hands, and especially the immigrants, who arrived in the North to the number of 800,000 during the war years, who shouldered the Union muskets.

Meanwhile, enormous profits were being made by war contractors. Among those famous fortunes founded during the Civil War were Armour in meat packing, Borden in dairy products, Carnegie in iron and steel, Marshall Field in merchandise, Huntington in merchandise and railroads, Remington in guns, Rockefeller in oil and Weyerhaeuser in lumber. Profiteering naturally contributed to inflation, and wages, without benefit of organized unions, trailed far behind skyrocketing prices. In purse as well as in person, then, it was "a rich man's war and a poor man's fight."

Among Lincoln's other difficulties in that summer of 1863 was the intrusion of France into Mexico, where Napoleon III hoped to set up a puppet government with the young Austrian Archduke Maximilian as his emperor. Little Napoleon had flagrantly violated the Monroe Doctrine, but there was not very much that Lincoln could do about it until after the war. Nor was there much that either Lincoln or Jefferson Davis could do about the defeatism and disloyalty that grew stronger in each camp with every passing month.

Some of the opposition to both presidents was provoked by the ruthlessness with which they enforced conscription. Some of it came from persons honestly convinced that peace could be achieved by negotiation, and some from those fainthearted or selfish persons for whom plotting or treason always has seemed the way of safety or profit. Thus both sides organized secret societies. In the Northwest the Knights of the Golden Circle terrorized loyalists with midnight raids or met with Southern spies to plot fifth-column uprising for which they really had no stomach, and in the South the Heroes of America gave more surreptitious aid and comfort to the North. On both sides, opposition was too formidable for either president to move against it.

Davis's chief difficulties came from states' rights governors such as Joseph Brown of Georgia, who suspended the draft and raised a militia of 10,000 men to defend his state alone. Governor Vance of North Carolina was only less obstructionist, and he acted in that fashion because his state was so full of antiwar sentiment that at one point there was open talk of seceding from the Confederacy. Much as the gentlewoman had been the South's chief recruiter, too many beloveds had been coming home in coffins. Mrs. Chesnut wrote: "Is anything worth it—this fearful sacrifice; this awful penalty we pay for war?"

The North's peace movement was more open and better organized. In the Northwest, where intense patriotism and open treason flourished side by side, it was led by those antiwar Democrats called Copperheads from their lapel insignia of an Indian head carved from a copper penny. A former Ohio congressman named Clement Vallandigham was the Copperhead leader. While in Congress the proslavery Vallandigham had taunted Republicans with the remark: "War for the Union was abandoned; war for the Negro openly begun, and with stronger battalions than before." While campaigning for governor of Ohio in 1863 he had characterized the war as being fought "for the purpose of crushing out liberty and erecting a despotism." Lincoln would have been content to let Vallandigham talk himself out, rather than make a martyr of him; however, the blunt General Burnside was now in command in Ohio and he had Vallandigham arrested, tried by a military court and sentenced to jail for the rest of the war. With keen good humor, Lincoln changed the sentence to banishment within the Confederacy. The Copperheads replied with a 40,000-member mass meeting in Lincoln's home town where they resolved "that a further offensive prosecution of this war tends to subvert the Constitution and the Government." They also assailed Lincoln's treatment of Vallandigham, to which he gave the grim answer: "Must I shoot a simple-minded soldier boy who deserts and not touch a hair of the wily agitator who induces him to desert?"

By then the North was shooting deserters a half dozen at a time, and with such solemnity and deliberation as would strike fear into the hearts of soldiers massed to witness the executions. Desertion was a problem for both sides—one out of nine enlistments in the South deserted, one out of seven in the North—but the Union army had to deal with defeatists who systematically encouraged soldiers to desert and mailed them packages containing the civilian clothes and railroad tickets that would facilitate their disappearance. Most despised deserters of all were the bounty jumpers, men who enlisted in one state or locality to claim a bounty, and then deserted to claim another one in a different place.

The bounty system was another Union headache. To reduce the number of men needed to be drafted from any state or city, bounties were paid to men who would volunteer. However, the bounties rose to as high as $1,000 per man after reluctant draftees began to bid against states and cities for the services of a substitute. Next there entered the inevitable middleman, the sly, grasping bounty broker who for a fee would find a man willing to enlist. Too often the broker operated like a waterfront crimp, getting his man drunk and inducing him to sign away his bounty rights for a pittance and then rushing him through the enlistment process. Some did not scruple to scour the slums of Europe for recruits. As a result, the dregs of society were often draped in Federal blue, to the indignation of one recruiting officer who protested against putting the uniform "upon branded felons; upon blotched and bloated libertines and pimps; upon thieves, burglars and vagabonds; upon the riff-raff of corruption and scoundrelism of every shade and degree of infamy which can be swept into the insatiable clutches of the vampires who fatten upon the profits of the execrable business." Naturally, the chief concern of such "soldiers" was how best to avoid fighting and how quickly to get out of uniform; and so, as the war grew older, they were treated with increasing harshness by a government that still had not the moral courage to draft outright all those shrinking, perfumed patriots who had purchased their own safety with these decrepit or debased human beings.

Although the South was not so hypocritical in waging a rich man's war and a poor man's fight, it nevertheless did discriminate to a lesser degree. Substitute-buying, though not as widespread, was permitted; and to the numerous exempt classes was added that of the plantation overseer at the rate of one to every twenty black slaves. This was the infamous "20-nigger law" which enraged the poorer whites, and helped to raise the rate of deserters and men absent without leave. In June of 1863 the proportion of absentees from the Confederate Army was nearing one-third, and President Davis proclaimed an amnesty for all who would return to their units. Few, however, came back.

52

■

Lee Moves North

AFTER THE ARMY OF THE POTOMAC resumed its old positions around Falmouth on the north bank of the Rappahannock, it began to become clear to everyone in blue down to the lowliest private that this "finest army on this planet" had not really been hurt but only humiliated once more. There was never a moment when Hooker's army had not had the power to destroy the Army of Northern Virginia. Even the barest minimum of hard fighting would have accomplished this, but the Northern host simply had not fought—as the casualties suggest.

Before the battle Lincoln had said to Hooker, "Put in all your men," as a reminder of what Burnside had failed to do. And Fighting Joe had let a third of his army stand idle. Between them the corps of Meade and Reynolds had lost fewer than 1,000 men, while Sickles and Sedgwick had each suffered four times as many. Yet Fighting Joe was quick to place the blame on Stoneman, Howard and Sedgwick. This was not only unjust— except for Stoneman—it was also untrue. Stoneman had indeed been incompetent and irresolute, if his casualties are any indication: 82 killed and wounded plus 307 missing—probably prisoners or deserters, for cavalry rarely rides into those artillery barrages that obliterate men. He had broken up his massed horsemen into small units and done nothing to hurt Lee. "Our only accomplishments," observed one of his disgusted troopers, "were the burning of a few canal boats on the upper James River, some bridges, hen roosts and tobacco houses." Hooker quite properly replaced Stoneman with the aggressive Alfred Pleasonton, but it must be remembered that it was Fighting Joe who sent away his horse and left himself fighting blind. But to criticize the faithful Sedgwick, who had tried to do all that Hooker asked of him, was not quite the essence of nobility in a defeated commander, while he also knew quite well that Howard's crumbled flank was eventually stabil-

472

ized and the Army of the Potomac still had an excellent chance to destroy the enemy. Only weeks later did Hooker admit: "I was not hurt by a shell, and I was not drunk. For once I lost confidence in Joe Hooker, and that is all there is to it."

Surprisingly, neither Lincoln nor Halleck seemed to have lost confidence in Joe Hooker, for they made no move to relieve him, except to place on him the temporary restriction of protecting Harpers Ferry and Washington.

Jubilation among the Graybacks below the river was in marked contrast to the gloom of the Bluebellies north of it. A feeling of invincibility blinded the Army of Northern Virginia to the true consequences of the deceptive victory at Chancellorsville: casualties again whittling the veteran troops of this always-outnumbered army; the loss of Jackson, the peerless field commander of the war and the hand to execute the daring designs issuing from the head of Lee; and, finally, the failure once again to capture or annihilate the Union's eastern army. This last was vital and would eventually be decisive. A succession of tactical victories however glorious or numerous is no substitute for that single slaying strategic stroke, and there was no one in Marse Robert's command to point out to him, as Hasdrubal had said to his brother Hannibal: "You know how to win victories, but not how to use them."

Nevertheless, by June of 1863 Lee was once again thinking of invading the North, a project he had been quietly contemplating even before Chancellorsville. He had never really believed in President Davis's strategy of defense, and now, having taken the measure of Hooker, he was eager to inflict on him that strategic victory which could win the war. Although Hooker in his present position was too strong for him, he reasoned that if he crossed the Potomac again he could lure him out of it into decisive battle. That is why he so eagerly accepted those raw conscripts to bring his strength up to more than 76,000 men, while thoroughly reorganizing his army into three corps under Longstreet, Ewell and A. P. Hill, with Stuart remaining in command of his oversized cavalry division. (At this time Confederate divisions and corps were still nearly twice as large as the enemy's, and it would not be until the last year of the war that attrition brought them down to the Federal level.) Each division was assigned a battalion of artillery and each corps given two battalions to use as corps ordnance.

There was some mild surprise at the selection of Ewell to lead Stonewall Jackson's old II Corps. When he commanded a division under Jackson, Richard Stoddart Ewell had been known as an eccentric, a bald-headed, forty-five-year-old bachelor whose hooked nose and habit of cocking his head to one side reminded those around him of a bird. Much about him seemed odd, not so much his inveterate profanity, but his habit of cursing with a lisp; and again not so much his ulcerous dispositon, but rather his attempt to soothe it with a diet of hulled wheat boiled in milk with raisins and honey. But then "Old Bald Head," as his troops called him, lost a leg at Groveton in August of 1862, and did not return to duty until May the following year as the "new" Ewell, supplied with three acquisitions: a wooden leg, religious faith leading him to lisp the Lord's name in prayer rather than in vain and a wealthy wife to soften his irascible personality. A widow, she had been married to a man named Brown, and with her fortune now at his own disposal, the new Dick Ewell was the soul of suavity, although he sometimes forgot himself and introduced his lady as "My wife, Mrs. Brown." Nevertheless, the talk around the campfires was whether or not Old Bald Head would prove to be a worthy successor to old Blue Light—and this, of course, could be answered only in the crucible of combat.

The appointment of A. P. Hill to command the new III Corps, however, did not go down too well with James Longstreet. Old Pete believed that Harvey Hill was best qualified for that post, observing later: "His record was as good as Stonewall Jackson's but, not being a Virginian, he was not as well advertised." There was more than just pique at not having been consulted on these selections behind Longstreet's complaint. Of the fifteen important commands in Lee's army, ten were held by generals from the Old Dominion, two by Georgians and one each by generals from Texas, South Carolina, and North Carolina—the latter having furnished a quarter of Lee's troops. Mississippi and Alabama with three brigades each and some of the finest fighting men in the South had no recognition at all.

Longstreet also encountered Lee's very definite Virginia bias when he advanced his proposal for winning the war. He saw the war as a whole, not a contest of separate theaters waged by separate commanders. He reasoned that the South still held interior lines and could thus move troops from point to point by railroad faster than the North could. He suggested that Lee could leave Ewell and A. P. Hill behind to contain Hooker, while taking Old Pete's own corps and all other available eastern formations west to unite them with the commands of Bragg, Buckner and Johnston and hurl the whole upon Rosecrans. Destruction of the Army of the Cumberland would stun the North and almost certainly compel the recall of Grant from Vicksburg.

Longstreet's proposal, visionary and original in that it was based on viewing the war as a whole, possessed great possibilities, even though it overrated the capacity of the South's railroads. But Lee declined to adopt it, not because of this less than decisive defect in transportation, but because he had drawn his sword to defend "my country"—Virginia. He therefore was unwilling to conduct operations outside its borders. Such parochialism, if it may be so described, was a serious shortcoming in a general who had been for some time the de facto supreme commander of Confederate forces in that he advised and counseled President Davis on all theaters, and eventually would become the actual general-in-chief.

Joined to this defect was an even graver shortcoming: a resigned and passive attitude toward the wretched state of the Confederate service of supply. Indeed, Lee's plan to invade the North again was based in part on the chronic failures and ineptness of the Rebel supply system, and he hoped to obtain food and clothing in Maryland and Pennsylvania. It is safe to say that the Army of Northern Virginia, though inspired by Chancellorsville and brilliantly reorganized by Lee, was the worst-fed and worst-clothed army in military history.

In fairness to Lee it must be said that the Confederacy—as Sherman had clearly seen—was simply not capable of waging modern war, and did not take into account its material deficiencies. It was a war entered under the hysterical guidance of a feudal ruling class fighting for its very life and wishfully believing that the heart could conquer the head, that spiritual power would overwhelm material power; and thus the dreadful suffering of their troops was not seen as cause for concern and correction but rather glorified as the unconquerable spirit of the South. It is also possible that Southern commanders including Lee, having been accustomed to seeing the men they now led—these valiant, hardy Pineys and Rednecks—wearing coarse clothing and subsisting on vile porridge in peacetime, were not quite so sorrowful to see them in rags and tatters and supplementing their sparse diet with nuts and berries during war. Rather the indomitable Graybacks are showered with praise and encomiums. They are "splendid scarecrows" or "magnificent ragamuffins." They are described as "ragged, slovenly, sleeveless, without a superfluous ounce of flesh upon their bones, with wild, matted hair, in mendicants' rags—and to think that when the battle flag goes to the front how they can and do fight!" Of them Lee would repeatedly make remarks such as: "There never were such men in an army before. They will go anywhere and do anything if properly led." But not fed. There is no record anywhere of constant and vigorous protests to Richmond about the quality and quantity of supply for the Army of Northern Virginia.

Indeed, the war had ravaged northern Virginia, but the Shenandoah was still productive; Longstreet, when on detached duty around Suffolk, had been amazed at the food, goods and forage he could collect in an area relatively untouched by the war. True, ardent states' righters such as Joe Brown in Georgia and Zebulon Vance in North Carolina had not been exactly selfless in their devotion to the Confederate cause, withholding supplies as well as troops, and in this the breakdown of the service of supply might have been the fault of President Davis. But Robert Edward Lee would never challenge or criticize Jefferson Davis, still less argue with him or dispute him. Indeed, throughout the war Lee only once showed any sign of disapproval of his commander in chief, and that quite properly was on the battlefield before Richmond in 1862 when Davis rode up followed by a lengthy cavalcade of officials and politicians. "Who are all this army of people," Lee asked in irritation, "and what are they doing here?" But that was an isolated incident, a necessary rebuke to the political arm interfering with the military, and it was never to be repeated. "I am a soldier," Lee said. "It is my duty to obey orders." True enough, but it was also his duty as an army commander and then as a supreme commander to complain to the various secretaries of war and even to Davis himself of the incredible hardships and privations being endured by his troops. In short, Robert Edward Lee was simply too submissive, too unwilling to wrestle in the foul and slippery arena of politics to demand on the pain of his resignation a commander's due: that his troops be adequately armed, fed and clothed.

Many of Lee's staff officers thought of him as a saint, and so he seemed with his unpretentious humility, his kindliness, his reluctance to give offense, his insistence on sharing the hardships of his soldiers, living in a tent no better than theirs, eating no better, even sending whatever dainties that came his way to the sick and wounded. He did this both to set an example to his officers and to gain the love and respect of his men, and he was eminently successful. As J. F. C. Fuller has said, he even "sanctified" his army, enrolling it in the noble cause, God's cause, if you will.

Just as Lee believed that God had placed the fate of the Confederacy in the hands of Davis, he also believed that He had given him this army as an instrument of divine justice. Here Lee appears as a kind of religious fatalist. But not as a saint, not one of those fierce and immensely practical men and women on fire with the love of God, giving it expression in caring for suffering humanity, founding hospitals and orphanages, tending the sick and feeding the poor, challenging emperors and kings, popes and cardinals, accepting martyrdom or exchanging their own persons for hostages and slaves—human beings submissive to no one but the will of God, following no example but that of Christ Himself. If Lee the good and gentle man had possessed something of this ferocity, this single-mindedness in his cause, he would have been a much better general and a far better supreme commander. Like Napoleon, he understood how to inspire troops, riding among them on his tall gray stallion to give them glory, but unlike Napoleon he would never say, "An army marches on its stomach." His fatalism did not lead him to control what he could control. "As soon as I order them forward in battle, I leave my army in the hands of God." To say as the cynical Bonaparte said, "God is on the side of the big battalions," would have seemed to him blasphemy.

Lee's fatalistic resignation to the suffering of his troops was rivaled by his appalling indifference to discipline. Just as his "reluctance to oppose the wishes of others, or to order them to do anything that would be disagreeable and to which they would not consent"—the words are those of his nephew, Fitzhugh Lee—he could not chastise these men whom he truly loved and admired. The only way an officer in the Army of Northern Virginia could establish authority or influence was by bravery in battle. He bought obedience by his blood. Punishment or the threat of it—in a word, a system of military justice—was not applied. Graybacks came and went as they pleased, often swarming over the countryside like foraging locusts. On September 22 of 1862 in Richard Ewell's division of more than 11,000 men, only 4,000 were present for duty. D. H. Hill repeatedly complained about the indiscipline of Lee's army, describing the Rebel battle line as a fragmented, convoluted crescent with "every man guiding on himself." Even Marse Robert himself wrote to Davis: "The greatest difficulty I find is in causing orders and regulations to be obeyed." He frequently explained to the War Department that he had halted some movement to collect stragglers.

Because of these serious defects in its commander, the army of 76,000 men that Lee planned to lead north, besides being the worst-fed and worst-clothed, was also the worst-disciplined army ever. Even worse, Lee the superb tactician, probably at this point in time the best in modern warfare and certainly the best ever in the annals of American arms, was not guided by a strategy matching his tactical skill. To shift over to the offensive to lure Hooker into decisive battle was, all things being equal, decidedly sound strategy. But all things were not equal. To do this Lee would be compelled to abandon his interior lines—the Confederacy's chief advantage next to the fighting prowess of its soldiers and the ability of its generals— and to spin out behind him a steadily lengthening line of communications vulnerable to enemy attack. Perhaps worse, Lee's poorly supplied army of 76,000 men would be on the offensive against Hooker's splendidly supplied host of 115,000, an almost exact reversal of the two-to-one superiority considered necessary in an invasion, in addition to the fact that the Rebels would be fighting in hostile territory and the Yankees on home ground.

James Longstreet had found none of this enchanting. He was still motivated by the conviction of his experience in Mexico: that it was better to receive attack than to deliver it. At Antietam he had said, "I wish we could stand still and let the damn Yankees come to us," and he had been pleased when Lee adopted a defensive stance there; satisfied again with the defensive at Fredericksburg where his corps took losses of less than 2,000 and gave 9,000. He was perhaps alone in his sour assessment of Chancellorsville: a victory won with casualties of three to four. By the remorseless arithmetic of war, four more such victories would leave Lee with almost nothing and Hooker with what Lee had in the beginning. He spoke of this when Lee announced his plans, but was unable to dissuade his chief. He then, as though he were of equal rank with Marse Robert, stipulated that the campaign "should be offensive in strategy but defensive in tactics, forcing the Federal army to give us battle when we were in a strong position and ready to receive them." Lee listened to him with his customary courtesy, but said nothing—even though he intended to follow no such course. Unfortunately for the Confederacy, Longstreet took his silence to mean consent.

On June 3 the "fabulous" Army of Northern Virginia began its movement west and north. Left behind to hold Fredericksburg and watch Hooker was A. P. Hill with three divisions.

Hooker's balloons had reported Lee's western movement and Hooker at once thought of attacking Hill across the river, and then of moving directly on Richmond. Lincoln and Halleck rejected both suggestions, insisting that Hooker's true objective was Lee's army. He should interpose his own between Marse Robert and the capital. Although irked by what he considered Lincoln's excessive concern for the safety of Washington, Hooker on June 5–6 sent Sedgwick across the Rappahannock to test Confederate strength. Hill struck back in such force that Sedgwick reported the ridge strongly held. Not quite satisfied with this report, Hooker dispatched Alfred Pleasonton—now a major general—on a scouting mission toward Culpeper in western Virginia.

Jeb Stuart with about 10,000 troopers was at Brandy Station near Culpeper with orders to march west on June 10. Before departing, he held a grand review of five brigades culminating in a grand finale complete with a mock attack by cavalry on horse artillery. It was so realistic with the booming and banging of cannon and pistols, the pounding of horses's hooves and the shrill yipping of the Grayjackets that some of Stuart's adoring lady friends in the grandstand fainted. Stuart was delighted, and he was transported when Lee arrived in Culpeper and rode over to Brandy to request a repeat of the review. It was done, but without the waste of gunpowder. Lee was also delighted, finding his young and favored friend "in all his glory."

Stuart did not feel exactly glorious when Pleasonton with his 10,000 horse burst upon him at Brandy Station. There then ensued the greatest and wildest cavalry battle of the war: saddle-to-saddle, saber-to-saber, mingling bugle calls and much confusion. Gradually Stuart gained the upper hand, and then Confederate infantry appeared. Pleasonton withdrew, having accomplished his mission, to report large concentrations of enemy infantry around Culpeper and Stuart preparing to ride west. Hooker, pleased to hear how well the Union cavalry had fought, was now certain that Lee was moving into the Shenandoah. He moved his army skillfully toward Manassas, after which A. P. Hill marched north to rejoin Lee. Meanwhile a Federal force moving slowly from Winchester to Harpers Ferry was struck by Ewell, losing a third of its numbers and all of its guns. The survivors with other small garrisons in the area concentrated on Maryland Heights above the Union arsenal.

At this point Jeb Stuart's shaken self-esteem was about to make trouble for Robert E. Lee. For the first time the dashing commander of dragoons was being criticized in the Confederate press and hooted at by the populace. Instead of the customary praise for what he had reported to be a "great victory" at Brandy Station, he was sharply attacked for allowing Pleasonton to surprise him and blamed for careless disposition of his troops in the interest of his showy grand review. Uncomplimentary remarks were made about all those ladies in the stands. People were saying he was a show-off and a lady-killer. The Richmond *Enquirer* said, "If he is to be the 'eyes and ears of the army,' we would advise him to see more and be seen less." Even his comrades were disgusted with him. Dorsey Pender wrote his wife: "The cavalry affair in Culpeper was a sad one. . . . I suppose it is all right that Stuart should get all the blame, for when anything handsome is done he gets all the credit." Stuart did not read those words, of course, but he did read and hear of similar outbursts. Because his ego was so large it was easily bruised, and he needed some glorious feat of arms to sooth it and restore his own romantic image of himself. It was partially rescued by three brisk battles with Federal horse at Aldie, Middleburg and Upperville, in which his troopers suffered 660 casualties compared to Federal losses of 827, but bruised again when, during the fighting at Aldie, he was at Middleburg surrounded by admiring ladies vying with one another to cut off his uniform buttons for souvenirs—only to be surprised once more by Yankee riders and put to ignominious flight. Something had to be done, and the opportunity came on June 23 when he received Lee's orders to detach two brigades to watch the gaps in the Blue Ridge and with the rest of his division "feel the right of Ewell's troops" across the Potomac. Given such wide latitude, Stuart next day rode east on his own—perhaps even another spectacular "ride around" the Federal army. Almost at once he became entangled with Union forces still south of the Potomac, and was then cut off from Lee. Marse Robert, now without information on the whereabouts of Hooker's army, assumed it was still below the river. But it wasn't. It was north of the Potomac around Frederick and its distraught commander was busily exchanging increasingly acrimonious messages with Lincoln and Halleck.

Hooker felt that Lincoln and Halleck were much too sensitive to the safety of the capital, that their concern was a millstone around his neck, one that Robert E. Lee gladly yanked from time to time by pretending to menace Washington from the Valley. He also thought that they were goading him into resigning. One after another his proposals had been rejected. Lincoln and Halleck both feared that Hooker might do something rash to silence growing criticism of him in the press. His desire to move on Richmond seemed a willingness to "swap queens"; Hooker to take Richmond, Lee to seize Washington. Hooker resented the rejection of his continued requests for reinforcements, when in fact he had been amply supplied with troops. At one point he even complained that Lee's army outnumbered his own! So he requested permission to withdraw the garrison on Maryland Heights and add its members to his army. This was the breaking point. Halleck replied that this post above Harpers Ferry had been fortified at great expense and was needed to watch Lee's line of communications.

Now Fighting Joe Hooker saw his chance—his out. His confidence was on the wane again and it is probable that he had no wish to try conclusions with Marse Robert once more. He had reached the point which the so-called Parkinson's Principle describes as "his own level of incompetence." Brave soldier, excellent corps commander, even skillful army chief that he was, the burden of responsibility was so heavy, so awful—he could lose the war in a day—that he could not bear it. So he asked to be relieved. His request was promptly granted. As his replacement Lincoln chose—to everyone's surprise—a general junior to both Reynolds and Sedgwick, a commander whom he admired as "A brave and able soldier, and a true man": George Gordon Meade.

53

■

George Gordon Meade

DURING THE THIRD WEEK of January 1816 the baptistry in the beautiful church of Nuestra Señora del Rosario in Cadiz, Spain, was ablaze with candlelight. A priest in a red cassock and white surplice stood next to the baptismal font, a silver ladle in one hand, a black leather service book in the other. Surrounding him were fashionably clad men and women— dark-eyed señoras in lace mantillas, their husbands dressed in suits of sober but rich cloth—people obviously drawn from the wealthy classes of Cadiz.

Behind the priest, holding the infant that was to be baptized, stood the child's father, Richard Worsam Meade, an American but for many years a leading exporter and merchant in Cadiz. Meade had been to the church on this mission many times before. Of his nine children, seven had been born in Cadiz.

This last was christened George Gordon Meade, born the last day of 1815. He had been named for his grandfather, the son of Irish immigrants who had become a wealthy Philadelphia merchant and a patriot who financed the Pennsylvania Bank's attempt to supply George Washington's army with food and clothing. Yet, by 1801, George Meade was bankrupt, although his son, Richard Worsam Meade, was rapidly acquiring his own fortune in Santo Domingo.

Richard Meade's success brought him an appointment as U.S. naval agent in Cadiz. There he lived sumptuously, waited on by liveried servants in a mansion lavishly decorated in Italian marble and housing one of the world's finest private art collections. Meade rose high in the royal favor when he placed his great wealth at the disposal of King Ferdinand in the fight against Napoleon. Although the Loyalists eventually won, by the end of the Peninsular War the royal treasury was bare. Meade's claims were ignored by the treasurer general, who considered they were phrased so insultingly that he threw the American into prison. Here began a cause célèbre between Washington and Madrid, and although Meade was freed in the end, he got none of his money back. In 1828, broke, heavily in debt, Meade, then living in suburban Washington, died at the age of fifty.

Margaret Meade was compelled to withdraw George from a fashionable and expensive military school in Philadelphia and enroll him in a less costly one in Baltimore. But even though he was graduated there with honors she simply could not afford to send him to a private university. So she hit upon the idea of applying to West Point for him, and in early July 1831, probably because of his studies at military schools, he was accepted.

George was sixteen when he arrived at West Point. He was near his mature height of slightly over six feet, slender, with brown hair and blue eyes and a hawkish nose that gave an aquiline cast to his aristocratic features. His fellow cadets remembered him as "dignified, courteous and gentlemanly, but rather reserved," or as a gracious youth "with the air of the highest breeding." Such judgments suggest that Meade's background, rather than his character or deeds, impressed his peers the most. Certainly he failed to fulfill his mother's expectations. In his first year he acquired 168 demerits. Few if any of these were for high or free spirits. Like Sherman after him, Meade detested drill, was careless in dress and allowed his equipment to rust or gather dust. He was not much of a soldier. As a student he was hardly better, but then his fear of being expelled and letting his mother down seized him and he improved, being graduated nineteenth in the 1835 class of fifty-six cadets.

Sent to the Seminole War, he saw no action, but did discover in himself an aptitude for topographical work and a keen eye for land that would one day make him an unrivaled expert at laying out camps and fortifications. Nevertheless, on October 28, 1836, having found the peacetime army life deadly dull, he resigned his commission. He did engineering work for a while with the Topographical Bureau, and fell in love with Margaret Sergeant, the oldest daughter of the distinguished Congressman John Sergeant, who had helped free Meade's father from jail. They were married December 31, 1840, Meade's twenty-fifth birthday, "amid a brilliant assembly." A few years later Congress passed a law excluding civilians from working for Topographical, and Meade was out of a job. Family influence came to his assistance. Through the influence of Congressman Henry A. Wise of Virginia he was reappointed a second lieutenant in the U.S. Army, assigned to Topographical, and although he was not happy to have lost six years' seniority he was pleased to have steady employment on which to support his wife and two sons.

The approach of the Mexican War brought him to Corpus Christi, Texas, where he impressed Zachary Taylor with his excellent maps and eye for land. It was Meade who laid out the American camp opposite the Mexicans at Matamoros on the Rio Grande. But he saw no action in the ensuing battles, although Taylor did have him breveted to first lieutenant.

After the war Meade continued his engineering work, building lighthouses and working on forts and bridges. But then in 1856 he was commissioned captain and ordered to Detroit to take charge of the Great Lakes Survey, moving there with his wife and family of seven children.

The task of surveying the bottoms of these immense inland seas—with a coastline equal to the one extending from Maine to Texas—had been begun in 1841 with no real comprehension of its magnitude. Nor could anyone have possibly foreseen the enormous demands the exploding American nation would make upon water transportation. Grain cargoes grew annually, supplanting the old fur trade, and Michigan's white pine lumber was very much in demand back east. Shiploads of iron ore from Minnesota's Mesabi Range had already passed through the Sault Ste. Marie Canal linking Lakes Huron and Superior and the first slab of steel had been rolled in Pittsburgh.

Nevertheless, in all the Great Lakes ship channels had to be marked, beacons and lighthouses built, harbors dredged, dangerous waterways converted into safe passages and shoals and rocks charted. Captain Meade understood the vastness of his project and gloried in its execution, even though Congress was niggardly with the funds needed to complete it. It is difficult to believe that in his first years his allowance was merely $25,000, although by 1859 he had quadrupled it to $100,000.

Meade was still in Detroit when the Civil War erupted. Ardently antislavery and devoted to the Union, he was nonetheless worried about his Southern family connections. That brother-in-law Congressman Wise who had been so helpful in gaining his readmission to the army had also become that Governor Wise who signed John Brown's death warrant. Meade's sister Elizabeth had married a Philadelphia banker named Alfred Ingraham but then moved to Kentucky and thence to Mississippi, where she became the mistress of an extensive plantation. Marianne Meade had married a member of a prominent South Carolina family, naval Lieutenant Thomas B. Huger. All of these relatives were ardent proslavery Southerners. Meade realized that these relationships could be held against him. Yet, when panicky politicians in Detroit called for a mass meeting at the post office where a crowd passed a resolution calling upon all officers—military and civilian—to make public renewal of their oath of allegiance to Washington, Meade refused to do so—and also with his officers absented himself from the oath-taking ceremony. When Michigan's superpatriot Zachariah Chandler—he of the witch-hunting Joint Committee on the Conduct of the War—heard of this, he became, in Meade's own phrase, "my bitterest enemy." All Meade's requests to the War Department for reassignment to combat duty went unheeded. At last his wife, who still had some political pull even though her congressman father was dead, enlisted Senator David Wilmot of Pennsylvania in her husband's cause, and on August 31, 1861, Meade was promoted to brigadier general and ordered to join McClellan's Army of the Potomac.

Meade commanded the Second Brigade in George McCall's division of Pennsylvania volunteers. Like so many veterans of Mexico, he distrusted volunteers, and although he found that their conduct justified his qualms he worked hard to put steel into their spines so that they fought well in McClellan's Peninsular Campaign. On one occasion Meade's ability to read the stars saved Fitz-John Porter's corps from marching straight into a Rebel trap, while at Beaver Dam and Gaines's Mill he earned a reputation as a front-line general of unflinching bravery. At White Oak Swamp he paid the price of his gallantry: two wounds, a painful one in the arm, and another seemingly minor one lower down. It was the second one that might have killed him. Meade did not realize how serious it was until he found his saddle bright with blood. He went hot with shame when he guessed that he had been shot in the back, but the surgeon restored his pride to him when he told him that he had probably turned in the saddle just as a sharpshooter above him squeezed the trigger.

Meade returned to duty in time for Second Bull Run under John Pope. He was not impressed with his old friend's handling of the Army of Virginia, nor by McClellan at Antietam, of which he later wrote: "We must encounter risks if we fight, and we cannot carry on war without fighting. . . . McClellan's vice . . . was always waiting to have everything just as he wanted before he would attack, and before he could get things arranged as he wanted them, the enemy pounced on him and thwarted all his plans." Meade thought less of Burnside, especially after Fredericksburg, when, with only 5,000 men in his division (he was now a major general), he made the only penetration of the day against the Rebel right. He complained bitterly that if he had been reinforced he would have rolled up the enemy's flank. Commanding a corps under Hooker at Chancellorsville he made his famous vehement but futile attempt to persuade Fighting Joe to live up to his nickname.

By then many of the perceptive officers in the Army of the Potomac were convinced that Meade was their ablest commander. His bravery was a watchword, along with his contempt for skulkers. He never hesitated to strike them with the flat of his saber to get them into line. At Fredericksburg, where two bullets passed through his hat and another through his horse's neck, he saw a fear-crazed soldier hanging back and ordered him onward. When the man aimed his musket at him, Meade struck him so forcefully on the shoulder with his sword that the blade snapped off at the hilt. The Chancellorsville debacle renewed army speculation about a possible successor to Hooker. Many generals were mentioned as likely to be the seventh commander to face "execution" as head of the ill-fated Army of the Potomac. Meade was among them, but he told his son George, now on his staff, that he did not have enough powerful friends at court. Besides, he really didn't want the job and there were plenty of others as competent as he was. Unknown to him, he did have a powerful friend: Abraham Lincoln.

On the night of June 27, 1863, George Gordon Meade lay down in his tent to get some sleep. He was almost frantic. He hadn't seen Hooker in two weeks. The army was scattered and no one seemed to know about any plans for it or the whereabouts of Lee's army. There were reports that Lee had invaded Pennsylvania. At last, Meade fell asleep. About three hours after midnight he felt a hand on his shoulder. He sat up and saw Colonel James A. Hardie of the War Department standing over him. Meade sleepily asked what he wanted. Hardie, in a fumbling attempt at humor, said he had come to give him trouble. Meade immediately guessed that Hooker had ordered his arrest.

Seeing his expression of alarm, Hardie lighted a candle and came to the point. He was astonished when Meade refused the high command. In agitation, Meade asked why his friend John Reynolds had not been chosen instead. He knew nothing of the army's present position or Hooker's plans. Hardie replied that all of these objections had been anticipated. Lincoln wanted Meade.

Meade began to put on his mud-stained uniform. "Well," he murmured, "I've been tried and condemned without a hearing, and I suppose I shall have to go to execution." Meade called for his son George. The trio rode to Hooker's tent, where the deposed commander appeared in dress uniform. He did not seem terribly shocked by the news that his resignation had been accepted. He and Meade discussed Lee's intentions. Hooker thought that because he had no bridging equipment Lee would not cross the Susquehanna to move on Harrisburg but, if he had invaded Pennsylvania, rather would turn southeast toward Baltimore and Washington. Meade said that if he knew Lee—as he did—he would cross the river at low water, which he did. Meade's surprise at the dispersion of the army angered Hooker. He made no mention of plans of his own, and Meade could see that he had none. No plans? No knowledge of Lee's whereabouts? No concentrated army? George Gordon Meade, like no commander of the major Union army before him, perhaps like few if any of on-the-spot-selected chiefs in all military history, was indeed looking into the little round mouth of the muzzle of "execution." Still he retained his composure, bade Hooker farewell and went outside the tent to his waiting son.

"Well, George," he said cheerfully, "I am now in command of the Army of the Potomac."

54

■

Prelude to Gettysburg

MARCHING RAPIDLY, by June 17 Lee's army was strung out a hundred miles, with Ewell's corps in the lead. Clearing the Potomac at Williamsport, Maryland, the Graybacks of Old Bald Head made for the Keystone State. To their great pleasure they were moving so fast over such good roads that some formations could boast of having had "breakfast in Virginia, whisky in Maryland and supper in Pennsylvania."

Entering "Pennsylvania Dutch" country they were amazed at the lush, manicured fields and fat cattle that they saw, the carefully kept farmhouses, silos and barns with those mystifying hexes on them. Frequently they mocked the stolid German farmers standing silently along the roadside. "Och, mine countree!" they called. "Here's your played-out rebellion!" Lee's ride through both states was like a triumphal procession. The appearance of the handsome gray-bearded patriarch astride his powerful gray charger usually produced a feeling of awe among the onlookers, best characterized by the girl wearing a Federal flag who cried, "Oh, I wish he was ours!" And when a man in Pennsylvania remarked, "What a large neck he has," a Butternut at once came back at him: "It takes a damn big neck to hold his head!"

The deportment of the Rebel columns was exemplary, for Lee, appealing again to the Almighty, had declared: "I cannot hope that Heaven will prosper our cause when we are violating its laws. I shall therefore carry on the war in Pennsylvania without offending the sanctions of a high civilization and of Christianity." Accordingly, his commissary officers were instructed to pay for any necessary requisitions—but in worthless Confederate money. His desire to contrast the discipline of his troops with the hideous rape of Fredericksburg by the Federals also was in part to encourage the peace movement in the North.

Jubal Early with Ewell's leading division may not have read these noble instructions, for when he arrived outside the Caledonia Ironworks owned by the ardent Abolitionist Thaddeus Stevens, he ordered it destroyed. Stevens's resident manager sought to dissuade him with the humane argument that to do so would only put several hundred people out of work and not hurt Stevens, since the business had been in the red for a decade. Shaking his head skeptically, "Old Jube" dryly observed, "That's not the way Yankees do business," and watched with immense satisfaction while the place was razed to the ground. Next confiscating all provisions and livestock, he headed east again toward York.

Although Lee's exact plans are not known, the movement of his troops now suggested that he was making for Harrisburg, capital of Pennsylvania, or trying to turn the enemy's right flank to descend on Baltimore. Because he had not heard from Jeb Stuart for days, Lee believed that the Federal army was still south of the Potomac, and still commanded by Joe Hooker—of whom he had little fear—and not by Meade, whom he respected.

Meade's own army did not feel that way. "What's Meade ever done?" the disgruntled men of the Army of the Potomac cried. The answer that he had shown himself a brave and able commander of a brigade, a division and a corps, was not satisfying to men aroused by Hooker's flamboyance or enchanted by McClellan's charm. They still dreamed of the day when McClellan would "save" the army a third time. Even Pope and Burnside, yes, even dowdy, poky Irvin McDowell, appeared dashing and soldierly alongside George Meade with his professorial, distant and patrician airs, his muddy boots and careless dress, his quick, waspish temper. "I know they call me a damned old goggle-eyed snapping turtle," Meade said, as he strove to concentrate his scattered command and gain some insight into Lee's intentions.

Neither glamorous nor magnetic, Meade nevertheless possessed the great virtue of decisiveness and he moved swiftly to concentrate his scattered command. By midafternoon he had decided against Hooker's plan for a westward movement against Lee's supply lines, choosing instead, as he wired Washington, "to move toward the Susquehanna, keeping Washington and Baltimore well covered, and if the enemy is checked in his attempt to cross the Susquehanna, or if he turns toward Baltimore, to give him battle." Meade's confidence was based upon a remarkably accurate intelligence report: "The enemy force does not exceed 80,000 men and 275 guns." This was achieved by careful scrutiny of Lee's army as it passed through Hagerstown and was only 5,000 men and three guns off the mark. Meade's own strength was well above 100,000 men, but as he continued his northeastward march skulkers dropping out of ranks and hiding in barns along the way reduced him to about 95,000 men. It has been suggested that Meade was fast losing his desire to find and fight Lee, but this belief is based chiefly on the nervous mannerisms that were a constant of his character. His order on the thirtieth to reconnoiter a defensive position along Big Pipe Creek was not a sign of hesitation but a sound engineer's hope that he might lure the enemy to attack him in a well-placed position. He also knew that Lee, whom he had met and admired in Mexico, was audacious enough to attempt it.

It has also been suggested that Meade may have had some qualms about his seven corps commanders, none of whom had led a formation of such size into battle at Antietam, and that the same could be said of all but two of the leaders of his nineteen infantry divisions. Fortunately, Meade had very early received the warm allegiance of the two men senior to him whom he had superseded. John Reynolds, his close friend and fellow Pennsylvanian, had immediately put on his dress uniform and come over to his tent to shake his hand. Reynolds, a handsome West Pointer beloved of his troops and admired by his officers, had been thought to be next in line, but he had gone to Washington to tell the president that he did not want the command without free rein. Meade's appointment had been his answer, and he accepted it with commendable grace. Uncle John Sedgwick might have been next, but Hooker's complaints about his "failures" at Chancellorsville had convinced Lincoln otherwise. Sedgwick had been riding in the woods with his staff when he received the news. Unable to conceal his dismay, he put spurs to his horse and led his aides on a wild gallop, before drawing rein and calmly trotting over to Meade's tent to shake his hand. His other veteran corps commanders were Howard and Slocum, of whom he approved, and Sickles, for whom he had little use. The new ones were Sykes, taking over Meade's old corps; and Hancock with Couch's.

George Sykes was a native of Delaware and a graduate of that illustrious West Point class of 1842 which contributed no fewer than a dozen corps and army commanders to both sides in the Civil War. Having fought the Seminoles and been breveted for gallantry in Mexico, Sykes's early service after Sumter was with regulars. "Sykes's Regulars" covered the Union rout at First Bull Run. A brave and able commander, esteemed by his troops, he was eminently competent to command a corps.

So was Winfield Scott Hancock, or Hancock "the Superb" as he was called after McClellan on the Peninsula cabled Washington: "Today Hancock was superb!" Tall, strongly built, extremely handsome, Hancock was also admired or abhorred for his versatility in the art of profanity, while the story of how he came to enter West Point might have been written by the author of *Black Beauty*.

Hancock's family lived in Montgomery County outside of Philadelphia. John Benton Sterigere had been a congressman from the district, riding over his constituency like a country doctor, mounted on a splendid horse which he came to love. After leaving Congress he gave the aging beast to a friend with the stipulation that it should be used only for light duty. To his horror one day in Philadelphia he saw it being mercilessly whipped by a cruel drayman. Demanding to know how he got the horse, he was told it had been bought for $75. Now Sterigere conceived a scheme of revenge upon his false, mercenary friend. He had learned the man planned to move from Delaware County to Montgomery to secure an appointment to West Point for his son. So Sterigere visited the incumbent congressman and secured from him a pledge to appoint no one but his nominee. Then he rode off to Hancock's home and offered the appointment to Hancock's father.

Hancock was only five feet five inches tall when he arrived on the Plains, promptly winning the affection of his fellow plebes by engaging in a fistfight with a much bigger upperclassman. But he grew nine inches in four years, so that upon graduation he stood six feet two inches tall, with a peaches-and-cream complexion and light blue eyes. Hancock was breveted for bravery in Mexico, serving with his old West Point friend first Lieutenant Lewis A. Armistead of Virginia, who had been dismissed from the Academy for hurling a plate at the head of Jubal Early. They were together again at the little California outpost of Los Angeles just before Sumter, and afterward at a farewell party given by Hancock for friends departing for service on either side of the Mason-Dixon Line.

No gathering can more poignantly portray the anguish with which these men of the little United States Army drew their swords for this war between brothers. Brigadier General Albert Sydney Johnston was there. As the midnight hour of departure approached he asked his wife to sing two old favorites: "Mary of Argyle" and "Kathleen Mavourneen." She did, weeping openly. Everyone wept. Armistead came to Hancock with his eyes streaming. Placing his hands on his shoulders, he said: "Hancock, good-bye. You can never know what this cost me, and I hope God will strike me dead if I am ever induced to leave my native soil, should worst come to worst."

By this he meant, like so many other Virginians, that he would fight only for his native state, and never attack the Federal government.

But at the end of June of 1863 he was with Robert E. Lee riding at the head of a brigade into Pennsylvania, while his old friend Winfield Scott Hancock was leading a corps in pursuit.

A mounting mood of apprehension and frustration had seized Robert E. Lee, chiefly because it had been so long since he had heard from Jeb Stuart. Lee did not even know that Meade had replaced Hooker or that for two days the blue host had been on the same side of the Potomac as his own force. It is possible that his anxiety was sharpened by recollection of how Hooker's decision to send his cavalry away from Chancellorsville had made Jackson's turning movement so much easier. All he knew was that three of Stuart's six brigades were scattered and the other three were with Stuart somewhere to the southeast. Never before had such a curtain of silence descended between Lee and his beloved young general. Again and again he asked his officers, "Can you tell me where General Stuart is?" or "Where on earth is my cavalry?"

The answer was that it was deep in the enemy's rear still struggling to get across the Potomac, still blocked by blue columns marching north, still unable to find a suitable ford unguarded. Again and again he had to fend off savage attacks of the newly aggressive Federal cavalry, and the ordeals and riding of the past few weeks had wearied his men and mounts. He had to make frequent stops to rest them, or to forage. At last he swung due north, making for Rowser's Ford, which he found deep, wide and wild. Stuart's six guns sank momentarily out of sight and the ammunition had to be carried across by his troopers. But at three o'clock on the morning of June 28, just as Hardie seized the sleeping Meade by his shoulder, Stuart's entire command "stood wet and dripping on the Maryland shore."

Now Stuart sought to carry out Lee's orders to put himself on Ewell's right flank, even though he had no idea where Ewell was. So he rode north making for the Susquehanna, hoping to meet him there. En route, along the chief Union supply route, he encountered a train of 150 mule-drawn enemy wagons at Rockville. "The wagons were brand new, the mules fat and sleek and the harness in use for the first time," a trooper recalled. "Such a train we had never seen before and did not see again."

Yelling wildly at sight of this rich prize, Stuart's Grayjackets swooped down on the train with such speed that they captured half the wagons at the first rush. The other half turned around and might have got away from the bone-weary Rebel horses had not one of them overturned to block the escape of all but twenty-five of them. An elated Stuart had taken 400 teamsters, 800 valuable mules, and 125 wagons laden with sugar, bacon, hams, hardtack, bottled whiskey and enough feed for Stuart's 5,000-horse command. Pausing only to parole his prisoners and feed both mounts and men, he pressed due north toward Hanover, Pennsylvania, roughly forty miles away.

On June 28 a Confederate spy informed Lee that Hooker's army had crossed the Potomac two days earlier. Marse Robert was shocked. His army was dispersed and offered to Hooker the opportunity to do to him what he had planned to do to Fighting Joe: defeat him in detail. At once he sent out orders for his army to concentrate around Cashtown, a little town about a half dozen miles west of Gettysburg. In conclusion, the spy casually mentioned that Meade had replaced Hooker. Again Lee was disturbed. Listening to his staff congratulating each other on the choice of another mediocre opponent, Marse Robert shook his head gravely and said: "General Meade will commit no blunder on my front, and if I make one he will make haste to take advantage of it."

Two days later the gray host was almost concentrated, Longstreet at Chambersburg and A. P. Hill and Ewell in the Cashtown area. Lee cautioned all his commanders not to bring on a battle until the entire army was united, a warning with which Major General Henry Heth in Ewell's corps did not exactly agree. Heth, a favorite of Jefferson Davis—and another one of those West Pointers who, with one general from V.M.I., commanded all of Lee's corps and divisions—was an inconsistent soldier: sometimes praised, sometimes blamed. He was also a distant cousin of Lee's and the only man in the army—apart from Lee's sons and nephew—whom Marse Robert called by his first name. Heth had heard that there was a supply of shoes in Gettysburg, and he sent Johnson Pettigrew with a brigade of infantry east from Cashtown to seize them. Pettigrew's men encountered Federal troopers along a creekbed west of town. Aware of Lee's instruction for caution, he prudently withdrew, establishing a bivouac midway between the two towns, before returning to Cashtown to report. Heth did not approve of such wariness, and he was eager to obtain those precious shoes for his unshod soldiers. So he went to Hill, who agreed that there could be no substantial enemy force in Gettysburg because the Federal army was still in Maryland. "The only force at Gettysburg is cavalry," he said, "probably a detachment of observation."

"If there is no objection," Heth said eagerly, "I will take my division tomorrow and go to Gettysburg and get those shoes."

"None at all," replied Hill.

■   ■   ■

That was on June 30. On the same day John Buford led his division of Federal horse into Gettysburg. Buford was a Kentuckian, a tough fighter and a soldier who liked his profession and had a keen eye for land. Hill had been correct in saying there were only enemy cavalry in Gettysburg, but not in deprecating them as "a detachment of observation." Buford had two full brigades. What was more, they were armed with the new Spencer seven-shot repeating carbine. With these, his troopers could get off twenty rounds a minute in comparison to a muzzle-loader's high of four. Moreover, his formations were outriders for John Reynolds's advance force of four corps numbering 41,000 men encamped within six miles of town, and he could count on quick reinforcement should a battle begin. Meade with the rest of his army had moved his headquarters to Taneytown, about a half dozen miles south of Reynolds and was as well concentrated as Lee.

So Buford's Bluejackets came clattering into this pleasant college town in open, rolling hill country with the high blue mass of the mountains rising above the western horizon. Buford saw at once that Gettysburg with its converging roads was much more important than its size. To hold it, he strung a strong picket line across the Chambersburg Pike on north-south McPherson's Ridge west of town, and another on roads to the north down which Ewell's corps was expected to march. That night he discussed the situation with Colonel Tom Devlin, whose troopers formed the picket lines. Devlin doubted that the Rebels were in the area in strength. He said that he could easily hold whatever enemy appeared in the area during the next twenty-four hours.

"No, you won't," Buford said sharply. "They will attack you in the morning and they will come booming—skirmishers three deep. You will have to fight like the devil until support arrives."

John Buford was a very apprehensive man that night. He kept his scouts patrolling to the west and north. He told his officers to stay on the alert: "Look out for campfires during the night, and for dust in the morning." He sent a warning of the situation to Meade, and was told to hold until Reynolds with his I Corps came up, followed by Slocum, Howard and Sickles. At last, under a bright moon, he fell asleep.

For want of a supply of shoes, two great armies groping for each other had just faintly touched fingertips. But through it they had found each other and perhaps the most momentous meeting engagement ever fought had just barely begun: a terrible titanic struggle around a pleasant little crossroads town over terrain in which neither army commander wished to fight—the Battle of Gettysburg.

55

■

Gettysburg: The First Day

O RDINARILY CAVALRY do not fight infantry, especially in defense of a position where all their shocking power is lost, or at least not without infantry support. But horse was all John Buford had and he spread his dismounted troopers out to either side of the pike with his six guns on the road behind them. Also to the rear were their horses, held by one man in every four. Unsupported by infantry, the Bluejackets probably could not hold out more than a few hours. But Buford did intend to give it all he had, and his men did have that five-to-one firepower superiority.

At dawn of July 1, 1863, the sun behind this thin blue line came up fiery red, promising humid heat and illuminating the top of South Mountain to the west. In that growing light the Federals could see the surface of Willoughby Run beneath them grow paler, and then the outlines of a long dun-colored column snaking toward them. Buford had been right: a heavy infantry attack with three-deep skirmishers flowing out to either side of the pike. Came the crash of Union guns and the sight of flying clods of dirt to the front, and then Heth's artillery went galloping into line and the sky above them blossomed with black puffs.

Several hundred yards to the rear of McPherson's Ridge rose Seminary Ridge, named for the Lutheran theological seminary on its crest. It was an ivy-covered red-brick building with a white bell tower.

John Buford rode back to this building and climbed the bell tower to study the battlefield. What he saw was not encouraging. More and more Graybacks kept flowing up the road and Heth had put more artillery on the far side of Willoughby Run. Rebel skirmishers were slowly working their way up from the brook toward the crest of the ridge, taking a withering fire from those stubby repeater carbines, losing men, but still coming on. Buford promptly sent couriers galloping off to tell Reynolds that the situation was worsening.

Reynolds needed no such warnings. He had heard the sound of gunfire, and while his men quickened their pace he rode rapidly ahead into Gettysburg and up to the seminary. Inside he saw a spurred boot descending the belfry ladder. "What's the matter, John?" he called up in a calm voice. "There's the devil to pay!" Buford replied, clambering down, his spurs tinkling. When Reynolds asked if Buford meant that he couldn't hold until his troops arrived, probably within an hour, he replied that he would try. With that Reynolds sent couriers galloping off to tell Sickles and Howard to join him at once and ordered an aide to ride to Meade at Taneytown with a verbal message: "Tell him the enemy are advancing in strong force, and that I fear they will get to the heights beyond the town before I can. I will fight them inch by inch, and if driven into the town I will barricade the streets and hold them back as long as possible." He then ordered Major General James Wadsworth to swing his division west below the town and get to Seminary Ridge by crossing fields. Wadsworth at fifty-five was white-haired but still vigorous. A lawyer and a political boss, he had run unsuccessfully for governor of New York against the Copperhead Seymour, disdaining to go home and campaign as beneath the dignity of a soldier. His men loved him for his concern for their welfare. Although he had only two brigades in his division they were among the best: one composed of one Pennsylvania and four New York regiments under Brigadier General Lysander Cutler and the other the celebrated Iron Brigade of three Wisconsin regiments, one from Indiana and another from Michigan, led by the fire-eating Solomon Meredith. Crossing the fields with their band playing "The Girl I Left Behind Me," they pulled their famous black slouch hats over their eyes against the morning sun.

Reynolds personally led Wadsworth's brigades from Seminary Ridge out the pike to McPherson's Ridge, where Buford's troopers had reached the breaking point. He put Cutler's brigade on the right and the Black Hats on the left. It was now ten o'clock and a critical moment arrived. Reynolds knew it. Turning in his saddle he urged the veterans trudging behind him into line to halt the Rebels scrambling up the ridge. "Forward, forward, men! Drive those fellows out of that! Forward! For God's sake, forward!" Below in an apple orchard a Confederate in an old stone barn drew a bead on the mounted general above him. He squeezed the trigger and Reynolds topplied off his horse. His aides turned him over and saw that behind his right ear was a half-inch hole. He gasped once, smiled—and died.

Now the stiff and formal Major General Abner Doubleday took command. Just as he did, Heth sensed that the rapid-firing Bluejackets above him were tiring and threw in his main body, two brigades under Joseph Davis and James Archer. Delayed momentarily by a fence, they splashed across Willoughby Run and began climbing the ridge—only to be struck to the ground by heavy, crashing volleys. This was not sporadic carbine fire but disciplined musketry. Through the smoke the stricken Confederates could see those famous black hats. " 'Taint no milishy," someone cried. "That's the Army of the Potomac!" Splashing back the way they came they were piled up against the fence and struck on the flank. Most got over the fence, however, except about seventy-five of them and General Archer, who was captured by a huge Irish private named Patrick Maloney. Delighted at the size of his catch, Maloney in his exuberance was not exactly deferential in his treatment of the general, who was taken to the rear and presented to Doubleday. "Archer!" his old army friend cried, extending his hand. "I'm glad to see you!" "Well, I'm not glad to see you by a damn sight," Archer replied coldly, keeping his hand by his side.

On the Federal right Heth's assault had been more successful. Davis, the nephew of the President, sent his men in on the double, determined to squelch those constant whispers of nepotism. They struck Cutler's soldiers not quite as prepared as the Iron Brigade had been. They had a much longer position to occupy and no covering wood to conceal them, and thus were not in position to receive the tumultuous, yelling onslaught of Davis's Graybacks. They fell back toward Seminary Ridge and the Rebels swept over McPherson's Ridge and down into the wide valley below. Here they charged into a deep but unfinished railroad cut, thinking it would lead them unseen into the Union rear. Instead they had blundered into a trap. The walls of the cut were too high and soon there were Federal rifles pointing down from both sides of the cut. Some 250 Rebels dropped their rifles in surrender, while those who sought to escape suffered grievously.

Doubleday was elated, and more so when his own division and John C. Robinson's—both from the dead Reynolds's corps—came marching in. But he was not so buoyant when Oliver Howard appeared on Seminary Ridge to take command of the battle. At noon his XI Corps—"the damned Dutchmen"—arrived under Carl Schurz, just in time to meet a new threat on the far right, or north, where Ewell had arrived from Carlisle.

Like Hill, Ewell was not with his troops, but riding at the rear of his column in his buggy, sulking like Achilles in his tent because Lee had recalled him from Harrisburg when the Keystone capital was within his grasp. His corps was not only not united but his three division commanders

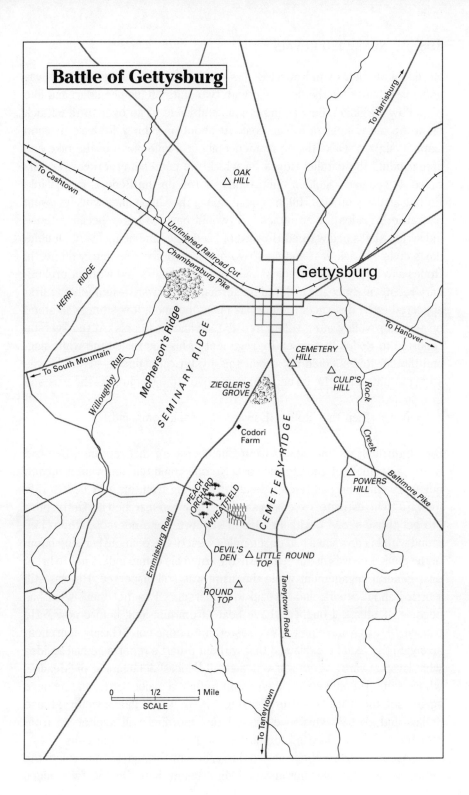

Battle of Gettysburg

To Harrisburg

To Cashtown

OAK HILL △

Unfinished Railroad Cut

Chambersburg Pike

HERR RIDGE

McPherson's Ridge

To South Mountain

Willoughby Run

SEMINARY RIDGE

Gettysburg

To Hanover

CEMETERY HILL △

CULP'S HILL △

Rock Creek

ZIEGLER'S GROVE

Codori Farm

CEMETERY RIDGE

POWERS HILL △

Baltimore Pike

Emmitsburg Road

PEACH ORCHARD
WHEATFIELD

DEVIL'S DEN
LITTLE ROUND TOP △

Taneytown Road

ROUND TOP △

0   1/2   1 Mile
SCALE

To Taneytown

were still on their own. Robert Rodes was one of these. Like Heth, he was going into battle for the first time with two stars on his shoulder; and like his fellow Virginian, he was impetuous and liable to go over to the attack upon the mere sight of a blue coat. At about one thirty Rodes's division came in sight of Oak Hill, an eminence about a mile north of the pike and commanding the parallel ridges on which the contending forces were arrayed. It seemed a golden opportunity to roll up the Federal right flank. Putting artillery on Oak Hill, he began raking the Union lines while massing his three brigades for an attack. He would have to hurry because those indiscreet shells had warned Howard of his danger and he had bent Doubleday's division back east and sent two of his own divisions hurrying north. Rodes saw all this. Nevertheless, without skirmishers and without preliminary reconnaissance, he ordered his formations forward—into what at first appeared to be destruction. Federals hiding behind a low stone wall stood up to pump volley after volley into the advancing Rebels. Alfred Iverson reported to Rodes that an entire regiment of his had raised the white flag, and though Rodes could not credit this hysterical estimate—Iverson was so demoralized that he turned command over to his adjutant—he was still in trouble.

It was then that Robert Edward Lee took command.

Riding through the mountains from Chambersburg that morning, Lee had heard the rumble of guns to the east. No one could tell him what it meant: not A. P. Hill who had risen pale and trembling from his sick bed to ride forward to investigate, except to say that Heth had marched on Gettysburg "to get those shoes," with Pender in support; nor Anderson, whom Lee found with his division a half dozen miles west of the ominously rising boom of the guns. Lee was disturbed. He had warned his commanders not to bring on a general engagement while the army was still dispersed. He was still worried about Stuart, and he said to Anderson: "I cannot think what has become of Stuart. I ought to have heard from him long before now." He paused. "He may have met with disaster, but I hope not." Gazing apprehensively up the road he explained that without Stuart's reports he had no idea what lay eastward, whether it was a small Federal detachment or Meade's whole army. He obviously did not want to fight a major battle, and he once again used the word "disaster," saying, "If we do not gain a victory, those defiles and gorges which we passed this morning will shelter us from disaster." Then he hurried forward toward the sound of the guns.

Ascending Herr Ridge at two thirty, he saw through his binoculars the entire battle as in a panorama unfolding below him. On the two ridges between himself and Gettysburg the Confederates and the Federals confronted one another. Heth had been repulsed on the Union left held by Doubleday's divisions, while Schurz with two of Howard's divisions had extended Doubleday's right to meet the threat from Oak Hill. Rodes's attack from that quarter had begun, but did not seem to be gaining momentum. At this point Henry Heth came riding up to Lee. Having heard that his famous cousin was on the field, he was eager to make amends for his failure, and he said:

"Rodes is heavily engaged. Had I not better attack?"

Lee was hesitant. "N-no, Henry," he said, and then, more firmly: "No. I am not prepared to bring on a general engagement today. Longstreet is not up." Suddenly the smoking panorama beneath him shifted dramatically. Rodes's right-hand brigade had found the point at which Doubleday had bent back his right flank and had struck him hard at this critical angle. Meanwhile, Rodes's reserve brigade dislodged the Federals from the stone wall where they had wrecked Iverson, while his left went plunging into a quarter-mile gap between Doubleday and Schurz. At this point, a host of Graybacks came roaring down the Harrisburg Road to hit Schurz's Germans on the right. It was Jubal Early's division from Ewell's corps.

Lee watched in quiet but mounting jubilation. Doubleday's eastern extension had begun to crumble and Schurz's was beginning to collapse at a much faster rate. Quickly changing his mind, he ordered A. P. Hill to send both Heth and William D. Pender crashing forward while Rodes and Early continued to drive the Federals. There was fierce fighting on the Union left to the south of the road. Here the Iron Brigade was posted, and here Heth was knocked unconscious by a shell fragment. Here also Doubleday had ordered Meredith to hold his position at all costs, and the valiant Black Hats almost did just that—until Pender's fresh troops entered the battle. Out of 1,800 men, there were only 600 unharmed Black Hats when the Iron Brigade fell back after Meredith, like Heth, was knocked senseless. On the Union right the Graybacks of Early had an easier time. Early's men simply crumpled Schurz's far right flank—and once again "the damned Dutchmen," so sullenly eager to erase the stain of Chancellorsville, took off in panicky flight: by squads and platoons at first, but then by whole companies and regiments.

Yelling fiendishly, the Rebels pursued them into Gettysburg, already crowded with Bluebellies fleeing from the north, where Ewell had begun to apply pressure. They gathered in prisoners by the hundreds, flushing them out of cellars and from behind walls. Still the blue flood was not entirely dammed and surrounded. Most of the fugitives, still clutching their weapons, went clawing up the side of a dominant height a half-mile south of town. It was called Cemetery Hill after the graveyard atop its plateau and Howard had wisely detached a division to occupy and fortify it. Here Federal guns were emplaced and fugitives halted and put into position, and here, Robert E. Lee knew, the Federals were gathering for another stand.

At some time after four o'clock on that July 1 of 1863, less than an hour after Pender had swept the Federals off Seminary Ridge, Lee stood on that height with his glasses focused on Cemetery Hill. He could see the blue masses arriving there, both from the north in Gettysburg and from the south as Meade's other corps began to come up. Guns were going into position and dirt was flying. To the east or what was now the Yankee right there rose another eminence slightly higher, Culp's Hill. Both were about a hundred feet above the town and connected by a precipitate saddle of rocky ground. Lee realized that he was studying what could quickly become an unassailable fortress.

He also realized that his sudden victory over the enemy had been more the result of tactical luck than of numbers or even skill on his part. He had been able to concentrate faster than Meade because of his good fortune in ordering a concentration around Cashtown and recalling Ewell from the north. He had not done that to prepare for this battle, indeed he had not desired it, but only to unite his army. So he had been able to get 25,000 men into line against only 20,000 of the enemy, and had suffered more casualties than he could afford: roughly 8,000 against 9,000, and half of these Federal losses were captives. Meade still had more than six full corps at his command, which, with his cavalry, would give him about 75,000 men when completely concentrated. Lee would have about 66,000 upon the arrival of Longstreet and Stuart, who had sent a courier to tell him that he was in Hanover and likely to arrive next day. It was clear that the tactical advantage gained by the Army of Northern Virginia that day would be clearly lost if the shaken Federal soldiers were allowed to recover their confidence, if heavy reinforcements and Meade himself arrived, and if Culp's and Cemetery hills could be fortified. Both by these considerations and the unquenchable ardor of his nature, Robert Edward Lee simply had to attack before nightfall could dissipate his momentum.

A. P. Hill agreed, but when Marse Robert asked him if he could renew the offensive, he declined. Only Anderson's division was fresh, but he was miles away. Heth's division had been devastated, with its commander still unconscious, and Pender's men were exhausted from their wild charge and howling pursuit. Because Lee knew that Hill was not a man to withhold himself or his men, he accepted this decision. It would have to be Ewell. Old Bald Head had Rodes holding his right above the town, Early in the center inside it and Edward ("Allegheny Ed") Johnson with Stonewall Jackson's old division marching eastward to take up a position on the left almost exactly in front of Culp's Hill. Johnson had suffered less and would be in better position. At about four thirty Lee sent word to Ewell "to carry the hill occupied by the enemy, if he found it practicable." It was a discretionary order typical of Lee in his unfailing courtesy and deference to the commander on the scene.

While Lee studied the battlefield, Longstreet rode up. He had arrived well ahead of his troops, who were marking time near Cashtown so that Johnson might use the only available eastward road. He too studied the panorama below, and when he lowered his glasses and turned to Lee he observed with evident satisfaction that the situation was ideal in which to put his cherished offensive-defensive scheme into effect.

"If we could have chosen a point to meet our plans of operation," he said, "I do not think we could have found a better one than this. All we have to do is throw our army around to their left, and we shall interpose between the Federal army and Washington. We can get a strong position and wait. . . . When they attack, we shall beat them, as we proposed to do before we left Fredericksburg, and the probabilities are that the fruits of our success will be great."

"No," Lee replied without hesitation, shaking his fist at Cemetery Hill. "The enemy is there, and I am going to attack him there."

"If he is there," Old Pete countered doggedly, "it will be because he is anxious that we should attack him: a good reason, in my judgment, for not doing so."

"No," Lee repeated decisively. "They are there in position, and I am going to whip them or they are going to whip me."

Longstreet said nothing, promising himself to renew the debate once he found his chief without his ardor aroused. At that moment a courier arrived from Ewell to say that Old Bald Head thought he could take Cemetery Hill if Hill attacked simultaneously from the west. Lee replied that the only support he could give was artillery. After Lee told Longstreet that he could not risk a general assault until Longstreet's I Corps arrived, Old Pete rode off to hasten his divisions' approach.

It was now five thirty and Lee remained on the ridge for another hour and a half, eagerly awaiting the start of Ewell's attack, turning from time to time to glance at the sun slowly sinking to his rear. At seven o'clock, with barely an hour of daylight remaining, he mounted Traveller and rode toward Gettysburg in search of Ewell and an explanation of this dreadful delay.

Back at Taneytown George Gordon Meade was not aware that a battle was being fought at Gettysburg. Like Buell at Perryville and Hooker at Chancellorsville, an atmospheric freak had put him in auditory isolation. Although the booming of the guns could be heard in Pittsburgh 150 miles west, the hills and ridges south of Gettysburg and the sultry heat had swallowed the sound of battle. Meade did not know that one was being fought until early afternoon when a newspaper correspondent galloped into camp on a lathered horse requesting the use of army telegraph to file his story of "the battle." Taken at once to Meade he reported that when he left the issue was still in doubt, adding the dolorous detail that Reynolds had fallen. Meade was appalled. John Reynolds, his friend and the man upon whom he hoped to depend during the early days of his command, was gone! So also might be one-fourth of his army, committed in an engagement he had not wanted, and over which he had no control.

Fortunately for Meade, Winfield Scott Hancock had arrived in Taneytown at noon. He ordered him to turn his corps over to Gibbon and ride to Gettysburg to take command. When Hancock reminded him that he was junior to Howard, Meade showed him a letter from Stanton specifying that in any such situation he would be sustained by himself and Lincoln. Thus forearmed, Hancock set out, riding in an ambulance at the start so that he might study maps of the area. Coming within earshot of the guns at three thirty, he shifted to horseback and rode hard for the battlefield, arriving on Cemetery Hill at four in time to perceive: "Wreck, disaster, disorder, almost the panic that precedes disorganization, defeat and retreat everywhere."

He also found Howard, slightly demoralized and understandably so. For the second time in two months he stared disaster in the face: of the two devastated Union corps, deducting skulkers as well as casualties, he had fewer than 8,000 men available. But if his reputation was in danger of being damaged a second time, his self-esteem was not. "Why, Hancock, you cannot give orders here," he exclaimed angrily when Hancock told him that Meade had placed him in command. "I am in command, and I rank you." After Hancock patiently explained Meade's instructions and Stanton's letter, he drew himself up stiffly and said: "I do not doubt your word, General Hancock, but you can give no orders while I am here." Anxious not to engage in a public squabble and thus further demoralize an already badly shaken army, and confident of his own ability to handle the prim and proper Howard, Hancock pretended to defer to him. Studying the new position, he said: "I think this is the strongest position by nature on which to fight a battle that I ever saw, and if it meets with your approbation, I will select this as the battlefield." When Howard nodded, he said: "Very well, sir, I select this as the battlefield."

Hancock was indeed well-named the Superb, for his presence on that height made a strong impression on both officers and men. He was like a tonic, just by his manly and confident bearing. "I remember," a Maine artilleryman wrote later, "even his linen, clean and white, his collar wide and free, and his broad wrist bands showing large and rolling back from his firm, finely moulded hands." And Carl Schurz could say: "His mere presence was a reinforcement, and everybody on the field felt stronger for his being there."

Hancock could also browbeat if needed, and thus, when he saw Culp's Hill unfortified even though it commanded Cemetery Hill, as well as Rebel patrols edging into a ravine in the rocky saddle between the two heights, he went at once to Doubleday and ordered him to occupy it immediately. When Doubleday demurred on the ground that his formations were fought out, Hancock roared at him in his parade-ground voice: "Sir! *I* am in command on this field! Send every man you have got!" So the remnants of the Iron Brigade went marching over to Culp's Hill, seizing it, and when the Rebel patrols found them there, they withdrew. Although Cemetery Ridge stretching away south from Cemetery Hill for about a mile was also occupied, the commanding height of Little Round Top still farther south was not—even though Hancock is supposed to have ordered this done. It lay there invitingly on the Federal left flank, just like the wood that screened Jackson's advance on Hooker's right at Chancellorsville. Otherwise Hancock's organization of the new Yankee position was indeed superb, and he got off a message to Meade stating that he considered his present position an excellent one for fighting a battle, "although somewhat exposed to be turned by the left." Whether or not that referred to Little Round Top is not known.

Meanwhile, more and more troops were arriving and being placed in position, steadily eroding Lee's superior numbers, and at seven o'clock even the reluctant Slocum appeared. He had heard that the battle was going badly and although he was willing to sacrifice his men, he was in no mood to take command from Howard as senior officer and thus have his name associated with defeat. To his immense relief he found Hancock in charge, although he was not enchanted when Hancock transferred command to him and rode back to Taneytown to persuade Meade to concentrate his entire army at Gettysburg.

■　■　■

Unless a victory be decisive, its unfelt results may become decisive another day and in another way. Thus Lee's triumph at Chancellorsville had deprived him forever of his right arm—Stonewall Jackson—and brought into the field against him the decisive Meade in contrast to the hesitant Hooker. If Jackson still commanded the II Corps and had received Lee's message to attack the Yankee right on Cemetery Hill before sundown "if practicable," it is almost certain that he would have attacked. To Stonewall the word "practicable" had a different meaning than it had to Old Bald Head. It meant a good chance of success, as he had shown at Fredericksburg until the Federal guns on Stafford Heights changed his mind. To Ewell it meant absolute certainty of success, and the sight of enemy fortifications growing stronger by the hour, and Lee's refusal to give him supporting troops, paralyzed his will. Moreover, Johnson's division did not arrive until after sundown, so that when Ewell conferred with Lee at twilight he was absolutely unwilling to move. The opportunity to crush a still dazed enemy had passed. Richard Ewell was simply no Stonewall Jackson.

Lee was obviously disappointed, and also plainly undecided where to launch his main attack next day. It had been his favorite maneuver to set the enemy up by attacking first with Jackson's corps and then finish him off with Longstreet's power punch. But Ewell—rather Early, who did most of his chief's talking—objected that an offensive on the Confederate left against the now well-entrenched Federal right did not seem wise. He favored an attack on the Rebel right, aimed at seizing the high ground in the Union rear. Lee bowed his head in thought. "Well, if I attack from the right," he said, musing aloud, "Longstreet will have to make the attack." He lifted his head. "Longstreet is a very good fighter when he gets into position and gets everything ready, but he is so slow." In silence Ewell and his commanders exchanged glances. It was a rare moment indeed when Robert E. Lee criticized a lieutenant in the presence of others. Marse Robert must be perplexed indeed!

He was, although he tentatively decided to strike the Union left with Longstreet while Ewell's corps stood ready to join him. Riding back to Seminary Ridge in darkness he changed his mind, ordering Ewell to bring his corps west and south to support Longstreet. This seemed to restore Old Bald Head's vocal powers, for he came in person to Lee's headquarters to protest. When he told Marse Robert that Johnson had reconnoitered Culp's Hill and believed he could take it, Lee was pleased. This would enable him to use his favorite one-two tactic: II Corps to set the enemy up, I Corps to punch him senseless. Even though he regretted finding the II's chief not nearly as fiery as his predecessor, it should work. Upon hearing Long-street's guns on the right commencing the assault on Cemetery Ridge, Ewell on the left would strike Culp's Hill. Notifying his staff that the attack would begin at first light July 2, he went to sleep.

Winfield Scott Hancock arrived in Taneytown about nine thirty, pleased to find that his message four hours earlier had convinced Meade that he should fight at Gettysburg. "I shall order up the troops," Meade said, and mes-sages went out to Sykes and Sedgwick, while Hancock prepared to resume command of his own corps. Meade did not go to the front at once, instead lying down to get some sleep. At 1 A.M. he mounted his horse and rode north with his staff for the battleground, arriving at Cemetery Hill two hours later. Bright moonlight flooded the cemetery itself, silvering the faces of blue-coated soldiers sleeping among the tombstones. In that light Meade made a brief inspection of Culp's and Cemetery hills, seeming satisfied with what he saw. As dawn began to break he watched Hancock's three divisions filing into line on Cemetery Ridge. He also received a message that Sykes was in Hanover and would arrive in a few hours. Sedgwick, farthest away with the largest of Meade's seven corps, could not be expected until late after-noon. However, the Army of the Potomac already seemed to be in good position. Sickles was on the left where Cemetery Ridge sloped down to low ground, Hancock on Sickles's right, then John Newton commanding Rey-nolds's corps, Howard on Cemetery Hill, Slocum opposite on Culp's Hill and Sykes eventually in reserve. In fact, the Army of the Potomac seemed so secure that many of its officers and men bragged openly about an impending Fredericksburg in reverse. Meade, however, was still hoping to attack on the right as soon as Sedgwick got there.

The sun rising behind the Federal host seemed to fall first on the heights of Little Round Top and then Round Top just south of Sickles. They commanded the Union position. Round Top, of course, was too thickly wooded and jumbled to be of much use. But Little Round Top was ideal for outflanking Meade. Except for a small Federal signal detail, it was unoc-cupied—and there was no one on Round Top.

56

■

Gettysburg: The Second Day

L EE AROSE at three oclock and ate breakfast in the dark. At first light he
sent Captain S. R. Johnston, a staff engineer, south from Seminary Ridge
toward the Round Tops to reconnoiter the area where his major blow would
fall. Longstreet arrived to report that McLaws and Hood were within easy
marching distance of the field and that George Pickett with his division
would arrive by nightfall. He also reopened the old offensive-defensive
debate, much to Lee's dismay. "No!" Lee replied emphatically. Longstreet
fell silent, although he was obviously undissuaded. A. P. Hill also came up,
still pale and shaken, but able to report that his whole corps was now in
place in the center of Lee's line. Next came Hood, to whom Lee said: "The
enemy is here, and if we do not whip him, he will whip us." Judging this
to mean that Lee was going on the offensive, Hood was surprised when
Longstreet took him aside and said: "The general is a little nervous this
morning. He wished me to attack. I do not wish to do so without Pickett.
I never like to go into battle with one boot off."

The plan that Longstreet opposed called for extending the Rebel right
south from Seminary Ridge to a point beyond the Union left held by Sickles
and then to attack north up the Emmitsburg Road, and it was to implement
this plan that Lee had sent Captain Johnston out on reconnaissance. When
McLaws appeared at eight o'clock Marse Robert explained it to him in
detail. Longstreet was silently pacing up and down while Lee spread a map
out on the ground, pointing to it as he told McLaws: "I wish you to place
your division across this road. I wish you to get there if possible withut
being seen by the enemy. Can you do it?" McLaws replied that he thought
he could, but would like to study the terrain first. Lee answered that he had
already dispatched a staff engineer to do just that. "I expect he is about
ready." By this he meant ready to make his report, but McLaws took it to

mean ready to set out. "I will go with him," he said. Longstreet, hearing this, ceased his pacing and interrupted sternly: "No, sir. I do not wish you to leave your division." Then Longstreet leaned over the map and with his finger traced a line perpendicular to the one Lee had drawn. "I wish your division placed so," he said. "No, General," said Lee, "I wish it placed just opposite." At this point the flustered McLaws, perhaps hoping to change the subject, declared that he would like to examine the ground Lee had mentioned. Once again Longstreet flatly ordered him to remain with his division, and Lee let the matter drop.

For Lee and his chief lieutenant to have become so deadlocked in a clash of wills while preparing to begin what could be the decisive battle of the war is incredible. For Lee to have permitted Longstreet to extend his prerogative as McLaws's corps commander to the brink of insubordination of his own chief is even further beyond belief. Finally, for Marse Robert to have accepted this rebuff in the interest of what appears to have been nothing more than his customary deference to the feelings of others, no matter how it might disrupt his plans, borders on the preposterous. How could Lee expect his plans to be executed with enthusiasm by someone who opposed them? It is of course possible that he considered relieving Old Pete, but hesitated to deprive himself of the services of his ablest corps commander, with no replacement able to carry that load really available. But there is no evidence to support such speculation. So there it was, not so much resistance to his chief's plan, but insistence on his own—and Lee said nothing.

After both Longstreet and McLaws had returned to their commands, Captain Johnson appeared to tell Lee that he had found the southern portion of Cemetery Ridge unoccupied, along with both Round Tops. Lee's dark eyes gleamed. "Did you get there?" he asked eagerly, and when Johnson replied that he had seen all this with his own eyes, Marse Robert became visibly excited. His plan to roll up the Federal left was not only feasible, it had every chance of success! Jubilant, Lee rode off to tell Ewell that upon hearing the sound of Longstreet's guns he was to make a strong demonstration against both Cemetery and Culp's hills, which, if success crowned Old Pete's attack on the Federal left, would be converted into all-out assault.

Upon his return to Seminary Ridge at eleven o'clock Lee's high spirits subsided somewhat when he found that Hood and McLaws were still in their standby rather than jump-off positions. Two hours had been lost, plus another half-hour delay requested by Longstreet. Thus it was not until eleven thirty that these two divisions began to move south under cover of

Herr Ridge for the attack that was to have begun "as early in the morning as practicable."

George Meade had set up headquarters in a small house beside the Taneytown Road, a half mile south of Cemetery Hill and thus at roughly the center of his curving three-mile line. He had been planning, once Sedgwick arrived, to attack with his right, but when Slocum reported that Culp's Hill was excellent for defense but not for offense, he changed his mind and busied himself with trying to divine his opponent's intentions. Knowing Lee's fondness for sudden surprises, he did not like the ominous silence in the enemy camp. He also did not like a message from Dan Sickles saying he believed himself to be dangerously exposed. No admirer of the political general's military judgment, he dismissed it with the remark, "Oh, generals are apt to look for the attack to be made where they are."

To the nervous Sickles this sounded too much like Hooker at Chancellorsville. On the far left of Meade's line, Sickles's sector was low, with even, marshy ground just short of Little Round Top. Since sunup he had been gazing in dismay at a knoll about 4,000 feet to his left front. Actually, it was only twelve feet higher than Sickles, but he could not help comparing it to Hazel Grove and the chaos that ensued after Hooker ordered him to abandon it. That was why he warned Meade, and why, dissatisfied with his reply, he rode to headquarters at midmorning to ask his chief if he were authorized to post his troops as he thought best. Meade replied that he was, but "within the limits of the general instructions I have given you," but he also instructed his artillery chief, Henry Hunt, to return to the sector with Sickles. Hunt thought Sickles's complaint was valid, but did not approve of his plan to advance his line to a peach orchard about a half mile to his front. This would create a dangerous salient, or bulge, in the Union line open to the interdiction of enemy artillery on either side, a sector so wide that his men would be spread thin to hold it. Hunt said he would discuss the matter with Meade, and rode back to headquarters.

Sickles was not satisfied, beginning to take counsel from his fears. Upon learning that Buford's cavalry assigned to patrol his left flank had been removed by Pleasonton and not replaced, he made up his mind to occupy the Peach Orchard. At three o'clock Sickles's III Corps moved out 10,000 strong, marching bravely westward, flags flying, bugles blaring, blue rank upon blue rank dressed with perfect parade-ground precision. Hancock's veterans on the right were impressed. "See how splendidly they march!" one of them cried. Hancock also saw them, dropping to one knee and leaning on his sword to watch. "Wait a moment," he said to Gibbon with a grim smile, "you'll see them tumbling back."

George Meade was dismayed when he heard Hunt's report, and he mounted his horse to ride out to the far left of his line. There he was simply appalled to find that Sickles had already occupied the new position a half mile to the west, with Andrew Humphreys's division on the right and David Birney's on the left. They formed a shallow, inverted V with the apex on the Peach Orchard. It was a most vulnerable salient, with all connection with Hancock on the right broken and the left dangling in mid-air. It could be attacked from three sides, as Meade told Sickles with his eyes full of wrath. Yet, he succeeded in controlling his terrible temper when he said: "General, I am afraid you are too far out." Even this remarkable understatement shook Sickles, who said he could hold if he had support, a stipulation never made heretofore, and then, sheepishly: "However, I will withdraw if you wish, sir." Meade was about to agree, when an earsplitting roar broke from the Confederate front. It was the beginning of Longstreet's assault, and his forty-six guns were baying in a rising, roaring symphony of steel. "I think it is too late," Meade said, almost absently, as though he were already weighing his options. Because Sedgwick had arrived, the situation was not that serious. He could put Uncle John's men, bone-tired after a blistering thirty-four-mile march, into reserve and thus free Sykes's rested divisions to support Sickles. "The enemy will not allow you," he added, his voice rising with the roar of enemy guns. "If you need more artillery, call on the reserve," he shouted. "The V Corps and a division of Hancock's will support—"

The terrified neighing of his mount drowned out Meade's last words. Rearing at the crash of a nearby gun, the horse had seized the bit in its teeth and bolted. Meade struggled to calm the fear-crazed beast, which for a moment seemed headed for the enemy line, at last reining him in and galloping back to headquarters, where he ordered Sykes to move with all speed to Sickles's left and Hunt to build up artillery there. As he did, another fierce cannonade began on the Federal right. Ewell, hearing Longstreet's guns, had joined the bombardment. Most of his shells struck Cemetery Hill where Federal guns were emplaced, converging in a cross fire with some of Longstreet's. Shells striking guns and gunners, splintering tombstones and shattering flesh, sent a ghastly mixture of steel and stone, bone and flesh flying through the air. So severe was the bombardment that a Massachusetts regiment that had been crouching behind a stone wall clambered over it to the enemy side where it was safer. A single shell-burst put twenty-seven men out of action, an incredible feat even for modern field artillery. Almost instantly, the Federal guns fired furiously in reply. Northeast of Culp's Hill they destroyed an entire Rebel artillery battalion, all but silencing Ewell's cannonade.

On the Union left held by Sickles, General Hunt had assembled battery after battery of his artillery reserve hub-to-hub to pour a murderous fire into Longstreet's guns. Following tactics developed at Antietam, they concentrated their fire on a single battery, smashing at it twenty to thirty guns at a time, silencing battery after battery. Still the Confederate gunners continued to fire, concentrating on Sickles's Bluebellies in the Peach Orchard and to either flank. Rather than fire counter-battery like the enemy and thus by their flashes and smoke give away their position, having the exact range, they lowered their muzzles and wrought a fearful destruction. And then there came the high, quavering yell of Hood's Graybacks pouring into the Devil's Den—a wicked jumble of huge boulders just west of Little Round Top—and Lee's attempt to turn Meade's left had begun.

Sedgwick's arrival with the biggest corps in the Army of the Potomac had tipped the scales decidedly in Meade's favor. Deducting yesterday's casualties and stragglers, he now had upwards of 80,000 men holding his curving three-mile line, giving him 27,000 to the mile or fifteen per yard—an enormous concentration by the standards of any war. Lee with the same deductions had about 50,000 effectives along a five-mile front, with 10,000 per mile or fewer than six per yard. Meade had 354 guns, Lee 154. Just as important, because Lee had chosen to be the attacker, he would be operating on exterior lines and would be compelled to move his troops greater distances from point to point, while Meade on interior lines would be deploying his faster. This factor, should Lee obtain a penetration, would increase his difficulty of maintaining or widening it; while the sector weakened by the obligation of providing reserves would be exposed to massive counterstrokes from Meade's superior interior forces.

Longstreet had been well aware of this when he offered his objections that morning, but now that Lee had rejected them and given his orders, he was, as always, the soul of obedience, although his still-sullen mood would not encourage him to anticipate his chief's orders. And he was sunk in gloom, his eyes sad and cast to the ground as he rode with his corps—less Pickett's division—under cover of Herr Ridge and then a thick wood to the jump-off position on the Yankee left.

Upon their arrival there, shortly after three o'clock, both Hood and McLaws were astonished to find that their massing point was occupied by the blue-coated divisions of Sickles's corps. McLaws was dismayed to discover that so far from being on the right of the Yankee left, he was in its center and his own right flank exposed. Obviously, Lee's plan conceived five hours previously was now badly flawed, and McLaws at once notified Longstreet. When he was told that there was only a regiment of infantry and one battery of artillery out there, he was incensed, replying that he knew better and had seen what he had seen—but without avail. Three times he protested, and three times he was told by Longstreet to attack north up the Emmitsburg Road as Lee had ordered.

Hood on McLaws's right felt the same way, but before protesting he sent out scouts to search for an alternative attack route. What they found amazed and delighted him: except for a small signal detail, the Round Tops and all the country south of them were unoccupied! At once Hood reported to Longstreet that it would be "unwise to attack up the Emmitsburg Road," requesting permission "to turn Round Top and attack the enemy in flank and rear." Longstreet replied: "General Lee's orders are to attack up the Emmitsburg Road." Thinking that his message had not been clear, Hood repeated his request—and back came that single, terse sentence. Grieving that he might be compelled to send his men into that dreadful Yankee nest in the Devil's Den, Hood again appealed. Such conduct on the part of Hood the valorous, Hood the valiant, might have suggested to Old Pete, doubtful as he still was about the operation, that something was indeed amiss. But the sentence came back like a rifle shot, after which Hood made a fourth request—only to be ordered by a staff officer to go forward without delay. It was now four o'clock, and as Hood got his offense going, Old Pete himself rode up and said: "We must obey the orders of General Lee."

Lee's instructions for the battle were for his formations to attack in echelons, or waves, so that the assault would roll steadily northward gathering strength. Thus Hood's division on the right would "begin the game" followed by McLaws to his left, then on his left Anderson of A. P. Hill's corps and finally Pender if needed. It would be brigade-by-brigade attacking, not whole divisions. Thus Evander McIvor Law's brigade on Hood's extreme right was to be the first to jump off—and it did. But the twenty-seven-year-old Law did not like his right aligned on the Emmitsburg Road to be exposed to a murderous fire from the Yankees in the Devil's Den. This was not from want of courage or skill, for this slender, handsome, thoughtful Alabamian was regarded by many of his seniors as the "best man in battle" in the Rebel army. What bothered him was the obvious bloodbath into which he was leading his five Alabama regiments. Being young enough not to be unduly reluctant to disobey orders, instead of attacking on the oblique, he charged directly north against the Devil's Den.

When the blue and the gray met in that confusing labyrinth of boulders and ravines, knit together by creeper and vine, a deadly game of hide-and-go-seek ensued. Like the Indian-fighting of old, soldiers hid behind trees to fire their weapons, taking potshots at figures flitting from stone to stone, or crept up on boulders to go leaping down on unsuspecting foemen beneath. In this maelstrom Hood fell with a shell fragment in his arm and had to be carried from the field on a stretcher. Meanwhile, a detachment of Federal sharpshooters in the wooded base of Round Top began picking off Law's Graybacks. At once he ordered twenty-seven-year-old Colonel William Oates to take two regiments and clean them out. It was done, and Oates's men, flushed with success, continued to climb the craggy height until they reached the top. Here Oates saw that Round Top was too heavily wooded to be of much tactical use, even though it was the tallest height in the area. But then he thought that if a battery of rifled guns could be manhandled up its steep sides the entire Union army could be blasted out of its stronghold. As he pondered this, a message arrived from Law ordering him to capture Little Round Top. Oates protested, but to no avail, and so he led his men downhill and across the valley separating the Round Tops. Just before he reached its base, he was joined by three more regiments. Forming in lines, they began to climb . . .

In the crucible of combat there is nothing more incalculable or more decisive in its effects than luck. Indeed, a commander's skill may be measured by the diligence with which he leaves nothing to chance; and yet Lady Luck, like Tinker Bell, can never be completely caged or contained—which may be why Napoleon always sought "lucky" colonels. On this fateful day in the history of the United States of America she seemed to have waved her wand over the men in gray the moment Dan Sickles began advancing his line a half mile west, thus opening gaps in Meade's left flank. But then Sickles's being where he was not supposed to be so disconcerted McLaws and Hood that another hour was lost in their fruitless appeals for a change in orders, after which Law decided to disobey orders, changing his attack route and ordering occupation of the vital Round Tops. That would have seemed to be enough caprice for one day, but then the fickle lady lifted her scepter once more and laid it upon the unprepossessing head of Gouverneur Kemble Warren.

It had been Warren who had tried to persuade Hooker to allow Meade and Couch to continue their assault from Chancellorsville on Lee's rear. At thirty-three he was still a brigadier and chief engineer of the Army of the Potomac. He commanded no troops, which was probably a good thing because this thin and frail-looking officer with the drooping mustache was obviously not the man to pick up a flag and cry, "Follow me!" But on this fateful day he supplied much more than heroics to the Union cause, coming to the crest of Little Round Top just at the moment when George Meade's horse bolted, and finding to his horror that, but for a handful of signalmen waving their long-handled flags, it was unoccupied. And from its barren crest cleared of timber only the preceding fall he could see the entire Union position as completely as though it had been drawn for him. Yelling to the signalmen to continue waving their flags as though nothing had happened, he hastened down the hill and there—by courtesy of Lady Luck once again—he met George Sykes bringing his V Corps out of reserve to reinforce Sickles. At his request Sykes detached Colonel Strong Vincent's brigade and sent it south to seize and fortify Little Round Top.

At twenty-six Vincent was the youngest brigade commander in the Union army, and also one of its ablest. Leading his men at a scramble up the side of a hill, he wisely deployed them well downhill to allow room for reinforcements behind him. Faint on the wind came the Rebel yell and then the Graybacks were in view climbing uphill, clambering over boulders. Behind boulders, the Bluebellies opened fire. As black-powder smoke pierced by gun flashes began to drift over the battlefield, Warren ordered up two guns of First Lieutenant Charles Hazlett's battery, and then went in search of more infantry.

On the Yankee far left Oates's own regiment—the 15th Alabama—seemed to be driving the 20th Maine under Colonel Joshua Chamberlain, former minister and Bowdoin professor. Half of Chamberlain's command—mostly lumberjacks and fishermen—were down under the repeated onslaught of Oates's valiant farmers. Chamberlain anticipated another attack which he knew could not fail, and so, to break it before it could gather momentum—like shattering a wave at its crest—he ordered a counterattack. "Come on!" he yelled, running toward the Rebel line barely 30 yards away. "Come on, boys!" After him came the color guard, flags fluttering in the smoke. Came a moment of hesitation, and then with a wild yell the Mainemen rose up and drove the startled Confederates back. They took 400 prisoners and were screaming "On to Richmond!" before Chamberlain could halt them and re-form.

On the far right the Graybacks seemed more successful, working their way around Vincent's right flank. Vincent himself was down with a bullet through the heart after crying, "Don't yield an inch!" Then the 16th Michigan gave way and the way seemed clear for the Confederates to claw their way to the crest. Above the battle Warren saw that crisis had come, and rode madly off in search of more infantry. Again Dame Fortune was kind. Warren found Stephen Weed's brigade marching west for the Peach Orchard and at the rear of the column his own old regiment—the 140th New York—now commanded by his friend twenty-three-year-old Colonel Patrick O'Rorke, a promising officer who had been at the top of his class at West Point. Warren ordered him to join Vincent, but O'Rorke protested that his orders were to help Sickles. Wasting no time to find Weed and get him to countermand that order, Warren shouted; "Never mind that, Paddy. Bring them up on the double-quick—and don't stop for aligning! I'll take the responsibility." Taking off at the dead run, the New Yorkers entered the battle with unloaded rifles and bayonets still in scabbards—yet they charged the Confederates surging up the hill. "This way, boys!" shouted O'Rorke. "This way!" It was an improbable counter-attack, but how could the startled Johnnies know that it was begun without blade or bullet—and they hesitated and withdrew. But then their first volley shattered the enemy and killed O'Rorke. Victory again seemed to wear gray, until Weed arrived with the rest of his brigade. Though Weed died with a sniper's bullet through his head, and the same marksman dropped Hazlett the artillerist dead across Weed's body, Oates could see that the Federals were too strong for him— especially after sweating Union cannoneers who practically hand-carried six three-inch rifles up the hill and into position began battering his reinforcements in the valley below.

It seemed to Oates that without help his five regiments fighting uphill against eight regiments supported by artillery could not possibly prevail, and he was certain of this estimate when a courier from Law told Major J. C. Rogers, who had succeeded to command of the 5th Texas, "General Law presents his compliments, and says to hold the place at all hazards." Rogers blew up. "Compliments, hell!" he roared. "Who wants compliments in such a damn place as this? Go back and ask General Law if he expects me to hold the world in check with the 5th Texas regiment?" With this, Oates realized that it was all over, and when the Mainemen launched a bayonet attack, as he said later: "We ran like a herd of wild cattle."

Little Round Top, thanks to Lady Luck and Gouverneur Warren, to Yankee valor at last matching Rebel dash, had been secured for the Stars and Stripes.

At one o'clock in the morning of July 2, Jeb Stuart set his ragged riders on the march for Gettysburg thirty miles away. It was their fifth night march in eight days, and the way they sat slumped in their saddles spoke eloquently of what they had endured. They were so exhausted that one trooper who tumbled sleeping from his horse slept on while sprawled across the fence that had broken his fall. At last in late afternoon they rode into Gettysburg, still clinging stubbornly to those 125 Yankee wagons. Stuart made for Lee's headquarters on Seminary Ridge. Marse Robert's face reddened at the sight of him and he lifted his arm as though in reproach, crying: "General Stuart, where have you been? I have not heard a word from you in days, and you the eyes and ears of my army!" Stuart was dismayed, so upset that he burst out eagerly, "I have brought you a hundred twenty-five wagons and their teams, General." Lee was not mollified. "Yes, General," he said sharply, "but they are an impediment to me now." Stuart seemed crushed, and Lee's manner softened. "Let me ask your help now," he said gently. "We will not discuss this longer. Help me fight these people."

While Hood's formations struggled to roll up the Federal far left, with special emphasis on the prize of Little Round Top, McLaws to the left of Hood waited impatiently to launch his own attack against the Bluebellies in the Peach Orchard. Longstreet held him back in hopes of duplicating his one-two punch at Second Bull Run, waiting for Sickles's corps to begin to crumble before applying the crusher on Birney and Humphreys. No one in McLaws's command was more impatient to charge than William Barksdale, still thirsting for glory after his Mississippi sharpshooters had held off the entire Union army at Fredericksburg. "General, let me go," he pleaded with McLaws. "General, let me charge." McLaws said no, but that was no acceptable answer for the tall Mississippian, and when Longstreet appeared he pointed to a battery at the apex of the Peach Orchard salient 600 yards away and said: "I wish you would let me go in, General. I will take that battery in five minutes." Longstreet declined with a smile. "Wait a little," he said evenly. "We are all going in presently."

But it was not until five thirty that he gave McLaws the nod, walking with his spearheads to the Emmitsburg Road where he waved them on with his hat, yelling like any Butternut in his deep, booming voice. The Graybacks charged toward a wheat field midway between the Peach Orchard and Little Round Top, striking Birney's division so hard that they began to roll the Yankees back. Their retreat was hastened after Dan Sickles fell with his right leg shattered beneath the knee by a shell fragment. Gasping, "Tell General Birney that he must take command," Sickles felt himself to be losing consciousness—until he heard a rumor that he was dead. Halting his stretcher-bearers, he ordered a cigar stuck in his mouth and lighted, puffing on it vigorously as though to send smoke signals that he was still alive. Thus with typical flamboyance did Dan Sickles depart the war, leaving for posterity an argument that still rages unsettled: did he by his creation of a bulge outside the Union line present a tactical advantage to Longstreet, when, if he had remained where he was, he could have devastated Old Pete's troops attacking up the Emmitsburg Road; or had his surprising presence in the Peach Orchard so unstrung Hood and McLaws that another precious hour was lost?

Whatever the answer—and there probably never will be a satisfactory one—the corps that dapper Dan left behind him was soon fighting for its very existence. On the western edge of the wheat field held by a brigade under James Barnes, the men in blue began to give away. Barnes ordered a retreat, crying: "It is too hot, my men cannot stand it!" With this the rest of Birney's division broke for the rear, despite their commander's efforts to halt them. Scenting victory, the yelling Rebels gave pursuit—until Hancock intervened. Having expected to see Sickles's troops "come tumbling back," he was ready for that eventuality, ordering John Caldwell to counterattack with his division. Caldwell gave it all he had, sending in his four brigades, and although they lost three of their commanders, they stopped the Graybacks cold, sending them flowing back westward through the trampled grain.

Now it was the turn of Humphreys, to Birney's right and opposite William Barksdale, trembling with excitement with his hat in his hand, his face "radiant with joy." Upon the command to charge, a wild yell arose from the Mississippians as they went streaming across the fields with such speed that they actually ran over the rail fences standing to either side of the road outside the Peach Orchard. The Federal battery standing there was taken not "in five minutes"—but in less than half that. As the boys from the Deep South followed their wild-eyed chief with the long white mane flowing behind him, they saw that he was pointing with his sword at the Yankees atop Cemetery Ridge a half mile away! The Peach Orchard could not satisfy Barksdale's thirst for glory—he wanted the Union line! His men responded valiantly to this vainglorious command, and both they and he were to suffer grievously for it. While a Federal brigadier assigned an entire rifle company to bringing down Barksdale, Hunt—the superb artillerist—unleashed the reception he had planned for just such a charge. Forty guns mounted on the ridge, supported by infantry Meade had rushed into the danger spot, began baying with iron tongues. Unmitigated slaughter ensued among the charging Butternuts. Even so, these were among the fiercest of the fierce-fighting Graybacks, and they overran the first line of artillery, where the gunners fought them hand-to-hand with rammer staffs and pistols—but the weight of metal was too much and the waiting blue infantry unneeded. With no one on either flank, Barksdale's men began flowing raggedly back the way they came, scourged by shellfire as they did and leaving half their number dead or wounded behind them—including their dying commander, his thirst for glory slaked at last.

Longstreet's corps had fought itself out. With customary bravery his brigades, outnumbered two to one in both men and guns, had tried to roll up the Federal left along Cemetery Ridge, and had come away with hardly more than the Devil's Den. Of their valor Longstreet would say: "I do not hesitate to pronounce this the best three hours fighting ever done by any troops on any battlefield." Perhaps true, even probably so—but the cost had been one-third of his attacking force, a price much too prohibitive to pay for a minor penetration made tactically useless by the Union guns on Little Round Top, no matter how much posterity might cherish the glory of capturing it. And so, with Longstreet's corps exhausted, Lee's rolling offensive passed leftward from Old Pete's men to those of A. P. Hill in the Confederate center.

Fighting Dick Anderson's division was next in line, and here the jumbled and piecemeal nature of Marse Robert's unusual "echeloned" attack was further complicated by a confusion in command. Hill had understood that his right-hand division was detached to Longstreet, or at least available to him, while Old Pete had interpreted Lee's vague orders to mean that Hill would be in support of him, and therefore still in command of his corps. Thus there was no direct control over Anderson, a commander accustomed to Longstreet's tight rein and now fighting for the first time under Hill's looser hand. As a consequence, his own control of his brigade commanders was similarly permissive, and in the outcome fatally so.

Cadmus Wilcox's Alabamians went driving for a point north of the Peach Orchard. Unknown to him and Anderson, he was charging the gap left by Sickles which Hancock had not had time to plug. Wilcox was followed by Colonel David Lang's three Florida regiments, supported on their left by Ambrose Wright's Georgia brigade. Carnot Posey had already dispatched three of his Mississippi regiments out front as skirmishers and was unaware that he was to charge with the fourth. To his dismay he discovered that he was not even covered on his left, where William Mahone was to be with his Virginians. But Mahone refused to come out of reserve. When Anderson sent Wilcox's adjutant to him to explain the situation he remained adamant, declaring: "I have my orders from General Anderson himself to stay here," paying no attention to the staff man's protest that "Anderson himself" had sent him there.

That was the beginning of the unraveling of the echelon plan, although at the outset of the Rebel onslaught it did not seem to matter. That was because of the élan with which the three attacking brigades pressed their charge. Wilcox in the center was making directly for that yawning gap on Hancock's left, driving the remnants of Humphreys's broken division before them. This was the critical moment perceived by Hancock himself, now in command of Sickles's corps as well as his own, when he rode among that backwashing blue tide and saw to his horror that Wilcox was on the verge of effecting a decisive penetration. He had already ordered up the divisions of John Gibbon and Alexander Hays, "but I saw that in some way five minutes must be gained or we were lost."

At that critical moment he saw the leading regiment of Gibbon's first brigade come marching four abreast over the crest of Cemetery Ridge. He rode forward, crying: "What regiment is this?"

"First Minnesota," replied Colonel William Colville.

Turning to point at the Alabama flag of Wilcox's charging Rebels, Hancock asked: "Colonel, do you see those colors?" When Colville said that he did, Hancock gave him the curt, cruel order: "Then take them!"

Because Colville's command had been stripped to supply skirmishers, he was down to 262 men. But they went charging forward with outthrust bayonets, straight at the oncoming Rebels. Wilcox's men were startled. Already winded by a mile run over stony ground, they recoiled briefly under the shock of this minuscule blue band. But then they came on with the customary wild yells and cut the Minnesotans to pieces. Colville and all but three of his officers were killed, yet when one of these led the forty-seven survivors back up the slope they had given a jubilant Hancock not five minutes but ten.

In that critical interval Gibbon had arrived with his remaining troops and taken position on the hill crest. From there they poured a devastating fire into Wilcox's oncoming Butternuts, and those of Lang on his left. Wilcox was also raked on his unprotected right by those batteries of Hunt that had earlier broken Barksdale. With no sign behind him of the reinforcements he had requested, he regretfully recognized reality and ordered a retreat. So did Lang.

And yet, a quarter mile to the north, Wright and his Georgians at that very moment had pierced the Yankee center. They had gone yelling up the slope of Cemetery Ridge, through the guns and onto the crest. But there they could not remain. Outflanked right and left by Gibbon and Hays, with no hope of help from the stalled Posey and the stubborn Mahone, or even Pender's division on his left, with Meade moving even more Bluebellies toward the penetration, Wright with half of his command gone faced either annihilation or encirclement—and so he ordered a slow but steady withdrawal down the slope and across the valley and the Emmitsburg Road.

Pender did not appear because Pender was gone, unhorsed by a shell fragment in his left leg which eventually led to its amputation and then the loss of his life. Doubtless Pender the valiant would have hurled his entire division into the hole in the Union line, hoping to exploit Wright's penetration. If he had, he might have succeeded, for it was weakly defended after Hancock moved Gibbon and Hays to the south to stop Anderson, and Meade shifted two of Newton's in the same direction. Even so, Lee's orders to Pender had been to assume a stance of discretionary support, and when Brigadier General James Lane, upon whom command devolved, witnessed what had happened to Anderson's adjoining brigades, he decided against the risk of attacking without support on his right. Hill might have ordered him forward, as he always did, but Hill was not there, having ridden north to confer with Rodes. And so the magic moment passed into the lamentable past, the limboland of lost opportunity, and as it did, the echeloned attack moved leftward again into the now eager hands of Richard Ewell.

Old Bald Head had been stung by Lee's complaint that he had failed "to pursue our advantage of yesterday." He was now eager to redeem himself, even though slightly restrained by Lee's orders to guard the Rebel left and make a demonstration the moment he heard Longstreet's guns, and thus hold the Yankees opposite him in place; and then, if success seemed likely, to join the assault himself. Hearing Old Pete's artillery at four o'clock, he did commence that bombardment of Cemetery and Culp's hills which only served to draw down upon his guns the higher and superior wrath of the Union ordnance.

Even so, what the now subdued Ewell did not realize was that he—not the Yankees—held the advantage of numbers. By one of those paradoxes common to battle, his failure to hold the Northern units to his front in place, by allowing both Hancock and Meade to strip them almost bare in order to contain the furious three-hour assault upon the Round Tops and Cemetery Ridge, he with his three divisions now faced only Howard's unreliable Dutchmen on Cemetery Hill and the remnants of Wadsworth's severely punished division: the survivors of the Iron Brigade and five regiments of upstate New Yorkers under George Greene, known fondly as "Pop" to his admiring troops because of his sixty-two years and his informal style of dress. There was also a brigade from sharp-eyed, sharp-tongued John Geary's division. Unaware of this numerical advantage, but very much conscious of the risks in attempting to storm such heights, Ewell at seven o'clock ordered the advance.

Rodes was on the right slightly west of Cemetery Hill, Early in the center opposite it and Allegheny Ed Johnson on the left below Culp's. Waving his thick hickory stick which earned him his other nickname of "Old Clubby," Johnson led his men against the formidable entrenchments that Greene had built. A savage fight ensued from dusk well into darkness, but Johnson was able to gain no more than a lodgment at the base of the hill.

In the center, Early achieved a deeper penetration, his Graybacks coming as they did against those jittery Dutchmen. Bursting through three successive Union lines, silencing their artillery, they drove these troops of Howard before them like frightened sheep, capturing many of them found "hiding in the pits for protection." For the third time one-armed Oliver Howard found himself facing disaster. Before he knew where the assault was made, he said, "our men and the Confederates came tumbling back together." Fortunately for him Hancock behind him on Cemetery Ridge heard the uproar of renewed battle to the north.

"We ought to send some help over there," he said to John Gibbon, who had taken over II Corps under Hancock's expanded command. "Send a brigade, send Carroll."

S. S. Carroll led a brigade in Hancock's old division, and he knew what his former chief expected of him. Marching briskly to the north, his men found themselves gradually engulfed in darkness magnified by drifting gunsmoke. Although delayed and slightly confused by this, the gloom obscured their blue uniforms and they appeared to be merely heavy masses of approaching infantry to Brigadier General Harry Hays, who at the moment was elated at having seized the crest of Culp's. Moreover, he was expecting reinforcements, and was, like so many Rebel commanders, mindful of what had happened to Jackson at Chancellorsville. Thus when these oncoming formations opened fire, he did not order it returned. Two more volleys staggered his two brigades, and when the flash of their guns illuminated the II Corps insignia on top of their forage caps, he realized to his dismay that they were Yankees and ordered his men to commence firing. It was too late, for other masses of enemy infantry and even Howard's fugitives were rallying to Carroll. If Hays had had the reinforcements he was expecting, even those three destructive volleys might not have dislodged him, but with the foe growing steadily stronger, he had no alternative but to withdraw.

As complete darkness closed upon the battlefield, only the Confederate dead remained on Culp's Hill.

57

■

Gettysburg: The Third Day

HISTORIANS OF THE CIVIL WAR are agreed that the Battle of Gettysburg was a study of two extremely different—even opposite—styles of command: Lee the audacious against the cautious Meade. Would the uncontrollable desire to come to grips with the enemy that so often seized Lee lead Marse Robert to make a fatal error—as he himself feared—on the careful Meade's front, or would the Union commander's innate caution cause him to miss a perceived opportunity? On that second night of the dreadful Battle of Gettysburg, the two commanders made their plans exactly along those lines, and so the greatest battle of the Civil War was to be determined by an excess of either flamboyance or taking care.

Although Lee had lost nearly 9,000 men on that July 2, 1863, to be added to the nearly 8,000 casualties of the preceding day, he was not as badly hurt as might be assumed. Moreover George Pickett's division of 4,600 men had arrived and gone into bivouac three miles away from the battlefield, and Stuart's three brigades of cavalry were also available to harry the fugitives of the collapsed Union army. In fact, only sixteen of Lee's thirty-seven infantry brigades had been committed that day, which presumably left twenty-one of them fresh for battle next day. So Robert E. Lee decided to attack once more, using these fresh troops. Accordingly, orders went out to Ewell to renew the assault on the left at dawn, with Johnson below Culp's Hill to be reinforced by two brigades from Rodes. Meanwhile, the army's artillery would be moved forward under cover of darkness. The centerpiece of Marse Robert's plan would be an assault on the Union center by Pickett, although he neglected to inform either Longstreet or Pickett himself of this decision. Lee also failed to confer with his corps commanders that night, although he did give instructions to Hill and

Ewell by courier. Shortly before midnight, he lay down in his tent on Seminary Ridge to get some sleep.

Across from Lee in the little cottage alongside the Taneytown Road no such confidence put George Gordon Meade to sleep. He had, of course, been buoyed by Warren's success on Little Round Top to his left and Hancock's firm stand in his center, so much so that he got off a jubilant message to Halleck: "The enemy attacked me about 4 P.M. this day, and, after one of the severest contests of the war, was repulsed at all points." At the time Meade wrote this dispatch, what he said was true, but not after Ewell attacked his right and Johnson, though repulsed at the crest of Culp's Hill, was able to occupy Slocum's abandoned trenches at its base. This meant the enemy now held lodgments left and right: the Devil's Den and Culp's Hill. To a man of Meade's cautious temperament this might be a prelude to disaster. Indeed, during only five days in command of the Army of the Potomac he had already lost more men than Hooker had lost in five months. So his jubilation gradually gave way to apprehension, and even though he had ordered Slocum to evict Johnson at daybreak, he began to regret his assurance to Halleck of remaining where he was and to think once again of occupying the far superior position along Big Pipe Creek. To this end, he ordered his chief of staff to draw up instructions for a withdrawal to that point. Then he also, probably to get himself off the hook with that hasty pledge to Halleck, summoned his seven corps commanders for a council of war.

Nine generals came, since Hancock had brought Gibbon along and Slocum fetched Williams. With Meade himself and his aides Butterfield and Warren also present, the tiny ten-by-twelve parlor was indeed crowded, with some corps commanders using the rickety bed for a couch and others even sitting on the floor. By eleven o'clock, just as Lee was retiring for the night, they had all arrived and the careful Meade submitted to them three questions.

These were: "1. Under existing circumstances, is it advisable for this army to remain in its present position, or to retire to another nearer its base of supplies? 2. It being determined to remain in present position, shall the army attack or wait the attack of the enemy? 3. If we wait attack, how long?" All nine generals agreed that the army should neither retreat nor attack, and on the third question of least importance their replies varied from the "Stay and fight it out" of the hesitant Slocum and the "Can't wait long" of the valiant Hancock. It was now midnight and the generals began to leave:

Sykes who would hold the far left, Sedgwick to be behind him in reserve, Hancock commanding both Sickles's III Corps and his own II which Gibbon still led in the center, Howard on Cemetery Hill and Slocum on Culp's. They clumped out of the cottage into a night so still that the chiming of the courthouse clock in Gettysburg a mile away could be clearly heard. As they left, Meade took Gibbon by the arm and said: "If Lee attacks tomorrow, it will be in your front," and when Gibbon asked why he thought so, he added: "Because he has made attacks on both our flanks and failed, and if he concludes to try it again it will be on our center." Gibbon never forgot that singularly accurate estimate, and years later would write: "I expressed the hope that he would, and told General Meade, with confidence, that if he did, we would defeat him."

As was his custom on the eve of a battle, Robert E. Lee arose early—at 3 A.M.—on that memorable morning of July 3, 1863, sharing his usual spartan breakfast with his staff. Daybreak was not but an hour away and Lee realized almost at once that he could not launch the dawn attack that he had planned. It would take a good two hours for Pickett to march his three brigades from his bivouac beside the Chambersburg Pike to their jump-off position on Seminary Ridge opposite the Union center on Cemetery Ridge. To strike at dawn they would have had to begin their approach march an hour ago. So Lee abandoned the daybreak attack, for this reason and perhaps also because to attack early or late was not an important consideration, although a late assault might be better in that it gave him more time to study the Federal position and the enemy less time to mount a counter-attack should he be repulsed. And so, not having informed Longstreet of his earlier intentions, he now did not tell Old Pete that his corps would make the main effort. Instead, he rode off to confer with him, after dispatching a courier to Ewell to instruct him to withhold his attack on the Federal right until ten o'clock or later. This vagueness, this lack of precision and coordination of his commands, had been strangely characteristic of Lee throughout this great battle and would remain so on its last day. As one aide had observed during the three-hour assault on Cemetery Ridge the day before: "The whole affair was disjointed. There was an absence of accord in the movements of the several commands." As Lee mounted Traveller and trotted off in the lengthening daylight in search of Longstreet, he heard the thunder of guns on the Federal right. He could not tell what they signified: whether Meade had gotten the jump on Ewell, or his courier had not arrived in time to forestall the Confederate dawn attack. Either way, it was not a good omen.

■ ■ ■

The gunfire Lee had heard came from four batteries of artillery that Slocum had posted on the northern slope of Powers Hill to begin his dawn attack on Johnson. Unable to advance his own guns across Rock Creek, Johnson ordered his troops to lie low in their trenches or among the rocks. Once the hour-long bombardment lifted, Old Clubby ordered them forward to seize control of the Baltimore Pike. But now that the Graybacks were visible, Slocum's guns began baying again, joined by another battery on Cemetery Hill. At this point a message arrived from Ewell telling Johnson to withdraw to await orders for a later attack to be coordinated with Longstreet's on the Federal center. Lee might have had that choice, but Johnson didn't. He was locked so intimately in seesaw battle that to attempt to disengage could be suicidal. In the end, the unopposed Union ordnance compelled him to withdraw, and Slocum repossessed the abandoned Rebel trenches.

Lee could now expect no help from his left, not even a diversion to pin the Federals down and prevent reinforcement of their center. Whatever Longstreet did that day would have to be done by himself.

Marse Robert found Old Pete shortly after sunrise in a field just west of Round Top. In contrast to the day before, he was in good spirits, and his greeting to Lee suggested why: "General, I have had my scouts out all night, and I find that you still have an excellent opportunity to move to the right of Meade's army and maneuver him into attacking us." As he had done before, Lee immediately set Longstreet straight. Pointing with his fist toward Meade's line, he said: "The enemy is there, and I am going to strike him." The light left the burly Georgian's face and his eyes were sad again. He seemed even more downcast when Marse Robert disclosed his plan for Longstreet to strike the Yankee left center with his entire corps. Old Pete argued that to withdraw McLaws and Law from the Devil's Den and the Wheat Field would be to expose his right to Union troops now held in check by these units. On reflection, Lee agreed: McLaws and Law would remain where they were, and instead support of Pickett would be provided by Heth and Anderson from A. P. Hill's divisions. This would shift the assault from Meade's left center on Cemetery Ridge to his right center. Even this did not satisfy Longstreet, who gloomily reminded Lee that Pickett's force of 4,600 men was the smallest in the army, and that Heth and Anderson, after the losses of the last two days, would be hardly larger. "General," he said to Lee in his final plea to abandon the offensive, "I have been a soldier all of my life. I have been with soldiers engaged in fights by squads, companies, regiments, divisions and armies, and should know as well as anyone what soldiers can do. It is my opinion that no fifteen thousand men ever arrayed for battle can take that position."

Lee made no reply, deepening his lieutenant's depression. Instead he began issuing orders for the battle. Pickett was to post his three brigades behind Seminary Ridge to the right of two of Anderson's brigades in support. To Anderson's left would be Heth's four brigades—now under J. Johnston Pettigrew, with Heth still incapacitated—supported by two brigades from Pender, still out of action with what became his mortal wound. These were led by Isaac Trimble, a sixty-one-year-old, fire-eating West Pointer who had been badly wounded at Second Bull Run. Twice Lee and Old Pete rode up and down this Confederate line, Longstreet still sunk in gloom, Marse Robert with rising enthusiasm. Nothing could discourage him, not even William Wofford's warning that "the enemy have had all night to entrench and reinforce." Yet the possibility of defeat was not completely out of mind, as he showed when A. P. Hill, who joined them, suggested that instead of using only eight of his thirteen brigades, he use them all. "What remains of your corps will be my reserve," he told Hill, "and it will be needed if General Longstreet's attack should fail."

George Edward Pickett had no such reservations. This Confederate dandy with the dubious distinction of having been graduated last in his West Point class of 1846 believed that his moment of glory had finally arrived. Breveted a lieutenant and captain for gallantry in Mexico, he had been wounded at Gaines's Mill on May 19, 1862, and seen no combat since. Leading his division—Virginians to a man—toward their assembly point, Pickett was on fire with zeal for this dangerous assignment, which he regarded as the last chance for a man nearing forty to gain the glory for which he hungered so passionately. Pickett had been described by a colleague as "dapper and alert," and he was indeed so with his small blue cap, huge buff gauntlets and blue cuffs on his neatly tailored gray uniform. Of medium height, slender and graceful on his sleek black horse, the gleam of his polished boots rivaling the glint of his golden spurs and the glitter of the double row of gilded buttons on his tunic, he was the essence of military elegance. Afoot or on horseback, he carried an elegant riding crop, his short beard and drooping mustache were carefully groomed and his hair fell to his shoulders in perfumed brown ringlets. Pickett's dandy airs—and his cockiness, as well—did not always delight his three brigadiers, all of whom were older than he was.

Richard Garnett was forty-five. A West Pointer and a fighter with a promising career ahead of him, he had succeeded Jackson as commander of the Stonewall Brigade—until Jackson's only defeat at Kernstown, where Garnett ordered a retreat to avoid annihilation. Stonewall put him under arrest for retreating without permission, and Garnett responded by demanding a court-martial. It dragged on interminably until Lee intervened and sent him back to duty.

James Kemper, the youngest at forty, had also been Pickett's superior until dapper George's friendship with Longstreet helped to bring him his second star. Kemper had been a lawyer and a prominent Virginia politician, active in military affairs in the House of Delegates and generally credited with preparing the Old Dominion militia for war. In oratory and even conversation he was bombastic—and boring—but in battle this valiant commander with the huge black beard had distinguished himself in every major battle since First Bull Run.

Lewis Armistead was the oldest at forty-six. A widower, he was both before and since his marriage a great ladies' man, although with his bald head and pepper-and-salt beard it is likely that his overtures were more successful before than since. But he still answered to the nickname "Lo"— short for Lothario. It was Armistead who had come to Winfield Scott Hancock with tears in his eyes on that departure night in Los Angeles, murmuring "Hancock, good-bye." He was aware that his old friend commanded a corps in Meade's army, but did not know that his troops were holding the Rebel objective. This was a little clump of umbrella-shaped trees atop Cemetery Ridge about one rolling green mile away from Seminary Ridge, behind which the Confederates were massed. Armistead and Garnett both stood on Seminary Ridge, studying this landmark. "This is a desperate thing to attempt," Garnett said quietly. "Yes it is," Armistead replied in the same low voice. "But the issue is with the Almighty, and we must leave it in His hands."

At twenty-eight Georgia-born Colonel Edward Porter Alexander was the most skillful artillerist in the Army of Northern Virginia. He commanded the 80 guns in Longstreet's corps which, with the 60 in A. P. Hill's, were to provide a full-throated bombardment of 140 pieces preceding Pickett's charge at that clump of trees. Alexander was a West Pointer who in 1859 had been the co-developer of the military wigwag (semaphore) signal system. He had fought or served in all of the Army of Northern Virginia's major battles since First Bull Run. On this late morning of that fateful Third of July, when the sound of Ewell's guns sputtering out to the east suggested that all now depended on Longstreet's attack, young Alexander received an astonishing and disturbing message from Old Pete: "If the artillery fire does not have the effect to drive off the enemy or greatly demoralize him, so as to make our effort pretty certain, I would prefer that you should not advise Pickett to make his charge. I shall rely a great deal upon your judgment to determine the matter, and shall expect you to let General Pickett know when the moment offers."

Alexander was incredulous. He had never doubted ultimate success, chiefly because the charge had been ordered by Lee. He, the artillery chief, had never before been asked to decide whether or not his bombardment had been successful; nor for that matter had any artillery chief in military history. Because of his youth he was unaware that Longstreet was asking him—between the lines—to join in protesting against the attack. Now, he was shaken: "Overwhelming reasons against the assault at once seemed to stare me in the face." So he got off a lengthy reply to Old Pete pointing out that because the enemy infantry was entrenched it was not possible to determine how badly it had been hurt, and that any alternative to the attack should be considered beforehand so that he would not waste his last stock of ammunition. Longstreet replied that Alexander's mission was to silence the Union artillery so that the Rebel infantry could advance. This was obvious, but the young artillerist also knew that this had never been done in the Civil War. Distraught, he went off to consult with Pickett, finding him so exuberantly confident that he replied curtly to Longstreet: "When our fire is at its best, I will advise General Pickett to advance."

Thus, right up until the moment he gave the order, "Let the batteries open," James Longstreet had done his utmost to prevent the assault that has entered history as Pickett's Charge. The first signal shot was fired at 1:07 P.M., and then, after a momentary delay, came the second; whereupon Alexander wrote later: "As suddenly as an organ strikes up in church, the grand roar followed from all the guns."

On Cemetery Ridge in the center of Hancock's line stood Gibbon with but three brigades, flanked on the left by Doubleday with two and Alex Hays with one. Barely 5,700 men held the position that Lee would strike with nearly three times that number. Even though Meade had warned Gibbon that the Rebel assault would come at him, he had made no effort to reinforce him, chiefly because he was so confident of Hunt's artillery enjoying a clear field of fire from Cemetery Hill to Little Round Top, and also because on reflection he recalled that Marse Robert preferred to strike the flanks rather than the center. Thus when Ewell's attack on the right was repulsed, he began to believe that the main blow would come at his left, where Sykes stood and behind him Sedgwick with a huge reserve. So he kept both in place.

At about noon the guns on the right fell silent, after which a strange almost eerie silence "as still as the Sabbath day" engulfed the men on Cemetery Ridge. Bluebellies who had taken cover clambered out of their trenches to lounge about, grumbling over their hunger and the heat. Suddenly there came that dreadful roar from across the narrow valley and then—like a thunderclap out of a sunny sky—that shower of shells burst upon them and the air seemed full of "murderous iron." "Down!" they cried, sprinting for their holes. "Down! Down!" General Hunt, standing on Little Round Top, thought the opening cannonade was "indescribably grand" and Gibbon considered it "the most infernal pandemonium" he had ever felt or seen, but those terrified Yankees quivering in their holes had no inclination for such professional, impersonal observation. Rather, it seemed to them that Hell itself was being hurled at them in flaming chunks. But then, gradually, it became clear that this dreadful weight of metal was no longer hitting their hill, but rather shrieking overhead to scourge the valley behind; and this knowledge that the enemy fire was punishing the generals as well as the rear-echelon troops instead of themselves, the customary cannon fodder, was a source of immense satisfaction to them and they recovered their aplomb.

Accurate at first, the Confederate fire—just as Alexander had anticipated—rapidly wreathed the enemy ridge in smoke so that the Rebel gunners were soon firing blindly. As they did, their recoiling gun trails dug deeper into the earth, thus elevating the gun barrels so that the angle of fire rose higher and higher. It struck the clerks and orderlies, ambulance drivers and other rear echelons, as well as the skulkers hoping to find sanctuary behind the ridge, killing and wounding them and driving them east and south in panic along the Taneytown Road and the Baltimore Pike. Most fortunate of all for this inaccurate Grayback fire were the errant missiles that fell upon General Meade's little white headquarters cottage. First the steps were carried away, then the porch collapsed, next a solid shot crashed through the front door barely missing Meade himself, another plowed through the roof and loft, filling the rooms below with flying splinters—after which the commanding general and his staff withdrew to the yard, where they beheld sixteen hideously mangled horses still tethered to a fence. Moving to a nearby barn, they vacated this after Butterfield was nicked in the neck by a shell fragment, finally moving to Powers Hill on the far right flank. Here they were safe, but out of control of the battle.

Meanwhile, the Yankees in the center of the ridge were still hugging the earth their mother, convinced "that nothing four feet from the ground could live"—until they perceived a most thrilling and astonishing sight. It was Winfield Scott Hancock, mounted on a splendid but occasionally rearing black horse, nonchalantly riding the length of his line as though those invisible missiles wailing and hissing around him were not the messengers of death. Some of his staff officers trailing behind him were not as much in love with danger, especially the one whose tractable mount Hancock commandeered after his own skittish steed became unmanageable—although this gentleman was happy to lead the frightened beast out of the impact area. Hancock, of course, was trying to encourage his soldiers, and when a brigadier protested, "General, the corps commander ought not to risk his life that way," Hancock replied disdainfully: "There are times when a corps commander's life does not count." Hancock continued his inspiring ride, gratified by the cheers of his admiring soldiers, but dismayed to find that General Hunt's guns on the ridge were not answering the Rebel fire.

Hunt had twenty batteries of just over one hundred guns in position from Little Round Top through the ridge to Cemetery Hill. He hesitated to fire counterbattery against the Rebels for fear that his gunners would shoot away their ammunition before the enemy infantry appeared. Accordingly, after ordering one six-gun battery on Little Round Top to maintain a deliberate fire on the enemy, he rode down to Cemetery Ridge to instruct the gunners there to remain silent while six batteries on Cemetery Hill to the north also maintained a steady fire. Thus a plunging crossfire from the heights on both extremities of the Yankee line would punish the Grayback batteries. Although Hancock had no quarrel with this provision, he did object to silence from his own sector, rather than the iron-tongued encouragement for his soldiers that would come from his own six batteries. So he countermanded Hunt's orders, as he had the right to do, but much to that worthy's displeasure. Those thirty-seven guns of Lieutenant Colonel Freeman McGilvery in artillery reserve, however, remained silent.

Meanwhile the Confederate cannonade continued unabated, especially in the vicinity of that target clump of umbrella-shaped trees on the ridge crest, and with such devastating effect that infantry were needed to replace the fallen gunners. They were, of course, "volunteered" in true army style. "Volunteers are wanted to man the battery!" a Massachusetts captain yelled. "Every man is to go of his own free will and accord. Come out here, John Dougherty, McGivern, and you Corrigan, and work those guns." It was done, and eventually McGilvery's batteries also opened up so that all the surviving Union guns were now thundering.

Hunt, now on Cemetery Hill, was pleased to see that so many of his cannon had escaped destruction, but disturbed that his answering fire might so shatter the enemy ordnance that the infantry assault would not materialize. This fear was shared by Major Thomas Osborn standing beside him, who asked if Meade did not hope to attack. When Hunt replied that he did indeed, Osborn said, "If this is so . . . I would cease fire at once, and the enemy could reach but one conclusion, that of our being driven from the hill."

Hunt agreed, ordering the batteries on the hill to cease fire, and then riding down to the ridge to do the same, although Hancock's badly mauled guns were allowed to maintain a sporadic fire. Eventually all the Union cannon fell silent, and after the Grayback guns did likewise at about two forty-five it seemed that the ruse had worked.

It had, at least in that the Rebel attack was not discouraged. Yet James Longstreet, who had thrown himself down to sleep after his exchange of notes with Alexander, had arisen still full of foreboding. Mounting his black horse with the roar of the artillery duel still in his ears, he rode to the edge of the woods in front of Pickett's men. Smoke swirled around the leaping Rebel guns, while the bellow of the outgoing shells was counterpointed by the roar of those arriving. The Yankee gunners were also firing high, but while their overshooting missiles spared the Confederate gunners, just as the Rebel projectiles missed the Union infantry, they scourged Longstreet's troops drawn up in the wood to the rear. Thus the pungent smell of powder mingled with the stench of death, and to the iron symphony of the guns and shells were added—like the high notes of violins—the screams of the stricken. Undisturbed by this customary clamor and confusion of battle, Longstreet silently sat his horse, waiting for George Pickett to come to his side. Before Pickett reached him, a courier rode up to Pickett and handed him a message; he read it as he approached Old Pete, handing it to him without a word. It was from Alexander and said: "General: If you are coming at all you must come immediately or I cannot give you proper support. The enemy's fire has not slackened materially, and at least 18 guns are still firing from the cemetery itself."

Longstreet read it and said nothing—even as the enemy fire began to subside. "General," Pickett asked, "shall I advance?" Again silence. Pickett did not move, his eyes on his beloved chief. Slowly Longstreet allowed his chin to sink onto his collar. That was his reply: the barest nod—if that. Hoping to elicit a direct order, Pickett said: "I shall lead my division forward, sir," but Old Pete said nothing. Still silent, Longstreet rode toward the Peach Orchard to confer with Alexander, while Pickett returned to his troops.

Alexander seemed elated when Longstreet rode up to him. He thought he had seen enemy artillery "on the cemetery" being moved to the rear. So had Longstreet. What neither realized was that the little clump of trees was not a cemetery, as Alexander had been told, and that the guns definitely taken to the rear did not number eighteen but only three. They belonged to a battered unit of Rhode Islanders, and Henry Hunt had given them permission to withdraw. Thus, more by accident than design, the Federal ruse of falling silent had led Alexander to believe that he had driven off the Union guns. It was now or never! So the young artillery chief thought when he dashed off another message to Pickett: "For God's sake, come quick! The 18 guns have gone. Come quick or my ammunition will not let me support you properly."

This message startled Longstreet. "Go and stop Pickett right where he is!" he cried. "And replenish our ammunition!"

"We can't do that, sir! The train has but little. It would take an hour to distribute it. . . ."

Old Pete seemed to waver. "I don't want to make this charge," he murmured in a hollow voice. "I don't believe it can succeed. I would stop Pickett now, but General Lee has ordered it and expects it." He paused significantly, as though hoping Alexander would agree with him. The youthful Georgian hesitated. This was too great a decision for him to express an opinion unless ordered to do so. And then the moment passed with the appearance of Garnett's brigade marching down Seminary Ridge to the jump-off point. Ahead of them rode their chief, too sick to walk, but wrapped in a blue overcoat astride a great black horse. Then Kemper's brigade emerged on his right. Finally Heth's men led by Pettigrew advanced into the open. There was a halt while lagging units caught up, while the long gray lines were dressed with parade-ground precision. A rising west wind shredded the gunsmoke and set nineteen battle flags to snapping briskly in the breeze.

"Sergeant," Lewis Armistead cried to a man in the 53rd Virginia, "are you going to put those colors on the enemy's works today?"

"I will try, sir, and if mortal man can do it, it shall be done."

"Armistead, hurry up!" Kemper shouted. "I am going to charge those heights and carry them, and I want you to support me."

"I'll do it!" cried the tall grizzle-beard. "Look at my line! It never looked better on dress parade."

"Up, men, and to your posts!" Pickett shouted, stirring the hearts of his Virginians. "Don't forget today that you are from Old Virginia."

On the left Pettigrew made the same appeal to his North Carolinians, calling to an officer: "Now, Colonel, for the honor of the good Old North State—forward!"

Beautifully dressed, the mile-long gray line stepped out, all flags unfurled, many flag officers mounted (because, like Garnett, they were all sick), starting forward on that rolling green three-quarter mile toward the silent ridge and that clump of trees. It was a stirring sight that lifted the heart of James Longstreet, even though he saw at once that his right could be enfiladed by the Union guns on Little Round Top. Dismounting, the burly Georgian sat hunched on a rail fence, watching his troops advance. He could see Armistead, whose brigade was to the rear of Kemper's and Garnett's in support, striding steadily forward with his cap perched on his high sword point.

It seemed to Old Pete that Cemetery Ridge was strangely still and silent in the July heat.

Atop the ridge the Federal gunners seized upon the lull in battle to clean their gun bores of gritty powder residue and to fill their caissons with the shells needed for the rapid-fire work ahead. Gun crews that had expended their supply of shells were issued canister, those deadly cylinders full of shot that do such dreadful work when fired point-blank into a charging foe. From Little Round Top came the wigwagged signal: "They are moving out to attack." It was as though a great sigh of relief passed through the ranks of Hancock's men. Upon the appearance of the toy-like long gray line on the other side of the narrow valley, a relieved Bluebelly cried: "Thank God! Here comes the infantry." He spoke for all foot soldiers everywhere, for the bullets of the enemy are much to be preferred to his rending, tearing artillery shells.

Now the spiraling gunsmoke clearly revealed the mile-long gray line steadily approaching: Pickett's three brigades on the right making for that tree clump, on the left six of them under Pettigrew and Trimble. Between Pickett's left and Pettigrew's right there yawned a quarter-mile gap.

On they came, blinking in the hot glare of the sun as they emerged from the gloom of the wood. Gradually their pupils contracted and they saw then what they had been asked to do. Three-fourths of a mile away across that narrow green basin stood the enemy with his fearsome guns and a clear field of fire. Into this they were moving with only their homespun butternut jackets to protect them, with scant hope of help from their own guns to the rear. On they came, shoulder-to-shoulder, aligned as never before, moving at a deliberate slow pace of a hundred yards a minute, neither yelling nor firing, for they had been forbidden to do either. This was not D. H. Hill's line "crooked as a ram's horn. Each rebel yelling on his own hook and aligning on himself." Perhaps this unique precision which was never to be repeated was like a bond strengthening them and intended to frighten the Yankees and even force them to retreat before they could unleash the hideous fire of those awful guns. And this did not come until three minutes after they had become visible to those amazed Bluebellies on the ridge.

Then the storm broke. Both flanks were taken in a murderous enfilading crossfire from Hunt's guns on Cemetery Hill to their left and Little Round Top to the right. From the blue center came the lesser scything of Hancock's artillery. Gaps small then huge began to appear in the neatly dressed lines. Men moving to fill them stepped over writhing, kicking comrades or motionless corpses. Now it was up to Pickett to close that quarter-mile gap to his left, and he did with the parade-ground order, "Left oblique!" It was neatly obeyed as though by steel-clad automatons rather than men of flesh and blood. But as they made that half-turn face to the left they were struck again by cannon fire, and even more severely when Pickett halted them in a swale halfway to the enemy ridge and parallel to it and gave them the incredible order to redress the line! How much better it would have been if this had been the Grayback ram's horn of old, fragmented and ragged and no easy target for the blue gunners. Even the Federal ground troops were astonished. "My God!" they cried in incredulity. "They're dressing the line!" But they came on again in perfect formation, and once more gaps appeared, especially at either flank of the entire line where shells struck at them end-on.

Seeing the bodies in gray and butternut strewn about the field and the constantly plunging flags, the blue-coated men behind the stone wall on the ridge were seized by a rising jubilation. Veterans of Burnside's bloodbath began shouting: "Fredericksburg! Fredericksburg!" Others remembering how the Rebels had taunted them there with cries of "Come on, Bluebellies! Come hyar!" began to shout: "Come on, Johnny! Keep on coming!"

Kemper's brigade on Pickett's right was fearfully punished by Little Round Top, and if the Federal shells passed overhead they exploded among Garnett's men. But on the Confederate left the fire from Cemetery Hill had an even more devastating effect. Here one of Pettigrew's brigades under Joseph Mayo came under the direct fire of twenty-nine Union guns. While they were so scourged, Alex Hays swung an Ohio regiment gatelike to take these staggered troops in enfilading fire on their left flank. This was more than they could endure, and they simply turned and fled, leaving behind them their dead, wounded and fallen flags, never stopping until they had reached the sanctuary of Seminary Ridge. Never before had such defection occurred in the Army of Northern Virginia, and half of these men were Virginians.

By then the gap between Pickett and Pettigrew had been closed, but with such a rush that the Graybacks crowding together were prime targets for the Union gunners. Yet the Rebels were still advancing. On the Confederate left Pettigrew's five brigades were mixed together, massed on a narrow front. Yet they scented victory and pressed on, yelling at last. Sheets of flame and bullets flew at them from Federal infantry behind the stone wall but they returned the fire. Birkett Fry urged his brigade forward, certain of success. "Go on!" he cried. "It will not last five minutes longer!" Just then he fell with a bullet in his thigh. On his right Garnett slumped from his horse dead. Kemper was mortally wounded with a bullet in the groin. This left Pickett with only Armistead as a brigade commander. Pettigrew was worse off: of his five brigadiers only Joe Davis, the nephew of Jefferson Davis, was still active; and Pettigrew was himself wounded after he crossed the Emmitsburg Road hurrying to the front. Though he remained in command, his division was out of control.

It soon became fiercely raked by enemy fire after Hays on the Union right at Ziegler's Grove just below Cemetery Hill neatly swung his rightmost regiment to join the Ohio regiment that had routed Mayo. Winfield Scott Hancock watched in delight as the two formations supported by two brass Napoleons poured an enfilading fire into the milling Rebels, multiplying their confusion and carnage. Shouting his approval, Hancock galloped south, hoping to get Doubleday on his left flank to duplicate the maneuver. As he rode he saw disaster looming in his center, just as it had the day before.

The Rebels had penetrated the Angle, a jog in the stone wall that had caused Gibbon's men to be posted 80 yards ahead of Hays's. As a result they were struck first by a flood of Graybacks, led by Armistead still waving his sword with a black hat balanced on its tip. Hancock had no way of knowing that this was his old friend, anxious as he was to find a unit to stem the tide. To his relief Colonel Arthur Devereaux, commanding a regiment in Gibbon's reserve, hailed him. "General, they have broken through! The colors are coming over the stone wall! Let me go in there!" Hancock reined his horse back on its haunches, turning in the saddle to see that the tall gray commander's hat had slipped down to his sword hilt, and that he was still waving his men on. "Get in there pretty God-damned quick!" he shouted, spurring his horse southward toward Doubleday. There to his immense relief he found that Brigadier General G. J. Stannard had anticipated his order and was wheeling two of his Vermont regiments in position to bear upon the Rebels overrunning the Angle. Company after company marched onto the Confederate flank, firing as they did, driving steadily northward to rip and tear Armistead's surprised Rebels and driving so close to them that the Union officers were able to add pistol fire to their musketry. "Glory be to God!" Abner Doubleday was crying, swinging his hat as Hancock rode up. "Glory be to God, see those Vermonters go it!"

Hancock waved his own hat in jubilation, but then a bullet passed through the pommel of his saddle and pierced his inner thigh, carrying with it bits of wood and a bent saddle nail. Two officers caught him as he fell from the saddle, gently lowering him to the ground while a tourniquet was fashioned from a knotted handkerchief wound tight with a pistol barrel. Examining his wound and the nail, Hancock wryly observed; "They must be hard up for ammunition when they throw such shot as that." When stretcher-bearers tried to carry him from the field, he refused to go, watching the critical action in the Angle.

There Armistead was urging his men forward before the Federals could close the gap. He had about 300 men following him. "Come on, boys," he cried, lifting his sword-held black cap aloft like a guide-on. "Give them the cold steel!" At that point the cap slid down the blade to the hilt, but the Graybacks surged forward, overrunning a pair of abandoned enemy guns. Armistead put a hand on the muzzle of one of them and was struck dying to the ground. Now all of Pickett's brigade commanders were down: Garnett dead, Armistead dying and Kemper apparently though not actually mortally wounded. But where was Pickett?

Throughout the famous charge that bears his name George Pickett was at his headquarters at the Codori farm on the Emmitsburg Road. As a division commander it was not necessary for him to be at the head of his troops, but rather behind them so as to coordinate their movements and to remain in touch with Longstreet. This is what Pettigrew was also doing on the left. When Longstreet sent Pickett word that he could have Cadmus Wilcox's brigades, he sent all three of his aides—one after another in the hope that at least one of them would get through—riding to order these formations forward. He did nothing thereafter. He was, in fact, useless. At this point in the military procedure and sense of honor then prevailing, it was incumbent upon him to mount his horse and ride forward to rally his men or at least to take command and give the appropriate orders to advance or withdraw. But he did not. Instead he rode to the rear, appearing at Longstreet's headquarters a dejected and defeated figure in sharp contrast to the bold and striking commander who had ridden so proudly toward Cemetery Ridge only a few hours earlier.

Pickett also complained that he was defeated because he had "no supports." This is most unfair to Colonel Alexander, who, more than any other officer on that field, did so much to support him. In the end, he was able to send eighteen guns forward—straight to destruction. That was the reason there were "no supports": the Rebel guns were in full view of the Union artillery above them and were simply smothered. That is why the stricken Armistead had no help when Devereaux's regiments struck his forlorn hope "pretty God-damn quick."

Reeling at first under the shock of their charge, the Rebels recoiled and came back. Hand-to-hand fighting ensued, but then the Bluebellies backed off to fire volley after volley into the close-packed gray mass, seeming to weave and undulate in the drifting smoke, through which could be caught glimpses of waving red flags. The smoke and the bits of red were all that Lee could see from his headquarters on Seminary Ridge.

Pickett's Charge was floundering in blood and broken bodies. All that had been gained was that shallow but short-lived penetration in the center. Both flanks, Pickett on the right, Pettigrew on the left, had been ripped and torn by Federal shells and canister, and then by the withering musketry of the blue regiments gate-swung by Stannard and Hays in what turned out to be an accidental double envelopment. On the left Pettigrew called for Trimble to support him with two brigades, and he did. But they were shattered by Federal artillery and of little use to Pettigrew, while the elderly Trimble was himself wounded again in the leg he nearly lost at Second Bull Run. Wilcox and Lang came across the valley to reinforce Pickett on the right in what became a limited advance, but one that did have the effect of compelling the now-wounded Stannard to order his Vermonters back into line to receive them. This eased the pressure on the Angle somewhat, although this wild, screaming, swearing, praying melee of men fighting with clubbed muskets and pistols, privates taking on officers and vice versa, continued for perhaps ten more minutes. Even Henry Hunt rode into it, emptying his revolver and crying, "See 'em! See 'em!" until his horse reared and fell kicking, pinioning the general beneath him.

The survivors of the flanking attacks were already moving across the valley, some running, others walking rapidly, pursued and still flayed by Yankee shells when the last of the Graybacks in the Angle joined the backward flood to Seminary Ridge. Pickett's Charge had lasted but an hour and had been utterly crushed. In all, the 12,500 Rebels actually engaged had suffered about 7,500 casualties, losses of 60 percent. In the five leading brigades casualties were 70 percent. Pickett had lost all three of his brigadiers, eight of his thirteen colonels and of all his officers above the rank of captain only one was unhurt. Pettigrew's casualties were nearly as severe. Almost as damaging to the Army of Northern Virginia was the fact that in Pickett's Charge it was the bravest who fell.

A rare ecstasy had seized the Bluebellies on Cemetery Ridge. General Hays and two aides rode triumphantly up and down the line, trailing captured Confederate colors in the dust. Even George Gordon Meade was exalted when he arrived on the battlefield. He could not believe it when he was told that the enemy attack had been repulsed in one hour. Reaching the crest and seeing the beaten gray tide flowing slowly back to the west, his hand jerked upward as though to seize his hat and wave it in elation. But then his innate sense of dignity prevailed and he merely waved his hand, breathing fervently, "Thank God!" Riding down the ridge Meade was greeted by cavorting, cheering soldiers and a band even played "Hail to the Chief," at which a war correspondent said to the Union leader: "Ah, General Meade, you're in very great danger of becoming President of the United States."

Perhaps, but George Gordon Meade at that moment was merely deeply thankful, contemplating neither the White House nor a counterattack upon his badly damaged enemy. This disappointed Winfield Scott Hancock, who had not yet left the field. Lying on his stretcher, he had already written a note to Meade urging just such a course—and it did seem the thing to do. Sykes's corps had been barely scratched and Sedgwick's huge corps in reserve had seen no action at all at Gettysburg. Surely, it appeared, these fresh formations had a very good chance of destroying Lee's badly disorganized and demoralized army. At the least it could have struck it a damaging blow with no fear of disengaging if thwarted. But Meade had no such plans. Hancock, meanwhile, had tears in his eyes upon the approach of an aide who handed him Lewis Armistead's watch, spurs and other personal effects. The aide had been with Hancock's old friend when he died, asking that these be given to him, and gasping: "Tell Hancock I have done him and my country a great injustice which I shall never cease to regret." So now it was no longer "Hancock, good-bye," but rather "Armistead, farewell," as the man who had done most to win the surpassing Union victory at Gettysburg was at last carried from the field, which, he proudly stated, "I did not leave . . . so long as a Rebel was standing upright."

■   ■   ■

Across the valley, the Army of Northern Virginia was sunk in gloom and mourning, all but James Longstreet, who, having seen his dire prophecy of disaster fulfilled, had recovered his hearty good nature and was methodically preparing to receive a counter-attack. Even Lee, though anguished, anticipated such an assault. When Pickett returned, he at once ordered him to put his division behind a hill and prepare to receive the Federals.

"General Lee," Pickett said, his eyes streaming tears, "I have no division, now. Armistead is down, Garnett is down and Kemper is mortally wounded."

"Come, General Pickett," Lee said, "this has been my fight and upon my shoulders rests the blame." Riding among his Butternuts, Lee cried to them so cheerfully, urging them so passionately to turn to receive the Yankees that they actually did regain their confidence, saying: "Uncle Robert will get us to Washington yet. You bet he will."

But after night fell and then rain with still no Federal attack, Robert Edward Lee at last gave way to the anguish that had seized his heart. Riding in the rain to his headquarters, his first cry was one of admiration. "I never saw troops behave more magnificently than Pickett's division of Virginians did today in that grand charge upon the enemy!" And then, the agony and the remorse: "And if they had been supported as they were to have been— but for some reason not yet fully explained to me, were not—we would have held the position and the day would have been ours." He paused, his voice rising and breaking: "Too bad! *Too bad!* OH, TOO BAD!"

If Lee's audacity had undone him, Meade's caution was now thwarting the resolve of his commanders to end the war that day. The first of these was the bellicose Pleasonton, who said to Meade: "I will give you half an hour to show yourself a great general. Order the army to advance, while I take the cavalry and get in Lee's rear, and we will finish the campaign in a week." Meade shook his head. "How do you know Lee will not attack me again?" he replied. "We have done well enough." Hancock also urged a prompt attack with the corps of Sedgwick and Sykes, but Meade merely responded with a warm verbal message thanking him for his services that day, and also avoiding the issue. But Meade was supported by Henry Hunt. Bruised and aching after being pulled out from under his horse, Hunt supported his chief without reservation: "A prompt counter-charge after combat between two small bodies of men is one thing, [but] the change from the defensive to the offensive of an army, after an engagement at a single point, is quite another." For Meade to attack in the belief that Lee was not prepared to receive him would be "rash in the extreme." Warren agreed. Thus, of the four generals most responsible for the Federal victory at Gettysburg, two supported Meade, while only one—the wounded Hancock—opposed him. The dead Reynolds, of course, could not vote.

It is difficult to fault Meade for this decision in the greatest battle of the war begun only three days after he took command of a scattered army. To the wisdom of Hunt's judgment must be added the terrible testimony of the Union casualties. They had numbered 23,049: 3,155 killed, 14,529 wounded and 5,365 missing. Of these last some were probably captured, more blasted to bits by shellfire, but most were skulkers. Also, next day Meade's army showed 51,414 present for duty, meaning that there were an additional 15,000 unaccounted for. Lee's casualties, of course, were more damaging in proportion to his inferior numbers: 3,903 dead, 18,735 wounded for a total of 22,638, with another 5,150 missing, of whom most were probably captured. Rebel losses then were closer to 28,000, but if Meade attacked immediately, Lee would be on the defensive again, and Robert Edward Lee the peerless defensive fighter was no general to strike with an army in no condition for prompt renewal of battle. Thus Meade's decision must be upheld, but not his slowness in following Lee to strike him at the opportune moment.

Elated at Meade's failure to come at him, Lee next day held his army in position to receive him—just as he had done with McClellan on the morrow of Antietam—and thus reasserted himself. Meanwhile his long convoy of wounded started to the rear. That night in a driving rain, the rest of Lee's army followed. Meade, meanwhile, spent that Fourth of July reorganizing. Next day he found Lee gone. He pursued him slowly. But William French with a detachment at Harpers Ferry on July 3 had surprised Lee's rear guard at Falling Waters in modern West Virginia and destroyed the bridge over the Potomac there. This left Lee trapped on the north bank with a swollen river at his back. Here was the chance to destroy him, for straggling and desertions had reduced Marse Robert to 35,000 men, with Meade now back up to 85,000, and he was low on ammunition. Still, he turned at Williamsport on July 7 and entrenched, meanwhile tearing down warehouses to bridge the river. On July 12, Meade approached him. His own caution deepened by the over-cautious French's advice not to strike Lee, he called a council of war. With his aggressive corps commanders— Reynolds, Sickles and Hancock—either dead or wounded, the vote was for not attacking. So Lee got his command safely over the river on the night of July 13–14, and although much of his rear guard was taken prisoner, the Army of Northern Virginia escaped.

Abraham Lincoln was most unhappy at Meade's failure to catch Lee.

"We had them within our grasp," he lamented. "We had only to stretch forth our hands and they were ours." True, but Lee's repulse at Gettysburg—costlier than the one at Antietam—ended forever Southern hopes for a victory on Northern soil which would bring help from abroad. Just as helpful to the Federal cause—perhaps even more—would be a decisive victory in the west, where Grant had begun the siege of Vicksburg.

58

■

The Siege and Fall of Vicksburg

V ICKSBURG WAS the key to the Mississippi, if not to the entire war. If it fell, the great waterway would be in Union hands, but if it held out, as Abraham Lincoln said: "We may take all the northern ports of the Confederacy and they can still defy us from Vicksburg. It means hog and hominy without limit, fresh troops from all the States of the far South, and a cotton country where they can raise the staple without interference." Vicksburg, however, was a very tough nut, especially from the water. It stood on high bluffs on the eastern bank commanding a great bend in the river, while on its eastern or landward side it was protected by the valley of the Yazoo, a watery labyrinth of swamps and bayous.

In the spring and summer of 1862 Commodore Farragut moved with his fleet up the Mississippi, receiving the surrender of Baton Rouge and Natchez and then, on May 18, imperiously summoning Vicksburg to surrender. From Brigadier General M. L. Smith, military governor of the city, came the reply: "Mississippians don't know, and refuse to learn, how to surrender. . . . If Commodore Farragut . . . can teach them, let [him] come and try." Farragut did come, did try—but did not, like Julius Caesar, conquer. His combined ordnance of two hundred guns and twenty-three mortars was enough to pulverize the city and to drive its inhabitants underground, but not enough to destroy its formidable defenses. An infantry assault up those steep and frowning bluffs would be suicidal. Vicksburg could be taken only by a massive land assault from the rear supported by a naval force blockading its front. So Farragut began dropping downriver, and as he did the Confederate ironclad *Arkansas* gave him a humiliating Parthian or parting shot.

Arkansas was a jerry-built ugly duckling hastily thrown together on the Yazoo River under the supervision of Isaac Newton Brown, a crusty old thirty-year veteran of the United States Navy who was the Rebel fleet's counterpart of Farragut. In mid-July, just as Farragut was promoted to admiral, Brown struck at the entire Union fleet, crippling the famous *Carondolet*. Next *Arkansas* swept between two startled Yankee flotillas moored on either bank, her ten guns spouting smoke and flame "to every point of the circumference, without the fear of hitting a friend or missing an enemy." But the Union ships were quick to reply, driving the bold Confederate off and severely damaging her, but not before she disabled one of the Ellet rams. Finally with sixty casualties, Brown drew off and steered to safety beneath the guns of Vicksburg.

Stung, his one-star nose out of joint, the new Union admiral prepared to chastise this impudent Rebel. But then on July 26, alarmed as the river began to fall rapidly in the summer heat, he sailed downriver before his ships could be grounded in low water.

Conquest of Vicksburg would have to await another year, and it would have to be done on land—which meant U. S. Grant.

After the Federal victory at Corinth in October 1862, Grant was told by Halleck, "Fight the enemy when you please." He immediately began to plan to lead his Army of the Tennessee in an overland assault on Vicksburg. As he did, he learned of an intrigue behind his back.

The political general John McClernand, a faithful War Democrat high in Lincoln's favor, had gone to Washington to ask the president to place him in command of a force to sail straight down the Mississippi and capture Vicksburg. McClernand told Lincoln that unless the great river were opened soon, the Northwest would drop out of the war. Eager for a victory, Lincoln consented—although he did not give McClernand exactly the carte blanche command he desired.

During the fall McClernand, fired by dreams of military glory, and then, of course, the White House, began recruiting dozens of regiments which he forwarded to Memphis to await his arrival. Grant learned of this through newspaper reports. He requested Halleck to clarify his own status, and Old Brains, who distrusted McClernand as much as Grant did, at once wired Grant that he had full command of all troops in his department. He also ordered the formations at Memphis to be formed into two corps, one to be commanded by Sherman, the other by McClernand. With this the opportunist in Illinois complained bitterly to Lincoln that he had been undone by a West Point conspiracy. But the President sided with Halleck and Grant.

As a result of this threat, Grant felt himself compelled to put his plans into premature operation. First he ordered Sherman to sail downriver from Memphis with the forces there before McClernand, who outranked Uncle Billy, could arrive to supersede him. Next, with 40,000 men he began advancing toward Vicksburg along the Mississippi Central Railroad. With Sherman moving by water and himself by land, Grant hoped that this pincers converging on Vicksburg would compel John Pemberton, now commanding there, to divide his already outnumbered force. Reaching Holly Springs, Grant established a forward base there, still confident of success. But then to his surprise he found Pemberton on his front with 20,000 Graybacks and solidly entrenched along the Yalobusha River at Grenada. Next he was dismayed at reports of devastating Rebel raids on his line of communication.

What had happened was that Joe Johnston, now commanding—or at least "coordinating"—Confederate forces in the West from Jackson, Mississippi, had ordered Nathan Bedford Forrest and Earl Van Dorn to wreck the enemy's line of communications. Forrest riding west from central Tennessee with 2,000 men tore up fifty miles of railroad and telegraph line, while Van Dorn riding north from Grenada with 3,500 troopers succeeded in getting behind Grant to destroy his base at Holly Springs. Deep in enemy territory without a supply line, Grant wisely called off his offensive. But his wire notifying Sherman of this decision could not move over downed telegraph lines, and thus, as Grant withdrew, Sherman confidently proceeded toward Vicksburg on the assumption that his chief's advance would occupy most of Pemberton's forces. A few miles north of the Confederate citadel city, he ascended the Yazoo River with his 32,000 men for an assault on the Rebels defending the vital high ground above Chickasaw Bayou.

On December 27 Union gunboats under David Dixon Porter went up the river shelling the bluffs, enabling Sherman's troops to disembark. That same day a heavy Union artillery bombardment struck the Confederate positions, but with little effect. By then, the force on the bluffs—also called Walnut Hills—had risen from 6,000 to 14,000. Nevertheless Sherman on the twenty-ninth rashly ordered a frontal assault. Two Union brigades charged across the bayou causeway to the foot of the bluffs, where they were struck by a plunging fire from Rebels invisible in rifle pits above them. Sherman promptly called off the attack, and the Battle of Chickasaw Bluffs ended in a Federal defeat. Casualties: for the South, 63 dead, 134 wounded and 10 missing; for the North, 208 dead, 1,005 wounded and 563 missing.

Grant's plans were now completely upset. Moreover, he could see that political considerations had ruled out the easier everland approach in favor of the more difficult but also more spectacular river route. Thus, with

Siege of Vicksburg

Memphis

Holly Springs

Helena

ARKANSAS

Mississippi Central Railroad

Yalabusha River

Grenada

Greenville

Greenwood

MISSISSIPPI

Mississippi River

Lake Providence

Yazoo River

YAZOO DELTA

Big *Black* *River*

MILLIKEN'S BEND

CHICKASAW BLUFFS

YOUNG'S POINT
Chickasaw Bayou

Vicksburg

CHAMPION'S HILL

Jackson

Bruinsburg

Port Gibson

Natchez

LOUISIANA

Mississippi

River

Port Hudson

Baton Rouge

0   25   50 Miles
SCALE

the chagrined McClernand still lobbying for command of the Mississippi, he requested and received it himself. On January 30, 1863, he arrived at Young's Point, about twenty miles above Vicksburg on the western bank.

Few generals have faced a more bleak outlook than Grant at that moment. Jefferson Davis had already hailed the defeat at Chickasaw Bluffs as proof that Grant would slink back to Memphis. Grant was himself still under the stigma of Shiloh, still rumored to be a drunkard and still the object of infamous attack in the Eastern press. He was also still suspected of bigotry because of his notorious "Jew Order" of December 17, 1862. During 1862, believing that "we cannot carry on war and trade with a people at the same time," both Grant and Sherman did their best to halt the illicit cotton trade through Memphis. They issued a stream of regulations tightening the issue of trade permits, banishing Southerners who refused to take the oath of allegiance, requiring all payments to be made in U.S. currency rather than the gold that could be converted into guns and banning suspicious Northern traders from Memphis. Many traders ignored these orders, among them some openly defiant Jews. When Grant's own father arrived in Memphis with three Jewish merchants seeking permits, his son lost his temper and issued this order: "The Jews, as a class violating every regulation of trade established by the Treasury Department, and also Department orders, are hereby expelled from the Department." Jewish leaders immediately denounced this "enormous outrage," punishing a whole race for the sins of a few; House Democrats, sensing a lovely issue, prepared to introduce a ringing denunciation of the order; until Lincoln, with customary balance, declaring that Grant had "proscribed a whole class, some of whom are fighting in our ranks," quietly rescinded the order.

On the military front, Grant's problems were that he was unable to turn back from the river approach, nor could he storm Vicksburg frontally or establish a base below the city until the spring rains ceased. Least of all, he could not sit still for four or five months to give his enemies proof of his "timidity" or to allow his army of 45,000 men to fall apart. Thus, to keep his men occupied, to perplex Pemberton in Vicksburg, and also just on the chance of finding a chink in the city's armor, he made four flanking attempts.

Opposite Vicksburg was a peninsula formed by the river's great hairpin bend. Soldiers and black contrabands under Farragut had begun to dig a channel through it the previous summer, but the work was abandoned when falling water compelled the Federal fleet to retire. Now Grant reasoned that if a canal could be cut through the peninsula it would bypass the city and allow his army to sail below it out of range of its guns. Sherman's corps went to work on the excavation in February, but after the canal was dug the Father of Waters refused to enter it. Grant next tried to deepen and connect a chain of lakes and streams winding west from Lake Providence 50 miles above the city to a reentry point 150 miles below it. This would provide a channel for gunboats and transports. Here also two months of hard work ended in failure.

A third course seemed most promising. This was to penetrate the watery jungle of the Yazoo Delta north of Vicksburg. Part of McClernand's corps led by gunboats went to Helena, four hundred river-miles above the hilltop citadel, and blew up a levee to float the gunboats into the flooded Delta rivers. Now the terrain and Confederate lumberjacks became the enemy. Moving over rivers scarcely wider than their beams, the gunboats were struck by low-hanging cypress and cottonwood branches which smashed smokestacks and swept everything above decks overboard. Rebel soldiers felled trees across the streams to block their passage. When the boats came under the gunfire of a fort hastily built near Greenwood, Mississippi, the Union commander, already nearing a nervous breakdown, called off the entire expedition.

David Dixon Porter led the fourth attempt himself in a flotilla of ironclads and transports carrying a division of Sherman's troops. But he encountered the same obstacles with the added annoyance of snakes, wildcats and raccoons dropping onto his decks from overhanging trees. Sailors armed with brooms were kept on watch to sweep them overboard. On March 20 Porter learned that a body of Confederate infantry was marching through the jungle to capture his entire force, and he notified Sherman: "Hurry up, for Heaven's sake. I never knew how helpless an ironclad could be steaming around through the woods without an army to back her." Sherman did come to the rescue, sending his men wading through waist-deep swamps to drive the Rebels off. Back-pedaling furiously, the gunboats returned to the Mississippi. And so a fourth failure was added to U. S. Grant's dismal record before Vicksburg.

Now a rising clamor of criticism of Grant erupted. Marat Halstead, editor of the influential Cincinnati *Commercial,* wrote to his friend Treasury Secretary Chase: "You do once in a while, don't you, say a word to the President, or Stanton, or Halleck, about the conduct of the war? Well, now for God's sake say that General Grant, entrusted with our greatest army, is a jackass in the original package. He is a poor drunken imbecile. He is a poor stick sober, and he is most of the time more than half-drunk, and much of the time idiotically drunk. . . . Grant will fail miserably, hopelessly, eternally." Chase passed the letter along to Lincoln, who said to his secretary: "I think General Grant has hardly a friend left, except myself." To a delegation of civilians who came to him to protest Grant's insobriety, he said: "If I knew what brand of whiskey he drinks I would send a barrel or so to some other generals." Lincoln simply refused to lose faith in a general "who will fight battles and win victories."

Yet, if the Cincinnati editor offered no evidence supporting the charge, a Wisconsin brigadier did, writing to his wife: "He tries to let liquor alone, but he cannot resist the temptation always. When he came to Memphis he left his wife at LaGrange, and for several days after getting here was beastly drunk, utterly incapable of doing anything. Quinby and I took him in charge, watching him day and night and keeping liquor away from him." They also telegraphed Julia to come to his side, and when she did Grant stopped drinking.

On the other hand Mary Livermore—later to be famous as a suffragette—led a Sanitary Commission delegation to Young's Point to investigate the rumors and found that Grant's "clear eye, clean skin, firm flesh and steady nerves . . . gave the lie to the universal calumnies then current." Under Secretary of War Charles Dana, sent by the unsatisfied Stanton ostensibly as an inspector of the pay service but actually to spy on Grant, came to the same conclusion, describing Grant as "the most modest, the most disinterested and the most honest man I ever knew, with a temper that nothing could disturb and a judgment that was judicial in its comprehensiveness and wisdom. Not a great man except morally; not an original or brilliant man, but sincere, thoughtful, deep and gifted with courage that never failed." And that was exactly what Grant's soldiers thought of him, too.

Yet the most telling evidence against Grant came from his friend and chief of staff John Rawlins and Sylvanus Cadwallader, a correspondent of the Chicago *Times.* While Grant invested Vicksburg from its landward side that summer Rawlins repeatedly had to take wine or whiskey away from him, once threatening to resign if he did not stop drinking. Cadwallader in his *My Three Years with Grant,* published thirty years later, wrote that while aboard the steamboat *Diligent* with Grant on the Mississippi: "I was not long in perceiving that Grant had been drinking, and that he was still keeping it up. He made several trips to the barroom of the boat in a short time, and became stupid in speech and staggering in gait." Cadwallader also reported having taken Grant's whiskey bottles away from him and heaving them into the river. He said he repeatedly tried to stop Grant from drinking, and was seldom successful.

Thus there seems to be no doubt that Grant did drink; usually from boredom or the depression that overcame him in the absence of Julia. It might have been a substitute for sexual satisfaction, or even just sexual companionship, for Grant was no alcoholic in the modern sense of a disease in persons so hopelessly addicted to drink that they become the despair and heartbreak of those who love and depend on them and cannot recover their health and happiness unless they swear off forever. Grant was a binge drinker. He could go without liquor for months, but when he started to drink he found it hard to stop. Yet whenever Grant was actively engaged or actually in combat he never sought support from the glass crutch. This may explain the sharply conflicting reports of those who observed the general: when Cadwallader found him stupefied and staggering, he was bored by the siege and drinking, and when Mary Livermore spoke of his clear eye and steady nerve, he was enthusiastic about upcoming operations and sober.

In those days drunkenness was abhorred as a shameful, sinful habit, and U. S. Grant fought hard to escape that stigma. His very struggle for self-discipline might have made him a better general, for it made of him a compassionate commander who could understand the shortcomings of those he led and also discipline them.

It is possible that Grant's four failures before Vicksburg so frustrated him that he reached for the bottle. But then he conceived a plan and was himself again. He had remembered that while he retreated from Grenada in the fall of 1862 he was "amazed at the quantity of supplies the country afforded. It showed that we could have subsisted off the country for two months . . ." In a word, he would not need a supply line. He could march his army down the western bank of the Big Muddy to a point below Vicksburg where a crossing to the eastern bank might be made. Grant's top generals, especially William Tecumseh Sherman, objected to such an advance. Sherman insisted that the only way to take Vicksburg was to return to Memphis and establish a secure supply line before starting over again along the line of the Mississippi Central. Grant could not be dissuaded, chiefly because he feared that such a delay would further depress the country's already sinking morale. No supply line, however efficient, could encourage the people, and only a victory could do that, he told Sherman. It must be done quickly "or our cause is lost." No victories had been won anywhere else (Gettysburg had yet to be fought) and they must "go on." So he ordered Sherman to make a diversion north of Vicksburg while he marched his army down the west bank opposite Bruinsburg. There he awaited the arrival of the Union fleet that was to run the gantlet of Vicksburg's guns so that it might carry his army across the river to the east bank safely below the hilltop citadel. On the night of April 16–17, 1863, that fleet under Admiral David Dixon Porter made its move.

With lights dowsed and engines silent, the ships began floating downstream. The dark wooded shores of the peninsula were on their right as they headed for the end of the hairpin turn. Reaching it, the Union fleet suddenly found itself illuminated by the flickering light of a house set ablaze on the peninsula and a calcium fire lighted on a Vicksburg hill. Stealth was not possible now, and Vicksburg's batteries were already booming. Thundering back with their own guns, the Yankees cracked on steam. One by one—armored gunboats, turtle-backed rams and steamboats belching fire and smoke from their tall funnels—the Union ships swept through the Rebel shot and shell. Soon the cotton bales that served as "armor" for some of the transports caught fire, and as the stricken *Henry Clay* staggered downstream she trailed a wake of fiery bunches of cotton that made Admiral Porter think "a thousand streamers were coming down." But all the other ships had come safely through. "When this was effected," Grant wrote, "I felt a degree of relief scarcely ever equalled since. . . . All that campaigns, labors, hardships and exposures from the month of December previous to this time that had been made and endured, were for the accomplishment of this purpose."

Meanwhile a Union cavalry raid deep into Mississippi began wrecking Pemberton's communication. This would forestall any attempt by the Rebel commander to oppose the movement to the east bank. Execution of the raid was given to the 1,700-man brigade of Colonel Benjamin Grierson, the most unlikely leader of mounted troops who ever sat in a saddle.

Eighteen months earlier Grierson had been a music teacher and bandmaster in Jacksonville, Illinois. When war broke out he joined the infantry because he feared horses, ever since one of them had kicked him in the head as a boy, leaving a lifelong scar. But the governor of Illinois assigned him to the cavalry, ignoring his protests. To his own amazement he became probably the Union's finest commander of mounted men in the West. His only music now was what he could coax from a Jew's harp he carried inside his blouse, along with a compass and a small map of the region he was to scourge. During the last two weeks of April he and his troopers swept through the entire state of Mississippi. They won several skirmishes, killing or wounding 100 Rebels and capturing another 500. They tore up fifty miles of track on the three different railroads supplying Pemberton, burning scores of freight cars and depots, until they rode at last into Baton Rouge, exhausted from sixteen days and six hundred miles of pillaging. By detaching small units from his main body to ride off into all different directions, Grierson had also lured most of Pemberton's depleted but still valuable cavalry and a full division of infantry into frustrated pursuit—frustrated because the Yankees were never in force where they were supposed to be. By this raid, which was easily of more strategic value than any of those by the redoubtable and much-more-famous Forrest, he had made it easy for Grant to get across the Big Muddy to the eastern bank.

So had Sherman's diversion. Landing a division near the site of his defeat at Chickasaw Bluffs, Uncle Billy made such a convincing demonstration there with artillery, gunboats and deploying of infantry that the position's commander desperately wired Pemberton for reinforcements—and the Vicksburg chief at once recalled 3,000 soldiers marching south to resist Grant.

On April 30 the crossing of the Mississippi was begun, and Pemberton was powerless to prevent it.

John Clifford Pemberton, the defender of Vicksburg, was the doughface par excellence of the Civil War. Born in Philadelphia on August 10, 1814, he entered West Point in 1833 and almost immediately fell under the spell of Southern cadets with all their grace and charm. Twice breveted for gallantry in the Mexican War, he married Martha Thompson of Norfolk, Virginia, to become even more deeply disposed to admire the South. A week after Sumter he resigned from the U.S. Army to join the Confederacy, while two of his brothers remained with the Union army. Jefferson Davis, pleased at this turnabout, rewarded him with a brigadier general's commission, and he rose rapidly to become a three-star general on October 10, 1862. Four days later he took command in Vicksburg.

Pemberton's rapid rise was due not to any exceptional military skill or brilliant campaigns, but rather to his friendship with Davis, again based more on delight at having a Yankee aboard than true admiration. Dull, absolutely incapable of arousing troops, he did have the virtue of unswerving obedience. This he converted into the defect of distrusting innovation, even when it was required to meet changing circumstances. Thus, when Grant crossed the Big Muddy he remained where he was, on static defense in Vicksburg.

Now Grant's daring came into play to match his farsightedness. Although he had about 33,000 men against Pemberton's 23,000, the enemy army in Vicksburg was linked to the interior by rail and could be easily reinforced or supplied. Grant decided to attack the city's rear, its supply base to the east in Jackson, then held by Joe Johnston with about 6,000 men. The Union chief proposed one of the most audacious moves in history: to cut loose from his base, seize Jackson, and then, still living off the land, turn west to invest Vicksburg. Thus, as Grant moved east toward Jackson, the bewildered Pemberton sallied from Vicksburg to "cut" the nonexistent Yankee supply line.

Grant had been right. He could live off the land. Civilians might be hungry in Mississippi, but the Yankee soldiers could seize what these penniless people could not buy. They stripped every plantation that they passed of what they needed: vegetables, hams, poultry, bread and milk. They were so thorough that when an irate planter on a mule rode up to complain to a division commander that his soldiers had robbed him of everything he owned, the general eyed his mount thoughtfully and said: "Well, those men didn't belong to my division at all, because if they were my men they wouldn't have left you that mule."

On May 12 as the Union army approached Jackson with Major General James McPherson's corps leading and Sherman following, McPherson was halted at Raymond by a Rebel brigade under John Gregg. A brisk firefight ensued, a confused and blundering battle fought for hours in the woods for possession of a bridge over Fourteen Mile Creek. Eventually McPherson with his superior numbers hurled Gregg back and the march on Jackson continued, with the Yankees suffering losses of 66 killed, 339 wounded and 37 missing, and the Rebels losing 72 killed, 252 wounded and 190 missing.

In Jackson Joe Johnston—having been promised reinforcements—was still at the head of only 6,000 men when, on May 14, 25,000 Yankees attacked out of a driving rainstorm. That was not nearly enough to hold, and the Rebels were rapidly routed out of their entrenchments and sent fleeing east—their commander with them. That night Sherman slept in Johnston's bed. Next day his troops began the work of destroying Jackson as a rail center. Tracks, cars and locomotives were destroyed, and all arsenals, factories, machine shops and foundries burned, so that hardly more remained to Jackson than chimneys standing lonely and stark, gaunt against the sky—and the Bluebellies gleefully renamed the town "Chimneyville."

Now Old Joe urged Pemberton to unite with his survivors and await the promised reinforcements which would make them Grant's equal in numbers. Vicksburg didn't matter now: Grant's army was the true objective. They could always reoccupy the river citadel after they had destroyed him. This was sound strategy, but the inflexible Pemberton replied that his orders were to hold Vicksburg and that was what he intended to do. Their disagreement became academic two days later when the fast-moving Grant marched out of Jackson, leaving Sherman to complete its destruction, and found Pemberton waiting for him at Champion's Hill, midway between Jackson and Vicksburg.

This was the key battle of the campaign: about 29,000 Yankees against 20,000 Rebels—not a terrible disparity either way, but it was also Grant against Pemberton. McClernand and McPherson made the assault, but while the usually aggressive McClernand dragged his feet on the left, McPherson's troops overwhelmed the Confederate right, completely collapsing this flank after a bloody battle of several hours' duration. Grant always believed that if McClernand had been more impetuous he could have destroyed the enemy. Even so, the Union army had inflicted casualties of 381 killed, about 1,800 wounded and 1,670 missing for a total of 3,851, against Federal losses of 410 dead, 1,844 wounded and 187 missing, for a total 2,441. Also Pemberton had lost an entire division, cut off when his demoralized main body fell back to the Big Black River about ten miles east of Vicksburg. There he held a strong position, holding doggedly to a bridge kept open for the return of the lost division. But unknown to Pemberton this formation was already marching east to join Johnston.

At the Big Black one of McClernand's brigades, chafing at having been denied a share in the glory of Champion's Hill, swept forward without orders to storm the bridge and shatter the Confederate left. Having lost about 1,750 men here against 200 for Grant, Pemberton ordered his troops into full retreat to Vicksburg. They entered the city May 17, so shocking its inhabitants by their appearance that one woman wrote, "I shall never forget the woeful sight. Wan, hollow-eyed, ragged, footsore, bloody, the men limped along unarmed . . . humanity in the last throes of endurance."

Grant, as relentless as ever, pursued, unimpressed by the renewed adulation descending upon him, much of it from former detractors. But he was pleased when he stood beside Sherman on the Walnut Hills gazing down at Chickasaw Bayou where the redhead had met bloody repulse and heard his chief lieutenant break the silence with the cry: "Until this moment I never thought your expedition a success! I never could see the end clearly until now. But this is a success, this is a campaign, if we never take the town!"

Grant intended to do that, too—immediately. Believing that Pemberton's dazed and demoralized army was now vulnerable to the knockout blow, without stopping to rest his own blown troops, he ordered a general assault on May 19. He did this so confident of success that he did not even bother to reconnoiter what was probably the most formidable fixed position of the Civil War. The terrain itself was of such a jumbled nature that it lent itself ideally to the fortifications begun a year ago when Farragut appeared below the city. A Rebel soldier who worked on these has best described the hills of Vicksburg: "After the Lord of Creation had made the big mountains and ranges of hills, he had left on his hands a large lot of scraps. These were all dumped at Vicksburg in a waste heap." Furthermore Grant's three-to-one superiority was greatly reduced by the necessity of building a line of contravallation to his rear to hold off any relief attempt by Joe Johnston. And this rearward line was twice as long as the enemy's to his front. Here he faced skillfully built and well-sited defenses stretching for seven miles along commanding ridges and anchored at each end on Vicksburg's 200-foot bluffs above the river. In a solid year of building and digging, Pemberton's soldiers had erected or emplaced redoubts, forts, redans, salients, lunettes and bastions, protected by overlapping fields of fire and connected by a complex of mutually supporting trenches. Unaware of these, unsuspecting that the supposedly stunned Graybacks within them had taken heart because of them, the Union attack swept forward in a soaring spirit of confidence—and was almost immediately shattered. The moment the Bluebellies came into the open they were struck to the ground, and Grant quickly canceled the operation.

But he launched another assault three days later. This time, having first gone over the enemy's defenses searching for soft spots—of which he found few—he then preceded the attack by a furious bombardment from two hundred guns on land and another hundred from Porter's ships on the river. Pleased to try again and bring the long campaign to an end, the Yankees struck with great spirit, but were again met by a horizontal rain of bullets and shells. This time, however, they gained a few lodgments— only to be driven back by counter-attacks. McClernand on the left, however, appeared to have made a solid penetration. He notified Grant that if the other two corps "would make a diversion in my favor" he was confident that he could expand it or even score a breakthrough.

Grant, already secretly planning to relieve McClernand when the opportunity appeared, was with Sherman when he received the message. "I don't believe a word of it," he said, but Uncle Billy protested that it might be worth a try. So he and McPherson rejoined the assault, while Grant sent reinforcements to McClernand. The result was complete and utter repulse which, Grant said later, "only served to increase our casualties without giving any benefit whatever."

Grant was furious. In three days he had lost more than 4,000 men, with 814 killed—and more than 3,000 of these casualties had been inflicted on the second attempt. Thus in three days he had lost almost as many men as in the previous three weeks. So, as was his wont, he found a scapegoat, reporting to Halleck: "General McClernand's dispatches misled me as to the real state of facts, and caused much of this loss. He is entirely unfit for the position of corps commander, both on the march and on the battlefield." U. S. Grant simply could not accept blame for failure. At Belmont it had been "excited" officers; at Donelson it had been McClernand; at Shiloh Lew Wallace and Prentiss, even though Prentiss probably prevented Grant's defeat; and at Iuka, it was Rosecrans's fault. Now it was McClernand again, and a few weeks later—on a technicality—he paid with his head for his foiled attempt to steal Grant's army.

This unpleasant trait in Grant probably also accounted for his reluctance to request a truce to bury his dead and succor his wounded. For days the stench of bodies burst quickly in that dreadfully humid Mississippi heat and the cries of the maimed, agonized both by wounds and by thirst, had been a torment in the nostrils and ears of the Rebels who had shot them down. Eventually on May 25 Pemberton appealed to him "in the name of humanity I have the honor to propose a cessation of hostilities for two and a half hours" for this purpose. Grant "acceded" to this request and it was done. Once again U. S. Grant could not show weakness, and thus the same man who could not ride across a battlefield because he could not endure the sight of blood, or could not eat a piece of meat not cooked to a char or stand the sight of someone abusing an animal without berating him or even attacking him with his fists, could allow his dead to putrefy and his wounded to suffer just so his opponent could not construe a request for a truce as a sign of softness. In any other pursuit such an attitude would indeed spring from an inhumanly heartless soul, but this was war—what Grant called "the business." To ask for the white flag of truce might also seem to be an admission of defeat, and thus encourage his foe while discouraging his countrymen, to say nothing of diminishing the brilliance of his so-far successful campaign. Grant would always take his losses stoically as though they were an occupational hazard to be accepted like any farmer contending with the weather or businessman calculating risks, and this is probably why he stayed away from the battlefield so that his compassion might not soften his resolve to get "the business" done.

Yet down at Port Hudson, Louisiana, below Vicksburg and the southern terminus of the 115 miles of Mississippi River still flying the Stars and Bars, almost the exact opposite reaction came from the inept Nathaniel Banks, commanding the Federal force there. Banks had about 30,000 men— including two black regiments of the Louisiana Native Guards—against the 7,000 Rebels under Major General Franklin Gardner, like Pemberton a

Northerner who had married South and chosen to fight for Dixie. On May 27 Banks's major assault came against the Confederate left, spearheaded by his black troops. They were shredded by the same kind of gunfire that had broken Grant's assaults on Vicksburg: about 2,000 Yankees downed compared to fewer than 300 Rebels. Banks, a political general unfamiliar with the heartless side of "the business," unhesitatingly asked for and was granted a truce to bury his dead and retrieve his wounded.

And so at Vicksburg, having "acceded" to Pemberton's suggestion, Grant did the same, confident that he would soon make up his losses. Within another week as he settled down to a state of siege he was back up to 71,000 effectives and informing Halleck: "The fall of Vicksburg and the capture of most of the garrison can only be a matter of time."

Vicksburg was caught in a trap. On the river, gunboats kept up a steady slow shelling of the city; on land, field artillery boomed away, the Union trenches spread their strangling arms wider and gun batteries wormed their way closer. Within the city, the garrison and the people lived like cave dwellers. Cave digging became a regular business, and a woman wrote: "The hills are so honey-combed with caves that the streets look like the avenues in a cemetery." Clothes and shoes wore out, and were replaced with homemade ones of rags. There was little to eat but corn bread and mule meat. Soldiers lived on spoiled bacon and bread made of pea flour. Those with hardy stomachs trapped and ate rats, comparing their flesh to spring chicken. When the tobacco gave out, they smoked sumac leaves. Throughout it all, there was hardly a glimmer of hope: the Union fleet held the river and Grant held the land. Yet the Vicksburg newspaper, reduced in size to a square foot and printed on wallpaper, continued to print encouraging headlines such as THE UNDA. .D JOHNSTON IS AT HAND or HOLD OUT A FEW DAYS LONGER. Johnston was not coming, a truth that disappointed of all people Ulysses S. Grant, who had said: "If Johnston tries to cut his way in we will let him do it, and then see that he don't get out. You say he has 30,000 men with him? That will give us 30,000 more prisoners than we now have."

Actually, the only attempt to relieve Vicksburg came from the west, not the east where Johnston was. Major General Richard Taylor, the son of President Zachary Taylor, diverted two brigades from the Port Hudson campaign to help Pemberton. One of them attacked the Union garrison at Milliken's Bend north of Vicksburg. The post was held by two regiments of black soldiers recruited from surrounding plantations and armed with old muskets. They fought with great bravery and with the help of Union gunboats drove the Rebels off. But the Graybacks, infuriated at the sight of armed slaves in blue uniforms, gave no quarter, murdering some of those that they captured and selling the rest into slavery, while bayoneting wounded ones. Charles Dana, still with Grant, said the valor of the black soldiers changed the minds of many white officers who had heretofore looked upon them with contempt.

The repulse at Milliken's Bend ended all hope for relief or reinforcement. Slowly Pemberton came round to the conviction that he could hold out only a few more days, especially after a petition signed "Many Soldiers" was delivered to him on June 27 stating: "If you can't feed us, you had better surrender, horrible as the idea is, than have this noble army disgrace themselves by desertion." Still Pemberton feared that Unconditional Surrender Grant would offer only harsh and dishonorable terms, until he learned two factors. One was that the Rebels had broken the Federal wigwag code and discovered that Porter had informed Grant that the navy wanted to avoid the troublesome, time-wasting task of transporting 30,000 prisoners northward up the river, and the other was that Grant wanted to set the Fourth of July for the capitulation date. "As a northern man," he told his staff, ". . . I know that we can get better terms from them on the Fourth of July than on any other date of the year." So Pemberton asked for terms and Grant responded generously, promising to parole the prisoners. On July 4, 1863, Pemberton surrendered.

To many Rebels to surrender on Independence Day was an egregious insult, for they, though in rebellion, still counted themselves descendants of those first Americans who had won the Revolution. They also feared humiliation. Yet the behavior of the Bluebellies marching into Vicksburg to raise the Stars and Stripes was exemplary. Rather than taunt their erstwhile enemies now so emaciated and forlorn, they actually showed how they admired them by sharing their rations and then—to the great delight of the Butternuts and the populace—breaking into the stores of food speculators who had hoarded food for higher prices, and piling them on the streets with the gleeful shout: "Here, Rebs, help yourselves!"

So the Fourth of July, 1863, went down into history as second only to the first one in national glory. In faraway Pennsylvania the high tide of Southern victory had turned to the ebb, and here in Vicksburg the Confederacy had been cut clean in two. In Washington Abraham Lincoln was jubilant, crying: "Grant is my man, and I am his the rest of the war!" When Gardner in Port Hudson heard the news he recognized reality and ran up his own white flag.

Now the Rail-Splitter could sigh with deep satisfaction: "The Father of Waters again goes unvexed to the sea."

59

■

Chickamauga and Chattanooga

THE NEWS OF THE DEFEATS at Gettysburg and Vicksburg struck the Confederacy like twin thunderbolts, although at first Gettysburg had been represented in the Southern press as a stunning success. The Charleston *Mercury* rejoiced in reporting "A brilliant and crushing victory," while the Richmond *Examiner,* presuming on its readers' credulity, calmly announced that Lee with 30,000 prisoners was marching on Baltimore. By the end of the month, however, both these journals and others with them reversed judgment full circle. "It is impossible for an invasion to have been more foolish and disastrous," the *Mercury* lamented. Thus the news of Vicksburg coming on Gettysburg's heels was truly shattering. "This surrender," said James Longstreet, "taken in connection with the Gettysburg defeat, was, of course, very discouraging to our superior officers . . . For myself, I felt that our last hope was gone, and that it was now only a question of time with us." Josiah Gorgas, the South's brilliant and tireless chief of ordnance, went further: "Yesterday we rode on the pinnacle of success. Today absolute ruin seems to be our portion. The Confederacy totters to destruction."

Nor was it lost upon perceptive Southerners what this latest subtraction in the arithmetic of war had done to Lee's army, while Meade's, as hydra-headed as ever, was back to full strength, and after the departure of Longstreet for the West, twice the size of Lee's 45,000.

Moreover both defeats came at a time when the Confederacy was struggling in the grip of corrosive inflation and facing the unpopular—indeed detested—remedy of taxation. In one year—from January 1863 to January 1864—the rate of three paper dollars for one gold dollar rose to eighteen or twenty paper dollars for one of gold, an inflationary rate of more than 600 percent. On April 24 the Confederate Congress passed a tax law so stern and far-reaching that it may be defined as confiscatory. An 8- to 10-percent tax was imposed on everything imaginable from bank deposits to the buying and selling of clothing, food and the metals of war to the licensing of every form of occupation or business to an income tax ranging from 1 percent on personal revenues $500 or less to 15 percent on those over $10,000. Thus the Richmond government had not only anticipated the Federal income tax by half a century, it had also made itself everybody's partner. To be so arbitrarily and comprehensively taxed was bitter medicine indeed, but to be subjected to such levies in the interest of prosecuting a losing war was to many Southerners simply unendurable.

Probably the most shocking consequence of the Yankee victories was their effect on Confederate foreign policy. Without a dramatic reversal of military fortune there was no longer any hope of help from Europe. The French scheme to mediate the war had already been rejected by Britain and Russia, and now these twin Union triumphs not only doomed all diplomatic efforts to secure Anglo-French intervention but also seemed to sink the so-far successful Confederate "commercial warfare" at sea. It had been hoped that the so-called "merchant" ships built clandestinely abroad, and then outfitted for war, would make these sea raiders a factor in Southern diplomacy. In effect, these nineteen warships imposed an open-sea blockade on Federal shipping, roaming the oceans in search of victims and either capturing or sinking them with their crews and cargoes. The most famous of these was the *Alabama,* under Captain Raphael Semmes. In its spectacular cruise of about twenty-one months *Alabama* took no fewer than sixty-four prizes with a total value of $6.5 million, never entering Confederate ports but always replenishing and refueling in neutral harbors from one end of the world to the other, until, on June 19, 1864, she was sunk by the USS *Kearsarge* off the French port of Cherbourg.

Unfortunately for Rebel diplomacy, *Alabama* and her sister seahawks were over-successful. Each loss of a Northern merchantman provoked a Yankee protest in London and Paris. Gradually, the Anglo-French narrowed their policy of permitting neutral nations to build ships for belligerents, the British finally seizing two Confederate ocean rams being built at Birkenhead. They also accepted Washington's extremely broad interpretation of what constituted contraband, a blow at the Southern policy of shipping supplies to Mexico which then could come overland to Texas. Richmond could not comprehend how Britain, the Mistress of the Seas, could allow the Yankees to twist her arm so successfully, but the answer was that these were times when the European balance of power was in a state of flux under the pressure of the *Risorgimento* in Italy, a new Polish uprising against

Russia and rumblings of a renewal of revolution in Germany. To preserve her freedom of maneuver, Britain simply could not even contemplate a war with the United States. Moreover Lord Palmerston could never forget those near catastrophic shipping losses at the hands of Yankee privateers in the War of 1812. Thus, until the Confederacy could again demonstrate decisive military strength, the Anglo-French would remain neutral. And after Gettysburg-Vicksburg this did not seem likely, certainly not in the West, which had erupted in battle once more.

After the Battle of Murfreesboro, William Rosecrans remained on the field while Braxton Bragg retired to the south and took up a position at Shelbyville-Wartrace. Bragg was determined to protect Chattanooga, a vital railroad junction controlling the Confederacy's east-west route. The trio in Washington which ran the war—Lincoln, Stanton and Halleck—were just as anxious to capture it, for here was the friendly center of Lincoln's land of heart's desire: east Tennessee. Throughout the winter this triumvirate did all possible to prod Rosecrans into action against Bragg and ultimately Chattanooga. But mules were more easily moved than Old Rosy. He merely exchanged cavalry raids with Bragg in which he came off somewhat better, losing only 3,000 men to Bragg's 4,000, while the Southern commander also saw Forrest humiliated by defeat and Morgan lost by capture. Neither side achieved anything lasting.

Meanwhile Rosecrans's self-proclaimed "victory" at Murfreesboro had convinced him that the art of war consisted in careful preparation. Conversely, the Washington triumvirate insisted upon his giving battle to Bragg to prevent him from going to Pemberton's assistance at Vicksburg. This, scoffed Old Rosy, was merely ridiculous. As May wore into June and Rosecrans began his sixth month of staying put at Murfreesboro—preparing and preparing—Halleck testily complained that their exchange of telegrams was putting a strain on the army's telegraph budget, after which his and Lincoln's dispatches became more and more acerbic. Threats of amputation by detaching some of Rosecrans's troops for service with Grant at Vicksburg, or of decapitation by relieving him outright made no impression on him, until, on June 16 an exasperated Lincoln ordered Halleck to ask him: "Is it your intention to make an immediate movement forward? A definite answer, yes or no, is required." Old Rosy replied: ". . . if immediate means tonight or tomorrow, no. If it means as soon as all things are ready, say five days, yes." That satisfied Washington, although when Old Rosy waited eight days rather than five before he started, he almost exhausted Lincoln's patience. But when he did move, he did so rapidly and brilliantly. First he sent Major General David Stanley's cavalry corps with Major General

Gordon Granger's reserve corps to move around the open or western flank of Shelbyville held by Polk, hoping to deceive Bragg into believing this was his main effort; after which his three other corps under McCook, Thomas and Crittenden would move through the mountain passes on the left or east to strike Hardee. The operation was conducted in rugged, exhausting terrain and over roads made muddy by rains so torrential that one soldier grumbled: "No Presbyterian rain, either—but a regular Baptist downpour." Still the Bluebellies stumbled on, and the maneuver succeeded in compelling Bragg to fall back on Tullahoma.

Rosecrans next sought to seize the Elk River crossings behind Bragg and thus isolate him from his base, but the Confederate commander just managed to avoid this trap, retiring over the Tennessee while leaving guns and supplies behind. On July 4 Bragg arrived in Chattanooga. Thus in nine days of rapid marches and skillful maneuvering, Old Rosy had forced the enemy to retire eighty-five miles and across the Tennessee at a cost of only 560 casualties, while inflicting similar losses on Bragg and capturing 1,634 enemy soldiers.

In Washington there was great rejoicing at this near bloodless victory sandwiched in between Gettysburg and Vicksburg, and Stanton on July 7 informed Rosecrans of these two great triumphs and said: "You and your noble army now have the chance to give the finishing blow to the rebellion. Will you neglect the chance?" Stung by this challenging question, which seemed to him just one more War Department goad, Old Rosy replied: "You do not appear to observe the fact that this noble army has driven the Rebels from Middle Tennessee. I beg in behalf of this army that the War Department may not overlook so great an event because it is not written in letters of blood." Whereupon he proceeded to tick off all the difficulties incumbent upon renewing the attack, among them replacement of a railroad bridge, laying new track, building new corduroy roads through seas of mud, Burnside's delay in moving against Knoxville on his left or eastern flank and the fact that Bragg's Army of the Tennessee now reinforced by Longstreet's corps outnumbered his own Army of the Cumberland about 66,000 to 54,000. He did not, of course, list his own advantages, not the least of which were his own generals, one of whom but for his generosity would have been his own chief: George Henry Thomas.

George Henry Thomas was born July 31, 1816, on a farm near Newsom's Depot in Southampton County, Virginia. The family homestead was in the notorious black belt of the state where slaves outnumbered whites three to two, and in which Nat Turner's Rebellion had risen. George's parents

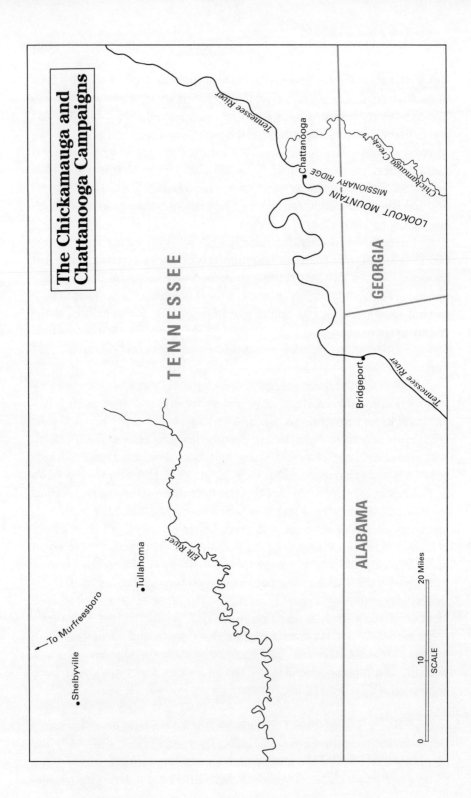

The Chickamauga and
Chattanooga Campaigns

were of Welsh and French stock, his father, John, having ancestors who migrated from Wales at the end of the seventeenth century and his mother, Elizabeth Rochelle, tracing her lineage to a French Huguenot forebear of that name.

As a boy George annoyed his parents by his fondness for frequenting the slave quarters to swap jokes with the blacks or to trade pilfered sugar loaves for the possums and raccoons they caught in the woods. His parents ordered him to stay away from the slaves, but he disobeyed them—even, against their wishes, teaching the black children the lessons he had learned at school and church.

It is likely that his disobedience was the defect of his virtues of independence of thought and extreme self-reliance. Because he was skillful with his hands he seemed to believe that he could master any trade or craft, going to the saddle maker's to learn how to make his own saddles or to the cabinet maker to discover how to fashion furniture. His outstanding trait was his deliberation. He would not be hurried or stampeded into rash or foolish reaction. His air of calm seldom deserted him, nor could he be frightened by any of the schoolyard bullies in the local academy which he attended, and where he was an outstanding student.

Actually, few youths George's age would dare to challenge him physically. He was extremely strong and upon maturity would stand a shade under six feet, broad-shouldered and brawny, and handsome with a fair complexion, wavy light brown hair and deep blue eyes.

In 1830 George's father died of an unexplained "farm accident." It was now up to George at fourteen to run the farm without the benefit of parental direction, but he did it with customary thoroughness. Yet, even though his skill with his hands was a valuable asset, he took no pleasure in it. He preferred a more exciting calling. A year later during Nat Turner's Rebellion he got all the excitement he wanted, riding from house to lonely house to warn the occupants of the approach of the marauding, murdering blacks, while his family fled through the woods to Jerusalem.

In the spring of 1836 Congressman John Young Mason nominated him for appointment to the U.S. Military Academy, and after George qualified, President Andrew Jackson, who had heard of his heroic ride, approved the appointment. George's classmates were impressed by his dignity and self-possession. When a hazing upperclassman burst into his room, he calmly told him: "Get out of here, or I'll throw you through the window." After being graduated twelfth in the 1840 class of forty-two cadets, Thomas was assigned to an artillery unit in New York Harbor. Although he had hoped to be a cavalryman, he soon became fond of cannon and became an expert artillerist. He also served in the Seminole War, but saw no action except on a patrol that skirmished briefly with a band of Indians, killing eight of them. The captain's report praised Thomas for "valuable aid and assistance."

It was five more years before Thomas heard a shot fired in anger again. This time it was in Mexico with his beloved artillery under Taylor, and he emerged from three battles breveted to captain. At home he was hailed as a hero and given a beautiful ceremonial sword.

Thomas returned to West Point after the war as an instructor in artillery, and later in the cavalry. Here the nickname "Old Slow Trot" was pinned upon him by cadets such as Sheridan, J. E. B. Stuart, O. O. Howard and George Washington Custis Lee. Thomas was a bit too heavy for an ideal commander of horse, and was always reluctant to urge his horse into a gallop that might leave it blown. Thus, when exercising his pupils on the plain, he did not conclude with an order for the wild gallop that they eagerly awaited, but frustrated them with the command, "Slow trot!"

But Thomas was moving at more than a slow trot when he met Frances Kellogg in the spring of 1852. The daughter of a wealthy upstate hardware merchant, she had come to the Plains to visit her cadet brother. She and George were married in November of that year and Thomas wore his ceremonial sword for the first time.

On July 21, 1855, Thomas was assigned to the 2nd Cavalry Regiment. With soldiers like Lee and J. E. B. Stuart he helped to make this hard-riding outfit famous. But in July of 1860 in an engagement with mounted Comanche horse thieves, an Indian arrow struck him full in the chest. With typical self-control, Thomas pulled the missile free and allowed the surgeon to dress his wounds.

They were severe and healed slowly in the desert heat. Granted a six-months' leave of absence, he went to New York for medical treatment. But his response was so slow that it seemed to him his career as an officer was at an end. He thought of teaching, applying for a vacancy at Virginia Military Institute, only to learn that it had been filled. By then, January of 1861, Lincoln had been elected and the states of the Lower South were leaving the Union to form the Confederacy. Thomas was bitterly resentful of the men responsible for the breakup, especially those in the North; and yet, with all his old friends making known their allegiance, North and South, he gave no hint of his own intentions. Recovering his health, he returned to the 2nd Cavalry quartered near Harrisburg. Reaching Carlisle Barracks, he heard the echo of the guns of Sumter, and he sent telegrams to his wife and his sisters announcing his decision to continue in the Federal service.

Many of his old Southern comrades were enraged by his "treachery." It was put about that he had chosen the North because he could not get a commission in the Confederate Army, which was obviously absurd. His friends in Southampton County said that if they could catch him they would hang him, and his maiden sisters promptly turned his picture to the wall, destroyed all his letters and wrote to him only to ask him to change his name. They told their neighbors that if George ever came home they would show him where to put his fine ceremonial sword. Thomas's attempts at reconciliation brought no reply, and he never came home again.

Only his wife knew how George Henry Thomas had wrestled with the problem that so many Southern officers, including Robert Edward Lee, had confronted: my state or the United States? "Whichever way he turned the matter over in his mind," said Frances Kellogg Thomas, "his oath of allegiance to his Government always came uppermost."

It was Thomas who had modestly protested against Halleck's order to take command of the Army of the Cumberland from Buell, for which act of generosity he still found himself a corps commander, but under Rosecrans, when it might have been vice versa. Still he was Old Rosy's chief corps commander, and he approved of the deliberate accumulation of mountains of supplies and hordes of horses by which Rosecrans prepared to advance on Chattanooga. Halleck, naturally enough, sternly disapproved, and the telegraphs clicked once again to Old Brains's peremptory orders to get going at once, and Rosecrans's sometimes sarcastic explanation of why this was not possible. At last, on August 16, after a rest and recuperation lasting only six weeks compared to the six months passed doing the same thing at Murfreesboro, Rosecrans began his march on Chattanooga. Only the day before Burnside had moved out of Cincinnati to make his lightning descent on Knoxville, abandoned by Buckner, which he captured on September 3. Moving just as rapidly and over terrain equally formidable, again maneuvering deftly, Old Rosy got his army safely across the Tennessee by demonstrating above Chattanooga while his main body crossed the river below the town. Once again deception and guile were his handmaidens. Keeping his main body well back from the river to screen his true intentions, he demonstrated upstream with three brigades. Every night they lighted hundreds of campfires to suggest great numbers of men. The ends of planks were sawed off and tossed into streams feeding the Tennessee to suggest that the Yankees were engaged in a massive boat-building program, an illusion enhanced by soldiers banging on empty barrels around the clock to simulate shipyard workers. Bragg could hardly be blamed if he did not anticipate a strong amphibious assault somewhere along the river. While he prepared to repulse it, Rosecrans got his army across the Tennessee, and on September 9 occupied the abandoned town.

It had been a masterful—and again almost bloodless—campaign, and the gateway to the heartland of the South was now in Yankee hands. East Tennessee at last seemed to be liberated with seizure of this city Lincoln called "fully as important as the taking and holding of Richmond." Actually this western bastion was the most naturally formidable of the two, with the broad silvery Tennessee serving it as a moat and the surrounding mountains and ridges as ramparts.

Now Rosecrans decided to pursue Bragg, believing that his withdrawal was actually a rabbity retreat, a misconception encouraged by those guileful Rebel "deserters" who poured into the Federal camp babbling with rolling eyes and twitching lips about the "demoralization" of Bragg's army. As one Rebel officer wrote years later: "The Confederate deserter was an institution which has received too little consideration. . . . He was ubiquitous, willing, and altogether inscrutable. Wherever he told the truth or a lie, he was always equally sure to deceive. He was sometimes a real deserter, and sometimes a mock deserter. In either case he was always loaded." These were indeed loaded and they encouraged Old Rosy in his conviction that his opponent was still all Bragg and no bite. So he resolved on headlong pursuit to catch and crush him, and because the terrain below Chattanooga was a most difficult land of huge ridges offering few passes, he divided his forces to facilitate their movement. But Bragg was not retreating. He was actually concentrating his army for battle, receiving reinforcements being rushed to him from Kentucky and Mississippi. Far away in Virginia, President Davis, at last conceding the importance of the West, had put James Longstreet and most of his corps aboard rickety trains and sent them by a roundabout route to Bragg's side. When they arrived in September, Bragg outnumbered Rosecrans by 70,000 to 60,000, and he saw that the Federal commander's rash dispersion was his own opportunity.

The battleground was to be in the valley of Chickamauga Creek. Here, Bragg first struck at the separated Union right under George Thomas and Alexander McCook. But the Confederate commanders, unaccustomed to any celerity from Bragg, moved with the usual deliberation and failed. Their failure alerted Rosecrans, who began frantically pulling his forces together on his left a few miles south of Chattanooga. Bragg evolved another plan: swing hard against the Union left before it could concentrate, driving it away from Chattanooga into a jumbled wilderness where it could be fragmented and beaten to death by bits.

Bragg as usual delayed, and Rosecrans rapidly moved Thomas's corps into position on the left of Thomas Crittenden's. So the Army of the Cumberland seemed prepared when Bragg began attacking on September 19, and the opening Confederate blows were blunted. Next morning the Rebels struck again, the right under the battling bishop Leonidas Polk coming against Thomas with crushing fury. Fighting desperately, the Federals held. But Thomas was hurt and he kept calling for reinforcements. Rosecrans tried to feed him a division from his quiet right flank, but the unit went astray and never reached Thomas. Thomas, however, renewed his pleas for help, giving Rosecrans the impression that a Confederate tidal wave was rolling against his left. In fact, Polk had been beaten back, and it was Rosecrans's right that was endangered.

Here James Longstreet had prepared his customary set-piece haymaker. Under cover of woods, he had formed his troops in a column of brigades. When they hit, they would hit in a series of hammer blows. And now, opposite Longstreet, chance was entering the battle.

Rosecrans had received an erroneous report that there was a gap to the right of his center. He ordered one division to "close up" on another to plug the gap, but the division commander, knowing that there was no gap, construed the "close-up" order to mean he should get behind the other division. So he pulled out of the line, leaving a gaping void, and as he did Longstreet's brigades came rolling into the hole.

They struck Union brigades as they were leaving the line, and they came yelling against them on their flanks. The result was sheer catastrophe. The Union right was swept away. Rosecrans, his staff, even Assistant Secretary of War Charles Dana were jostled off toward Chattanooga on a struggling flood of soldiers, ambulances, baggage wagons and artillery. When Dana saw the devout Rosecrans crossing himself in supplication, he concluded that all was lost.

But all was not lost. George Thomas, the solid general from Virginia, was hanging on. While Longstreet and Polk eagerly closed around him, he reorganized around Horseshoe Ridge. Longstreet might cry jubilantly, "They have fought their last man and *he* is running," but the fact was that the Federals were rallying, tightening their lines beneath the smoke, waving their flags defiantly at the oncoming Rebels. In the hollow of a hill, Thomas stood feeding his horse corn, impassively following the battle. At one point Thomas told a colonel that his hill must be held at all costs, and the colonel replied: "We'll hold it, General, or we'll go to heaven from it."

The hill held, Thomas held—like a rock, to receive the immortal nickname of "the Rock of Chickamauga"—and the Army of the Cumberland was saved from destruction. That night Thomas retired, and the Confederates failed to pursue. Nevertheless, the South was thrilled to hear of Bragg's great victory at the Battle of Chickamauga. It seemed that he had turned the tide in the West, and even the price of 18,450 Confederate casualties as against 16,170 Union losses seemed not too high to pay for such a great reversal of fortunes. Moreover, Bragg had Rosecrans's army penned up in Chattanooga, and it seemed only a matter of time before the Federals capitulated.

Unfortunately for the South, Bragg had also succeeded in bringing U. S. Grant into the field against him.

News of the defeat at Chickamauga and fears for the safety of the Army of the Cumberland all but panicked the Washington government. Two full army corps were immediately detached from Meade and sent west under Joe Hooker, while Sherman was ordered east from Memphis with part of the Army of the Tennessee. Finally, Lincoln named Grant chief of all Union forces between the Allegheny Mountains and the Mississippi,* with the option of choosing Rosecrans or Thomas to command at Chattanooga. Grant chose Thomas, until, on October 23, he arrived there himself.

Grant was then still suffering from an extremely painful leg injury suffered in New Orleans in September 1863. After the fall of Vicksburg he had gone down the Mississippi, perhaps to show that the Father of Waters was now his, as well as to enjoy himself socially and to bask in the admiration of the Yankees now in control of the river cities. It was a triumphal procession worthy of a Roman conqueror, banquets and receptions by the literal dozen as he sailed down the great river. In New Orleans Nathaniel Banks staged a magnificent grand review in Grant's honor ten miles outside of town. Riding back on a borrowed powerful war horse—the sort of dangerous mount he loved to bend to his will—he entered the city and its traffic still galloping. As he did so he came close to a carriage or a streetcar—Grant himself said it was a locomotive—so that the frightened horse reared, throwing him. Although his mount arose unhurt, Grant lay dazed on the street where General Thomas Kilby Smith's following horse—another powerful beast—struck him, sinking its hoof into the calf of his leg. He was taken to St. Charles Hotel, where he lay for a week in an agony he has himself described: "My leg was swollen from the knee to the thigh, and the swelling almost to the point of bursting, extended along the body up to the armpit. The pain was almost beyond endurance. I lay at the hotel ... without

---

*Except for the force in New Orleans under Banks.

being able to turn myself in bed." Of course Grant's enemies and traducers were quick to put it about that he had been drinking, else how could Grant the consummate horseman allow himself to be thrown? His defenders explained that it was an uncontrollable accident caused by a soft spot in the street surface of crushed fish shells. The fact that neither his wife, Julia, nor his trusted chief of staff, John Rawlins—in whose company Grant never drank—were not with him lent some credence to the charge that he had been imbibing. But the charge has never been proved, and Grant, though still limping, was certainly under the influence of nothing but his own clear and incisive mind when he arrived in Chattanooga to take charge of the battle. He found the Union forces caught in a trap and in danger of being starved into surrender. A vast Confederate semicircle enclosed the Federals. It ran around Chattanooga from the Tennessee upstream, following the heights of Missionary Ridge south and then swinging west again to Lookout Mountain and a bit beyond to the Tennessee. To the north of the Union rear ran wild, mountainous country penetrated only by a single cart track. Thus there was no way out if a retreat were contemplated, and no way in for supplies.

The situation could hardly have been worse, and for Grant, whose spirit thrived on adversity, that was tantamount to never being better. Almost at once he determined to open a supply line. On the night of October 26 about 1,500 Federals surprised a Rebel force at Brown's Ferry to the west, seized a beachhead and threw a pontoon bridge over the river. From here, Joe Hooker led a march overland to Bridgeport, the Union supply depot on the Tennessee. Thus was opened the famous "cracker line" over which troops and supplies came into Chattanooga. Bragg, failing to grasp the importance of this breach in his investing line, did little to retake Brown's Ferry. Instead, he detached Longstreet and 15,000 badly needed veterans, sending them 150 miles north to attack General Burnside in Knoxville.

Now Washington actually did panic, bombarding Grant with shrill requests to do something to relieve Burnside. On November 7 Grant asked Thomas to attack Bragg's right flank so as to compel him to recall Longstreet. Thomas, however, grimly alluded to the fact that he had not enough mules or horses (10,000 of them had died during the siege) to draw a single piece of artillery. Grant agreed to wait until Sherman arrived. In the meantime the Battle of Knoxville became a foot race between Longstreet's and Burnside's commands.

■　　■　　■

On the night of November 14 Longstreet's Graybacks crossed the Little Tennessee and went marching north toward Knoxville. Burnside at once left the city to organize the withdrawal of his IX and XXIII corps in Old Pete's path. Traveling northeast on parallel routes, the blue and the gray hosts were like shadowing columns throughout the fifteenth, and a race began between them to reach the crossroads at Campbell's Station. Whoever arrived first at this strategic intersection on the Kingston road to Knoxville would be able to repulse or capture the other. Burnside won—by fifteen minutes—fighting a delaying action until nightfall, when, behind a cavalry screen, he retreated safely into Knoxville. Longstreet came up to besiege the city, but it held out, repelling a number of half-hearted attacks, until Longstreet withdrew on the night of December 4. By then Grant had begun his attack upon Bragg at Chattanooga.

Sherman arrived in Chattanooga still saddened by the death from typhoid fever of his son, nine-year-old Willy, his namesake and first-born, "that child on whose future I based all the ambition I ever had." Not even his succession to the command of the Army of the Tennessee assuaged his grief and deep sense of loss, although when Grant disclosed his plan of attack to him his fighting spirit rose. Grant hoped to bring off a double envelopment. Hooker was to strike the Confederate left at Lookout Mountain while Sherman hurled himself at the Rebel right on the upper end of Missionary Ridge. In the meantime, Thomas's men were to put the pressure on the center at Missionary Ridge to prevent Bragg from reinforcing his flanks.

The battle began November 24, 1863, with Hooker meeting immediate and spectacular success. His men outnumbered the Rebels by five or six to one, and they swarmed up Lookout Mountain's rocky slopes and meadows to drive the defenders off the summit. Below them, war correspondents gazed in enchantment at the mountaintop alive with the winking of thousands of deadly fireflies, and then after a fog drifted in between valley and crest, giving Lookout a circlet of smoke infused with flame, the phrase "battle fought above the clouds" was born. Actually, Hooker had not done much more than knock Bragg's left anchor loose.

Meanwhile on the right, Bragg's men were breaking Sherman's attack into fragments. Here, there was not one continuous ridge as Grant and Sherman believed, but a jumble of separated small hills. The Rebels fought from behind excellent fortifications, sometimes rolling big boulders down upon their luckless attackers. With nightfall, Sherman had not made much of a dent in Bragg's right.

Next day, November 25, the double assault was renewed. This time

Hooker's men descended the other side of Lookout Mountain and blundered into futility on a wooded plain, while Sherman once again could get nowhere on the right. In fact, Sherman was so convinced that Bragg was reinforcing from his center that he asked Grant for help. Grant's reply was to order Thomas to press forward against the Rebel center on Missionary Ridge.

Here were bristling lines at the foot of the five-hundred-foot hill and on its crest. Thomas had some doubts about taking even the rifle pits at the bottom, but Grant prodded him forward. Standing on a hill smoking a cigar, Grant watched Thomas's men start for the blazing pits. Into a tangle of felled trees they poured, 20,000 strong, breaking through in several places to strike the dismayed Rebels on opened flanks and exposed rear. In an instant, the Confederates broke and fled up the ridge. Into the abandoned pits jumped the aroused Federals, men of the Army of the Cumberland who had fought hard at Chickamauga only to find themselves the butt of endless needling by the unbeaten dandies of Sherman's and Hooker's units. Now they looked eagerly up the ridge to the Confederate guns.

Cocky little Phil Sheridan, resplendent in dress uniform, sat his horse and looked at the guns. He drew a flask from his pocket and toasted a group of Confederate officers above him, crying, "Here's to you!" At once, the Rebel guns roared at Sheridan, striking close enough to shower him and his officers with dirt. Sheridan's face darkened. "I'll take those guns for that!"

And then, suddenly and in a rush, the Federals went charging up the ridge, straight into a storm of enemy fire, and right before the incredulous eyes of U. S. Grant on his hilltop. Wheeling in anger, Grant snapped: "Thomas, who ordered those men up the ridge?"

"I don't know," Thomas replied slowly, and then, addressing one of his corps commanders, Gordon Granger: "Did you order them up, Granger?" Slowly at first came the answer, "No, they started up without orders," and then, with a flash of pride: "When those fellows get started all hell can't stop them!"

Growling something to the effect that someone would suffer if the attack failed, Grant turned to watch the charging Cumberlands, and saw to his delight that all hell indeed could not stop them. The great battle line was now a series of **V**'s struggling upward behind fluttering battle flags, for the regiments were racing each other for the crest. Ahead of them all raced the 24th Wisconsin led by its youthful adjutant Arthur MacArthur, soon to be famous as "the boy colonel of the West." Waving the regimental colors, crying "On, Wisconsin!" his face smoke-blackened and his uniform wet with mud and blood, young MacArthur triumphantly planted his flag on the crest of the ridge, for which gallant feat he was awarded the Medal of Honor, the nation's highest military honor and one which MacArthur's more famous and more decorated son Douglas sought for half a century with an unrequited passion. On through the fire and smoke came the following units, sometimes pausing for breath, but sweeping inexorably closer until Confederate astonishment turned to alarm, then to fear—and they broke and ran. Jubilant Federals chased them, beckoning their comrades forward and calling, "My God! Come and see them run!"

Butternuts had never before been routed like this, but they had been through much, these weary fighters of Bragg's army. So they gave completely away, a two-mile hole was punched in Bragg's center, and the Battle of Chattanooga ended with Bragg retreating into Georgia and the Union forces in full possession of the West.

Chattanooga, with 5,820 Union casualties and 6,600 Confederate, also placed the reputation of U. S. Grant beyond reach of his numerous traducers. It seemed to Abraham Lincoln that in Grant he might have found the dedicated killer that he had been seeking for nearly three frustrating and agonizing years; a master of martial arithmetic who would soothe "the tired spot" inside the president. "Nothing touches the tired spot," he was given to saying in a sad voice, and once, returning from one of those horseback rides that seemed to restore his spirits, he was urged by a friend to find more time for such rest and relaxation. "Rest?" he repeated, shaking his head dolefully. "I don't know. . . . I suppose it is good for the body. But the tired part is *inside,* out of reach."

Perhaps Grant could reach it, but first, there were questions to be asked about him. Would he, like Pope and Halleck, those other Lochinvars who came out of the West, prove to be a fizzle like Pope or another "mere military clerk" like Old Brains? It did not appear so; but yet, there was another, far more important question: had his military glory turned his head? In a word, did he seek the White House? Lincoln had already said of himself, "When the Presidential grub once gets into a man, it hides well." Was it inside Grant, quietly eating away? Already he was being wooed by prominent leaders of both parties. Lincoln was too much of a realist not to understand that the war could always produce a military hero whose glory would outshine all true presidential qualifications. So he made inquiries, and was gratified to be told by friends of the general that for the present at least he had no such aspirations, that he was above all a soldier who believed he had no right to discuss politics at all. Lincoln laughed at Grant's wry remark that after the war he might run for mayor of Galena so that he might improve the sidewalk between his house and the railroad station. But that had been some time ago; what of now? From another friend of the general came a letter from Grant containing an unreserved disclaimer: "My only desire will be, as it has been, to whip out rebellion in the shortest way possible, and to retain as high a position in the army afterwards as the Administration then in power may think me suitable for."

Lincoln was now satisfied, although the phrase "Administration then in power" suggested to him that the simple soldier from the West might not be as artless as he seemed, for his own administration and the Republican Congress were then, in those early months of 1864, trembling on the edge of an abyss. On February 1 Lincoln had issued a presidential order drafting "five hundred thousand men to serve for three years or during the war." Heavy battlefield losses and the approaching expiration of enlistments of those volunteers who had rallied to the colors two and three years ago had made such an unpopular course imperative. Such an enormous levy also indicated that the campaigns of 1864 might be bloodier and costlier than all that were now history. How would the voters respond? Defeat at the polls in November of this presidential year could cause the greatest turnaround in the history of the young nation: loss of the White House, the congressional committee chairmanships, access to the fattest pork barrel ever as well as to the enormous spoils that would become available when the South was ultimately crushed two or three years hence. To avert this, either absolute victory or a complete reversal of military fortune must be achieved before November 1864. The Republican majority in Congress had demonstrated that it understood this when, after rejecting a bill to revive the rank of lieutenant general, it reconsidered and approved it, leaving it to Lincoln to name him. He did: U. S. Grant, and on March 2 Congress confirmed the nomination, while Lincoln summoned Grant to Washington to take command of all the Federal armies.

60

■

The Gettysburg Address

A S THE SUMMER OF 1863 turned toward fall the limited hospital facilities of Gettysburg were taxed far beyond their capacity to care for
twenty thousand wounded men of both sides. So it was decided that as soon
as they were able to move, they would be sent to superior hospitals in York,
Washington, Baltimore and Harrisburg. This seemed to solve the problem
of caring for these suffering soldiers, until a conscientious medical inspector
submitted a report excoriating the venal railroad companies hired to trans-
port the men: ". . . the railroad companies," he reported, "who got the only
profit of the battle, and who had the greatest opportunities of ameliorating
the suffering of the wounded, alone stood aloof and rendered no aid." The
trains were incredibly unclean, he said, there were no medical attendants,
no water and not even straw for the wounded to lie upon—"absolutely
nothing but the bare cars, filthy from the business of transporting cattle and
freight."

Widespread indignation succeeded this report, and the railroads were
compelled to provide clean trains with decent living quarters, while a medical officer was detailed to accompany each train, water coolers were provided along with bedpans and medicines, and soon there were six trains
daily carrying the convalescing soldiers away from Gettysburg. Within
three weeks 16,000 of them were thus transported, and the little Pennsylvania town seemed able to care for the remaining 4,000.

On the battlefield itself, of course, there were grisly reminders of the
carnage. Among the boulders and the gullies of the Devil's Den alone were
strewn the deteriorating bodies of the slain, while elsewhere the rains and
winds had stripped the shallow graves of their covering earth, exposing the
rotting corpses to the dissolving rays of the sun as well as to the hunger
of scavenger birds and carnivorous small animals. Governor Andrew Curtin

of Pennsylvania was horrified by what he saw during a visit to the battle-field, setting in motion a proposal for the governors of all the eighteen Northern states whose men had fought at Gettysburg to combine to provide a proper cemetery.

The idea took hold and by mid-August funds had been raised and the state of Pennsylvania had purchased seventeen acres on Cemetery Hill and the work of constructing the cemetery was begun. It was decided to bury the fallen by states, one plot for Virginians, another for Jerseyans, and so on. By the fall the cemetery had been built and the dead interred beneath neat rows of white crosses. Governor Curtin now thought of dedicating the cemetery, and so invited the famous orator, Edward Everett of Massachusetts, to be the principal speaker on October 23. He also invited General Meade. Everett replied that he could come, but would need more time to fulfill certain commitments and also to compose an appropriate speech. So Curtin postponed the ceremony to November 19. Meade, meanwhile, had declined the honor, observing that he was too busy with the Army of the Potomac. As an afterthought, on November 2, Curtin also invited President Lincoln, but only in a minor capacity, of course. "It is the desire that after the oration, you, as Chief Executive of the nation, formally set apart these grounds to their sacred use by a few appropriate remarks." In other words, don't talk too much, Abe, and don't crack any jokes.

When news that the President would appear at Gettysburg appeared in the media, it provoked a storm of outrage. A ceremony honoring the fallen certainly should not be sullied by what would almost certainly be a partisan political speech, cried many hostile editors. There were also leading Republicans who thought that Lincoln's appearance could really do no harm since he was already quite a dead duck politically. Thus Thaddeus Stevens quipped, "Let the dead bury the dead." Lincoln himself brushed off the invective and ridicule by remarking, "I am used to it." Meanwhile, in the press of affairs of state, social necessities such as the wedding of Chase's daughter Kate to wealthy young Senator William Sprague of Rhode Island, and his own anguish—compounded by Mary's hysteria—when young Tad was laid low by a mysterious fever, the president had little time to devote to his speech. Indeed, he had done nothing on it when he departed Washington on November 18 in a special four-car train carrying himself and his staff, three cabinet members, the French and Italian ministers, army and navy officers, and his close friend Ward Lamon. Sitting for about an hour swapping stories with the others in a drawing room, he finally got to his feet to excuse himself with the remark, "Gentlemen, this is all very pleasant, but the people will expect me to say something to them tomorrow, and

I must give the matter some thought."

Arriving at sundown in the overcrowded little college town, he spent the night at the home of Judge David Wills, along with Everett and Governor Curtin. In the morning he found that the crowd of sightseers had risen to 15,000 people thronging the streets in quest of breakfast or prowling the battlefield searching for souvenirs. At ten o'clock a procession led by Lincoln on horseback began to form on the town square. He wore his customary black suit with the stovepipe hat and white gloves. Behind him walked or rode the other dignitaries, governors, Generals Gibbon and Doubleday, congressmen and his own party. They crowded together on the platform, waiting for Everett, who was late. His appearance created a stir on the platform and among the crowd. Tall, white-haired, and nearing seventy, his was still an imposing presence, this celebrated orator whose achievements and offices read like a litany of success: former governor of Massachusetts, minister to Britain under Tyler, successor to Daniel Webster as Fillmore's secretary of state, president of Harvard, and in 1860 John Bell's running mate on the Constitution Union ticket. "Mr. President," he said with a graceful bow to the tall man slumped in thought in his chair, and Lincoln glanced up in response. "Mr. Everett," he said in acknowledgment, and the celebrated orator began his speech.

It continued for two hours in the high-flown rhetoric of the day, laced with classical quotations, some attributed, others not, filled with a review of the war and its causes, the speaker's voice like Galahad's strength seeming to grow ever stronger, finally ending on the peroration: "Down to the latest period of recorded time [Shakespeare], in the glorious annals of our common country there will be no brighter page than that which relates the Battle of Gettysburg." It was on the whole the sort of pedestrian bombast that passed for brilliant oratory in those days, and when it ended the crowd burst into prolonged applause; probably as much because it had ended as for any other reason, and Lincoln, who had put on his wire-rimmed spectacles to read his own speech while Everett drew to a close, arose and began to speak in "a sharp, unmusical treble voice."

"Fourscore and seven years ago our fathers brought forth upon this continent a new nation, conceived in liberty and dedicated to the proposition that all men are created equal. Now we are engaged in a great civil war, testing whether that nation, or any nation so conceived and so dedicated, can long endure. We are met on a great battlefield of that war. We are met to dedicate a portion of it as the final resting place of those who here gave their lives that that nation might live. It is altogether fitting and proper that we should do this. But in a larger sense we cannot dedicate, we cannot consecrate, we cannot hallow this ground. The brave men, living and dead, who struggled here, have consecrated it far above our poor power to add or detract." A polite scattering of applause was overridden at this point as Lincoln continued. "The world will little note, nor long remember, what we say here, but it can never forget what they did here. It is for us, the living, rather, to be dedicated here to the unfinished work that they have thus far so nobly carried on. It is rather for us to be here dedicated to the great task remaining before us, that from these honored dead we take increased devotion to that cause for which they here gave the last full measure of devotion; that we here highly resolve that these dead shall not have died in vain; that the nation shall, under God, have a new birth of freedom; and that government of the people, by the people, for the people, shall not perish from the earth."

Lincoln sat down to delayed, scattered and barely polite applause. Indeed he had almost completely finished his speech before the throng realized that he was speaking, everyone watching a photographer setting up to take Lincoln's picture—which he missed—while preparing to endure another marathon address such as the one that had preceded it. Few people really heard what he said, and many felt cheated—like the photographer— and might have been inclined to agree with the Chicago *Tribune*'s report on the speech next day: "The cheek of every American must tingle with shame as he reads the silly, flat and dishwatery utterances of the man who has to be pointed out to intelligent foreigners as the President of the United States." Lincoln himself was most unhappy. Seated again next to Lamon, he used a prairie image of a plow not cutting cleanly through the soil: "Lamon, that speech won't *scour*. It is a flat failure and the people are disappointed."

But there were those who saw the pure prose and the serene perfection of "my little speech" as Lincoln called it, among them a Cincinnati editor who described it as "the right thing in the right place and a perfect thing in every respect," as well as, to his enduring credit, Edward Everett who wrote to Lincoln next day: "I should be glad if I could flatter myself that I came as near the central idea of the occasion, in two hours, as you did in two minutes." Later Lincoln made some minor changes in his text, chiefly of syntax but never of substance, so that the Gettysburg Address memorized by so many hundreds of millions of American schoolchildren— South as well as North—was slightly different from the original.

It had indeed *scoured* the sacred soil of Gettysburg.

61

■

From the Wilderness
to Petersburg

TUESDAY, MARCH 8, 1864, dawned in Washington cold, raw and gusty,
bearing no sign that the vernal equinox—the first day of spring—was
less than two weeks away. At Willard's Hotel two blocks down Pennsylvania Avenue from the White House the lobby was thronged with the
customary crowd of contract hunters, office seekers, generals and admirals
"on station" in the capital or passing through to new assignments. Few of
them seemed to notice when a slightly built two-star general in a faded
blouse cut full in the skirt, a high-crowned blue hat set square on his head,
threaded his way to the registration desk accompanied by a thirteen-year-
old boy. One bystander who watched his progress, however, recorded what
he saw: ". . . rough, light-brown whiskers, a blue eye and rather a scrubby
look withal . . . as if he was out of office and on half pay, with nothing to
do but hang around the entry of Willard's." He also thought the general had
the look of a man fond of the glass.

To the blasé clerk behind the polished oak of the registration counter
here was yet another among that multitude of faceless flag officers beseeching him—if not exactly begging—for a room for the night. Well, yes, there
was a vacant small room on the top floor, he replied, condescendingly
spinning the register toward the supplicant. The general signed, and the
clerk spun the book back, reading as he did: "U. S. Grant & Son—Galena,
Illinois."

His eyes bugging, the clerk struck the bell with such force that its
clang brought a squad of bellboys on the run, while riveting the eyes of the
startled lobby idlers upon this nondescript soldier who could compel such
respect from such a lofty personage as the room clerk at Willard's. That
worthy was now the soul of unction, wringing his hands like an obsequious
Uriah Heep, changing the reservation from that tiny top-floor room to the

splendor of Parlor 6, the best suite in the house, where Presidents-elect and visiting princes were wont to dwell. Without a word, Grant beckoned to young Fred and the two passed silently through that buzzing throng. But when he entered the dining room later, holding Fred by the hand as though to protect him from the capital's contamination, and quietly took his place at a small table, he saw to his dismay that everyone there knew who he was. Came the cry, "Three cheers for Lieutenant General Grant!" and the room resounded and the very chandeliers seemed to quiver at the thunderous response, while the table pounding that next ensued actually did cause the silver, the glasses and china to shake. Obviously embarrassed, Grant arose, awkwardly brushed his lips with his napkin, bowed—and sat down. Mercifully, his admirers allowed him to finish his meal in peace, but when he arose the same noisy and unwelcome adulation—compounded by the now familiar ordeal of having to run a gantlet of hearty handshakes—accompanied him to the door.

Back in Parlor 6 he found an invitation from Lincoln to come to the White House. Unaware that the president reserved Tuesday nights for his weekly receptions, presuming that his commander in chief wanted to confer with him, he walked up to the Executive Mansion and entered the front hall. By then the crowd, larger than usual because word had spread that Grant would appear, had for the most part moved into the brilliantly lighted East Room. But there was still "a stir and a buzz" in the hall when "it was whispered that General Grant had arrived." Lincoln moved to greet him, taking his hand and remarking: "Why, here is General Grant. Well, this is a great pleasure." They shook hands warmly and chatted. Grant pulled awkwardly at his lapel and lowered his eyes shyly. But they were steady when his glance met Lincoln's. It was a good start.

Lincoln turned Grant over to Secretary of State Seward, who presented him to a beaming Mary Lincoln. Giving Grant her arm, she led him on a promenade through the crowded East Room. Her husband followed at a distance, sometimes stopping to chat with a favored guest, his eyes full of amusement staring steadily over the heads of the crowd at the blushing, sweating hero. Soon the guests shed their decorum in an outburst of cheering that Navy Secretary Welles found "rowdy and unseemly." Many admirers rushed eagerly up to the general with outstretched hand so that his five-foot eight-inch figure was hidden from sight. Someone cried, "Stand up so we can all have a look at you." With that Grant stepped up on a red plush sofa, looking out in consternation at the mass of upturned faces. "It was the only real mob I ever saw in the White House," a capital correspondent wrote later. "People were caught up and whirled in the torrent which swept through the great East Room. Ladies suffered dire disaster in the crush and confusion; their laces were torn and crinolines smashed, and many got up on sofas, chairs and tables to be out of harm's way or to get a better view of the spectacle." Even the president was upstaged—though unintentionally—by the unassuming Grant. Official and social Washington had been charmed by this ingenuous general, so different from his predecessors to whom their friendship or patronage had seemed so important, but had been so fatal. By his shyness he had kept them at a distance from which it would be difficult to interfere in his plans or to make of him a social lion frittering away his time.

U. S. Grant was indeed shy, but ingenuous or guileless he was not. He was quite aware that he could not succeed without the support of Congress, and could not therefore offend its members by operating from a headquarters in the West, as his close friend William Tecumseh Sherman urged him to do. The volatile redhead, always motivated by an over-simplified detestation of politicians and all things political, warned him that the wily men of Washington would exploit him for their own ignoble ends and ultimately destroy him. Much as Sherman admired his friend and chief, he believed that his very simplicity of character which undergirded his military success would be a fatal flaw among such selfish, unscrupulous men. Grant considered this advice, but quickly realized that the West was not the place from which to conduct the war. Its twin focuses were in Washington and Richmond, the residences of the rival presidents. Jefferson Davis in Richmond embodied the rebellion, but if the Confederate capital had to be seized to crush it, it could only be done by conquering its defending armies.

To do this, Grant would remain in the East in constant touch with Washington, but he would not reside there. In just three days in the capital he had had a surfeit of adulation and invasion of his privacy, so much so that he declined to attend Mary Lincoln's banquet in his honor. When Lincoln protested, "Mrs. Lincoln's dinner without you would be *Hamlet* with Hamlet left out," Grant replied: "I appreciate the honor Mrs. Lincoln would do me, but time is very important now. And really, Mr. Lincoln," he added frankly, "I have had enough of this show business."

So he left that night on a westbound train to confer in a Cincinnati hotel room with Sherman. Together they worked out a plan for destruction of the Confederate Army. Basically, as Sherman said later: "He was to go for Lee and I was to go for Joe Johnston," who had replaced Braxton Bragg in the West. Grant would hold Lee by constant attack, while Sherman maneuvered against Johnston and gradually drove him back toward Atlanta. Thus neither Confederate force could help the other, and each would be worn down until one or the other was crushed, and then both Union armies would unite to destroy the survivor. Thus also, the Confederacy would be exposed to attrition—to the "arithmetic of war"—those high casualties that though they might be less than the Union's could not be endured by the Rebel armies.

The problem of command of the Army of the Potomac now held by Meade had been solved during a visit to his headquarters at Brandy Station. At first Grant had believed that the only way to correct the Eastern army's continuing lack of verve and audacity was to remove the Pennsylvanian. But after he conferred with him alone he was so impressed by Meade's modesty and his offer to step down in the interests of cohesion and his willingness to serve wherever placed that Grant changed his mind. This proposal, Grant said, gave him "even a more favorable impression of Meade than did his great victory at Gettysburg." For his part, Meade wrote his wife: "I was much pleased with Grant. You may rest assured he is not an ordinary man."

So Meade remained in command of the Army of the Potomac, but Grant would accompany it in the field. It was a unique arrangement, and yet for the most part it turned out to be workable, even though an occasionally disenchanted Meade would sometimes wonder in letters to his wife if he were not, after all, a supernumerary. It was also inevitable that the Eastern army would come to be known as Grant's army, and by his continued presence did often come under his direct control. Grant was also still the general-in-chief, to the humiliation of Henry Halleck, his old superior and sometime enemy who was now reduced to chief of staff. But when Lincoln in the presence of Old Brains had pinned that third star on Grant's shoulder, Grant had betrayed not the slightest sign of satisfaction. Gloating was not in keeping with Grant's simple character. He had gotten the chief command, the plan was his and the war in effect was his. To make it total he ordered Ben Butler to take the Army of the James against Richmond and a Shenandoah army under Franz Sigel to move on Staunton and threaten Lee's railroads. Phil Sheridan was also brought east to command Grant's cavalry. In the simplest terms, the pressure was to be applied everywhere and made unbearable. Lee would not be permitted to maneuver, and he would be thrown on the defensive with the inevitable results.

In eight weeks, then, U. S. Grant put together his war machine, oiled and geared it, and on May 4, 1864, he sent it clanking toward the foe.

Lee's army had passed a frightful winter. The men were in rags, half-starved and freezing in their miserable huts along the Rapidan. Food was so scarce that when Lee had guests one day he could serve nothing but stringy bacon and cabbage. Because there was obviously not enough bacon to go around, the diners politely declined it. Next day there was even less to eat. Lee, remembering the untouched bacon, asked his steward about it and was told that it had been borrowed in the first place and had already been returned to its hungry owner.

Shortages in hay and fodder also caused the death of thousands of horses. When Longstreet left for Georgia, he was not able to take his guns, and half the animals in Jeb Stuart's horse artillery were dead.

During those early months of 1864 the Confederacy found itself at bay and fighting for survival, so much so that President Davis, buffeted by inflation, betrayed by discontent and disloyalty, his armies undone by desertion, and his own authority thwarted seemingly everywhere by the states' righters, at last bit the bullet and on February 3 asked Congress to suspend the writ of habeas corpus. For close to three years maintenance of this cornerstone of freedom had been the stick with which Davis might flog Lincoln, who had not hesitated to take this drastic step, and had thus been able to deal as harshly as he pleased with dissent and discontent. But now Davis found himself unable to enforce conscription or deal with traitors in the face of writs issued by hostile judges protecting offenders from prosecution. Davis's request was acrimoniously debated for twelve days in a secret session of Congress before it was finally and reluctantly approved—but only for six months. As could be anticipated, howls of protest arose from the states' righters, chiefly Vice President Stephens. "Georgians, behold your chains!" an Athens newspaper cried, and it seemed that the entire Lower South would unite in a massive program of civil disobedience. In inflammatory language, Mississippi, Georgia and Louisiana passed resolutions against the act, and North Carolina went so far as to pass a law nullifying it. Everywhere, it seemed, the loss of liberty was being lamented by fiery leaders who should have known better: that states' rights themselves could not be upheld except on the point of Rebel bayonets, and that without successful conscription there would not be enough Graybacks to do it.

For a time, Davis had been encouraged by a decline in Federal numbers and a corresponding increase in Confederate strength that reduced the Union's advantage to less than two to one in soldiers. But then Lincoln had called for "500,000 more," and Davis had found no alternative but to ask for suspension of the writ.

From the Army of the Tennessee, meanwhile, came a far more drastic proposal to keep the Confederate Army up to strength. It was born in the brain of Irish-born Pat Cleburne, once an Arkansas lawyer and now considered to be the best division commander in both armies. Cleburne saw that the manpower shortage and slavery were twin millstones around the Southern neck, and he proposed to get rid of them both by emancipating the slaves and enlisting them in the army. This, he informed his fellow generals in Johnston's Western army, would transform the "dreaded weakness" of bondage into a source "of strength," adding: "We can do this more effectually than the North can now do, for we can give the Negro not only his own freedom, but that of his wife and child, and can secure it to him in his old home." Cleburne's fellow commanders were stunned and then outraged, and Johnston advised them to let the matter go no further. Cleburne agreed not to pursue his plan, but Richmond eventually heard of it with the effect that the gallant and skillful Irish general never rose to higher command. President Davis, closer to the realities of the situation, was not so shocked, although he realized how much louder the politicians would howl if they ever got wind of Cleburne's proposal. But he did not in his own mind reject it. Like Lincoln putting Emancipation on hold, he reserved it as a course to be considered when all seemed lost.

Incredibly enough, the Confederate soldiery in those dark and divisive winter months of 1864 lost nothing of their confidence, especially those in Lee's Army of Northern Virginia. On April 6 a jubilant Marse Robert had divined Grant's plans, and he impatiently awaited Grant's anticipated movement across the Rapidan. As the weeks passed and the Yankee juggernaut seemed to grow in strength and arms until it outnumbered Lee's command of 60,000 two to one, he seemed to recover his old combativeness, saying to a member of his staff: "Colonel, we have got to whip them! We *must* whip them!" He smiled wanly as though in relief. "It has already made me better to think of it." Lee's confidence was infectious. After all, his men and officers reasoned, Bobby Lee *had* whipped the Yankee generals before—all six of them—and this Grant would be the seventh. James Longstreet once again was a dissenter from this roseate view. He had been Grant's friend at West Point, had been in attendance at his wedding and later became related to him by his own marriage—and had also served against him in the West. "We must make up our minds to get into line of battle and stay there," he said, "for that man will fight us every day and every hour until the end of the war." Here, once again, was Old Pete's reluctance to deliver rather than receive an attack. Lee, however, contemplated no such static defense, but was thinking offensively. First he ordered Beauregard to defend Richmond against Butler and scraped together a scratch force to hold off Sigel in the Valley. Marse Robert planned to attend to Grant personally, letting him cross the Rapidan and hitting him with all his strength as the ponderous slow Union army crawled through the steaming green tangle of the Wilderness.

As Lee had correctly judged, Grant had chosen that route. Lee's army was too strong to be taken by frontal assault, and although his left flank would be easier to reach by marching through favorable terrain, it would unmask Union communications. An advance on his right, however, would cover those lines and Washington as well while threatening Lee's. It would also place the Army of the Potomac closer to Butler's Army of the James. These considerations outweighed the major drawback of passing through the same Wilderness that had blinded Hooker the previous year. So Grant chose to cross the Rapidan on Lee's right flank, believing that he could move swiftly through the Wilderness in one day and thus with his two to one superiority be free to maneuver against Marse Robert in open country.

At midnight of May 3 the three Federal corps under Sedgwick, Warren and Hancock began marching toward the Rapidan fords. Behind them Burnside's corps protected the railroads. Meade had divided his cavalry, with one division moving ahead of each column. These were Grant's first mistakes. If he had begun his march at nightfall rather than four hours later at midnight, and used his cavalry to seize the exits from the Wilderness to protect his army's passage, he probably would have achieved his objective of passing through that dreadful labyrinth in a single day. As it turned out, even though Grant, to hasten his passage, had taken with him only essential supplies, the trains lagged behind so that early in the afternoon of May 4 Hancock in the lead and Warren behind him had to halt to let them close up. Here they offered Robert E. Lee an excellent target.

Marse Robert could not have hoped that Grant would be bogged down so soon in unfamiliar and tangled terrain which could cancel out his superior numbers and splendid artillery. Yet Lee's own deployment was poor. During the winter it had been necessary to scatter his underfed army to make the problem of feeding it easier. On May 4 it was still dispersed in three corps: Longstreet at Gordonsville forty-two miles away, A. P. Hill about half that distance along the Orange Plank Road and Ewell moving along the Orange-Fredericksburg Turnpike only a few miles away from Warren. Stuart's cavalry was still at Fredericksburg. If Lee had had his entire army concentrated on that afternoon of May 4, or even on the morning of May 5, it is quite possible that he could have destroyed Hancock and Warren. One explanation for this delay is that Lee's intelligence could not convince Marse Robert that Grant's army was twice as large as his own. So it was that once again a meeting engagement, or at least a chance encounter—

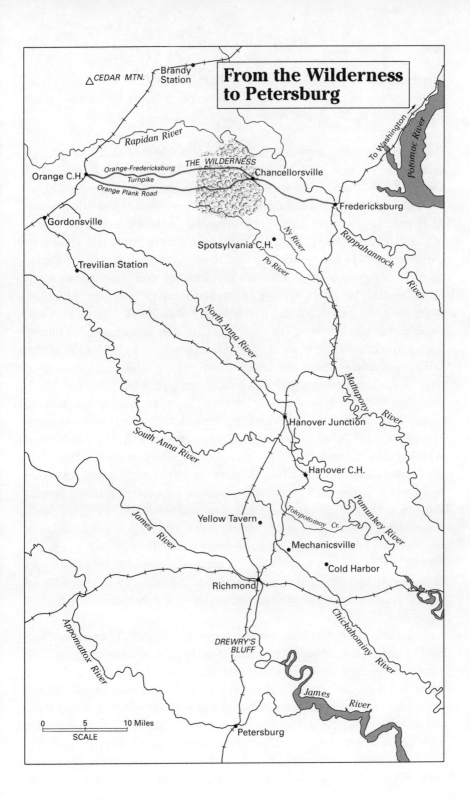

△ CEDAR MTN.

Brandy
Station

From the Wilderness
to Petersburg

Rapidan River

THE WILDERNESS

Orange-Frederiksburg
Turnpike

Orange C.H.

Orange Plank Road

Chancellorsville

To Washington

Potomac River

Fredericksburg

Gordonsville

Ny River

Spotsylvania C.H.

Rappahannock

Po River

Trevilian Station

River

North Anna River

Mattapony

River

South Anna River

Hanover Junction

Hanover C.H.

James River

Yellow Tavern

Totopotomoy Cr.

Pamunkey River

Mechanicsville

Cold Harbor

Richmond

DREWRY'S
BLUFF

Chickahominy River

Appomattox River

James River

0   5   10 Miles

SCALE

Petersburg

Ewell's collision with Warren on the Orange-Fredericksburg Turnpike at seven o'clock in the morning of May 5—was to touch off another great struggle: the Battle of the Wilderness.

Only a year ago the armies of Lee and Hooker had swirled through this maze of swamp and swale, leaving it a monster burial ground. Here eyeless sockets stared from the bleached skulls of men and horses, there a skeletal hand or leg rose from a half-finished grave; every thicket was strewn with rusty guns and canteens and every bush seemed to blossom with rotten bits of bloodstained clothing. Even the bullet-nicked trees bore mute testimony to the savagery of Chancellorsville, and the entire scene startled the Federals of Gouverneur Kemble Warren's corps as that unit came poking south from the Rapidan. They quickly recovered from their horror, however, when they blundered into the Butternuts of Dick Ewell's corps who had come marching east along the turnpike. Gradually this chance encounter built up into full-scale conflict, the opening notes of the Battle of the Wilderness, and within a few hours it had become a blind, black struggle over which neither commander exercised much control.

In a field near Wilderness Tavern, U. S. Grant sat on a stump, smoking a cigar and whittling on a stick, issuing the orders that fed more and more soldiers into the fight. In the Confederate rear, Robert E. Lee calmly rode with A. P. Hill as that general's corps came rushing up on Ewell's right. Lee also sent orders for Longstreet to hurry up from Gordonsville, forty-two miles away. So the battle grew and grew, the Rebels trying to get around the Union army, the Federals building up their left flank to contain them. Soon rolling clouds of smoke intensified the forest gloom. Now soldiers merely fired blindly into the smoke and murk, others groped their way forward or crawled on their bellies. A horizontal rain of bullets three feet high swept the battlefield. Then the woods took fire, and the crackle of flames mingled with the wild screams of men and animals being burned alive.

By midafternoon Grant had the corps of Sedgwick, Warren and Hancock, right to left, opposed to Ewell and Hill. He resolved to crush the Confederate right under Hill and sent Hancock crashing forward. Once again, the Wilderness was the Rebel ally. It quickly fragmented solid formations into bits, while the outnumbered Confederates—better woodsmen, who knew every path and fastness by heart—riddled the Union attack. By nightfall, however, two of Hill's divisions were badly battered.

That night Lee realized that he had met his most aggressive adversary. All day long the Federals had attacked, attacked, attacked, never surrendering the initiative and never once giving Lee the opportunity to maneuver. He had been held in place as never before, and now his right flank was badly damaged. Still, he hoped that Longstreet would arrive next day in time to turn the tide. Early on May 7, however, the roar of enemy guns told Lee that Hill's weakened divisions were once again being assaulted.

Lee mounted Traveller and rode toward the guns. He galloped through stragglers, and then, to his mounting alarm, through a butternut flood pouring away westward. Lee's right was shattered. Not since Antietam had he faced such a crisis. Lee rode back to consult A. P. Hill and to look anxiously for Longstreet. Hill shouted at his artillery to fire off twelve loaded guns before withdrawing the pieces from danger. The guns bucked and roared and hurled shells into the woods and the approaching Federals only 200 yards away. Smoke swirled around Lee. The Federals came on, and then, through the smoke behind him, Lee saw a score of ragged soldiers dash forward with muskets in their hands.

They were Texans. Texans! That meant they were from John B. Hood's famous brigade in Longstreet's corps. Longstreet had arrived! In rare excitement Robert E. Lee spurred Traveller forward through the gun pits. He came up with his advancing reinforcements as though to lead them forward. "Go back, General Lee, go back!" they cried. He ignored them, and they shouted: "We won't go on unless you go back!"

Persuaded at last, Lee reined in Traveller, waved his hat at the onrushing Texans, and rode back to see Longstreet. That stolid general bluntly told Lee to go farther behind the lines, and then came forward himself to stop the Yankee attack—and to be wounded badly by the fire of his own men.

So the Battle of the Wilderness ended as Antietam had ended, with the eleventh-hour arrival of reinforcements to save Lee's crumbling right. Would it also end as had all other drives on Richmond? Would the Army of the Potomac turn north, recross the river and regain Washington to refit and regroup before shuffling south again? It seemed so to many of the Union soldiers lying weary and heart-broken in the darkness. When they were ordered to take the road, it seemed only that the command to retire had come sooner than usual. It was another Chancellorsville, they told each other. Then they came to a crossroads. If they turned left, they would be retreating again. They turned right, and suddenly those tired men lifted their heads and a great cheer rose in the night. They capered in the dust and tossed their caps in the dark and shouted with a wild fierce joy until U. S. Grant reined in his great war horse Cincinnati and told his staff to tell the men to stop cheering or else the enemy would realize that the Army of the Potomac was slipping away south.

Neither Lee nor Grant had fought with distinction, only with determination; and if casualties measure victories, then Lee had won: Union losses were between 15,000 and 18,000, Confederate estimated at between 7,750 and 11,400. Casualties, however, measure only the costs of battle. It was Grant who was the victor. He had achieved his objective: he had held Lee, had fixed him, had thrown him on the defensive. All Lee's moves hereafter were to be in response to Grant's. Yet Grant the slugger was stalking Lee the boxer and must inevitably become bruised and lacerated, while the very success of Grant's policy was to call forth from Lee all that mastery of defensive warfare which was uniquely his. A field engineer by education, Lee had spent decades building forts and dredging rivers. He had a marvelous feel for terrain and here, in the Wilderness, he was fortifying his own back yard. "When our line advances," an aide of Grant's wrote, "there is the line of the enemy, nothing showing but the bayonets, and the battle-flags stuck on top of the works. It is a rule that when the Rebels halt, the first day gives them a good rifle pit; the second a regular infantry parapet with artillery in position; and the third a parapet with an abattis in front and entrenched batteries behind. Sometimes they put this three days' work into the first twenty-four hours." Thus did the King of Spades make bloody woe of Grant's progress south, and on that very night that the Union chief sideslipped left to come up under Lee's right at Spotsylvania Court House, Lee shifted right to race him for that position. The Confederate commander won, and on May 8 Grant found his path once again blocked.

It was blocked because the Confederate advance guard had marched with lightning speed and because the Union cavalry had dawdled clearing the road through Spotsylvania. Meade blamed this failure on Sheridan, and when the little cavalry chief appeared at his headquarters the towering commander of the Army of the Potomac lost his temper with a roar that could be heard by every orderly with a pretext for being within hearing distance. Black-eyed Phil Sheridan, five feet five inches of pure pugnacity, yelled back with an insubordinate vigor that rattled the chain of command and warmed the orderlies' hearts. It was Meade's fault, Sheridan shouted, because Meade countermanded his orders and used his cavalry as scouts and errand boys rather than as a fighting corps. What Sheridan wanted, Sheridan shouted, was to go out and whip Jeb Stuart clear out of his saddle. Somewhat startled, Meade took the dispute to Grant, and Grant asked: "Did Sheridan say that? Well, he generally knows what he is talking about. Let him start right out and do it." So Grant ordered Sheridan to "cut loose from the Army of the Potomac, pass around the left of Lee's army and attack his cavalry." He was also to cut Lee's communications. Thus, shortly after noon of May 8 the entire cavalry corps—13,000 strong—was assembled under Sheridan to make a wide swing around the Union right and then make a bee-line for Richmond. This mass of mounted men and their artillery did not go off at a jingling trot but rather at a walk. It moved over the roads like a long, thick, blue constrictor undulating and twisting with power. Once it encountered a Rebel skirmish line. There was a fire-fight and troopers came tumbling back. Sheridan asked them, "Cavalry or infantry?"

"Cavalry," came the answer.

"Keep moving, boys—we're going on through," Sheridan replied. "There isn't enough cavalry in all the Southern Confederacy to stop us!"

The troopers cheered, Sheridan waved his little black porkpie hat, and the great constrictor began undulating again.

In the meantime, the Battle of Spotsylvania had swelled from an advance-guard encounter into a rolling, roaring eight-day battle which eventually embroiled both armies. While the conflict developed, Lee skillfully en-trenched himself between the Po and Ny rivers in a line roughly resembling an inverted V. This enabled him to put most of his troops on the line and to move them to and from either face of the upside-down V as the situation required. Trees and underbrush concealed most of his works and his skir-mish line was pushed far enough forward to prevent Union scouts and officers from reconnoitering it. This made it difficult for Grant to gauge the extent of the opposition, and with Sheridan's cavalry gone he was, like Lee at Gettysburg, fighting nearly blindfolded.

Confederate sharpshooters also kept Federal artillery at a respectful distance, or pinned down those gunners rash enough to drag their pieces within sniping range. On May 9 John Sedgwick tried to rally his nervous artillerists by standing erect among the pinging bullets and crying, "Don't duck, they couldn't hit an elephant at this distance!" A minute later Sedg-wick was down and dying with a sniper's bullet under his left eye. Command of his corps passed to Horatio Wright, and it was Wright who seems to have decided that the weakest point of Lee's heretofore impregnable line was the west face of the V, or "the Mule Shoe," as the Rebels called it. Although the works there were strong, they could be enfiladed by Union artillery, and there was a stand of trees that would enable a Federal force to come within 200 yards of the works undetected. It seemed to Wright that the Mule Shoe could be taken by a sudden silent rush, and he organized a special force of twelve regiments under an intense young colonel named Emory Upton.

Upton was among the most professional commanders in the Union army. Free to criticize, he was himself very hard to fault because of his capacity for taking pains. He planned his assault carefully, taking his commanders forward to study the ground, organizing four lines of three regiments each. The first line was to pierce the outermost Confederate line and widen the gap so that a second line could rush through to assault the second Rebel position. The last two lines were to form a reserve, lying down beneath the Confederate breastworks until called for.

Late in the afternoon of May 10, 1864, Union artillery began pounding the Rebel positions. At 6:15 P.M., Upton's blue lines charged and drove straight through as planned. But then the Rebel guns scattered the Union reserve, which had formed in the open contrary to orders, and Upton was left isolated inside the Confederate position. He hung on until nightfall, assisted by another attack from the Federal right, and then withdrew. Yet he had proved that the salient at the Mule Shoe could be penetrated. Obviously, a larger force might break it and split Lee's army in two. That was what U. S. Grant meant when he said to Meade: "A brigade today— we'll try a corps tomorrow."

It was two days later and with two full corps that Grant attacked the Mule Shoe. Hancock's corps came straight down against the tip of the V while Wright's hammered away at the western face, and throughout that day and night of May 12, 1864, there raged probably the most vicious battle ever fought on American soil, and possibly one of the most ferocious fought anywhere. It was worst on Wright's front, "the Bloody Angle," as it was called. It was hand to hand. Men fired muskets muzzle to muzzle, and struck at each other with battle flags. The Rebels ran their guns right up to the parapets and sprayed double canister shot into rank after falling rank of Yankees. Fence rails and logs in the breastworks were actually splintered by the hail of Minié balls, and trees over a foot and a half in diameter were cut in two by them. Skulls were smashed with clubbed muskets, men were stabbed to death by swords and bayonets thrust between the logs of the parapets separating the forces, and the wounded were entombed alive by the crush of dead bodies toppling upon their wriggling, helpless forms. Night fell and a fierce rainstorm broke, and still the struggle convulsed the Bloody Angle until at last, at midnight, both sides sank on their arms in exhaustion.

At the point of the V, meanwhile, it appeared that Hancock's massed Federals had won the day. They bore straight down on the Mule Shoe, broke it, captured artillery pieces and took prisoners, and swept on until momentarily checked by an incomplete line of breastworks. Here Robert E. Lee came riding on Traveller, faced once again with disaster. He rode straight to the center of the division commanded by John Gordon, and Gordon thought that "Lee looked a very god of war." Then Lee turned his horse's head as though to lead the desperation charge needed to shatter Hancock's advancing front.

At once Gordon spurred his horse across Traveller's front and grasped Lee's bridle. Lifting his voice deliberately so that his men might hear, Gordon said: "General Lee, you shall not lead my men in a charge. No man can do that, sir." Turning to his men, Gordon asked if they would fail Lee. "No, no, no!" they roared back, "We'll not fail him!" Turning back to Lee, Gordon shouted: "You must go to the rear," and his men echoed him with a thundering shout: "General Lee to the rear, General Lee to the rear!" Crowding around the beloved Marse Robert, some clutching his bridle, others holding his stirrups, they forced Traveller around with such vehemence that Gordon believed that if Lee had resisted they would have carried both horse and rider to the rear. But Lee submitted to their pressure, and Gordon's division rolled forward with cyclonic force to shiver Hancock's lines and eventually force the Federals out of most of the Mule Shoe.

In the meantime, attacks by Warren on the Federal right and Burnside on the left were also repulsed. Lee hurried construction of a new line at the base of the Mule Shoe. By nightfall the Confederate position was out of danger.

By then also Jeb Stuart had overtaken Sheridan's cavalry at Yellow Tavern about ten miles above Richmond. Outnumbered two to one, Stuart tried to hold off the Union horse until infantry reinforcements could arrive from Richmond. But the Federals were too strong, they were scattering the Rebels aside, and Stuart personally led a mounted countercharge. As he did, a dismounted Yankee trooper ran past him, fired his pistol at him—and vanished. Stuart slumped in the saddle, gravely wounded.

That had been on May 11, and Sheridan's cavalry had broken through, riding through Richmond's outer defenses and eventually making a complete circuit of Lee's army. On the night of the twelfth, while the Mule Shoe battle still raged, Lee learned that Stuart was dying. Lee's voice was trembling when he told his staff: "He never brought me a piece of false information." Later, he was told that Stuart had died. Grief-stricken, Lee retired to his tent with the remark: "I can scarcely think of him without weeping." It was a black night for Robert E. Lee, who had lost his right arm, Jackson, a year ago and tonight "the eyes and ears of the army." Jackson dead, Stuart dead, Longstreet wounded, A. P. Hill sick and Ewell weakening. All the old faces were vanishing. Two of his corps were in the hands of men as yet untried to high command: Richard Anderson and Jubal Early. Yet Lee must hang on—and he did, assisted by four days of rain that enmired Grant's subsequent attempts to burst the Rebel line.

Nevertheless, Ulysses S. Grant had not given up. His casualties at Spotsylvania totaled between 17,000 and 18,000 against between 9,000 and 10,000 for Lee. Yet on May 19 he sat down to write his famous report: "I purpose to fight it out on this line if it takes all summer."

On the following night he sideslipped left again in another attempt to draw the King of Spades outside his invincible earthworks.

Although Grant was successfully holding Lee while Sherman in Georgia had begun to drive Johnston before him, Union movements elsewhere were being decisively defeated. Ben Butler's advance on Richmond was blocked by Beauregard at Bermuda Hundred, after which Butler allowed himself to be trapped on the Bermuda Hundred peninsula, corked up neatly in a bottle, as Grant phrased it, thus releasing troops to Lee. In the Shenandoah Valley, Franz Sigel, a Union general by virtue of his abhorrence of slavery, had met John Breckinridge at Newmarket and been defeated in a battle distinguished by the fighting of a corps of cadets from Virginia Military Institute. It was now up to Grant alone to keep the pressure on his opponent. He did, compelling Lee, in fact, to follow him; yet never succeeding in drawing Marse Robert out into the open.

Lee's counter to Grant's second sideslip was to move into another V-shaped position prepared the previous winter inside the steep-banked North Anna River. Again Lee was able to move troops from face to face of the V, making such clever use of the terrain that if Grant tried to move from flank to flank he would have to cross the river twice. Grant had no desire to be so discomfited, and after a few days of light skirmishing he sideslipped left again. Skirmishing once more to Totopotomoy Creek, he stepped left a fourth time and finally came up against Lee at a place called Cold Harbor.

Cold Harbor was neither chilly nor a port but a crossroads taking its name from a tavern that served only cold food. It was near the 1862 battlefields called the Seven Days. Fighting on June 1 and 2 had not been fierce. On the first the Federals did not launch their assault until 6 P.M. when Wright and William ("Baldy") Smith attacked. They made some gains in the beginning, but then the Confederate defenses stiffened and both Union corps entrenched in their advanced position. On the second Grant had scheduled his attack for early morning, but troop movements, replenishment of ammunition and the fatigue caused by that extremely hot day produced delays so that the assault was postponed until 5 P.M. Once again the attack was put off, this time because of the approach of rain. During these two days Grant thought he detected a lack of élan in Lee's usually spirited army and it was from this, together with no sign of any serious offensive action, that he concluded that Lee was beaten. Accordingly, he scheduled an all-out assault for June 3.

Lee was far from being beaten and was supremely confident, even though confined to his tent by an illness. The fact that he led only 60,000 against Grant's 110,000 did not daunt him, and he had given no sign of offensive intention simply because he was so impressed by the natural defensive features of Cold Harbor that he was content to remain there. Both of his flanks were anchored on rising streams and the terrain was such that the Graybacks could achieve a maximum of firepower with a minimum of protection. Without imposing fortifications such as those of Spotsylvania and the North Anna, the enemy might be beguiled into believing that they confronted a vulnerable foe. Actually the seven miles of Confederate front was integrated—linked and joined with overlapping fields of fire. Lee had not been indolent those first two days but rather busy constructing it. And the Yankees were deceived, or at least not alarmed. Neither Grant nor Meade had reconnoitered Lee's front, an unpardonable oversight in both, and in Meade a contradiction of his cautious character to which was joined an engineer's eye the equal of Lee's. Instead, Meade's order postponing the June 2 attack had said: "Corps commanders will employ the interim in making examinations of the ground on their front and perfecting the arrangements for the assault." Baldy Smith was "aghast" at this instruction since it seemed to imply "the utter absence of any military plan." He was right.

The soldiers in the Federal army seemed to be possessed by an even deeper sense of foreboding, for a young officer noticed that on the rainy night of June 2 many of them had taken off their blouses and were mending them. Closer examination revealed that they were actually writing their names and addresses on slips of paper and pinning them to their tunics so that their bodies would be identified and their fate made known to their families.

Next day the Yankees advanced with a deep-throated roar—shouting, "Hurrah! Hurrah!"—and that seemingly silent and lonely landscape ahead of them came alive with flame and smoke and a scything rain of bullets struck them. "It seemed more like a volcanic blast than a battle," one survivor recalled, "and was just about as destructive."

Grant was attacking all along the line rather than massing at a single point. Like Lee at Gettysburg and Burnside at Fredericksburg he had failed to grasp the new and awesome superiority of the defense. As a result the Battle of Cold Harbor was a Union slaughter.

Charge after charge was broken up, some in less than a quarter hour. In one sector an outraged company commander, believing that his men had basely taken cover, ran over the field indignantly prodding them with his sword until he realized that they were all dead. Taken in their flank by enemy fire, some Union formations collapsed one upon another like falling dominoes. Across their entire front all the Bluebellies could see was the black slouch hats of the Rebels and their muzzle flashes piercing the smoke. Whenever that withering fire seemed to be subsiding, the pinned-down Yankees got up on all fours to scratch out a depression in the earth with their bayonets. Gradually they sank out of sight and when couriers came crawling out to them with orders to renew the assault they simply refused to go forward. And with good reason: in less than an hour Grant lost 7,000 men against 1,500 for Lee, and he finally called off the assault.

It was a shocking defeat, the only battle in which Grant did not inflict upon Lee casualties roughly equal to his own, and thus achieve his objective of whittling Marse Robert, and it was made more doleful by the cries of "Water, water, for God's sakes, water!" breaking from the parched and agonized lips of Grant's wounded outside the Confederate lines. Lying there moaning in blistering heat, they could not be retrieved by their comrades because of the dreadful fire of Rebel sharpshooters. Lee, anxious to compel Grant to admit defeat, refused to call them off; and it was not until June 5—two days after the dreadful slaughter—that Grant sent an aide inside Lee's lines with a letter suggesting a cease-fire be called to allow stretcher-bearers to succor his wounded. Lee insisted that "a flag of truce be sent, as is customary." Next morning Grant wrote Lee that stretchers and white flags would go out that day, but Lee replied that he would agree to this only if a request were made under a flag of truce, otherwise: "I have directed that any parties you send out be turned back." It was not until the night of June 7 that a truce was agreed upon, and by then it was too late, for almost all of the Federal wounded were dead.

Here, once again as at Vicksburg, was Grant's reluctance to show weakness; although this time it was sharpened and perhaps excused by his awareness that Lincoln's political fortunes were then at their nadir, that all the savants were predicting he would not only not be reelected but probably not even renominated. His refusal to ask for a truce, then, was not calloused indifference to the suffering of his soldiers, as some historians have maintained, but rather unwillingness to have a white flag misconstrued as an admission of a defeat that would encourage the Northern peace movement and discourage Lincoln's supporters. He simply did not want to be the instrument of his chief's downfall. What would history say of such a commander? War is an extension of foreign policy and in war men die, sometimes for objectives absolutely invisible or incomprehensible to them—such as an attempt to test or probe the enemy's front by attacks in which men seem to perish pointlessly—and a decision to allow soldiers to die rather than risk the defeat of a policy for which the war is being fought, although seemingly infinitely heartless, simply cannot be condemned on humanitarian grounds. War, as Clausewitz said, may be "part of the social province"— but it is not humane. Above all war presumes the breakdown of law and civility so that the customary moral canons do not always apply. One of these is the true maxim that the end does not justify the means. Yet, if war is to be judged morally, it is only by its objectives: i.e., its ends, whether they be moral or immoral. Inasmuch as no nation in history ever has or ever will admit to marching in an evil cause, the commanders of either side seeking victory can be motivated by nothing higher than military necessity. Lee wanted to force Grant to admit defeat and thus help divide the North politically. Grant shrank from such a concession for reasons already cited, knowing full well that his reluctance would be criticized. If the situation had been reversed, with Lee the loser, even the gentle Marse Robert would have done the same.

The true tragedy of Cold Harbor was that gallant young men in blue were sent into battle without plan or preparation, and it was one of those apprehensive soldiers who made their own "dog tags" the night before who wrote the epitaph for that awful carnage. The last entry in his bloodstained diary read:

"June 3. Cold Harbor. I was killed today."

Cold Harbor closed a month of battle such as neither the Army of Northern Virginia nor the Army of the Potomac had ever before experienced. Many Union soldiers and some officers saw nothing but senseless slaughter. "For thirty days it has been one funeral procession past me," cried the sensitive General Warren, "and it is too much!" It was not too much for U. S. Grant. True enough, he would one day write: "I have always regretted that the last assault at Cold Harbor was ever made." Though shaken, he was not dismayed, and he saw in his defeat proof that frontal assault against Lee would never succeed. Instead, he decided to attack Lee's rear, to move all the way down to the south bank of the James River and cut off Lee's source of supply.

Here was an audacity worthy of Robert E. Lee. Grant was going to break contact with the watchful Lee and march undetected into Lee's rear, moving through Lee's own country swarming with Lee's own spies. To do this he must march fifty miles through swamps and across two rivers—including the half-mile-wide tidal James—always risking attack from that masterly commander whose favorite tactic was to strike an army on the move. Yet Grant had confidence in himself and his men, and he believed that the Rebel army was no longer capable of those lightning adjustments that once had been its specialty. Whittling his sticks, gazing thoughtfully through clouds of cigar smoke, Grant formulated his plans.

First, a force under Sheridan went into the Shenandoah Valley to disrupt Lee's supply lines there. Next, Meade prepared a second line of entrenchments to the rear of Cold Harbor under cover of which the army might slip away. Then Baldy Smith was ordered to take his corps by water up the James to seize Petersburg, holding it until Grant arrived with his main body.

Petersburg was the key to Grant's scheme. It was a vital rail junction lying twenty-odd miles south of Richmond. If it fell and the Shenandoah line were blocked, Richmond could not be held and the specter of starvation would drive Lee's army into the open for a finish fight.

On the night of June 12 the Army of the Potomac began slipping away, moving as much like clockwork as is possible for 100,000 human beings. Every crossroad was strongly held to screen the army's movements. The James was spanned by one of the greatest military bridges in history, a pontoon crossing 2,100 feet long, built to resist a strong tidal current and to adjust to a four-foot tidal rise and fall. Even Confederate gunboats on the upper James were contained. It was truly a magnificent maneuver, and Lee was left in the dark.

On the morning of June 13 his scouts reported the enemy trenches at Cold Harbor were empty. Lee did not know exactly where to look for Grant's vanished army. He had already moved to check the Union build-up in the Shenandoah, and he had also sent Jubal Early there to threaten Washington and play the old game of panicking the North. Thus Lee was looking north while Grant was moving south, and he had weakened himself at a time when he needed to be strongest.

Beauregard, holding the Petersburg defenses, had divined Grant's intentions and had pointed out that Petersburg was in great danger. Eventually Lee came to realize this, and when he did he began rushing reinforcements south in a race against time.

From the Union viewpoint, all depended now on Baldy Smith. He arrived with his corps by water at Bermuda Hundred on July 14 and was reinforced by a division of black troops and one of cavalry. He had about 10,000 men, but Beauregard had only about 2,200 holding Petersburg. If Smith moved swiftly, he could crack Beauregard's thinly held defenses and walk into the city. But it was not until 4 P.M. of July 15 that he ordered his attack. Then it was discovered that the artillery horses had been sent to water, and another two hours passed before the supporting guns could be hauled into position. Finally, with a division of Rebels marching madly to Beauregard's rescue, with Hancock's corps coming toward Smith, the Federal assault began.

The Rebels were overrun, and the black troops were so jubilant that they danced in triumph around their captured cannon. Petersburg was Smith's for the taking, but he decided to hold what he had and wait for Hancock. When Hancock did arrive, Smith advised him not to attack, and so these fresh, eager soldiers merely relieved Smith's weary men. They had marched toward Petersburg crying, "We'll end this damned rebellion tonight!" but after they realized that the golden chance had gone glimmering and that tonight's weak enemy would be tomorrow's strong foe, they cursed and ground their teeth in anguish. "The rage of the enlisted men was devilish," a soldier wrote. "The most bloodcurdling blasphemy I ever listened to I heard that night, uttered by men who knew they were to be sacrificed on the morrow."

With the eternally true instincts of cannon fodder, the men were right. During the night Beauregard moved all his troops from Bermuda Hundred across the Appomattox River to reinforce Petersburg. This unbottled Butler, who could have placed himself between Richmond and Petersburg and perhaps, like Baldy Smith, won the war. But Butler only justified Beauregard's contempt for him, making a few token moves before retiring in the face of reinforcements from Lee. In the meantime, Beauregard's Butternuts held off three entire Federal corps the next day, the sixteenth. They did the same on the seventeenth. On the eighteenth Beauregard pulled back and the Union assault struck thin air. By the time the Federals regrouped, Lee had arrived with more reinforcements and Petersburg was too tough to storm.

Thwarted by his subordinates, baffled by Beauregard, Grant settled down to a siege.

62

■

The Beginning of the End

A SIEGE, Robert E. Lee had said, would make it "a mere question of time" for the Army of Northern Virginia. Yet time was exactly what the Army of the Potomac was not supposed to grant the enemy.

Abraham Lincoln needed a quick victory, one that would come soon enough to influence the presidential election. Not only Lincoln's office was at stake on November 8 but the very fate of the nation as well: the election would also be a vote for or against continuing the war, and if the North said no to the war, that meant that the Union stood dissolved, perhaps permanently.

Discontent and disenchantment were spreading, and for different reasons. On the one hand were those radical Republicans who thought the war was not being fought hard enough, and they had already nominated John Charles Frémont as their own candidate for president. Such a splinter party could not fail to hurt Lincoln, who had been nominated by the so-called Union Party and had chosen a War Democrat, Andrew Johnson of Tennessee, as his running mate. On the other hand were those Peace Democrats, Copperheads, strict Constitutionalists and others who thought the war ought to be waged less harshly or else abandoned outright. Then there was the great bulk of the people who favored prosecution of the war but were dismayed by the sight of so many limbless veterans and the sound of so many funeral bells, and were wondering if the South was not actually unconquerable.

The Confederacy did seem unshaken in the summer of 1864. It was in truth a hollow shell, its insides eaten away by economic ills, but most people only saw that hard outer rind. Grant may have done exactly what he had proposed to do in fixing Lee on the defensive, but to many Northerners it appeared that he had only advanced to the James at the cost of a stunning butcher's bill of 60,000 men. Nor did Sherman seem to have done much better against Johnston.

True, Sherman did not suffer so many losses and he had driven Johnston deeper and deeper into Georgia. Yet Johnston's army, his true objective, remained undefeated; and because the Rebels gathered in reinforcements as they retreated, it had grown even stronger. By the middle of July 1864, Sherman had reached the outskirts of Atlanta, but he seemed to be stalled there.

At the same time, Jubal Early came bursting out of the Shenandoah to menace Washington. This, of course, turned out to be only a passing scare. "Old Jube" knew very well that if he took his men into Washington he probably would never come out again, and after Grant calmly sent a corps north by water to attack him, Early quickly turned about and headed for home. Still, this last play of Robert E. Lee's capital card had not helped Northern war nerves. Nor were they eased when Grant made his last attempt to take Petersburg by literally blasting his way in.

The 4th Pennsylvania Regiment under Lieutenant Colonel Henry Pleasants was composed mainly of soldiers from the hard coal regions of Schuylkill Country, the same breed of Irish miners who had so bitterly resented the draft. One of them in the presence of Pleasants had pointed to a Rebel redan or artillery bastion about 150 yards to his front and said: "We could blow that damned fort out of existence if we could run a mine shaft under it." Pleasants was intrigued, reporting the remark to his superior officer, who passed it upward to Burnside who spoke of it to Meade. Meade liked the idea, as much for the chance to keep some bored men busy as for its likelihood of success. But his engineers did next to nothing to help Pleasants and his eager miners. With no tools forthcoming, Pleasants improvised—making picks with the help of regimental blacksmiths, barrows for moving dirt from hardtack boxes, cutting timbers and planks for shoring up the gallery walls and roof inside a wrecked sawmill, and even borrowing a theodolite—an instrument for measuring angles—from Washington.

Because the tunnel under the fort was to be more than 500 feet long, Pleasants was assured by the engineers that it could not go more than 400 feet without ventilation shafts, which would be visible to the enemy. Once again Pleasants improvised. Installing an airtight canvas door at the shaft entrance, he built a square wooden pipe from just outside the door and underneath it, extending it as the tunneling progressed. A fireplace near the sealed door sent heated air up its camouflaged chimney, creating a draft that drew the stale air from the far end of the shaft, pulling in fresh air through the wooden pipe.

The miners started digging on June 25, burrowing into the steep bank of an abandoned railway cut out of sight of Rebel lookouts. They worked in shifts around the clock inside a gallery five feet high, four feet wide at the bottom and two feet at the top. On July 17—22 days after they began tunneling—they completed a shaft 511 feet long directly under the Confederate outwork and only twenty feet above their heads. They could hear the enemy soldiers walking and talking as they dug a lateral powder chamber to both sides, 75 feet long under both the bastion and the trenches flanking it. By July 23 all the pick-and-shovel work was finished and Pleasants began bringing in 320 kegs of black powder weighing twenty-five pounds each. This monster four-ton charge was placed in four connected magazines and so sandbagged as to direct the explosion upward. At the final moment, Pleasants did not receive the insulated wire and galvanic batteries he had requested. Still undaunted and improvising, he secured two fifty-foot fuses, spliced them together, attached one end to the charge at the end of the shaft, and ran the remainder as far toward the entrance as it would go; after which he filled the last forty feet of tunnel with close-packed, tamped-down earth so as to contain a backlash and give himself—the fuse lighter—a good chance to sprint to safety. Pleasants and his hard-working miners had done what they promised to do, and it was now up to the generals.

Burnside was in command of the operation. Of his four divisions he chose one consisting of black soldiers hitherto assigned only to guard duty. It was led by Brigadier General Edward Ferrero, and selected because Burnside—an ardent Abolitionist—wanted to give the blacks a chance to prove themselves. For two weeks these two black brigades had been rehearsing their part in the assault. Once the charge was blown and the fort and adjoining trenches obliterated, they were to rush into the crater and expand the gap so that the three following divisions would be able to pass through it and charge into Petersburg itself. Meade and Grant had become so enthused about the prospect of this bizarre scheme that they had assigned close-up support of no fewer than 144 fieldpieces—mortars and siege guns—more than had been massed by either side at Gettysburg. Moreover Grant had directed Hancock's corps supported by Sheridan's cavalry to make a diversion toward Richmond above the James and so draw off Rebel formations from Petersburg. The feint worked, even though Sheridan was bested by Hampton in a four-hour cavalry battle, so that five of Beauregard's eight divisions in Petersburg were sent north of the James. This left the Little Creole with only 18,000 men to defend the besieged city.

This was good news for Burnside, but the bad—nay, the horrendous—news was yet to come. Twelve hours before the charge was to be blown a courier arrived bearing an order from Meade, approved by Grant, for a white division to spearhead the assault rather than Ferrero's well-rehearsed blacks. Here was reverse racism. Grant had already shown at Cold Harbor how sensitive he was to the political fortunes of his commander in chief, and here, as he testified during an investigation, he thought: "If we put the colored troops in front and [the attack] should prove a failure, it would then be said, and very properly, that we were shoving those people ahead to get killed because we did not care anything about them." Perhaps, but this fear of Abolitionist wrath erupting with the presidential election but four months away could also put the entire operation in jeopardy. None of the white soldiers had been rehearsed for the spearhead assignment. To substitute them for the blacks who had, down to a man, understood what was required, and who were also enthusiastic at this chance to excel, could unravel everything. Moreover Burnside was known to have black sympathies and it was he—not Meade or Grant—who chose Ferrero's division. Burnside did protest along these lines, but got nowhere. He was also so shaken by the order that he could not decide which of the three white divisions should lead the assault. So he ordered Brigadiers Robert Potter, Orlando Wilcox and James Ledlie to draw straws—and Ledlie won. Rather, when Ledlie won, the Union lost, for this artillerist had no knowledge of infantry tactics and still less of combat.

In darkness the four divisions were marched into line: Ledlie's in front, Potter's next, then Wilcox and Ferrero last. Elsewhere along the Federal line the men of the other corps stood ready, along with the artillery troops, standing by their loaded guns with taut lanyards. Shortly after three o'clock in the morning of July 30 Pleasants entered the tunnel to light the fuse. The charge was to be blown at three thirty. Ledlie's leading troops glanced nervously at the dark sky ahead. Burnside watched the hands of his watch creep toward the appointed hour. So did Meade and Grant. Three thirty came and went. Still no blast. So did 4 A.M. In another half hour the red edge of the sun was visible to the Union rear. Grant was so disgusted he was about to order Burnside to make the assault without the explosion. Pleasants was distraught. A brave lieutenant and sergeant—by name Harry Reese and Jacob Douty—accompanied him back into the shaft. It was found that the fuse had burned out at the splice. They cut and relit it—and fled for the tunnel entrance 150 yards away, emerging just before the 8,000-pound charge erupted at 4:44 A.M.

"A slight tremor of the earth for a second," an observer wrote, "then the rocking as of an earthquake, and, with a tremendous blast which rent the sleeping hills beyond, a vast column of earth and smoke shoots upward to a great height, its dark sides flashing out sparks of fire, hangs poised for a moment in mid-air, and then, hurtling down with a roaring sound, showers of stones, broken timbers and blackened human limbs, subsides—the gloomy pall of darkening smoke flushing to an angry crimson as it floats away to meet the morning sun."

Behind Ledlie's men crouching in awe the gunners pulled their lanyards and a second roar succeeded the first. Caught between these two cataclysms, the spearheading Bluebellies simply went to pieces and broke for the rear en masse. Surprisingly their officers were able to rally them quickly and within ten minutes had them moving toward the enemy. But as they scrambled over the parapets they found that Burnside had been so shaken by the change in orders that he forgot to clear away the defensive obstacles there. Instead of advancing on a broad front as planned—one brigade following the other—they were jammed into a passage barely ten feet wide, and then, after this struggling file had advanced about a hundred yards they saw what lay before them and stopped short. Here was a monster crater about 170 feet long, 60 to 80 feet wide and 30 feet deep, filled with rubble and sprawling Graybacks, with others writhing in its midst or wandering about dazed. In all 278 Rebels were killed, but the Yankees did not rush forward to kill more but rather busied themselves helping the survivors. Merciful as this might have been, it was not war and the more they dallied the more time Beauregard had to re-form his troops and bring up reinforcements.

To rally the Yankee spearhead was not quite possible inasmuch as General Ledlie had taken cover in a bombproof where he tried to sustain his failing courage with a bottle of rum cadged from an army doctor. So Potter's and Wilcox's blue lines also swept forward to join the confusion in the crater, and then it became apparent that all three divisions could not climb out of this trap thirty feet deep. Since no one had given thought to this eventuality, no scaling ladders had been provided. Next the fourth division—Ferrero's blacks—entered the battle. But they did not descend into the trap but swung around it, making for the high ground ahead of them, singing as they advanced: "We looks like men a-marching on, We looks like men of war." Unfortunately they ran straight into the Graybacks counterattacking under Major General William Mahone. "Capture the Yanks!" these men cried, and then, when they sighted the blacks: "Kill the niggers!" Ferrero was not there to rally his own men, having decided to share Ledlie's bombproof and refreshments. Of his 4,000 men, 1,327—a solid third—were killed or wounded. Now the Rebels had completely recovered and were delivering a plunging fire into the ghastly confusion of the crater below. It was just like—there is no better image—shooting fish in a barrel; and at last Meade called off this fiasco known as the Battle of the Crater after suffering losses of 4,400 men.

It probably would not have ended that way but for Grant's misplaced anxiety for his chief's political fate, Burnside's jittery nerves and the refusal of Meade's engineers to cooperate in what was really not a bizarre plan at all but an ingenious idea that, if carried out properly and with the same dogged devotion that motivated Pleasants and his miners, had a very good chance of success. U. S. Grant never explained why, in his concern for a black bloodbath that would arouse the Abolitionists, he did not balance against this the chance of a spectacular stroke that could end the war or at least result in a smashing victory that would rescue Lincoln's plummeting fortunes.

As it was, some of the more sordid details of the newest defeat, such as the drunken perfidy of Ledlie and Ferrero and the deliberate bayoneting of black Union soldiers trying to surrender by Graybacks insane with fury at the sight of black men in uniform, helped to nourish Northern defeatism to the extent that Horace Greeley could announce flatly: "Mr. Lincoln is already beaten. He cannot be re-elected." Lincoln himself was deeply pessimistic. On August 23 he mystified his Cabinet by asking its members to sign a folded paper which would probably have flabbergasted them had they read it. It said:

> This morning, as for some days past, it seems exceedingly probable that this administration will not be re-elected. Then it will be my duty to so co-operate with the President-elect as to save the Union between the election and the inauguration; as he will have secured his election on such ground that he cannot possibly save it afterward.

In effect, "such ground" was virtual Copperhead control of the Democratic Convention gathered at Chicago that month. Led by Clement Vallandigham, who had slipped back into the North, the Peace Democrats denounced the war in the most violent terms and poured personal vituperation on the head of Lincoln. In the immemorial American way delegates took the convention floor to shout that free speech had been suppressed, and one of them avowed that his right to speak his mind openly had been denied on "the infamous orders of the gorilla tyrant that usurped the Presidential chair." In the end George Brinton McClellan was nominated on a peace platform. McClellan did not actually accept that platform, however, only the support of those who formulated it. And as August ended it appeared that universal war weariness would put Little Mac in the White House.

With hindsight it can be seen that the flood of Federal misfortune—rather of apparent misfortune—had turned to the ebb long before Vallandigham and his bellicose pacifists made common cause with the pacific warrior McClellan. As the month of August began, the Southern facade began to crack and bulge under the strain of inexorable Federal pressure, and the first fissure appeared at Mobile.

Mobile had always seemed to Ulysses S. Grant one of the cornerstones of Confederate power. In 1863 he had told Halleck that an expedition from Mobile could detach Mississippi, Alabama and most of Georgia from the Confederacy. After he took command on March 9, 1864, Grant had wanted to seize Mobile so as to threaten Johnston in his rear while Sherman pressed him on the front. The troops for such an expedition were then on the Red River Campaign under Nathaniel Banks. Their mission was to invade Texas for the sake of cotton and of frightening Napoleon III out of Mexico. However, they were defeated by the Rebels at Sabine Crossroads, Louisiana, on April 8, 1864, and Grant thereafter changed his plan.

Mobile, meanwhile, became an objective of the Union navy. It was the Confederacy's last port on the Gulf of Mexico and it sheltered a Rebel gunboat flotilla and the big ironclad ram *Tennessee*. On August 5 a Federal fleet of wooden sloops, monitors and gunboats under Admiral Farragut entered Mobile Bay.

Farragut had climbed into the rigging of his flagship *Hartford* for a better view, and the ship's skipper, remembering the admiral's attacks of dizziness, had had him lashed there as a precaution. From the leading ship, *Brooklyn,* came a warning that the bay was filled with mines (torpedoes they were called then), and from Farragut came the famous reply: "Damn the torpedoes! Four bells! Captain Drayton, go ahead! Jouett, full speed!" One by one the Rebel gunboats were sunk, the ram *Tennessee* was crippled and captured, and on August 23, the day of Lincoln's deepest pessimism, Fort Morgan was taken by assault.

The Confederacy, severed east from west by Union possession of the Mississippi, was now nearly shut off from the sea. As the month ended, William Tecumseh Sherman tried to cut it again, north from south.

Grant's orders to Sherman were "to move against Johnston's army, to break it up, and to get into the interior of the enemy's country as far as you can, inflicting all the damage you can against their war resources." To do this Sherman now commanded 98,000 men and 254 cannon in the Military Division of the Mississippi based at Chattanooga. This force was divided into three armies—the Cumberland under Thomas; the Ohio under John Schofield; the Tennessee under James McPherson—and four cavalry divisions. Schofield had been transferred from Missouri, where he had served brilliantly as chief of staff to Nathaniel Lyon. If his advice to retreat had been followed at Wilson's Creek a sharp Union setback might have been avoided and Lyon might be still alive. Short, plump and scholarly, Schofield had been graduated from West Point seventh in the class of 1853, had taught philosophy and physics and hoped someday to "work out the mathematical interpretation of all the phenomena of physical sciences, including electricity and magnetism." McPherson was considered by many officers—especially Grant and Sherman—to be the most promising young general in the Union army. Handsome and brilliant, he had been graduated from West Point first in the class of 1853. Still a bachelor at thirty-six, he had planned to marry Miss Emily Hoffman of Baltimore in the winter of 1864. But Grant told him that as an army commander charged with getting his divisions ready for hard fighting, he could not have leave just then, but would have to wait a while. Thus when Sherman got his armies moving toward Georgia and Joe Johnston on May 7, 1864, McPherson was still unmarried but hopeful of placing his ring on his beloved Emily's finger the following winter.

Johnston with his Army of Tennessee was then in Dalton about twenty-five miles below Chattanooga. He had two corps under Hood and Hardee, and a third under Leonidas Polk was en route from Mississippi. When Polk arrived, Johnston would have a total of 53,000, including cavalry under Joseph Wheeler. "Fighting Joe," as he was called, was a leader of mounted men as dashing and nearly as successful as Nathan Bedford Forrest. His most daring exploit was his series of raids on Rosecrans's communications in late 1862, bottling up Old Rosy in Chattanooga during a two-day circuit in which he captured 1,000 men, burned all or part of four wagon trains, seized enough weapons to arm a brigade and inflicted hundreds of thousands of dollars of matériel losses on the enemy. He and his troopers were of great value to Johnston as Sherman approached with his mighty host, enabling Old Joe to make repeated tactical withdrawals to escape the hammer blows aimed at him by the Union general. Always Sherman gave rapid pursuit, but there was no real battle until the one at Resaca on May 14–15, in which Thomas repulsed an advance by Hood. Still sideslipping, Johnston turned and gave battle from naturally advantageous positions atop mountains named Lost, Pine and Brush. Two weeks of fierce fighting ensued, and on June 14 the gallant bishop-general Leonidas Polk lost his life. Sherman's attempt to turn Johnston's right compelled Old Joe to retreat once more, this time to Kenesaw Mountain. There Sherman, frustrated by his fruitless flanking movements, decided to launch a frontal assault, regretting it almost immediately after his Bluebellies were struck to the ground by a storm of shot and shell. In this brief encounter Sherman lost 2,000 men compared to Johnston's casualties of 500. Resuming his sidestepping, the redhead forced Johnston to abandon one by one all the natural barriers he had occupied until a crossing of the Chattahoochee River by Schofield's troops on July 8 removed the last such obstacle between Sherman and Atlanta.

On July 9 Johnston received a delegation sent by Davis from Richmond to impress upon Old Joe the president's dissatisfaction with his delaying campaign. Davis must have known that this was the only tactic possible in the face of a foe so superior in every way as Sherman, but he, like Lincoln, was also in political trouble and needed a spectacular victory. Moreover, he still disliked Johnston, as became obvious when one of the delegates quoted Davis as saying that "if he were in your place he could whip Sherman now."

"Yes," Old Joe replied with icy scorn. "I know Mr. Davis thinks he can do a great many things other men would hesitate to attempt. For instance, he tried to do what God failed to do. He tried to make a soldier of Braxton Bragg, and you know the result. It couldn't be done."

Eight days later, on July 17, Davis replaced Johnston with Hood.

". . . Mr. Davis had an exalted opinion of his own military genius," U. S. Grant was to write. "On several occasions during the war he came to the relief of the Union army by means of his *superior military genius.*"

One of these occasions was his putting Hood in the place of Johnston, a skilled professional fighting a classic delaying action and actually prepared to make Sherman pay at least two more months for possession of Atlanta, and then intending to draw him still farther away from his base. Valiant and indomitable though John Bell Hood was, he simply was incapable of exercising high command.

Born in Kentucky June 1, 1831, the son of a distinguished physician who had founded his own medical school, Hood early in life by his love of the outdoors and of stories about Indian-fighting ancestors showed no fondness for study or to follow his father into the medical profession. He wanted West Point, and he got it. At six feet two inches and massively built with wide shoulders and a deep chest, handsome with tawny blond hair and dreamy deep blue eyes that were often sad in repose, he was indeed a striking physical specimen. Graduated forty-fourth among the 55 cadets of the class of 1853, he was delighted to find himself in the elite 2nd Cavalry Regiment with such famous officers as Albert Sidney Johnston, Robert E. Lee and George Thomas. Here he also showed a fondness for local country lasses he encountered on the frontier, so much so that Colonel Lee told him: "Never marry unless you can do so into a family which will enable your children to feel proud of both sides of the house."

During his service against the Indians he also made it plain that his unconquerable fighting spirit was not matched by military sagacity. Chasing marauding Comanches, he pressed on with such élan that his band of twenty-five troopers dwindled to seventeen, and he was led into a trap surrounded by a hundred screaming, shooting "hostiles" outside a ring of blazing grass. An arrow pierced his hand and he calmly broke it and pulled the pieces free. Then he led a valorous charge that drove the Indians off. For this he received a commendation for bravery, rather than a deserved reprimand for recklessness, and thus was convinced early in his career that victory—and with it advancement—is to be achieved more by the heart than by the head.

After Sumter Hood adopted Texas as his home state and came to Richmond seeking high command, which he received by dint of his all-out assault upon the hearts of the influential ladies of the capital, and his ability by his mere presence to subdue the riotous, undisciplined men of the 4th Texas Regiment. Of this feat Mary Chesnut wrote: "When Hood came with his sad Quixotic face, the face of an old Crusader, who believed in his cause, his cross and his crown, we were not prepared for such a man as [being] the beau-ideal of the wild Texans." He was indeed, and soon he had a brigade of them, and as they entered battle crying, "Hood! Hood! Hood!" they became by their blazing valor as celebrated as Jackson's famous Stonewall Brigade. After his left arm was crippled at Gettysburg, Hood lost his right leg at Chickamauga, and was compelled to enter battle strapped to his horse, like El Cid, the very apotheosis of valor.

And yet when William Tecumseh Sherman heard that Hood had replaced Johnston, he was delighted.

To impress President Davis, Hood on July 20 promptly attacked Sherman at Peachtree Creek about three miles north of Atlanta, using the plan that Johnston had prepared for just that purpose. This was to strike Thomas with the corps of Hardee and Polk, now commanded by Alexander Stewart, a tall, professorial man with wavy short hair and a big belligerent nose.

Known as "Old Straight" to his men, Stewart's war record read like a roll call of the Western battles. While these two formations struck at Old Slow Trot to the northeast, the rest of the Army of Tennessee held the fortifications of Atlanta against Schofield and McPherson to the east. As might be expected of soldiers led by Hood, the Rebels attacked with great spirit, but they were met with Yankee determination and undone by poor coordination between Hood and Hardee and the necessity to withdraw Pat Cleburne's division from the assault to help the forces defending against McPherson. Peachtree Creek was a small battle with large casualties: Hood lost 4,796 of the 19,000 men he sent into action, and Sherman 1,779 from his 20,000 engaged.

Undaunted by his losses, Hood prepared to attack again. This time he prepared a bold and promising plan. It was based upon exploiting McPherson's relative isolation from the rest of Sherman's army, as well as his lack of a cavalry screen. Stewart's corps was to confront Thomas and Schofield, holding them in place, while Benjamin Cheatham's corps struck McPherson frontally as he moved west toward Atlanta from Decatur. Cheatham was a former Tennessee farmer with a battle record the equal of Stewart's as he successively commanded a brigade, a division and now a corps. Meanwhile, Hardee's corps and Wheeler's cavalry were to attempt to turn McPherson's left flank by a march deep into his rear, and thus destroy the Union Army of the Tennessee.

On the night of July 21, Hood began the offensive by ostentatiously retiring from his outer defenses into the fortifications of Atlanta. Thinking the Gate City was being evacuated, McPherson's spearheads advanced westward along the Decatur Road. On the morning of the twenty-second they were struck hard by Rebel skirmishers of the divisions of W. H. T. Walker and William Bates. The Graybacks came on in strength, but because of errors by Hardee and Walker they found that they had not marched far enough to the east to get around McPherson's flank. Thus they were twice driven back by the Bluebellies of Grenville Dodge's corps, and during the repulses General Walker was killed.

McPherson was at lunch when he received reports that his left was in danger. Mounting his horse, he galloped off to the sound of cannon followed by his orderly. En route he ordered up a brigade toward what appeared to be a dangerous gap between Dodge's corps and that of Francis Blair. McPherson was bent low over his mount's withers to avoid being swept from the saddle by low-hanging branches. So was his orderly. Graybacks who had come through the yawning gap opened fire and a bullet pierced McPherson's back traveling upward toward his heart. He fell heavily from the saddle, and so did the orderly, knocked from his seat by a branch. "Are you hurt, sir?" the orderly asked. "Oh, orderly, I am," McPherson replied in agony as he buried his face in the dust, quivered once—and died. Next the orderly felt himself being yanked erect by his belt while a Rebel snarled, "Git to the rear, you Yankee son-of-a-bitch!" Then a captain rode up, astonished by the sight of the two-star Yankee general lying dead in all his military finery. "Who is this lying here?" he asked the grief-stricken orderly. "It is General McPherson, sir," the orderly sobbed. "You have killed the best man in our army."

Still the Confederate attack threatened to exploit the breach between Dodge and Blair—until the reserve brigade ordered up by McPherson came slamming into the close-packed gray ranks, driving them back. Next General John Alexander Logan, Abraham Lincoln's friend and the best of his political generals, took command of the Army of the Tennessee. Waving his black, bell-crowned hat, his long jet black hair and his guardsman's mustache flying in the wind, Logan rode among the embattled Bluebellies crying, "Will you hold this line for me? Will you hold this line?" "Black Jack!" the men chanted in reply, "Black Jack!" Gradually the Army of the Tennessee stiffened and held in the face of Hardee's assaults, and Hood, who had delayed committing Cheatham until midafternoon, finally sent him into action bolstered by 5,000 Georgia militia. But the strike came too late. Had it occurred earlier, the faltering Army of the Tennessee might have been destroyed. Thus the Battle of Atlanta ended in a smashing Union victory. Federal losses were 430 killed, 1,559 wounded for a total of 1,989, plus 1,733 missing. Confederate casualties were estimated at 7,000 dead and wounded plus another thousand missing.

This was the clinching battle of Sherman's Atlanta campaign, but the redhead was too grief-stricken by McPherson's death to exult in it. He wept openly in the presence of his staff, yet his anguish was in no way comparable to the agony of McPherson's fiancée, Emily Hoffman. Daughter of a strongly Southern family which had disapproved of her engagement to a Yankee general, she heard a relative cry: "I have the most wonderful news— McPherson is dead!" With this Emily fled to her room where she remained for a year with curtains drawn, silently consuming the three trays of food placed daily outside her door—seeing and speaking to no one. Sherman poured out his heart to her in a long letter: "I yield to no one on earth but yourself the right to exceed me in lamentations for our dead hero. Rather the bride of McPherson dead than the wife of the richest man in Baltimore . . . I see him now, so handsome, so smiling, on his fine black horse, booted and spurred, with his easy seat, the personification of the gallant knight."

Hood now withdrew his own battered Army of Tennessee into the defenses of Atlanta, while Sherman cautiously pursued. Making no attempt to attack the city's formidable fortifications, he laid it under siege and a steady bombardment, drawing his noose ever tighter. For another month or so there ensued around the Gate City a series of infantry battles and cavalry raids and counter-raids. Hood's sortie at Ezra Church on August 28 was hurled back, and his assault on Sherman's flank at Jonesboro on August 31–September 1 was repulsed with heavy losses. Hood's casualties were 1,725 killed and wounded, compared to Sherman's 179. This was a battle Hood could not afford to lose, and it convinced him that Atlanta was doomed. On September 1 his rear guard marched out of a city half wrecked by Federal artillery and retiring Rebel dynamiters, and on the following day the jubilant Federals marched in. A few days later William Tecumseh Sherman made his famous report, beginning: "So Atlanta is ours, and fairly won."

News of the fall of Atlanta electrified the North. It stunned the soft-war forces which had rallied around McClellan and silenced the plotters in Lincoln's own party who had been secretly preparing to repudiate the president in favor of "some candidate who commands the confidence of the country." Down at Petersburg, an overjoyed U. S. Grant ordered a loaded 100-gun salute fired at the Rebel batteries.

Obviously, the Union's pressure on the Confederacy was becoming unbearable, and before the month was over it had opened another seam in the beautiful and prosperous Shenandoah Valley.

Here was one of the South's great assets. It not only provided food and forage for Lee's army but aimed a dagger at the Federal heart in Washington. Because the Valley ran southwest to northeast, a Confederate army marching down it would be moving directly toward the Union capital; but a Union army ascending the Shenandoah would only be going farther away from Richmond. Again and again Lee had taken advantage of this geographical accident. Stonewall Jackson and others had gone repeatedly into the Valley to frighten Washington and draw Union troops away from Richmond for the Northern capital's defense. It might almost be said that Lee defended Richmond in the Valley, just as he also supplied his army from there.

Of these facts U. S. Grant was well aware. He wanted the Valley cleared of Rebels and an army of hungry Federals to "eat out Virginia clear and clean as far as they go, so that crows flying over it for the balance of the season will have to carry their provender with them." The man eventually selected to carry out this mission was Philip Sheridan.

At first Grant had ordered that no houses were to be burned and that the Valley's inhabitants—many of them pacifists with a religious horror of war—though notified to move, were to be treated justly. Sheridan echoed these instructions. However, such compassionate reservations are not possible to an army ordered to make "a desert" of a lush and smiling garden, and it is difficult not to suspect that they were advance disclaimers for the excesses that both Grant and Sheridan must have known were inevitable.

One reason that excesses were inevitable was that by the summer of 1864 the American Civil War had followed the logic of warfare, which argues that when the enemy does not quickly submit, then more and more brutal means must be brought to bear to compel his submission. A thickening fog of hatred had also descended upon both camps, especially after both sides learned of the horrible treatment of their captured soldiers. There were also atrocities committed by both sides, and again the South led the way with the burning of Lawrence, Kansas, by Colonel William Quantrill's raiders. Irregular bands such as Quantrill's were another reason that the soldiers of Sheridan's Army of the Shenandoah were not going to fill the hypocritical bill of a gentle desolation. Many of these guerrillas operating in the Shenandoah were little better than outlaws. Deserters and desperadoes, they had no stomach for the battle line but preferred the sudden midnight swoop and the quick getaway; and they were detested as much by Confederate commanders as they were dreaded by Federal soldiers. The fires of hatred, then, had crept into that last calm crevice of war: the breast of the common soldier. Johnny Reb and Billy Yank had openly fraternized from Vicksburg to Petersburg, swapping jokes and comic taunts and trading Confederate tobacco for Yankee newspapers and coffee. But now they hated, if not each other, at least the other side; and in this growing mood of savagery the Union picked up the red-hot iron of total war and pressed it down hard on the Shenandoah.

The results were red and smoking scars. From mountain to mountain billowing clouds of smoke shut out the sun by day, and by night the shadows danced and flickered in the light of glowing bonfires. Stacks of hay and straw were burned, barns filled with harvested crops were set blazing, all supplies of use to man or beast were set afire and all cattle were driven off. Everywhere that Sheridan's troops lifted the torch they were met by throngs of weeping old men, women and children, but the work of scorching the enemy's earth went on inexorably. As a Union chaplain wrote: "The time had fully come to peel this land and put an end to the long strife for its possession."

The strife, however, was far from over. Alarmed, Lee sent Jubal Early to drive Sheridan out of the Valley. Early was a descendant of an old Virginia family that had migrated from England in the middle of the seventeenth century. A good student, he might have been graduated from West Point much higher than his rank of eighteenth but for his hot temper, his sloppy dress, and an aberrant horror of touching brass. His classmates remembered him best for his mess-hall fistfight with Lewis Armistead. Early fought in Florida and Mexico, after which he fell in love with a beautiful young Philadelphia debutante whose life he had saved by riding into a rain-swollen stream to pluck her from a sinking carriage. He had hoped to marry her, until she sent him a newspaper clipping describing her wedding to someone else. This soured Old Jube. Tall, thin, hard-drinking, with a rasping wit to deliver his misanthropic gibes, he became one of the best of Lee's band of able lieutenants, receiving his third star just before setting out in pursuit of Sheridan. Early was also impetuous, and he did not hesitate to hurl his 15,000 lean veterans against Sheridan's 45,000.

The two forces met at Winchester, where Early caught Sheridan's advance guard and drove it back. Riding forward on his great black horse Rienzi, Sheridan built up his battle line and pressed the Rebels back. Not since the days of Fighting Phil Kearny had Federal soldiers seen a Union general so far forward. Waving his little flat hat, crying out, "Come on, boys, come on," disdaining enemy fire, laughing when a shell burst directly overhead, the fiery little general on the big horse infused his army with a dash and daring hitherto unknown among the Federals of the Shenandoah. Just before dusk, a splendid Union cavalry charge struck the Confederates in their left flank and rear to roll them back—and Winchester was another Union victory to lift Lincoln's reviving political stock still higher. Three days later, on September 22, Frémont withdrew from the presidential race.

Sheridan pursued Early up the valley, still spreading devastation as he moved, and still harassed by the attacks on his supply line made by the masterful Confederate partisan chieftain John Mosby. Mosby played on Sheridan's line like a virtuoso, forcing the Union general to detach large bodies of troops to protect his rear.

By mid-October Sheridan's army was encamped at Cedar Creek, twenty miles south of Winchester. Sheridan had gone to Washington for a brief visit. He did not think that the twice-beaten Early would dare attack his powerful army. On the night of October 18, Sheridan was back in Winchester—and the daring Early had already made up his mind to strike the Union left at Cedar Creek the next morning. Out of the misty dawn the Confederates poured on that memorable October 19, 1864, rolling back the surprised Federals and threatening to rout Sheridan's entire army. Up in Winchester, an officer awakened Sheridan and told him he had heard artillery. "It's all right," Sheridan said, explaining that a scouting force was "merely feeling the enemy." Two and a half hours passed before Sheridan was mounted on Rienzi, and it was then that he heard the roar of artillery to the south. Leaning forward in his saddle, he heard it grow at a rate indicating that his own army must be falling back. He had heard:

> The terrible rumble, grumble and roar
> Telling the battle was on once more—
> And Sheridan twenty miles away!

Sheridan did not go galloping wildly all the way down that road, as Read's poem says, but he did urge his horse forward into the frantic backwash of a beaten army. Wagon trains, sutlers and camp followers, walking wounded and artillery wagons, stragglers and skulkers, all flowed back toward Winchester, their hurry and their fright eloquent of a disaster at the front. Sheridan rode faster now, coming at a gallop in front of some fifty mounted men. Now he saw real soldiers retreating, and he drew rein to shout at them: "Turn back! Face the other way! If I had been here with you this morning this wouldn't have happened." On he rode, crying, "Turn back! Turn back!" swinging his little cap and calling for more and more speed from the tireless Rienzi. Then he fell silent, his face setting into stone while his piercing black eyes took on the dull red stubborn glint of a spirit defiant in defeat.

Suddenly, Sheridan had reached the battlefield. Across the battle line he galloped while a thunderous great cheer broke from the throats of his army. "Sheridan! Sheridan!" his soldiers shouted, as though the mere repetition of his name would avert disaster. Such emotional outbursts rarely occur on modern battlefields, but there were men there who swore that Sheridan's presence meant: "No more doubt or chance for doubt existed; we were safe, perfectly and unconditionally safe, and every man knew it."

Regrouped, revitalized, the Union army swept forward; and it was irresistible. The redoubtable Jubal Early and his veterans could not contain such furious waves of blue, and the fact of Sheridan's ride was thus equal to the legend: by his sudden appearance the Union general turned defeat into victory and closed the Shenandoah to the South forever.

Mobile, Atlanta, the Shenandoah, they were names that stuck in the minds of Northern voters going to the polls on that fateful November 8, 1864. There, with ballots not bullets, the real battle was being fought.

There, in an event unique in history, a democracy engaged in a dreadful civil war was electing a president. At Washington on that rain-swept night Abraham Lincoln awaited the result in the war telegraph office. He was confident. He told of another rainy election night, when he had lost to Stephen Douglas. Walking home on a slippery hogback, "my foot slipped from under me, knocking the other one out of the way, but I recovered myself and lit square, and I said to myself: 'It's a slip and not a fall.'" Toward midnight Abraham Lincoln knew that he had been reelected. Well-wishers besieged the telegraph office with a brass band and demands for a speech.

"It is no pleasure to me to triumph over anyone," Abraham Lincoln said, "but I give thanks to the Almighty for this evidence of the people's resolution to stand by free government and the rights of humanity."

63

∎

Fort Fisher: Sherman's March

A S THE YEAR 1864 came to a close the Civil War possessed all those hideous features that make the Medusa of modern war. It had begun with gay flags and blaring bands and pink-cheeked farm boys in baggy red pants, and it was ending with sabered pigs and burnt barns and weeping women shoved rudely aside by gaunt men with hollows in the cheeks where innocence once had bloomed.

Along the way the Civil War had introduced the breech-loading rifle, barbed wire, hand grenades, winged grenades, wooden wire-bound mortars, rockets and even booby traps. Magazine rifles were invented and also the Requa machine gun. At Mobile the Confederacy had built a submarine, the 35-foot *R. L. Hunley,* which was propelled by a screw worked from the inside by eight men, and on February 17, 1864, the *Hunley* torpedoed and sank the U.S.S. *Housatonic* and went down with her. The first battle of ironclads had been fought between *Monitor* and *Merrimac,* while on land there were armored trains as well as land mines. Trench warfare as grim and dirty as any in World War I had already started outside Petersburg, and poison gas was foreshadowed by the Confederate officer who toyed with the notion of a stink-shell to give off "offensive gases" and cause "suffocating effect." Flag and lamp signaling also was used, as well as field telegraph, while both sides maintained observation balloons. In fact, "the meanest trick of the war" occurred when the North captured a Rebel balloon made of silk dresses donated by patriotic ladies. Finally, the restless mind of Ben Butler had come up with the forerunner of the flame thrower, a "small garden engine" squirting Greek fire. "Also he is going to get a gun that shoots seven miles and taking direction by compass, burn the city of Richmond with shells of Greek fire." In this, the concepts of Big Bertha and of fire bombing are rolled into one, and Butler may have been unique in

615

thinking of constructing an auger to bore a tunnel five feet in diameter and thus dig his way into Richmond. Except for tanks, airplanes and atomic bombs, then, the foundations for the arsenal of modern warfare had been laid; and yet, while the means of killing and maiming the enemy were being improved, the barbaric practice of mistreating his captured soldiers was allowed to continue.

Some 408,000 soldiers of both sides fell into the hands of their enemy during the Civil War, and of these about 56,000 died in agony and neglect in the remote prison camps of North and South. At the time this shameful record produced bitter and mutual recrimination, and although the controversy continues to rage until this day, it would seem that these unfortunate prisoners of war were not the victims of deliberate brutality born of malice, but rather of inefficiency and inexperience. Granting that individual cruelty among captors always has and always will be encountered in any prison compound anywhere, the suffering inflicted upon the captive soldiers of both sides was much more the result of short-sightedness and lack of resources than of deliberate policy. North and South went to war without a single prison camp capable of holding more than a handful of men. Dixie expected no war, Yankeeland anticipated a short, quick one. Because the early battles were small, the few soldiers captured could be held in obsolete forts, county jails or converted factories and warehouses. If these facilities became overcrowded, informal exchanges of prisoners were made, often on the very battlefield, or paroles granted. A paroled soldier would be set free on his signed promise not to take up arms again. But the Confederacy, already feeling the burden of feeding its army let alone prisoners, soon pressed for a formal cartel, as agreements on the exchange of prisoners are called. This Lincoln was reluctant to grant, for it would imply recognition of the Confederate government. When it was agreed that negotiations were to be between armies, an exchange cartel was accepted on July 22, 1862: thus, a private for a private; a non-commissioned officer for two privates; a lieutenant, four; and a commanding general, sixty.

This agreement lasted for ten months, breaking down over the South's threat to execute or reenslave captured blacks, and its duplicity in the handling of parolees. After Grant paroled 30,000 Rebels at Vicksburg, he and his countrymen were enraged to learn that some of them were fighting at Chickamauga, for the South had arbitrarily declared them exchanged when actually they had not been. The South also refused to treat blacks as prisoners of war or to stop arming paroled soldiers, although at the end of 1863 the Confederacy did indicate a willingness to exchange black captives who were legally free when they enlisted. But, insisted the chief of the Confederate Bureau of War: "We cannot on any principle allow that *our property* can acquire adverse rights by virtue of the theft of it." More to the point, Secretary of War Seddon had earlier directed that "we ought never to be inconvenienced with such prisoners . . . summary execution must therefore be inflicted on those taken."

Such a policy guided deliberate massacre of surrendering blacks at the Crater, Poison Spring and at Fort Pillow, where Nathan Bedford Forrest massacred about 100 blacks, declaring: "The river was dyed with the blood of the slaughtered for two hundred yards. . . . It is hoped that these facts will demonstrate to the Northern people that negro soldiers cannot cope with Southerners." A Federal sergeant has described another massacre of blacks at Plymouth on the North Carolina coast in April 1864:

> All the negroes found in blue uniform or with any outward marks of a Union soldier upon him was killed—I saw some taken into the woods and hung—Others I saw stripped of all their clothing, and they stood upon the bank of the river with their faces riverwards and then they were shot—Still others were killed by having their brains beaten out by the butt end of the muskets in the hands of the Rebels . . .

Lincoln and his cabinet repeatedly pondered their dilemma: if they retaliated—even against guilty Rebel prisoners—they would set in motion a dreadful cycle of blood-for-blood. But they did threaten it, and eventually such pressure brought about the South's decision to regard freed blacks from the North as bonafide prisoners of war. This did not mean equal treatment, for they were usually assigned to latrine details or other onerous duties.

Actually the North was not as outraged by the treatment of black prisoners as by the suffering of all Union captives. The harvest of prisoners reaped by the Confederate armies as both Grant and Sherman pressed their relentless attacks of 1864 were just too much for the South's jerry-built prisons and stockades to handle. The same bloody battles had also filled the prison camps of the North to overflowing, so that conditions there deteriorated to the extent that Rebel suffering, sickness and death began to rival the ordeal of the Southern camps.

But no prison—North or South—could even compare to the daily portion of death, disease, starvation rations, brutality and executions that characterized the camp at Andersonville in southwest Georgia. By August of 1864 some 33,000 Yankee prisoners were herded into a stockade of

twenty-six acres—about 34 square feet to a man. (By comparison, at El-
mira, New York, the worst of the Federal prisons, 9,600 captives lived
inside a forty-acre enclosure, an average of 180 square feet per man—and
all of them dwelt in barracks.) There were no barracks at Andersonville, not
even tents. Food and even water was scarce, and any man daring to slake
his thirst in the scummy green surface of a little stream that ran through
camp soon found his face so swollen that he could not see. Others fell sick
of eating poisonous root to supplement starvation rations consisting of a
pint each of wormy peas and meal plus a strip of moldy bacon daily.
Everyone was black from the greasy smoke of resinous pine wood used for
cooking. Without shade, in a Deep South summer and with no shelter
except what they could rig from sticks, blankets and odd bits of cloth,
ravaged by dysentery, dropsy, scurvy and malaria, more than a hundred
prisoners died each day during that dreadful summer. All together 13,000
of the 45,000 men eventually imprisoned there died or were shot.

Shooting prisoners became common after the arrival of Captain Henry
Wirz, who has been described by John Ransom in his famous diary: "Is not
a very prepossessing looking chap. Is about thirty-five or forty years old,
rather tall, and a little stoop-shouldered; skin has a pale, white-livered look
with thin lips. Has a sneering sort of cast of countenance. Makes a fellow
feel as if he would like to go up and boot him . . ." Wirz was fond of roaming
the camp with a guard detail searching for escape tunnels. If he found one
the men digging it were shot. He also circumscribed the camp with a "dead
line" about twelve or fourteen feet inside the wall on which the young boys
and elderly men employed as Confederate guards were stationed. If a
Yankee came too close to the dead line he was summarily shot dead by
these trigger-happy misfits.

Although dignitaries and ranking officers frequently visited Andersonville—among them Howell Cobb, now a general—no humane voice was
raised in protest. Indeed an Atlanta newspaper in August declared: "During
one of the intensely hot days of last week more than 300 sick and wounded
Yankees died at Andersonville. We thank Heaven for such blessings." When
such comment was read in the North it provoked a storm of anguished
demands for retaliation or renewal of exchange, or the president was attacked for sacrificing thousands of white soldiers just to protect a few
blacks. But Lincoln could no more desert the principle that the blacks were
bonafide Union soldiers than he could revoke Emancipation. He did, however, permit a limited retaliation whereby the rations of Southerners in
Federal prison camps were reduced to the level of the Confederate army's
issue. In practice, however, Rebel soldiers seldom received the full official

issue, so that their captive countrymen actually were eating better than they were.

The exchange impasse continued until January 1865, when the South, hoping soon to begin recruiting black slaves for its own army, suddenly found the "barbaric" Yankee policy acceptable. The cartel began functioning again and within the next three months thousands of prisoners were exchanged each week, until the end of the war liberated everyone.

Except for Andersonville and the unspeakable Captain Wirz, it is not true to suggest that the Confederacy deliberately mistreated its captives. The fault lay rather with the South's deficient economy. A nation unable to feed its own soldiers and civilians properly cannot be expected to feed enemy prisoners better, and if it cannot supply enough tents to shelter its own troops should it build barracks for the enemy's? Because the South had constantly anticipated the renewal of the cartel it made no long-range plans for its prison system, and this also contributed to its inefficiency. But the claims of Jefferson Davis and Alexander Stephens that the suffering in Southern prisons was caused by Lincoln's refusal to exchange prisoners unless Union blacks be considered bonafide soldiers, or that the death rate in Southern prisons was actually lower than in those of the North must be emphatically rejected. The first assertion rests upon the conviction that black slaves were *property,* and the second upon such dubious facts as the supposed horrors of Federal camps such as Johnson's Island, Ohio. In truth, the death rate at Johnson's Island was 2 percent, while it was 29 percent at Andersonville—and there was no Captain Wirz at Johnson's Island. Figures that suggest an overall death rate of 15.5 percent in the Southern prisons and 12 percent in those of the North are based upon an estimate of 194,743 captured Yankees compared to 214,865 prisoners from Dixie. In actuality, there were far more Federals than that number taken prisoner, but the South's prison records were either lost, destroyed or not even kept.

But if Andersonville and Captain Wirz were to be removed from this sordid story of misery, neither side would have much to brag about. Nor would the North feel very proud of having introduced the Hitlerian tactics of *schrecklichkeit*—frightfulness—during Sherman's march through Georgia.

Of all the remarkable leaders of the Civil War the most original was William Tecumseh Sherman. Many military historians acclaim him as the first of the modern strategists. Certainly he was the first to see that industrialized war shifted the target from the military to the economic and moral. A nation must be struck in its capacity to fight and its will to fight, Sherman reasoned.

This meant bypassing its armies and attacking its industrial potential and its population; this meant nothing less than deliberate desolation and demoralization: this was *schrecklichkeit*.

The man who conceived this strategy was not, as the descendants of his Southern victims maintain, the reincarnation of Attila the Hun. He was rather an unusually perceptive, gifted and complicated human being, in whose character and career can be found perhaps more marks of genius than in those of any other American commander before or since. Chief of all, he cared nothing for human respect. He wore rumpled, muddy, mismatching uniforms; he conceded a russet beard to the chin fashions of the day but kept it close-cut; he was tall, lanky, awkward, given to shoving his hands into his pockets or rubbing up his thatch of coarse red hair; his face was wrinkled, his nose pointed and red, and his little eyes black and sharp. "Uncle Billy," as the soldiers called Sherman, talked rapidly in a high voice about a host of subjects, his features often all but obscured by clouds of "seegar" smoke and his clothing covered by a fine film of cigar ash. One young lieutenant who met him thought him the "ideal Yankee," while admitting that he had "experienced almost an exhaustion from the excitement of his vigorous presence."

In Sherman were combined so many seemingly conflicting qualities that he would seem to have been crippled by that foolish passion for consistency that is called "the hobgoblin of little minds." Actually he was balanced: quick in thought and careful in detail, visionary in planning and practical in execution, dynamic yet reflective, warmhearted but coolheaded. Sherman was one of those unique double personalities who are at once the man who thinks and the man who feels. Neither gained the ascendancy, but such a struggle between head and heart must necessarily carry a man very close to insanity, and so it was no wonder that he was often thought "crazy" or that he, too, was touched with that divine discontent which sank him deep in despondency or sent him soaring to the heights of inspiration.

By the fall of 1864 he knew this well enough to make one of the boldest gambles in military history. By then, Hood had shown that he could prevent Sherman from destroying his army. By then also, Sherman had learned that his long supply line back to Louisville was becoming a costly nuisance. First Nathan Bedford Forrest had gone into Tennessee to tear up railroads and cause enough trouble to compel Sherman to send Thomas and 30,000 men back to Nashville to contain him. Then Hood himself had begun to maneuver against the Union supply line north of Atlanta, hoping to draw Sherman north. Hood did not hurt the supply line much, but neither did Sherman ever catch Hood in a finish fight. Finally, with the boldness born of desperation, Hood began marching his entire army toward Tennessee in the belief that Sherman would now have to abandon Atlanta and come after him.

Sherman's response to Hood's gamble was an even bolder decision. He proposed to ignore the enemy army and attack instead the spirit of the South. He decided to abandon his supply line and lead some 60,000 men from Atlanta to Savannah and the sea. An army of human locusts would devour the food so badly needed by Lee's hungry soldiers in Petersburg and then destroy what they could not eat or carry off. They would make the people of Georgia feel the harsh hand of war in their very homes, and they would make the entire South feel helpless at the sight of a Union army moving unchecked through its heartland. "I can make the march, and make Georgia howl!" Sherman told Grant, and eventually both Grant and Lincoln agreed.

On November 15, then, as Hood marched north toward Tennessee, Sherman set his face in the opposite direction: the seacoast. First, however, he burned Atlanta. It is said that Sherman intended to wreck and burn only railroad installations and factories, that he wanted to spare shops and stores and private homes. Nevertheless, as the South still maintains with much justice, Sherman's soldiers were "a mite careless with powder and fire," and most of Atlanta went up in flames.

Nor were Sherman's soldiers very careful about property rights as they moved on a sixty-mile front through a rich land where the harvest was in, the barns were stuffed with corn and forage, smokehouses bulged with hams and bacon, and the fields were full of cattle. Each morning each brigade detached a forage company of about 50 men to comb the countryside a few miles to either side of the brigade's line of march. Seizing farm wagons and carriages, they loaded them with bacon, eggs, cornmeal, chickens, turkeys and ducks, sweet potatoes—whatever could be carried off—and delivered their loads to the brigade commissaries at the end of each day. Meanwhile, other units drove off livestock. What they could not take, they killed. To save ammunition, they sabered pigs and poleaxed horses and mules between the ears. From sunup to sundown lean veterans accustomed to hardtack and salt pork gorged themselves on ham and yams and fresh beef, and as they advanced across the state they grew fat and sleek. So did the blacks to whom they gave the plantation masters' food, and who frolicked on the heels of the advancing host in the living embodiment of the famous ditty:

Say Darkies has you seen old Massa
Wid de muffstache on his face
Go long de road sometime dis mornin'
Like he gwine to leave de place?

De massa run, ha-ha!
De darkey stay, ho-ho!
I tink it must be Kingdom Coming
And de yar ob Jubilo.

It was indeed the Year of Jubilo for the blacks, just as for Sherman's laughing veterans the march had become a picnic promenade, but to the South it seemed a wanton and barbaric ruin that cried out to heaven for vengeance. From wing to wing sixty miles apart there rose columns of smoke as the advancing army trailed its own somber clouds of destruction. Warehouses, bridges, barns, machine shops, depots and factories were burned. Not even houses were spared, especially not by the "bummers," those deserters, desperadoes and looters, North and South, who were drawn to the march for the sake of spoil. These were the men who forced old men and helpless women to divulge the secret places where silver, jewelry and money were hidden. They danced with muddy, hobnailed boots on snow-white linen or gleaming table tops, smashing furniture with gun butts, slashing feather beds with sabers and shattering windows and mirrors with empty bottles. Sherman, who might have restrained them, did little to stop them. "War is cruelty, and you cannot refine it," he had told the people of Atlanta, and it was his intention to demonstrate that the Confederacy was powerless to protect its people against it.

Railroad-wrecking was another object of the march, and to this, Sherman wrote, "I gave my personal attention." After the rails had been pried up they were heated over bonfires of crossties and then twisted around trees to be left useless, and the countryside was festooned with "Sherman hairpins" or "Jeff Davis neckties." Thus like a flow of molten lava sixty miles wide and three hundred miles long, the Union army marched to the sea.

Meanwhile, General Hood had begun a successful drive into Tennessee. On November 29–30 near Franklin he nearly trapped a Federal army under John Schofield, but the Federals eventually escaped after savage fighting which caused the death of five Confederate generals—among them the gallant Pat Cleburne. Hood pursued toward Nashville, where Thomas blocked his path. Thomas, in fact, was in position to destroy Hood; and a jittery U. S. Grant ordered him to do so before the Rebel army could bypass

Nashville and invade the North. Such a maneuver might upset all Grant's plans and thus prolong a war that seemed on the verge of being won. But the stolid Thomas moved in his own good time, so slowly, in fact, that Grant resolved to relieve him. On December 15, however, Thomas struck Hood with such fury that the Confederate army was sent south in headlong retreat. That was the South's last gasp in the West, and six days later, when Sherman's sleek tatterdemalions jubilantly pitched camp outside Savannah, the death rattle of the Confederacy was clearly audible on both sides of the Mason-Dixon line. Within another month the last link with the outside world was cut.

Fort Fisher at the mouth of the Cape Fear River in North Carolina guarded the port of Wilmington a few miles upstream, the Confederacy's last outlet to the sea. Almost nightly Rebel blockade-runners slipped past Fisher's protective guns bringing to Wilmington those vital cargoes without which the South could not live. Two days before Christmas of 1864 a Federal invasion fleet stood outside the Cape Fear preparing to storm the fort. Admiral David Dixon Porter commanded the fleet, while two divisions of Union troops numbering some 6,500 men were under Benjamin Butler.

Why the safely-reelected Abraham Lincoln should have allowed such an important command to pass to this woefully inept political general is difficult to comprehend. Butler by his harsh hand in New Orleans had already made it almost impossible for the president to launch his cherished Reconstruction program in Louisiana. He had alienated New Orleans by publicly hanging a man convicted by a drumhead court of helping to tear down an American flag, and then infuriated the entire South by his infamous Woman Order threatening to jail as a whore any woman showing contempt for a Federal soldier. Jefferson Davis had responded to this last by issuing an order that if Butler were captured he should be executed on the spot, and now, it seemed to the 1,371 aroused Graybacks holding Fort Fisher, that that opportunity was at hand.

But Ben, with his penchant for innovation—not to say crack-brained schemes—was not going to risk capture by an amphibious assault on the fort, but rather was going to blow it up. To do this the overage gunboat *Louisiana* had been stripped to resemble a blockade-runner, and stuffed with 215 tons of gunpowder, all above the water line to maximize the explosion. A skeleton crew would run her as close to the sprawling fort as her eight-foot draft allowed, and then set the clockwork fuses ticking before rowing away to safety. Simultaneously with the explosion Butler's troops would be landing between the fort and Wilmington ready to march blood-lessly down into the remains.

On the night of December 23 *Louisiana* dropped anchor about 250 yards offshore of the fort. At 11:48 the fuses were started and the crewmen made their escape. Twelve miles offshore the sailors aboard Porter's sixty warships cast their eyes anxiously toward the starlit stretch of beach front-ing the fort. Porter gazing at his watch was vexed when the hands passed the anticipated eruption time of 1:18. Minutes passed.... Then at 1:40 there came an encompassing and instantaneous flash of light illuminating even the far-off fleet, followed by a rumble sounding like hardly more than a deep cough and then a tremendous cloud of black smoke appeared on the land-ward horizon. "As it rose rapidly in the air," a *New York Times* correspon-dent reported, "[it] presented a most remarkable appearance, assuming the shape of a monstrous waterspout, its tapering base seemingly resting on the sea. In a very few minutes it passed us, filling the atmosphere with its sulphurous odor, as if a spirit from the infernal regions had swept by us."

A firecracker could hardly have done less damage. Inside the fort some soldiers thought they felt a rumbling such as is caused by a passing railroad train, and one Rebel on duty told his relief that he believed that one of the Yankee ships had burst a boiler. Porter was so mortified that he spent the afternoon hurling an estimated 10,000 shells at the fort—the heaviest naval bombardment of the war—while Fisher answered with 622. Ashore, one Rebel was killed and 22 wounded, while at sea 83 Union sailors were killed or wounded, half of them when five of their own guns blew up.

On the following morning—Christmas Day—Porter continued the onslaught, chiefly to pin down the Confederates while 2,000 of Butler's soldiers came ashore under Major General Godfrey Weitzel. Approaching the fort they were struck by a hail of canister, next finding themselves on the edge of a mine field. When captured Rebels told Weitzel that a full division was marching down from Wilmington to strike the Yankee rear he sent word to Butler on his headquarters tug, and Ben promptly ordered his men back to their ships. The last of them were taken aboard on December 27 and the entire fleet returned to Hampton Roads with everyone from Porter down to the lowliest tar and foot-slogger blaming Ben Butler for its ignominious failure.

So did Lincoln and Grant, who now agreed that since Butler was no longer of political use, his military liability had ceased to be bearable, and on January 7 he was relieved of his command—replaced next day by Major General E. O. C. Ord.

On that same day Admiral Porter took another huge fleet south to

Fort Fisher. This time the troops numbered 8,000 and were commanded by the capable Major General Alfred Terry. This time also the furious three-day bombardment from Porter's 627 guns firing a total of 20,000 shells at the fort was much more accurate and effective. Rebel guns were silenced and defensive works shattered. When Braxton Bragg in Wilmington ordered Robert Hoke with 6,000 men to strike the Federal rear, the Federals built a defensive line to hold them off while the assault on the fort continued. Hoke was halted, and though Bragg was repeatedly appealed to for help by Colonel William Lamb commanding Fort Fisher, he refused to order Hoke forward on the ground that the Federal line was too strong. On January 15, 1865, Lamb surrendered Fort Fisher to the triumphant Yankees. He had lost a total of about 500 men killed and wounded, against Porter's combined losses of 1,341—but the loss of Fort Fisher sealed off Wilmington and cut off Dixie from the outside world.

Twelve days earlier, William Tecumseh Sherman had begun his campaign to sever the Carolinas from the Confederacy for good.

Sherman had planned to take Savannah by frontal assault, but Hardee, in command in the Georgia capital had been carefully watching his enemy's movement, and on December 20 skillfully withdrew to head north to concentrate with other Confederate remnants. Sherman did not immediately pursue, temporarily content to wire Lincoln on December 22: "I beg to present you, as a Christmas gift, the city of Savannah, with 150 heavy guns and plenty of ammunition, and also about 25,000 bales of cotton."

The redhead was far from content with this triumph. Having made Georgia howl as promised, he now hoped to make South Carolina—heart and home of the rebellion—writhe and squirm. On January 3, 1865, he began his movement into the Palmetto State.

This was no picnic parade, no soldier's lark like the march through Georgia, but rather a grueling, chattering, soaking, exhausting progress across flat swampy lowlands criss-crossed by many rivers swollen by the frequent rains of a typical low-country winter. Joe Johnston who had been recalled to take command of the remnants of Hood's Western army, watched Sherman's steady advance from a distance and marveled that he was moving as rapidly through flood and mud as he had over the dry roads of Georgia. Of this he wrote: "I made up my mind that there had been no such army in existence since the days of Julius Caesar."

Nor soldiers. Laughing at their ordeal, wise-cracking that "Uncle Billy seems to have struck this river end-ways," Sherman's ragged Bluebellies sloughed steadily north. When rivers in flood barred their path, they built bridges; when roads were washed away, they built new ones, until it seemed that these indomitable, ingenious Yankees were determined to corduroy their own path all the way from Savannah to Charleston. When it appeared that everything on wheels had become enmired in mud, entire regiments were detailed to haul the vehicles free by hand ropes. In one unit commended for its work, a soldier replied: "Yes, we got the mules and the wagons out, but we lost a driver and a damn good whip down in that hole."

All along the way the Bluebellies gleefully set fire to towns and plantations—for this was South Carolina, where it all began—or burned down beautiful stands of towering white pines and great spreading live oaks just to see them burn in tongues of yellow, red, and blue and hear their resin sizzle and snap. By day the Yankees marched under a pall of smoke while at night they gathered singing around campfires glinting only palely in the greater glare of burning buildings and forests.

Where there had been no personal animus in Georgia, there was the deepest resentment in South Carolina and most of the arson was deliberately vindictive rather than in accordance with Uncle Billy's military objective of destroying the Army of Northern Virginia's bread basket. Thus every night when mounted foragers cantered into camp trailing hundreds of wagons loaded with foodstuffs, as well as buggies and carriages, in the morning after the food had been consumed the vehicles were set ablaze. Probably not one house in ten escaped destruction, and the Federals were particularly exultant when, an Illinois soldier reported, on finding an especially prosperous plantation: "The rich were put in the cabins of the Negroes; their cattle and corn were used for rations, their fences for corduroy and camp fires and their barns and cotton gins for bonfires. It seemed to be decreed that South Carolina, having sown the wind, should reap the whirlwind."

Such destruction boded ill for Charleston, the fiery heart of Dixie where the Ordinance of Secession had been passed. News of Sherman's depredations and the rapid approach of his scourging blue host served to thicken the flood of civilians scurrying west for the state capital of Columbia and sanctuary. But Sherman merely feinted at the Queen City, satisfied with cutting across all its communications while he swung west for the state capital. Even Charleston's defenders abandoned the city, and it fell easily to Union forces which had striven so unsuccessfully for nearly four years to capture it. Eventually a great ceremony would be held there and out on Fort Sumter, when the invalided Robert Anderson, now a two-star general, would raise the colors he had hauled down four years previously.

Now the fate reserved for Charleston fell in all its fury on Columbia.

Confederate cavalry held the city, but only weakly. At the first sign of Federal determination to attack, they galloped away. Sherman's troops marching in were startled by the numerous small fires seeming to burn everywhere. Then a great wind sprang up gathering all the little blazes into a huge single consuming holocaust, and Columbia, like Atlanta, was all but reduced to a pile of ashes. The splendid discipline that had restrained Sherman's troops in Savannah was nowhere evident in Columbia. One witness wrote: "The scene as witnessed at sundown beggared description, for men, women and children, white and black, soldiers and citizens, many of whom were crazed with drink, were all rushing frantically and aimlessly through the streets, shouting and yelling like mad people." Sherman always maintained that the fire was started in cotton bales by retreating Rebels, while the Confederates angrily replied that Uncle Billy's men deliberately set fire to the city in a spirit of revenge. History will never know how the fire started, but it is true that Sherman and his generals struggled to regain control of their men and control the blaze. In the end, Columbia was all but destroyed. Years later, with the calm of retrospect, General Slocum was to observe: "A drunken soldier with a musket in one hand and a match in the other is not a pleasant visitor to have about the house on a dark, windy night, particularly when for a series of years you have urged him to come so that you might have an opportunity of performing a surgical operation on him."

Thus the Palmetto State did quiver and burn under the avenging hands of Sherman's army, and yet, when the blue forces marched into North Carolina on March 7, that spirit had completely vanished. Sherman had ordered his officers to "deal as moderately and fairly by North Carolinians as possible." There would be no more looting or burning of private property and any soldier caught in such acts would be shot. Nearing Goldsboro, Sherman began to encounter opposition. Although Joe Johnston commanded a ghostly host of shadow soldiers—Hood's broken remnants, the men Hardee had pulled out of Savannah, whatever units below Virginia were able to rally to the Rebel cause—he was still determined to delay Sherman in his march toward Grant. There was a sharp little fight at Averysboro, and a bigger one at Bentonville on March 19, when Johnston struck at Sherman's exposed left wing, but Old Joe simply did not have the strength to harm his opponent, retreating after Sherman sent in reinforcements. In despair Johnston wrote to Davis: "I can do no more than annoy him." Even that small solace vanished after Schofield, marching east from Tennessee, joined Sherman in Goldsboro, thus raising Uncle Billy's strength to 80,000 well-fed, well-motivated and even cocky veterans. Johnston could do absolutely nothing, even when Sherman halted his advance to confer with Lincoln and Grant at City Point.

The three men met March 28–29. All were aware that one more campaign would be needed to end the war. Both generals were eager to hear from the president what sort of terms they could offer the defeated enemy. Sherman said later that Lincoln favored a clement attitude. Once the Rebels laid down their arms he was ready to grant them full rights as citizens of the United States. He was eager to begin Reconstruction, especially this spring, with Congress not in session and not due to reconvene until December. This would give the president a head start on the Jacobins. But Sherman gave no details of the president's plans, except to say that they imbued both himself and Grant with a spirit of conciliation.

64

■

The End at Appomattox

JEFFERSON DAVIS was not the man to listen to his own death rattle. Unbending die-hard or eleventh-hour savior, he would not in either case be conscious of impending defeat. As the year 1864 came to a close the Confederacy had shrunk to the Carolinas and Virginia; Hood's army was a wreck, Sherman was poised to march north to join Grant's swelling Army of the Potomac, and Sheridan was ready to ride down to Petersburg with all his immense and veteran horsemen. Surely the South, for all its splendid fighting spirit, should fight no longer. Its economy was crippled, and its government so powerless to wage war that even the gentle Robert E. Lee raged against congressmen who "do not seem to be able to do anything except to eat peanuts and chew tobacco, while my army is starving." Lee's army was also cold and poorly clothed, and its ranks were dwindling. Desertions were now at their height, because when Sherman menaced a hearth in Georgia or the Carolinas he twisted a heart at Petersburg. Moreover, as Grant inexorably extended his lines to his left, the outnumbered Lee had to move right to contain him, and this thinned his lines. Yet Jefferson Davis had no thought of capitulation.

The Confederate president, a son of the eighteenth century, if not an earlier age, still saw the war as a contest between armies, soldier to soldier, not as a conflict between nations in which capacity to fight is paramount, or a war between democracies in which the will to fight is major. Attrition and blockade had scuttled the Confederate capacity, while hunger, defeat and calculated frightfulness had worn down the will. Southern morale had also been weakened by disputes over Davis's frequent suspensions of the writ of habeas corpus, and many a brave Butternut left the trenches and headed home after being informed that the Confederate commissary was stripping his farm of food and animals. Under these conditions a peace movement was begun under the leadership of Davis's archfoe and obstructionist, Vice President Alexander Stephens. Davis agreed to ask for a peace conference, but actually only in the hope of provoking a harsh statement of Union war aims that would stiffen the Southern spine.

On February 3, 1865, Stephens and two others met Lincoln and Seward on the *River Queen* in Hampton Roads. Stephens proposed that the two camps make peace to join in evicting the French from Mexico in defense of the Monroe Doctrine. Lincoln replied that he could not enter negotiations unless the Confederacy agreed to return to the Union and abolish slavery. Such proposals, of course, could not even be considered by the Confederates—and the war went on.

It continued with Johnston recalled to block Sherman's northward march through the Carolinas, and with Robert E. Lee at last the Confederate commander in chief. Popular resentment against Davis's conduct of the war had led to creation of this position, but the gesture came as the hands of the clock neared midnight. Lee knew that the Confederacy was teetering on the edge of disaster. Desertions had so drained his armies that the Confederacy passed a law conscripting slaves. With splendid irony the South offered blacks the equal opportunity of fighting shoulder to shoulder with whites to preserve their own enslavement.

Nevertheless, Jefferson Davis was determined to go down to utter defeat rather than accept any terms that did not recognize Southern independence, and because it was not Lee's habit to challenge the president on matters of policy, Lee also decided to fight on. Ever the gambler, he resolved on a last, desperate chance: a breakout from Petersburg followed by a lightning march south to join Johnston and overwhelm Sherman, after which both armies would return north to defeat Grant. General John Gordon, the hero of Spotsylvania, was ordered to lead the assault on Union-held Fort Stedman directly east of Petersburg. An hour before daylight on March 25, 1865, the Rebels attacked.

They went in with a silent rush, surprising and seizing Stedman and sending a spearhead ahead to pierce the Federal secondary line. If they could widen their breakthrough and hold it, Lee's army could pour through the breach and get clean away to North Carolina. But the Federals rallied. Forts to either side of Stedman refused to fall, a counter-attack was launched on Stedman, and Union artillery shattered the Rebel front. By midmorning Lee's last sally had been broken and hurled back with losses of 5,000 men. Now it was the turn of U. S. Grant.

Before Gordon's attack Grant had seen that he must crush Lee's right flank, seizing the roads and railways by which the Confederates might escape south. Heavy rains had delayed putting his plan into operation, but after Philip Sheridan arrived at Petersburg with all his cavalry Grant began to move swiftly.

On March 29 a full corps began striking Lee's right, while Sheridan led a corps of cavalry and one of infantry in a wide sweep toward Five Forks still farther to the Rebel right. If he could get in behind Lee, he would cut off the Confederate escape and practically guarantee Lee's defeat. Lee reacted swiftly, sending Pickett to oppose him. On March 31 the Confederates halted Sheridan's forces short of Five Forks at a place called Dinwiddie Court House. But the little Union general was not defeated. He had wisely retired to await reinforcements, and Grant sent him Warren's corps.

Next day Sheridan chafed at Warren's delay. Sheridan smelled victory; he could win the war that day, and he cried aloud: "This battle must be fought and won before the sun goes down!" In simple terms, Sheridan wanted to crush and scatter Pickett's force and seize the Southside Railway to his rear. Unknown to Sheridan, Pickett was not with his troops but was enjoying himself at a shad bake while his men were fighting and dying, a dereliction of duty so infuriating to Lee that he relieved him of his command. If Sheridan could capture the railroad this day it would be all over with Lee and probably for the Confederacy.

At last Warren's veterans began moving into line. Sheridan was everywhere among them. When one of his skirmish lines was staggered and seemed ready to fall back, he galloped toward his faltering soldiers, shouting, "Come on—go at 'em—move on with a clean jump or you'll not catch one of them!" A soldier beside him was hit in the throat. "I'm killed!" he cried, blood spurting thickly from his jugular vein. "You're not hurt a bit!" Sheridan roared. "Pick up your gun, man, and move right on!" Obediently, the soldier trotted forward—and fell dead. Now the battle line was formed, and Sheridan shouted: "Where's my battle flag?" It was brought forward, and the general raised his little swallow-tailed red-and-white banner high over his head and rode black Rienzi up and down the line.

A bullet pierced the flag, and the sergeant who had brought it fell. Sheridan rode forward, spurring his horse toward the Rebel earthworks. After him came the yelling Federal infantry. Sheridan put Rienzi over the works in a splendid leap, and his infantry swarmed in after him. Now a perfect rage of battle had come over Sheridan, in the midst of which he relieved the unfortunate Warren of his command. It was brutal, it was probably not just, but Sheridan realized with Grant that the end of the war was within the Union grasp, and a general should be ready to press forward as obediently as the private whose lifeblood poured from his throat.

"What I want is that Southern Railway," Sheridan roared repeatedly. "I want you men to understand we have a record to make before the sun goes down that will make Hell tremble!"

Capture of the vital railway that day was not to be. Yet Pickett's force had been completely shattered and Five Forks fell to Sheridan. A jubilant Grant cabled the information to Lincoln, who relayed the information to the press. For the next few days an eager North read with drawn breath of the progress of that single win-the-war battle that had eluded the nation for four years.

Next day, April 2, Grant attacked all along the line. Row upon row of Federal gun batteries began baying in a voice of rolling thunder, hurling a dreadful weight of death and destruction upon the Rebel positions. Then came silence. Thousands upon thousands of Federal soldiers moved forward. Slowly, with a gathering rush, they struck the Confederate lines, and in the weakened center they tore them apart. One by one clusters of Rebel muskets winked out in that predawn darkness, and black gaps opened in the Southern line. Into the open spaces rushed the Federals, widening them, and a quarter hour after Wright's corps attacked in the center a decisive breakthrough was achieved.

To the rear A. P. Hill heard of the penetration while discussing the battle with Lee. He rode forward, to receive a bullet in the heart and strip from Lee yet another of his great lieutenants. Tears in his eyes, Lee called upon Longstreet. But Old Pete and his valiant men could not stem the rising Federal tide.

As the Sunday of April 2, 1865, grew lighter, Lee prepared to abandon Petersburg. He still hoped to join Johnston. It was a forlorn hope, and Lee doubtless knew it, yet his sense of duty kept him loyal to President Davis's designs. As 30,000 red-eyed and starving survivors of the Army of Northern Virginia began streaming west, Lee dictated the long-dreaded telegraph to the War Department.

Meticulously dressed in gray, cold as a marble statue, Jefferson Davis sat in the family pew at St. Paul's Episcopal Church. Surrounded mostly by women, many dressed in black, Davis heard the preacher say: "The Lord is in His holy temple; let all the earth keep silence before Him." Into that churchly silence there crept the tinkle of spurs. An officer holding his saber came striding down the aisle. He handed Davis a paper. The president unfolded it and read: "I advise that all preparation be made for leaving Richmond tonight. I will advise you later, according to circumstances."

With tight-lipped calm, Davis pocketed Lee's message of doom and walked majestically from the church. Going to the War Department, he telegraphed Lee that to move the Confederate government that night would "involve the loss of many valuables." Lee received the protest in the field, and angrily tore it to bits with the remark: "I am sure I gave him sufficient notice." Regaining his composure, he notified Davis that it was "absolutely necessary" to move that night.

Richmond learned swiftly that the government was fleeing. Throughout that Passion Sunday civilians fought government clerks for possession of carts and wagons, carriages and gigs, while crowded streets echoed to rolling wheels or the rumbling of departing trains. The Confederate treasury—less than a half-million dollars in bullion—was placed in charge of a battalion of naval cadets. Civilians able to flee joined the government exodus. Those who could not locked their doors and closed their shutters and sat down in despair to await the Yankee invasion. Night fell and the city began to tremble to the detonation of bridges and arsenals.

Soon the city was afire. So was neighboring Manchester. They blazed like beacons in the dark while the James lay glittering between them. Inevitably, those people of Richmond whom inflation and food shortages had transformed into wild, half-starved creatures turned to looting. Commissary depots were full of supplies never delivered to Lee's hungry army, and now that they were left unguarded they were broken into and plundered. Barrels of whiskey were also found, and soon there were drunks capering in the reflected flames of burning cotton or tobacco warehouses. Then the mob began breaking into shops and storehouses, sotted women fought each other for ostrich plumes, drunken men shot each other over boots and sashes. So the flames and the frenzy spread, and soon the only safe place in Richmond was in the green hills of Capitol Square. Here women in shawls clasped frightened children to their bosoms, and here, while the night winds whipped the fires, as tall flames roared and drunken revelers shrieked, like a shower of sparks from a falling building, the capital of the Confederacy collapsed.

Next morning, April 3, troops from the Army of the James under Major General Godfrey Weitzel entered the ruined capital. A small guidon was raised over the State House, erstwhile capitol of the Confederacy, by Major Atherton H. Stevens, Jr., of Massachusetts. Among the weeping citizens who watched, peering through their shutter chinks, was Mrs. Mary Fontaine, who wrote: "I saw them unfurl a tiny flag, and I sank on my knees, and the bitter, bitter tears came in a torrent." At eight fifteen in the City Hall General Weitzel accepted surrender of the city. "Then the Cavalry thundered at a furious gallop . . . Then the infantry came playing 'The Girl I Left Behind Me', that dear old air that we heard our brave men so often play; then the negro troops playing 'Dixie'." Now the streets were swarming with people, many of them jubilant blacks, the men hugging each other, the women kissing. Throughout the early morning the looting continued, and the flames flickered on, until the Federal troops took charge so that the thieves were either arrested or frightened off and the fires subdued. By midafternoon Richmond was quiet again, no longer the Confederate capital but a Federal city forevermore. Eventually, President Lincoln who had been to Petersburg would arrive in Richmond, and to General Weitzel's question about how to treat the conquered people in his charge, the Rail-Splitter gave his famous reply, "If I were in your place, I'd let 'em up easy—let 'em up easy."

There was little of such sentiment in the Federal capital, however, when the telegrapher at Fort Monroe dit-dotted out the historic message: "We took Richmond at 8:15 this morning." Never before or since has the white city on the Potomac rocked and reverberated to such scenes of jubilation. Church bells pealed, fire engines clattered and clanged, railroad locomotives and riverboats screamed and whistled, while batteries of artillery thundered in a seemingly endless 800-gun salute: 300 for Petersburg, 500 for Richmond—with 100 more from the navy's massive Dahlgrens. Children dismissed from school added to the general gaiety, joined by government clerks given the day off. Everywhere were the newspaper "extras" with exultant bold, black banner headlines, an explosion of printer's ink led by the *Star*'s firecracker string: GLORY!!! HAIL COLUMBIA!!! HALLELUJAH!!! RICHMOND OURS!!! People who did not know each other embraced and kissed, friends-turned-enemies buried the hatchet, while casual acquaintances swore eternal fidelity as all of them marched through the streets arm-in-arm singing. And of course there was much of that artificial exaltation found in bottles with every bar jam-packed and the patrons vying with one another to buy a round of drinks. One newsman declared: "A more liquorish crowd was never seen in Washington." Nor was a more vindictive one. When Stanton asked a crowd what should be done with Richmond, there came the universal vengeful cry: "BURN IT! BURN IT! LET HER BURN!"

There was more of the same—much more—on the following night when the formal celebration called "the Grand Illumination" was held. Throughout the day workmen had been swarming over the public buildings preparing them for the gala. The Capitol glittered from basement to dome under a huge gaslighted sign upon which was emblazoned the biblical quotation: THIS IS THE LORD'S DOING, IT IS GLORIOUS IN OUR EYES. All the surrounding buildings were similarly bedecked from the Marine barracks to the lonely lunatic asylum on the hill. As they began to shine brighter in the gathering night a huge throng surrounded the speakers' platform in front of the Patent Office, where gas jets atop its granite pillars spelled out the word U N I O N. Here District Judge David Carter began the festivities—not to say verbal lynching—by describing Jefferson Davis as "the flying rascal out of Richmond," a theme echoed and expanded upon by Vice President Andrew Johnson. After he mentioned Davis and his listeners shouted, "Hang him! Hang him!" he quickly agreed with the remark, "Yes, I say hang him twenty times." Nor was there any of his chief's mild and merciful recipe, "Let 'em up easy," in his own prescription for treatment of the Confederate leaders. To a man their property would be confiscated, and then: "I would arrest them, I would try them, I would convict them and I would hang them. . . ."

A great roar of delight rose into the night, and thus began in Washington to the sound of popping corks and gurgling liquid, music and song, by the light of candles, gas and fireworks, a saturnalia of joy and hate that lasted until dawn.

Robert E. Lee had a head start of one day in his race against the tenacious Grant. With this advantage, Lee believed he could get his army to Danville, the pleasant little city on the Dan River to which Jefferson Davis had already moved the government. Here he could be joined by Johnston.

On April 3 it did not seem to Lee that Grant was pursuing too rapidly. That night his ragged veterans staggered into Amelia Court House, twenty-one miles west of Petersburg. There, to his dismay, Lee found not a single ration to feed 30,000 agonizingly hungry men. He had no recourse but to halt next day while forage wagons searched the countryside for food. In the meantime, the day's head start was lost. Federal cavalry were everywhere. Close behind them hurried three eager corps of Union infantry, marching a few miles south of Lee on a straighter, parallel route. That night of April 4 some of Sheridan's riders menaced Amelia.

On the morning of April 5 the forage wagons came in, and Lee saw with concealed despair that they were nearly empty. His men must march now on their nerves alone, their hearts nourished by Lee's spirit but their bellies empty and growling with hunger. Another delay ensued: Ewell and Anderson were slow in closing up. Finally, the army moved south from Amelia Court House—and found Federal infantry and cavalry barring the way.

There was nothing left to do but to shift west toward Farmville, where there was hope of receiving rations from Lynchburg. This meant a night march that killed a good part of Lee's army. It was a slow stumble over crowded roads made by men with leaden limbs, men who moved like sleepwalkers. Many fell out never to return. Many were captured by Federal cavalry, which never left off nipping at Lee's heels. Grant was clinging to Lee's army, and he would not let go.

Still, Lee pressed on. On April 6 the Federals caught up at a place called Sailor's Creek. Here they overwhelmed Gordon, who was covering the Confederate trains, capturing the greater part of Lee's wagons, and here, as Lee watched in agony, they broke Ewell's and Anderson's corps. Sitting on Traveller and holding a red battle flag, Lee saw the wreck of shattered regiments come backwashing toward him, and he cried aloud: "My God, has the Army been dissolved?" That day Lee lost between 7,000 and 8,000 men. That night Lee's army was down to 15,000 muskets and sabers to oppose 80,000 Federal infantry and cavalry. On April 7, however, his pale and pinched veterans struggled into Farmville, where they received their first rations since the retreat began. From Farmville, Lee continued his withdrawal. He got safely across the Appomattox River and burned the bridges behind him. Some of them were saved by the Federals, however, and once more Union cavalry began to bite on Lee's rear. That night Lee received Grant's invitation to surrender. He handed it to Longstreet, who replied: "Not yet."

There was still hope. If Lee could get to a place called Appomattox Station, he could feed his men from four trains of food from Lynchburg, and then swing south to safety at Danville.

On April 8 Lee was forced to fight another rear-guard action to save his remaining wagons. As he did, Sheridan's cavalry and infantry under E. O. C. Ord swept past his southern flank and drove into Appomattox Station. They captured Lee's ration trains and put themselves across his line of march. That night Lee's army reached Appomattox Court House. Below them, across their path, lay Sheridan's force. If it was only cavalry, it might be brushed aside and the army yet saved. But if infantry were there in force, the Army of Northern Virginia would be doomed.

April 9, 1865, was a Palm Sunday. Very early that morning Robert Edward Lee put on a new gray uniform, a sash of deep red silk, the jeweled sword given him by ladies in England, beautiful red-stitched spurred boots and long gray gauntlets. An officer expressed surprise, and Lee said: "I have probably to be General Grant's prisoner and thought I must make my best appearance."

To the east, riding anxiously toward Appomattox over sloppy roads came a slender brown-bearded man wearing a mud-spattered private's blouse. His face was strained, for he had a bad headache and had been up all night bathing his feet in hot water and applying mustard plasters to his neck and wrists. Still, Ulysses S. Grant was hopeful that today would see an end to four years of blood and agony.

Yet Palm Sunday was beginning with the roar of guns. Down from Appomattox Court House charged the Butternuts under General Gordon. They brushed aside the Federal outriders, and saw a solid blue phalanx of glittering bayonets to the rear. The Army of Northern Virginia had come to the end of the road. Back to Lee went Gordon's message that he could do nothing without reinforcements. "Then," said Robert E. Lee calmly, "there is nothing left for me to do but to go and see General Grant, and I would rather die a thousand deaths!"

It was the end. With cries of anguish, protesting men and officers clustered around Lee. One general proposed that the army disperse and turn to guerrilla warfare. Lee replied that to do so would make mere marauders of his soldiers and inflict anarchy upon the South. He was prepared to sacrifice his own invincible pride for the safety of his country, and as the messages went out to Grant, Phil Sheridan opposite Lee grew impatient. He had massed both his men and horse with the passionate cry: "Now smash 'em, I tell you, smash 'em!" Now his bugles blew and his blue lines leaned forward, and out from those pitiful gray ranks huddled beneath a host of battle flags a lone rider galloped. He carried a flag of truce and he told Sheridan that Lee was waiting to see Grant in the McLean House.

Skeptical at first, Sheridan finally ordered a cease-fire. Dazed, the two armies sat down and contemplated each other. In the spring stillness they suddenly heard bird song rather than bullets. Then General Grant rode up to Sheridan. He inclined his head toward the village and asked, "Is General Lee up there?" Sheridan said, "Yes," and Grant said, "Well, then, let's go up."

They "went up" to that McLean House which, ironically, had brought the war full circle. It was at the home of Wilmer McLean that Beauregard made his headquarters during the First Battle of Bull Run. To get away from the war, McLean sold out and moved to Appomattox. Now it was in McLean's front parlor that Grant met Lee.

Grant came in alone and saw Lee with two aides. Taking off his yellow thread gloves, Grant stepped forward to shake Lee's hand. He was aware of his own mud-stained appearance and Lee's splendor, but he gave no sign of it. Both men sat at tables while a half dozen of Grant's generals entered with tinkling spurs and clanking sabers to stand behind their chief. Lee gave no sign of disapproval of their presence.

Grant spoke: "I met you once before, General Lee, while we were serving in Mexico, when you came over from General Scott's headquarters to visit Garland's brigade, to which I then belonged. I have always remembered your appearance, and I think I should have recognized you anywhere."

"Yes," Lee said, "I know I met you on that occasion, and I have often thought of it and tried to recollect how you looked, but I have never been able to recall a single feature."

Grant talked eagerly of Mexico, perhaps to soften the impact of the request that he must make, and Lee, probably anxious to be done with the ordeal of surrender, brought him back gently with the words: "I suppose, General Grant, that the object of our present meeting is fully understood. I asked to see you to ascertain upon what terms you would receive the surrender of my army."

Without changing countenance, with not a hint of exultation or gloating in his voice, Grant quickly outlined his terms: ". . . the officers and men surrendered to be paroled and disqualified from taking up arms again until properly exchanged, and all arms, ammunition and supplies to be delivered up as captured property."

Next Grant set down his terms in writing. Lee read them, courteously corrected an unintentional oversight, and agreed. There was, however, the matter of the horses, which were the private property of his cavalrymen and artillerists. Would the men be permitted to retain them? At first Grant said that the terms allowed only officers to keep private property, but then, seeing how much this request meant to Lee, he promised "to let all the men who claim to own a horse or mule take the animals home with them to work their little farms."

Lee was relieved and grateful. "This will have the best possible effect on the men," he said. "It will be very gratifying and will do much toward conciliating our people." In Grant's generosity Lee saw not a vindictive but a compassionate conqueror.

Robert E. Lee knew then that the South had fallen. Even though the army which he formally surrendered a few minutes later was only his own, even though combat might sputter on until May 26, the fighting soul of the South died with Lee's signature on that Palm Sunday of 1865.

After he signed, Lee arose and shook hands with Grant. He bowed to the others in the room and strode silently out the door. On the porch of the McLean House he paused to draw on his gauntlets. He gazed sadly toward the hillside where his little army lay, faithful and fearless to the last. Twice, with slow and savage ruefulness, Lee drove his fist into his palm. Then, crying for Traveller in a hoarse and choking voice, he mounted and rode out of sight.

65

.

Lincoln's Assassination

N EXT MORNING as a rainswept dawn broke over Washington, the
booming of guns again informed the capital's residents of a great victory: the surrender of Lee's army. This time, however, the city did not go
quite as mad as it had exactly a week ago upon reports of the fall of
Richmond, chiefly because the rain was so fierce and the streets so muddy,
and there were only 500 explosions compared to the 900 then. Eventually,
however, as the downpour slackened, the streets did become thronged
"with people singing and cheering, carrying flags and saluting each other,
hungering and thirsting for speeches." Above all they wanted to hear from
the president, who had returned to the White House and was in high spirits
when, at breakfast, the Treasury Department clerks celebrated another day
off by serenading him with the national anthem.

He was still excited from Grant's triumphal telegram of the night
before, in which exalted mood he was joined by Tad, now fully recovered
from his mysterious fever. "Let Master Tad have a Navy sword," Lincoln
wrote to Navy Secretary Welles, and then to Stanton: "Tad wants some
flags. Can he be accommodated?" He was, and the happy youngster jubilantly waved a Rebel battle flag when a detail of sailors dragged six boat
howitzers up Pennsylvania Avenue, firing blanks as they approached the
White House. There a crowd had gathered, cheering Tad lustily and then
his father when he made his smiling appearance at the window. "Speech!"
they cried. "Speech!" But he put them off, promising to deliver one the
following night. Then a thought seemed to strike him, and he called down
to them: "I see you have a band of music with you." A voice answered, "We
have two or three." Lincoln proposed closing the occasion by having the
band play "Dixie". "I have always thought 'Dixie' one of the best tunes I
ever heard," he said. "Our adversaries over the way attempted to appropri-

ate it, but I insisted yesterday that we fairly captured it." The crowd laughed, and a band played the enemy's favorite tune in lively style, after which they went all-out on "Yankee Doodle", and then the crowd broke up and drifted away.

An even larger throng was back on the White House lawn the following night as the president delivered his promised speech. It was a misty evening, but the new illuminated dome of the Capitol was visible. In the distance across the Potomac, Robert E. Lee's Arlington plantation was bright with colored candles and exploding rockets, the light flickering on the dark upturned faces of scores of former slaves singing "De Yar ob Jubilo".

Lincoln's speech was read by the light of a candle held by an aide behind him. As he spoke the president let his handwritten sheets fall to the balcony floor, where Tad scrambled to collect them. The audience, once buzzing with animated conversation punctuated by laughter, soon fell silent, and then restive. It was a puzzling address. It was almost as though Lincoln were musing aloud as he struggled with the "knotty problems" of Reconstruction and readmission of the wayward sister states. Soon the mist changed to a drizzle and then to rain. Some listeners left in boredom, but most remained—although shifting uneasily as Lincoln began to discuss enfranchisement of the freed black slaves. When he endorsed limited black suffrage in Louisiana, and expressed sympathy with the bondsman's desire for the vote, one of them turned in rage to his companion and snarled:

"That means nigger citizenship! Now, by God, I'll put him through!"

So spoke John Wilkes Booth that rainy night of April 11, 1865.

John Wilkes Booth was born April 26, 1838, in Bel Air, Maryland, the son of a famous acting family, among them himself, his father—known as "Junius the Elder"—and two brothers, Junius Jr. and Edwin. John studied drama in Baltimore, where he made his stage debut. He quickly established himself as a rising young Shakespearean star, especially in the South, where unreserved acclaim from genteel audiences established a bond between himself and the Dixie aristocracy. Strikingly handsome, he enchanted audiences North and South with his rich, musical voice, his spectacular acrobatics, and those quick changes of mood from tenderness to rage which probably sprang from his own personal alternations from joy to depression. But it was the South above all that he loved, and he told his sister Asia that he wished to be known as a Southern actor.

After Sumter his love of Dixie was expressed in militant Confederate sympathies, so that one day he could say to Asia: "If the North conquer us, it will be by numbers only."

"If the *North* conquer *us?*" Asia repeated in gentle reproach "We are *of* the North."

"Not I!" Booth cried fiercely. "Not I—so help me God! My soul, life and possessions are for the South."

It was a natural consequence that Booth's love of the Confederacy should produce in him a violent hatred of Abraham Lincoln, whom he considered to be the vilest of tyrants, the bloody-handed enemy of liberty. "You will see Lincoln made a King in America," he swore to his brother Edwin.

Hating Lincoln and Abolition, he also despised the black bondsman and celebrated slavery as the greatest gift "that God ever bestowed upon a favored nation."

Thus the reelection of Lincoln in 1864 and the rise in the fortunes of the Union army drove John Wilkes Booth almost insane, until he conceived the great plan of kidnapping the tyrant in the White House and taking him to Richmond to hold him for ransom of all the Rebel prisoners. To do this he recruited from the dregs of Washington and Baltimore society a band of followers; misfits and drifters bound to him by their common allegiance to the South and hatred of Lincoln. There was baby-faced John Surratt, who had once studied to be a Catholic priest, proud in his boyish way of the toothbrush of manly whiskers sprouting from his chin. George Atzerodt, a German immigrant with a heavy accent, was a brawny wagoneer with a scraggly beard. Samuel Arnold and frail Michael O'Laughlin had been Rebel soldiers and boyhood chums of Booth. Little Davy Herold was a slight simulacrum of value only because he clerked in the drugstore where the Lincolns bought their medicines. Finally, Lewis Powell (alias Paine, alias Wood) was a hulking ne'er-do-well from Florida who claimed to have fought at Gettysburg and to have ridden with Mosby. Booth found him roaming the streets of Washington and chose him for his strength and violent nature. With such followers, who might well have suited John Brown, the first mad murderer who was a chief cause of the war, this second homicidal maniac planned to end the struggle in Dixie's favor.

For weeks the conspirators studied maps and plans of the White House. They trailed the president on his carriage or horseback rides or on his frequent visits to the theater, always kept at a frustrating distance by the heavy cavalry detail the watchful Stanton assigned to guard his chief. The only real opportunity came on March 4, 1865, Inauguration Day, when Booth himself held the tyrant in plain view from a railing above the inaugural platform. "What an excellent chance I had to kill the president," he cried afterward in anguished regret. Booth was ready a few days later but the plan to kidnap Lincoln fizzled when he failed to appear at the point where Booth and his band lay in wait.

After that failure, O'Laughlin, Surratt and Arnold broke away from Booth, but the other three remained. It was to Davy Herold that Booth spoke on that rainy night of Lincoln's speech, vowing that the president must be murdered. By Good Friday he had decided that Vice President Johnson and Secretary of State Seward also must go. Atzerodt was to kill Johnson and Powell to assassinate Seward. Booth would personally account for Lincoln and thus the top executive trio in the United States would be removed. By accident that very April 14 became the Day.

On that morning John Wilkes Booth went to Ford's Theater to pick up his mail. From Harry Ford, co-owner of the theater, he learned that the Lincolns were to attend *Our American Cousin* that night. On fire with excitement Booth made his preparations. Either he or a fellow conspirator (probably himself because he was so well-known there) went to Ford's to drill a small peephole in the door of the state box so that Lincoln could be seen in his rocking chair. Next the door to the corridor leading to the box was fixed so that it could be barred from inside. All was now in readiness.

Ford's Theater still stands on Tenth Street between E and F Streets N.W., looking exactly as it did on that memorable Good Friday night of 1865: a three-story brick building filled with cane-bottomed chairs on the main floor as well as the two balconies. The Lincolns came there often, as well as visiting Grover's and other theaters in the city. Mary adored plays and Lincoln found them wonderfully relaxing, especially comedies. Tragedies he read in private to ponder on them.

It was a foggy night when the Lincolns, accompanied by Clara Harris and her fiancé, Major Henry Rathbone, drove in their carriage to Ford's. Gaslights on the street corners gleamed eerily in the mist. In the theater were perhaps a thousand persons—Washington dignitaries, generals and admirals, socialites—when the Lincoln party appeared to receive a standing ovation and hear the strains of "Hail to the Chief". They proceeded to the state box and sat down. Lincoln wore his customary black, Mary a gray silk dress and matching bonnet. She rested her hand on her husband's knee. To their right were Clara Harris and Major Rathbone. At sight of them, Harry Hawk, the male lead, ad-libbed the line: 'This reminds me of a story, as Mr. Lincoln would say," and the crowd laughed good-humoredly. Lincoln leaned forward, eager for comedy and a relaxing evening.

■　　■　　■

At eight o'clock that night Booth and his trio of accomplices met at the Herndon House on Ninth Street, less than a block from Ford's. They rehearsed their plan to strike down the North's three leading men, and then broke up. Booth rode to Ford's, where he dismounted in an alley behind the theater and handed the reins to Edman Spangler, a scene-shifter and an accomplice. Booth was dressed as usual in a black felt hat and high black boots with spurs, and carried a derringer and a dagger concealed in his clothes. He passed the doorkeeper who knew him with the quip, "You don't need a ticket, Buck," and entered the blazing lobby. The third act was in progress and the lobby clock read ten after ten. Crossing to the door to the main floor he opened it to study the crowd. The sight of Lincoln in the state box seemed to satisfy him, and as he closed the door he seemed less nervous.

Booth knew *Our American Cousin* by heart and planned to strike when the exit of two actresses left Harry Hawk on stage alone. The moment was near, and Booth climbed the stairs humming, entering the corridor to the state box. It was dark and empty. John Parker, who was to guard Lincoln that night, had either gone to the gallery to watch the play or outside for a drink. Booth lowered his head to peer through the peephole. He could see the back of Lincoln's head. Mary was next to him with her hand in his, then the affianced couple. On stage the fortune-hunting Harry Hawk had been both rejected as a suitor by the girl he sought to marry and insulted as a social boor by her mother. As both women exited, he called out: "Don't know the manners of good society, eh?" It was Booth's cue. "Wal, I guess I know enough to turn you inside out, old gal, you sockdologizing old mantrap—"

Booth opened the door, took a step and shot Abraham Lincoln in the back of his head with his derringer. A horrified audience heard the report and turned to see a scuffle in the state box. Booth slashed Rathbone's arm with his dagger and leaped from the box, his spur catching in a flag causing him to crash on the stage and break his left shinbone just above the ankle. Now the audience was astonished. It was the actor John Wilkes Booth! Was this all a part of the play? But then Booth cried, or muttered—no one was ever sure—the Virginia state motto: *"Sic semper tyrannis"*—Thus always to tyrants. Lunging awkwardly at Hawk, he clambered to his feet and hobbled off the stage, leaving the theater by the back door, mounting his mare and galloping off into the night.

Inside Ford's was in an uproar. "The president is shot!" Clara Harris screamed, while Mary Lincoln began shrieking hysterically: "Help! Help! Help!" Below people were yelling, pushing each other into the aisles, even rushing for the exits in fear that the assassination of Lincoln might be the signal for a general massacre. Two doctors fought each other to reach the state box, and the first there sought to revive Lincoln with mouth-to-mouth resuscitation. But there was nothing to revive. Booth's bullet had destroyed Lincoln's brain, lodging behind his right eye, and he was dying. So said Dr. Charles A. Leale, assistant surgeon U.S. Volunteers, only twenty-three years old but already an expert on gunshot wounds: "His wound is mortal," Leale said. "It is impossible for him to recover."

Leale, two other doctors, and four soldiers bore the body across crowded Tenth Street—where an officer had to draw his sword to force a path through the throng—and into Petersen's boarding house. Here they passed down a narrow hallway to a dingy little room of a War Department clerk named William T. Clark. They laid the tall president diagonally across a short four-poster bed, on top of a red-white-and-blue counterpane with fierce eagles at the corners. A boarder lighted a hissing gas lamp, illuminating the little room in ghastly green light. Lincoln had lost blood and brain matter and his right eye was now badly swollen and discolored. Three more doctors arrived, including Surgeon General Joseph Barnes. They could do nothing. More dignitaries crowded into the tiny room, the green light flickering on their anxious faces. A trembling Sumner sat next to Lincoln, taking his limp hand in his own. . . . Andrew Johnson (Atzerodt had lost his nerve and never tried to kill him) arrived, unnerved himself by the vast power of the office about to devolve upon him. . . . Naval Secretary Welles took station beside the bed to watch "the giant sufferer." "He had been stripped of his clothes," Welles wrote later. "His large arms, which were occasionally exposed, were of a size which one would scarce have expected from his spare appearance. His slow, full respiration lifted the bedclothes with each breath he took." Now Lincoln's calm face began to twitch. The upper right side of his face turned purplish and the eye with the bullet behind it began to bulge from its socket. Mary Lincoln screamed in horror and had to be led from the room. Everywhere there was the sound of muffled weeping. A newsman said Sumner, still seated beside his friend, still holding his hand, lost control of himself. "He was sobbing like a woman, with his head bowed down almost on the pillow of the bed on which the President was lying."

Secretary of War Stanton came close to breaking down when he saw the face of his beloved chief whom he had once despised as "the original baboon." But he controlled himself to take charge of the situation, setting up headquarters in a small sitting room adjacent to the Petersen House's front parlor. There, assisted by a Federal judge, he began interviewing witnesses. Then came word that Secretary Seward had also been attacked by a knife-wielding assailant. This was the powerful and unbalanced Florida drifter, Lewis Powell, who found the secretary in bed, where he had been since he was thrown from a carriage on April 5 and severely injured. His shoulder had been dislocated and his jaw broken on both sides, but the iron frame binding his jaw had helped to save him, deflecting Powell's slashes aimed at his throat. "I'm mad! I'm mad!" Powell cried as he dashed from the room, having also wounded four members of Seward's household, including his son.

Panic might have ensued in the capital had not Stanton "instantly assumed charge of everything near and remote, civil and military, and began issuing orders in that autocratic manner so superbly necessary to the occasion." Among other measures, Stanton stopped traffic on the Potomac and the railroads, warned the Washington Fire Brigade to stand by for mass arson, ordered Grant back to the capital to command its military defenses, and then—having established Booth as the wanted assassin—alerted guards along the Canadian border and all major eastern ports to be on the lookout for suspicious persons trying to flee the country.

Booth's guilt had been demonstrated within four hours of his escape. First, his one-shot derringer had been found on the floor of the state box, and after that there were so many witnesses who knew Booth coming forward to identify him as the man who had leaped from the box that identification was certain. But Stanton could not believe that Booth had acted alone. And what about Seward? Abolitionist and Dixie-hater that he was, Stanton convinced himself that the famous matinee idol was merely an actor at the center of a wide-scale Confederate plot, and that here was a heaven-sent opportunity to lay still another stripe across the back of the fallen South. So he issued his alert and description of Booth with this possibility uppermost in his mind.

Meanwhile Stanton made repeated visits to the room in which Lincoln lay, and in which it was clear that his time was fast approaching. His stertorous groans shook Stanton, and the screams and hysteria of Mary Lincoln all but unnerved him. "Doctor, save him!" she implored the physicians, or else: "Bring Tad. He will speak to Tad, he loves him so." She frequently leaned forward from a chair beside the bed to place her mouth close to Lincoln's and once, when a frothy roar broke from his lips, she shrieked and fell backward in a faint. At last her piercing screams were too much for Stanton and he ran into the death room crying sternly: "Take that woman out, and do not let her in again."

Finally, when that dreadful Good Friday of 1865 had passed into history, and dawn of April 15 fell bleakly upon the throng gathered in the rain outside the Petersen House, Mary Lincoln was allowed into the room where her husband was breathing his last. At 7:22 A.M. Surgeon General Barnes pulled the sheet over Lincoln's face.

The sore spot had been soothed at last.

66

■

Honest Abe Goes Home

T HE ASSASSINATION of Abraham Lincoln stunned the Union as had
no other event in the young nation's eighty-nine-year history. It was as
though the shock waves of a moral earthquake were rolling across the
country. Admirers and traducers—critics who had ridiculed the president
as a "gorilla tyrant" or denounced him as a stupid, inept incompetent or
damned him as a dictator and an enemy of liberty—lamented his murder
with deep and moving grief.

On Wednesday, April 19, the president lay in state in the East Room
of the White House. His coffin, barely big enough to contain his long body,
rested on a flower-covered catafalque. All but traces of the horrible purple
swelling around his eye had been effaced by the embalmer. His head lay on
a white satin pillow, his face pale, a faint smile seeming to be frozen on his
lips. Even in death that unbeautiful but noble face was eloquent of a great
capacity for suffering and an infinite compassion. Upstairs Mary Lincoln lay
weeping and hysterical, on the edge of madness. Her son Tad sought to
soothe her, though stricken himself. Throwing his arms around her neck,
he pleaded: "Don't cry so, Momma! Don't cry, or you will make me cry,
too! You will break my heart." But Mary could not control herself and was
unable to attend the services downstairs.

In the hushed and dimly lighted East Room, festooned in black crepe
like all adjoining rooms, Robert Lincoln stood at one end of the coffin, his
face nearly as pale as his dead father's. Ulysses S. Grant was at the other
end, a black mourning crepe on one arm, staring sadly at a cross of white
lilies. He began to weep openly on this "the saddest day of my life." Now
the principal mourners began arriving. President Johnson came in accompanied by his entire cabinet. Edwin Stanton's eyes were reddened by his grief.
So were Sumner's, present with almost all of his congressional colleagues.

Soon nearly 600 mourners had crowded into the East Room: almost all official Washington, generals and admirals, the diplomatic corps, Lincoln's cavalry escort and his secretaries.

Services conducted by four ministers began at about eleven o'clock in the morning. Upon their completion a dozen veteran reserve corps sergeants hoisted the coffin onto their shoulders and carried it out into bright sunlight and the waiting funeral carriage. Slowly, with church bells tolling and minute guns firing, with bands playing dirges, the procession moved up Pennsylvania Avenue led by a detachment of black troops. Behind them was the carriage and then a riderless horse and then the mourners in their funeral garb, walking in slow, measured cadence. Soon wounded soldiers from nearby hospitals joined the procession, some of them hobbling on crutches, many in bandages. Some 4,000 black citizens followed, marching hand in white-gloved hand, forty abreast, curb to curb, tall silk hats on their heads. Reaching the Capitol, the procession halted while the sergeants carried the coffin into the rotunda to place it upon another catafalque, where it lay in state. Next day thousands upon thousands of mourners filed slowly past the open bier to pay their last respects. Throughout the day there was the sound of muffled weeping.

On April 21 a nine-car funeral train decorated with Union flags stood waiting at the station. A hearse carried Lincoln's coffin to it, where it joined the coffin of Willie Lincoln, which had been removed from its Georgetown grave and brought to the train. Now the locomotive train whistle blew and the train lurched gently forward, its bell tolling regularly as it began the 1,600-mile journey to Springfield, Illinois, and the plot where little Edward Lincoln lay buried. Along the route thousands of sad Americans—many with their children—gathered in mournful silence to either side of the railroad to watch the funeral train pass. In New York City 85,000 people watched the passage of the funeral cortege through the streets. Here Walt Whitman, the great poet, was sobbing uncontrollably at the passing "of him I love." That night in the statehouse at Albany additional thousands walked silently past the open coffin. In Cleveland the dead president lay in state in Monument Park to be viewed by 150,000 mourners from Ohio, Michigan and Pennsylvania. That night puffing westward to Indiana the yellow light of bonfires to either side of the tracks flickered on the faces of mourners standing silently in the rain. At last the train carrying Lincoln and Willie home sped across the prairies to Springfield. There father and son joined little Eddy beneath the sod. As Edwin Stanton remarked when Abraham Lincoln drew his last breath:

"Now he belongs to the ages."

67
.
Johnston Surrenders:
End of the Assassins

WILLIAM TECUMSEH SHERMAN was about twenty miles above
Raleigh, North Carolina, when on April 14 he received a message from
Joe Johnston requesting a truce to discuss peace terms. Uncle Billy was
delighted, replying: "I am fully empowered to arrange with you any terms
for suspension of hostilities between the armies." He added that he hoped
to extend to Johnston the same generous terms Grant had given Lee.
Between them, the two commanders arranged for a meeting on April 17
between the Confederate position at Hillsboro and Sherman's headquarters.
As the Union chief was boarding his train, a telegraph operator came
clattering down the depot stairs with word that a coded message was
coming over the wire. Would the general wait? He would—and this was one
of the most fortuitous waits of the Civil War, for when the telegrapher
returned with the message decoded Sherman saw that it was from Stanton
and had been a full two days in transit. It said:

> PRESIDENT LINCOLN WAS MURDERED ABOUT 10 O'CLOCK LAST
> NIGHT IN HIS PRIVATE BOX AT FORD'S THEATER IN THIS CITY . . .

Stanton added that Andrew Johnson was ready to take the oath of office and
also—still sniffing the wind for a Confederate plot—warned Sherman that
"an assassin is also on your track . . ." Ignoring the secretary's typical
alarm, Sherman stuffed the flimsy in his pocket and swore the telegrapher
to secrecy. At Durham he and his staff changed to horses to ride toward
Johnston, encountering him and his entourage about five miles out. They
were a picturesque contrast: the tall forty-five-year-old redhead with his
close-cropped russet beard, as plain and unpretentious a man as ever lived,
and the small, neat Southerner thirteen years his senior, his silvery imperial

and mustache perfectly groomed and his gray uniform immaculate. They found a roadside farmhouse owned by a man named James Bennett who granted them permission to use it.

Once they were alone, Sherman took the flimsy from his pocket and gave it to Johnston. Huge beads of perspiration formed on Old Joe's forehead, and he denounced the assassination as "the greatest possible calamity to the South." His eyes full of appeal, he said that he hoped Sherman did not suspect the Confederate government of complicity in the crime. Sherman recalled later that he assured Johnston that he could never believe that Lee or any other Rebel officer would be capable of plotting assassination, "but I would not say as much for Jeff Davis . . ." Johnston made no reply, and the two generals began to negotiate.

Almost at once they reached an impasse. Sherman could not agree to any proposal leading to negotiations between civil authorities, the very basis upon which Davis had authorized the meeting, probably in the expectation that this would torpedo all truce talks. Johnston quickly broke the barrier by proposing that he and Sherman "make one job of it," by settling "the fate of all armies to the Rio Grande." This meant all men still under arms including those west of the Mississippi. When Sherman questioned Johnston's authority to make such a commitment, Old Joe replied that he possessed it and could have it certified by Secretary of War John Breckinridge in their presence. Sherman demurred. He could not deal with a member of the Rebel cabinet, he said. But then Johnston reminded him that Breckinridge could join them in the capacity of a Confederate general. The three of them could meet tomorrow and work it all out. Sherman agreed.

Uncle Billy returned to Raleigh wrestling with the delicate problem of how best to inform his men of Lincoln's murder without arousing their thirst for vengeance. He was aware that "one single word by me would have laid [Raleigh] in ashes . . ." Fortunately, the army had been on good behavior in North Carolina, so much so that one Illinois private wrote: "Discipline was now so good that the men didn't know themselves." So he ordered all units into their camps before releasing a bulletin carefully absolving the Confederacy of any complicity in the crime. It worked, even though one private wrote home: "The army is crazy for vengeance [and] if we make another campaign it will be an awful one."

William Tecumseh Sherman was in a cheerful mood when he entered the Bennett house the following day. He was no longer the Sherman of Southern legend—"a mite careless with powduh and fiah"—but the Sherman of Atlanta, who had told Southerners "when peace does come you can call on me for anything. Then will I share with you the last cracker and watch with you to shield your homes and families against danger from every quarter." He would today take Johnston up on that proposal to "make one job of it" and settle "the fate of all armies to the Rio Grande." Johnston seemed to sense this attitude when he entered the room with Breckinridge. But the Confederate secretary of war and former vice president of the United States was in a foul mood. He had gone without a drink for days and had had to satisfy this unrequited craving with a double dose of his other addiction: chewing tobacco. He was chewing vigorously, his long piratical mustaches bobbing up and down, his face dark, when the ebullient Sherman opened one of his saddle bags and drew forth a bottle. "Gentlemen, it occurred to me that perhaps you were not overstocked with liquor, and I procured some medical supplies on my way over. Will you join me before we go to work?" Breckinridge's face cleared with a beatific smile and he spat his quid of tobacco into his hand, hurling it into the fire while accepting a glass of water to rinse out his mouth. Then, emptying the tumbler to fill it with bourbon, he swallowed it with a great sigh of satisfaction, stuffing a fresh quid into his mouth. Then the negotiations were renewed.

Sherman was astonished by Breckinridge's knowledge of international and constitutional law, and the eloquence of his silver tongue, loosened as it had been by that Olympian draft. At one point Uncle Billy pushed his chair back in protest. "See here, gentlemen—who is doing this surrendering anyhow? If this thing goes on, you'll have me sending a letter of apology to Jeff Davis." It is possible that Sherman, already in such a conciliatory mood, might have been influenced beyond good sense by Breckinridge's superior skill and experience in negotiation. At any rate, he at once settled down to writing out his terms in straightforward, soldierly fashion. At one point, seemingly stymied, he arose to reopen the bottle of bourbon. Breckinridge, like Pavlov's dog, at once smiled and threw away his quid again. But there was to be no second slaking of his thirst. Sherman absently poured out a few fingers of liquor, recorked the bottle, and stood at the window sipping thoughtfully before he returned to the table to finish his "Memorandum, or Basis of Agreement." Finally he laid down his pencil with the remark, "That's the best that I can do."

It was enough, far more than enough—outdoing Grant's generosity at Appomattox by a margin wide enough to make Johnston's eyes glow with hope. He was in high spirits when he left the Bennett house with Breckinridge clutching his copy of the Memorandum. But the former vice president's face was again dark and dour, and when Johnston asked him what he thought of Sherman he said: "He is a bright man, a man of great force. But, General Johnston," he continued, his voice rising, "General Sherman is a hog. Did you see him take that drink by himself?" When Old Joe suggested that perhaps Uncle Billy had been just absent-minded, Breckinridge shook his head fiercely and declared: "No Kentucky gentleman would have taken away that bottle. He knew we needed it, and badly."

William Tecumseh Sherman's terms had been far from hoggish, as he learned to his dismay within a few days when he found his friend U. S. Grant on his doorstep. Both President Johnson and Edwin Stanton had been enraged by the Memorandum. Stanton saw in it a bid by Sherman for the "Copperhead nomination for President," and also, shifting his scent of conspiracy from the Confederacy itself to Uncle Billy, according to Secretary Welles, "expressed fears that Sherman, at the head of his victorious legions, had designs on the government itself." Grant was called in, and though he vigorously defended his friend, he agreed that the terms which repeatedly encroached upon the civil authority and made no mention of the South's slaves whatsoever, "could not possibly be approved." So Grant was ordered to North Carolina to explain the situation to Sherman, which he did, making no mention of the new president's indignation or Stanton's paranoid suspicions. He also showed him a copy of a War Department order he had received in March while still in front of Petersburg, which said: "You are not to decide, discuss or confer upon any political question. Such questions the President holds in his own hands; and will submit them to no military conference or conventions." Upon reading it, Sherman dryly observed that if a copy of this order had been sent to him, "It would have saved a world of trouble," and promptly notified Johnston that Washington had vetoed the Memorandum. In what can only be described as an ultimatum he gave Old Joe forty-eight hours to surrender "on the same terms as were given General Lee"—or else. . . .

This is what Davis had correctly anticipated and he rejoiced even as he approved the now-rejected Memorandum. Johnston, dismayed, turned next to Breckinridge for advice and was told to fight on. This a man of Joe Johnston's deep and essential humanity could not do, and he met again with Sherman in the Bennett house where an agreement was finally negotiated on the terms proposed by the North. When Sherman offered to issue ten days' rations to Johnston's 25,000 paroled Graybacks to feed them on their homeward journeys, Old Joe was so moved that he said "the enlarged patriotism manifested in these papers reconciles me to what I previously considered the misfortune of my life—that of having had to encounter you in the field."

In such mutual self-esteem the two generals parted, and the American Civil War—but for sporadic skirmishing by diehards in the West—was at an effective end. Other capitulations—notably Kirby Smith's west of the Mississippi—would follow, while many a Rebel still clad in butternut or gray set his face toward the setting sun bound for Texas, the American west or Mexico. Where the great cavalry leader Nathan Bedford Forrest, surprisingly enough, opted to return home to Tennessee—where he eventually founded the Ku Klux Klan—thus risking possible prosecution for the massacre of blacks at Fort Pillow, another chief of irregulars, Jo Shelby, led most of his mounted Butternuts across the Rio Grande. Others crossed into Canada like Jubal Early, who finally returned to Virginia still defiantly "unreconstructed," while a few like James Longstreet counseled his fellow officers to recognize reality by applying for pardon and accepting reunion, for which wise advice he was mercilessly castigated as an unspeakable scalawag by a group of officers known as the Virginia Cabal, which, searching for a scapegoat to blame for the Lost Cause—preferably one not from the Old Dominion—settled on the burly Georgian whose chief crimes seemed to have been his conduct at Gettysburg and his friendship with Grant. Jefferson Davis, of course, could accept no such reconciliation. Captured in Georgia while fleeing for Texas—where he hoped to reestablish a Confederate government—and basely and falsely charged with trying to escape wearing his wife's clothes, he was imprisoned in Fort Monroe for two years while Washington tried to decide what to do with him. A treason trial was intended, but as passions cooled, and the news that the Confederate president had been brutally and barbarically placed in irons raised a public outcry, North as well as South, he was finally given his release. But he would not sue for pardon, even to give Mississippi a non-Reconstructionist seat in the Senate, because he firmly believed until his death in his eighty-second year that his cause had been noble, just and even Godly. Robert Edward Lee, though deprived of his citizenship, still, like Longstreet, advised his fellow Southerners to forget their bitterness and become loyal Americans again. Spurning prestigious job offers, he became president of Washington College in Lexington—later renamed Washington & Lee— where, though an innovative educator as he had been at West Point, he was also, for all his reputation as the gentle warrior, an uncommonly stern headmaster.

Thus for all the bloodthirsty cries of "Hang 'em!" breaking from the throats of superpatriots in the podiums and pulpits of the North, no citizen or soldier of the defunct Confederate States of America was ever prosecuted for treason, and the only Southern war criminal convicted and executed was Captain Henry Wirz, for his murderous neglect and exploitation of Union prisoners at Andersonville. And even as Sherman and Johnston brought the bloodshed to its effective end on that momentous April 26, 1865, John Wilkes Booth was at last run to earth.

On Easter Sunday, April 16, an enormous man hunt had begun for Booth and his accomplices. Stanton pressed all the War Department's resources and personnel into the search: soldiers, civilians and Secret Service agents. Within a week the dim-witted Powell, the drunken Atzerodt, Arnold, O'Laughlin and scene-shifter Edman Spangler were all arrested and locked in irons in the hold of an ironclad anchored in the Potomac. But Booth and Davy Herold were still at large.

After shooting Lincoln, Booth had ridden over the Navy Yard Bridge into backcountry Maryland. Herold overtook him there and the pair rode at high speed for the Mason-Dixon Line. Confederate sympathizers in Maryland helped them on their way with food and drink. Dr. Samuel A. Mudd of Bryantown, another friend of the Rebellion, set Booth's injured leg and fashioned a pair of crude crutches for him. Moving through thickets and swamps, coming so close to Stanton's pursuers that they could hear the rattling of soldiers' sabers, they got across the Potomac and took refuge in a barn on Richard H. Garrett's tobacco farm near Port Royal on the Rappahannock. There in the early morning of April 26 a column of Union cavalry and War Department detectives converged on them. They were ordered to surrender. Herold came out with his hands up, but Booth cried out defiantly:

"Well, my brave boys, you can prepare a stretcher for me."

The barn was set on fire to smoke him out. Troopers peering through the chinks between the barn boards could see Booth hobbling about with a carbine in one hand and a revolver in another. One of them—probably Sergeant Boston Corbett of the 16th New York Cavalry—opened fire and Booth fell mortally stricken. Dragged from the smoking barn, he was laid out on the grass outside, where he gasped: "Tell my mother . . . tell my mother that I died for my country." Two hours later he was dead, and his body carefully sewed in a bag was brought to Stanton. The secretary was understandably upset about how to dispose of the remains. He feared quite reasonably that some Rebels or their friends might try to seize it and glorify it, exalting the assassin at his victim's expense. Indeed the Dallas *Herald* had already proclaimed: GOD ALMIGHTY ORDERED THIS EVENT! and the Chattanooga *Rebel* said: "Abe has gone to answer before the bar of God for the innocent blood he has permitted to be shed." So Stanton had Booth secretly buried under the floor of a former prison at the Washington Arsenal. In

1869, with the Rebel cause definitely dead, the War Department had the body disinterred and delivered to Booth's family, who had it buried in Green Mount Cemetery in Baltimore.

Stanton's agents also apprehended Dr. Mudd and Mary Surratt, the mother of John Surratt, who had fled to Europe, and also proprietor of the boarding house where the conspirators had met. Trials were begun before a secret military court of nine officers. Powell, Atzerodt, Herold and Mrs. Surratt were all convicted of conspiracy to kill Lincoln and hanged. Although the court had recommended clemency for Mrs. Surratt because of her age and sex, President Johnson said that he had not seen the court's recommendation. But Judge Advocate General Joseph Holt, who prosecuted the cases, said that Johnson had not only read it but had muttered, "She kept the nest that hatched the egg." Dr. Mudd, O'Laughlin, Arnold and Spangler were convicted of the same charge but the first three were sentenced to life imprisonment at hard labor and Spangler to six years. Sent to a penal colony on an island off Florida, O'Laughlin died there, while in 1869 the others were pardoned by Johnson. John Surratt, meanwhile, returned to Baltimore about that time and became an auditor, giving a lecture in 1870 in which he denied complicity in the murder plot but boasted about participating in the scheme to kidnap Lincoln. He was neither harmed nor heeded, and so ended in the summer of 1865 the last grim chapter in the saga of the Civil War.

Before then the bright chapters had begun: on May 10 President Johnson declared all armed resistance at an end; and on the twenty-third and twenty-fourth a grand review of the Grand Armies of the Republic was held in Washington. Grant stood in the reviewing stand while Meade on the first day led the Eastern army in its march-past and on the second Sherman paraded his Western veterans. On May 29 Johnson issued a proclamation of amnesty and pardon to all persons who directly or indirectly participated in "the existing rebellion," with a few exceptions. These were the wealthy, those who had left Congress or the armed forces to serve the Confederacy, governors of Southern states, and so on; and these could apply to the president for clemency. Johnson, much to the chagrin of the Jacobins, who had sought more severe penalties, was most generous with his pardons.

So ended what was then the bloodiest and most dreadful war in history. In round numbers (exact computations of casualties in any war is simply not possible) the Union host of 2 million men was reduced by 640,000 men, and the 750,000 Confederates who took the field by about 450,000. Actually killed in battle were 110,000 Federals to 94,000 Rebels, but the figure soars after that with men dying of every disease known in those days, in prisons, or in non-combatant accidents. North-South total losses are put by the authoritative Thomas L. Livermore's *Numbers and Losses in the Civil War* at 623,026 dead and 471,427 wounded. Even though such exactitude can be questioned by any historian familiar with the vicissitudes of computing casualties, they are close enough to be considered authentic. There had been no fewer than 10,000 recorded military actions, 76 full-scale battles, 310 engagements, 6,337 skirmishes and numerous but uncounted forays, sieges, raids and expeditions. Like in no other war ever, there was a truly amazing proportion of general officers killed in action: 47 out of 583 Union flag officers; 77 of 425 from Dixie.

Thus the war begun by the North to preserve the Union had done so, just as a by-product of the conflict had eradicated the evil that was its root cause: chattel slavery. Emancipation, however, had by no means made blacks equal with whites. As one freed Alabama slave remarked. "I don't know nothin' 'bout Abraham Lincoln, 'cept they say he sot us free. And I don't know nothin' 'bout that, neither." Rather, Emancipation had inadvertently created a nation divided between first-class citizens who were white and second-class citizens who were black—just as Lincoln had feared and which he had hoped to avoid by his cherished plan of colonization. But it could hardly have been otherwise, granting that the African slaves, through no fault of their own, had been deliberately kept ignorant, illiterate and unskilled and therefore were not immediately ready to assume the duties of responsible, productive Americans. That would take time and understanding.

So slavery was succeeded by a policy of segregation across the Southern countryside, and in the teeming black slums of the Northern cities by the same de facto if not authorized injustices. Yet from prolonged pain and great convulsions come new perceptions and new directions. The Civil War had indeed shocked the American nation as never before or since. It was a rare household that had not in some way suffered, and for decades the presence of limbless veterans on the streets of the towns and villages would remind Americans of that sacrifice. At first there may have been barely more than glimpses of what social good might come from all this agony. They would grow into true visions and purpose while over the decades Southerners and Northerners ceased to despise each other under the binding pressure of growth and expansion, and settlers from both regions migrated into those very western lands the organization of which either to slavery or to freedom had provoked the conflict. Unifying tendencies were also present in two small foreign wars and three major ones, although a fourth—in Vietnam—was actually divisive. But before Vietnam the impact of the greatest struggle—World War II—in which blacks were drafted to fight for a freedom which they did not possess applied a shock and an impetus toward civil rights at least as great as the Civil War. The black community became so enraged at this final indignity that they breathed a new life and fire into the hitherto moribund National Association for the Advancement of Colored People, which, assisted by conscience-stricken whites, conducted a remarkably peaceful and successful demand for what belonged to them by birthright. This was officially acknowledged in the historic decision of the United States Supreme Court in 1953 outlawing segregation in schools, which was followed by laws against discrimination. True though it may be that hatred and prejudice cannot be legislated out of existence, or that the struggle against racial injustice is not over—if it ever will be—it is nevertheless safe to say that as this twentieth century draws to a close the civil rights movement for full equality will continue to gather momentum.

The Civil War, then, destroyed both the concept of secession and slavery. After it the United States truly became "one nation indivisible" and the American ideal of "freedom and justice for all" was put on the road toward reality.

Selected Bibliography

Ambrose, Stephen E., *Halleck: Lincoln's Chief of Staff.* Baton Rouge: Louisiana State, 1962.

Baker, Jean H., *Mary Todd Lincoln.* New York: W. W. Norton, 1987.

Ballard, Michael B., *A Long Shadow: Jefferson Davis and the Final Days of the Confederacy.* Jackson: University Press of Mississippi, 1988.

Beringer, Richard E., Herman Hattaway, Archer Jones, and William N. Still, Jr., *Why the South Lost the Civil War.* Athens: University of Georgia Press, 1986.

Bishop, Jim, *The Day Lincoln Was Shot.* New York: Harper & Row/Perennial, 1964.

Boothe, F. Norton, *Great Generals of the Civil War and Their Battles.* New York: Gallery, 1986.

Bridges, Hal, *Lee's Maverick General: Daniel Harvey Hill.* New York: McGraw-Hill, 1961.

Bushong, Dr. Millard Kessler, *Old Jube: A Biography of Jubal Early.* Boyce: Carr, 1955.

Cadwallader, Sylvanus, *Three Years with Grant.* New York: Knopf, 1955.

Carter, Hodding, *The Angry Scar: The Story of Reconstruction.* New York: Doubleday, 1939.

Catton, Bruce, *Mr. Lincoln's Army.* New York: Doubleday, 1952.

——— *Glory Road.* New York: Doubleday, 1952.

——— *A Stillness at Appomattox.* New York: Doubleday, 1953.

——— *This Hallowed Ground.* New York: Doubleday, 1956.

Coddington, Edward H., *The Gettysburg Campaign.* New York: Scribner's, 1968.

Coggins, Jack, *Arms and Equipment of the Civil War.* Garden City, N.Y.: Doubleday, 1961.

Cleaves, Freeman, *Meade of Gettysburg.* Norman: University of Oklahoma Press, 1960.

——— *Rock of Chickamauga: The Life of General George H. Thomas.* Norman: University of Oklahoma Press, 1949.

Congdon, Don, ed., *Combat: The Civil War.* Secaucus N.J.: Blue & Gray Press, 1985.

Commager, Henry Steele, ed., *The Blue and the Gray.* New York: Bobbs-Merrill, 1950.

Cooling, Benjamin Franklin, *Forts Henry and Donelson: The Key to the Confederate Heartland.* Knoxville: University of Tennessee Press, 1987.

Cornish, Dudley Taylor, *The Sable Arm: Black Troops in the Union Army.* Lawrence: University Press of Kansas, 1987.

Davis, Burke, *Stonewall.* New York: Holt, Rinehart and Winston, 1964.

—— *The Long Surrender.* New York: Random House, 1985.

Davis, William C., *Duel Between the First Ironclads.* New York: Doubleday, 1975.

Davis, William C., and Bell I. Wiley, eds., *The Image of War: 1861–1865,* vol. I, *Shadows of the Storm.* New York: Doubleday, 1981.

—— vol. II, *The Guns of '62.* New York: Doubleday, 1982.

—— vol. III, *The Embattled Confederacy.* New York: Doubleday, 1982.

—— vol. IV, *Fighting for Time.* New York: Doubleday, 1983.

—— vol. V, *The South Besieged.* New York: Doubleday, 1983.

—— vol. VI, *The End of an Era.* New York: Doubleday, 1984.

Dowdey, Clifford, *The Land They Fought For: The Story of the South as the Confederacy.* New York: Doubleday, 1955.

Downey, Fairfax, *Clash of Cavalry: The Battle of Brandy Station.* New York: McKay, 1959.

Dulles, Foster Rhea, *The United States Since 1865.* Ann Arbor: University of Michigan Press, 1959.

Dyer, Frederick H., *A Compendium of the War of the Rebellion,* 3 vols, *Regimental Histories.* New York: Thomas Yoseloff, 1959.

Eaton, Clement, *A History of the Southern Confederacy.* New York: Macmillan, 1954.

—— *The Growth of Southern Civilization.* New York: Harper & Row, 1961.

—— *Jefferson Davis.* New York: The Free Press, 1977.

Eckenrode, H. J., and Bryan Conrad, *George B. McClellan: The Man Who Saved the Union.* Chapel Hill: 1941.

Esposito, Col. Vincent J., *West Point Atlas of American Wars,* vol. I. New York: Praeger, 1959.

Faust, Patricia, ed., *Historical Times Illustrated Encyclopedia of the Civil War.* New York: Harper & Row, 1986.

Foner, Eric, *Reconstruction: America's Unfinished Revolution.* New York: Harper & Row, 1988.

Foote, Shelby, *The Civil War: Sumter to Perryville.* New York: Random House, 1958.

—— *The Civil War: Fredericksburg to Meridian.* New York: Random House, 1963.

—— *The Civil War: Red River to Appomattox.* New York: Random House, 1974.

Freeman, Douglas Southall, *Lee: An Abridgement of the Four-Volume Biography.* New York: Scribner's, 1961.

Fuller, Maj. Gen. J.F.C., *Grant and Lee.* Bloomington: Indiana University Press, 1957.

Genovese, Eugene D., ed., *The Political Economy of Slavery: Studies in the Economy and Society of the Slave South.* New York: Vintage, 1967.

Glatthaar, Joseph T., *The March to the Sea and Beyond: Sherman's Troops in Georgia and the Carolinas.* New York: New York University Press, 1985.

Grant, U.S., *Personal Memoirs.* New York: Chas. L. Webster, 1894.

Gonan, Gilbert, and James W. Livingood, *A Different Valor: The Story of General Joseph E. Johnston.* New York: Bobbs-Merrill, 1956.

Hassler, Warren W., *McClellan: Shield of the Republic.* Baton Rouge: Louisiana State University Press, 1957.

Hattaway, Herman, and Archer Jones, *How the North Won.* Chicago: University of Illinois Press, 1983.

Filler, Louis, *The Crusade Against Slavery.* New York: Harper & Row, 1960.

Harwell, Richard B., *The War They Fought.* New York: Longmans, 1960.

Hebert, Walter H., *Fighting Joe Hooker.* New York: Bobbs-Merrill, 1944.

Hoehling, A.A. and Mary, *The Last Days of the Confederacy.* New York: The Fairfax Press, 1981.

Keller, Allan, *Thunder at Harper's Ferry.* Englewood Cliffs, N.J.: Prentice-Hall, 1958.

Johnston, R.M., *Leading American Soldiers.* New York: Holt, 1907.

Kerby, Robert L., *Kirby Smith's Confederacy: The Transmissippi South.* New York: Columbia University Press, 1972.

Ketchum, Richard M., ed., with narrative by Bruce Catton, *American Heritage History of the Civil War,* 2 vols., New York: American Heritage, 1960.

Kimmel, Stanley, *Mr. Lincoln's Washington.* New York: Coward-McCann, 1957.

Kraus, Michael, *The United States to 1865.* Ann Arbor: University of Michigan Press, 1959.

Leckie, Robert, *The Wars of America,* New York: Harper & Row, 1981.

—— *Great American Battles.* New York: Random House, 1968.

Lewis, Lloyd, *Captain Sam Grant.* Boston: Little, Brown, 1950.

—— *Sherman: Fighting Prophet.* New York: Harcourt, Brace, 1932.

Linderman, Gerald F., *Embattled Courage: The Experience of Combat in the American Civil War.* New York: The Free Press, 1987.

Lewis, Thomas A., *The Guns of Cedar Creek.* New York: Harper & Row, 1989.

Leech, Margaret, *Reveille in Washington.* New York: Harper, 1941.

Long, E.B., *The Civil War Day by Day: An Almanac.* New York: Doubleday, 1973.

McElroy, John, *Andersonville: A Story of Rebel Military Prisons.* Toledo: Locke, 1879.

McFeely, William S., *Grant.* New York: Norton, 1981.

McPherson, James M., *Battle Cry of Freedom: The Era of the Civil War.* New York: Oxford University Press, 1988.

McWhiney, Grady, *Braxton Bragg and Confederate Defeat.* New York: Columbia University Press, 1969.

—— and Perry D. Jamieson, *Attack and Die: Civil War Military Tactics and the Southern Heritage.* Birmingham: University of Alabama Press, 1982.

Miers, Earl Schenck, *The Last Campaign: Grant Saves the Union.* Philadelphia: Lippincott, 1972.

Mitchell, Reid, *Civil War Soldiers: Their Expectations and Their Experiences.* New York: Viking, 1988.

Moore, Ben Perley, *Life of Burnside.* Providence, R.I.: Reid, 1882.

Morison, Samuel Eliot, *The Oxford History of the American People,* New York: Oxford University Press, 1965.

Naval History Division, Navy Department, *Civil War Naval Chronology 1861–1865.* Washington: 1971.

Nevins, Allan, *Fruits of Manifest Destiny: 1847–1852.* New York: Scribner's, 1947.

—— *A House Dividing: 1852–1857.* New York: Scribner's, 1947.

—— *Douglas, Buchanan and Party Chaos: 1857–1859.* New York: Scribner's, 1950.

—— *Prologue to Civil War: 1859–1861.* New York: Scribner's, 1950.

—— *The Improvised War: 1861–1862.* New York: Scribner's, 1959.

—— *War Becomes Revolution: 1862–63.* New York: Scribner's, 1960.

—— *The Organized War: 1863–1864.* New York: Scribner's, 1971.

—— *The Organized War to Victory: 1864–65.* New York: Scribner's, 1971.

Oates, Stephen B., *With Malice Toward None: The Life of Abraham Lincoln.* New York: New American Library, 1977.

—— *The Fires of Jubilee: Nat Turner's Fierce Rebellion.* New York: New American Library, 1975.

—— *To Purge This Land With Blood: A Biography of John Brown.* Amherst: University of Massachusetts Press, 1984.

—— *Abraham Lincoln: The Man Behind the Myth.* New York: Harper & Row, 1984.

O'Connor, Richard, *Sheridan the Inevitable.* New York: Bobbs-Merrill, 1953.

—— *Hood.* Englewood Cliffs, N.J.: Prentice-Hall, 1949.

Osborn, Thomas, *The Fiery Trail: A Union Officer's Account of Sherman's Last Campaigns.* Knoxville: University of Tennessee Press, 1986.

Piston, William Garrett, *Lee's Tarnished Lieutenant: James Longstreet.* Athens: University of Georgia Press, 1987.

Potter, David M., *The Impending Crisis: 1848–1861.* New York: Harper & Row, 1976.

Ransom, John, *John Ransom's Andersonville Diary.* Middlebury: Eriksson, 1963.

Robertson, James I., *General A. P. Hill.* New York: Random House, 1987.

—— *Soldiers Blue and Gray.* Columbia: University of South Carolina, 1988.

Roehrenbeck, William J., *The Regiment That Saved the Capital.* New York: Thomas Yoseloff, 1961.

Roland, Charles P. *Albert Sidney Johnston: Soldier of Three Republics.* Austin: University of Texas Press, 1964.

Sandburg, Carl, *Abraham Lincoln: The Prairie Years and the War Years.* New York: Harcourt, Brace, 1954.

———— *Storm over the Land: A Profile of the Civil War.* New York: Harcourt, Brace and World, 1942.

Sobol, Donald J., *Two Flags Flying: Fifty Dramatic Stories of the Civil War.* New York: Munk, 1960.

Sommers, Richard J., *Richmond Redeemed: The Siege at Petersburg.* New York: Doubleday, 1981.

Stampp, Kenneth, ed., *The Causes of the Civil War.* New York: Simon & Schuster, 1974.

Stuart, George R., *Pickett's Charge.* Cambridge: Riverside, 1959.

Swanberg, W.A., *Sickles the Incredible.* New York: Scribner's 1956.

Swinton, William, *Decisive Battles of the Civil War.* New York: Promontory Press, 1986.

Thomas, Emory M., *Bold Dragoon: The Life of J. E. B. Stuart.* New York: Harper & Row, 1986.

———— *The Confederate Nation: 1861–65.* New York: Harper & Row, 1979.

Trefousse, Hans L., *Ben Butler.* New York: Twayne, 1957.

Tucker, Glenn, *Hancock the Superb.* Indianapolis: Bobbs-Merrill, 1960.

Wellman, Paul I., *The House Divides: The Age of Jackson and Lincoln from the War of 1812 to the Civil War.* New York: Doubleday, 1966.

Werstein, Irving, *Kearny the Magnificent.* New York: John Day, 1962.

Wert, Jeffrey D., *From Winchester to Cedar Creek: The Shenandoah Campaign of 1864.* Carlisle: South Mountain Press, 1987.

West, Richard S., Jr., *Mr. Lincoln's Navy.* New York: Longmans, 1957.

Wheeler, Richard, *Witness to Gettysburg.* New York: Harper & Row, 1987.

———— *Sword over Richmond.* New York: Harper & Row, 1987.

Wiley, Bell Irvin, *The Life of Billy Yank.* New York: Bobbs-Merrill, 1951.

———— *The Life of Johnny Reb.* New York: Bobbs-Merrill, 1943.

Williams, Kenneth P., *Lincoln Finds a General,* 6 vols. New York: Macmillan, 1952.

Williams, T. Harry, *Beauregard: Napoleon in Gray.* Baton Rouge: Louisiana State University Press, 1954.

Wilson, Edmund, *Patriotic Gore.* New York: Oxford University Press, 1962.

Wyeth, John Allan, *That Devil Forrest.* New York: Harper, 1959.

Index

Abolitionism, 28–29, 47, 55, 57, 77, 184, 388
Adams, Charles Francis, 124–25, 157, 427
African slave trade, 12
Agriculture: in the South, 24–25
Alabama, 84, 87–88
Aldie, battle of, 479
Alexander, Edward Porter, 455–56, 527–28, 529, 531–32, 537
Amnesty, 656
Anaconda Plan, 158, 200–212, 232
Anderson, Richard: and Chancellorsville, 458; as a corp commander, 592; and Gettysburg, 498, 500, 511, 517–18, 519, 525, 526; and the Kelly's Ford battle, 438, 439, 440; and the Sailor's Creek battle, 636; and the Spotsylvania Court House battle, 592; and the surrender of the Confederacy, 635
Anderson, Robert: and the capture of Charleston, 626; as a commander in the West, 153, 176; and Fort Sumter, 110, 111–12, 136, 139–42; and the Kentucky invasion, 176–77; promotion of, 153
Andersonville, Georgia [prison], 617–18, 654–55
Andrew, John A., 150–51, 464
Annapolis, 153
Antietam, 371–75, 376–87, 478
Appomattox, 636–39
Apportionment, 28
Archer, James J., 401, 496
Arkansas, 110
Arkansas [ironclad], 542–43
Arlington Heights, battle of, 153
Armistead, Lewis A., 490, 527, 532, 533, 535, 536, 538, 539, 612

Army of the Cumberland. *See name of specific general or battle*
Army of the James. *See name of specific general or battle*
Army of the Mississippi. *See name of specific general or battle*
Army of Northern Virginia. *See name of specific general or battle*
Army of the Ohio. *See name of specific general or battle*
Army of the Potomac. *See name of specific general or battle*
Army of the Tennessee. *See name of specific general or battle*
Army of Virginia. *See name of specific general or battle*
Arnold, Samuel, 642, 643, 655, 656
Asboth, Alexander, 256, 257
Assassinations/assassination attempts, 121–22, 641–46, 648, 650–51
Atlanta, Georgia, 607–10, 621–22
Atzerodt, George, 642, 643, 645, 655, 656
Averell, William Wood, 434, 435

Baker, Edward D., 192–93, 194
Ball's Bluff, battle of, 191–95
Banks, Nathaniel, 315–16, 328–30, 352, 555–56, 568–69, 604
Barksdale, William, 407, 409, 515, 516–17
Barlow, Francis, 381, 382
Barnes, Joseph, 645, 646
Barnwell, Robert W., 116
Barrow, Bennett, 17
Bates, Edward, 126–27